# TRUSTS IN
# LATIN AMERICA

# TRUSTS IN LATIN AMERICA

## NICOLAS MALUMIAN

OXFORD
UNIVERSITY PRESS

*Oxford University Press, Inc., publishes works that further Oxford University's objective of excellence in research, scholarship, and education.*

Oxford   New York
Auckland   Cape Town   Dar es Salaam   Hong Kong   Karachi   Kuala Lumpur   Madrid   Melbourne
Mexico City   Nairobi   New Delhi   Shanghai   Taipei   Toronto

With offices in

Argentina   Austria   Brazil   Chile   Czech Republic   France   Greece   Guatemala   Hungary   Italy
Japan   Poland   Portugal   Singapore   South Korea   Switzerland   Thailand   Turkey   Ukraine
Vietnam

Copyright © 2009 by Oxford University Press, Inc.

Published by Oxford University Press, Inc.
198 Madison Avenue, New York, New York 10016

Oxford is a registered trademark of Oxford University Press
Oxford University Press is a registered trademark of Oxford University Press, Inc.

Library of Congress Cataloging-in-Publication Data

Malumián, Nicolás.
  Trusts in Latin America / Nicolás Malumián.
    p. cm.
  Includes bibliographical references and index.
  ISBN 978-0-19-538821-3 ((hardback) : alk. paper)
  1.  Trusts and trustees—Latin America.  2.  Security (Law)—Latin America.  I. Title.
  KG184.M35 2009
  346.805'9—dc22                                                                 2009015319

1 2 3 4 5 6 7 8 9

Printed in the United States of America on acid-free paper

**Note to Readers**

This publication is designed to provide accurate and authoritative information in regard to the subject matter covered. It is based upon sources believed to be accurate and reliable and is intended to be current as of the time it was written. It is sold with the understanding that the publisher is not engaged in rendering legal, accounting, or other professional services. If legal advice or other expert assistance is required, the services of a competent professional person should be sought. Also, to confirm that the information has not been affected or changed by recent developments, traditional legal research techniques should be used, including checking primary sources where appropriate.

*(Based on the Declaration of Principles jointly adopted by a Committee of the American Bar Association and a Committee of Publishers and Associations.)*

You may order this or any other Oxford University Press publication by
visiting the Oxford University Press website at www.oup.com

I dedicate this book to my wife Andrea
and my son Bautista

# Contents

Acknowledgments . . . . . . . . . . . . . . . . . . . . . . . . . . . **xxi**

Translation Note . . . . . . . . . . . . . . . . . . . . . . . . . **xxiii**

Introduction . . . . . . . . . . . . . . . . . . . . . . . . . . . **xxv**

**Part I**

**General Aspects** . . . . . . . . . . . . . . . . . . . . . . . . . . .1

**Chapter 1: Antecedents** . . . . . . . . . . . . . . . . . . . . . .3

    **A.** The Trust in Roman Law . . . . . . . . . . . . . . . . . . .3

        1. *Fideicommissum* . . . . . . . . . . . . . . . . . . . . .4

        2. *Fiducia* and *Pactum Fiduciae* . . . . . . . . . . . . .5

        3. The Fall into Disuse of the *Fiducia* . . . . . . . . . . .6

    **B.** Evolution of the Trust in Continental Civil Law . . . . . . . . . . .7

    **C.** Trusts in England . . . . . . . . . . . . . . . . . . . . . . .8

    **D.** Trusts in the United States . . . . . . . . . . . . . . . . . 11

**Chapter 2: Trusts in Latin America** . . . . . . . . . . . . . . . . . **15**

    **A.** Adoption of Trust Statutes in Latin American Countries . . . . . . . 16

        1. Adaptation of U.S. Trust to Latin American Civil Law by
           Mexican Jurists. . . . . . . . . . . . . . . . . . . . . 16

    **B.** The Nature of the Latin American Trust . . . . . . . . . . . . . . 19

        1. Theory of the Irrevocable Agency Instruction . . . . . . . . . . . 20

        2. Theory of the Unfolded Property . . . . . . . . . . . . . . 20

        3. Theory of the Unholder Special-Purpose Patrimony . . . . . . . . . . 20

        4. Theory of the Trustee's Special-Purpose Patrimony. . . . . . . . . . 21

        5. Trust Agreement, Trust Property, and Special-Purpose Patrimony . . . . . 22

    **C.** Comparison of Anglo-Saxon and Latin American Trusts . . . . . . . . . 23

        1. Common-Law and Civil-Law Traditions . . . . . . . . . . . . . . 23

        2. Latin American and U.S. Trusts. . . . . . . . . . . . . . . . . . 24

        3. Sources of the Trust Law in Latin America . . . . . . . . . . . . 26

    **D.** The Hague Convention on the Law Applicable to Trusts and on
    Their Recognition and the Latin American Trust. . . . . . . . . . . . 27

    **E.** Parties to the Trust Agreement . . . . . . . . . . . . . . . . . . . 29

        1. The Grantor . . . . . . . . . . . . . . . . . . . . . . . . . . . 29

        2. The Trustee . . . . . . . . . . . . . . . . . . . . . . . . . . . 30

        3. The Beneficiary . . . . . . . . . . . . . . . . . . . . . . . . . 32

        4. The Protector . . . . . . . . . . . . . . . . . . . . . . . . . . 32

        5. Coexistence of Various Roles in the Same Person . . . . . . . . . . 32

    **F.** Creation and Termination of Trusts . . . . . . . . . . . . . . . . . 34

        1. Ways of Creation of Trusts . . . . . . . . . . . . . . . . . . . . 34

        2. Causes of Termination of Trusts . . . . . . . . . . . . . . . . . 35

        3. Effects of the Termination of the Trust . . . . . . . . . . . . . . 38

    **G.** Responsibility, Rights, and Duties of the Trustee. . . . . . . . . . . . 39

        1. Executing All the Necessary Actions to Accomplish
        the Trust Purposes . . . . . . . . . . . . . . . . . . . . . . . . 39

        2. Diligence of a Good Businessperson, Good Paterfamilias,
        or Diligent Administrator. . . . . . . . . . . . . . . . . . . . . 39

        3. Adequate Identification of Trust Assets and Rendering of Accounts. . . . 41

        4. Trustee's Liability for Trust Debt . . . . . . . . . . . . . . . . . 41

        5. Trust Secret and Criminal Responsibility . . . . . . . . . . . . . 42

        6. Trustee's Fees and Reimbursement of Expenses . . . . . . . . . . 42

        7. Termination of Office of the Trustee . . . . . . . . . . . . . . . 43

    **H.** Compared Tax Treatment of Trusts in Latin America. . . . . . . . . . 43

        1. Responsibility of the Trustee for Trust Taxes . . . . . . . . . . . 46

**Chapter 3: Securitization in Latin America.** . . . . . . . . . . . . . . . **47**

    **A.** Mortgage Securitization in the United States as a Model
    for Latin America . . . . . . . . . . . . . . . . . . . . . . . . . . 48

        1. Ginnie Mae . . . . . . . . . . . . . . . . . . . . . . . . . . . 50

    **B.** Definition and Advantages of Securitization in Latin America . . . . . . . 51

        1. Advantages of Securitization in Latin America . . . . . . . . . . . 51

    **C.** Risks and Credit Enhancement . . . . . . . . . . . . . . . . . . . . 52

        1. Credit Enhancement . . . . . . . . . . . . . . . . . . . . . . . . 54

    **D.** Public Offer of Trust Securities . . . . . . . . . . . . . . . . . . . 56

        1. Previous Authorization . . . . . . . . . . . . . . . . . . . . . . 57

        2. The Trustee as Securities Underwriter . . . . . . . . . . . . . . 58

## Chapter 4: Trusts versus Other Types of Contractual Arrangements and Legal Vehicles . . . . . . . . . . . . . . . . . . . . . . . . 61

    **A.** Simulated Agreement . . . . . . . . . . . . . . . . . . . . . . . . 61

    **B.** Bailment . . . . . . . . . . . . . . . . . . . . . . . . . . . . . . . 62

    **C.** Agency . . . . . . . . . . . . . . . . . . . . . . . . . . . . . . . . 63

    **D.** Pledge and Mortgage . . . . . . . . . . . . . . . . . . . . . . . . 64

    **E.** Usufruct . . . . . . . . . . . . . . . . . . . . . . . . . . . . . . . 65

    **F.** Corporation . . . . . . . . . . . . . . . . . . . . . . . . . . . . . 66

    **G.** Foundations . . . . . . . . . . . . . . . . . . . . . . . . . . . . . 67

        1. Private-Interest Foundations . . . . . . . . . . . . . . . . . . . 68

## Chapter 5: Types of Latin American Trusts . . . . . . . . . . . . . . 71

    **A.** Administration Trusts . . . . . . . . . . . . . . . . . . . . . . . . 71

        1. Charitable Trusts . . . . . . . . . . . . . . . . . . . . . . . . . 72

        2. Business Trusts . . . . . . . . . . . . . . . . . . . . . . . . . . 72

    **B.** Guarantee Trusts . . . . . . . . . . . . . . . . . . . . . . . . . . 73

    **C.** Governmental or Public Sector Trusts . . . . . . . . . . . . . . . 74

    **D.** Testamentary Trusts . . . . . . . . . . . . . . . . . . . . . . . . 75

        1. Forced Heirship . . . . . . . . . . . . . . . . . . . . . . . . . . 76

        2. Distinction between Fiduciary Substitution and Trust . . . . . . . 76

    **E.** Project Finance Vehicle . . . . . . . . . . . . . . . . . . . . . . . 79

    **F.** Other Types of Trust . . . . . . . . . . . . . . . . . . . . . . . . 80

## Part II

## Country-by-Country Analysis . . . . . . . . . . . . . . . . . . . . . . 81

## Chapter 6: Argentina . . . . . . . . . . . . . . . . . . . . . . . . . . 83

    **A.** Overview . . . . . . . . . . . . . . . . . . . . . . . . . . . . . . . 84

        1. Antecedents . . . . . . . . . . . . . . . . . . . . . . . . . . . . 84

2. Sources for Drafting Law No. 24441 . . . . . . . . . . . . . . . 85

3. Definition . . . . . . . . . . . . . . . . . . . . . . . . . . . . . 86

4. Requirements of the Trust Agreement . . . . . . . . . . . . . 87

**B.** The Grantor . . . . . . . . . . . . . . . . . . . . . . . . . . . . . . 88

**C.** The Trustee . . . . . . . . . . . . . . . . . . . . . . . . . . . . . . 89

1. Rights and Duties of the Trustee . . . . . . . . . . . . . . . . 90

2. Trust as a Separate Patrimony . . . . . . . . . . . . . . . . . 92

3. Criminal Responsibility of the Trustee . . . . . . . . . . . . . 94

4. Termination of the Office of the Trustee . . . . . . . . . . . . 94

5. The Financial Trustee . . . . . . . . . . . . . . . . . . . . . . 95

**D.** The Beneficiary . . . . . . . . . . . . . . . . . . . . . . . . . . . . 95

1. The Residual Beneficiary (*Fideicomisario*) . . . . . . . . . . . 96

**E.** Securitization and Financial Trust . . . . . . . . . . . . . . . . . 97

1. Securitization . . . . . . . . . . . . . . . . . . . . . . . . . . 98

2. Financial Trust Instrument . . . . . . . . . . . . . . . . . . . 99

3. Trust Securities . . . . . . . . . . . . . . . . . . . . . . . . . 101

**F.** Particular Cases and Experience . . . . . . . . . . . . . . . . . 104

1. Public Sector Trusts . . . . . . . . . . . . . . . . . . . . . . . 104

2. "Cost Contribution" Real Estate Trusts . . . . . . . . . . . . 105

**G.** Tax Treatment . . . . . . . . . . . . . . . . . . . . . . . . . . . . 105

1. Federal Income Tax . . . . . . . . . . . . . . . . . . . . . . . 105

2. Value-Added Tax . . . . . . . . . . . . . . . . . . . . . . . . 106

3. Gross Revenue Tax . . . . . . . . . . . . . . . . . . . . . . . 106

4. Other Taxes . . . . . . . . . . . . . . . . . . . . . . . . . . . 106

**Chapter 7: Belize** . . . . . . . . . . . . . . . . . . . . . . . . **107**

**A.** Overview . . . . . . . . . . . . . . . . . . . . . . . . . . . . . . . 108

1. Definition . . . . . . . . . . . . . . . . . . . . . . . . . . . . 109

2. Applicable Law . . . . . . . . . . . . . . . . . . . . . . . . . 109

3. Creation and Duration . . . . . . . . . . . . . . . . . . . . . 110

4. Invalid Trusts . . . . . . . . . . . . . . . . . . . . . . . . . . 110

5. Independence from Foreign Laws . . . . . . . . . . . . . . . 111

6. Powers of the Court . . . . . . . . . . . . . . . . . . . . . . . . . 112

7. Assets That May Be Transferred in Trust . . . . . . . . . . . . 113

**B.** The Settlor, the Beneficiaries, and the Purposes of the Trust . . . . . . . 113

1. The Beneficiary . . . . . . . . . . . . . . . . . . . . . . . . . . 113

2. The Letter of Wishes . . . . . . . . . . . . . . . . . . . . . . . 114

3. Charitable Trusts . . . . . . . . . . . . . . . . . . . . . . . . . 115

4. Noncharitable Trusts . . . . . . . . . . . . . . . . . . . . . . . 115

5. Revocation, Termination, and Failure . . . . . . . . . . . . . . 115

6. Variation of Trusts . . . . . . . . . . . . . . . . . . . . . . . . 117

**C.** The Trustee and the Protector . . . . . . . . . . . . . . . . . . . . . . 117

1. Trustee . . . . . . . . . . . . . . . . . . . . . . . . . . . . . . 118

2. Appointment, Removal, and Resignation of the Trustee . . . . . . . 118

3. Powers of the Trustee . . . . . . . . . . . . . . . . . . . . . . 119

4. Duties of the Trustee . . . . . . . . . . . . . . . . . . . . . . . 120

5. Fees and Reimbursement of Expenses . . . . . . . . . . . . . . 123

6. Breach of Trust . . . . . . . . . . . . . . . . . . . . . . . . . . 124

7. Case Law . . . . . . . . . . . . . . . . . . . . . . . . . . . . . 125

**D.** International Trusts . . . . . . . . . . . . . . . . . . . . . . . . . . . 126

1. Creation of a Register of International Trusts . . . . . . . . . . . 126

2. Trust Agent . . . . . . . . . . . . . . . . . . . . . . . . . . . . 127

3. Exemptions of International Trusts . . . . . . . . . . . . . . . . 128

**Chapter 8: Bolivia** . . . . . . . . . . . . . . . . . . . . . . . . . . **129**

**A.** Definition and Overview . . . . . . . . . . . . . . . . . . . . . . . . 129

**B.** The Grantor . . . . . . . . . . . . . . . . . . . . . . . . . . . . . . . 131

**C.** The Trustee . . . . . . . . . . . . . . . . . . . . . . . . . . . . . . . 131

**D.** The Beneficiary . . . . . . . . . . . . . . . . . . . . . . . . . . . . . 133

**E.** Securitization . . . . . . . . . . . . . . . . . . . . . . . . . . . . . . 133

1. Legal Framework . . . . . . . . . . . . . . . . . . . . . . . . . 133

2. The Stock Market Act . . . . . . . . . . . . . . . . . . . . . . . 134

3. Tax Treatment . . . . . . . . . . . . . . . . . . . . . . . . . . . 136

**Chapter 9: Brazil** . . . . . . . . . . . . . . . . . . . . . **137**

  **A.** Overview . . . . . . . . . . . . . . . . . . . . . . . . . 137

  **B.** Guarantee Trusts (*Alienação Fiduciaria en Garantía*) . . . . . . . . . . . 138

    1. Trust Transfer in Guarantee of Personalty Ruled by Law No. 4.728 of
      1965—The Capital Markets Act (*Ley do Mercado de Capitais*) . . . . . 142

    2. Realty Trust Transfer in Guarantee
      (Law No. 9.514 of 1997 Chapter II) . . . . . . . . . . . . . . . . . 143

    3. Aeronautic Code . . . . . . . . . . . . . . . . . . . . . . 145

    4. Transfer of Creditors Rights in Guarantee . . . . . . . . . . . . . 146

  **C.** Realty Mutual Funds (Law No. 8.668 of 1993) . . . . . . . . . . 146

  **D.** Inheritance Trust (*Fideicomisso or Substituição Fideicomissária*) . . . . . 148

  **E.** Securitization (Law No. 9.514 of 1997 Chapter I,
    Sections IV, V, and VI) . . . . . . . . . . . . . . . . . . . . . 149

    1. CRI . . . . . . . . . . . . . . . . . . . . . . . . . . . 149

    2. Securitization Trusts . . . . . . . . . . . . . . . . . . . . 150

    3. The Fiduciary Agent . . . . . . . . . . . . . . . . . . . . . 152

**Chapter 10: Chile** . . . . . . . . . . . . . . . . . . . . **153**

  **A.** Overview . . . . . . . . . . . . . . . . . . . . . . . . . 153

    1. Trust Property . . . . . . . . . . . . . . . . . . . . . . . 154

  **B.** The Trustee . . . . . . . . . . . . . . . . . . . . . . . . 156

  **C.** The Beneficiary . . . . . . . . . . . . . . . . . . . . . . . 156

  **D.** Securitization . . . . . . . . . . . . . . . . . . . . . . . . 157

  **E.** Securitization Companies . . . . . . . . . . . . . . . . . . . 160

    1. Separate Patrimonies . . . . . . . . . . . . . . . . . . . . 161

    2. Full Disclosure . . . . . . . . . . . . . . . . . . . . . . . 162

    3. Liquidation . . . . . . . . . . . . . . . . . . . . . . . . 163

  **F.** Tax Treatment . . . . . . . . . . . . . . . . . . . . . . . . 164

**Chapter 11: Colombia** . . . . . . . . . . . . . . . . . . **167**

  **A.** Overview . . . . . . . . . . . . . . . . . . . . . . . . . 167

  **B.** Commercial Trusts . . . . . . . . . . . . . . . . . . . . . 169

    1. Legal Framework . . . . . . . . . . . . . . . . . . . . . . 170

    2. Special-Purpose Patrimony . . . . . . . . . . . . . . . . . . 171

3. Real and Personal Relations Created by Trusts . . . . . . . . . . . . 171

4. Formalities and Prohibited Stipulations of Trust Instruments . . . . . . 172

5. Termination of the Trust . . . . . . . . . . . . . . . . . . . 173

**C.** The Trustee . . . . . . . . . . . . . . . . . . . . . . . . 174

1. Duties of the Trustee . . . . . . . . . . . . . . . . . . . 174

2. Resignation and Removal of the Trustee . . . . . . . . . . . . 175

**D.** The Grantor and the Beneficiary . . . . . . . . . . . . . . . . 176

**E.** Particular Cases and Experiences . . . . . . . . . . . . . . . . 177

1. Real Estate Trusts . . . . . . . . . . . . . . . . . . . . 177

2. Guarantee Trusts . . . . . . . . . . . . . . . . . . . . 177

3. Investment Trusts and Mutual Funds . . . . . . . . . . . . . 178

4. Securitization Trusts . . . . . . . . . . . . . . . . . . . 179

**F.** Tax Treatment . . . . . . . . . . . . . . . . . . . . . . . 179

**Chapter 12: Costa Rica** . . . . . . . . . . . . . . . . . . . . **181**

**A.** Overview . . . . . . . . . . . . . . . . . . . . . . . . . 181

1. Termination of the Trust . . . . . . . . . . . . . . . . . . 182

2. Invalid Trusts . . . . . . . . . . . . . . . . . . . . . . 183

**B.** The Trustee . . . . . . . . . . . . . . . . . . . . . . . . 183

1. Appointment . . . . . . . . . . . . . . . . . . . . . . 184

2. Powers and Duties . . . . . . . . . . . . . . . . . . . . 184

3. Investments Carried Out by the Trustee . . . . . . . . . . . . 186

**C.** The Beneficiary . . . . . . . . . . . . . . . . . . . . . . . 187

**D.** Tax Treatment . . . . . . . . . . . . . . . . . . . . . . . 187

**E.** Securitization . . . . . . . . . . . . . . . . . . . . . . . 188

1. *Peñas Blancas* Hydroelectric Project Securitization Trust . . . . . . . 189

2. Other Projects . . . . . . . . . . . . . . . . . . . . . . 190

**F.** Particular Cases and Experience . . . . . . . . . . . . . . . . 191

1. Real Estate Trusts . . . . . . . . . . . . . . . . . . . . 191

2. Conservation of Wildlife Trusts . . . . . . . . . . . . . . . 191

3. Guarantee Trusts . . . . . . . . . . . . . . . . . . . . 191

4. Public Sector Trusts . . . . . . . . . . . . . . . . . . . 191

**Chapter 13: Ecuador** . . . . . . . . . . . . . . . . . . . . . . **193**

    **A.** Overview . . . . . . . . . . . . . . . . . . . . . . . . . . . 193

    **B.** Fiduciary Transactions: Civil Trust, Fiduciary Mandate,
and Commercial Trust . . . . . . . . . . . . . . . . . 194

    **C.** Commercial Trusts . . . . . . . . . . . . . . . . . . . . . 195

        1. Definition of Commercial Trust as a Special-Purpose Patrimony . . . . 196

        2. Commercial Trust Instrument . . . . . . . . . . . . . 197

        3. Rendering of Accounts . . . . . . . . . . . . . . . . . 199

    **D.** The Grantor . . . . . . . . . . . . . . . . . . . . . . . . . 199

    **E.** The Trustee . . . . . . . . . . . . . . . . . . . . . . . . . . 200

        1. Resignation and Substitution . . . . . . . . . . . . . 202

    **F.** The Beneficiary . . . . . . . . . . . . . . . . . . . . . . . 203

    **G.** Tax Treatment . . . . . . . . . . . . . . . . . . . . . . . . 203

    **H.** Securitization . . . . . . . . . . . . . . . . . . . . . . . . 204

    **I.** Tax Treatment of Securitization . . . . . . . . . . . . . 208

**Chapter 14: El Salvador** . . . . . . . . . . . . . . . . . . . **211**

    **A.** Overview . . . . . . . . . . . . . . . . . . . . . . . . . . . 211

    **B.** The Grantor and the Beneficiary . . . . . . . . . . . . 214

    **C.** The Trustee . . . . . . . . . . . . . . . . . . . . . . . . . . 214

        1. Appointment . . . . . . . . . . . . . . . . . . . . . . . 215

        2. Rights and Duties . . . . . . . . . . . . . . . . . . . . 215

        3. Substitution . . . . . . . . . . . . . . . . . . . . . . . 216

    **D.** Tax Treatment . . . . . . . . . . . . . . . . . . . . . . . . 217

**Chapter 15: Guatemala** . . . . . . . . . . . . . . . . . . . **219**

    **A.** Overview . . . . . . . . . . . . . . . . . . . . . . . . . . . 220

        1. Definition . . . . . . . . . . . . . . . . . . . . . . . . . 220

        2. Trust Creation Formalities . . . . . . . . . . . . . . . 220

        3. Separate Patrimony . . . . . . . . . . . . . . . . . . . 221

        4. Termination and Maximum Period of Trusts . . . . . . . . . 222

        5. Prohibited Trusts . . . . . . . . . . . . . . . . . . . . 223

    **B.** The Grantor . . . . . . . . . . . . . . . . . . . . . . . . . 223

  **C.** The Trustee . . . . . . . . . . . . . . . . . . . . . . 223

  　1. Rights and Duties . . . . . . . . . . . . . . . . 224

  　2. Causes of Removal . . . . . . . . . . . . . . . 225

  **D.** The Beneficiary and the Residual Beneficiary . . . . . . . . . . 225

  　1. Rights of the Beneficiary . . . . . . . . . . . . . 225

  **E.** Tax Treatment. . . . . . . . . . . . . . . . . . . . 226

  **F.** Public Sector Trusts . . . . . . . . . . . . . . . . . 226

  **G.** Particular Cases and Experience . . . . . . . . . . . . . 227

  　1. Housing Promotion Trusts . . . . . . . . . . . . 227

  　2. Agriculture Promotion Trusts . . . . . . . . . . . 227

  　3. Guarantee Trusts. . . . . . . . . . . . . . . . 228

  **H.** Securitization and Investment Trust Agreement . . . . . . . . 228

  **Chapter 16: Honduras** . . . . . . . . . . . . . . . . **231**

  **A.** Overview. . . . . . . . . . . . . . . . . . . . . . 232

  **B.** The Grantor and the Beneficiary . . . . . . . . . . . . . 233

  **C.** The Trustee . . . . . . . . . . . . . . . . . . . . . 234

  **D.** Securitization . . . . . . . . . . . . . . . . . . . . 237

  **E.** Tax Treatment. . . . . . . . . . . . . . . . . . . . 239

  **Chapter 17: Mexico** . . . . . . . . . . . . . . . . . **241**

  **A.** Overview. . . . . . . . . . . . . . . . . . . . . . 242

  　1. Formalities, Registration, and Enforceability of
  　　Trust Instruments . . . . . . . . . . . . . . . 244

  　2. Trust Termination . . . . . . . . . . . . . . . 245

  **B.** The Grantor . . . . . . . . . . . . . . . . . . . . 247

  　1. The Technical Committee . . . . . . . . . . . . 247

  **C.** The Beneficiary. . . . . . . . . . . . . . . . . . . 248

  **D.** The Trustee . . . . . . . . . . . . . . . . . . . . . 249

  　1. Credit Institutions . . . . . . . . . . . . . . . 249

  　2. General Rules on Trustees . . . . . . . . . . . . 252

  　3. Relevant Case Law. . . . . . . . . . . . . . . 253

  **E.** Guarantee Trusts . . . . . . . . . . . . . . . . . . 254

**F.** Experience and Particular Cases . . . . . . . . . . . . . . . . 258

    1. Trusts in the Restricted Zones (*Fideicomisos de Zonas Prohibidas*) . . . 258

    2. Governmental or Public Sector Trusts . . . . . . . . . . . . . . 260

    3. Trust of Shares of Financial Entities under Restructuring . . . . . . . 260

**G.** Securitization . . . . . . . . . . . . . . . . . . . . . . . . . 261

**H.** Income Tax . . . . . . . . . . . . . . . . . . . . . . . . . 265

**Chapter 18: Panama** . . . . . . . . . . . . . . . . . . . . . . **267**

  **A.** Overview . . . . . . . . . . . . . . . . . . . . . . . . . . 269

    1. Trust Instrument . . . . . . . . . . . . . . . . . . . . . . . 270

    2. Separation of Trust Patrimony . . . . . . . . . . . . . . . . . 271

    3. Beneficiaries . . . . . . . . . . . . . . . . . . . . . . . . 271

    4. Termination of the Trust . . . . . . . . . . . . . . . . . . . 272

    5. Trust Confidentiality and "Know Your Client" Rules . . . . . . . . . 272

    6. Applicable Legislation and Change of Jurisdiction of the Trust . . . . . 273

    7. Trust for the Liquidation of Corporations . . . . . . . . . . . . . 273

  **B.** The Trustee . . . . . . . . . . . . . . . . . . . . . . . . . 273

  **C.** Tax Treatment . . . . . . . . . . . . . . . . . . . . . . . . 276

    1. Panamanian Source Income . . . . . . . . . . . . . . . . . . 276

    2. Tax Rates . . . . . . . . . . . . . . . . . . . . . . . . . 277

    3. Trusts with Assets Outside of Panama . . . . . . . . . . . . . . 277

    4. Trusts with Panamanian Source Income . . . . . . . . . . . . . 277

    5. Pension Funds . . . . . . . . . . . . . . . . . . . . . . . 278

    6. Guarantee Trusts . . . . . . . . . . . . . . . . . . . . . . 278

  **D.** Private-Interest Foundations . . . . . . . . . . . . . . . . . . 279

    1. Main Regulations of the Foundations Act . . . . . . . . . . . . . 279

    2. The Foundational Act . . . . . . . . . . . . . . . . . . . . 281

    3. The Foundation Council and Controlling Bodies (Protector) . . . . . . 283

    4. Termination of the Foundation . . . . . . . . . . . . . . . . . 286

    5. Change of Domicile of the Foundation (*Redomiciliation*) . . . . . . . 286

    6. Taxation . . . . . . . . . . . . . . . . . . . . . . . . . 287

**Chapter 19: Paraguay** . . . . . . . . . . . . . . . . . . . . . **289**

   **A.** Overview . . . . . . . . . . . . . . . . . . . . . . . . . . . 290

      1. Legal Framework . . . . . . . . . . . . . . . . . . . 290

      2. Central Bank of Paraguay as Trust Regulator . . . . . . . . . . . 291

      3. Transference of Assets to a Trust . . . . . . . . . . . . . 292

      4. Illegal Trusts . . . . . . . . . . . . . . . . . . . . . 293

      5. Separation of the Trust Patrimony . . . . . . . . . . . . 293

      6. Termination and Liquidation of Trusts . . . . . . . . . . . . 294

   **B.** The Grantor . . . . . . . . . . . . . . . . . . . . . . . . 296

   **C.** The Trustee . . . . . . . . . . . . . . . . . . . . . . . . 297

      1. Trustee Substitution . . . . . . . . . . . . . . . . . . 297

      2. Rights and Powers of the Trustee . . . . . . . . . . . . . 298

      3. Duties of the Trustee . . . . . . . . . . . . . . . . . . 298

      4. Trustee's Fees . . . . . . . . . . . . . . . . . . . . . 301

      5. Trustee Resignation . . . . . . . . . . . . . . . . . . 301

   **D.** The Beneficiary and the Residual Beneficiary . . . . . . . . . . . . 302

   **E.** Securitization Companies . . . . . . . . . . . . . . . . . . 303

   **F.** Tax Treatment . . . . . . . . . . . . . . . . . . . . . . . 305

      1. Value-Added Tax . . . . . . . . . . . . . . . . . . . 305

      2. Stamp Duty . . . . . . . . . . . . . . . . . . . . . 306

      3. Notary Rights . . . . . . . . . . . . . . . . . . . . . 306

   **G.** Particular Cases and Experience . . . . . . . . . . . . . . . 306

      1. Investment Trusts . . . . . . . . . . . . . . . . . . . 306

      2. Guarantee Trusts . . . . . . . . . . . . . . . . . . . 308

      3. Real Estate Trusts . . . . . . . . . . . . . . . . . . . 308

      4. Securitization Trusts . . . . . . . . . . . . . . . . . . 308

**Chapter 20: Peru** . . . . . . . . . . . . . . . . . . . . . . . **311**

   **A.** Overview . . . . . . . . . . . . . . . . . . . . . . . . . . 312

      1. Trust as a Separate Patrimony . . . . . . . . . . . . . . 313

      2. Formalities of the Trust Instrument . . . . . . . . . . . . 313

3. Duration of a Trust. . . . . . . . . . . . . . . . . . . . 314

4. Invalid Trusts. . . . . . . . . . . . . . . . . . . . . . 314

5. Termination of Trusts. . . . . . . . . . . . . . . . . . 315

6. Testamentary Trusts . . . . . . . . . . . . . . . . . . 315

7. Guarantee Trusts. . . . . . . . . . . . . . . . . . . . 316

**B.** The Trustee . . . . . . . . . . . . . . . . . . . . . . . . 316

1. Rights and Duties of the Trustee . . . . . . . . . . . 317

**C.** The Grantor and the Beneficiary . . . . . . . . . . . . . 319

1. The Beneficiary . . . . . . . . . . . . . . . . . . . . 319

**D.** Securitization. . . . . . . . . . . . . . . . . . . . . . . 320

1. Securitization Trusts . . . . . . . . . . . . . . . . . 322

2. Formalities of the Securitization Trust Instrument. . . . . . . . . . 322

**E.** Securitization Companies. . . . . . . . . . . . . . . . . 323

1. Separate Patrimony . . . . . . . . . . . . . . . . . . 325

2. Securities Backed with the Securitization Trust Assets . . . . . . . . 325

3. Termination of the Trust . . . . . . . . . . . . . . . . 326

4. Special-Purpose Companies . . . . . . . . . . . . . . 327

5. Securities Offering and Risk-Rating. . . . . . . . . . . 328

**F.** Tax Treatment. . . . . . . . . . . . . . . . . . . . . . . 328

1. Income Tax . . . . . . . . . . . . . . . . . . . . . . 329

2. General Sales Tax . . . . . . . . . . . . . . . . . . . 330

3. Municipal Taxes . . . . . . . . . . . . . . . . . . . . 330

**Chapter 21: Uruguay.** . . . . . . . . . . . . . . . . . . **331**

**A.** Overview. . . . . . . . . . . . . . . . . . . . . . . . . 332

1. Definition of Trust . . . . . . . . . . . . . . . . . . . 333

2. Trust as a Separate Special-Purpose Patrimony. . . . . . . . . . . 334

3. Assets That May Be Transferred to a Trust . . . . . . . . 335

4. Trust as Agreement, Separate Patrimony, and Trust Property . . . . . . 335

5. Registration of the Trust Instrument . . . . . . . . . . 336

6. Termination . . . . . . . . . . . . . . . . . . . . . . 337

7. Insufficiency of the Trust Assets . . . . . . . . . . . . 339

**B.** The Grantor . . . . . . . . . . . . . . . . . . . . . . . . . . . 340

**C.** The Trustee . . . . . . . . . . . . . . . . . . . . . . . . . . . 340

    1. Registry of Professional Trustees . . . . . . . . . . . . . . . 341

    2. Penalties . . . . . . . . . . . . . . . . . . . . . . . . . . . 341

    3. Multiple Trustees and Trustee Substitution . . . . . . . . . . . 342

    4. Standard of Trust Services . . . . . . . . . . . . . . . . . . 342

    5. Duties of the Trustee . . . . . . . . . . . . . . . . . . . . . 342

    6. Prohibitions That Affect the Trustee . . . . . . . . . . . . . . 343

    7. Trustee's Fees . . . . . . . . . . . . . . . . . . . . . . . . 343

    8. Termination of the Office of the Trustee . . . . . . . . . . . . 344

**D.** The Beneficiary . . . . . . . . . . . . . . . . . . . . . . . . . 345

**E.** Guarantee Trusts . . . . . . . . . . . . . . . . . . . . . . . . . 346

    1. The Montevideo Airport Guarantee Trust . . . . . . . . . . . 347

**F.** Testamentary Trusts . . . . . . . . . . . . . . . . . . . . . . . . 347

    1. Forced Heirship in Uruguay . . . . . . . . . . . . . . . . . . 347

**G.** Financial Trusts . . . . . . . . . . . . . . . . . . . . . . . . . . 349

    1. Securitization in Uruguay Before the Trust Law . . . . . . . . . 349

    2. Current Situation . . . . . . . . . . . . . . . . . . . . . . . 350

    3. Trust Securities . . . . . . . . . . . . . . . . . . . . . . . . 351

    4. The Trust Securities Holders' Meeting . . . . . . . . . . . . . 351

**H.** Tax Treatment . . . . . . . . . . . . . . . . . . . . . . . . . . . 352

    1. Nonfinancial Trusts . . . . . . . . . . . . . . . . . . . . . . 353

    2. Financial Trusts . . . . . . . . . . . . . . . . . . . . . . . . 353

    3. Guarantee Trusts . . . . . . . . . . . . . . . . . . . . . . . 353

    4. Offshore Trusts . . . . . . . . . . . . . . . . . . . . . . . . 354

    5. Tax Benefits . . . . . . . . . . . . . . . . . . . . . . . . . 354

    6. Tax Treatment and Responsibility of the Trustee . . . . . . . . 354

    7. Foreign Beneficiaries . . . . . . . . . . . . . . . . . . . . . 354

    8. Tax Secret . . . . . . . . . . . . . . . . . . . . . . . . . . 355

**Chapter 22: Venezuela** . . . . . . . . . . . . . . . . . . . . **357**

    **A.** Overview . . . . . . . . . . . . . . . . . . . . . . . . . 358

        1. Testamentary Trusts . . . . . . . . . . . . . . . . . 359

        2. Termination . . . . . . . . . . . . . . . . . . . . . . 360

        3. Competent Courts and Sanctions . . . . . . . . . . 360

    **B.** The Trustee . . . . . . . . . . . . . . . . . . . . . . . . 361

        1. Duties of the Trustee . . . . . . . . . . . . . . . . . 362

        2. Acceptance, Removal, and Resignation . . . . . . . 364

        3. Regulation of Investments . . . . . . . . . . . . . . 364

    **C.** The Grantor and the Beneficiary . . . . . . . . . . . . 366

        1. The Beneficiary . . . . . . . . . . . . . . . . . . . . 366

    **D.** Particular Cases and Experience . . . . . . . . . . . . 367

        1. Club Administration Trusts . . . . . . . . . . . . . 367

        2. Realty Trusts . . . . . . . . . . . . . . . . . . . . . 367

        3. Savings Funds Trusts (*Fideicomiso de Fondos de Ahorro*) . . . . . . 367

        4. Savings Bank Trusts (*Fideicomisos de Caja de Ahorro*) . . . . . . . . 367

        5. Social Benefits Trusts (*Fideicomiso de Prestaciones Sociales de Antigüedad*) . . . . . . . . . . . . . . . . . . . . . . 368

        6. Trusts for Carrying Out Projects . . . . . . . . . . . 368

        7. Guarantee Trusts . . . . . . . . . . . . . . . . . . . 368

        8. Investment Trusts . . . . . . . . . . . . . . . . . . . 368

        9. Housing Plan Trusts . . . . . . . . . . . . . . . . . 369

      10. Retirement Plan Trusts . . . . . . . . . . . . . . . . 369

      11. Life Insurance Trusts . . . . . . . . . . . . . . . . . 369

**Bibliography** . . . . . . . . . . . . . . . . . . . . . . . . **371**

**Index** . . . . . . . . . . . . . . . . . . . . . . . . . . . . **375**

# Acknowledgments

I would like to thank several people without whom this book would not have been a reality.

First, gratitude and appreciation goes out to Pat Grube for his wonderful help in the preparation of this book. His patience and guidance made this book possible.

I would like to especially thank all my Latin American colleagues, mentioned in the corresponding chapters, who helped me in my research and understanding of the different jurisdictions. In particular, I thank Thaís Cíntia Cárnio for the excellent material she provided me.

I also thank my European colleagues who explained trust regulations in continental Europe to me; in particular I would like to thank Benedetta Ubertazzi for sending me her issues on trusts in Italy and Spain.

Finally, I would like to thank Hugo Tordoni for his wonderful help in the translation of several materials, his corrections to the manuscript, and most important, the long discussions on the best way to express my ideas in English, and Steve Rosberg and Jeremy Vogler for reading the manuscript and making valuable comments.

# Translation Note

This book is based on case law, statutes, administrative decisions, as well as books and articles from jurists originally written in Spanish or Portuguese. To capture the essence of the ideas expressed in the sources examined, a literal translation has been avoided where possible. It must be noted that not only was it necessary to "translate" from Spanish or Portuguese to English, but also from civil law to common law. Accordingly, the author concentrated more on concepts with a view to helping the reader understand the key points addressed in the text.

In particular, the term "securitization" is used throughout this book for the Spanish terms *securitización, titulización, titulización,* or *bursatilización*; the terms "section" and "article" are issued as perfect synonyms for *artículo*; either "settlor" or "grantor" is used interchangeably to translate *fiduciante, constituyente,* or *fideicomitente,* and "trustee" for *fiduciario.* Similarly, either *beneficiario* or *fideicomisario* (residual beneficiary) is translated as "beneficiary" unless the context requires otherwise. Finally, the right of *dominio,* the most complete right of ownership under the continental law, is simply translated as "ownership" unless the context requires otherwise; and *derecho real* is translated as "real right" and/or *jus in rem* and *derecho personal* as "personal right" and/or *jus ad rem.*

# Introduction

The fact that the antecedents of trust under the common-law system contrast with the relative historical dearth of it in Latin America, and because Latin American laws are based on the civil-law tradition, most English-speaking practitioners and scholars are led to think that there is no actual relevance of the trust in the region. Nevertheless, today there is an extensive use of business trusts and guarantee trusts in Latin America, and anyone who wants to make business in the region (i.e., as an investor, a creditor, or as a purchaser of goods from Latin American providers) needs to know how to use a trust as a business vehicle or a guarantee scheme.

The first Latin American jurisdiction to adopt the trust, as it is known today, was Mexico, and it did so in 1932.[1] There were countries, such as Argentina, with laws that contained some provisions concerning the "trust property," but it was not used because of a lack of adequate legal framework.[2] Based on the Mexican experience, the express trust has made its way from north to south into the laws of most Latin American countries, with the exception of a few countries, such as Chile.[3]

---

[1] Acosta Romero and Almazán Alaniz explained that "it is evident that the trust does not have a long history in [Mexico]. It is a concept from abroad, one of the first that was included in our law [in the twentieth century;] there were several attempts in the first three decades but they were unsuccessful, like the 1926 Act, but it was definitely included in the 1932 Securities and Credit Transactions General Act (*Ley General de Títulos y Operaciones de Crédito*), which in a certain way copied the [U.S.] trust, of course, under the influence of Pierre Lepaulle's works, which was very important as was the participation of Pablo Macedo." MIGUEL ACOSTA ROMERO & PABLO R. ALMAZÁN ALANIZ, TRATADO TEÓRICO PRÁCTICO DE FIDEICOMISO 1 (1999). There were some legal antecedents in Mexico, but they were not actually used.

   As explained in Chapter 18 on Panama, although Panama had the first trust law in Latin America (Law No. 9 of 1925 replaced by Law No. 17 of 1941, which was in turn replaced by current trust Law No. 1 of 1984) written by Ricardo J. Alfaro, the trust began to be actually used after the enactment of the current act in 1984.

[2] The 1869 Argentine Civil Code (which is still in force, albeit with several major amendments) regulated fiduciary property in its § 2662. Nevertheless, it was necessary to wait until 1995, in which year Law No. 24441 established the trust as it is known today.

[3] As explained in the relevant chapters, after Mexico's experience, specific regulations on trust were incorporated in Colombia in 1941, Honduras in 1950, Venezuela in 1956, Costa Rica in 1961, Brazil in 1965, Guatemala and El Salvador in 1970, Bolivia in 1977, Panama in 1984, Ecuador in 1993, Argentina in 1995, Peru and Paraguay in 1996, and Uruguay in 2003.

The most common legislative technique has been the enactment of a trust act or the modification of the civil or commercial code. These rules allow the creation of business trusts, guarantee trusts, or trusts with any other purpose with a wide range of possibilities and flexibility. The notable exception to the general trust regulation trend is Brazil. Through the enactment of several specific statutes, Brazil adopted several kinds of guarantee trusts that can only be applied for specific purposes (i.e., a guarantee trust over real estate assets and a guarantee trust over movable assets), and there is no law regulating trusts for other purposes than guarantee. Put differently, in Brazil there is no general regulation of administration trusts that could be used for several purposes, but there exists a specific set of rules for guarantee trusts.

In those countries where there is no legal regulation of the trust at all (as in Chile), or where the trust is not regulated on a general basis, but for the specific purpose of serving as a guarantee (as in Brazil), it should not necessarily be understood that administration trusts are forbidden or illegal. Nevertheless, such "trusts" do not enjoy the necessary legal protections and would probably be transactions based exclusively on the confidence that the grantor places in the trustee and not special-purpose patrimony (i.e., the trust is not a separate fund of the trustee but part of his or her own property). In other words, if there is no specific trust statutory regulation, there is no separation between the trustee's own estate and the trust assets.

Although at first glance it could be thought that the Latin American trust was derived from the Roman *fiducia* or *fideicomissum* (as examined below), the Latin American trust as it is known today was actually inspired by the U.S. trust, and it is a relatively "new" creature under continental law (i.e., the system of law prevailing in Latin America). Put differently, the model followed by Latin American legislators was the modern U.S. trust. Nevertheless, the differences between common law and continental law has led to an "adaptation" process. In this vein, the following points should be considered: (a) continental law never had a separation such as the one that existed between common law and equity; (b) continental law is based on statutes (codes are an attempt to regulate by statute all the relevant issues on certain matters, such as the civil code, the commercial code, the mining code, etc.); (c) the only form contemplated by the statutes is the express trust (which in several countries must be a written instrument); and most importantly, (d) the Latin American experience is not as rich and evolved as it is in the United States.

It should be pointed out that the Latin American countries had to adapt the trust to their legislation without comparison to such forms under European continental law given the fact that most European countries did not regulate the trust.[4]

---

4    France regulated the trust (*fiducie*) only in 2007 with Law No. 2007-211 of February 19, 2007, which modified the French Civil Code. That means that all the Latin American trust acts analyzed in this book were enacted previously to the French regulation of trusts. It must be pointed out that the current French *fiducie* is very different from the common-law trust and the Latin American trust. The main differences are: (a) the settlor (*constituent*) of a *fiducie* can only be a corporation subject to corporation tax (i.e., it cannot be an individual, a partnership, or a tax pass-through legal entity), (b) the *fiducie* cannot have charitable purposes. Furthermore, in France, only banks and insurance companies can be trustees (*fiduciaries*), although this is different from the common-law practice, it the rule in several Latin American countries. Regarding

The trust is widely used in Latin America today because it has proved to be an excellent legal vehicle for investments, an individual's wealth protection scheme, and a legal device for securing obligations or securitizing cash flows and other assets. If well-structured from a tax and legal perspective, the trust can be an efficient mechanism for ensuring that certain assets are subject to the accomplishment of a particular purpose. This makes the uses of the trust virtually limitless.

The characteristics shared by all of the trust regulations in each Latin American country are highlighted in Part I. In Part II, you will find a country-by-country comparative analysis of Latin American trusts that outlines the differences and special characteristics of each jurisdiction.

---

fiducie and a translation to English of the relevant sections of the French Code see Laurent Chambaz, *Is France Adopting Trust Wholesale? The Answer Is "Not, But . . ."*, 13 TR. & TRUSTEES 255 (2007).

Spain, Italy, Germany, and Switzerland do not have trusts regulation. In relation to the situation of Spain *see* Benedetta Ubertazzi, *The Trust in Spanish and Italian Private International Law—Part II*, TR. & TRUSTEES 13 (1) 7–13 (2007). *Also see* Sonia Martin, *Trusts in American Law and Some of Their Substitutes in Spanish Law: Part II*, 13 TR. & TRUSTEES 242 (2007). It must be pointed out that Italy, the Netherlands, and Switzerland ratified the Hague Convention of July 1, 1985, on the Law Applicable to Trusts and on their Recognition (with entry into force January 1, 1992). The application of the Convention does not imply the introduction of a trust regulation but only the recognition of foreign trusts and, as stated in its article 11, "shall imply, as a minimum, that the trust property constitutes a separate fund, that the trustee may sue and be sued in his capacity as trustee, and that he may appear or act in this capacity before a notary or any person acting in an official capacity. In so far as the law applicable to the trust requires or provides, such recognition shall imply, in particular: (a) that personal creditors of the trustee shall have no recourse against the trust assets; (b) that the trust assets shall not form part of the trustee's estate upon his insolvency or bankruptcy; (c) that the trust assets shall not form part of the matrimonial property of the trustee or his spouse nor part of the trustee's estate upon his death; (d) that the trust assets may be recovered when the trustee, in breach of trust, has mingled trust assets with his own property or has alienated trust assets. However, the rights and obligations of any third party holder of the assets shall remain subject to the law determined by the choice of law rules of the forum."

Regarding Italy, although there is no trust regime, it has certain statutory rules regarding trust, settlor, and beneficiary taxation (Law No. 296/2006 articles 74–76). Regarding trust in Italy, *see* Benedetta Ubertazzi, *The Trust in Spanish and Italian Private International Law—Part I*, TR. & TRUSTEES 12 (10) 14–19 (2006). For an analysis of the tax treatment of trusts in Italy see Nicola Saccardo, *Taxation of Trusts in Italy*, 6 TR. Q. REV. 21 (2008). *Also see* Luigi Belluzzo & Alessandro Belluzzo, *Trusts Find a Tax Rule within the Italian Financial Bill 2007*, 13 TR. & TRUSTEES 262 (2007).

Regarding tax matters in Switzerland, the Federal Tax Authorities published guidelines on the taxation of trusts and trustees with connections to Switzerland in Circular No. 20 on March 27, 2008, (an English translation is *available at* www.step-ch-fl.com/pinboard/_rcs/common/attachments/p_filename_519.pdf).

# PART I

# General Aspects

# Chapter 1

# Antecedents

A. The Trust in Roman Law  3
  1. *Fideicommissum*  4
  2. *Fiducia* and *Pactum Fiduciae*  5
  3. The Fall into Disuse of the *Fiducia*   6
B. Evolution of the Trust in Continental Civil Law  7
C. Trusts in England  8
D. Trusts in the United States  11

It must be pointed out again that the modern-day Latin American trust is based on U.S. trust law, which in turn is derived from English law. Furthermore, as we examine in this chapter, the English trust derived, directly or indirectly, from the Roman *fidei-commissum* and the *fiducia*. Therefore, the study of trusts must commence with the Roman antecedents.[1] The antecedents provide elements to understand the nature and characteristics of the Latin American trust.

## A. THE TRUST IN ROMAN LAW

Regarding the trust in Roman law,[2] the first distinction that must be made is between the Roman trust as a testamentary (*mortis causa*) disposition called *fideicommissum,*

---

1  Both terms are derived from the common root in the word "*fides*" which, in Latin, means trust or confidence. The reason for this "coincidence" is that it was necessary to trust in the trustee to execute a trust. The Latin word "*fides*" is the root of *fideicommissum* (a commission based on confidence), *fiducia,* and *pactum fiduciae* (an agreement based on confidence). These terms gave birth to the Spanish terms *fideicomiso* and *fiducia* used nowadays, as well as the concept of "fiduciary duties" in English.

2  For the purposes of this book, I will consider Roman law as the rules and general principles in force since the foundation of Rome (753 B.C.) to the death of Emperor Justinian (565 A.D.). Needless to say that during such a long period of time, there were major changes in the law in

on the one hand, and the Roman trust as an *inter vivos* agreement (*pactum fiduciae* or *fiducia*), on the other.

## 1. *Fideicommissum*

In Rome, the *fideicommissum* was a commission (*commissum*) based exclusively on the honor and good faith of the trustee (*fides*) without any legal action that allowed claim to its execution. It was instrumented by a testamentary (*mortis causa*) disposition by which the grantor directed the trustee to deliver certain property to a third party who was not capable of receiving the trust property directly under the prevailing testamentary law.[3] According to Roman law, among others, the following designees could not be favored by a will: municipalities, poor persons, foreigners, personas that were not citizens, and unmarried persons.[4]

The beneficiary of the assets held in trust by the trustee under the *fideicomissum* had no legal action to exercise his or her rights under the trust to obtain the assets that were granted to him or her under the arrangement. It was a pure *fiducia*ry duty, in which the trust was absolute. The absolute nature of such trust subjected the arrangement to potential abuse by the trustee. After this first stage, the *fideicomissum* had an evolution that could be summarized as follows:

a. The emperor Augustus created a legal action against the trustee. He directed the Roman consuls to intervene in the most egregious cases to force the trustee to observe the trust agreement that he had signed.
b. The aforementioned actions were so common that the emperor Claudius had to name two *praetors* for the specific purpose of monitoring these actions (called *praetor fideicommissarius*).
c. The emperor Justinian established that the beneficiary of the *fideicomissum* had a personal right to claim the assets held by the trustee.
d. Under the emperor Nero, and because of Trebelio's Senatus Consultum[5], the beneficiary was considered an heir with the same rights and duties.

---

force (in fact this period comprises the Roman kingdom, republic, and empire). Some scholars are of the opinion that Roman law is the compilation of laws made by Emperor Justinian in the sixth century, which since its edition by Dionisio Godofredo in Geneva in 1583 is known as the *Corpus Iuris Civilis*. This compilation has four parts: (a) the *Codex Iustinianus* with the rules in force by then; (b) the *Digesta* or *Pandecta,* the compilation of case law; (c) the *Institutiones,* an explanation of the main principles of law; and (d) the *Novellae,* the rules that entered into force after the compilation. Luis Rodolfo Argüello, Manual de Derecho Romano: Historia e Instituciones 3, 21, 109 (3rd ed. 2007). For a comment on the *Corpus Iuris Civilis* in English and an analysis of its relevance for the civil-law system see John Henry Merryman, The Civil Law Tradition: An Introduction to the Legal Systems of Western Europe and Latin America 6–10 (2nd ed. 1985).

3    *See* Ricardo D. Rabinovich-Berkman, Derecho Romano 750 (2001).
4    *See* Héctor Turuphial Cariello, El Fideicomiso 29 (2000).
5    "Senatus Consultum" can be translated as "Senate Advice," a resolution of the Roman Senate directed to magistrates to be applied (simply suggestions in the first stages of Roman history

In short, under Roman law the *fideicommissum* was used mainly in the inheritance context to circumvent the onerous restrictions of Roman hereditary law.[6] The *fideicomissum* allowed testators to achieve indirectly that which they could not achieve directly given the strict nature of Roman inheritance laws. This indirect disposition capability eventually led to the demise of the *fideicommissum,* especially in legal systems in which hereditary succession was strictly regulated.

After the fall of the Roman Empire, the *fideicomissum* was used for the sole purpose of keeping certain real estate properties within the family and can be called "fiduciary substitution." In other words, a perpetual inheritance order was created to avoid the sale of the real estate property object of the fiduciary substitution. This creation of a "privilege" or special inheritance order would be rejected during the French Revolution eliminating the trust from the Napoleonic Code.[7]

## 2. *Fiducia* and *Pactum Fiduciae*

Under the *fiducia* there was an actual transfer of property to the trustee,[8] and an obligation (based on confidence) to transfer such property to a third party after a period of time, or when a condition was satisfied. The Roman trust agreement (*pactum fiduciae*) effected a transfer of property to the trustee but with the obligation to give the trust property to a third party in the future.

There were two kinds of fiducia, *fiducia cum amico* and *fiducia cum creditore.*[9] The *fiducia cum amico* is the more ancient of the two. Under this kind of *fiducia,* an asset was transferred to a trustee with the obligation to transfer it to the settlor or a third party. Diniz explained that "*fiducia cum amico* was an agreement based on

---

but then mandatory) that were named after the Emperor that made the consult, or as in the case of the Trebelian's Senatus Consultum, named after the Consul that chaired the meeting in which the Senate established the rule (in the case of the Trebelio's Senatus Consultum, Consul Maximo Trebelio). Some scholars are of the opinion that the original Trebelio's Senatus Consultus only dealt with the responsibilities of the trustee in relation with the debts of the estate and that was in a latter estage that it was modified and unified with others Senatus Consultum to comprise several more issues in relation with trust regulations in Rome.

6    Hess et al. explained that "Roman law prohibited giving property by will to certain persons, for example, to persons who were not Roman citizens. The Romans developed the custom of devising property to one capable of taking it, with a request that the devisee deliver the land to a desired devisee who was incompetent to take it directly. This was the creation of a fideicommission. The obligation of the devisee to the desired beneficiary in this relationship was not at first legally enforceable, but it later became so. This confidence was analogous in many ways to the English trust or use, but differed in that it arose by will only and was limited to one purpose." Ami Morris Hess, George Gleason Bogert & George Taylor Bogert, The Law of Trusts and Trustees 18 (3rd ed. 2007).

7    Cariello, *supra* note 4, at 31, 33.

8    *See* Rabinovich-Berkman, *supra* note 3, at 559. *Also see* Argüello, *supra* note 2, at 265–266 quoted below.

9    These concepts can be found in the actual works of several Latin American scholars that use these expressions to refer to the administration trust and the guarantee trust.

confidence only, and not a [guarantee], under which a settlor transferred his assets to a friend (*amicus*), under the condition that they were transferred back when certain circumstances terminated, such as the risk to die in a war, a trip, political events, etc."[10] In short, the *fiducia cum amico,* was an agreement with a "friend" for the administration of assets during a certain period of time.

Conversely, the *fiducia cum creditore* was a guarantee, considered by several authors as the first formal guarantee of Roman law.[11] This legal form originated in the commercial context because of the lack of credit guarantees. The *fiducia cum creditore* involved the transfer of an asset for the purpose of guaranteeing a loan or other kind of credit. The trustee was recognized as the creditor of the loan, and the trust property was in the trustee's favor.

The key difference between the *fiducia cum creditore* and the *fiducia cum amico* is that the latter was created in favor of the grantor or a third-party beneficiary and not in favor of the trustee, whereas the former was a guarantee in favor of the trustee.

During the period of time in which there was no legal action to demand restitution of the trust property, the debtor under a *fiducia cum creditore* arrangement had to trust solely in the good faith of the creditor. As explained, when the *actio fiduciae* was granted in Rome, the grantor could legally force the trustee (the creditor) to return the trust property or to indemnify against damage caused. Nevertheless, the grantor could not get back the trust assets if they had been sold by the trustee to a third party. Conversely, trustees had in their favor the *actio fiduciae contraria,* a legal action to obtain payment expenses incurred during trust administration and to be indemnified against damages suffered in their capacity as trustees.

The legal risks that the grantor endured under the *fiducia* were caused by the disproportionate rights enjoyed by the trustee under the arrangement. Such an unbalanced legal arrangement led to the eventual extinction of the *fiducia* and the development of other legal forms, such as the *pignus* (pledge) and the *hyphoteca* (mortgage). These later-developed arrangements had similar purposes, but with a far greater legal protection for the debtor (that is, the transferor of the assets in a *fiducia cum creditore*).

## 3. The Fall into Disuse of the *Fiducia*

To summarize, the *fiducia cum amico* and the *fiducia cum creditore* were the two original forms of *fiducia*. These forms eventually weakened and were replaced by other arrangements. The former, as it was based on the trustee's good faith, suffered from a lack of certainty of the grantor's rights. The latter, the *fiducia cum creditore,*

---

10   4 Maria Helena Diniz, Curso de Direito Civil Brasileiro 582 (23rd ed. 2008).

11   Diniz explained that "the first real guarantee in the history of law was the *fiducia* (which did not survive), under which the debtor transfers to his creditor the property of an asset, which would be returned when the credit were paid. Therefore, such guarantee does not protect the debtor, which could never get his assets back because he has no means to prevent his creditor from selling the assets . . . the *pignus* [pledge] avoided these problems, because it was not the transfer of the property but of the possession of the assets." *Id.* at 471.

was substituted by other forms, especially the *pignus* and *hyphoteca* as guarantees.[12] In conclusion, the *fiducia* became obsolete and was eventually dropped under the Justinian code.[13]

## B. EVOLUTION OF THE TRUST IN CONTINENTAL CIVIL LAW

A scheme similar to the *fiducia* was adopted under ancient German law in the form of the *salman* (*manus fidelis*). This arrangement involved a trustee (*trehuhänder*) that had title to the property, but beneficial ownership was in favor of a third party. Under ancient German law, the rights of the *salman* over the trust property were limited to the purpose of the trust. If trustees failed to accomplish their obligation or breached the agreement, the grantor and successors had a legal action to claim the trust property, even where the trustee had disposed of the property to a third party. Nevertheless, a trust as it is understood today was not developed in Germany—the *treuhand* being different from the trust.[14]

The Roman *fiducia* also had some successors under ancient French law, but its form was quite different, and it was later omitted from the French civil code at the beginning of the nineteenth century. Regarding the reasons for the omission of trusts in the Napoleonic Code, Turuhpial Cariello explained that "in France, during the ancient regime, fiduciary substitutions were a usual practice, being called simply substitutions and the assets affected by them, substituted assets. Substitutions were used by the aristocracy to keep the concentration of wealth and family assets with the firstborn sons so as to keep their political influence, which, obviously, would be damaged with family assets and titles distributed among several sons and daughters, weakening their powers in relation to the sovereign and other feudal lords."[15] Cariello further explained that the assets were received by the firstborn son (*maior natu*) with the condition that he transfer them to his firstborn son, and so on. Therefore, a perpetual inheritance order

---

12     Argüello explained that the *fiducia, pignus* (pledge), and *hypotheca* (mortgage) are three kind or guarantees in rem used in the Roman law. The most ancient form of guarantee in rem is the *fiducia cum creditore,* under which the debtor delivers the property of an asset to the creditor, through the emancipation or the *in iure* cession, entering into the agreement (*pactum fiduciae*) that the creditor was subject to the obligation in confidence (*fides*) to return the property of the asset to the debtor once the credit was paid. A legal action was created in favor of the creditor to claim the restitution of the property of the asset (*action fiduciae*), but it does not allow the claim of the asset from third parties that acquired it. The pledge guarantee replaced this one because of the possibility of abuse by the creditor. ARGÜELLO, *supra* note 2, at 265–266.

13     Diniz concludes that the *fiducia* was used often in the classic era of Roman history but was later abolished by the emperor Justinian, and consequently not adopted by the contemporary codes based in Roman law such as the Brazilian Code of 1916. DINIZ, *supra* note 9, at 582.

14     Turuphial Cariello explained that if the *treuhander* transfers the property, the beneficiary has no action against the person who acquired it unless the beneficiary can proved the complicity of the acquirer; the assets are subject to the claims of the creditors of the treuhander, and in the event of bankruptcy, they can be foreclosed. Furthermore, the applicable rules in the event of death of the treuhander are unclear. CARIELLO, *supra* note 4, at 48–49.

15     *Id.* at 87.

was created. The liberal ideas of the French Revolution attacked this system, and in 1792 the legislative assembly prohibited fiduciary substitution, and although there was a limited return, section 896 of the Napoleonic Code prohibited the fiduciary substitutions.[16] The confusion between the trust and fiduciary substitutions[17] led to the idea of the prohibition of trusts in all the countries that used the Napoleonic Code as a model (such as most Latin American countries).[18] Regarding France, it was necessary to wait until 2007 to have a trust regime (*fiducie*) established by Law No. 2007-211 of February 19, 2007, that modified the French civil code (which, as previously explained, has major differences with Latin American common law and trusts).

The Napoleonic civil code is particularly relevant for the purposes of understanding the evolution of Latin American trusts because this code was followed by most Latin American countries.

## C. TRUSTS IN ENGLAND

Hess et al. explain that "the generally accepted view is that uses were modeled after the *treuhand* or *salman* developed under the Germanic [l]aw."[19] German scholars of the nineteenth century, who took the form from the Roman *pandectistas,* considered the *fiducia* to have a dual effect: an external and visible effect (the transmission of the ownership of an asset) and a hidden effect not evident to third parties (the agreement to return the assets, and consequently not sell them to third parties). Accordingly, there were two legal effects: the transfer of the assets from the grantor to the trustee and the obligation of the trustee in favor of a third party (the beneficiary). Under this interpretation, it is understood that this is the concept of trust that was adopted by the English law.[20] Conversely, Hess et al. state that another previously accepted "view was the development of the Roman *fideicommissum.*"[21, 22]

---

16  *Id.* at 87–88.

17  Chalhoub explained that the Latin American trusts derive from the Anglo-Saxon trust. During the Middle Ages, the use of the Roman trust was a means to segregate the patrimony of a family in the hands of a few of its members. The abuse of the trust led to a reaction against it during the French Revolution, which in turn led to the prohibition of the trust in the Napoleonic Code, which was adopted as a model by most Latin American countries. Nevertheless, it was a mistake to confuse all the trusts with the fiduciary substitution (that is a way to avoid the inheritance law using a trust). Luis A. Chalhoub, *Estudio Comparativo entre el Fideicomiso y la Fundación de Interés Privado en la Legislación Panameña, in* ALGUNAS CONFERENCIAS SOBRE EL FIDEICOMISO, LAS FUNDACIONES DE INTERÉS PRIVADO Y SUS USOS EN PANAMÁ 89–90 (2005).

18  The United States also reacted against "dynastic trusts" but in a completely different fashion. Most states simply enacted rules against perpetuities and/or allowed the trustee to sell the trust assets. *See* LAWRENCE M. FRIEDMAN, A HISTORY OF AMERICAN LAW 252–254 (2nd ed. 1985).

19  HESS ET AL., *supra* note 5, at 18.

20  *See* JOAQUÍN DE ARESPACOCHAGA, EL TRUST, LA FIDUCIA Y FIGURAS AFINES 18 (2000).

21  HESS ET AL., *supra* note 5, at 18–19.

22  Regarding the influence of Roman law in current UK law, Hillaire Belloc express that "the first essential fact that must be learnt about the history of England is the Roman foundations of our society" and adds that English laws and institutions derive without interruption from the

It was in England where the trust, in its modern conception, evolved into a legal form. The trust, similar to many legal concepts under common law, was shaped during the centuries by the division between equity and common law, case law, scholars' works, and the parliamentary work that led to several statutes.

The *use,* which is the predecessor of the trust, involved a transfer of real estate property to an individual, with the instruction to benefit the transferor or a third party. This transfer could be *inter vivos* or *mortis causa.* Although there were lawful reasons for the use, several authors point out that in many cases this mechanism was used to achieve illegal results.[23]

From the inception of the use to the development of the trust, four distinct, evolutionary periods can be identified. The first of these periods started with the adoption of the first uses through the fifteenth century. The next period ended with the enactment of the Statute of Uses in the sixteenth century. The third period reached into the second half of the seventeenth century, with the advent of the first trusts. Finally, the last period involved the development of the modern day trust.

Uses appeared in England prior to the Norman Conquest, but it was during the Middle Ages that the religious orders made a wide application of it, especially the Franciscans who applied them for the purpose of circumventing the Statute of Mortmain.[24] Toward the end of the thirteenth century, grantors transferred property to individuals who were capable of owning property in their own right, but under the belief that possession would be accompanied by the transferee's solemn promise of using the property for religious purposes.

In a first stage, the beneficiary of the trust was not protected by the common-law courts because there was no body of law recognizing such relationship. Uses and trusts were purely based on confidence with legal right. If trustees wished to appropriate the property granted in trust, they could do so.[25] This was a situation similar to the one existing at the first stage of Roman law, but because of the existence of a division

---

entrance of England in Roman civilization. HILLAIRE BELLOC, HISTORIA DE INGLATERRA: DESDE LOS ORÍGENES HASTA EL SIGLO XX 7 (2008).

23    "English jurists centuries ago suggested that the parents of the trust were fraud and fear and that the court conscience was its nurse." HESS ET AL., *supra* note 5, at 19.

24    The Statute of Mortmains (1217) prevented religious orders from being the owners of real estate properties. To avoid this act, the religious orders of the Middle Ages initially used trusts to benefit from the donations they received, which were made to a third party for the benefit of the religious orders.

      Black's Law Dictionary reads: mortmain acts "had for their object to prevent land getting into the possession or control of religious corporations, or, as the names indicates, *in mortua manu* [in dead hands]. After numerous prior acts dating from the reign of Edward I, it was enacted by the statute 9 Geo. II, c. 36 (called the "Mortmain Act" *par excellence*), that no lands should be given to charities unless certain requisites should be observed. Some traces of these laws remained until 1960." BLACK'S LAW DICTIONARY 1012 (6th ed. 1990).

25    "Early English law was extremely rigid. Forms and technicalities were strictly observed. The courts of common law gave no remedy unless a writ fitted exactly to the case could be found. As a result, the introduction of new remedies through the law courts was a matter of great difficulty. They rarely recognized a new type of property interest." HESS ET AL., *supra* note 17, at 24.

between common law and equity, it took a completely different course. Under Roman law, a legal action was created, and the obligations of the trustee became legally enforceable. In the case of the English trust, common-law courts did not change its arrangement, but courts of chancery recognized the existence of an obligation between the trustee and the beneficiary and gave it legal effect based on equity. Put differently, for the court of chancery, the obligations generated by the trust granted a right of equity character, which obliged the trustee to fulfill the trust or confidence of the sett-lor, in benefit of the beneficiary. In short, the court of chancery granted to the beneficiary the property in equity of the trust assets.[26] Therefore, the trustee was the legal owner and the beneficiary the owner in equity.[27]

In 1535, Henry VIII enacted the Statute of Uses with the purpose of suppressing the uses. Under this act the *feoffee*[28] or trustee was deprived of his legal interest, giving the beneficiary the legal property, and thereby changing the use in direct possession. It was argued that the real objective of the Statute of Uses was to abolish the uses to prevent the feudal lords' loss of rights and probably to attack religious orders, which were the beneficiaries of the uses. Nevertheless, the Statute of Uses did not have the desired effect because many cases remained outside its jurisdiction (e.g., uses on assets that were not real estate, or uses over uses) and were recognized and protected by the court of chancery.[29] This act was finally repealed in 1925.[30]

A relation known as *trust* existed in England before the Statute of Uses. Trusts were divided into two classes: the active or special and the simple or general. An active trust

---

26     It is a usual explanation of this decision that the chancellor, who at that time was an ecclesiastic would not tolerate the injustice of permitting a trustee to violate the obligation he had made in good faith.

      Turuphial Cariello explained that up to sixteenth century most chancellors were priests. Cariello, *supra* note 4, at 31–33.

      Johnson explained that even by 1815 approximately one-half of them were priests. Paul Johnson, El Nacimiento del Mundo Moderno 404 (1999).

27     The dual system of common law and equity was maintained up until 1875, in which both were merged by the Judicatura Acts (1873–1875) in one judicial system. From that moment on, any English court would be competent to hear actions based on the common law or in the equity, giving the parties the right to invoke one law or the other in the same suit and before the same judge. In the event of conflict, the rules of equity prevailed.

28     During the historical development of the trust, its participants were named in different ways, the old feoffor came to be known as the settlor or grantor, the old feoffee came to be known as the trustee, and the old *cestui que use* came to be known as the beneficiary.

29     Sheridan explained that "the statute was curiously worded; it did not abolish uses, nor was it intended to do so. For the statute to operate, it was necessary that one person should be 'seized' to the use of another. There was therefore no difficulty in holding that it did not apply to uses of leaseholds, copyholds or chattels. Furthermore, whilst a grant of land to A to the use of a corporation was within the statute, a grant of land to a corporation to the use of A was outside it. More important was the principle that the statute did not apply to active uses, i.e., those where the feoffee had some positive duty to perform, such as the collection of rents and profits. Trusts for sale were therefore outside the statute. Lastly, the statute did not apply where A was [seized] to the use of himself; it was essential that he be [seized] to the use of another." L. A. Sheridan, The Law of Trusts 27 (12th ed. 1993).

30     *See* Hess et al., *supra* note 5, at 28.

was when the trustee had the property for a period of time with the active obligation to fulfill certain conditions. However, if the transfer of land to the trustee was with the sole purpose of giving it to another one, but without any other obligation, such as to fulfill a condition, care, or administer the trust, this type of arrangement was known as a general or simple trust. After the Statute of Uses was issued, the term "trust" was applied to any interest held by a person in benefit of a third one.

Finally, the trust was shaped by English case law and statutes,[31] and, as described by Sheridan, "has gone abroad wherever English law has gone (including the United States of America)."[32]

## D. TRUSTS IN THE UNITED STATES

The process of the creation of the U.S. law on trusts can be summarized by saying, as Calvi and Colment expressed for U.S. law in general, that "there was no abandonment of important principles or abrupt break with the English system, although adjustments were made to suit the new environment."[33] The 13 original states of the union adopted the English trust law and adapted it to the new environment.

Hess et al. said that "by the end of the [eighteenth] century, when trusts came into more common use in America, the English system had been well developed and was adopted almost in its entirety by the American colonial and early state chancellors."[34] In other word, as early as the eighteenth century, the trust was well established in America.

Friedman explained that trust litigation was fairly sparse in the early nineteenth century. "Except for marriage settlements, living trusts were probably not common. Most trusts were short-term, 'caretaker' trusts, created to protect some weaker member of the family. . . . Frequently, too, a man would set up a trust to avoid passing property on to a bankrupt son or son-in-law."[35]

---

31    Hess et al. claimed that "to a considerable extent trust law has been codified in England since 1850 to meet changing conditions with regard to business and the law of property. The Trustee Act (1925), the Judicial Trustee Act, the Public Trustee Act, the Perpetuities and Accumulations Act (1964), and the Variation of Trusts Act have codified a large portion of the law applicable to private trusts. In addition various statutes applying to charitable trusts remove many areas of administration from more direct control by courts of equity." HESS ET AL., *supra* note 5, at 32–33.

For a description of the current trust law in England see E. H. BURN & G. J. VIRGO, TRUSTS & TRUSTEES: CASES & MATERIALS (6th ed. 2002).

32    SHERIDAN, *supra* note 27, at 5.

33    JAMES V. CALVI & SUSAN COLEMAN, AMERICAN LAW AND LEGAL SYSTEMS 33 (4th ed. 2000). The authors further maintained that one hallmark of the new system was the merging of law and equity, and the power afforded to a single judge to render both types of remedies in the appropriate cases (as opposed to the parallel court systems).

34    HESS ET AL., *supra* note 5, at 31.

35    FRIEDMAN, *supra* note 16, 251.

Compare with Hess et al. who claimed that "[t]he first state reports show that despite the relative poverty and newness of America, trusts were involved in litigation with fair measure of frequency." HESS ET AL., *supra* note 5, at 31.

The development of trusts in the United States, a federal country with fifty states, each with its own case law and statutes, created the need for the unification of the trust concepts. As a response, the American Law Institute[36] gathered the rules concerning the trust emerging from the judicial decisions and acts issued by each state in the *Restatement of the Law, Trusts.*[37] The first *Restatement of the Law, Trusts* was finished and published in 1935; in 1948 a supplement containing several actualizations were made, but the growth of the trust and the resulting law rendered a new version of the *Restatement* essential.[38] Hess et al. held that "a Restatement of the Law of Trusts was prepared by the report for the subject, Professor A. W. Scott, with the aid of a group of advisors. . . . The Restatement of Trusts does not deal with business trusts or trusts used for security purposes.[39] It also does not deal with constructive trusts unless the constructive trust arises as a result of attempting to create an express trust or as the result of the express trust itself. Some types of trusts are dealt with in other restatements. The Restatement of Trusts also does not deal with conflicts of law."[40]

The work was later enlarged and modified in several points, in the *Restatement of the Law Second, Trusts* (adopted and promulgated in 1957 and published in 1959). Finally, a *Restatement of the Law Third, Trusts,* updated, amended, and with new sections, was published by the American Law Institute in separate volumes: (a) in 1992 a preliminary volume (*Prudent Investor Rule*) was published; (b) volumes 1 and 2 were

---

36   This Institute was organized on February 23, 1923, being composed of two kinds of members, those elected for life and the official members. The official members are: (a) the members of the Supreme Court, (b) the highest hierarchy judges from the U.S. Court of Appeals, (c) the presidents of the highest Courts of several states and the Columbia District, (d) the president and members of the Executive Committee of the American Bar Association, (e) the presidents of the State Bar Associations, (f) the president of the National Conference of Commissioners on Uniform State Laws, (g) the presidents of societies such as the American Society of International Law, and (h) the deans of the schools that are members of the Association of American Law Schools. William Draper Lewis, *Introduction* to Restatement of the Law of Trusts, at vii–viii (American Law Institute, 1935).

37   The aim of the Institute in preparing the Restatement was to present an orderly enunciation of the general *common law* of the United States, including in this term not only the law developed by the court's decisions, but also that law developed from the moment of the application by the courts, of the state laws that had been in force during several years with a general scope. The authority of the Institute supported the accuracy of the statements on the law that were made. These have to be seen not only as the result of professional opinion, but also as the law expression by the professionals of the law. American Law Institute, Restatement of the Law of Trusts, vii–viii (1935).

   "The Restatements consists of 'black letter' sections where the portion of the law in question is stated, followed by comments and illustrations. The generally prevailing rule of case law is stated on a given subject, and where a conflict exists, the [American Law Institute] selects the view which is deemed sounder in principle or possibly more expedient." Hess et al., *supra* note 5, at 82.

38   Herbert F. Goodrich, *Introduction* to 1 Restatement of the Law Second, Trusts, at vii & ix (American Law Institute 1959).

39   A further comment on this issue can be found later when comparing U.S. trusts with Latin American trusts.

40   Hess et al., *supra* note 5, at 82.

adopted and promulgated in 2003; and (c) volume 3 was adopted and promulgated in 2007.

It should be stressed that the *National Conference of Commissioners on Uniform State Laws*[41] prepared several law models on trusts to be adopted by the states, with different degrees of success: the *Uniform Fiduciaries Act,* the *Uniform and Principal Act,* the *Uniform Trustee's Accounting Act,* the *Model Prudent Man Investment Act,* the *Uniform Trustee's Powers Act,* the *Uniform Probate Code,* and the *Uniform Commercial Code.*[42] Nevertheless, the major development in trust regulation in the United States was the enactment by the National Conference of Commissioners on Uniform State Laws in 2000 (amended in 2001, 2003, 2004, and 2005) of the Uniform Trust Code, which was adopted by several states,[43] and the enactment of other uniform acts that affect trust regulation.

To sum up, trusts have been a well-known legal device for more than two centuries. This vast experience was seen by Latin America, and there were attempts to adapt the trust to the Latin American continental system as explained in Chapter 2. Nevertheless, by the time the Mexican jurists were working on the Mexican trust regulations, there was no unified legislation model, nor restatement of the law of trusts available; they based their work on the law of each U.S. state and the relevant U.S. scholars.

---

41    As explained in its website, "The National Conference of Commissioners on Uniform State Laws has worked for the uniformity of state laws since 1892. It is a nonprofit unincorporated association, comprised of state commissions on uniform laws from each state, the District of Columbia, the Commonwealth of Puerto Rico, and the U.S. Virgin Islands. Each jurisdiction determines the method of appointment and the number of commissioners actually appointed. Most jurisdictions provide for their commission by statute. There is only one fundamental requirement for the more than 300 uniform law commissioners: that they be members of the bar. While some commissioners serve as state legislators, most are practitioners, judges, and law professors. They serve for specific terms, and receive no salaries or fees for their work with the Conference." NATIONAL CONFERENCE OF COMMISSIONERS ON UNIFORM STATE LAWS, *available at* www.nccusl.org (March 25, 2009).

42    GEORGE T. BOGERT, TRUSTS 16–17 (6th ed. 1987).

43    Adopted (in some cases with substantial amendments) by: Alabama, Arizona, Arkansas, District of Columbia, Florida, Kansas, Maine, Missouri, Nebraska, New Hampshire, New Mexico, North Carolina, North Dakota, Ohio, Oregon, Pennsylvania, South Carolina, Tennessee, Utah, Virginia, and Wyoming.

# Chapter 2

# Trusts in Latin America

A.  Adoption of Trust Statutes in Latin American Countries  16
    1.  Adaptation of U.S. Trust to Latin American Civil Law by
        Mexican Jurists  16
B.  The Nature of the Latin American Trust  19
    1.  Theory of the Irrevocable Agency Instruction  20
    2.  Theory of the Unfolded Property  20
    3.  Theory of the Unholder Special-Purpose Patrimony  20
    4.  Theory of the Trustee's Special-Purpose Patrimony  21
    5.  Trust Agreement, Trust Property, and Special-Purpose Patrimony  22
C.  Comparison of Anglo-Saxon and Latin American Trusts  23
    1.  Common-Law and Civil-Law Traditions  23
    2.  Latin American and U.S. Trusts  24
    3.  Sources of the Trust Law in Latin America  26
D.  The Hague Convention on the Law Applicable to Trusts and on
    Their Recognition and the Latin American Trust  27
E.  Parties to the Trust Agreement  29
    1.  The Grantor  29
    2.  The Trustee  30
    3.  The Beneficiary  32
    4.  The Protector  32
    5.  Coexistence of Various Roles in the Same Person  32
        a.  Grantor-Beneficiary  32
        b.  Grantor-Trustee (Declaration of Trust)  33
        c.  Trustee-Beneficiary  34
F.  Creation and Termination of Trusts  34
    1.  Ways of Creation of Trusts  34
    2.  Causes of Termination of Trusts  35
        a.  Accomplishment or Complete Impossibility of Accomplishment
            of the Purposes of the Trust  35
        b.  The Agreement between the Grantor and the Beneficiary  35

    c. Expiration of Period or Fulfillment of Condition  35
    d. Revocation by the Grantor  36
    e. Insufficiency of the Trust Assets  36
    f. Legal Actions by Creditors of the Settlor  36
    g. The Sole Trustee Being the Sole Beneficiary  38
    h. As a Result of Death or Legal Incapacity of the Trustee
       Declared by a Judge Unless the Trust Instrument Appoints a
       Substitute Trustee  38
  3. Effects of the Termination of the Trust  38
G. Responsibility, Rights, and Duties of the Trustee  39
  1. Executing All the Necessary Actions to Accomplish the Trust Purposes  39
  2. Diligence of a Good Businessperson, Good Paterfamilias, or Diligent
    Administrator  39
  3. Adequate Identification of Trust Assets and Rendering of Accounts  41
  4. Trustee's Liability for Trust Debt  41
  5. Trust Secret and Criminal Responsibility  42
  6. Trustee's Fees and Reimbursement of Expenses  42
  7. Termination of Office of the Trustee  43
H. Compared Tax Treatment of Trusts in Latin America  43
  1. Responsibility of the Trustee for Trust Taxes  46

## A. ADOPTION OF TRUST STATUTES IN LATIN AMERICAN COUNTRIES

As most of the legal systems in Latin American countries were based on European continental civil law, and in particular the French Napoleonic Code,[1] it must be stressed that the Latin American trust did not derive from such system. The concept of the Latin American trust (called *fideicomiso* or *fiducia*) was not founded on Roman law antecedents but on an adaptation of the U.S. trust.

### 1. Adaptation of U.S. Trust to Latin American Civil Law by Mexican Jurists

Beyond any debate on the role played by various Latin American jurists who took part in the trust adaptation to the Latin American law, the work of Mexican jurist

---

[1]    "In the nineteenth century, the principal states of Western Europe adopted civil codes (as well as other codes), of which the French Code Napoleon of 1804 is the archetype . . . A European of Latin American civil code of today clearly demonstrates the influence of Roman law and its medieval revival . . . In civil law nations . . . the influence of Roman civil law is much more pervasive, direct, and concrete than it is in the common-law world. We have no reception of Roman law." JOHN HENRY MERRYMAN, THE CIVIL LAW TRADITION: AN INTRODUCTION TO THE LEGAL SYSTEMS OF WESTERN EUROPE AND LATIN AMERICA 10 (2nd ed. 1985).

Pablo Macedo must be stressed. He drafted what would become the first operative trust legislation in Mexico, an undoubted influence on trust legislations in all of Latin America.[2]

In a preliminary work to the translation of Pierre Lepaulle's works,[3] Pablo Macedo expounded on the genesis of Mexican trust legislation, commenting on the most influential jurisprudence.

Pablo Macedo thought highly of Emilio Velasco's work, as it was related to the instances of trusts held previously to the *Ley General de Títulos y Operaciones de Crédito* (Securities and Credit Transactions General Law), mostly by American and English investors in railroads and other infrastructure works. Additionally, after Batiza (the Mexican author), Macedo critiqued Toribio Esquivel Obregón's stance and commented on the bills of Jorge Vera Estañol and Enrique C. Cree.

Finally, Macedo took special interest in the Panamanian scholar Ricardo J. Alfaro and his classic book.[4] He drew up a bill that was adopted as Panamanian law in 1925. This bill considered the trust "an irrevocable mandate by virtue of which certain assets are transmitted to a person, called the trustee, for him to dispose of them in accordance to the settlor's mandate, for the benefit of a third party, called the beneficiary."[5] Although this is a very important antecedent in the development of trusts in Latin America, as explained in Chapter 18 on Panama, this law was not used in practice and was abrogated.

Regarding the legislative evolution in Mexico, on November 24, 1924, the first antecedent of the trust was introduced with the creation of the "trust banks" in the *Ley General de Instituciones de Crédito y Establecimientos Bancarios* (Credit and Banking Establishments General Law).

---

2   This is not the first trust act in Latin America, such merit corresponds to Ricardo J. Alfaro's 1925 Law of Panama as explained in Chapter 18. But this law was not used, and then it was replaced (and in turn, the second law was replaced) with a law similar to, by then, the Latin American model based on the Mexican experience.

3   I refer to the study on the Mexican Trust by Pablo Macedo as an analysis of the translation of Pierre Lepaulle's treatise.

Sheridan affirms that "M. Pierre Lepaulle did much to explain the trust to continental jurists" and that "one consequence of the reception of trust in civil-law countries has been the elaboration of theories, concerning the nature of the trust, which seem strange to the Anglo-American equity lawyers. Of those theories, that of Lepaulle is possibly the most widely known, and it has directly influenced trust legislations in several countries, particularly that of Mexico." L. A. SHERIDAN, THE LAW OF TRUSTS 5, 37 (12th ed. 1993). As explained in this chapter that although Pierre Lepaulle's theory was a great influence, it was not adopted by Mexican law. Therefore, as explained in detail when dealing with the nature of trust, it is not the prevailing theory in Latin America.

4   The book is entitled: *El Fideicomiso: Estudio Sobre la Necesidad y Conveniencia de Introducir en la Legislación de los Pueblos Latinos Una Institución Nueva, Semejante al Trust del Derecho Inglés.* The title of the book could be translated as follows: TRUST: STUDY ON THE NEED AND CONVENIENCE OF INTRODUCING A NEW LEGAL STRUCTURE IN LATIN AMERICAN LAWS SIMILAR TO THE TRUST IN ENGLISH LAW (Imprenta Nacional, Panama 1920).

5   Section 1 of Law Nr. 9 of 1925 of Trust Institution, published in official gazette Nr. 4567 of January 29, 1925.

On June 30, 1926, the *Ley de Bancos de Fideicomiso* (Trust Banks Law) was passed. This piece of legislation was modeled after the Alfaro Law (which becomes evident after considering that its article 6 established that "trust is an irrevocable mandate by virtue of which certain assets are delivered to the bank in its capacity of trustee for it to dispose of them, or its proceeds, according to the will of the one doing that delivery, called settlor, in the benefit of a third party, called beneficiary").

On August 31, 1926, only a few months subsequent to the *Ley de Bancos de Fideicomiso* (Trust Banks Law), a new *Ley General de Instituciones de Crédito y Establecimientos Bancarios* (Credit Institutions and Banking Establishments General Law) was passed, which adopted the same concept of trust as irrevocable mandate as the Trust Banks Law, thereby upholding the model of the Alfaro Law. Pablo Macedo, quoting Roberto Molina Pasquel (*Los Derechos del Fideicomisario,* 108, 1946) held that no trust as such was held by any Trust Bank while this law was in force. In other words, although there was a trust law in place, no use was made of it.

On June 28, 1932, the new *Ley General de Instituciones de Crédito* (Credit Institutions General Law) was passed, followed by the *Ley General de Títulos y Operaciones de Crédito* (Securities and Credit Transactions General Law) on August 26, 1932. Both laws were conceived jointly and must be analyzed as complementary. The first regulated the trustee and the second, the trust itself. These regulations broke away from the Alfaro Law and the conception of trust as irrevocable mandate, being the first example of the notion of Latin American trust as it is known today. Macedo explained that he proposed the articles of the Securities and Credit Transactions General Law, which was to become Title II, Chapter V, entitled Of Trusts, accepted by the Drafting Commission of the Law, for which articles he is fully accountable and the one and only author.

After commenting on the doctrine and the regulatory antecedents mentioned above, Macedo went on to comment on the articles of the regulations relevant to trusts. It is interesting to emphasize the notion of the trust and trust property as adopted by this Mexican scholar, inasmuch as this is the notion to be adopted subsequently by the various Latin American legislations. Macedo explained that

> This is the first point in which the legislator followed the ideas already expounded by Professor Pierre Lepaulle. . . . [T]he idea of the trust property is fundamental in Lepaulle and, hence, in the Law, since it is on those assets—no longer belonging to the settlor, but which no longer belong to either the trustee or the beneficiary—that the trust legal structure is based. Are these assets without an owner? That is Lepaulle's conclusion. Not concurring with such a conclusion, which does not enjoy unanimous acceptance, we do not reject it either, as we did not wish to construct a new type of trust property, or propose a division of property into, for example, legal and economic. We limit ourselves to granting title to the settlor, not granting the status of full property to trust property. The reason for such a decision is that the deeper our survey delved into the matter, the more numerous the theories upheld by the different authors consulted became. . . . Based on the principle that the Law must not teach but rule, and that it is not a didactic manual but a body of precepts, a choice was made to present the trust with the greatest clarity possible, both in contents and effects, leaving it up to case law decisions and case law to study the matter and propose. . . . Moreover, what the Securities and Credit

Transactions General Law aimed at was to diverge from Dr. Alfaro's theory, already rejected by then and unable to overcome later criticism, regardless of the efforts made by the author, even by means of corrections and additional explanations.[6]

In brief, although a first antecedent of the Latin American trust can be found in the writings of the distinguished Dr. Alfaro, Latin American legislation broke away from his notion of irrevocable mandate (later, an irrevocable mandate with asset transfer) and adopted the idea of trust property with a particular end, property of the trustee (albeit a *sui generis* property limited by the objectives of the trust). The scholar who drew up the first and most influential law in Latin America was Pablo Macedo who, even while somehow following the ideas of Lepaulle, created the most successful and widespread legislation in Latin America.

The rapid growth in the trustees business in Mexico and the benefits of the use of the trust for its domestic economy showed to the remaining Latin American countries the need for trust regulation.[7] Trust legislation moved from north to south in the following order: Colombia (1941), Honduras (1950), Venezuela (1956), Costa Rica (1961), Brazil (1965), Guatemala and El Salvador (1970), Bolivia (1977), Panama (1984), Ecuador (1993), Argentina (1995), Peru and Paraguay (1996), and Uruguay (2003).

## B. THE NATURE OF THE LATIN AMERICAN TRUST

The assimilation of the trust by Latin American countries was not an easy task. The main obstacle was the difficulties of transferring to a civil-law concept an Anglo-Saxon concept based on a law system in which two parallel classes of property coexisted. One of the aspects that made the inclusion of the trust in the jurisdictions of the continental or civil law difficult, was the principle of *numerus clausus* in the subject of *jus in rem,* which did not allow the creation of new real rights (*jus in rem*) that were not specifically contemplated in the law. Therefore, if there was no statute to create trust property (different from ordinary property), such kind of property could not be created by agreement. Continental law did not have a similar or equivalent separation of the law to the one existing between common law and equity law.

To include the trust in continental law a complete new legal concept was created. In this vein, one unique feature of trusts in Latin America is that they implied creating a special-purpose patrimony, with the trust property separated from the trustee's own property. The trust implied not only unfolding the property into a legal or formal one (in the hands of the trustee) and a substantial or economic benefit (in the hands of the beneficiary), but it also created a special-purpose patrimony as will be addressed below in detail.

---

6   PABLO MACEDO, *El fideicomiso mexicano*, in xxv–xxvi TRATADO TEÓRICO Y PRÁCTICO DE LOS TRUSTS (Porrua Ed. 1975).

7   Another cause of introduction of the U.S. trust in certain Latin American countries was the consulting services performed by Professor Edwin Walter Kemmerer (1875–1545) in favor of several Latin American countries. The services and its reports are usually called *Misión Kemmerer* and quoted as such by several Latin American scholars.

In this sense, there were many efforts to adapt this concept, proposing different theories to justify it. In the next sections, the main theories that tried to explain the nature of the trust in the Latin American continental law will be covered.

## 1. Theory of the Irrevocable Agency Instruction

Ricardo Alfaro, the Panamanian jurist, made the first serious attempt to explain the concept of the trust under the Latin American law. He thought that the Anglo-Saxon trust could be explained under the Latin American legislation as an agency contract with certain particular characteristics. This agency contract had the particularity of being irrevocable, because as it was well-known, the general rule was that the agency was revocable. So the trustee appeared, in this way, as the administration of certain assets on behalf of a third one, without a real property transmission, only having the legal representation of the grantor, which kept that title. That is to say, the trustee was considered a person who only acted on behalf of another.

The authors criticized this theory arguing that in a trust the trustee acts in relation to a trust property that belongs to him or her. On the contrary, the agent acts in relation to the property of a third person. After this criticism, Alfaro made a statement adding to his definition that the trust was an irrevocable agency that transferred some assets to the trustee and/or agent. This theory was very influential in the first Panamanian trust law and in one of the first Mexican trust laws but does not have current practical application.

## 2. Theory of the Unfolded Property

There was also an attempt to view the trust as an institution in which the original property right unfolded into two new contemporary property rights, invested in different individuals and which had the same object. That is to say, the trustee has the legal property of the assets, and the beneficiary has the economic property of them. When the trust finished, these two characteristics reunited in the same individual.

Although this theory attempted to explain the nature of the Anglo-Saxon trust, it was not enough to achieve an adaptation of the trust concept to the civil-law countries. Furthermore, this theory was criticized for considering the personal right owned by the beneficiary of the trust property as a real property right. The main reason to put aside this theory is that it simply does not reflect the legal status of the trust in most Latin American countries.

## 3. Theory of the Unholder Special-Purpose Patrimony

This theory held that trusts are a patrimony "without owner" that should be used to carry out certain activity or to reach some particular end. The key element of the trust is the application of assets to a particular purpose. Put differently, under this theory a trust is a "special-purpose patrimony" (in Spanish, *patrimonio de afectación*) that does not require someone to be its owner, but is sufficient if the desired aim is stated by an instrument. The trustee not being the owner of the properties, not only is he or she unable to use the trust property in his or her own benefit, but also he or she is obliged to use and administer it only for the purpose determined by the grantor. Furthermore, under this theory, the trust patrimony would not be affected by the bankruptcy of the grantor, the trustee, or the beneficiary.

Pierre Lepaulles, who created this theory, explained that "if the need of a patrimony and an affectation are essential conditions for the creation and the life of a trust, we cannot escape to the conclusion that: the trust is an affected patrimony. . . . Trust is a legal institution that consists in a patrimony independent of any person and whose cohesion derives from an affectation freely made within the law and the public policy."[8]

Although this was a major advancement and the basis for the current explanation of trusts in civil-law tradition countries, this theory did not describe the legal status of the trust patrimony that was owned (in trust property) by the trustee. It was not a patrimony without owner, and this was rejected by the Mexican legislator and was not receipted by the rest of the Latin American laws.

## 4. Theory of the Trustee's Special-Purpose Patrimony[9]

This theory was the result of the evolution of the theories described above, was the one adopted by most scholars to explain the concept of trust, and best fits trust regulations in Latin America.

The unholder patrimony theory was criticized because this theory held that the existence of a patrimony always required a holder. It stated that the existence of several patrimonies was possible, but always with a person as the owner of all of them.

These theorists believed that the trust was a special kind of patrimony. This patrimony was the total mass of existing and potential rights that belonged to a person (trustee) and tended to a specific purpose in benefit of a third person (beneficiary). This was not the "ordinary" patrimony of the trustee (the trustee's own estate) but a "trust patrimony," a separated patrimony that had an objective, a purpose: it is a special-purpose patrimony.[10] The trust instrument created a special-purpose patrimony. The principle of unity (in Spanish, *univocidad*) of the patrimony of continental law

---

8   Pierre Lepaulle, Tratado Teórico Práctico de los Trusts: En Derecho Interno, En Derecho Fiscal y en Derecho Internacional 23–24 (1975).

9   In Spanish, *patrimonio de afectación*.

10  Relating to the different denominations used by the doctrine and laws to refer to the trust patrimony, the terms "autonomous" (in Spanish, *autónomo*), "for a destiny" (in Spanish, *de destino*), "separate" (in Spanish, *separado*) are used without much distinction. Nevertheless, complete identity seems not to exist among all the mentioned categories. They vary in the level of independence between the "ordinary" patrimony of the trustee, in relation to the trust patrimony. In the laws of different countries of Latin America that adopted the trust, they have been named in different ways. For example, in Mexico and Honduras, they use affected assets (in Spanish, *bienes afectos*); in Colombia and Costa Rica, separate or autonomous patrimonies.

stated that every person had a patrimony, and that every patrimony belonging to a person was broken. A trustee could have as many patrimonies as trust agreements he or she held.

A trust patrimony differed from the trustee's estate, because it was under a determined mandate to be used for a special purpose. In other words, the trustee's ordinary patrimony was not subject to any mandate or assignment, but each trust patrimony was under a special assignment that is different from the rest of the patrimonies. This mandate or assignment is the key to identifying and differentiating trust patrimonies.

Likewise it was affirmed that for this patrimony to be a "separate patrimony" it was an essential condition that an Act is passed to establish this kind of patrimony as the object of a special treatment. Most of the Latin American jurisdictions follow this theory and have special trusts acts passed by its parliaments.

It should be noted that as the trust patrimony is separated from the ordinary patrimony of the trustee, any liability that arises in relation to one patrimony does not affect the other. This principle was also established in most Latin American laws. Put differently, as the trust property is a separated patrimony, it cannot be executed by the trustee's or grantor's creditors.

The existence of a trust property is essential for the existence of a trust.[11] The trust implies a relation between the trustee and the trust property in benefit of a third party (the beneficiary).[12] As to the nature of trust ownership, this is an "imperfect" one.[13]


## 5. Trust Agreement, Trust Property, and Special-Purpose Patrimony

In short, under Latin American law, the term "trust" refers to:

a. A contract or a will (trust instrument by which property interests are vested in the trustee)
b. A special-purpose patrimony (affected to the fulfillment of a special purpose and which has the trustee as the owner) that is constituted by the assets under trust property
c. The trust property, an *in rem* right

The interaction of these three concepts is the following: The trust agreement involves the transfer of ownership on certain assets from the grantor to a special-purpose

---

11  Same solution under U.S. law: A trust cannot be created unless a trust property exists.

12  Same solution under U.S. law. *Cf.* 1 American Law Institute, Restatement of the Law Second, Trusts 191 (1959).

13  Property can be divided into two species: perfect and imperfect ownership. Perfect or ordinary ownership can be characterized as the perpetual real right of one person over a thing. Imperfect ownership is subordinated to last only until the occurrence of a resolutory condition, or until the expiration of a period, but regarding the transfer of a thing to a third party. Indeed, fiduciary ownership is imperfect property not only because it is subject to a time limit, but also because the trustee is subject to the express limitations emerging from the contract and to the implied limitations emerging from the object of the trust.

patrimony that is owned by the trustee, and simultaneously, the creation of a personal right in favor of the beneficiary, whose obligor is the trustee as owner of the said special-purpose patrimony.

## C. COMPARISON OF ANGLO-SAXON AND LATIN AMERICAN TRUSTS

### 1. Common-Law and Civil-Law Traditions[14]

The following points should be considered when comparing common-law and civil-law traditions in those aspects that are relevant to trust law:

a. The continental law never had a separation similar to the one that existed between common law and equity.
b. The role of judges in common law as "law-maker" as compared to the role of judges in civil law as "law-finder"—Merryman explained that

> The system of checks and balances that has emerged in the United States places no special emphasis on isolating the judiciary, and it proceeds from a philosophy different from that which produced the sharp separation of powers customarily encountered in the [c]ivil [l]aw world. It is important to emphasize this point and to understand why this was the case. In France the judicial aristocracy were targets of the Revolution not only because of their tendency to identify with the landed aristocracy, but also because of their failure to distinguish very clearly between applying law and making law. . . . In the United States and England, on the contrary, there was a different kind of judicial tradition, one [in] which judges had often been a progressive force on the side of the individual against the abuse of power by the ruler, and had played an important part in the centralization of governmental power and the destruction of feudalism. . . . The legislative power is by definition the lawmaking power, and hence only the legislature could make law. . . . The result of all this is that the accepted theory of sources of law in the civil tradition recognizes only statutes, regulations and customs as sources of law. This listing is exclusive. It is also arranged in descending order of authority. A statute prevails over a contrary regulation. Both a statute and a regulation prevail over an inconsistent custom.[15]

c. Continental law is based on statutes (i.e., codes regulate by statute all the relevant issues on certain matters, such as the Civil Code, the Commercial Code, the Mining

---

14      For a comparison of both systems of law see MERRYMAN, *supra* note 1, at 3–4. The author explained that "the civil law tradition is both the oldest and the most widely distributed. The traditional date of its origin is 450 B.C., the supposed date of publication of the XII Tables in Rome. . . . The date commonly used to mark the beginning of the common law tradition is A.D. 1066, when the Normans defeated the defending natives at Hastings and conquered England."

15      MERRYMAN, *supra* note 1, at 15–16, 23–24.

Code, etc.) and on the interpretation made by scholars and professors.[16] On the common-law system, Calvi and Coleman, expressed that "today's practitioners, laypersons, and judges routinely use codes, such as the Internal Revenue Code or the Penal Code, but they use them primarily as references or collections of statutes; the interpretation of the statutes is left to the judicial and administrative branches. Some of the codes are merely reenactments of judicially established rules, such as the various codes of criminal and civil procedures and the Uniform Commercial Code. . . . Nevertheless, judges remain the most potent and powerful component of the American legal systems."[17] Although not completely impossible, it is not to be expected that trusts are created or substantially ruled by court decisions in civil-law countries if there is no express statutory trust regulation[18] as commented on below.

d. As a general rule, no punitive damages could be imposed under most Latin American countries.[19]

## 2. Latin American and U.S. Trusts

To summarize, the main differences between Latin American and U.S. trusts are:

a. Trusts in Latin America are mainly business[20] and guarantee trusts, whereas in the United States, most practitioners consider trusts as an institution in the field of gratuitous transfers.[21] This seems to be a huge difference, but taking into account

---

16   "The teacher-scholar is the real protagonist of the civil law tradition. The civil law is a law of professors. By the way of contrast, although the influence of law professors and legal scholarship may be growing in the United States, judges still exercise the most important influence in shaping the growth and development of the American legal system." MERRYMAN, *supra* note 1, at 56–57.

    All Latin American Codes are the work of scholars such as the Argentine scholar Dalmacio Vélez Sársfield, who drafted the 1869 Argentine Civil Code (still in force, albeit with several amendments) or the Venezuelan jurist Andrés Bello (born in Caracas, died in Chile), who drafted the Chilean Civil Code of 1855 that was adopted by Ecuador in 1861 with minor amendments. RICARDO D. RABINOVICH-BERKMAN, PRINCIPIOS GENERALES DEL DERECHO LATINOAMERICANO 209 (2006).

17   JAMES V. CALVI & SUSAN COLEMAN, AMERICAN LAW AND LEGAL SYSTEMS 35 (4th ed. 2000).

18   The best example of the importance of Codes in Latin America is the huge effort made by Brazil to enact its new and unified Civil and Commercial Code, which replaced the previous 1916 Code and several Acts on particular matters. The new Brazilian Civil Code (Act No. 10.406 of January 10, 2002) entered into force on January 11, 2003, and it was drafted by a commission headed by the prestigious Brazilian jurist Miguel Reale.

19   One exception is the Argentine Consumers Protection Law No. 24.240 § 52 bis (as amended) that provides that the judge may impose punitive damages.

20   Schemes such as the Massachusetts Trusts.

21   John H. Langbein explained that "[i]n the culture of Anglo-American law, we think of the trust as a branch of the law of gratuitous transfers. That is where we teach trusts in the law school curriculum, that is where we locate trusts in the statute books, and that is where American lawyers typically encounter the trust in their practice. The trust originated at the end of the

that several states have business trust acts, the difference is not so large. Testamentary trusts are almost unknown in Latin America (mainly because of forced heirship rules), whereas they are widespread in the United States.

b. As the Latin American continental law never had a separation similar to the one that existed between common law and equity, it is simply impossible to consider the Latin American trust as a relationship under which a beneficiary has a right "in equity" or equivalent. Furthermore, the rule in civil-law tradition is that *jus in rem* can only be created by law. In other words, if there is no statute that provides the existence of trust property, such a concept cannot be created by agreement between parties. From a practical perspective the trust generates a division of the property in the formal ownership of the trustee (or legal title) and benefits flowing hence (or beneficial interest) in the hands of the beneficiary. Along these lines, the beneficiary is the person who is entitled to the economic benefits emerging from the trust assets. From a legal perspective, the trustee is the owner of real right of fiduciary or trust property, and the beneficiary is the holder of a personal right to a credit against the trustee acting as such.

c. The only form of trust contemplated by the Latin American trust statutes is the express trust (which in several countries must be a written instrument). No implied trust is ruled by trust acts in Latin America and, as the Latin American trust experience is not as rich and evolved as it is in the United States, there is no such thing as the case law creation of implied trusts or other kind or trusts. This has to be compared with paragraph 407 of the Uniform Trust Code, which provides that "except as required by a statute other than this [Code], a trust need not be evidenced by a trust instrument, but the creation of an oral trust and its terms may be established only by clear and convincing evidence."

d. The Uniform Trust code allows the trust in favor of an animal (*in re* Trust for Care of Animal 408), which would not be valid under most Latin American laws.

---

Middle Ages as a mean of transferring wealth within the family, and the trust remains our characteristic divide for organizing intergenerational wealth transmission when the transferor has substantial assets or complex family affairs . . . *The Restatement (Second) of Trusts*, the most authoritative exposition of American trust law, exemplifies our tradition of thinking about the trust exclusively as a branch of the law of gratuitous transfers. Austin W. Scott, the reporter, excluded commercial trusts from the Restatement on the ground that "many of the rules" of trust law are inapplicable in commercial settings. Scot offered no support for that claim, which is mistaken. The familiar standards of trust fiduciary law protect trust beneficiaries of all sorts, regardless of whether the trust implements a gift or a business deal (unless, of course, the terms of the transaction expressly contraindicates). Indeed, one of the great attractions of the trust for the transaction planner who is designing a business deal is the convenience of being able to absorb these standards into the ground rules for the deal, merely by invoking the trust label. . . . My theme in this [e]ssay is that the American legal intellectual tradition, which characterizes the trust as a branch of the law of gratuitous transfers, is at odds with the reality of American trust practice. In truth, most of the wealth that is held in trust in the United States is placed there incident to business deals, and not in connection with gratuitous transfers. It will be seen that well over 90 percent of the money held in trust in the United States is in commercial trusts as opposed to personal trusts." John H. Langbein, *The Secret Life of Trust: The Trust as an Instrument of Commerce*, 107 YALE L.J. 166 (1997–1998).

e. The Uniform Trust Code 602(a) establishes that "unless the terms of a trust expressly provide that the trust is irrevocable, the settlor may revoke or amend the trust." Latin American law provides that for *inter vivos* trusts, the rule is that they are irrevocable unless the settlor expressly reserves the right to revoke the trust. In short, the rule regarding the assumption of the revocability of the trust is exactly the opposite.

f. Another practical difference is that in several countries of Latin America only banks or special purpose companies can be trustees, whereas in the United States the rule is that any person can be trustee.

g. A great difference between the trust model in the United States and in Latin America is that in the United States the general rule is that the settlor can be the trustee. This is because U.S. law permits the creation of a trust by a unilateral act, that is to say, there is no obstacle for the existence of a trust in which the grantor and the trustee are the same person. In Latin America, for example, some jurisdictions, such as Bolivia, Brazil, Chile, and Peru, allow securitization companies, if certain conditions are met, to create trusts in which they are settlors and trustees.[22] Nevertheless, the general rule is that the grantor and the trustee cannot be the same person.

h. The legislation in Latin America does not foresee the protector concept. Nevertheless, the creation of one is not forbidden and, for example, in Mexico, the existence of a "technical committee," whose functions are determined by the grantor, is foreseen by the law. In short, although there are no special provisions in the law regarding protectors, there is no legal obstacle to create this concept in a trust agreement.

i. Finally, many Latin American laws provide in an express and clear fashion that the agreement that created a trust is a contract (nevertheless, this is not the case in all jurisdictions, and there is some debate as to the nature of the trust agreement). Conversely, Langbein explained that U.S. "black letter law has resisted the insight that trusts are contracts. The second *Restatement* of 1959, declares: 'The creation of a trust is conceived of as a conveyance of the beneficial interest in the trust property rather than as a contract.'"[23]

## 3. Sources of the Trust Law in Latin America

Most probably, if a U.S. lawyer is requested by a foreign colleague to provide information on trust regulation in the United States, he or she would send to his or her colleague the Uniform Trust Code, the *Restatement of the Law Third, Trusts,* and several state statutes (which are applicable only to the corresponding jurisdiction),

---

22    In the case of Argentina, although it used to be permitted under certain conditions by the CNV rules (the Argentine equivalent to the SEC rules), these rules were changed, and today there cannot be a settlor that acts as trustee.

23    John H. Langbein, *The Contractarian Basis of the Law of Trusts*, 105 YALE L.J. 628, 660 (1995). As the author explained, the article quoted "sets forth the grounds for understanding the conventional three-party trust as a prevailing contractarian institution. More is at stake in this choice between contract and property formulations of the trust than mere labeling" and that "the modern trust is preeminently a management device for separating ownership and enjoyment; the trust deal sets the terms under which that trustee administers and applies the assets."

the leading cases, and a book on case law. Conversely, if the civil-law practitioner receives the same request most probably his or her foreign colleague would receive one or several books written by scholars that deal with a description of the statues, trust regulations of each country, and the opinion of the scholars on such statutes and regulations. It seems that the common-law and the civil-law lawyers have done something completely different, but in essence both types of lawyers have done the same: They sent the information from the most important sources of trust law in their countries.

In Latin America (civil-law jurisdictions), the sources of the trust law are:

a. Statutes: the civil codes, commercial codes and specific acts.[24]
b. Case law, but only understood as the application of the general rules contained in the statutes to particular cases.[25] Put differently, case law is closer to a clarification of the statutes than an independent source of law.[26]
c. General principles of law—general rules that are usually determined by scholars.
d. Custom, which is only applicable if it does not contravene the previous sources. It is usually used in commercial cases and in some labor cases.
e. Legal doctrine (the work of scholars)—authors are key to understanding the law on trusts in Latin America. They are quoted by courts, and they provide a logical explanation of the other sources of law and elaborate the general principles of law.

## D. THE HAGUE CONVENTION ON THE LAW APPLICABLE TO TRUSTS AND ON THEIR RECOGNITION AND THE LATIN AMERICAN TRUST

The Convention of July 1, 1985, on the Law Applicable to Trusts and on their Recognition entered into force on January 1, 1992, drafted by the Hague Conference on Private International Law.[27] Although Argentina, Brazil, Chile, Ecuador, Mexico, Panama,

---

24  This is the reason every chapter of Part II of this book begins with the description of the applicable statutory law. Furthermore, the key importance of the statutory law determines that if there is no specific law or sections of the civil or commercial codes, as it happens in Nicaragua, no comment will be made on the trust law in that jurisdiction.

25  Therefore, I will summarize the main cases I found in my research.

26  The exception to this rule is the case of Brazilian *Súmulas* described in Chapter 9 on Brazil. Under Brazilian law, a *Súmula* is a summary that records a pacific or majority interpretation made by a court in relation to a particular matter. It has the double purpose of publishing the court criteria and of promoting the uniformity of court decisions. According to § 103-A of the Brazilian Constitution, *Súmulas* issued by the *Supremo Tribunal Federal* are binding for all other courts after their publication in the Official Gazette.

27  The full text of the convention, a complete list of countries that ratified it, and the full list of the members of the Hague Conference on Private International Law can be found at the website of the Hague Conference on Private International Law, *available at* http://www.hcch.net. As explained in the website (as of March 23, 2009) the Hague Conference on Private International Law is an intergovernmental organization, whose purpose is "to work for the progressive unification of the rules of private international law (article 1 of the Statute of the Hague Conference). The principal method used to achieve this goal consists in the negotiation

Paraguay, Peru, Uruguay, and Venezuela are members of the Hague Conference on Private International Law,[28] none of them, nor any other Latin American country, ratified the Convention under analysis. This does not mean that a foreign trust would not be recognized. On the contrary, because of the existence of trust regulations in Latin American countries, the trust would be recognized as a existing and valid legal scheme.

Article 2 of the Convention provides that "for the purposes of this Convention, the term 'trust' refers to the legal relationships created—*inter vivos* or on death—by a person, the settlor, when assets have been placed under the control of a trustee for the benefit of a beneficiary or for a specified purpose. A trust has the following characteristics: (a) the assets constitute a separate fund and are not a part of the trustee's own estate; (b) title to the trust assets stands in the name of the trustee or in the name of another person on behalf of the trustee; (c) the trustee has the power and the duty, in respect of which he is accountable, to manage, employ or dispose of the assets in accordance with the terms of the trust and the special duties imposed upon him by law. The reservation by the settlor of certain rights and powers, and the fact that the trustee may himself have rights as a beneficiary, are not necessarily inconsistent with the existence of a trust."[29] It must be pointed out that the Latin American trust does comply with all these characteristics.

Article 11 of the Convention establishes that the recognition of a trust "shall imply, as a minimum, that the trust property constitutes a separate fund, that the trustee may sue and be sued in his capacity as trustee, and that he may appear or act in this capacity before a notary or any person acting in an official capacity. In so far as the law applicable to the trust requires or provides, such recognition shall imply, in particular: (a) that personal creditors of the trustee shall have no recourse against the trust assets; (b) that the trust assets shall not form part of the trustee's estate upon his insolvency or bankruptcy; (c) that the trust assets shall not form part of the matrimonial property of the trustee or his spouse nor part of the trustee's estate upon his death; (d) that the trust assets may be recovered when the trustee, in breach of trust, has mingled trust assets with his own property or has alienated trust assets. However, the

---

and drafting of multilateral treaties, called 'Hague Conventions.' Between 1893 and 1904 the Conference adopted seven international Conventions, all of which have been subsequently replaced by more modern instruments. From 1951 to 2005 the Conference adopted 36 international Conventions [including the Convention of 1 July 1985 on the Law Applicable to Trusts and on their Recognition]. Until 1960 the Conventions were drafted only in French; since then they have been drawn up in French and English."

28  Regarding the participation of Latin American countries, Alfred E. von Overbeck explained that, among others, experts from Argentina and Venezuela participated in the special commission that adopted the preliminary draft of the Convention, and the government of Argentina made comments on the draft. Additionally, Argentina, Uruguay, and Venezuela sent representatives, and Panama sent an observer, to the fifteenth session of the Hague Conference in which the convention draft was discussed. The Argentine representative was part of the subcommittee in charge of the final clauses. Alfred E. von Overbeck, *Explanatory Report on the 1985 Hague Trusts Convention, in* 2 The Proceedings of the Fifteenth Session (1984): Trusts—Applicable Law and Recognition 371 (1985).

29  Article 2 of the The Convention of July 1, 1985, on the Law Applicable to Trusts and on their Recognition.

rights and obligations of any third party holder of the assets shall remain subject to the law determined by the choice of law rules of the forum."[30] As mentioned before, it is reasonable to think that Latin American judges would recognize trusts as existing and valid legal schemes. Therefore, all the consequences of such recognition would follow. Nevertheless, it seems that the rigid and complex inheritance and matrimonial assets protection rules, most of them considered public policy of the country (not derogable by voluntary act), may impair the recognition that "the trust assets shall not form part of the matrimonial property of the trustee or his spouse nor part of the trustee's estate upon his death." In fact, this situation is contemplated in article 15 of the Convention, which laid down the rule that "the Convention does not prevent the application of provisions of the law designated by the conflicts rules of the forum, in so far as those provisions cannot be derogated by voluntary act, relating in particular to the following matters: (a) the protection of minors and incapable parties; (b) the personal and propri-etary effects of marriage; (c) succession rights, testate and intestate, especially the indefeasible shares of spouses and relatives; (d) the transfer of title to property and security interests in propertythe protection of creditors in matters of insolvency; (f) the protection, in other respects, of third parties acting in good faith. If recognition of a trust is prevented by application of the preceding paragraph, the court shall try to give effect to the objects of the trust by other means." Article 18 provides that "the provisions of the Convention may be disregarded when their application would be manifestly incompatible with public policy (*ordre public*)."

## E. PARTIES TO THE TRUST AGREEMENT

Trusts can be created by will, by an agreement, and in certain particular cases, by the unilateral act of one person acting as settlor and trustee. The trust agreement has been the object of long scholarly controversy, one of the aspects being who the parties of such agreement are.

From a strictly technical point of view, only the grantor and the trustee are parties to the trust agreement. Conversely, although the trust agreement is in the benefit of the beneficiary and the residual beneficiary and in certain jurisdictions they should accept the benefit, they are not parties of the agreement. The trust is created between the grantor and the trustee by the sole act of executing an instrument. That is why there could be up to four possible participants (grantor, trustee, beneficiary, and residual beneficiary), but only two parties (grantor and trustee).

### 1. The Grantor

The grantor is the party who transmits the property of the assets and instructs the trustee to fulfill a purpose related to those assets. The general rule is that the grantor

---

30   Article 11 of the The Convention of July 1, 1985, on the Law Applicable to Trusts and on their Recognition.

only has power of disposition over the trust assets until the moment of the transfer of the trust property. Regarding *inter vivos* trusts, after the manifestation that creates a trust to transfer the property, the power of the grantor over the transferred assets is only historical. That is why the analysis of the grantor's role must be based mainly in his or her capacity to transmit the property and to express his or her will of creating a trust. However, the grantor can break this rule and reserve rights to him or herself; the most important one would be to revoke the trust. Other rights that the grantor can reserve for him or herself are: to add more beneficiaries, to determine the investments the trustee must do, or to have the power of veto in certain decisions. In fact, one of the great advantages of the trust is its versatility and the possibility of creating a special-purpose patrimony that is tailored to the parties, and the faculties of the grantor are no exception to this rule. As a general rule, there is no need to provide in the trust instrument the right of the grantor to require the trustee to render accounts, because it is an obvious consequence of his or her capacity to demand the performance of the task committed to the trustee. Nevertheless, a clear stipulation with a detail of the way it should be done is highly advisable.

As trusts are used as legal vehicles for businesses, it is not surprising that a trust could have several settlors. This situation could be the result of:

a. Several settlors are co-owner of the asset that is transferred to the trust.
b. Several settlors transfer different assets to the trust at the moment of the execution of the trust instrument.
c. The most common case is that in which an initial settlor created the trust executing an agreement with the trustee, and then another settlor adheres to the trust agreement under the terms and conditions established in it.
d. A particular case is the introduction of a new settlor if such a case is not regulated by the trust agreement. As a general rule, this is not possible, and the trustee should reject such a pretension of a third party asking to be a settlor of the trust. Nevertheless, there are situations such as the insolvency of the trust (and therefore the impossibility to accomplish its purposes) that may create an exception to the general rule.

## 2. The Trustee

The other intervening party is the trustee, which is the party who owns the trust property in order to fulfill the purpose established by the grantor. In succeeding sections, the role and characteristics of the trustee in each jurisdiction will be explained. Here the existence of large differences in relation to the possibility of being a trustee in Latin America is explored.

Although it will be explored in detail in Part II, one of the aspects in which there are more differences between U.S. and Latin American trust law is the one related to the persons authorized to act as trustee:

a. In Argentina any person can be trustee, with the exception of: (i) financial trusts, that is, trusts used for securitizations, that require an authorized financial trustee, and (ii) the trustee wanting to make a public offer of his or her services, that requires previous licensing. There is no restriction to be a trustee as long as the trust does not have as its purpose to carry out a securitization, or the trustee does not advertise his or her services.

b. In Belize, any person who has the capacity to own and transfer property can be the trustee of a trust.

c. In Bolivia, only banks can be trustees.

d. In Colombia, only trust companies, which have as their sole activity being trustees and especially authorized by the bank's superintendence can be trustees.

e. In Costa Rica any individual or legal entity capable of acquiring rights and contracting obligations may be a trustee.

f. In Ecuador, only "fund and trust management companies" (*Administradoras de Fondos y Fideicomisos*), and certain government companies: the State Bank (*Banco del Estado*) and the National Finance Corporation (*Corporación Financiera Nacional*) are authorized to act as trustees.

g. In El Salvador only banks or authorized credit institutions may be trustees.

h. In Guatemala only banks established in the country, credit institutions, and "private investment companies" with authorization by the Monetary Committee (*Junta Monetaria*), may become trustees.

i. In Honduras, only authorized banking institutions may act as trustees.

j. In Mexico, only credit institutions can be trustees of any kind of trusts. Insurance companies and stock exchange brokers can only be trustees of trusts whose object is related to their activity. Regarding guarantee trusts, there is broader criteria, and the following can be trustees of guarantee trusts: credit institutions, insurance institutions, bail institutions, stock exchange brokers, financial corporations of multiple object included in the General Organizations and Auxiliary Credit Activities Act section 87-B (*Ley General de Organizaciones y Actividades Auxiliares de Crédito*), general depositaries, and credit unions.

k. In Panama, any natural or legal persons may be trustees. However, the relevant license must be secured if the activity as trustee is pursued professionally.

l. In Paraguay, only specialized departments of banks and corporations with the exclusive purpose of being trustees authorized by the Central Bank of Paraguay may act as trustees.

m. In Peru, only the following are authorized to act as trustees: (i) the *Corporación Financiera de Desarrollo* (COFIDE), a state owned financial institution), (ii) banking companies, financial companies, municipal savings and credit banks, municipal people's credit banks, entities for the development of small- and micro-sized companies (EDPYMEs), savings and credit cooperatives authorized to raise resources from the public, rural savings and credit banks, exchange services companies and funds transfer companies; (iii) fiduciary services companies (corporations that have as sole object and activity to be trustees); and (v) insurance and reinsurance companies.

n. In Uruguay any person can be trustee, with the exception of: (i) financial trusts, that is, trusts used for securitization, which require a financial trustee duly authorized, and (ii) professional trustees (any person who is the trustee of five or more trusts in any calendar year will be considered a professional trustee).

o. In Venezuela, only banking institutions and insurance companies may be trustees if they are granted the corresponding authorization.

In short, the general rule in Latin America is that only specialized companies or banks can be trustees. This is exactly the opposite of the general rule in the United States where any person can be trustee.

## 3. The Beneficiary

The beneficiary, as mentioned earlier, is not a necessary party to the trust agreement, which capacity is represented by the grantor and the trustee. However, taking account of the fact that the trust contract is in the beneficiary's benefit, it would be advisable that he or she signs the trust instrument accepting the advantages flowing from it as well as any obligation that it could impose on him or her.

Only Argentina makes a distinction in its law between the beneficiaries (the one who benefits during the life of the trust) and the residual beneficiary (the one who receives the assets when the trust terminates). All other jurisdictions do not give an specific name to these two parties and simply use the terms "beneficiary" or "residual beneficiary" for both. The sole fact that the law does not establish two different names does not mean that there is a prohibition to create two or more categories of beneficiaries, but any special right should be determined by the trust instrument.

## 4. The Protector

As mentioned when comparing U.S. trusts and Latin American trusts, laws in Latin America do not foresee the concept of protector. Nevertheless, the creation of one is not forbidden and, for example, in Mexico, the existence of a "technical committee" whose functions are determined by the grantor, is foreseen by the law. In short, although there are no special provisions in the law regarding protectors, there is no legal obstacle to create this concept in a trust instrument.

As mentioned before, the grantor can reserve for him or herself several rights. Furthermore, the grantor can stipulate in the trust instrument that these rights will be exercised by a third party, someone he or she appoints who deserves his or her confidence. This is particularly important in jurisdictions in which the trustee can only be a bank, because this allows the settlor to have a natural person to control the trust.

## 5. Coexistence of Various Roles in the Same Person

a. *Grantor-Beneficiary* In this type of trust, the person transferring the assets and creating the trust (the grantor) and the person receiving the benefits of the trust assets (the beneficiary) is the same person. It is possible to ask, then, why the trust ownership is transferred to a third party if the economic benefit of the transferred assets will be retained.

Although several possible reasons exist, the most common ones are the wish for a professional administration of the assets and the possibility of gathering several parts under one secure legal structure that enables carrying out a given common project.

The typical example of grantor-beneficiary trusts in Latin America is to be found in the case of small- or medium-size construction projects. An example could be as follows: One of the parties transfers a parcel of land in trust to a trustee, constituting a trust in which the incorporation of other grantors is contemplated. The transfer of the parcel of land is in exchange for the right as beneficiary and residual beneficiary to a part of the income of the project. Another person contributes the execution of the construction, a third person contributes cash, and a fourth contributes the service of sale of the units to be built. The trustee receives the contributions in trust from all the grantors and carries out the construction which, once finished, will permit the sale of the units. When the execution of the project is terminated, the grantors will receive the net amount from the sales in the proportion originally agreed on (generally in proportion to their contributions).

The trusts with grantors-beneficiaries are far more flexible than corporations because they permit, among other features, the distribution of different powers to the trustees, for example, in the form of the creation of a committee for trustee control or one which the trustee should consult with regard to certain subjects (i.e., the indebtedness of the trust above a certain amount or with a certain purpose). In the case of a corporation, functions do not admit modifications. Additionally, the constitution and liquidation procedures of corporations could prove too rigid and costly for a single project. Furthermore, in certain jurisdictions trusts are pass-through entities for tax purposes.

*b. Grantor-Trustee (Declaration of Trust)* As mentioned before, one difference between the trust model in the United States and Latin America is that in the United States the general rule is that the settlor can be the trustee. This is because U.S. law permits the creation of a trust by a unilateral act; that is to say, there is no obstacle for the existence of a trust in which the grantor and the trustee are the same person.

In Latin America, some jurisdictions, such as Bolivia, Brazil, Chile, and Peru, allow securitization companies, if certain conditions are met, to create trusts in which they are settlors and trustees.[31] Nevertheless, the general rule is that the grantor and the trustee cannot be the same person.

---

31  In the case of Argentina, although it used to be permitted under certain conditions by the CNV rules (the Argentine equivalent to the SEC rules), these rules have been changed, and today there cannot be a settlor that acts as trustee. At first, the regulations of the CNV (General Resolution No. 271/95) acknowledged the trust by unilateral act, so long as they obtained the authorization to place the securities to be issued by means of a public offering. Nevertheless, arising from the scholarly criticism generated by this method, the CNV sanctioned Resolution No. 296/97 (Official Gazette, August. 26, 1997); § 1 imposed the current wording. Thus, the current CNV regulations read: "No trusts by unilateral act shall be created, these being those where the persons of the grantor and the beneficiary merge. The unilateral trusts in existence today, and those with participation certificates and/or debt securities already issued, may continue until the lapse of the periods for which they have been authorized in each case. Two cases were reported under the previous regulations of banks which employed this mechanism,

*c. Trustee-Beneficiary* In Latin America it is possible for the grantor to be one of or the only one of the beneficiaries. Nevertheless, there are restrictions relating to the possibility of being trustee and beneficiary. In this sense, not only in the United States, but also in Latin America in general (with the exception of the particular cases below), the only trustee of a trust cannot be the only beneficiary of the trust.

The explanation under Latin American law for the aforementioned prohibition is that if a person has the formal property as well as the economic benefit of the property, there is no trust, because there is no separation of both items. It cannot be sustained that a person has the trust property in favor of him or herself because it would be the same as saying that he or she has duties with him or herself. If he or she has the property of the assets without being tied to any limit, there is no trust. Some countries consider that such a situation would lead to a null and void trust (e.g., Mexico and Paraguay), others rule that although he or she was appointed beneficiary, the trustee would not benefit from the trust (Costa Rica), and others rule that the trust is terminated (Panama).

In general, Latin American Laws prohibit one person from being the trustee and the beneficiary of a trust, excepting guarantee trusts, for example in Argentina[32], Brazil, Mexico[33] and Uruguay (if the trustee is a bank).

## F. CREATION AND TERMINATION OF TRUSTS

### 1. Ways of Creation of Trusts

In Latin America (as in the United States) the trust can be created by means of:

a. A declaration of the property's owner having the trust property in favor of a third person. In this case a trust would be created by a unilateral act (an act executed by one party only), without the transfer of the property to a third person. It has already been pointed out that this situation is related to certain particular cases that only

---

generating trusts in which they acted as grantors and trustees, the holders of the trust securities issued being the beneficiaries."

32  As there is no express rule, it is a matter of discussion if in a guarantee trust the trustee can be the beneficiary of the guarantee. There have been court decisions in relation to guarantee trusts in which the trustee was the beneficiary of the guarantee, and the courts did not declare the trust null and void. In Argentina, the law expressly prohibits the trustee from being the residual beneficiary, but it does not provide a rule regarding the situation of the trustee who is beneficiary (and not a residual beneficiary). It must be considered that Argentine law is the sole one in Latin America that distinguishes between the beneficiary (the one who gets the profits of the property during the existence of the trust) and the residual beneficiary (the one who receives the property at the end of the trust). However, it is understood that, with the exception of guarantee trusts, the trustee cannot be the sole beneficiary.

33  The trustees of guarantee trusts can be at the same time beneficiaries of the trust if the trust has as its purpose to guarantee credits of the trustee. In such a case, the parties must agree to the terms and conditions to settle possible interest conflicts.

occur in some Latin American countries, under certain very special conditions (securitization trusts).

b. A transfer *inter vivos* by the owner of a property to some other person such as the trustee in benefit of the same grantor or of a third person. This case is the most traditional of the trust agreements and the most used in Latin America.

c. The transfer by the will of the owner of a property to another person as a trustee in benefit of a third one. The testamentary trust is specifically foreseen in the majority of the Latin American laws. Although this point will be commented on in more detail when dealing with the classification of trusts, it can be advanced that this kind of trust is subject to the formalities of wills and can have a bigger or smaller development depending on the degree of forced heirship existing in that country.[34]

## 2. Causes of Termination of Trusts

Considering the causes of termination of trusts in each country, it can be concluded that the major causes for the termination of trusts in Latin America are as follows:

*a. Accomplishment or Complete Impossibility of Accomplishment of the Purposes of the Trust* If it is considered that a trust is a special-purpose patrimony, it is obvious that the accomplishment or the complete impossibility to accomplish the purposes of the trust would mean that the trust is senseless and must be terminated.

An example of complete impossibility of accomplishment of the trust purposes is the complete loss of the trust assets. These cases are rare, and in most cases, if the trust instrument is not clear on who must determine the impossibility, give rise to a debate over whether the impossibility is total or partial, or even if it exists at all.

*b. The Agreement between the Grantor and the Beneficiary* If the person who created the trust and the person who receives its benefits agree to terminate the trust, there is no reason to object to such an agreement. The sole caveat to this rule is that the trustee has the right to receive a fee during the life of the trust, and he or she has a right to receive a compensation for the reduction of the duration of these services.

*c. Expiration of Period or Fulfillment of Condition* A trust can be terminated owing to the expiration of its period, the fulfillment of the resolutory condition to which it has been subjected, or the lapse of the maximum legal period (which is usually between twenty and thirty years, with Mexico as the country with the longest maximum period of fifty years).

If the stipulated resolutory condition has not occurred once the maximum legal term has elapsed, it is reasonable to consider it accomplished for all legal purposes.

---

34  It should be considered that there are countries such as Argentina where 80 percent of the assets are a forced portion of the issue. Therefore, little room is left for wills and/or testamentary trusts.

*d. Revocation by the Grantor* The trust will be terminated by the revocation of the settlor if he or she expressly reserved that power.[35] There are two possible solutions regarding the effects of the revocation: It can be retroactive, so that the acts carried out by the trustee are subject to the condition that the trust is not revoked, or it can have no retroactive effects, and the acts carried out by the trustee are still valid despite the revocation.

In testamentary trusts, by virtue of the fact that it is dealing with a last will disposition only effective subsequent to the testator's death, and that the transfer of assets would not take place until that time, the will could be revoked and render the future creation of the trust ineffective despite the fact that such a power had not been provided in the trust instrument. Wills are essentially revocable acts, and this condition does not change although the will provides the creation of a testamentary trust.

*e. Insufficiency of the Trust Assets* The insufficiency of the trust assets for the satisfaction of obligations is a cause of impossibility to accomplish the trust purposes that is ruled in detail by several jurisdictions. Absent other remedies provided by the settlor or the beneficiary according to trust provisions, liquidation of the trust assets will be effected by the trustee.

The experience during the financial crisis that affected several business trusts is that if the project that is being carried out by the trust is an interesting one for investors, there will be the possibility to include new settlors. As this will mean changing the conditions of the previous settlors-beneficiaries, their consent would be necessary. From a practical perspective, it is wise to rule this case in the trust instrument to avoid discussions at such a critical moment (i.e., lack of funds and uncooperative settlors-beneficiaries that are dealing with several urgent issues as a result of a crisis).

The rule has an obvious rationale, if there are no means to accomplish the trust objectives, there is no reason for the existence of the trust.

*f. Legal Actions by Creditors of the Settlor* All Latin American countries have anti-fraud provisions that provide that should there be a transfer of assets by a grantor with a view to injure one or several of his or her creditors, such creditors may require the revocation of the contracts or agreements carried out by the debtor, which injure or defraud his or her rights. In other words, if a trust is created by a settlor with the purpose of injuring his or her creditors, such trust in invalid and can be terminated by a judge.

To exercise the antifraud legal proceeding the usual requisites are:

a. The debtor is insolvent. This standing is presumed from the time he or she files for bankruptcy.
b. The injury to the creditors results from the very act of the debtor, or that he or she was insolvent before.

---

35    I refer to the comparison between the U.S. trust and the Latin American trust in relation to the existence of the inverse criteria in the Uniform Trust Code of the United States.

c. The credit, by virtue of which the action is started, dates back before the debtor's act. This condition will not be required in the case of dispositions previous to a slaying, which aim at preventing the murderer from facing liability with his or her own property.

Some jurisdictions state that the revocation of the trust transfers carried out by the debtor will only be in the interest of the creditors who had requested it and for the amount of their credits. Therefore, the whole trust is not considered null and void but just "inexistent" in relation to the creditors who were successful obtaining the anti-fraud measures. Nevertheless, the general effect is that once the transfer to the trustee is qualified by the court as "a fraudulent act by the debtor," it is revoked, and the properties transferred to the trust by the debtor must be returned to his or her patrimony.

The intent of the debtor to defraud his or her creditors by means of acts to their detriment is presumed from his or her insolvency. The complicity of a third party in the fraud of the debtor is also presumed if the former was in knowledge of his or her standing at the time of dealing.

If the insolvent's act injuring the creditors was of a gratuitous nature (charity), it may be revoked at their request, even when the person to whom those assets had passed was not in knowledge of the debtor's insolvency. Instead, if the creditors' action was directed against an onerous act by the debtor (e.g., a sale), it is requisite for the revocation of the act that the debtor intended by that means to defraud his or her creditors, and that the third person with whom he or she contracted was a party to the fraud. These regulations must be considered in relation to the trust transfers according to the ultimate object sought. Put differently, although the trust transfer is not technically speaking of a gratuitous or onerous character, it is reasonable to interpret that if there is no compensation for the grantor, the rules applicable to gratuitous acts must be applied and, should the grantor receive a compensation, those applicable to onerous acts must be applied.

If the trustee transfers the trust assets to a third party, the creditors' action will only be permissible:

a. If the transfer has been carried out gratuitously; or
b. If it was in exchange for consideration, if the purchaser had taken part in the fraud.

On the subject of the effects of the insolvency by the grantor on the trust transfer, although many legislations do not expressly address this issue, it is safe to assume that trust transfers should probably not be an exception to the provisions of the Bankruptcy Act that provides that the following are ineffective with respect to creditors after the insolvency is declared:

a. Gratuitous acts
b. Anticipated payment of debts
c. The mortgage, pledge, lien, or any other guarantee or preference with respect to outstanding obligations that originally did not enjoy that security

*g. The Sole Trustee Being the Sole Beneficiary* As explained before, if the sole trustee is the sole beneficiary, a trust has not been established, but it is instead ordinary ownership. Nevertheless, this rule has the exception of the guarantee trust, in which the sole trustee (a creditor of the settlor) could be the sole beneficiary of the guarantee. It can be argued that it is not an exception to the principle because usually the settlor of a guarantee trust is the residual beneficiary of the trust assets in case he or she fulfills the obligation guaranteed by the trust.

*h. As a Result of Death or Legal Incapacity of the Trustee Declared by a Judge Unless the Trust Instrument Appoints a Substitute Trustee* This is a particular rule of Uruguay that does not have a counterpart in other Latin American regulations. Other Latin American laws rule that the incapability of the trustee to continue acting as such simply means that the trust assets are transferred to another trustee, and the trust is not affected.

It is assumed that if the trustee is an individual, unless the substitution of the trustee is expressly regulated in the trust instrument, the trustee is essential for the trust. Therefore, if the trustee dies or his or her legal incapacity is declared, the trust is terminated. As an obvious conclusion, in Uruguay, if an individual is appointed as trustee, his or her replacement must be ruled in the trust instrument to avoid that his or her death or declaration of legal incapacity frustrates the objectives of the trust.

## 3. Effects of the Termination of the Trust

After trust termination, the trustee will be under an obligation to deliver the trust assets to the beneficiary or to his or her successors. In practice the delivery of the assets takes several days, and in the case of trusts with major and diverse assets, even months. For example, if several real estate properties were transferred, a long period would be necessary to carry out the delivery because registration of the new owner must be complied with at the relevant registry.[36]

The trustee is under an obligation to close the trust dealings on hand with due diligence and cannot interrupt his or her activity abruptly. This entails that the trust assets would continue to be a separate patrimony until delivery of the assets to the residual beneficiaries designated in the trust contract is effected, so that the trustee remains bound to the proper administration of the trust.

Where the trust has expired and the trustee entertains doubts as to the scope of his or her duties (i.e., acceptance of payment of a credit with reduction or grace period), it would be appropriate to seek advice from the residual beneficiary, who is the person entitled to the assets. If such directions are not forthcoming within a reasonable period, the trustee should act in accordance with the general standards of the pertinent line of business.

---

36    In certain countries the law expressly established that actual transfer is not required for the trustee to convey the ownership of the trust assets because it is automatic at the end of the trust.

## G. RESPONSIBILITY, RIGHTS, AND DUTIES OF THE TRUSTEE

### 1. Executing All the Necessary Actions to Accomplish the Trust Purposes

The basic and obvious obligation of the trustee is to carry out the settlor's instruction, that is, to do his or her best to fulfill the trust purposes. From this duty, several others derive. The trustee cannot sell or encumber the trust assets beyond the purposes of the trust. In other words, the trustee may dispose or encumber the trust assets when the trust instrument allows him or her, without the trustee or the beneficiary's consent being necessary, unless agreement to the contrary. Where the assets were disposed of or encumbered beyond the powers granted in the contract or without the appropriate consent, the trustee would be incurring civil and criminal responsibility.[37]

One of the trustee's primary responsibilities is to protect and defend the trust assets because trust assets are essential to accomplish the trust purposes. As with the trustee's liabilities for damages to third parties, the trustee must evaluate which protection steps, both de facto and de jure, are appropriate according to the type of assets. Regarding de facto steps, the trustee must have an appropriate insurance policy and/or derived agreements covering the other risks that could affect the trust assets. Regarding the legal protection of the assets, the trustee is empowered to exercise all the acts necessary for the defense of the trust assets, both against third parties and against the beneficiary. The court may authorize the grantor or the beneficiary to start actions in lieu of the trustee, when the latter did not do so in time, and there are no sufficient grounds for the delay or omission.

The trustee could defend the trust assets against the beneficiary because the latter is entitled to nothing except a right to receive certain considerations stated in the trust instrument, but is not entitled to the trust assets directly.

### 2. Diligence of a Good Businessperson, Good Paterfamilias, or Diligent Administrator

In addition to the provisions of the trust instrument, which usually indicates the rights and duties of the trustee, Latin American laws provide that the trustee must conform with the duties imposed by statute or the trust instrument and the law, with the prudence and diligence of a good businessperson, a good paterfamilias, or a diligent administrator acting by virtue of the confidence reposed on him or her.

There is no definition of good businessperson,[38] good paterfamilias, or diligent administrator, but there are general rules of prudence and due diligence. They are

---

37    Where assets are acquired from trustees, it is strictly necessary to read the trust contract in detail to ensure that they is not acting beyond their powers (*ultra vires*).

38    Case law has established that "the yardstick of conduct assessment . . . 'diligence of the good businessman,' imposes the forecasting of happenings which are not unusual within the context of the activity in question according to common experience." National Commercial Court of Appeal of Buenos Aires-Argentina [CNCom. Room D], 9/9/1995, "Estancias Procreo Vacunos S.A. v. Lenzi," (Arg.).

special standards higher than the one applicable to an ordinary person. Not surprisingly, the standard is similar to the criteria emerging from paragraph 804 of the Uniform Trust Code, which provides that "a trustee shall administer the trust as a prudent person would, by considering the purposes, terms, distributional requirements, and other circumstances of the trust. In satisfying this standard, the trustee shall exercise reasonable care, skill, and caution. Furthermore, paragraph 806 of the Uniform Trust Code states a rule that would also be applicable to Latin American trustees when it provides that "a trustee who has special skills or expertise, or is named trustee in reliance on the trustee's representation that the trustee has special skills or expertise, shall use those special skills or expertise."[39] Obviously, the standard is not the same for a professional trustee as a trustee who has no special qualification.

One of the essential duties under the umbrella term of "the good businessperson" is the requirement to act with transparency, that is, the trustee must be able to offer a clear account and rationale of his or her deeds. This duty is best illustrated by the duty to render accounts and performance reports, and by the necessity to rely on documented professional assistance to back the trustee's decisions in technical matters. Several specialists must be called on (e.g., legal and fiscal advisors), and it is necessary to have formal written opinions to document the reasons the trustee deems relevant.

The trustee's diligence is measured relative to the performance of the grantor instructions, the aim the grantor has in sight at the time of the agreement. Therefore, it is of the utmost importance that this aim be stated clearly to avert undesired situations. The trust, depending on the type of assets transferred and the object sought for them, may involve a mere guardianship or preservation of assets or an active transaction. This is not foreign to accounting—in the first instance it will suffice to show that the assets have been preserved, whereas in the second, the criteria followed in the conduct of the business transaction must be indicated in detail. Accounting and its significance in relation to the trustee's liability will be examined further below.

It should be pointed out that it is common practice to include clauses in the trust instruments stating that, in the event of doubt, the trustee may and must seek direction and, where an answer is not obtained within a reasonable period, he or she will not be liable for any omission to act. The significance of this type of clause is revealed if the fact is considered that the trustee receives a compensation far inferior to the amount of the assets he or she administers and, therefore, of the responsibility he or she assumes. As a result, it is essential for the trustee to reduce the risks relating to the transaction and associated with the resolution of unforeseen situations for his or her activity to be economically viable.

The situation of the trustee in the event of doubt is different depending on the country:

a. In some Latin American countries, the trustee is subject to the legal obligation to request instructions from a judge or an administrative authority.
b. In other countries, such as Mexico, a special committee that provides advice to the trustee (and he or she has no responsibility if he or she acts based on such advise) is ruled by law.

---

39    Uniform Trust Code, Article 8 "Duties and Powers of Trustee," ¶ 806.

c. Finally, other countries do not expressly provide that trustees should resort to third parties, such as official control bodies, or a technical committee as in Mexico, for them to make the decisions in unforeseen cases, thus freeing the trustee from liability for the consequences of such acts.

Finally, the trust instrument may not exempt the trustee from the liability or tort that either him or herself or his or her subordinates (such as employees) could incur. The trustee is liable either if the damage is the result of his or her involuntary tortuous acts (i.e., negligent, reckless, or ignorant of the matters he or she should necessarily know) or if it is voluntarily tortuous, that is, with intent to injure.

## 3. Adequate Identification of Trust Assets and Rendering of Accounts

Another aspect relating to the proper performance of the trustee's duties is the strict requirement to maintain the trust assets separately. This duty materializes in the keeping of separate accounts, duly recorded and, according to the amount or type of assets, audited by qualified professionals. Most laws set forth that any record relating to trust assets in a balance sheet must indicate the trust character of the property with the rubric "in trust" (*en fideicomiso*).

The trust instrument may not dispense the trustee from the duty to render accounts, which may be requested by the beneficiary; in all cases the trustees must render accounts to the beneficiaries with a periodicity not in excess of one year (in some countries the maximum period is six months).

The trust instrument could include the duty to render accounts in favor of other interested parties, or even third parties. Nevertheless, the grantor is entitled to request accountings even when this has not been provided in the trust instrument because it is in his or her power to remove the trustee in the face of poor performance of his or her duties, or to be summoned in the event that such a request is made by the beneficiary. Also, in most cases, it would not be viable to claim reasons of privacy or commercial confidentiality to deny the grantor the required accounting, as he or she is the one who gave rise to the trust assets and stipulated their object.

The trustee should receive the assets clearly identified in the trust instrument, which entails the need for an initial inventory. In addition, it is essential to keep accounts and, where the amounts involved or the activity carried out warrants it, to have an independent outside audit, according to the market's common practices. This is further proven by the fact that accounts are of the essence when dealing with amounts of money, which cannot be otherwise identified.

## 4. Trustee's Liability for Trust Debt

Because of the nature of the special-purpose patrimony, the trustee's assets cannot be reached for the obligations incurred in performance of the trust, which may only be satisfied with the trust assets. The sole exception to this rule is tax liability. It is essential that the trustee always state that he or she is acting in his or her capacity as such, so that his or her own estate is not involved. Should the situation lend itself to confusion, the other party to the agreement could intend to reach the trustee's own personal property.

## 5. Trust Secret and Criminal Responsibility

An essential duty is that of loyalty to the confidence placed in the trustee and the duty to honor the confidentiality of commercial or personal information that has been entrusted him or her or which he or she has obtained in the performance of his or her duties. The statement is clear that the trustee is under the rule of professional confidentiality, a violation of which represents a criminal offense, apart from the civil liability for the damages incurred.[40] Few countries provide specific criminal offense regulations for unfaithful trustees (e.g., Argentina[41] and Paraguay), but all Latin American countries have criminal rules that may be applicable to such cases.

## 6. Trustee's Fees and Reimbursement of Expenses

Except for express stipulation to the contrary in the trust agreement, the trustee is entitled to the reimbursement of expenditures and to a fee. If that was not fixed in the trust instrument, it will be fixed by the court in taking account of the nature of the grantor instructions and the importance of the duties to be performed.

It is common practice in several countries to stipulate in the trust instruments a fee based on a percentage of the assets, together with some variable compensation linked to the success or the importance of the duties performed. An initial setup fee could also be granted for the special duties required by the trust's start-up.

This is one of the key aspects of trust contract drafting and one that has been the cause of many controversies. It is crucial to determine the calculation basis,

---

40 It should be noted that that is the general rule.
41 Section 173 of the Argentine Criminal Code subsection 12, which refers to: "the trustee . . . who in his own benefit or that of a third party encumbered, disposed of or otherwise acted to the detriment of the assets and thus defrauded the rights of the cosigners." Thus, the grantor, the beneficiary, and the residual beneficiary are protected from the possibility of the trustee disposing fraudulently of the assets subject to the agreement. The term "cosigners" is construed in the sense of all those directly interested or participating in the agreement, and not in the stricter sense of "parties" to it. The cited article 173 lays down the special cases of fraud, referring to article 172 in reference to the applicable penalties. Article 172 prescribes that "the person who defrauded another by means of an assumed name, false capacity or qualifications, pretended influence, confidence abuse, or by posing as holding assets, credit, duties, business or negotiation, or by means of any other hoax or deceit, will be penalized with from six months to one year imprisonment."

the different applicable percentages, the time of calculation, and the time of payment of the stipulated fee to avoid any inconveniences.

## 7. Termination of Office of the Trustee

The trustee will terminate his or her office because of any of the following:

a. Removal of the authorization of a licensed trustee
b. Termination of the trust
c. Judicial removal because of nonperformance of duties
d. Death or legal incapacity declared by the court, in the case of individuals
e. Dissolution, in the case of legal persons
f. Bankruptcy or liquidation
g. Resignation, only if expressly allowed by the trust instrument[42]
h. Lack of payment of trustee fees or reimbursement of trustee expenses

If any of the preceding situations occur, the trustee will be replaced by the substitute designated in the trust instrument in accordance with the procedure indicated therein. In the event of no such provision being made or the designated trustee declining, the court may appoint a substitute trustee.

One topic of several debates, because it is not regulated by the law, is who is the responsible party for the payment of the expenses of the trustee substitution. This point must be specifically addressed in the trust instrument.

As mentioned before, the provisions in the trust instrument to appoint a substitute trustee are especially important in Uruguay, because in the event of the death of the trustee if there are no such provisions, the trust will terminate.

## H. COMPARED TAX TREATMENT OF TRUSTS IN LATIN AMERICA[43]

Given the diversity of political systems and practical solutions regarding trust taxation, it is impossible to find tax rules applicable to the totality of Latin American countries. Nevertheless, an attempt will be made to sketch some general principles and their main exceptions.

The first aspect to be considered in tax matters is that Latin America comprehends centralized as well as federal countries. In countries belonging to the first group, two levels of taxation may be observed, that is, the municipal and the federal or national levels. Federal countries (Argentina, Brazil, and Mexico) exhibit three levels

---

42    In those Latin American countries where the capacity to act as trustee has been restricted to certain entities (i.e., banks), the existence of regulations prohibiting the trustee to resign are the general rule.

43    This part of the chapter, duly adapted and updated, is based on my lecture in the Latin American Congress on Trust (*Congreso Latinoamericano de Fideicomiso* [COLAFI]) in 2004.

of taxation: the national or federal, the state or provincial, and the municipal. Based on the existence of an intermediate layer of government with taxing authority (the state or provincial one), a greater impact and fiscal complexity is to be expected in federal countries. Further, from a practical perspective, knowledge of the province or state involved becomes relevant in determining the tax treatment applicable to the trust. Put differently, it is not sufficient to know that a certain trust will have assets in Brazil; it is necessary to know whether those assets will be located in the Federal District (Brasilia) or in one of its 26 states, as the local sales tax may be substantially different.

Secondly, it must be noted that most countries tax worldwide source income, whereas others (Costa Rica, Panama, and Uruguay) only tax national source income. If a trust is located in a jurisdiction taxing worldwide source income, it must pay taxes on its profits in that jurisdiction, as well as on those originating in its activities performed or capital placed outside of that jurisdiction. The exception are the three countries mentioned above, in which trusts must only be taxed on the profits obtained within the country. For example, if a trust is created in Uruguay, and that trust only obtains profits originating in Brazil, it will not be taxed in Uruguay because there are no profits from a Uruguayan source. Conversely, if that same trust were to be established in Peru (or any other country with the worldwide source rule), it would be taxed on its profits originating abroad, and it should pay taxes in Peru.

Concerning the treatment of the trust as a taxable entity in itself, it should be stressed that the fact that the legislation of certain countries grants trusts fiscal standing (in other words, that the trust is a passive subject that should pay taxes) is totally independent from the fact that that same legislation may not grant it legal standing. For example, although Ecuador is the sole country in Latin America granting legal standing to a trust, it is not the only one that considers trusts passive subjects of income tax. The dissociation of the two concepts does not occur only in trust matters but in a multiplicity of fiscal subjects that are not legal subjects.

For the sake of clarity, it is possible to summarize the existing models in three groups of trust tax systems:

a. The first involves regarding trusts as corporations for tax purposes, that is, a subject of the tax that must be paid by the trustee itself at the same tax rate as corporations.[44] In this case, the trust is considered a business vehicle or corporation, which must itself be taxed.
b. The second alternative is considering that the trust is inexistent to tax purposes, that is, that the settlor is the subject of the tax, as if the trust had never been created. This is the solution that is generally adopted for guarantee trusts, in which, even though there is a trust property, there is considered to be no separate legal structure for tax purposes. It is rather like constituting a mortgage or a pledge: It does not imply the creation of a new taxpayer.

---

44  As a general rule individuals are subject to progressive tax rates, whereas corporations are subject to flat rates.

c. The third system maintains that the trust obtains profits but that it must not pay taxes, but rather that the taxes must be attributed to other parties, such as settlors or the beneficiaries. The trust is a pass-through vehicle. The difference with the previous alternative is that if the income obtained by the trustee was exempted for the beneficiary (if it had been obtained directly), the use of the trust would mean the loss of such advantage. The beneficiary is earning a gain arising from a trust and not the income obtained by the trust itself (as would be the case in the second alternative).

Latin American countries have not adopted one common solution. For example:

a. Colombia and Mexico attribute profits to the beneficiaries.
b. Peru attributes profits to the settlor.
c. Argentina offers a mixed solution: The trust is subject to taxation unless the settlor is the same person as the beneficiaries, in which case taxation is attributed to those subjects.
d. Guatemala, Uruguay, and Honduras consider the trust a taxpayer.
e. Ecuador considers the trust a subject of taxation, but it allows profits to be attributed to the beneficiaries by means of a stipulation in the trust instrument.

One of the items that has aroused the most debate is the treatment that should be granted to the trust transfer of assets. Evident as it may seem, this transfer is not the onerous sale or cession of an asset but the transfer by the settlor to constitute or enlarge the trust fund. In neither of these respects is there any legislative uniformity in Latin America; however, it could be said that the trust transfer, as a general rule, is either not reached or exempt. For example:

a. In Honduras, transfer to the trust does not qualify as a sale.
b. In Peru, the transfer of assets to a commercial trust qualifies as a sale for tax purposes only if it is agreed that the asset will not return to the settlor. Nevertheless, in no case is the transaction taxed with the general sale tax.
c. In Guatemala, the transfer of assets to a trust is exempt from any taxation, as is the return of assets to the settlor.
d. In Ecuador, trust transfer is exempt from any taxation, and the return of the asset to the settlor in the same condition in which it was transferred (e.g., in a guarantee trust, in which the guaranteed obligation is complied with) is also exempt.
e. In Argentina, it is thought, at the national or federal level, that any transfer to a trust is a sale. Nevertheless, at the provincial level the criterion is that a sale exists providing the trust transfer is for consideration.

Regarding value-added tax, trusts are considered taxpayers. This is because this tax tends to disregard the existence of legal standing to qualify as taxpayers the "sets of assets aimed at a certain end" (such as trusts, which are special-purposes patrimonies). This implies that the trust will be responsible for the payment of the corresponding tax.

As to real estate, automobile, or patent tax, and such other taxes as financial transactions or debit or credit tax, the trust is taxed, and the trustee is responsible for its payment.

## 1. Responsibility of the Trustee for Trust Taxes

In tax matters, the general rule that establishes that the trustee's own estate cannot be affected by trust obligations, except for guilt or neglect, is altered, because the trustee is designated responsible for the trust debt, either jointly responsible or simply directly responsible for any tax payments of the trust. In other words, the trustee must answer with his or her own estate for any taxes omitted by the trust.

It is noteworthy that some jurisdictions, such as Peru, determine that the trustee will only be responsible from the time that the tax authorities require, so that only from that time will interest accrue, and he or she will not be held accountable for fines. However, the central problem remains, as the settlor finds him or herself exposed to the tax authorities' actions once the trust has been liquidated.

From a practical perspective, good fiduciary practices impose adequate tax planning, understood as the analysis and consensus of the trustee, the settlor, and the beneficiaries regarding the tax criteria to be followed. Should this task not be conducted, the trustee could see him or herself in the dilemma of having to choose between a conservative criterion (safeguarding his or her responsibility before the tax authorities, but exposing him or herself to the claims of the beneficiaries) or an aggressive criterion (safeguarding his or her responsibility before the beneficiaries, but exposing him or her to a future claim by the tax authorities). Besides, this evaluation must contemplate the existence of liquid funds for the payment of tax because, in the absence thereof, assets will have to be resorted to or debt incurred, both of which circumstances could incur the responsibility of the trustee should they not be expressly foreseen.

# Chapter 3

# Securitization in Latin America

A. Mortgage Securitization in the United States as a Model for Latin America  48
    1. Ginnie Mae  50
B. Definition and Advantages of Securitization in Latin America  51
    1. Advantages of Securitization in Latin America  51
C. Risks and Credit Enhancement  52
    1. Credit Enhancement  54
D. Public Offer of Trust Securities  56
    1. Previous Authorization  57
    2. The Trustee as Securities Underwriter  58

Given the voluminous amount of material that exists with respect to securitization in general, especially in the United States, this chapter will concentrate on the aspects or the subjects that are relevant to Latin America.[1] You will find a brief explanation of many aspects from a Latin American perspective. The countries with the most experience are Mexico, Brazil, and Argentina (in order of importance), although there are securitizations in all Latin America.[2]

---

[1] In relation to securitization in Latin America, *see* Hela Cheikhrouhou, W. Britt Gwinner, John Pollner, Emanuel Salinas, Sophie Sirtaine & Dimitri Vittas, Structure Finance in Latin America: Channeling Pension Funds to Housing, Infrastructure, and Small Businesses (2007).

[2] Jacob Gyntelberg et al. explained that "the development of domestic securitization in Latin America is a very recent phenomenon. Although there has been a significant expansion since 2003, the market as reflected by its size, continues to be in its infancy. . . . According to Fitch Ratings, in 2006, the market just reached [US$16 billion]. . . . The main leading assets in the region are future flows, real estate related transactions and consumer loans. . . . Real estate related transactions are particularly important in Colombia, where they represent a third of the total market, and in Mexico. In the region, most of the bulk of credit-linked obligations is done in the Mexican market. In Brazil and Argentina, the securitization of personal and consumer loans (receivables to chain retailers, supermarkets and regional banks) has become very popular, surpassing MBSs as the asset with the second-largest securitized volume." Jacob Gyntelberg,

In the first three points of this chapter, the history of securitization in the United States is outlined. Although it is quite obvious, it should be stressed that the relevance of this matter lies in the fact that U.S. securitization was the model for Latin American legislations (i.e., securitization companies that try to reproduce the Ginnie Mae and Fannie Mae model) and that today the U.S. market creates the future trends in the region.[3]

The reason for including this chapter and other comments on securitization in Latin America is that the legal vehicle par excellence for securitizations in the region is the trust.[4] It can be a financial trust (as in Argentina and Uruguay), a securitization trust (as in Peru, Bolivia, and Brazil), or a trust that is the basis for the issuance of participation certificates (as in Mexico), but in any case with the basic model of a trust.


## A. MORTGAGE SECURITIZATION IN THE UNITED STATES AS A MODEL FOR LATIN AMERICA

To help the United States revive from the 1930 depression, the U.S. Congress created the *Federal Housing Administration* (FHA) through the *National Housing Act* in 1934. Title II of this act established, as one of the principal functions of the FHA, the granting of insurance on mortgage credits given by private investors and foresaw the creation of material mortgage associations. These associations had to be private companies ruled by the FHA, and their main purpose was to buy and sell the mortgages to be insured by the FHA. Under this authority the Federal National Mortgage Association (Fannie Mae), was created on February 10, 1938.

The initial purpose of Fannie Mae was to finance the mortgage credits insured by the FHA, which were widely accepted by investors. As a result of 1948 modifications, the FHA lost its capacity to create entities, and title III of the 1934 National Housing Act became Fannie Mae's organic law.

After the World War II, the demand for homes increased enormously. As a response to this situation, the U.S. Congress passed the *Serviceman's Readjustment Act* in 1944. This act gave the Department of Veterans Affairs the authority to guarantee the credits to the veterans without an initial payment and or requirements of insurance premium payments.

In 1968, the U.S. Congress passed the *Housing and Urban Development Act,* which established Ginnie Mae, with the purpose of guaranteeing loans granted by other

---

Eli Remolona & Camilo E. Tovar, *Securitization in Asia and Latin America Compared*, in EXPANSION AND DIVERSIFICATION IN SECURITIZATION YEARBOOK 2007, at 390 (Jan Job de Vries, Robbé & Paul Ali ed., 2008).

3　For example, in 2001 the Mexican federal government created the *Sociedad Hipoteca Federal*, "a state-owned development bank and guarantor which has the mandate to foster the development of the primary and secondary mortgage markets. This institution has 'full faith and credit' of [the] federal government on risks taken through 2013 and must be self[-]supporting afterwards." *Id.*

4　The sole exception is Brazil, in which, although securitization trusts exist and are used, specific closed-end mutual funds (*Fundos de Investimento em Direitos Creditorios*) are the preferred structure.

federal agencies. However, it also recharacterized Fannie Mae as a "government-sponsored" private organization. In fact, what the act did was separate Fannie Mae into two organizations: the Fannie Mae of private property and the Ginnie Mae of public property.

When Fannie Mae was created by the U.S. Congress in 1938 to support the home-building industry, it was authorized to buy only loans guaranteed by the FHA in order to supply funds for mortgages. In 1944, *Fannie Mae* obtained the authorization to be involved in the loans granted by the Veterans Administration, another governmental agency under the Lyndon Johnson presidential administration. In 1954, Fannie Mae was partially privatized, and in 1968, it became totally private. Two years later, in 1970, the shares of Fannie Mae began to be listed in the New York Stock Exchange (NYSE) and the Pacific Stock Exchange. That same year, President Nixon signed legislation authorizing Fannie Mae to purchase conventional mortgages. This enabled Fannie Mae to buy mortgages in dollar amounts beyond traditional government loan limits, reaching out to a broader cross section of Americans. Along the same line, in 1972 Fannie Mae made its first purchase of a nonfederally backed mortgage, beginning the secondary market of mortgages. Since 1972, the Fannie Mae mortgage program has exploded not only in size but also in the variety of products. In 1981, Fannie Mae started to buy *adjustable rate mortgages* (ARMs). In the 1980s Fannie Mae began its business of mortgage-backed securities (MBSs).

During the 1980s and 1990s, Fannie Mae diversified the nature of the mortgages granted and also the kind of securities issued. In 1987, it established the first *real estate mortgage investment conduit* (REMIC) fund. By 1992, it was the biggest issuer and warrantor of mortgage-backed securities, overwhelming Ginnie Mae and Freddie Mac[5] because of its size.

Fannie Mae has two main business lines: (a) the purchase of mortgages and mortgage-backed securities, in both cases, financed by the issuance of debt to a minor rate and, (ii) the grant of onerous warranties to credits granted by third parties for the purchase of lodgings for one or several families.

One of the greatest innovations in the Fannie Mae business was the beginning of mortgages with adjustable interest in the middle of the 1980s. With two-digit interest rates, these mortgages captured almost 65 percent of all mortgages. Fannie Mae began to buy adjustable rate mortgages in 1983, and the next year it issued the first security in this kind of mortgage. Fannie Mae removed to a great extent the credit risk of the securities issued guaranteeing the payment of the mortgages that back their payment.

As mentioned earlier, at the end of the 1980s, the market of the mortgage-backed securities made another push forward with the introduction of a new and more efficient vehicle with several types of securities: the REMIC fund (also known as collateralized mortgage obligation [CMO]). This market developed and offered a variety of REMIC securities with different yields and risks.

---

5    The Federal Home Loan Mortgage Corporation (FHLMC, or "Freddie Mac," also known, since 1976, as the Mortgage Corporation) is a federal company. It was established in 1970 by title III of the *Emergency Home Finance Act* with the goal of increasing funds available for mortgages and giving mortgage investors bigger flexibility.

As a result of the financial crisis that caused severe losses to Fannie Mae and Freddie Mac, on September 6, 2008, the U.S. Department of the Treasury agreed to provide up to $100 billion of capital as needed to ensure Fannie Mae's continuation, which implied virtually the (re)nationalization of Fannie Mae.

## 1. Ginnie Mae

As previously noted, Ginnie Mae was created in 1968 as a wholly owned corporation within the *Department of Housing and Urban Development* (HUD). Its purpose is to serve low-to-moderate–income home buyers. The primary function of Ginnie Mae is to operate a mortgage-backed security (MBS) program. Ginnie Mae does not issue, sell, or buy MBSs or purchase mortgage loans. Ginnie Mae's MBSs are issued by approved private institutions. The underlying mortgages are insured by the *Federal Housing Administration* (FHA) or by the *Rural Housing Service* (RHS), or they are guaranteed by the *Department of Veterans Affairs* (VA).

Because of its guarantee, investors in *Ginnie Mae* securities are assured timely payments of scheduled principal and interest due on the pooled mortgages that back their securities. The payments also include any prepayments and early recoveries of principal on the pooled mortgages. These payments are guaranteed even if borrowers or issuers default on their obligation.

The payments to investors occur monthly.[6] These payments are called "modified pass-through" payments because, through Ginnie Mae's MBS program, money is passed from the borrower through to the investors in the Ginnie Mae securities. It is "modified" because if the amount collected from the borrowers is less than the amount due, the issuer modifies the pass-through to add on an amount from its corporate funds to make the payment complete.

Unlike Fannie Mae, Ginnie Mae remains a part of the federal government. As such, the Ginnie Mae guarantee is backed by the full faith and credit of the United States.

Ginnie Mae securities are some of the most widely held and traded mortgage-backed securities in the world. Historically, 95 percent of all FHA and VA mortgages have been securitized through Ginnie Mae.

As mentioned before, both Fannie Mae and Ginnie Mae were the models for the creation of securitization companies and banks acting as trustees of securitization trusts in Latin America. Nevertheless, with the exception of NAFIBO in Bolivia, no state-owned securitization company ever had a similar relevance in its country as Fannie Mae and Ginnie Mae do in the United States. The main securitization companies or banks acting as financial trustees in Latin America are not state-owned.

---

6    It should be borne in mind, from the financial point of view, that one key dissimilar element of a mortgage-backed security and a typical debt instrument is the form of the principal amortization. Generally, a typical debt instrument pays the total amount of its principal at the time of maturity, whereas the mortgage-backed security amortizes the capital along its life with periodic payments.

## B. DEFINITION AND ADVANTAGES OF SECURITIZATION IN LATIN AMERICA

As a preliminary comment, it should be said that the term "securitization" came from the transformation of loans into securities. This transaction gave birth to asset-backed securities (in Spanish, *títulos de deudas respaldados con activos*), that is to say, guaranteed by assets or cash flows. Securitization can be defined as the financial transaction by means of which a liquid asset is obtained, such as publicly placed securities, from an illiquid asset (such as loans or cash flows, among others), which are isolated in a special purpose vehicle.[7]

One of the reasons for the development of securitization in Latin America was the existence of pension funds administrators, such as the Bolivian, Chilean, Costa Rican, Colombian, Ecuadorian, Panamanian, Peruvian, and Uruguayan *Administradoras de Fondos de Pensión* (AFPs) or *Administradoras de Fondos de Ahorro Previsional* (AFAPs) with abundant resources that must be invested in securities.[8]

## 1. Advantages of Securitization in Latin America

With relation to the advantages of securitization, it should be noted that although they seem to be the same worldwide, in the particular case of Latin America, the main ones are:

a. The grantor could solve the problem of the mismatch of financial terms in the cases in which he or she is financed in the short-term and grants long-term financing.

---

7   Securitization is defined by Brazilian law (which created the neologism "securitição" in Portuguese) in Law No. 9514 of 1997, which states that securitization of real state credits is the "operation by which these credits are expressly linked to the issuance of certain securities by means of a document arisen from a securitization company."

Porras Zamora defined securitization as a process by means of which capital assets of slow rotation are transformed into cash through the issuance or securities backed on such assets and the placement of the securities in the market. JORGE PORRAS ZAMORA, EL FIDEICOMISO EN COSTA RICA, NOCIONES Y PRODUCTOS BÁSICOS 98 (1998).

The Commission formed in Costa Rica by Executive Decree No. 27127—MP-MIVAH, June 27, 1998, defined the securitization of mortgages as a mechanism that allows the recycling of tied-up resources in mortgages. For that purpose, long-term financial instruments are issued: (a) guaranteed by those mortgages that must satisfy specific conditions of quality and standardization, and (b) with financial conditions similar to the original mortgages conditions.

8   It has been said that "AFPs are growing fast in several Latin American countries, and annuity providers will start to grow as the fully pension systems mature. As of December 2005, Latin America's AFPs have more than US$300 billion in assets under management, or about 10–15 percent of gross domestic product (GDP) in countries where reforms were fairly recent and close to 60 percent in Chile (excluding annuity providers), the first country to move to a parallel defined benefit pillar may not achieve such large fully funded pensions, even when their systems mature, but AFPs (and soon annuity providers) are sizable and growing fast in these countries as well. They are an important class of domestic investors and a large source of capital for highly creditworthy investments." CHEIKHROUHOU ET AL., *supra* note 1, at xiv.

For example, there are financial entities that receive thirty-day deposits and grant loans for five-year periods. When these five-year loans are transferred to a trust in exchange for cash, the grantor uses securitization as a tool to handle this financial mismatch. The trust will have the same five-year period loan, but it will issue securities for the same time length.

b. It allows the excessive exposition to credit risks in a particular geographical region or industry to diversify. For example, a loan portfolio that is only composed of mortgages in a certain region of a country or in a certain industry could be securitized to transfer that risk to the investors in those securities. With the proceeds of the transfer to the trust, the grantor could, eventually, purchase securities related to some other kind of portfolio of assets. Although the same result could be achieved through a credit derivative, regulatory and tax reasons may lead to the use of securitization instead of derivatives.

c. It may allow the rating agencies to obtain a better risk-rating than a direct debt bonds issuance. This advantage is very important in the case of companies that cannot place their own securities in the international markets because of low ratings based on the sovereign risk of the country in which they operate but, for example, have cash flows in hard currencies from foreign countries. Furthermore, when the market requires high rates of interest as a result of bad ratings, this mechanism arises as the most suitable one to obtain a good reduction of interest rates in comparison with an ordinary debt issuance. There are several examples of successful securitization of cash flows arising from exports.[9]

d. Securitization allows the grantor to obtain financing granted by institutional investors such as pension funds, insurance companies, and mutual funds. This produces a reduction of the financial expenses, and it could create a positive image of the issuer in the market, thus allowing the diversification or widening of financing sources.

e. It can produce a reduction of the debt ratios of the grantor. This advantage can be clearly seen in the cases of securitization of loans that were financed through the issuance of debt. Securitization allows the transfer of the loans and the repayment of the associated debt.

f. Depending on the structure of the securitization and the negative pledges imposed on the grantor by its lenders, securitization could allow the grantor to obtain financing without breaking contractual covenants.

g. In the case of banks subject to equity-to-loan restrictions, securitization allows them to continue granting loans at the same pace without the need of new capital contributions by the shareholders.

## C. RISKS AND CREDIT ENHANCEMENT

Some risks depend on the kind of assets transmitted to the trust, and others are systematic ones and depend on the market in which the securitization is carried out.

---

9    Some of these cases of securitizations have been carried out with vehicles in foreign jurisdictions to avoid the sovereign risk of the country in which the company is operating.

With loans, the main risks that could affect the securitized trust assets and jeopardize the repayment of the issued securities are the following:

a. The inexistence or illegality of the loans that were transferred to the trust.
b. The delay in the collection of the interest and principal repayment of the loans or the bankruptcy of the collector agent. It should be stressed that the appointment of a backup servicer is usual (and a requirement of certain rating agencies).
c. The delay in the foreclosure of the guarantees (i.e., mortgages) because of the inefficiency of the administrator, judicial delays, or the enactment of laws that make the foreclosure of loans illegal.
d. The precancellation of loans and/or leasing contracts as a result of interest rate changes.

As can be seen, in securitization of loans, the analysis is focused on the trust assets and not in the originator because his or her bankruptcy does not affect the trust (except if he or she is also the servicer or collector agent). As the assets are isolated in the trust, the trust securities do not depend on the financial health of the grantor.

With trusts that have cash flow as an underlying asset,[10] performance risk must be evaluated. In this kind of trust, there is no economic independence between the grantor and the trust. When there is bankruptcy of the one who has to render the services or to generate the assets that are reattributed with the cash flow transferred in trust, this cash flow will be interrupted, and the trust will not be able to meet its obligations. As can be expected, these risks affect the credit rating of the trust securities. Put differently, the economic status of the company that generates the cash flow is essential in this kind of trust. One of the key points to consider is the position of the company in the market. New competitors or changes in the conditions may determine the reduction of its share and, therefore, of the cash flow transferred to the trust.

With real estate projects or direct investment funds (i.e., investments in forestry, mining or any other finance[11] project instrumented with trusts), the internal risks of each activity must be considered, for example, torts (including environmental damage), risk of noncompletion (because of the lack of or delay in municipal permits), market risks (decrease in price or lack of demand for the units that are constructed), availability

---

10　As examples of securitization of cash flows that have been conducted in Latin America, the following can be mentioned: air ticket sales, rents of commercial places, highway tolls, prepaid medical services, retail sales, educational establishment fees, exports, taxes, public services fees, sport or entertainment show tickets, and so on.

There are projects in which the developer is not the owner of the assets and will never be, but he or she only has the right to collect a fee from the future users of the construction. An example is the contract for the concession of highways, which gives the concessionaire the right to collect a toll from the users, but whose properties belong to the state. In is these cases, it useless to try to collect the credits granted through the sale of the assets because they are state-owned, and not the concessionaire's property. The only possible guarantee is the transfer of the tolls to a guarantee trust. Therefore, the risk analysis must be focused on the toll cash flow, not in the assets that produce it.

11　Trusts are one of the best legal vehicles for project finance structures.

risk, or prices of the raw materials of the project, and so forth. A very important risk is that of incompletion. This is because the sale of the assets half constructed probably would not cover a meaningful part of the debt amount. As will be explained when the guarantee trust is discussed (Chapter 5, Section B), the trust has a main advantage in relation to the other guarantees, namely, that it allows lenders to step in and replace the developer and/or the builder of the project to finish it successfully.

The main systematic risks are: fiscal and regulatory issues, political instability, inflation, currency risk, restrictive legislation (there is a clear tendency to overregulate), and financial crisis of the countries of the region.[12]

## 1. Credit Enhancement

The most common form of credit enhancement of trust securities is the creation of two kinds of securities: a senior piece and a subordinated piece. The total of funds is first used to pay the senior securities, and the remaining part of the funds is used to pay the subordinated piece. In a scenario of scarcity of funds, the subordinates piece takes the first loss. Consequently, the higher risk of the subordinated securities should be rewarded with a higher interest rate or percentage of income. This structure is used because it does not imply a disbursement by the grantor and allows him or her to substantially reduce the interest rate paid by the senior piece. This simple solution allows the issuer, who most probably would by all or a portion of the subordinate piece, to have a security that can be purchased by institutional investors and obtain finance from them.

In very simple terms, trusts allow efficient risk management because each risk could be allocated to the party that better knows and better manages it. Therefore, this allows the participation of investors who are only willing or prepared to run certain risks, but not others. The risk that one investor does not want is allocated to another (with the financial reward for it).

Other forms of credit enhancement usually used in Latin America are the following:

a. A third party guarantee in favor of the trust or the trust securities holders. In Latin America it is very common to have guarantees granted by the headquarters of the issuer (subsidiary of an U.S. or European company), which permits a substantial reduction in the interest rate.[13]

---

12  *Cf.* Esteban C. Buljevich & Mariano A. Fabrizio, *Securitization in Latin America*, *in* EXPANSION AND DIVERSIFICATION IN SECURITIZATION YEARBOOK 2007, at 190 (Jan Job de Vries Robbé & Paul Ali eds., 2008).

13  Jacob Gyntelberg et al. explained that the IFC has offered partial credit guarantees for corporate bonds in Mexico (microfinance and municipalities) and Colombia (Davivienda Bank). Gyntelberg et al., *supra* note 2, at 390.

b. The obligation of the grantor to replace any given loan that is not paid in due time. This structure is traditional in the case of securitizations of loans by local banks and avoids delays in the foreclosure of the guarantees of the loans securitized. By these means, the grantor and not the trust, suffers those delays. The obligation of replacement of defaulting loans could be of all the defaulted loans or up to a certain sum.

c. Overcollateralization through the transmission to the trust of more assets than the strictly necessary to repay the trust securities: The assets that remain in the trust after the cancellation of the principal and interest of the trust bonds are transferred to the grantor in his or her role of residual beneficiary.

d. The creation of a guarantee trust with additional cash flow or assets. This point follows the same concept as the previous one: It is based on the affectation as a guarantee or more assets than those needed to pay the obligations of the trust. The use of a second trust as guarantee instead of increasing the amount of assets of the principal trust is based on tax and regulatory reasons.

e. The creation of a sinking fund with the amounts in cash reserved by the trustee (i.e., at the moment of payment of the assets to the grantor, the trustee reserves the necessary amounts of funds to make the first payment of interest and/or certain expenses of the trust).

f. Insurance of political risks granted by private companies (monoproduct or multiproduct) or international organisms such as the Overseas Private Investment Corporation (OPIC).[14]

---

14    OPIC, a governmental agency from the United States, helps U.S. business invest outside of the United States, when this is an economic or strategic interest. The most important tools of this agency are political risk insurance and the loans granted to help U.S. taxpayers invest and compete in more than 140 emergent markets and developing countries. "The OPIC insurance contract—Andino, Buendía and Kime explain—is used as a reference due to the fact that it is the most developed insurance contract for the transactions in the capital markets." Diane Audino, Rosario Buendía & Kevin Kime, *Los Seguros de Riesgo Político Pueden Mejorar las Transacciones Estructuradas*, *in* TITULIZACIÓN EN AMÉRICA LATINA 2000, 43 (2001). According to its principle declaration, the OPIC mission is to move and facilitate the participation of U.S. private capital in the economic and social development of the less developed countries, and their transition from a domestic to an open economy. OPIC aids U.S. investors through four main activities to promote investments outside the United States and reduce risks associated therewith. These activities are: (a) To secure American investments against political risk, (b) to finance business through loans and guarantees, (c) to finance private investments funds to invest in certain businesses, and (d) to defend the interest of the U.S. commercial community against third countries. In Latin America, several operations have been conducted with OPIC guarantees, which have shown to be an useful tool to reduce risks and the financial cost for the issuer. A main point in the analysis of this kind of hedge, as in any insurance contract, is its scope. OPIC does not cover credit risk, but risks related with the transfer of currency from the debtor's country to a foreign country. Eventually, other political risks are covered, such as the expropriation risk and the nonconvertibility of the local currency to a foreign currency risk. However, delays after the submission of the request until payment should be taken into account. Furthermore, it should be considered that in certain cases the insurance does not cover the total amount of the payments the issuer has to make. Further information is available at www.opic.gov.

g. In trusts with exportation cash flows as underlying assets, one of the main concerns of international investors in Latin America is currency risks (associated with the devaluation of the local currency and the creation or modification of the exchange control regimens); one of the best credit enhancement tools is the creation of an offshore trust that receives cash flow from abroad. This structure reduces the risk of the country because the cash paid from abroad to the local exporter is deposited in a foreign account under a foreign trust.

h. Hedging interest rates with derivatives or credit risk with credit derivatives: These instruments are usually granted by related companies because they are too expensive to be economically feasible.

i. The appointment of a backup servicer.[15]

The credit enhancement methods mentioned above could be used in isolation or together. Using one or another depends on the characteristics of the transaction and the rating agency requirements.

## D. PUBLIC OFFER OF TRUST SECURITIES

Securitization is associated with the issuance of securities and its placement through a public offer. Therefore, this section is a general discussion on the main public offer rules in Latin America.[16] The first and basic rule is that public placement of securities

---

15   Although the duty to administer the assets is the trustee's, it is common that this duty be delegated to the grantor (because of his or her knowledge of the administered portfolio, not to affect the commercial relation of the grantor with his or her clients) or to a third party: the servicer. The servicer is in charge of, among other possible aspects: (a) the collection of the transferred credits or funds flows; (b) the recording and analysis of the payment patterns of loan debtors or the development of the transferred funds flows to be able to know the trends and allow for the appropriate steps to be taken or trigger the contractual clauses provided for those instances; (c) the prompt initiation of the collection actions in cases of delinquency; and (d) the preparation of reports on the status of the portfolio or funds flow. A backup servicer is expected to take charge of the portfolio management in the event the original servicer is unable to perform his or her task, as this is a requirement with certain risk-rating agencies. This is a replacement in the event the original servicer suffers voluntary or involuntary bankruptcy, is disqualified in any way, and so forth.

16   Although there is no clearance and settlement system of securities transactions that covers all Latin American jurisdictions, there are systems with national coverage in certain countries, and many of them have agreements with Depository Trust Company or DTC (a member of the U.S. Federal Reserve System, a limited-purpose trust company under New York State banking law and a registered clearing agency with the U.S. Securities and Exchange Commission, more information in www.portaldtc.com) and Euroclear. For example, the *Caja de Valores S.A.* in Argentina, the Institute for the Deposit of Values of Mexico (*SD Indeval*), Brazil's *Central de Custodia e Liquidação de Títulos* (CETIP), Venezuela's *Caja Venezolana de Valores*, Colombia's *Depósito Centralizado de Valores* (DECEVAL) , and Peru's CAVALI ICLV S.A.

requires the previous approval of the equivalent to the Securities and Exchange Commission (SEC) in each country.[17]

## 1. Previous Authorization

A public offering is deemed as an offer made to the public generally or to particular groups or sectors to carry out any agreement involving securities. It may be conducted by the issuers or by sole partnerships or companies dedicated exclusively or nonexclusively to the trading of securities, by means of personal offers, publications, radio and television broadcasts, cinema projections, posters, signs or bills, circulars, and printed notices, or any other method such as Internet offering.

In most Latin American jurisdictions, the authorization of public offerings follows the same criteria as that at the U.S. federal level: It is to grant adequate, immediate, and truthful information to the investor ("full disclosure") for him or her to make an informed decision, with full knowledge of the positive or negative facts that will affect his or her placement of funds.

The issuance of securities to be placed through the public offering procedure would entail the admission of that company to the public offering regime, from which time it is mandatory to, among other things:

a. Inform on an immediate basis any occurrence or situation, whether positive or negative, which as a result of its significance could affect: (i) the normal course of the issuer's business, (ii) its accounting statements, or (iii) the quotation or offering of its securities.
b. Submit the last three financial statements audited at the time of the request, and thereafter submit them on a quarterly basis.
c. Submit a personal report on the members of the board of directors.
d. Submit the details of any shareholder with more than a 5 percent stake in the company, of those who made irrevocable contributions and of the controlling or controlled companies.

Where assets are transferred to a financial trust that makes public offering of its trust securities, the grantor need not be admitted to the public offering regime. Only the aspects that could affect the issued security should be reasonably described (e.g., the asset transferred into the trust and how the different circumstances affecting the investor would impact the securities).

Securities issuers and those persons offering the securities and the persons signing the prospectus of a publicly offered securities issuance will be responsible for all the information included in such prospectuses. The brokers participating as organizers or underwriters in a securities purchase or the sale of a public offering must diligently

---

17    Any natural or legal person participating in public offerings of negotiable securities without the pertinent authorization can be penalized with warning, fine, disqualification, suspension, and/or prohibition from carrying out public offerings.

review the information contained in the relevant prospectuses. The experts expressing their opinions on certain parts of the prospectus (e.g., tax advisors) will only be liable for such portion of the information as they have issued opinions on.

Regarding insider trading, it is established that trustees, directors, administrators, managers, auditors, controlling shareholders, and professionals of any entity authorized for public offerings of securities, and brokers and intermediaries in public offerings, including trustees, and, generally, any person who by virtue of his or her position or activity possesses intelligence regarding a fact that has not been publicly revealed yet and which, given its importance, is susceptible to affecting the placement or the course of the trading being carried out through authorized publicly offered securities must observe strict confidentiality and refrain from trading until such information has a public character and must not take advantage of the confidential information stated therein to obtain, for themselves or others, any kind of benefits, whether they derive from purchase or sale of securities or any other transaction relating to the public offering regime.

In relation to market manipulation and deceit, it is ruled that issuers, intermediaries, investors, or any other participants in negotiable securities must refrain from conducting, in their own names or a third party's, in initial offerings or secondary markets, practices or conducts that intend or permit the manipulation of prices or volumes of negotiable securities, rights or term agreements, or futures and options, altering the normal course of supply and demand; they are under the particular obligation to observe legal and procedural regulations.

In addition, such persons must refrain from incurring deceitful practices or conducts that may unduly influence any participant in the said markets, regarding the purchase or sale of any publicly offered negotiable security, whether through the use of hoaxes, false or inaccurate statements, or those in which essential facts are omitted, or through any act, practice or course of action that may have deceitful and injurious effects on any person in the market.

## 2. The Trustee as Securities Underwriter

First, it should be made clear that although the duties of trustee, issuer, and underwriter are conceptually different, they are ordinarily fulfilled by the same entity and are very much linked to one another.

The underwriting can take two basic modes depending on the risk assumed by the underwriter:

a. *Firm commitment:* The underwriter undertakes to purchase the securities in order to place them on the market. If the subsequent placement was not successful, the underwriter will not be able to return the securities to the issuer. Where the underwriter undertakes to purchase the securities that were not placed on the market but without a deposit of the funds to the issuer before the securities go on the market, the underwriting is a standby one because of its latency until the placement with a remnant is completed.

b. *Best efforts:* The underwriter only commits to make his or her best efforts to place the securities object of the agreement. The underwriting agreement generally contains clauses permitting the underwriter to withdraw from the transaction without liability if: (i) adverse material changes exist in the market in which the placement is to take place (a material adverse change [MAC] clause), (ii) an adverse change exists in the issuer's conditions, (iii) a statement by the issuer is declared false, and (iv) the necessary legal and tax opinions are not received by the due date.

If the trustee remains with trust securities at the end of the placement, that would mean that the trustee is beneficiary of the trust. Such a situation represents a problem in most Latin American jurisdictions, and it is avoided by simply not celebrating firm commitment underwritings but only best efforts ones.

# Chapter 4

# Trusts versus Other Types of Contractual Arrangements and Legal Vehicles

A. Simulated Agreement  61
B. Bailment  62
C. Agency  63
D. Pledge and Mortgage  64
E. Usufruct  65
F. Corporation  66
G. Foundations  67
    1. Private-Interest Foundations  68

In this chapter, the differences and similarities between the trust and other contractual arrangements and legal vehicles in the civil-law tradition will be analyzed. This chapter attempts to impart clearer understanding of the trust and to determine the rules that should be applicable in those hard cases in which there are no specific statutory rules. Furthermore, this chapter should help the reader gain a deeper understanding of the nature of the Latin American trust, and the concept of the trust as a special-purpose patrimony.

## A. SIMULATED AGREEMENT

In the simulated agreement there is a real will and a declared one, without convergence between them. The simulation takes place when the actual intention of an agreement is covered under the mere appearance of another. Therefore, the agreement contains provisions that do not reflect the real will of the parties. One common example of simulated agreement is the one that transfers assets to interposed people, who are not really the ones for whom they are constituted or transmitted.

The simulated agreement is the one that has a different appearance from reality. There is a contrast between the external form and the objectives of the parties. In other words, the simulated contract attempts to create a formal expression in discrepancy with the reality of the substantial will of the parties.

The simulation is total when the signed agreement in completely false, and it is a partial simulation when it is forms an agreement with an appearance that hides in part the real aims.

Some scholars from civil-law countries in which there were no trust regulations expressed that the trust was a simulated contract, that is, there was an appearance of a transfer or property, but the actual business was a mere agency. This, obviously, is completely wrong. In a trust agreement, the actual will and the declared one coincide, and both are expressed in the trust instrument. Put differently, the business done is the one wished by the parties. There is no mere appearance different from the reality. In short, in simulated contracts there is a discrepancy between the real will and the one declared that the trust does not have.

## B. BAILMENT

It is important to compare trusts with bailment (or deposit) because both concepts have many elements in common. However, there are substantial characteristics that distinguish both of them.

There is a deposit when one of the parties obliges him or herself to keep a movable or immovable asset, which the other gives him or her, onerously or for free, and to return the same and identical thing. Nevertheless, not every time something is kept is there a deposit. To be a deposit, custody of the asset is the main purpose. For example, there could be a mandate or agency contract in which an asset is transferred, and it is not a deposit because the main purpose is not the custody of the asset, but the execution of a lawful business.

The main difference between a deposit and a trust is precisely the inexistence of a trust property. To analyze this point in detail, the two main kinds of deposits should be considered in comparing this contract with the trust:

a. Regular deposit: The same deposited asset should be returned, and it is not enough to return one of the same kind and in the same amount. For example, if I make a deposit of my car I should receive my car back and not a car of the same characteristics. The bailee of a regular deposit differs from the trustee because he or she is not the owner of the deposited assets but only the holder. He or she has no property right over the deposit asset but mere tenancy.

b. Irregular deposit: In the irregular deposit, the bailor receives back an asset that has the same characteristics of the originally deposited one but is not necessarily the same. The classic example is the deposit of a sum of money or of a commodity— the depositor will receive the same sum of money (plus interest if proper) or the same amount of the commodity with the same characteristics. As far as he or she is concerned, the keeper of an irregular deposit has the ordinary property and not a trust property of the assets deposited. In other words, in an irregular deposit the depositor has a credit against the depositee, and the latter has the property of the asset in deposit.

From a practical viewpoint, however, in most of the cases the trustee must perform a trust instruction that will be much more complex than the instructions the depositee or bailee should follow. In this situation, the trustee would probably have more discretion and responsibilities in relation to the trust assets than the keeper in relation to the deposit assets.

## C. AGENCY

Agency as a contract exists when a party gives the other the power, which is accepted, to represent, to the effect of executing in his or her name and by his or her account a lawful business, this task being done in a free or onerous way.

Although in the mandate, as well as in the trust, there is an instruction for a person to engage another in certain business, the main difference is that the agent does not have the property of the asset, whereas in trusts there is always transmission of a trust property.

The agent acts on behalf and in the name of the person who granted the power of attorney, whereas the trustee does not act on behalf of the grantor, but in his or her role of trustee of the trust property. Therefore, the activity of the agent affects the patrimony of the mandator. The contracts executed by the agent within the limits of his or her powers, and in the name of the mandator, the same as the obligations, are considered as done by the mandator personally. On the contrary, the activity of the trustee affects the trust assets, a patrimony separated from the grantor and trustee assets.

As a general rule, the following differences can be found in all of Latin America regarding the legal regulation of trusts and agencies:

a. The mandate is finished by the death of the mandator and/or the attorney, whereas the trust is not affected by the grantor or the trustee's death, excepting that it was already foreseen as a specific reason in the trust deed (or in the case of Uruguayan law when the replacement procedure of the trustee is not stipulated in the trust instrument).
b. The mandate is revocable by the mandator, whereas in the trust the power of revocation of the trust by the settlor must be expressly foreseen to exist, and its irrevocability is assumed.
c. The attorney can delegate a third party to execute the received instruction unless expressly prohibited, whereas in the trust the rule is the prohibition of delegation by the trustee.[1]
d. The attorney must consult the mandator in the case of doubt, but a trustee must consult the administrative or judicial authorities in certain jurisdictions, or the trustee must make the decision alone.

---

[1] The Uniform Trust Code ¶ 807 established the rule of the delegation of the trust responsibilities: "A trustee may delegate duties and powers that a prudent trustee of comparable skills could properly delegate under the circumstances."

The differentiation between mandates and trusts was expressly considered by the Convention on the Law Applicable to Agency, which determined the applicable legislation to international relations established when a person, the intermediary, has power to act, acts, or has the intention to act on behalf of another person, the one represented. The convention will be applied when the intermediary acts in his or her own name or in the name of the represented one, this being his or her habitual or occasional activity. This Convention established in its article 3 that "the trustee shall not be regarded as an agent of the trust, of the person who has created the trust or of the beneficiary."[2]

To summarize, both agency and trust have in common that a command, order, or direction is given by one person to another. Nevertheless, all trusts imply the existence of a trust property and a trustee acting in relation to it, whereas under agency the agent is acting on behalf of the mandator.

Although it is explained in the corresponding chapters in Part II, it is worth mentioning that some Latin American countries such as Colombia, Ecuador, and Paraguay have fiduciary transactions that do not involve the transfer of property, which are called "fiduciary mandates." Even though in some cases they are regulated jointly with trusts, fiduciary mandates are agency contracts and not trusts. They do not involve the creation of a special-purpose patrimony and, in case a certain asset is needed to carry on the fiduciary mandate, a bailment is used.

## D. PLEDGE AND MORTGAGE

Although pledges, mortgages, and guarantee trusts could be considered guarantees on realty (or guarantee *jus in rem* rights), there are some important differences among them:

a. It is obvious that a trust does not necessarily have the aim of a guarantee; it may have many other objectives.
b. Mortgages and pledges are always *inter vivos* contracts, whereas guarantee trusts can be created by a will (although this is not a common case). Any kind of assets can be transmitted in trust property, no matter if they are corporeal things or incorporeal rights, whereas pledges or mortgages, by definition, can only be executed on movable or real property. For example, guarantee trusts can be used to secure an obligation with a future cash flow, which is impossible with a pledge or a mortgage because these two require a corporeal thing (some Latin American countries allow the pledge of cash flows). Before trusts, in most jurisdictions it was legally impossible to secure a credit with a cash flow. An example of these trusts is highway construction with financing that was guaranteed with a large cash flow.

---

2    Paragraph (b), of article 3 of the Convention on the Law Applicable to Agency signed in The Hague on 1978 that entered into force in 1992 (ratified by Argentina, France, Netherlands and Portugal). The full text can be found at www.jurisint.org/doc/html/ins/en/2000/2000jiinsen36. html.

c. One of the most important points to be considered when treating the guarantee trust is the criminal responsibility of the participants. If a debtor transfers the trust property of a cash flow and keeps their collecting activity, he or she will become the administrator of a third-party asset (the creditor). Therefore, if the collected funds were not given in time and form, he or she could have criminal responsibility related to the fraudulent administration. This creates a substantial difference with an ordinary debt default, which is not a criminal offense.

d. The trust assets could be foreclosed extrajudicially. This situation represents a very important advantage with respect to pledges or mortgages. The creditor has no need to enter a judicial process to recover the invested capital. Avoiding the juridical process by directly selling out the trust assets, the trustee will increase the value of the asset as an object of guarantee, because the costs and time of the recovery of the asset in guarantee will be smaller than in a judicial process. Nevertheless, seeking for celerity and economy in the realization of the business, good practices indicate a quite simple and transparent proceeding must be established to allow the trustee, in the event of default of the creditor, to sell out the trust assets in the best possible way, but at the same time, in such a way as is fair to avoid debtor's objections. Trust property is more flexible, as different methods of administration and disposition could be stipulated. In short, the guarantee allows a private selling out of the assets given in trust, whereas in the pledge and the mortgage, judicial participation is required through public auction.

e. The asset given in guarantee trust comes to be the trustee's property, that is to say, the trust ownership of the assets is transmitted, forming with them a special patrimony separate from the trustee, grantor, and beneficiary, whereas in the pledge and the mortgage, the assets remain in the debtor's patrimony, subject to natural, juridical, and economic movements.

To summarize, there are very significant differences between the guarantee trust and pledges and mortgages.[3] The main one is the possibility of a private liquidation of the trust assets in the event of default of the debtor.

## E. USUFRUCT

The usufruct is the real right (*jus in rem*) to use and enjoy a thing that belongs to another without altering its substance.

The usufruct implies a division of the ownership in favor of the usufructuary, generating a remainder proprietary (*nudo propietario*) who will have the full property at the end of the usufruct. In this respect, no separate patrimony is in existence constituted by the asset, which is the object of the usufruct, nor an assignment to fulfill by the usufructuary. On the contrary, a trust involves a special-purpose patrimony that is to be devoted to the fulfillment of a goal (the trust assignment). More importantly, in the

---

3  For a list of advantages of the guarantee trust in comparison to pledges and mortgages, see section B, Guarantee Trusts, in Chapter 5, Types of Latin American Trusts.

usufruct there is no instruction from the one who transfers the usufruct to the one who receives it. The usufruct is in the benefit of the holder of the right, whereas the trust is in the benefit of a person (beneficiary) that is not the holder of the title (trustee).

## F. CORPORATION

Because in Latin American the most widely used trust is the business trust, it is common for a foreign practitioner to ask when to use a trust and when to use a corporation as a legal vehicle for business. The general answer is that the corporation would be the right vehicle to carry out an activity, and the trust is the adequate legal vehicle for a particular project. Most probably, in the case of a business trust there will be a settlor and beneficiaries structure, under which several settlors will make asset contributions to a trust to benefit (usually in the same proportion of the contributions) from the trust development of a project.[4]

From a purely formal point of view, the main difference between a trust and a corporation is that the latter is a legal person, whereas the former is a special-purpose patrimony. Other differences are as follows:

a. A trust is a flexible plan that allows the creation of several committees and the distribution of powers among the settlors and beneficiaries. For example, it may be stipulated in the trust instrument that one or several settlors will have a power of veto on certain decisions of the trustee, such as the sale of certain assets, any contract that would imply a payment superior to a certain amount of money, the modification of certain characteristics of the project, the indebtedness of the trust above a certain amount or with a certain purpose, and so forth. In comparison a corporation is far less flexible and does not allow the distribution of specific powers among the shareholders, and the function of the board of directors does not allow modifications.
b. In certain countries, corporations can only make dividend distributions if there are liquid earnings, whereas trusts are not subject to this restriction.
c. In most Latin American countries, a corporation must have at least two shareholders, whereas trusts can be created by one settlor.

---

4    Langbein explained, referring to the U.S. law, that he finds it "useful to think of the trust as a competitor, locked in a sort of Darwinian struggle against other modes of business organization and finance, in particular the corporation, but also the partnership and the various techniques of secured finance. The challenge is to understand why the trust prevails when it does. I shall point to four key attributes of the trust device that entice the transaction planner: (1) the protection of beneficial interests in the event that the trustee becomes insolvent; (2) the ease with which the trust lends itself to favorable conduit-type taxation; (3) the protective regime of trust fiduciary law; and (4) the trust's flexibility of design in matters of governance and in the structuring of beneficial interest." John H. Langbein, *The Secret Life of Trust: The Trust as an Instrument of Commerce*, 107 YALE L.J. 179 (1997–1998).

d. The constitution and liquidation procedures of corporations could prove too time consuming, rigid, and costly for a single project.

e. Furthermore, in certain jurisdictions trusts are pass-through entities for tax purposes.

## G. FOUNDATIONS

The traditional definition of foundations (in Spanish, *Fundaciones*) states that foundations are legal entities established by one or several founders for charitable, educational, religious, scientific, health, relief of the poor, political, or other benevolent or general social-benefit purposes, and not for profit, being the recipients either the community as a whole or an unascertainable and indefinite portion hereof.[5] Foundations usually have income tax and value-added tax exemptions and are allowed to receive donations that are tax deductible for the donors. They usually require the approval of the government to be created.

Foundations are legal entities different from corporations, partnerships, and other commercial vehicles, which have a separate legal regime. The main difference is that foundations have no owners. Put differently, there are no shareholders, partners, or members of the foundation. A foundation is managed by a board or council whose initial members are chosen by the founder and then by the same board (or a third party determined by the foundation bylaws). In most Latin American countries, foundations are under the permanent control of the government and, in the event of dissolution, a foundation's assets cannot be distributed to members of the board, founders, or any other related individual, excepting a charitable institution, or they become state-owned assets.

Charitable foundations are a legal vehicle widespread in Latin America used by those who want to make a charitable endowment—few Latin American countries have specific rules for charitable trusts, and even fewer have a tradition of setting up such trusts. There are also famous examples in the United States, such as the Ford Foundation or the Rockefeller Foundation.

The main difference between a foundation and a charitable trust is that foundations are legal entities (not just a separate patrimony) and have a long tradition in Latin American countries. The main similarity can be found in section 1 of the Panamanian Foundations Act, which establishes that "the creation of a foundation implies the affectation of a patrimony to certain objectives or purposes expressed in the foundational act. The initial patrimony can be increased by the founder or by any other person."[6] Certainly, this provision helps to explain the parallelism between private-nterest foundations and asset-protection trusts, both being legal schemes that allow the creation of a patrimony effected for certain purposes.

---

5   The definition has not changed much since Roman law, which considered a foundation as a legal person that has as its main object to administer assets for a certain purpose, in general, a charitable or religious one. *See* Luis Rodolfo Argüello, Manual de Derecho Romano: Historia e Instituciones 164–165 (3rd. 2007).

6   Section 1 of Act No 25 of June 12, 1995 of Panama that rules Private Interest Foundations (Official Gazette No. 22,804 of July 14, 1995).

## 1. Private-Interest Foundations

Foundations as defined in the preceding section can be called "public-interest foundations" and must be differentiated from "family" or "private-interest foundations." Private-interest foundations are not created to benefit the community as a whole or an unascertainable and indefinite portion of it but to benefit certain individuals as established by the founder. They do not require express authorization, only the registration of a foundational act.

The sole country in Latin America that has a "private-interest foundation regime" and, therefore, the sole country in which such foundations can be legally created, is Panama. All the other countries request for the existence of a foundation that the interest that is served by the foundation is a public one (charitable purposes). In general, Latin American countries allow public-interest foundations but not private-interest ones, Panama being the sole exception.

Private-interest foundations are analogous to asset-protection trusts with the difference that a foundation is a legal entity, and a trust is but a separate patrimony. The comparison between a Panamanian private-interest foundation and a trust can be summarized as follows:

a. Unlike trusts, foundations are legal entities.
b. Instead of a trust deed, there is a foundation bylaw that must be registered so that the legal entity is created. In Panama there are shelf foundations available. Regarding the substantial aspects, both instruments (the trust deed and foundation bylaws) deal with the same issues (mainly the administration and rules for the distribution of assets), and both the trustee and the members of the board are subject to fiduciary duties.
c. A foundation may not be involved in business activity directly on a permanent basis, but it can be the sole shareholder of a corporation that is permanently involved in such activities.
d. Trusts are well known in the common-law tradition countries. The question that arises is if this is an advantage or a disadvantage. The points to be considered are: (i) practical aspects such as a further delay in opening a bank account (although under current standards and because of "know your client" requirements, the opening of a bank account is a time-consuming process both for trusts and foundations); (ii) there is a higher degree of uncertainty on the decision of a common-law judge on the validity and enforceability of a foundation; and (iii) a common-law creditor of the founder would have more difficulties to determine his or her rights against the foundation.
e. Panamanian private-interest foundation law specifically addresses the issue of the forced heirship rules of the jurisdiction of the domicile of the founder and states that the Panamanian judge would not consider such rules applicable to the foundation.
f. Foundations are legal entities, and as such, there is no new concept involved (as there is in trusts, which involve the creation of a separate patrimony) if they acquire real estate assets in jurisdictions in which the trust is not recognized (either

in the internal law or as a result of the ratification of the 1984 Hague Convention on Trusts. In other words, it would be much simpler to explain that a foundation is the owner of a real estate property to a judge who does not know trusts than to explain the concept of trust property.

Further detail on Panamanian private-interest foundations will be provided in Chapter 18.

# Chapter 5

# Types of Latin American Trusts

A.  Administration Trusts  71
    1.  Charitable Trusts  72
    2.  Business Trusts  72
B.  Guarantee Trusts  73
C.  Governmental or Public Sector Trusts  74
D.  Testamentary Trusts  75
    1.  Forced Heirship  76
    2.  Distinction between Fiduciary Substitution and Trust  76
E.  Project Finance Vehicle  79
F.  Other Types of Trust  80

The trust is a flexible concept of changeable characteristics. Although the U.S. law has no special classification of trusts, it permits different forms that lend themselves to classification. Scholars distinguished between discretionary trusts, participation trusts, active and passive trusts, express trusts, implicit trusts, executed trusts, resulting trust, and constructive trusts, among others. The classification made in Latin America by scholars and by the statutes and regulations is different from the one in the United States. A description of the different kinds of trusts in Latin America and their particular characteristics follow.

## A. ADMINISTRATION TRUSTS

The main classification of trusts in Latin America distinguishes between administration and guarantee trusts. In turn, administration trusts can be divided into two subclasses: (a) those that involve a charity act with the aim of benefiting third parties, and (ii) those that intend to organize a business for profit.

## 1. Charitable Trusts

These trusts could be compared with a donation, which instead of ending in a single act transmitting an asset, remains during a period of time for the benefit of a third party. For example, if I donate a building to a school, there is a single act, but if I create a charity trust with that same building as an underlying asset in favor of the same school, the benefit will be received by the school during the life of the trust. Charity trusts should fulfill the rules related to nonlucrative acts, such as rules concerning formalities of donations and substantial rules regarding forced heirship.

This kind of trust is growing in popularity in Latin America. The most common case is the one in which a trust is created to help indeterminate but determinable individuals, such as a scholarship for the best student of a certain university. The benefit (i.e., an amount of money) could not be donated at the time because it is not known who will be the best student in the future. Therefore, a charity trust is the best alternative. In some countries (e.g., Colombia, Costa Rica, El Salvador, Honduras, Mexico, and Paraguay), this kind of trust is excluded from the maximum legal term for trusts.

As explained when comparing trusts with foundations, in Latin America there is a long tradition of using foundations instead of trusts to effect a patrimony for a charitable cause. Nevertheless, as the foundation is subject to many more legal restrictions and is far less flexible than a trust, trusts have been increasingly used in the last years.

## 2. Business Trusts

Business trusts and guarantee trusts are the most widely used kind of trusts in Latin America. In the case of business trusts, the basic structure is the one in which several settlors are the beneficiaries of one trust (in the same proportion of the contribution as settlors), which was formed to develop a project. The most common examples are trusts for the development of small- or medium-sized businesses in: (a) commodities production (soy bean, berries, cattle, oleic corn, etc.), (b) real estate (apartments, units in fenced neighborhoods, hotels, etc.), (c) forestry, and (d) vineyards. The trust is usually created by an agreement between the first settlor or beneficiary and the trustee, and other settlors or beneficiaries adhere to the trust afterwards.

Trusts in which the settlors are also the beneficiaries are an ideal vehicle for investment projects because of their versatility, their tax treatment (in several jurisdictions the trust is not subject to income tax, but the grantors-beneficiaries are), and the existence of a limitation of liability (settlors and beneficiaries are not responsible for the trust debts).

In this kind of trust, the trustee's essential duty is the management of the trust assets so that they make a profit that will be distributed to the beneficiaries. Put differently, in the investment trust, trust assets should be applied to the development of a project to increase the trust patrimony, and the trustee is the one responsible for doing so. Having said that, it is common to appoint an "operator" or "manager," who provides the administration services and technical know-how that the trustee does not possess. For example, if a bank is appointed as trustee (it must be kept in mind that in several

Latin American countries only banks can be trustees), and the trust is for forestry, it is necessary to appoint a person who provides all the necessary services and know-how to administer the timber owned by the trust.

## B. GUARANTEE TRUSTS

Guarantee trusts can be defined as those by which assets are transferred to the trustee to guarantee a debt; the creditor could be the trustee and/or a third party. In the event of nonfulfillment, the creditor would be paid with the proceeds of the trust assets, which should be sold out. The difference between a guarantee trust and other trusts, is the nature of the beneficiary's right, which in the guarantee trust is to secure an obligation and not an actual payment.

The Costa Rican Code of Commerce, which will be considered in detail in Chapter 12, expressly disposes in the second paragraph of its article 648 that "a trust on assets or [guarantee] rights on an obligation of the grantor with the beneficiary can be constituted. In that case, the trustee can proceed to the sale or auction of the assets in case of [nonfulfillment], all in accordance with what is settled in the contract." It should be underscored that there is a similar norm in several Latin American countries.

The Colombian guarantee trust, Decree No. 653 of 1993, establishes that when the total loan is guaranteed through an irrevocable trust constituted by an authorized entity, the value of the sellout assets that will be given in guarantee cannot be less than one and a half the value of the loan and its benefits. The trust instrument must establish that the trustee will be obliged to sell the necessary assets to pay in the event the issuer does not pay in time the amount of the principal or the interests of the holders. With the product of the sale, the trustee will proceed to pay the holders directly or through the entity that has been designated as the manager of the issue.

In Brazil, there are no general regulations of trust, but several concepts of trust in guarantee are regulated.

In Mexico, the guarantee trust has been defined as the one that has the aim of guaranteeing debts on behalf of a client (grantor), in favor of the commission merchant's office or any other third-party creditor (beneficiary), through adding real estate, shares of corporations or other assets to the trust, which are transmitted to the bank (trustee) through establishing in the trust instrument a conventional proceeding of guarantees' foreclosure in the event of nonfulfillment.[1]

Although some of these points have already been mentioned when comparing the guarantee trust with pledge and mortgage, the advantages of the guarantee trust as compared to other guarantees is summarized below:

a.  The foreclosure procedure is a nonjudicial one.
b.  The assets that are assumed in the guarantee cannot be affected by third parties (such as other creditors of the debtor) because they are not the property of the debtor.

---

1   MIGUEL ACOSTA ROMERO & PABLO R. ALMAZÁN ALANIZ, TRATADO TEÓRICO PRÁCTICO DE FIDEICOMISO 397 (1999).

c. It allows the collateralization of several debts—it being far simpler to change the creditor (no registration with a public registry is needed).

d. The grantor does not necessarily have to be the debtor, and the trustee does not necessarily have to be the creditor.

e. Several assets that in most Latin American countries cannot be the object of a pledge or mortgage can be transferred as guarantee (such as a cash flow emerging from services to be provided).

f. Businesses that form an economic unit can be combined in a trust as collateral. Therefore, it is the ideal plan for a project finance.

g. In the case of construction or real estate development projects, the key advantage of the guarantee trust compared to the mortgage is that the creditor is not simply allowed to sell the land with the uncompleted construction (which would probably have a value far inferior than the amount invested), but the creditor can appoint a new construction company or developer, complete the construction, and sell the final units or the finalized project with a higher chance of recovering the funds granted. There are several successful cases in Latin America in which the trust allowed the continuation of projects that were severely affected by a crisis, and halted projects in which the creditor only had a mortgage.

One of the most frequently asked questions is whether it makes any sense to have a guarantee trust plus a mortgage on a construction project. As mentioned before, the guarantee trust would permit the creditor to step into the project if the construction goes bankrupt. And it does make sense to have a mortgage if there is credit to the trust for the construction, because the mortgage would allow to someone to be a preferred creditor in relation to other creditors of the trust.

The main downside of a guarantee trust compared to a mortgage or a pledge is that, eventually, the debtor may start legal actions, and the judges of certain jurisdictions may not be as familiar with the guarantee trust as they are with "traditional" guarantees, such as mortgages and pledges. This risk can be reduced in part by an arbitral clause that allows that any conflict be discussed in front of arbitrators who are aware of the characteristics of guarantee trusts.

To summarize, the guarantee trust has been used in Latin American law with proven versatility and utility.


## C. GOVERNMENTAL OR PUBLIC SECTOR TRUSTS

Governmental or public sector trusts are those in which the federal, provincial, or local state is the grantor, beneficiary, or both at once. In this kind of trust, the state, directly or by means of its agencies, in its role as grantor, transmits the assets or affects public funds to pursue a licit public-interest object.

Few jurisdictions specifically regulate the public trust, and there is no specific regulation that expressly makes this kind of trust clear, despite the importance they have nowadays. Most Latin American countries issued rules to provide adequate control on public trusts' assets and activities (such as Mexico) or to establish limits on the creation of public trusts unless there is a specific statute (as in Costa Rica and Argentina).

These kinds of trusts are subject to public administrative law and, therefore, are in some way under a different set of rules than the ones applicable to all the rest of the trusts. Unless specifically mentioned, in this book does not address the rules applicable to public sector trusts.

## D. TESTAMENTARY TRUSTS

As said before, the trust can also be set up by a will, done in some of the forms specifically foreseen for such acts. In such instances, it depends on each country's statutes to determine if a trust exists or not until the moment when the trustee accepts the position and operates the transfer of the trust property. In this sense, if the original trustee will not accept the task, it is necessary to follow the rules fixed in the contract for the election or assignment by a judge of a substitute trustee.

The testamentary trust is the last will disposition by which a person (testator-settlor) transfers certain assets to another one (trustee), who obliges him or herself to administer the trust property in benefit of the party designated in the will (beneficiary).

One of the particular points of the testamentary trust is the lack of possibility, in the event of nonacceptance or inexistence of the beneficiary for any other reason, of the assets returning to the grantor because he or she has died. Considering this case, if there is no substitute beneficiary expressly designated by the settlor, the reasonable solution is to submit the trust assets to the common rules of inheritance law as if the trust had never been created.

As mentioned earlier, irrevocability is the rule, and to be revocable a trust instrument must have an express provision, being the essence of the will the possibility of its revocation, it is not necessary that the testator had reserved the faculty of doing so in order for the will to be revocable. In short, although the rule for the *inter vivos* trust is its irrevocability, except if it has a contractual disposition which expressly states the contrary, the rule with testamentary trusts established by wills, is the revocability of the will until the death of the testator. In fact, if the testator revokes a will in which a trust is established for the moment of his death, he is not revoking an existing trust but just a potential or future one.

One possible use of the testamentary trust is the trust transfer of the payment that is made by a life insurance company for the death of an insured, to be managed by a professional who delivers the profits to the beneficiaries appointed by the insured. This allows, in the event of the death of the insured, the beneficiaries to enjoy a more efficient professional administration of the assets than they could do possibly because of their lack of ability or experience in this matter.

From a practical point of view, it should be stressed that testamentary trusts are not used in Latin America: The main reason is the existence of forced heirships that do not leave much room for estate planning. Most estate planning is done with trusts or private-interest foundations in a different jurisdiction from the testator's (as explained in the section on private-interest foundations in Chapter 18 on Panama) and in relation to assets not located in the country of the owner.

## 1. Forced Heirship

Testamentary trusts are not successful in countries with a low proportion of available assets for the testator, such as Argentina, where law stipulates that the children have the right to a forced heirship[2] of 80 percent. According to this, a person who has children can only dispose of 20 percent of his or her patrimony in his or her will because the remaining 80 percent is subject to forced heirship. Uruguay has similar rules. In other countries (such as Panama), there is no forced portion, or it is much more reduced, giving more possibilities to the application of the concept.

> Forced heirship forms an important part of the succession law of most civil law jurisdictions in Latin America and continental Europe. In essence, it gives the surviving spouse, children and/or other relatives of the deceased person, fixed shares of his or her estate. The consequences of forced heirship violations are not uniform among the countries that have this legislation. In some jurisdictions, the offending transfers of property may be treated as void from the very outset so that no title passes. In other legal systems, the transfers may be treated as merely voidable. The far more common paradigm, however, is not to invalidate the transfer at all but rather to "claw-back" into the estate any offending gifts that might have been made by the deceased person during their lifetime. . . . The Hague Convention on Trusts . . . by Act 15, expressly requires subscribing states to honor "(mandatory) succession rights, especially indefeasible shares of spouses and relatives." This is a clear and pointed reference to forced heirship rights and the succession laws that frame them. Needless to say, [anti-forced heirship] regimes as exemplified by the Bahamas model, run in the opposite direction, being designed to give primacy of the trust and the beneficial interests created [thereunder] over forced heirship rights.[3]

This explains why Guernsey, which ratified the Hague Convention, made express provision for the nonrecognition of foreign judgments and the exclusion of foreign inheritance laws. Guernsey is a peculiar jurisdiction that has a forced heirship regime (based on Norman customary law), but its courts recognize as valid a trust in breach of foreign forced heirship law.

## 2. Distinction between Fiduciary Substitution and Trust

Although many of the ideas regarding fiduciary substitution were already expressed in previous sections of this book or will be in Part II, the aim of this section is to bring all

---

2   Forced heirship is the part of the patrimony of the constituent of which some close relatives cannot be deprived, by a will or a donation, without a fair cause of disinheritance.

3   Wendy Warren, *Anti-Forced Heirship Regimes*, 16(10) STEPJOURNAL 51 (Nov. 2008).

of them together in a coherent explanation. As mentioned when discussing the anteced-ents of trusts, after the fall of the Roman Empire, the *fideicomissum* was used for the sole purpose of keeping certain real estate properties within the family and received the name of "fiduciary substitution." In other words, a perpetual inheritance order was cre-ated to avoid the sale of the real estate property object of the fiduciary substitution.

This indirect disposition capability eventually led to the demise of the *fideicommis-sum,* especially in the civil-law system in which hereditary succession was strictly regulated. *Fideicommisum* derived in the fiduciary substitution that was abolished by the French Revolution. Along this line of reasoning, Cariello explained that in France, during the ancient regime, fiduciary substitutions were a usual practice, being called simply substitutions and the assets affected by them substituted assets. Substitutions were used by the aristocracy to keep the concentration of wealth and the family assets with the firstborn sons so as to keep their political influence, which, obviously, would be damaged with the distribution of their properties and the titles they held among several sons and daughters, thus weakening their powers in relation to the sovereign and other feudal lords. Cariello further explained that the assets were received by the firstborn son (*maior natu*) with the condition that he transfer them to his firstborn son, and so on. The liberal ideas of the French Revolution attacked this system, and in 1792 the Legislative Assembly abolished fiduciary substitution. The Napoleonic Code section 896 reasserted the Assembly criteria and prohibited fiduciary substitutions.[4]

The confusion between trusts and fiduciary substitutions led to the idea of the prohibition of the trust in all the countries that used the Napoleonic Code as a model (such as most Latin American countries).[5]

When trusts were introduced in Latin American countries, several legal stipulations were included to avoid the possibility that they were used to avoid the public policy inheritance law using trusts as devices for fiduciary substitutions.

Technically speaking, a fiduciary substitution is a legal scheme similar to a trust in which the trust property is in favor of the trustee, but with the limitation that it cannot be sold, but must be used and kept in favor of someone predetermined by the trust instrument (e.g., a firstborn child). Nevertheless, the same effect can be achieved with a trust in which the trustee is a corporation, and the beneficiary is replaced at the moment of his or her death by his or her firstborn child.[6] With these kinds of trusts in

---

4    HÉCTOR TURUPHIAL CARIELLO, EL FIDEICOMISO 87–88 (2000).

5    Chalhoub explained that during the Middle Ages, the Roman trust was used as a means to
     segregate the patrimony of a family in the hands of a few of its members. The abuse of the trust
     led to a reaction against it during the French Revolution, which in turn led to the prohibition of
     the trust in the Napoleonic Code that was adopted as model for most Latin American countries.
     Nevertheless, it was a mistake to confuse all the trusts with the fiduciary substitution (using a
     trust is a way to avoid the inheritance law). Luis A. Chalhoub, *Estudio Comparativo entre el
     Fideicomiso y la Fundación de Interés Privado en la Legislación Panameña, in* ALGUNAS
     CONFERENCIAS SOBRE EL FIDEICOMISO, LAS FUNDACIONES DE INTERÉS PRIVADO Y SUS USOS EN PANAMÁ
     89–90 (2005).

6    Although the maximum period of time of trust may represent a limit, in most Latin American
     countries such period of time can be renewed, and it is unclear if the trust instrument can allow
     the trustee alone (without the approval of the beneficiaries) to do it.

mind, the legislators of Latin American countries adopted several solutions to avoid fiduciary substitution:

a. Prohibition (as in Bolivia and Colombia) of those trusts in which the benefit is vested in various persons who must successively be substituted as a result of the death of their predecessor: In short, if a trust provides that the beneficiary will be replaced because of his or her death by another beneficiary in a line that has no end, such trust is simply illegal.
b. Limitation: In Costa Rica, the fiduciary substitution is valid as long as the beneficiaries are alive or already conceived at the grantor's death. In Peru, it is valid as long as the substitution is carried out in favor of persons existing at the time the right of the first appointee is made good. And in Venezuela, as long as the substitution is carried out in favor of persons in being when the first beneficiary's right is obtained[7].
c. Brazil is a very particular case because fiduciary substitution exists but is limited to one degree. Put differently, it is null and void to appoint a residual beneficiary of the residual beneficiary.[8] In such a case, the heir (*fiduciário*) would be the owner of the assets without restriction.[9] In short, the Brazilian Civil Code allows appointing an heir to the heir. It is not a trustee as conceived in common law and in most Latin American countries, because the trustee can use the property in his or her own benefit with the sole restriction of transferring it to a third party at the moment of his or her death, at a certain date, or at the moment of the accomplishment of a condition. Another main difference with a trustee is that there are several cases in which the heir becomes full owner (holds an ownership without the restriction of transferring to a third party). Therefore, this legal institution is not a trust as understood under common law and the other Latin American jurisdictions, but a fiduciary substitution as understood in ancient Roman law.[10]
d. In Chile, section 745 of the civil code prohibits the creation of two or more successive trust properties in such a way that, once the trust has been restored to a person, he or she acquires it with the encumbrance of restoring it to another at a later time. This is the way to avoid fiduciary substitutions in Chilean law. If two or more successive trust properties were actually created and the trust property was acquired by one of the appointed beneficiaries, the expectancy of the others would be expired forever. It must be pointed out that this is an exception to the general rule in Chilean law (and almost all Latin American laws) that a prohibited stipulation is null and void.

---

7   This is a way to avoid the fiduciary substitution explained in Chapter 1, Section A,1 and Section B, and in Chapter 5, Section D,2.
8   Civil Code § 1959.
9   *Id.*
10  Diniz explained *fideicomisso,* expressing that it is a kind of revocable ownership (it can be used by the owner, but it is subject to a limited period of time) created *mortis causa* under which the heir has the duty to transfer the assets received as inheritance after certain conditions are accomplished. 4 Maria Helena Diniz, Curso de Direito Civil Brasileiro 330–331 (23rd ed., 2008).

Regarding U.S. law, Friedman referred to the "dynastic" use of trusts:

> [T]hrough trusts and settlements, a testator who so wished could bind an estate within his family for as long as the law would permit. How long was that? There was a limiting doctrine, called the rule against perpetuities. The rule, which had reached full flower in England in 1800, was at least nominally in force in the United States. The New York revision of 1827–[18]28 modified the rule and made it even more stringent. The New York statutes on trusts were, as we have seen, antidynastic. Only caretaker trusts were intended to survive the onslaught of reform, although the point was blunted by later amendments. Neither in New York, nor in Michigan, Wisconsin, or Minnesota, which borrowed the code, were the rules to stamp out the dynastic trust ever fully carried out. The drafting of the New York code had a specific image in mind, a specific type of dynasty. They were thinking of the great English landed estates. Under a settlement of long-term trust, such an estate was "tied-up" in a family in two senses: [N]o current member of the family had the right to sell his interest, nor could anybody, including the trustee, treat land and improvements as market commodities; land and family were tied tightly together.[11]

Even today, certain scholars identify trust (*fideicomiso* or *fiducia*) with fiduciary substitution, in particular in civil-law tradition countries in which trust (*fideicomiso* or *fiducia*) is not regulated, such as Spain.[12]

In short, trust (in Spanish, *fideicomiso* or *fiducia*) as it is known today in Latin America is completely different from fiduciary substitution, which is still limited or prohibited, whereas trust is a flexible legal institution that can be used for multiple purposes as shown in this chapter.

## E. PROJECT FINANCE VEHICLE

Trusts as project finance vehicles offer the utmost transparency and security by virtue of the fact that the assets will only be applied to the selected project, based on the principle of professional management of the funds by the trustee, with the investor and the administrator's independence.

In the past, the two most frequent examples of direct investment funds were forestry trusts and real estate development trusts. Nowadays, the most frequent cases are agriculture trusts and those related to the export of commodities.

Regarding project finance, trusts present clear advantages over corporations because of the following:

a. More flexibility exists in terms of restrictions to payments to third parties (i.e., no payment of benefits to sponsors until full payment of debt).
b. The application of funds is specific to one end in the trust, whereas the board of directors of a corporation could assume responsibilities and apply the funds to

---

11    LAWRENCE M. FRIEDMAN, A HISTORY OF AMERICAN LAW 252–255 (2nd ed. 1985).
12    *See* ANTONIO DOMINGO AZNAR, EL FIDEICOMISO Y LA SUSTITUCIÓN FIDEICOMISARIA (1999).

other ends. This is a natural consequence of the fact that corporations are a legal vehicle to transact business generally and are not themselves specific projects.

c. The trust permits the creation of tailor-made offices, such as a committee comprised of members with different functions and powers (e.g., the need for one of the creditors and/or sponsors to be consulted in certain issues, or his or her right to veto, etc.). This allows the utmost freedom in the distribution of duties. In the case of a corporation, certain rigidity exists as imposed by the functions that may or may not be exercised by the corporate organs, which would amount to a problem in the face of specific cases.

d. As a general rule, trusts are simpler to create and liquidate than corporations. Nevertheless, this depends on the type of vehicle under analysis (e.g., with or without public offering of its securities, duration of the project, etc.).

e. Trusts permit investors to focus on the analysis of the project's fund flow and should any of the participants pose a problem, they may be replaced so that the project is completed and operates successfully. The natural outcome is to permit project financing that otherwise would not have been obtained, as its promoter would not meet the required conditions.

## F. OTHER TYPES OF TRUST

Other kinds of trust are those used

a. To implement programs in companies of shared property in favor of workers, as the one implemented in light of the privatization of state-owned companies.

b. To create mutual funds, or, as in the Brazilian and Argentinean cases, as a legal vehicle for mutual funds in real property.

c. To rebuild financial entities in trouble: These kind of trusts are used when the authorization of financial entities to operate is suspended or revoked, and a central bank takes over the reorganization and/or liquidation.

To summarize, the trust is a very flexible and versatile legal scheme that allows the implementation of different aims safely and has been used with several administration and surety purposes.

# PART II

# Country-by-Country Analysis

# Chapter 6

# Argentina

A. Overview 84
   1. Antecedents 84
   2. Sources for Drafting Law No. 24441 85
   3. Definition 86
   4. Requirements of the Trust Agreement 87
B. The Grantor 88
C. The Trustee 89
   1. Rights and Duties of the Trustee 90
   2. Trust as a Separate Patrimony 92
   3. Criminal Responsibility of the Trustee 94
   4. Termination of the Office of the Trustee 94
   5. The Financial Trustee 95
D. The Beneficiary 95
   1. The Residual Beneficiary (*Fideicomisario*) 96
E. Securitization and Financial Trust 97
   1. Securitization 98
   2. Financial Trust Instrument 99
      a. Transference of Credits to the Trust 99
      b. Trust Assets Insufficiency 100
   3. Trust Securities 101
F. Particular Cases and Experience 104
   1. Public Sector Trusts 104
   2. "Cost Contribution" Real Estate Trusts 105
G. Tax Treatment 105
   1. Federal Income Tax 105
   2. Value-Added Tax 106
   3. Gross Revenue Tax 106
   4. Other Taxes 106

## A. OVERVIEW

The regulation of the trust in Argentina was established in January 1995, by the Housing and Construction Financing Act (Law No. 24441) which, as its name suggests, had as its main objective the creation of the legal instruments to facilitate the financing of housing construction. The Law created the financial trust as the vehicle of securitization of mortgages and the ordinary trust as the vehicle for small-to-medium-sized real estate projects. The object of Law No. 24441 is to attract capital without any third-party intermediation for producers wishing to develop production and construction projects, facilitating funding, and reducing its cost. This procedure also permitted investment by the public, generally in activities that would otherwise be closed to it. Furthermore, this form of project implementation permitted extension to international capital markets.

The 2001–2002 Argentinean crisis created the perfect conditions for trusts to boom. The lack of bank financing and the lack of confidence in banks, plus the extraordinary boost in construction, agriculture, forestry, mining, and other commodities made the trust the ideal vehicle for investors to develop projects in those fields. The investors were settlors and beneficiaries of the trust, the trustee was responsible for administering the assets (or a third party that was hired by the trustee), and the trust deed was the document in which the project was described in detail. Under these conditions, the ordinary trust became a widespread and well-known business vehicle for projects.

In short, Argentina was one of the last countries in Latin America to adopt a trust regulation (the sole country after Argentina that created trust regulation was Uruguay in 2003), but it made an intensive use of it, compensating its short history with a fast, widespread use of the trust.

## 1. Antecedents

Before Law No. 24441, it was possible to create trusts in Argentina under a civil code article,[1] but lack of adequate regulation and unfamiliarity with the concept resulted in its scant use. Nevertheless, some scholars encouraged the use of the trust prior to the enactment of Law No. 24441.[2]

---

1   Article 2662 of the Argentine Civil Code, drawn up by the Argentine Jurist Dalmacio Vélez Sarsfield at the end of the nineteenth century, stated in its original drafting (then modified by Law No. 24441): "Fiduciary ownership is the one acquired in an 'individual' trust, subordinated to last but until the occurrence of a resolutory condition, or until the lapse of a resolutory period, for the effect of restoring the thing to a third party."

2   In 1982, Carregal claimed that in Argentina trusts "have enjoyed an exceedingly limited use and, in this way, after more than a century since the enactment of the Civil Code, the applications of [a]rticle 2662 are but few." Therefore, he added that "experience is almost nonexisting, in spite of the absence of insurmountable obstacles in our legislation in order to put them into practice at once." MARIO A. CARREGAL, EL FIDEICOMISO: REGULACIÓN JURÍDICA Y POSIBILIDADES PRÁCTICAS 13, 38 (1982).

Isolated cases of trust creation prior to Law No. 24441 were based on Civil Code article 2662, as well as in particular acts. It is worth pointing out that "for instance, in the liquidation of the former City of Buenos Aires Transportation Association,[3] toward 1958, Laws No. 14065 and 14501 employed the legal concept of the trust," among other cases.[4]

Several drafts of acts of the National Congress included the regulation of the trust. One of the most prominent was the draft of the Trust Law, drawn up in 1969, by a committee of prestigious jurists. Unlike the current rules, it was noteworthy that in this draft the assets subject to trust were limited to imported equipment or assets included in housing programs, and the possible trustees were confined to financial institutions.

In addition, Law No. 18061, or the Financial Institutions Act, modified by Law No. 20574, provided the possibility of investment banks and financial institutions acting as "trustees." It should be noted that articles 22 and 24 of the current Financial Institutions Act (Law No. 21526), in keeping with the foregoing antecedents, maintained the power granted these entities to act as trustees.

Another instance of the use of the trust concept prior to Law No. 24441 is found in Law No. 23696 and its Regulatory Decree No. 584/93, which deemed trusts as the means to implement employee-shared ownership programs of privatized companies.

## 2. Sources for Drafting Law No. 24441

Regarding the sources considered in the drafting of Law No. 24441, the presidential *Message of Presentation* to the Argentine National Congress of the bill to become Law No. 24441 claimed that "it is hardly necessary to note that this is a concept long called for by the legal doctrine and by economic operators, since the brief regulation that the Civil Code introduces touching trust property is absolutely inadequate, which has given rise to numerous drafts which attempted to regulate it." Further, the president stressed that the text attached (what would become Law No. 24441) "followed the substance of the Civil Code reform bill (prepared by the committee appointed by the Executive Power by Decree [No.] 468 of March 19, 1992), which in turn had as a source the Commerce Code of the Republic of Colombia, the Credit Securities and Transactions General Act of the United States of Mexico (*Ley General de Títulos y Operaciones de Crédito de los Estados Unidos Mexicanos*), Law No. 17/1941 of the Republic of Panama, and the Civil Code of Quebec (Canada), sanctioned on December 18, 1991"[5] and "Law [No.] 19301 (which modified the Securities Market

---

3    In Spanish, *Corporación de Transportes de la Ciudad de Buenos Aires*.

4    ELÍAS P. GUASTAVINO, LA PROPIEDAD PARTICIPADA Y SUS FIDEICOMISOS 22–23 (1994). The author detailed various cases of legal rules that bore some of the features of the trust.

5    Bonfanti explained that the Code "sanctioned in 1991 comprises more than a hundred articles written both in French and English; e.g., [a]rticle 1260 *De la nature de la fiducie* or *Nature of the trust,* which underscores (i) the creation of a special-purpose patrimony; (ii) intended for a particular object; and (iii) administered by a trustee." Mario A. Bonfanti, *Significado Actual del Fideicomiso* 780 J.A. (1999-III).

Act, Law [No.] 18045 (*Ley de Mercado de Valores*) of the Republic of Chile. The bill clearly provides that the trust assets constitute a separate patrimony, as it is with trusts in Anglo-Saxon law."[6]


## 3. Definition

Law No. 24441 defines the concept of "trust" in article 1, stating that a trust shall exist when a person (the grantor) transfers the trust property of certain assets to another (trustee), who undertakes to exercise it in the benefit of the person designated in the trust instrument (beneficiary) and to transmit it on the accomplishment of a period or condition to the grantor, to the beneficiary, or to the residual beneficiary.

The trust may be created by will or by means of an *inter vivos* act (contract). The contractual type of trust encompasses two subspecies: the ordinary and the financial. The ordinary trust, which is the type provided in the definition of the prior paragraph, and the financial trust, which is no more than an ordinary trust that complies with two requirements: (a) that the trustee be a financial trustee (financial institution or authorized company), and (ii) that the beneficiaries' rights be evidenced in securities. The financial trust is the legal vehicle for securitization in Argentina.

Flowing from the definition, for there to be a trust it is a sine qua non requirement that there exist some assets with ownership that is transferred from one party to the other to accomplish a certain object because of which there must be: an asset, two parties, and a set of directions to the trustee. Each of these elements will be analyzed in detail later in this chapter. It is for now sufficient to say that the trust is a will or contract that creates a special-purpose patrimony; namely, an asset or set of assets that are specifically devoted to one purpose in an act that may be *inter vivos* or testamentary. The trust is not a legal entity in Argentina, but is a segregated patrimony owned and administered by the trustee.[7]

When creating a trust in Argentina, the transfer of ownership and the creation of a special-purpose patrimony is a necessary condition for the accomplishment of the object sought by the parties. Although cases where a similar end could be accomplished by other means (e.g., agency or bailment), no such legal certainty would exist for the parties as with the trust, and that could entail the failure of the transaction or sought-after object. In other words, the creation of a special-purpose patrimony is a necessary requirement for an agreement to qualify as a trust, and this patrimony is an object sought by the parties. Therefore, there is no such thing as an "excess of means" to accomplish a result.

As the testamentary trust (or trust created by will) is not used in Argentina because of the high proportion of assets subject to forced heirship (80 percent in cases where the person drafting the will has at least one child), this chapter will focus on the contractual trust or trust created by contract. Furthermore, as most trusts in Argentina are

---

6   Antecedentes Parlamentarios 821 (1995).

7   The sole country in Latin America in which the trust has legal personality is Ecuador. This particularity is explained in Chapter 13 on Ecuador.

used as a legal vehicle to carry on a real estate, forestry, agriculture, or some other kind of project, and that means the existence of several settlors and beneficiaries, a special point will be made about contractual trusts with several participants.

## 4. Requirements of the Trust Agreement

Under Argentine law, the *inter vivos* trust instrument must include the following:

a. *The identification of the assets under trust property:* The trust instrument must record the identification of the assets to be transferred to the trustee and, in the event of impossibility of such identification at the time of the creation of the trust, the requirements and characteristics that the assets must meet. For example, in an agricultural trust the asset that is transferred at the creation of the trust is cash, but most probably the contract would state that any settlor could transfer other assets, such as the right to use a portion of land, fertilizer, agricultural services, and so forth.

b. *The definition of the method whereby other assets may be incorporated into the trust:* As I understand it, this point is linked to the possibility that the original grantor, subsequent to the execution of the trust contract, may transfer the trust ownership of more assets, or where a trust has multiple grantors, without all of them simultaneously signing it. The case could be posed of a trust where the original grantor gives rise to the agreement, and other grantors subsequently join him or her, under prearranged terms, acquiring certain rights in exchange for their trust contribution. This is the ordinary way to create a trust with several grantors to avoid the need of all the them being present at the outset of the trust.

c. *The period or condition to which the trust ownership is subjected:* In no case may it be in excess of thirty years from its creation, unless: (a) the beneficiary lacks legal capacity (i.e., because of mental disability), in which case the trust may continue until his or her death or the termination of his or her disability; or (b) it is a forestry trust, in which case the trust could last until the completion of the forestry project.

As a practical matter, the definition of the maximum period of thirty years permits the trust to be the legal scheme to implement the use of realty by a person different from the owner. It should be stressed that under Argentine law the maximum rental period is ten years, the usufruct of realty in favor of legal persons cannot be longer than twenty years, and the lease[8] has no maximum period, but requires the existence of a purchase option that may not be desired by the parties that want to have a legal mean to use realty but not to transfer the property of it.

d. *The recipient of the trust assets on termination of the trust:* The law requires the designation of the recipient of the assets on the termination of the trust in the trust instrument. If, because of exceptional circumstances, it came to pass that the trust assets could not be delivered to the residual beneficiary nor to his or her

---

8    As used in Argentina, the term "leasing" refers to a rental agreement with a purchase option in all cases, "rental" being substituted where there is no such option.

successors, the grantor must be consulted. If consulting the grantor was not possible (e.g., because of death), and no criterion flowed from the contract to solve the situation, the assets must be delivered to the heirs of the grantor, because the trust would have lost its original reason for being. If this latter possibility were not possible either, it would be a *res nullius,* and the relevant rules should be applied.

From a practical perspective, two recommendations are in place here: the first is the provision of successive residual beneficiaries, the last of which should be one or several institutions that, it may be reasonable to assume, will continue to exist in the foreseeable future; the second point is that, in the face of a scenario where the course of action to be followed is unclear, the trustee should resort to payment into court to be discharged from any liability.

e. *The powers and duties of the trustee and the method for his or her substitution if he or she terminated in office:* This item will be covered later in this chapter (Section C, 4) when dealing with the trustee.


## B. THE GRANTOR

This is the party of the trust agreement who transfers the ownership of the assets and gives the trustee the instructions to follow in relation to those assets.

The general rule is that the grantor only enjoys powers of disposition on the trust assets until the time the trust ownership is transferred. Therefore, any analysis of the role of the grantor must be based on his or her ability to transfer the ownership and manifest his or her intent of creating a trust. Nevertheless, as under Latin American law the trust is a contract,[9] a grantor might reserve rights for him or herself. The most important right is that of revoking the trust, but it is possible to think of his or her reserving the right to change the beneficiary and/or residual beneficiary, add other unforeseen beneficiaries, determine the investments to be made by the trustee, or enjoy the power of veto in certain decisions, among others. Indeed, one of the advantages of the trust is its versatility and the possibility of creating a special-purpose patrimony governed by tailor-made rules set by the parties involved. Further, the mirror image of the trustee's duty to render accounts is the power of the grantor to enforce them, a natural consequence of his or her ability to demand the accomplishment of the charge he or she entrusted. In any case, and although nothing was established in the trust instrument, the settlor will have the right to request the rendering of accounts by the trustee.

Although Law No. 24441 addresses the "grantor" in the singular, nothing in particular prevents the existence of multiple grantors. This situation may be caused by: (a) a fiduciary contribution originally made jointly (e.g., grantors of an asset held jointly); (ii) a plurality of grantors provided by the trust instrument, but not executed jointly (e.g., grantors in an investment project known and encouraged by the existence

---

9   Note the difference with U.S. law under which trust is not considered a contract by most authors.

of other grantors who enter the trust at different times); or (iii) a subsequent contingency. In relation to item (iii), in the face of a situation of economic or financial stress, it will be the trustee's responsibility, based on good businessperson standards and considering the grantor instructions that he or she must perform, to elect between: (a) accepting a new grantor, (b) receiving a loan, or (c) simply dissolving the trust for considering impossible the accomplishment of the trust object. Where no exceptional economic or financial circumstance existed, it would not seem correct for the trustee to accept the contribution of a new grantor, unless the original instructions expressly or by implication so provided.

## C. THE TRUSTEE

As stated earlier, the contractual trust encompasses two kinds: the ordinary and the financial. First, the general requirements regulating the trustee's performance in an ordinary trust will be addressed, and then the specific rules governing the performance of the trustee of a financial trust will be discussed. Overall, all types of trustees are subject to the same rules as to their performance. The major dissimilarity is the capacity required of one or the other to be eligible to the trusteeship. Any person may be an ordinary trustee, but only some may be financial trustees (banks, companies, and branches authorized by the National Securities Commission).[10] This is a particular case of Argentina (and Uruguay, which used Argentine rules as the main source of its legislation) because in most Latin American countries only certain companies can be trustees.

As noted, the trustee is the party who exercises the fiduciary ownership to perform the grantor instructions. In Argentina, ordinary trust trustees are divided into two classes: (a) ordinary trustees and (b) public ordinary trustees. Law No. 24441 article 5 sets forth as a general rule that "the trustee may be any natural or legal person." However, if such a trustee were willing to offer his or her services publicly, he or she would qualify as a public ordinary trustee, and it is worth mentioning that there is an exception to the general principle, as only banks and legal entities registered in the Ordinary Trustees Public Registry with the National Securities Commission may offer their services as trustees publicly.

To summarize, the general rule is that anyone can act as an ordinary trustee. Nevertheless, to make a public offer of services as trustee (i.e., advertising in a newspaper offering services as trustee), a registration with the National Securities Commission is necessary, with the exception of banks; and such registration is also needed (but with higher requirements) to be a financial trust trustee.

In addition to what was explained in Part I, the following sections will focus on the special features of the trustee's responsibility under Argentine law.

---

10    The National Securities Commission (*Comisión Nacional de Valores*) is the Argentine equivalent of the American SEC. Argentina copied the U.S. model of public offering control. *See* Nicolas Malumian & Federico Barredo, Oferta Pública de Valores Negociables (2007).

## 1. Rights and Duties of the Trustee

As mentioned earlier in this chapter, provisions of article 4 of Law No. 24441 require the trust agreement to indicate the rights and duties of the trustee and the method of substitution should he or she abandon office. Furthermore, article 6 sets forth that "the trustee must conform with the duties imposed by statute or contract, with the prudence and diligence of a good businessman acting by virtue of the confidence placed in him."[11]

"A good businessman," maintains Carregal, "is not necessarily the one who conducts good business but he who adopts all the precautions dictated by deliberation and wisdom."[12] Hayzus claimed that "the law emphasizes a level of personal responsibility regarding a special standard—that of the prudence and diligence of the good businessman, called upon to assume and comply in good faith with the task at hand, within the circumstances proper to the agreement."[13]

There is no abstract median concerning the good businessperson generally, but rather the law demands an adequate qualification to manage the concrete transactions in which the trustee is involved. Case law established that "the yardstick of conduct assessment . . . 'diligence of the good businessman,' imposes the forecasting of happenings which are not unusual within the context of the activity in question according with common experience."[14]

It should be stressed that Argentine legislation, unlike that of other Latin American jurisdictions, does not expressly provide that trustees should resort to third parties, such as official control bodies, or a technical council as in Mexico, for them to make decisions in unforeseen cases, thus freeing the trustee from liability for the consequences of such acts.

The relevant legislation to serve as basis for an analysis of the liability of the trustee is provided by articles 512[15] and 902[16] of the Argentine Civil Code. Professional liability is greater for public ordinary trustees and financial trustees, because of the qualification required for the performance of their functions.

Another aspect relating to the proper performance of the trustee's duties is the strict requirement to maintain the trust assets separately. This duty materializes in the keeping of separate accounts, duly recorded and, in accordance with the number or type of assets, audited by qualified professionals. It should be borne in mind that article 1 of

---

11    Section 6, Nacional Law No 24441 (published in Oficial Gazette of January 16, 1995).
12    Carregal, *supra* note 2, at 96.
13    Jorge R. Hayzus, Fideicomiso 49 (2000).
14    National Commercial Court of Appeal of Buenos Aires [CNCom. Room D], 9/9/1995, "Estancias Procreo Vacunos S.A. v. Lenzi," (Arg.).
15    Section 512 of the Civil Code defined fault (lack of due diligence), establishing that "the debtor's fault in the performance of his or her duties consists in the omission of those procedures demanded by the nature of the duty, and which corresponded to the circumstances of the persons, time and place."
16    Section 902 of the Civil Code established that "the greater the duty to act with prudence and full knowledge of matters, the greater the liability deriving from the possible outcome of those acts."

Decree No. 780/95, which regulates Law No. 24441, sets forth that any record relating to trust assets in a balance sheet must indicate the trust character of the property with the rubric "in trust" (in Spanish, *en fideicomiso*). This point is related to the separation of debts and liabilities of the trust assets and the trustee's own personal assets, which has been addressed above (Section A3) and will be addressed again further on (Section C2).

Article 7 of Law No. 24441 provides in its first part that "the (trust) contract may not dispense the trustee from the duty to render accounts, which may be requested by the beneficiary in accordance with contractual provisions . . . in all cases the trustees must render accounts to the beneficiaries with a periodicity not in excess of one year."[17]

The trust instrument could include the duty to render accounts in favor of other interested parties, or even third parties. Nevertheless, it is reasonable to understand that the grantor is entitled to request accountings even when this has not been provided in the trust contract because it is in his or her power to remove the trustee in the face of poor performance of his or her duties, or to be summoned in the event that such a request is made by the beneficiary. Also, in most cases, it would not be viable to claim reasons of privacy or commercial confidentiality to deny the grantor the required accounting, as he or she is the one who has given rise to the trust assets and has stipulated their object.

Based on the provisions of the Argentine Commercial Code applicable to accounting, it may be construed that trusts should receive the assets clearly identified in the trust instrument (as required by law), which entails the need for an initial inventory. In addition, it would be essential to keep accounts and, where the amounts involved or the activity carried out warrants it, to have an independent outside audit, according with the market's common practices (good businessperson's common practice). This is further proven by the fact that accounts are of the essence when dealing with amounts of money, which cannot be otherwise identified.

Law No. 24441 article 7 also states that the trust agreement may not exempt the trustee from the liability or tort which either he or she or his or her subordinates (such as employees and directors among others) could incur. The trustee is liable either if the damage is the result of his or her involuntary tortious acts, that is, with negligence, recklessness, or ignorance of the matters he or she should necessarily know, or if it is voluntarily tortious, that is, with intent to injure.

In Argentine law, the general rule is the legal impossibility of dispensation of voluntary tort (the intent to injure) in contracts, with the possibility of dispensation of fault (lack of diligence or skill). Nevertheless, because of article 7, the trustee could not be dispensed of his or her fault in the trust agreement. Put differently, the trustee is subject to a higher standard than the ordinary one.

The foregoing article 7 also sets forth that the trustee cannot be exempted in the trust instrument "from the prohibition of acquiring the trust assets for himself." As it will be elaborated further in this chapter, this provision entails the prohibition of the trustee

---

17    First paragraph of Article 7, Law No. 24441

from being the residual beneficiary, and certain scholars have construed this as further barring the trustee from being the beneficiary.

Law No. 24441 article 17 provides that the trustee may dispose or encumber the trust assets when the trust contract allows him or her, without the trustee or the beneficiary's consent being necessary, unless there is agreement to the contrary. Where the assets were disposed of or encumbered beyond the powers granted in the trust instrument or without the appropriate consent, the trustee would be incurring the criminal responsibility explained further below.

As a practical matter, two comments are in place: (a) Article 17 allows wide latitude to afford the business the particular profile sought by the parties; and (ii) where assets were acquired from a trustee, it is strictly necessary to read the trust instrument in detail to ensure that he or she is not acting beyond his or her powers (*ultra vires*).

Law No. 24441 article 18 provides that the trustee is empowered to exercise all the acts necessary for the defense of the trust assets, both against third parties and against the beneficiary. The court may authorize the grantor or the beneficiary to start actions in lieu of the trustee, when the latter did not do so in time, and there are no sufficient grounds for the delay or omission.

Regarding trustee's fees, Law No. 24441 article 8 provides that "except for stipulation to the contrary, the trustee is entitled to the reimbursement of expenditures and to a fee. If that had not been fixed in the contract, it must be fixed by the [c]ourt taking account of the nature of the grantor instructions and the importance of the duties to be performed."

It is common practice to stipulate a fee in the trust instrument based on a percentage of the assets, together with some variable compensation linked to the success or the importance of the duties performed. An initial setup fee could also be granted for the special duties required by the trust's start-up.

This is one of the key aspects of trust agreement drafting and one that has been the reason for many controversies. It is crucial to determine the calculation bases, the different applicable percentages, the time of calculation, and the time of payment of the stipulated fee to avoid any inconveniences.

## 2. Trust as a Separate Patrimony

Along the same lines as the discussion in Part I of this book about the nature of the special-purpose patrimony, article 16 of Law No. 24441 in its first section states that "the trustee's assets cannot be reached for the obligations incurred in performance of the trust, which may only be satisfied with the trust assets." The exception to this rule is tax liabilities. The trustee is responsible for trust taxes until they expire, regardless of the trust having been liquidated.

It is essential that the trustee always state that he or she is acting in his or her capacity as such, so that his or her property (not trust assets but his or her own) is not involved. Should the situation lend itself to confusion, the other party to the agreement could intend to reach the trustee's own personal property.

In no case must the trustee affect nor dispose of his or her own personal property for compliance with the trust instrument unless he or she expressly grants a surety or guarantee. The obligations incurred in the execution of the trust should be satisfied with the trust assets exclusively, in accordance with the provisions of Law No. 24441 article 16.

In relation to the responsibility of the trustee for the debts of the trust, it must be pointed out that Argentine Civil Code section 1113 provides that "the liability of one who has caused an injury extends to the damages caused by his subordinates, or by the things he uses or keeps in his care. In the event of damages caused by things, the owner or tenant, to be exempted from liability, must show that there was no liability on his part; but if the damage had been occasioned by the risk or defect of the thing, he will only be partially or totally exempted from liability by proving the liability of the victim or of a third party for whom he is not held accountable. If the thing had been used against the owner or tenant's express or imputed intent, he will not be held liable." Therefore, as a general rule, if a third party were injured by the trust assets, the trustee would be liable for his or her indemnification. Nevertheless, the last part of article 14 of Law No. 24441 states that the aforementioned responsibility "is limited to the value of the trust asset whose risk or defect was the cause of the damage if the trustee could not reasonably have insured against that."

The wording of that section of the Civil Code could create certain practical problems, because the condition for the objective liability limitation to operate (if the trustee had not managed to take out reasonable insurance) is very difficult to establish, considering that in insurance the appraisal normally hinges on the return-to-cost ratio considerations. It is hard to establish when it should be deemed that a "reasonable impossibility" of insurance exists, thus raising the question as to the possible application of an unlimited liability.

Doubts also exist in terms of the value to be considered as the limit of the trustee's liability. This is so because the market value of the thing could be taken as being either that at the time of coming into the trust, or prior to or subsequent to the injurious act, among other alternatives. Having said this, the most central discussion would revolve around whether the "thing" that caused the particular damage should be considered, or the entire trust assets whereof the "thing" causing the damage is but a part. For example, if a machine valued at $100, which is part of a trust property of $1000, causes damage valued at $300, the question arises whether that damage would only be redressed partially, or whether the other trust assets could be affected. My view is that the concept of "thing" must be construed as all the trust assets at the time of the event.

To sum up, if the thing had not been insured, the liability limitation to the value of the trust thing would not operate, and the trustee would respond with all his or her personal property unless he or she demonstrated that it was impossible for him or her to insure it. This limitation to the amount of the damage to be redressed applies only in the cases of objective liability (that not based in fault), not in the cases where guilt or fraud exists, in which case the trustee must respond with all of his or her property.

## 3. Criminal Responsibility of the Trustee

Law No. 24441 added to the Argentine Criminal Code article 173(12), which refers to: "the trustee . . . who in his own benefit or that of a third party encumbered, disposed of or otherwise acted to the detriment of the assets and thus defrauded the rights of the co[]signers." Thus, the grantor, the beneficiary, and the residual beneficiary are protected from the possibility of the trustee disposing fraudulently of the assets subject to the agreement. The term "cosigners" is construed in the sense of all those directly interested or participating in the agreement, and not in the stricter sense of "parties" to it.

The cited article 173 lays down the special cases of fraud, referring to article 172 in reference to the applicable penalties. Article 172 prescribes that "the person who defrauded another by means of an assumed name, false capacity or qualifications, pretended influence, confidence abuse, or by posing as holding assets, credit, duties, business or negotiation, or by means of any other hoax or deceit, will be penalized with six months to one year imprisonment."

No parliamentary antecedents of the inclusion of this criminal concept in the Argentine Codes exist beyond a passing mention in the *Message of the Executive Power to Congress*.


## 4. Termination of the Office of the Trustee

Under the provisions Law No. 24441 article 9, the trustee will terminate in his or her office on the basis of the following:

a. Judicial removal caused by nonperformance of duties, at the grantor's instance, or at the request of the beneficiary, with summons served to the grantor
b. Death or incapacity declared by the court, in the case of individuals
c. Dissolution, in the case of legal persons
d. Bankruptcy or liquidation

If any of the situations delineated above came to pass, the trustee would be replaced by the substitute designated in the trust agreement, in accordance with the procedure indicated therein. In the event of no such provision being made or the designated trustee declining, the court will appoint as trustee one of the entities authorized to act as financial trustees.

One key issue in trust agreement drafting is that referring to the possibility of resignation by the trustee. It is customary to incorporate a clause allowing the trustee to resign his or her position but with the obligation to remain in office until a new trustee has been appointed and an orderly transfer of the assets has been completed. It is also frequently stipulated that the expenses of transferring the assets will be charged to the trust.

The vital importance of this item will become apparent when the fact is considered that the agreement is based on confidence reposed in the trustee and the difficulty in replacing the trustee in the case of noncommercial trustees designated by virtue of a special relation with the trustee.

In those Latin American countries where the capacity to act as trustee has been restricted to certain entities (i.e., banks), the existence of regulations prohibiting the trust to resign are the general rule. In the Argentine case, the trustee could resign even though the instrument says nothing in that respect, but that would only be possible if reasonable grounds existed.

## 5. The Financial Trustee

As has been said, one of the characteristic features of financial trusts is that the trustee is a bank or a company (subsidiary or branch) specifically authorized by the National Securities Commission to act as financial trustee.

To obtain registration in the Financial Trustees Registry, compliance with the following requirements must be proven: (a) net assets in excess of US$1,000,000; (b) state in its corporate purpose its performance as trustee; and (c) adequate administrative organization to render the service.

No company that is not expressly authorized to act as financial trustee may include in its name or otherwise use the term "financial trustee" or any such other terminology prone to generate confusion.

## D. THE BENEFICIARY

As explained, from a practical perspective the trust generates a division of the property in the formal ownership of the trustee—or legal title—and benefits flowing hence—or beneficial interest—in the hands of the beneficiary. In this reckoning, the beneficiary is the person who is entitled to the economic benefits emerging from the trust assets. From a legal perspective, the trustee is the owner of a real right of fiduciary or trust property, and is held in favor of the beneficiary.

The beneficiary is not a necessary party to the trust agreement, which capacity is represented by the grantor and the trustee. However, taking account of the fact that the trust agreement is in his or her benefit, it seems generally advisable that he or she signs the trust instrument accepting the advantages flowing from it as well as any obligation that it could impose on him or her. In the case of financial trusts, there is a consideration in favor of the beneficiary, which is the payment for the acquisition of the securities issued by the trust, and the natural form of evidencing his or her acceptance is by signing a securities purchase agreement.

The fundamental regulation regarding agreements in favor of third parties is Argentine Civil Code article 504, which sets forth that if an advantage in favor of a third party has been established, this third party may request the satisfaction of that obligation, had he or she accepted it and informed his or her acceptance to the obligor before it is revoked. In a trust agreement, the whole agreement has as its sole objective to bring about that obligation by the promisor before the beneficiary. Therefore, all of the trust agreement should be accepted by the beneficiary. Case law has acknowledged the character of the trust agreement as an agreement in favor of a third party and the ensuing power of the beneficiary of demanding compliance thereof once the agreement has been accepted.

As regards the specific regulations of Law No. 24441, article 2 provides that the trust agreement must individualize the beneficiary, who may be a natural or legal person who may or may not exist at the time of the agreement; in the latter case, the data permitting his or her future identification must be recorded in the trust instrument. More than one beneficiary may be appointed, who except for provision to the contrary, will benefit equally; substitute beneficiaries may be appointed for the event of declination, resignation, or death. If no beneficiary accepted, all of them resigned, or did not come into being, the grantor will be deemed the beneficiary. The beneficiary's right may pass by *inter vivos* acts (a transfer of rights) or *mortis causa* (will), except for provision to the contrary by the grantor.

Based on the fact that the trustee is the sole owner of the trust assets for the duration of the trust, the beneficiaries are only creditors of an obligation to give, and any defense of the trust assets is not in their own name but subrogating the trustee's rights. Case law, in a case where the grantor was also the beneficiary of the right over the proceeds of the realization of the trust assets (shares of a corporation) has held that "true as it may be that the trust assets are exempted from the individual or joint action of the trustee's creditors . . . however, the challenged decision did not order attaching the trust assets . . . but the income of its alienation. Therefore, the right to the 'contingent' income of the sale of the shares makes up the property of the debtor, so that that right is susceptible of being attached."[18] In this manner, it is made clear that the trust assets are not exposed to the possible contingencies of the grantor and/or beneficiary, but the latter's rights are part of his or her property and may be attached, without affecting the trust.

To sum up, the trust is an agreement in favor of a third party (the beneficiary). Even though great latitude exists regarding his or her appointment, the beneficiary must be singled out, and the pertinent acceptance must be available for the agreement to be enforceable by the same.

## 1. The Residual Beneficiary (*Fideicomisario*)

First, a terminological comment is in order. In several Latin American legislations, the name of *fideicomisario* is given to the person who is the beneficiary of the income of the trust without distinction from the one who receives the trust assets at the expiration of the agreement. Under Argentine law, the *fideicomisario* or residual beneficiary is the party who is entitled to receive the assets on termination of the trust.

---

18    National Commercial Court of Appeal [CNCom. Room D], 29/4/1997, "Manoukian, Ricardo v. Derymant SA," (Arg.).

This participant (strictly speaking not a party to the agreement as explained regarding the beneficiary) is distinguished from the beneficiary (in Spanish, *beneficiario*), who is the one receiving the income of the trust assets for the length of the trust's life. As understood, this differentiation between beneficiary and residual beneficiary enriches the concept and does not detract from its possibilities because, as shall be seen, no conflict whatsoever exists in the same person being beneficiary and residual beneficiary.

By virtue of Law No. 24441, the agreement must necessarily contain the recipient of the assets on termination of the trust, so that must include indication of the residual beneficiary.

## E. SECURITIZATION AND FINANCIAL TRUST

Securitization transactions may be carried out under several legal forms in Argentina, the financial trust being the sole one actually employed. Although securitization may be conceived as rising from closed-end mutual fund structures or special-purpose companies issuing debt securities, regulatory and tax reasons render these vehicles inappropriate means. In this light, financial trusts are tailor-made vehicles for securitizations as they permit isolation of the assets affected to the repayment of the securities from risks alien to the transaction.

Law No. 24441 article 19 defines financial trusts as those trusts subject to the rules of ordinary trusts, where the trustee is a financial institution or a company specifically authorized by the National Securities Commission to act as financial trustee, and the beneficiaries are the holders of certificates of participation in the fiduciary ownership or of asset-backed trust debt securities. From the legal definition, it follows that the key features of the financial trust are two: (a) the character of the trustee, which must be a financial institution or a company specially authorized to perform as financial trustee;[19] and (b) the form of evidencing the rights of the beneficiaries (securities).

The National Securities Commission is the authority that dictates regulatory requirements on financial trusts that make public offer of securities. Although the public offering of the trust securities is not a requirement for the trust to be financial, case law and the National Securities Commission consider that their intervention is confined to those cases where financial trusts conduct a public offering of their securities.

To sum up, that trust that meets the requirements set forth by Law No. 24441 article 19 is a financial trust. Namely, (a) that its trustee be a financial trustee, and (b) that its beneficiaries hold their rights in securities. Public offering is not a legal requirement of financial trusts; it is, however, one of the requirements for the application of a favorable legal system of rules and involves the intervention of the National Securities Commission.

---

19    See the item on financial trustees (Section C5 in this chapter).

# 1. Securitization

The first securitization was made by the then-named *Banco Hipotecario Nacional* (National Mortgage Bank) (later privatized and called *Banco Hipotecario SA*) in 1995. After this first experience, the securitization market grew at a fast pace until the 2001–2002 Argentine economic crisis, but a few years later it recovered. However, in 2008, the international financial crisis and the abrogation of the pension funds damaged the securitization market.[20] The assets being securitized changed after the first securitization from mortgages, car pledges, and leasing contracts to consumer credits and credit card coupons.

Since 1995, securitization has been employed in Argentina by several banks and companies with a view to securing funds and applying them to granting more loans or to their specific activities.[21] Regarding the assets liable to securitization, they may be divided into credits (mortgages, pledges, personal loans, export receivables or sale of goods) and credit rights (rents, toll collection, university fees, etc.). It could be claimed that it is possible to securitize any future funds flow by means of a financial trust.

As to the structure of the transaction, on the transfer of the assets to the trust, the grantor directs the financial trustee to issue trust debt securities and/or participation certificates to be placed in the capital market. With the revenue of the placement of the securities, the company is compensated for the transfer of the rights ceded to the trustee.

From the grantor's viewpoint, this is a trust transfer paid out of the funds obtained from the placement of securities. In turn, from the beneficiary's point of view, it may be appreciated that he or she has paid a sum of money for the security representing his or her beneficial interest. As there was a transfer of assets in exchange for cash in arm's length conditions, in the event of bankruptcy (under the antifraud rules explained earlier) there should be no problem. This is the reason that it could be supported that, from a legal standpoint, financial trusts generate a bankruptcy remote vehicle. In Argentina, courts have focused primarily on the consideration obtained by the seller of the assets as a primary factor for determining if there has been a true sale and not recourse against the transferor for the losses of the trust because of credit defaults.

In this transaction, the grantor obtains the present value of the transferred rights or loans, and the securities holders participate (in their role as creditors in the case of trust

---

20     In December 2008, the amount placed in financial trust securities was US$300 million (with 31 trusts), which represents a decrease of 24 percent in comparison with December 2007 (US$97 million less than the US$397 million issued in December 2007). Nevertheless, the amount of financial trust securities placed in 2008 was US$3,068 million (with 244 issuances) versus US$2,768 million (with 243 issuances) in 2007. Therefore, there was an increase of 11 percent (US$300 million) in 2008. Regarding the underlying assets of the financial trusts, 90 percent were consumer loans or credit card coupons, 7 percent car pledges, and 3 percent agriculture projects.

21     Jacob Gyntelberg et al. explained that "during the 1990s Argentina was the largest of the local structured finance market." Jacob Gyntelberg, Eli Remolona & Camilo E. Tovar, *Securitization in Asia and Latin America Compared, in* Expansion and Diversification in Securitization Yearbook 2007, at 390 (Jan Job de Vries Robbé & Paul Ali eds., 2008).

debt securities holders, or in their role as participants in the business in the case of participation certificate holders) in the returns emerging from the transferred credits.

## 2. Financial Trust Instrument

As to the contents of the financial trust agreement, Law No. 24441 article 20 provides that "the trust instrument must include the provisions of [a]rticle 4 [discussed in the section, *Requirements of the Trust Agreement* (Section A4 of this chapter) ] and the issuance terms of the participation certificates or debt securities." The particular comments applicable to financial trust deeds are as follows:

It is common practice to establish that the duration of the financial trust will extend until total payment of the service of the trust securities has been made according with their issuance terms, once the liquidation of remaining assets and liabilities has been conducted, if any. These clauses presuppose that the trust will exist for as long as the securities issued thereby. However, the period will not exceed the term set in Law No. 24441 article 4(c), which is thirty years from creation, except for forestry funds.

There is complete freedom to establish the causes of termination of the trust, among which may be mentioned by way of example: (a) adverse substantial alteration of market conditions, (b) changes in tax law, (c) the precancellation of the credits constituting the underlying trust asset; or any other reason forcing termination of the financial trust.

Once the payment of the service of the trust securities has been fully met and all other liabilities of the trust cancelled (deductible expenses, taxes, etc.), the remaining trust assets will be transferred to that person designated in the agreement as residual beneficiary, whether it is the grantor him or herself, the beneficiaries or a third party, or his or her successor.

Except for provision to the contrary in the issuance agreement, the trust assets will be the only payment source of the trust securities and of the obligations incurred in carrying out the trust, so that the trustee does not expose his or her assets in the issuance of the trust securities. The National Securities Commission has imposed the inclusion of a model paragraph expressly stating so in the offering memorandum, for the benefit of the potential securities purchasers.

*a. Transference of Credits to the Trust*  An issue arising in securitization processes in Argentina is that the transfer of credits requires the notice to the transferred debtor by a "public act"[22] for the transfer to be fully enforceable before third parties. This requirement may create practical difficulties because of the times and costs involved.

To solve this problem, Law No. 24441 provided in articles 70, 71, and 72 a particular system that permits the transfer of credits without a public notification act so long

---

22  *Cf.* Article 1467 of the Argentine Civil Code. There being no uniform opinion as to what should be construed by the expression "public act" because it is not defined in the Civil Code. It is construed to include notifications carried out by public notaries, among others.

as there is "contractual provision to that effect." In addition, Law No. 25248 of Leasing Agreements provides that the grantor may always transfer current or future credits or purchase option exercise price to the securitization of the rights emerging from the leasing agreements and, for their securitization, he or she may transfer them in the terms of the cited articles.

Article 70 of Law No. 24441, in conjunction with articles 71 and 72, set forth that their provisions will be enforced where rights are transferred as parts of a credit portfolio to secure the issuance of securities by public offering. Thus, this transfer may be carried out by a single act, identifying each credit and its amount, interest, and securities. Where appropriate, they will be recorded in the relevant registries (i.e., mortgages or pledge registries).

Law No. 24441 article 72, in its turn, prescribes that in the cases provided by article 70: (a) no notice to the transferred debtor is necessary provided there is contractual provision to that effect in the document of the credit that is being transferred; the transfer will be effective from the date it is performed; (b) the only exception against the assignee will be that based on the invalidity of the credit relationship or documented payment prior to the transfer, and (c) where a financial institution issues securities secured by a securities portfolio deposited with it, the entity will be the trust owner of the assets.

Therefore, as a practical matter, it is advisable in credit transactions to include the clauses allowing their subsequent securitization without the requirement of notice by public act.

The prohibition of transferring the credit not having been agreed on and there being no agreement of disposition to a certain person, a valid challenge to their transfer could only be based on circumstances relating exclusively to the assignee or, otherwise, with the grantor's breach of contract. The credit may be transferred even against the transferred debtor's consent because, should his or her consent be necessary, the force of this agreement would in fact be voided, impairing its primary characteristic, that is, negotiability of the credits, the mobility of economic relationships.[23]

*b. Trust Assets Insufficiency* In the assumption that the trust assets are insufficient to face the obligations of the financial trust, in accordance with articles 16 and 23 of Law No. 24441, the trustee's assets are not susceptible to claims relating to the obligations incurred in carrying out the trust, which will only be satisfied with the trust assets.

As has been noted, Law No. 24441 article 16 provides that "the inadequacy of trust assets to meet these obligations will not give rise to bankruptcy. In this assumption, and absent other remedies provided by the grantor or the beneficiary under contractual stipulations, the trustee will proceed to its liquidation, disposing of the trust assets and delivering the proceeds to the creditors, according with the preference provided for the bankruptcy; in the case of financial trusts, the provisions of [a]rticle 24 will control,

---

23    National Commercial Court of Appeal of Buenos Aires [CNCom. Room A], 21/5/1999, "Premafin SA v. Total Austral SA," (Arg.).

where applicable." Article 24 provides that for financial trusts such rules may regulate, *inter alia,* over the following:

a. The transfer of trust assets as a whole to another trustee
b. The modifications of the issuance agreement, which may encompass remission of a part of the debts or the modification of periods, methods or initial terms
c. Changes in the administration of the trust assets until termination of the trust
d. The liquidation method of the trust assets
e. The appointment of the person who will be in charge of liquidating the assets as a whole or of the assets that make it up
f. Any other respect determined by the general meeting of trust securities holders relating to the administration or liquidation of the trust

The constitution of the general meeting of the trust securities holders will be deemed valid when securities holders representing at least two-thirds of issued capital in circulation were present; it is possible to act by attorney. Agreements must be carried by the favorable vote of securities holders representing, at least, an absolute majority of the issued capital in circulation, except where modifications of the issuance agreement are involved, which may concern the remission of part of the debts or the modification of the periods, methods or initial terms; in this case, two-thirds of the issued securities will be deemed a majority.

If a quorum was not reached in the first summons, a new general meeting must be called, to be held within thirty days following the date arranged for the general meeting that did not take place; this second general meeting will be deemed valid with however many holders present.

Under the cited rules, the trustee is responsible for carrying out the liquidation process. The guideline in this respect is the contractual provisions and the Bankruptcy Act. Given that this law provides that liquidation will take place "absent other remedies provided by the grantor or the beneficiary under contractual provisions," even if such provisions did not exist, it would be prudent for the trustee to turn to the grantor, the beneficiary, and the residual beneficiary with the purpose of enabling them to assist the trust and avert its liquidation.

Finally, liquidation is not exempt from the rule of necessary documented accounting to the beneficiaries and grantor by the trustee, so that it must be conducted in such an orderly fashion as to allow a subsequent account and documentation of the actions and criteria followed.

## 3. Trust Securities

Certificates of participation in the trust property and trust debt securities were created by Law No. 24441 as the way to document the rights of the beneficiaries of financial trusts, as is established in the second paragraph of article 19, "they will be deemed securities and may be the object of public offerings."

One of the key features of financial trusts is that the beneficiaries are title holders of certificates of participation or debt securities, backed by the assets thus transferred. This is reflected not only in the definition in article 19 of Law No. 24,441, but also in article 20 of the law providing that the financial trust agreement must include the issuance terms of the securities.

The trust securities issued as trust debt securities will grant a right to the reimbursement of the face value of the security and, if appropriate, to the payment of an interest established in the issuance terms of the respective series and type of trust debt security. Interest may be based on a fixed or floating rate and will accrue from the date established for that series and class, or from a different date, as agreed on in the relevant issuance agreement.

Participation certificates will grant a right to participate partially or totally in the trust income, once all the deductible expenses have been deducted and/or other charges effected under the terms of the agreement.

Participation certificates may only be issued by the trustee. Instead, the debt trust securities may be issued by the trustee or by third parties, as appropriate. Nevertheless, despite the existence of a legal option in relation to the debt securities issuer, in practice, for tax reasons, in nearly the totality of cases the issuer has been the trustee. This is so because of the opinion of the tax authority, based on a literal construction of Law No. 24441 article 83, which only in the case of debt securities issued by the trustee certain fiscal benefits will be applied, such as exemption from income tax and value-added tax.[24]

In view of the above discussion, if the debt securities were issued by the trustee, his or her assets would not be exposed to claims deriving from obligations incurred in the execution of the trust, which would only be satisfied with the trust assets. In this case, the offering memorandum must include the following rubric: "The trustee's assets are not exposed to claims deriving from obligations incurred in the execution of the trust. These obligations will be satisfied exclusively with the trust assets, as provided by [a]rticle 16 of Law [No.] 24441."[25]

Law No. 24441 states that different classes of participation certificates may be issued with different rights, but the same rights must be granted within each class. The issue may also be divided into series, with respect to which, it must be said, no prohibition exists similar to that contained in Law No. 23576 article 2 on negotiable obligations limiting the issuance of new series insofar as the previous ones have not been subscribed.[26] Within each series, one or more classes of trust securities may be issued, having different types of participation or credit rights in the trust, among others:

a. Seniority or subordination for the collection of the proceeds of the trust, or the distribution of the trust cash flow

---

24    Regulation 11/97 (DAT) of the Argentine Tax Authorities.

25    This rubric is established by the Rules of the Argentine National Securities Commission (*Comisión Nacional de Valores*), in Chapter XV, Section 2.2, Article 13 and Section 2.3. and Article 15 (these Rules can be found at the official site of the said Commission: www.cnv.gov.ar)

26    Article 2 *in fine* of Law No. 23576 and its amendment on negotiable obligations (a kind of corporate debt bond) established that "new series of the same class may not be issued so long as the previous ones are not completely subscribed."

b. Limitation of participation rights to a certain agreed-on income or revenue

c. Right to certain guarantees

The final combination of different classes of trust debt securities and/or participation certificates permits the creation of "tailor-made" securities for the several funds borrowers in the capital market, allowing for a better placement of the securities owing to the design of the funds outlay generated by the trust ("waterfall"). Further, the trust securities may be placed with or without discount.

Law No. 24441 does not expressly state that different classes of debt securities may be issued. This results from the clarification provided by the amendment to the civil code introduced by Law No. 24441 article 76, which attaches a last paragraph to article 3876 of the code that states that "the subordination of the creditor's rights may be agreed upon until other current or future debts by the debtor are met partially or totally." This subordination of certain creditors involves the possibility of issuing senior debt in relation to other indebtedness (subordinate debt) to create different types of debt securities granting different rights and involving different risk levels.

By virtue of the fact that hybrid securities could be issued, that is, whose payment share certain characteristics with securities and others with participation certificates, it is understood that the substance-over-form rule must be followed to determine their nature (debt or equity). Consequently, the following criteria would be useful to determine whether debt or equity is being dealt with: (a) the denomination given to the securities, (b) the presence or absence of a fixed maturity date, (c) the source of repayment, (d) the right to require the payment of the amount given to the trust and its income, (e) whether the funds contribution entitles to participation in the management of the trust, (f) subordination level of the right of the contributor of the funds relative to other creditors, (g) intent of the parties, (h) existence of adequate capitalization (thin capitalization test), (i) the trust's ability to obtain loans from financial institutions in similar conditions, (j) extent to which the funds were applied to acquire capital assets, (k) default by the debtor without seeking a refinancing agreement, and (l) harmony or discrepancy of interests between the holders of participation certificates and the contributor of the funds. These and other pertinent factors must be taken into account and evaluated, not simply added mathematically.

Argentine case law has claimed that those transactions that may not be considered normal indebtedness by reason of "their exceedingly high amount relative to capital and free reserves . . . or even relative to the value of their fixed assets and to the volume of their transactions at the time when it is conducted, as well as the untimeliness in servicing, the absence of a fixed time for the repayment of principal and, meaningfully, of real or personal securities for the required loan" may not be treated as such for tax purposes.[27]

In brief, there is no limit to the structuring of different types of securities designed for particular investor niches nor for the creation of securities with mixed, fixed, or variable yields.

---

27    Federal Tax Court [Court B, Judges Agustín Torres, Pedro José Pagani & Beatriz González de Rechter], 16/9/1980, "Hauni Latinoamerciana S.A.I.C / appeal-Income Tax," cause 169-I (Arg.).

Trust securities may be issued as evidenced in paper (certificated), in individual sheets of shares, or global certificates, or as a record in a book (book-entry form or uncertificated). Certificated trust securities (printed on paper) must include at the back a summary of the trust terms and conditions and may or may not have coupons for the collection of service. To be noted, in the case of uncertificated securities, such a transcription must figure in the subscription agreements. In no case will the transcription be exempt from the obligation to present every investor with a copy of the issuance prospectus, if he or she so wished.

Trust securities may be traded through the joint deposit system or by any other international clearing system, such as Cedel or Euroclear or any other system agreed on in the relevant issuance agreement.

## F. PARTICULAR CASES AND EXPERIENCE

Some instances of transactions implemented by means of trusts shall now be addressed.

### 1. Public Sector Trusts

Law No. 24441 did not specifically regulate public trusts; that is, that trust in which the government (federal, provincial, or municipal), directly or by means of state-owned entities acting as grantor, transferred the title of its public or private assets or affected public funds to carry out a lawful object of public interest.

Although this type of trust fits the contractual structure regulating trusts generally, it is preceded by *a sui generis* legal procedure commencing with the legal act that validates trusts (law, decree), fixes its objects and features, and determines the terms and conditions whereto the agreement will be subject. Nowadays, the federal state and its agencies cannot transfer assets to trusts, with the exception of the *Banco de la Nación Argentina* (the state-owned Bank of the Argentine Nation) and the *Banco de Inversión y Comercio Exterior SA* (BICE) (export bank, also state-owned).

An example of a national public trust is the one created by Decree No. 286/95, whereby the executive power constituted a trust fund for the development of the provinces (similar to United States). Such a trust fund was aimed primarily at assisting province banks subject to privatization and furthering the privatization of province corporations.

Further, another example of a public trust was that created by Decree No. 675/97, called Corporate Capital Trust Fund. Such a fund was initiated with the purpose of facilitating the nationwide development of the less favored small-company sector.

To the preceding examples must be added those trusts created by the provinces, for example, with the rights emerging from the tax participation scheme to secure the issuance of province public securities. Nowadays, this kind of trust is broadly used by provinces and municipalities.

## 2. "Cost Contribution" Real Estate Trusts

Since 2002, Argentina has seen a boom of trusts organized by real estate developers as vehicles for real estate projects. The developer looks for a suitable place and designs the project. Once the number of units is determined (i.e., apartments of a building), the developer creates a trust with one settlor and starts to raise the necessary funds looking for other settlors. Each settlor will contribute the necessary amount of cash to purchase land and erect the building in the proportion of the unit he or she has the right to receive as beneficiary of the trust. In other words, all the settlors are beneficiaries (and obviously vice versa). They have the obligation to make a contribution of a certain amount of money to cover a certain percentage of the cost of the project, and they have the right to receive certain units.

The advantages of this kind of trusts are the same as the ones described in the point related to trusts for the structuring of project finance, with the difference that these "cost contributions" are ideal legal vehicles for small to medium projects, and there are no third parties buying the units or providing a cash flow for the repayment of debt. In fact, in most of these projects there is no debt or other leverage mechanism involved. The fact that the trust is not selling the units to third parties does not mean that the settlor-beneficiary could not sell his or her rights as such to a third party and in that way make a capital gain or receive the apartment and then sell it with a capital gain.

## G. TAX TREATMENT

Argentina is a federal country and as such there are three levels of taxation: federal or national level, provincial or state level, and municipal or local level. In the following section on the tax treatment of trusts, the focus will be placed on national income tax and then on national value-added tax and provincial gross revenue tax.

## 1. Federal Income Tax

The general rule is that corporations are subject to a 35 percent tax rate and that dividends are not subject to tax. In principle, trusts are subject to the same tax treatment, with the exception of trusts in which the settlor is the beneficiary and is an Argentine tax resident (not a foreign beneficiary of the trust). Put differently, regarding federal income tax trusts should be divided in

a.  Ordinary trusts, in which the settlor is the beneficiary and is an Argentine tax resident. The trust is a pass-through entity not subject to tax; the settlor-beneficiary must include in his or her tax return the benefits arising from the trust.
b.  Ordinary trusts, in which the settlor is not the beneficiary or the settlor is the beneficiary but is a foreign resident: These kinds of trusts are subject to a 35 percent tax

rate at the trust level, as if it were a corporation, and benefits arising from the trust are not subject to withholding tax (and in the case of a foreign resident not subject to withholding tax).

c. Financial trusts, which are subject to the tax at a 35 percent tax rate but are allowed to deduct as an expense interest payments (because of trust debt bonds). Trust debt securities are exempted from tax for Argentine individuals and foreign residents as long as they are publicly offered with the previous authorization of the National Securities Commission.

## 2. Value-Added Tax

There are no differences as to the tax treatment of trusts based on the kind of trust. Tax treatment depends on the activity carried on by the trust. The general tax rate is 21 percent. The sole exemption that is particularly relevant for trusts is the one on interest paid by debt trust securities whose interest will not be subject to tax as long as they are publicly placed with the previous authorization of the National Securities Commission.

## 3. Gross Revenue Tax

This is a provincial tax that depends on the location in which the trust carries on an activity. Argentina has 23 provinces and a federal district (Buenos Aires City), and each one has its own gross revenue tax that taxes gross revenue (as a general rule no expense is deductible) at rates that range from 1 percent to 5 percent. There are few rules regarding trusts, but it is reasonable to understand that all trusts are subject to this tax in accordance with the activity carried on.

## 4. Other Taxes

It should be considered that at the provincial level there is a stamp duty (with rates of approximately 1 percent of the value of the deed) and national taxes such as the tax on bank account credits and debits and the national asset tax (similar to the alternative tax), which is paid in cases where no income tax is paid.

From the patrimonial taxation perspective, it must be stressed that trusts and beneficiaries must consider two federal taxes: a) Personal Wealth Tax (0.5 percent of the assets of the tax paid annually by the trustee on behalf of the beneficiaries); and b) Minimum Pressumed Income Tax at a 1 percent rate over the assets of the trust. This tax must be assessed every fiscal year but it must only be paid in case it is higher than income tax, and in case it is actually paid, it represents a tax credit against the federal income tax for the following ten years (after this period of time the credit expires).

# Chapter 7

# Belize[1]

A. Overview  108
    1. Definition  109
    2. Applicable Law  109
    3. Creation and Duration  110
    4. Invalid Trusts  110
    5. Independence from Foreign Laws  111
    6. Powers of the Court  112
    7. Assets That May Be Transferred in Trust  113
B. The Settlor, the Beneficiaries, and the Purposes of the Trust  113
    1. The Beneficiary  113
    2. The Letter of Wishes  114
    3. Charitable Trusts  115
    4. Noncharitable Trusts  115
    5. Revocation, Termination, and Failure  115
    6. Variation of Trusts  117
C. The Trustee and the Protector  117
    1. Trustee  118
    2. Appointment, Removal, and Resignation of the Trustee  118
    3. Powers of the Trustee  119
    4. Duties of the Trustee  120
    5. Fees and Reimbursement of Expenses  123
    6. Breach of Trust  124
    7. Case Law  125
D. International Trusts  126
    1. Creation of a Register of International Trusts  126
    2. Trust Agent  127
    3. Exemptions of International Trusts  128

---

1    I thank the kind help of Rishi Alain Mungal, who provided some excellent material, in particular, an excellent summary on Belize's trust case law that is included in this chapter.

## A. OVERVIEW

Although Belize does not qualify as a Latin American country because of its history, its official language (English instead of Spanish or Portuguese), and its English common-law tradition, it has been included in this book because of its location and the opportunity to make a comparison with Latin American trusts.

Belize is one of the few countries (with Panama and Uruguay, to a lesser degree), out of the ones analyzed in this book, that is a good jurisdiction to host a trust with asset-protection objectives for foreign grantors and beneficiaries. Therefore, a section of this chapter will be devoted to the Belize International Trust as regulated since 2007.

The Belize Trusts Act was passed in 1992[2] and amended in 2007 (referred to as the Trusts Act); its focus is to provide a very efficient asset-protection trusts jurisdiction.[3]

When looking for the right offshore jurisdiction to create a trust, several points are considered. From a Latin American settlor point of view, the main one is a solid anti–forced-heirship legal regime that allows the settlor to provide for the distribution of his or her estate according to his or her wishes and not the rules established in the jurisdiction in which he or she is domiciled. Neither the Panamanian trust (the Panamanian Private Foundation has a different regime, as will be noted in Chapter 18) nor the Uruguayan trust has such a regime. Therefore, Belize is the sole country out of the ones analyzed in this book that provides an anti–forced-heirship regime for trusts.[4]

---

2    *"Trust Act 1992 (1992 Act)* is based on the *Trusts (Guernsey) Law 1989,* as amended, incorporating substantial amendments and innovations. The *1992 Act* was developed and drafted by Milton Grundy and Dr. Philip Baker of Grays Inn Chambers, London, and American legal advisors. Prior to the *1992 Act,* the principal trust legislation was the *Trusts Act 1923 (1923 Act).* With the exception that the *1923 Act* continues to apply to trusts created prior to the commencement of the *1992 Act,* the *1992 Act* repealed the *1923 Act.* . . . In 2000, a revised act was published as *The Trust Act Chapter 202 Revised ed. 2000."* Glen CH Wilson, *Belize, in* STEP DIRECTORY AND YEARBOOK 539 (2008).

3    *Cf.* Denis Kleinfeld, *Choosing an Offshore Jurisdiction, in* 1 ASSET PROTECTION STRATEGIES: PLANNING WITH DOMESTIC AND OFFSHORE ENTITIES 79–80 (Alexander A. Bove, Jr., ed., 2005).

4    Wendy Warren explained that "the past 20 years have seen the proliferation of anti-forced heirships (AFH) legal regimes in offshore financial centers to provide wealthy individuals with the option to leave their wealth to whomever they choose. . . . The Bahamas was one of the first jurisdictions to introduce AFH legislation with revised legislation in 1996, resolving the question as to whether forced heirship rights applied while a settlor was still alive. A telling fact is that in the 20 years since AFH regimes first came into being, there has not been a single reported instance in which a trust established in an AFH jurisdiction has been successfully attacked in litigation purely on the basis of forced heirship considerations." Wendy Warren, *Anti-Forced Heirship Regimes,* 16(10) STEPJOURNAL 51 (Nov. 2008).

# 1. Definition

The Trusts Act provides that a trust exists where a person (known as "a trustee") holds or has vested in him or her, or is deemed to hold or have vested in him or her, property[5] that does not form, or that has ceased to form, part of his or her own estate:

(a) for the benefit of any person (known as "a beneficiary"), whether or not yet ascertained or in existence; or

(b) for any valid charitable or non[ ]charitable purpose, which is not for the benefit only of the trustee; or

(c) for such benefit as is mentioned in paragraph (a) and also for any such purpose as is mentioned in paragraph (b).

# 2. Applicable Law

The proper law of a trust shall be: (a) the law expressed by the terms of the trust or intended by the settlor to be the proper law; (b) if no such law is expressed or intended, the law with which the trust has its closest connection at the time of its creation; or (c) if the law expressed by the terms of the trust or intended by the settlor to be the proper law, or the law with which the trust has its closest connection at the time of its creation, does not provide for trusts or the category of trusts involved, then the proper law of the trust shall be the law of Belize.

In ascertaining the law with which a trust has its closest connection, reference shall be made in particular to: (a) the place of administration of the trust designated by the settlor, (b) the situs of the assets of the trust, (c) the place of residence or business of the trustee, and (d) the objects of the trust and the places where they are to be fulfilled.

The terms of a trust instrument may provide for the proper law of the trust or the law governing a severable aspect of the trust to be changed from the law of one jurisdiction to the law of another jurisdiction. Where the proper law of a trust or the law governing a severable aspect of a trust is changed from the law of another jurisdiction (here called "the old law") to the law of Belize, no provision of the old law shall operate so as to render the trust void, invalid, or unlawful, or to render void, invalid, or unlawful any functions conferred on the trustee under the law of Belize. Where the proper law of a trust or the law governing a severable aspect of a trust is changed from the law of Belize to the law of another jurisdiction (here called "the new law"), no provision of the law of Belize shall operate so as to render the trust void, invalid, or unlawful or to render void, invalid, or unlawful any functions conferred on the trustee under the new law.

---

5     Section 67 of the Trusts Act established that "property" means property of any description, wherever situated, including any share therein, and it, includes rights and interests whether vested, contingent, defeasible, or future.

These regulations related to the law that regulates the trust are especially relevant in relation to forced heirship regulations of the settlor and the beneficiaries. The application of Belize law means the application of the rules that allow the creation of a trust by a foreign settlor that provides for the distribution of his or her estate in a different way than the one established as public policy by the law of the jurisdiction of his last domicile.

## 3. Creation and Duration

A trust, other than a unit trust, may be created by oral declaration, or by an instrument in writing (including a will or codicil), by conduct, by operation of law, or in any other manner whatsoever. A unit trust may be created only by an instrument in writing.[6]

No formalities or technical expressions are required for the creation of a trust provided that the intention of the settlor to create a trust is clearly manifested.

A trust (other than a trust by operation of law) involving land situated in Belize shall be unenforceable unless evidenced in writing.

With the exception of trusts established exclusively for a charitable purpose or purposes that have no limit to their duration, the maximum duration of a trust shall be 120 years from the date of its creation, and the trust shall terminate on the 120th anniversary of the date of its creation unless it is terminated sooner. The rule of law known as the rule against perpetuities[7] shall not apply to any trust to which this section applies.

The terms of a trust may direct or authorize the accumulation of all or part of the income of the trust for a period not exceeding the maximum duration of the trust.

## 4. Invalid Trusts

Subject to the provisions of the Trusts Act, a trust shall be valid and enforceable in accordance with its terms.

A trust shall be invalid and unenforceable:

a. To the extent that (i) it purports to do anything contrary to the law of Belize; or (ii) it purports to confer any right or power, or impose any obligation the exercise of which, or the carrying out of which, is contrary to the law of Belize; or (iii) it has

---

6     Section 67 of the Trusts Act defined the unit trust as "a trust established for the purpose, or having the effect of, providing, for persons having funds available for investment, facilities for their participation as beneficiaries under the trust in any profits or income arising from the acquisition, holding, management or disposal of property."

7     The "rule against perpetuities" is defined by Black's Law Dictionary as: "Principle that no interest in property is good unless it must vest, if at all, no later than 21 years, plus period of gestation, after some life or lives in being at time of creation of interest." BLACK'S LAW DICTIONARY 1331 (6th ed. 1990).

                                                           **TRUSTS IN LATIN AMERICA**

no beneficiary identifiable or ascertainable (unless the trust was created for a valid charitable or noncharitable purpose).

b. To the extent that the court declares that: (i) the trust was established by duress, fraud, mistake, undue influence or misrepresentation; or (ii) the trust is immoral or contrary to public policy; or (iii) the terms of the trust are so uncertain that its performance is rendered impossible (provided that a charitable purpose shall be deemed always to be capable of performance); or (iv) the settlor was, at the time of its creation, incapable under the law in force in Belize of creating such a trust.

Where a trust is created for two or more purposes of which some are lawful and others are not, or where some of the terms of a trust are invalid and others are not: (a) if those purposes cannot be separated or the terms cannot be separated, the trust is invalid; (b) if those purposes can be separated or the terms can be separated, the court may declare that the trust is valid as to the terms that are valid and the purposes that are lawful.

Where a trust is partially invalid, the court may declare what property is to be held subject to the trust.

Property provided by a settlor and as to which a trust is invalid shall, subject to any order of the court, be held in trust by the trustee for the settlor absolutely or, if he or she is dead, as if it had formed part of his or her estate at his or her death.

## 5. Independence from Foreign Laws

Where a trust is created under the law of Belize, the court shall not vary it, set it aside, or recognize the validity of any claim against the trust property pursuant to the law of another jurisdiction or the order of a court of another jurisdiction in respect to: (a) the personal and proprietary consequences of marriage or the termination of marriage; (b) succession rights (whether testate or intestate), including the fixed shares of spouses or relatives; or (c) the claims of creditors in the event of insolvency. This is a key provision regarding the strength of the Belizean trust as an asset-protection scheme.

The rule above shall subsist and shall have effect notwithstanding domestic provisions of the Law of Property Act section 149 (which normally makes voluntary transfer of property to avoid creditors voidable), the Bankruptcy Act section 43 (which normally makes settlements generally voidable if the settlor becomes bankrupt up to ten years after the settlement was made) and the provisions of the Reciprocal Enforcement of Judgments Act (thereby nullifying any effect of a foreign judgment on a Belize trust or the transfer of assets into the trust).

Kleinfeld explained that

A trustee in bankruptcy has the right under the Bankruptcy Act to set aside a trust in certain circumstances but, to this general right, there is an exception. That is, it cannot be exercised where the claim giving rise to it was made pursuant to the law of another jurisdiction. This prohibition cannot be circumvented by bringing action in the other jurisdiction and then seeking to enforce the order of the foreign court under the Reciprocal Enforcement of Judgments Act. In effect, the Statute of Elizabeth[8] has been repealed and the statute of limitations period to challenge a disposition of assets into trust effectively is zero.[9]

## 6. Powers of the Court

The court has jurisdiction in respect to any matters concerning a trust where: (a) the proper law of the trust is the law of Belize; (b) a trustee of the trust is resident in Belize; (c) any property of the trust is situated in Belize; and (d) any part of the administration of the trust is carried on in Belize.

On the application of a trustee, a beneficiary, a settlor, or his or her personal representatives, a protector (in the case of a trust established for a charitable purpose), the attorney general or, with the leave of the court, any other person, the court may

a. Make an order in respect to (i) the execution, administration, or enforcement of a trust; (ii) a trustee, including an order as to the exercise of his or her functions by a trustee, the removal of a trustee, the appointment, remuneration, or conduct of a trustee, the keeping and submission of accounts, and the making of payments, whether into court or otherwise; (iii) a protector, including an order appointing a protector; (iv) a beneficiary, or any person connected with a trust; (v) any trust property, including an order as to the vesting, preservation, application, surrender, or recovery thereof.
b. Make a declaration as to the validity or enforceability of a trust.
c. Direct the trustee to distribute, or not to distribute, the trust property.
d. Make such order in respect to the termination of the trust and the distribution of the property as it thinks fit.
e. Rescind or vary an order or declaration under the Trusts Act, or make a new or further order or declaration.

Where the court appoints or removes a trustee under this section: (a) it may impose such requirements and conditions as it thinks fit, including provisions as to remuneration and requirements or conditions as to the vesting of trust property; (b) subject to the court's order, a trustee appointed by the court has the same functions, and may act in all respects, as if he or she had been originally appointed a trustee.

If a person does not comply with an order of the court under the Trusts Act requiring him or her to do anything, the court may, on such terms and conditions as it thinks fit, order that the thing be done by another person, nominated for the purpose by the court,

---

8    The Statute of Elizabeth was codified in 1487 and established that "[a]ll deeds of gift and chattels, made of to be made in trust to the use of that person or persons that made the same deed or gift, be void and of none effect." Similar statutes have been enacted in several of the U.S. states. Richard W. Hompesch II, *Domestic Asset Protection Trusts—More Might than First Appears, in* 1 ASSET PROTECTION STRATEGIES: PLANNING WITH DOMESTIC AND OFFSHORE ENTITIES 79–80 (Alexander A. Bove, Jr., ed., 2005).
9    Kleinfeld, *supra* note 3, at 80.

at the expense of the person in default (or otherwise, as the court directs), and a thing so done has effect in all respects as if done by the person in default.

A trustee may apply to the court for directions as to how he or she should or might act in any of the affairs of the trust, and the court may make such order as it thinks fit.

The court may order the costs and expenses of, and incidental to, an application to the court under the Trusts Act to be paid from the trust property, or in such manner and by such persons as it thinks fit.

## 7. Assets That May Be Transferred in Trust

Any property may be held by or vested in a trustee on trust. In other words, there is no limitation on the kind of assets that can be held on trust. A trustee may accept property to be held on trust from any person. A trustee shall not be bound to accept property to be held on trust, but where a trustee accepts property subject to the performance of an obligation, the trustee shall be deemed to have given to the obligee an undertaking to perform that obligation for good consideration.

Where a settlor declares a trust regarding property he or she does not own at the time of the declaration, then: (a) the trust is incompletely constituted at the time of the declaration, and no rights or duties arise thereunder; but (b) if the settlor subsequently receives property that was the intended subject matter of the declaration of trust, the court shall at the instance of the beneficiary or the trustee (and whether the beneficiary has given consideration for the declaration of trust or not) compel the settlor to transfer that property to the trustee or to hold that property on the terms of the trust.

## B. THE SETTLOR, THE BENEFICIARIES, AND THE PURPOSES OF THE TRUST

Any person who has under the law of Belize the capacity to own and transfer property may be the settlor of a trust. The settlor may also be a trustee, a beneficiary, or a protector of the trust.

## 1. The Beneficiary

A beneficiary shall be identifiable by name or ascertainable by reference to a relationship to some person (whether or not living at the time of creation of the trust) or otherwise by reference to a description or to a class.

The terms of a trust may (a) provide for the addition of a person as a beneficiary or the exclusion of a beneficiary from benefit under the trust; (b) impose an obligation on a beneficiary as a condition of benefit under the trust.

Where a trust is in favor of a class of persons then, subject to the terms of the trust: (a) the class closes when it is no longer possible for any other person to become a member of the class; (b) a woman older than sixty years of age shall be deemed to be no longer capable of bearing a child; and (c) where the interest of the class relates to income, and no member of the class exists, the income shall be accumulated and retained until a member of the class exists or the class closes.

A beneficiary may (a) disclaim his or her whole interest under a trust; or (b) subject to the terms of the trust, disclaim part of his or her interest under a trust (whether or not he or she has received some benefit from his or her interest).

Subject to the terms of the trust, a disclaimer: (a) shall be in writing; (b) may be temporary; and (c) may, if the disclaimer so provides, be revoked in the manner and under the circumstances specified therein.

The interest of a beneficiary is personal property. This clarification of the trust law has several connotations, the main one being that the beneficiary has no direct rights over the trust assets. The trust law adds that subject to the terms of the trust, the interest of a beneficiary may be sold, pledged, charged, transferred, or otherwise dealt with in any manner whatsoever.

The terms of a trust may make the interest of a beneficiary: (a) subject to termination; (b) subject to a restriction on alienation of or dealing in that interest or any part of that interest; or (c) subject to diminution or termination in the event of the beneficiary becoming insolvent or any of his or her property becoming liable to seizure or sequestration for the benefit of his or her creditors. Such a trust shall be known as a protective or a spendthrift trust.

Where any property is directed to be held on protective or spendthrift trust for the benefit of a beneficiary, the trustee shall hold that property: (a) in trust to pay the income to the beneficiary until the interest terminates in accordance with the terms of the trust or a determining event occurs; and (b) if a determining event occurs, and while the interest of the beneficiary continues, in trust to pay the income to such of the followings (and in such shares) as the trustee in his or her absolute discretion shall appoint: (i) the beneficiary and any spouse or child of the beneficiary; or (ii) if there is no such spouse or child, the beneficiary and the persons who would be entitled to the estate of the beneficiary if he or she had then died intestate and domiciled in Belize.

A "determining event" shall mean the occurrence of any event or any act or omission on the part of the beneficiary (other than the giving of consent to an advancement of trust property) that would result in the whole or part of the income of the beneficiary from the trust becoming payable to any person other than the beneficiary.

Any rule of law or public policy that prevents a settlor from establishing a protective or a spendthrift trust of which he or she is a beneficiary is hereby abolished.

## 2. The Letter of Wishes

The settlor of a trust may give to the trustee a letter of his or her wishes or the trustee may prepare a memorandum of the wishes of the settlor with regard to the exercise of any functions conferred on the trustee by the terms of the trust.

A beneficiary of a trust may give to the trustee a letter of his or her wishes or the trustee may prepare a memorandum of the wishes of the beneficiary with regard to the exercise of any functions conferred on the trustee by the terms of the trust.

Where a trust is in favor of a class of persons, then a member of that class may give to the trustee a letter of his or her wishes, or the trustee may prepare a memorandum of the wishes of that member with regard to the exercise of any functions conferred on the trustee by the terms of the trust.

Where a letter of wishes or a memorandum of wishes is given to or prepared by the trustee of a trust then: (a) the trustee may have regard to that letter or memorandum in exercising any functions conferred on him or her by the terms of the trust; but (b) the trustee shall not be bound to have regard to that letter or memorandum and shall not be accountable in any way for his or her failure or refusal to have regard to that letter or memorandum.

No fiduciary duty or obligation shall be imposed on a trustee merely by the giving to him or her of a letter of wishes or the preparation by him or her of a memorandum of wishes.

## 3. Charitable Trusts

For the purposes of the Trust Act, the following purposes shall be regarded as charitable: (a) the relief of poverty, (b) the advancement of education, (c) the advancement of religion, (d) the protection of the environment, (e) the advancement of human rights and fundamental freedoms, and (f) any other purposes that are beneficial to the community.

A purpose shall not be regarded as charitable unless the fulfillment of that purpose is for the benefit of the community or a substantial section of the community, having regard to the type and nature of the purpose.

A purpose may be regarded as charitable whether it is to be carried out in Belize or elsewhere, and whether it is beneficial to the community in Belize or elsewhere.

## 4. Noncharitable Trusts

A trust may be created for a purpose that is noncharitable provided that: (a) the purpose is specific, reasonable and capable of fulfillment; (b) the purpose is not immoral, unlawful or contrary to public policy; and (c) the terms of the trust provide for the appointment of a protector who is capable of enforcing the trust and for the appointment of a successor to any protector.

If the attorney general has reason to believe that there is no protector of a trust for a noncharitable purpose or the protector is unwilling or incapable of acting, he or she may appoint a person to be protector of the trust, and such person shall from the date of appointment exercise the functions of protector of the trust.

## 5. Revocation, Termination, and Failure

The general rule is that, unless a trust makes provision for revocation, then the trust shall be irrevocable. A trust and any exercise of a power or discretion under a trust may be expressed to be capable of revocation (in whole or in part) or of variation. No such revocation or variation shall prejudice anything lawfully done by a trustee in relation to the trust before he or she receives notice of the revocation or variation.

Subject to the terms of the trust, if a trust is revoked in whole or in part, the trustee shall hold the trust property, or the part of the trust property that is the subject of the revocation, in trust for the settlor absolutely or, if he or she is dead, as if it had formed part of his or her estate at death.

With the exception of charitable trusts, and subject to the terms of the trust and to any order of the court, where: (a) an interest lapses, (b) a trust terminates, or (c) there is no beneficiary and no person (whether or not then living) who can become a beneficiary in accordance with the terms of the trust, the interest or property concerned shall be held by the trustee in trust for the settlor absolutely or, if he or she is dead, as if it had formed part of his or her estate at death.

Where trust property is held for a charitable purpose and: (a) the purpose has been, as far as may be, fulfilled; (b) the purpose cannot be carried out at all, or not according with the directions given and to the spirit of the gift; (c) the purpose provides a use for part only of the property; (d) the property, and other property applicable for a similar purpose, can be more effectively used in conjunction, and to that end can more suitably be applied to a common purpose; (e) the purpose was laid down by reference to an area which was then, but has since ceased to be, a unit for some other purpose, or by reference to a class of persons or to an area which has for any reason since ceased to be suitable or to be practicable in administering the gift; (f) the purpose has been adequately provided for by other means; (g) the purpose has ceased to be charitable (by being useless or harmful to the community or otherwise); or (h) the purpose has ceased in any other way to provide a suitable and effective method of using the property, the property, or the remainder of the property, as the case may be, shall be held for such other charitable purpose as the court, on the application of the attorney general or the trustee, may declare to be consistent with the original intention of the settlor.

Where trust property is held for a charitable purpose, the court, on the application of the attorney general or the trustee, may approve any arrangement that varies or revokes the purposes or terms of the trust or enlarges or modifies the powers of management or administration of the trustee, if it is satisfied that the arrangement: (a) is now suitable or expedient and (b) is consistent with the original intention of the settlor.

On the termination of a trust, the trust property shall be distributed by the trustee within a reasonable time in accordance with the terms of the trust to the persons entitled thereto. Nevertheless, the trustee may retain sufficient assets to make reasonable provision for liabilities (existing, future, contingent, or other).

Without prejudice to any power of the court and notwithstanding the terms of the trust, where all the beneficiaries are in existence and have been ascertained, and none is a person under legal disability or a minor,[10] or the trust is a protective or spendthrift

---

10   Defined by § 67 of the Trust Act as a person who has not attained full age under the law of his domicile.

trust, and all beneficiaries are in agreement so to do, they may require the trustee to terminate the trust and distribute the trust property as the beneficiaries direct.

## 6. Variation of Trusts

The court may, on the application of any beneficiary, the trustee, the settlor or his or her personal representatives, or the protector of a trust, approve on behalf of: (a) a minor or a person under legal disability having, directly or indirectly, an interest vested or contingent, under the trust; (b) any person unborn; (c) any person who is presently unascertained, but who may become entitled, directly or indirectly, to an interest under the trust as being (at a future date or on the happening of a future event) a person of any specified description or a member of any specified class; or (d) any person, in respect to an interest that may accrue to him or her by virtue of the exercise of a discretionary power on the failure or determination of an interest under a protective or spendthrift trust, any arrangement that varies or revokes the terms of the trust or enlarges or modifies the powers of management or administration of the trustee, whether or not there is another person with a beneficial interest who is capable of assenting to the arrangement.

A settlor may create a trust (in whatever form and by whatever name it is known) of a type recognized by the law or rules of his or her religion or nationality, or which is customarily used by his or her community, provided that: (a) there is a recital to that effect in the instrument creating the trust; and (b) the trust is of a type approved by the attorney general by order published in the Gazette. This trust may provide that the trustee shall hold the trust property: (a) for a period not exceeding 120 years, to pay or apply the income and capital thereof for the maintenance, education, advancement or benefit of the family of the settlor, and/or for the purpose of performing acts or services in honor of the settlor or the ancestors of the settlor; and (b) thereafter for the advancement of the settlor's religion, or for such other charitable purpose as the settlor may specify or, if the settlor has not specified a charitable purpose, for such charitable purpose as the trustee shall determine.

The instrument creating a trust may be written in a language other than English, provided that a version in the English language certified by the original trustee to be a true translation is appended to the instrument.

## C. THE TRUSTEE AND THE PROTECTOR

The terms of a trust may provide for the office of protector of the trust. The protector shall have the following powers: (a) (unless the terms of the trust shall otherwise provide) the power to remove a trustee and to appoint a new or additional trustee; and (b) such further powers as are conferred on the protector by the terms of the trust or of this Act.

The protector of a trust may also be a settlor, a trustee, or a beneficiary of the trust. In the exercise of his or her office, the protector shall not be accounted or regarded as a trustee.

Subject to the terms of the trust, in the exercise of his or her office a protector shall owe a fiduciary duty to the beneficiaries of the trust or to the purpose for which the trust is created.

Where there is more than one protector of a trust then, subject to the terms of the trust, any functions conferred on the protectors may be exercised if more than one-half of the protectors for the time being agree on its exercise.

A protector who dissents from a decision of the majority of protectors may require his or her dissent to be recorded in writing.

## 1. Trustee

Any person who has under the law of Belize the capacity to own and transfer property may be the trustee of a trust. The trustee may also be a settlor, a beneficiary, or a protector of the trust.

Unless the terms of the trust provide for a greater number, the minimum number of trustees shall be one.

A trust shall not cease to be valid only on the ground that there is no trustee or fewer than the number of trustees required by the terms of the trust.

Where there is no trustee or fewer than the number of trustees required by the terms of the trust, the necessary number of new or additional trustees shall be appointed, and until the minimum number is reached, the surviving trustee (if any) shall act only for the purpose of preserving the trust property.

Except in the case of a trust established for a charitable purpose: (a) the number of trustees shall be not more than four; and (b) if at any time there are more than four persons named as trustees, only the first four persons so named shall be the trustees of the trust.

Where the terms of a trust contain no provision for the appointment of a new or additional trustee, then: (a) the protector (if any); or (b) the trustees for the time being (but so that a trustee shall not be required to join in the appointment of his or her replacement); or (c) the last remaining trustee; or (d) the personal representative or liquidator of the last remaining trustee; or (e) if there is no such person (or no such person willing to act), the court, may appoint a new or additional trustee.

Subject to the terms of the trust, a trustee appointed under this section shall have the same functions and may act as if he or she had been originally appointed a trustee.

## 2. Appointment, Removal, and Resignation of the Trustee

On the appointment of a new or additional trustee, anything requisite for vesting the trust property in the trustees for the time being of the trust shall be done.

Where there is no trustee resident in Belize, a beneficiary may apply to the court for the appointment of a person resident in Belize and nominated in the application as an additional trustee. The court: (a) if satisfied that notice of the application has been served on the existing trustee; (b) having heard any representations; and (c) having ascertained, that the person nominated is willing to act, may appoint that person as an additional trustee.

No person shall be obliged to accept appointment as a trustee, but a person nominated as trustee who knowingly intermeddles with the trust property shall be deemed to have accepted appointment as a trustee.

A person who has not accepted and is not deemed to have accepted appointment as a trustee of a trust may, within a reasonable period of time after becoming aware of his or her nomination as trustee: (a) disclaim his or her appointment by notice in writing to the other trustees of such trust (if any); or (b) if there are no such other trustees or such other trustees cannot be contacted, apply to the court for relief from his or her appointment, and the court may make such order as it thinks fit.

A person nominated as a trustee who does not disclaim his or her appointment within a reasonable period of becoming aware of his or her nomination shall be deemed to have accepted appointment as a trustee.

A trustee other than a sole trustee may resign by notice in writing to his or her cotrustees. A trustee shall cease to be a trustee immediately on: (a) the delivery of a notice of resignation to the cotrustees; (b) his or her removal from office by the court; (c) his or her removal from office by the protector of the trust; or (d) the coming into effect of or the exercise of a power under a provision in the terms of the trust under, or by which he or she is removed from, or otherwise ceases to hold, his or her office.

A person who ceases to be a trustee shall do everything necessary to vest the trust property in the new or continuing trustees.

When a trustee resigns or is removed: (a) he or she shall duly surrender all trust property held by or vested in him or her or otherwise under his or her control; and (b) he or she may require that he or she be provided with reasonable security for liabilities (existing, future, contingent, or other) before surrendering the trust property.

A former trustee shall not be liable to any trustee or to any beneficiary or other person interested under the trust for any act or omission in relation to the trust property or to his or her functions as a trustee, except for any liability: (a) arising from a breach of trust to which the trustee (or, in the case of a corporate trustee, any of its officers or employees) was a party or was privy; and (b) in respect to an action to recover from the trustee (or, in the case of a corporate trustee, any of its officers or employees) trust property, or the proceeds thereof in his or her possession or under his or her control.

## 3. Powers of the Trustee

The Trust Act establishes the fundamental rules: (a) interest of a trustee or protector in the trust property is limited to that which is necessary for the proper performance of the trust; and (b) the trust property does not form part of the trustee's or protector's estate. These limitations do not apply as long as the trustee or protector is also a beneficiary and in the measure of his or her interest as a beneficiary.

Where a trustee or protector becomes insolvent, or on his or her property becoming liable to distrait, seizure, sequestration, or similar process of law, his or her creditors shall have no recourse against the trust property except to the extent that the trustee or protector him or herself has a claim against it or a beneficial interest in it.

A corporate trustee may (a) act in connection with a trust by a resolution of the corporate trustee or of its board of directors or other governing body; or (b) appoint an officer or employee to act on its behalf in connection with the trust.

A trustee is not, in the absence of fraud, affected by notice of any instrument, matter, fact, or thing in relation to a trust if he or she obtained notice of it by reason of his or her acting or having acted as trustee of another trust.

A trustee of a trust shall disclose to his or her cotrustees any interest that he or she has as trustee of another trust if any transaction in relation to the first-mentioned trust is to be entered into with the trustees of the other trust.

Where, in a transaction or matter affecting a trust, a trustee informs a third party that he or she is acting as trustee, a claim by the third party in respect to the transaction or matter shall extend only to the trust property. If the trustee fails to inform the third party that he or she is acting as trustee: (a) he or she incurs personal liability to the third party in respect to the transaction or matter; and (b) he or she has a right of indemnity against the trust property in respect to his or her personal liability, unless he or she acted in breach of trust. These rules shall not prejudice any claim for breach of warranty of authority.

A bona fide purchaser for value without notice of a breach of trust: (a) may deal with a trustee in relation to trust property as if the trustee were the beneficial owner thereof and (b) is not affected by the trusts on which the property is held.

A third party (a person other than a settlor, trustee, protector, or beneficiary of the trust) paying or advancing money to a trustee is not concerned to see: (a) that the money is needed in the proper exercise of the trust functions; (b) that no more than is so needed is raised; or (c) that the transaction or the application of the money is proper.

## 4. Duties of the Trustee

A trustee shall in the execution of his or her functions: (a) act with due diligence, (b) observe utmost good faith, (c) act to the best of his or her skills and abilities, and (d) exercise the standard of care of a reasonable and prudent person of business.

A trustee shall carry out and administer the trust in accordance with the Trust Act and, subject thereto, in accordance with the terms of the trust.

A trustee shall owe a fiduciary duty to the beneficiaries of the trust, the members of a class for whose benefit the trust was established, or the purpose for which the trust was established. Where a fiduciary duty is owed to a purpose for which a trust was established, that duty may be enforced by the protector of the trust or (in the case of a trust established for a charitable purpose) by the attorney general.

A trustee shall, subject to the terms of the trust and to the provisions of the Trust Act: (a) ensure that the trust property is held by or vested in him or her or is otherwise under his or her control; and (b) preserve and, so far as is reasonable, enhance the value of the trust property.

Except with the approval of the court or in accordance with the terms of the trust or the provisions of the Trust Act, a trustee shall not: (a) derive, directly or indirectly, any profit from his or her trusteeship; (b) cause or permit any other person directly or indirectly to derive any profit from his or her trusteeship; or (c) on his or her own account enter into any transaction with his or her cotrustees or relating to the trust property that may result in any such profit.

The trustee of a trust shall keep accurate accounts and records of his or her trusteeship.

A trustee shall keep trust property separate from his or her own property and separately identifiable from any other property of which he or she is a trustee.

A trustee shall so far as is reasonable and within a reasonable time of receiving a request in writing to that effect provide full and accurate information as to the state and amount of the trust property and the conduct of the trust administration to: (a) the court; (b) the settlor or protector of the trust; (c) in the case of a trust established for a charitable purpose, the attorney general; (d) subject to the terms of the trust, any beneficiary of the trust who is of full age and capacity; and (e) subject to the terms of the trust, any charity for the benefit of which the trust was established. The main difference with most Latin American laws is that there is no mandatory rendering of accounts on a periodic basis but just in the event of a request.

Subject to the provisions of the Trusts Act and to the terms of the trust, and except as is necessary for the proper administration of the trust or by reason of any other act, the trustee of a trust shall keep confidential all information regarding the state and amount of the trust property or the conduct of the trust administration.

A trustee is not (subject to the terms of the trust and to any order of the court) obliged to disclose documents that reveal: (a) his or her deliberations as to how he or she should exercise his or her functions as trustee; (b) the reasons for any decision made in the exercise of those functions; and (c) any material on which such a decision was or might have been based. A substantial difference with most Latin American laws is that the trustee is not subject to the obligation to explain the reasons for his or her decisions and actions.

Subject to the terms of the trust, where a trust is established for one or more beneficiaries or purposes (whether concurrent or consecutive), a trustee (other than a trustee who is also a beneficiary) shall act impartially as between these beneficiaries and purposes.

Subject to the terms of the trust and the provisions of the Trusts Act, a trustee shall have, in relation to the trust property, all the powers of a beneficial owner.

Subject to the terms of the trust and the provisions of the Trusts Act, a trustee shall exercise his or her functions only in the interests of the beneficiaries or for the purpose for which the trust is established and in accordance with the terms of the trust.

Where the terms of a trust provide that the trustee may add or remove beneficiaries or purposes for which the trust is established, then if such power is exercised properly and on the basis of valid considerations the exercise of the power shall not be regarded as a breach of the duty of the trustee under the trust.

A trustee may sue and be sued as trustee.

The terms of a trust may require a trustee to consult or obtain the consent of another person before exercising any functions under the trust.

Where he or she considers it necessary or desirable in the interests of the good administration of the trust, a trustee may consult a lawyer, accountant, investment advisor, or other person in relation to the affairs of the trust.

A person shall not, merely by virtue of giving or refusing his or her consent to the exercise of any functions or being consulted in relation to the affairs of a trust, be deemed to be a trustee or to owe a fiduciary duty to the beneficiaries of the trust.

Subject to the terms of the trust and to the provisions of the Trusts Act, a trustee may invest any money requiring investment in any investment or property of whatsoever nature and wheresoever situated and whether producing income or not and whether involving any liability or not and on such security (if any) as the trustee shall in his or her absolute discretion think fit as if the trustee were the absolute owner thereof.

Where the terms of a trust or any other instrument provide that any money requiring investment shall only be invested in "authorized trustee investments" (or any similar expression), then the money shall be invested only in such investments as are specified in the First Schedule of the Trust Act.[11]

A trustee may not delegate the exercise of his or her functions unless permitted to do so by the Trusts Act or by the terms of the trust. Except where the terms of the trust provide to the contrary, a trustee may (a) delegate the management of trust property to and appoint investment managers whom the trustee reasonably considers to be qualified to manage the investment of the trust property; (b) appoint and employ any lawyer, accountant or other person to act in relation to any of the affairs of the trust or to hold any of the trust property; and (c) authorize any such manager or person to retain or receive any commission or other payment usually payable for services of the description rendered.

A trustee shall not be liable for any loss arising to the trust from a delegation or appointment or from the default of any such delegate or appointee, provided that the trustee exercised the standard of care of a reasonable and prudent man of business in: (a) the selection of the delegate or appointee; and (b) the supervision of the activities of the delegate or appointee.

---

11    Mainly: (a) securities issued by, or the payment of interest that are guaranteed by, the government of Belize, the United Kingdom, the United States of America, or any territory within the Commonwealth; the African Development Bank, the Asian Development Bank, the Caribbean Development Bank, the European Economic Community, the European Investment Bank, the International Finance Corporation, the International Monetary Fund, or the International Bank for Reconstruction and Development; (b) deposits with a company registered under the Companies Act that is a licensed financial institution within the meaning of the Banks and Financial Institutions Act; (c) debentures issued by a quoted company; (d) units in a quoted unit trust; (e) quoted shares; (f) freehold property situated in Belize and leasehold property situated in Belize of which the unexpired term at the time of the investment is not less than forty years, and mortgages of such freehold or leasehold property.

## 5. Fees and Reimbursement of Expenses

A trustee shall be entitled to be reimbursed out of the trust property all expenses properly incurred by him or her in connection with the trust.

Subject to the terms of the trust, an individual trustee engaged in any profession or business shall be entitled to charge and be paid all usual professional or other charges for business transacted, time spent and acts done by him or any partner or employee of his or her or of his or her firm in connection with the trust, including acts that a trustee not being engaged in any profession or business could have done personally.

Subject to the terms of the trust, a corporate trustee shall be entitled to such remuneration as may from time to time be agreed in writing between such corporation and the settlor or protector or (in the absence of such agreement) in accordance with its standard terms and conditions as to the administration of trusts current from time to time.

Where the terms of a trust provide that a trustee shall not receive any payment for acting as such, payment may nevertheless be authorized: (a) by the court or (b) by some or all of the beneficiaries of the trust provided that a beneficiary may not authorize such payment if the beneficiary: (i) is a minor or a person under legal disability, (ii) does not have full knowledge of all material facts, or (iii) is improperly induced by the trustee to authorize such payment. Where only some of the beneficiaries authorize payment to a trustee, the payment shall be made out of the share of the trust property, which in the opinion of the trustee is referable to the interests of those beneficiaries who so authorize payment.

Subject to the terms of the trust, a trustee may, without the consent of any beneficiary, appropriate trust property in or toward satisfaction of the interest of a beneficiary in such manner and in accordance with such valuation as he or she considers appropriate.

Subject to the terms of the trust and to any prior interest or charge affecting the trust property, where any property is held by a trustee in trust for any beneficiary for any interest whatsoever: (a) while the beneficiary is a minor, the trustee (i) may, at his or her discretion, pay to the parent or guardian of the beneficiary or otherwise apply the whole or part of the income attributable to that interest for or toward the maintenance, education or benefit of the beneficiary and (ii) shall accumulate the residue of that income as an accretion to the trust property and as one fund with the trust property for all purposes (b) provided that the trustee may, while the beneficiary is a minor, apply those accumulations as if they were income of the then current year, and (c) if the beneficiary is no longer a minor and his or her interest has not yet vested in possession, the trustee shall thenceforth pay the income attributable to the interest to the beneficiary until his or her interest vests in possession or terminates.

Subject to the terms of the trust, a trustee may in his or her discretion pay or apply trust property for the advancement or benefit of any beneficiary whose interest in the trust has not yet vested in possession provided that (a) any trust property so paid or applied shall be brought into account in determining the share of the beneficiary in the trust property; (b) no such payment or application shall be made which prejudices any person entitled to any prior interest unless such person is of full age and consents to the payment or application or (if such person is not of full age) the court consents; and (c) the part of the trust property so paid or advanced shall not exceed the presumptive share of the beneficiary in the trust property.

## 6. Breach of Trust

Subject to the provisions of the Trusts Act and to the terms of the trust, a trustee who commits or concurs in a breach of trust[12] is liable for (a) any loss or depreciation in value of the trust property resulting from the breach and (b) any profit that would have accrued to the trust had there been no breach.

A trustee may not set off a profit accruing from one breach of trust against a loss or depreciation in value resulting from another.

A trustee is not liable for a breach of trust committed by another person prior to his or her appointment or for a breach of trust committed by a cotrustee unless (a) he or she becomes, or ought to have become, aware of the breach; and (b) he or she actively conceals the breach, or fails within a reasonable time to take proper steps to protect or restore the trust property or to prevent the breach.

Where trustees are liable for a breach of trust, they are liable jointly and severally.

A trustee who becomes aware of a breach of trust shall take all reasonable steps to have the breach remedied.

Nothing in the terms of a trust shall relieve a trustee of liability for a breach of trust arising from his or her own fraud or willful misconduct.

A person who derives a profit from a breach of trust or who obtains property in breach of trust shall be deemed to be a trustee of the profit or property, unless he or she derives or obtains it in good faith and without actual, constructive, or implied notice of the breach of trust. This person shall deliver up the profit or property to the person properly entitled to it.

Without prejudice to the personal liability of a trustee, trust property that has been charged or dealt with in breach of trust, or any property into which it has been converted, may be followed and recovered unless: (a) it is no longer identifiable; or (b) it is in the hands of a bona fide purchaser for value without actual, constructive, or implied notice of the breach of trust.

A beneficiary may relieve a trustee of liability to him for a breach of trust or indemnify a trustee against liability for a breach of trust, unless the beneficiary: (a) is a minor or a person under legal disability, (b) does not have full knowledge of all material facts, or (c) is improperly induced by the trustee to act in the trustee's benefit.

The court may relieve a trustee wholly or partly of liability for a breach of trust where it appears to the court that the trustee has acted honestly and reasonably and ought fairly to be excused for the breach of trust or for omitting to obtain the directions of the court in the matter in which the breach arose.

---

12  Section 67 of the Trust Act provides that "breach of trust" means a breach of any duty imposed on a trustee by this Act or by the terms of the trust.

Where a trustee commits a breach of trust at the instigation, at the request or with the concurrence of a beneficiary, the court (whether or not the beneficiary is a minor or a person under legal disability) may impound all or part of his or her interest by way of indemnity to the trustee or any person claiming through him or her.

No period of limitation or prescription applies to an action brought against a trustee (a) in respect to any fraud to which the trustee was a party or was privy or (b) to recover from the trustee trust property or the proceeds thereof: (i) held by or vested in him or otherwise in his or her possession or under his or her control or (ii) previously received by him and converted to his or her use. The period within which an action founded on breach of trust may be brought against a trustee is (a) three years from delivery of the final accounts of the trust or (b) three years from the date on which the plaintiff first has knowledge of the breach of trust, whichever period first begins to run. Where the plaintiff is a minor or a person under legal disability, the period mentioned in this paragraph does not begin to run until his or her minority or disability, as the case may be, ceases.

## 7. Case Law

Recent case law up to early 2008 confirmed that the Belize courts strongly upheld the trust's statutory asset-protection provisions including the choice of Belize law as proper law of the trust, freedom from outside interference, and the obligation to comply strictly with Belize law and trust terms. Among the orders granted were:

a. No disclosure—that if any trustee of the Belize trust is ordered, requested, or required, whether by an order of a foreign court or other foreign institution, to disclose any information relating to the state of or the amount of the trust property originally settled or today remaining in the Belize Trust Fund ("the Trust Fund"), or in respect to the conduct of the administration of the Belize Trust Fund, to any authority or party directly or indirectly involved in the foreign proceedings, and/or to such other persons related to the Belize Trust Fund as the said court may determine on further application, the trustee is hereby directed not to do so unless ordered to do so by a judge of the Supreme Court of Belize; provided, however, that the trustee shall remain free to continue to provide such financial information to persons related to the Belize Trust Fund from time to time as shall be necessary for them to meet their foreign tax filing and tax-paying obligations.

b. No surrender or payment over of assets by the trustee—that if any trustee of the Belize Trust Fund is ordered, requested, or required, whether by an order of a foreign court, or otherwise, to surrender, deliver, transfer, pay over, disgorge or in any way part with any of the Trust Fund, to any authority or party directly or indirectly involved in the foreign proceedings, and/or to or at the direction of such other person including persons related to the Belize Trust Fund as the said court may determine on further application, the trustee is hereby directed not to do so unless ordered to do so by a judge of the Supreme Court of Belize.

c. No surrender or payment over of assets by settlor—that if the trustee of the Belize Trust Fund is requested or required by persons related to the Belize Trust Fund to surrender, deliver, transfer, pay over, disgorge or in any way part with any of the Trust Fund to any authority or party directly or indirectly involved in the foreign proceedings, and/or to or at the direction of such other person including persons related to the Belize Trust Fund as the said court may determine on further application, the trustee is hereby directed not to do so unless ordered to do so by a judge of the Supreme Court of Belize.

d. No compelled change of fiduciaries or signatories—that in the event there is an attempt on the part of any authority or party directly or indirectly involved in the foreign proceedings or otherwise to remove and/or replace and/or add any trustee and/or any protector under the Belize Trust Fund, and/or to change or to compel the change of any signatory currently applicable to financial accounts held by the Belize Trust Fund, then any such attempt shall be ineffective until this court shall have an opportunity to have a hearing thereon if so required or permitted by this court, and/or to otherwise rule thereon, and the trustee is hereby directed to immediately seek further directions from this court prior to complying with or responding in any way to any such attempt.

## D. INTERNATIONAL TRUSTS

As mentioned at the beginning of this chapter, on June 15, 2007, the Trusts (amendment) Act came into force. The most relevant rules are the following:

An "international trust" means a trust where: (a) the settlor is not resident in Belize; (b) no beneficiary is resident in Belize; (c) the trust property does not include any land situated in Belize; (d) the law of Belize is selected as the proper law of the trust; and (e) in the event of a purpose trust, the purpose or object of the trust is to be pursued or performed outside of Belize.

An international trust may be created only by an instrument in writing. Every declaration of trust (or deed of settlement) creating an international trust shall be signed by the trustee(s) (and the settlor in the case of a deed of settlement) and authenticated by notary public or other similar authority if executed outside Belize.

## 1. Creation of a Register of International Trusts

A register of international trusts was established under the jurisdiction and control of the International Financial Services Commission. The trusts register will contain the following information: (a) name of the trust, (b) date of settlement of the trust, (c) date of registration of the trust, (d) name(s) of the trustee(s), (e) name of the protector (if any), and (f) name and address of the trust agent.

The necessary particulars for all international trusts must be registered within ninety days of their date of creation (which period may be extended on the discretion of the Registrar of International Trusts). Registration of the trust document itself is not mandatory.

A registered international trust shall be issued a numbered certificate of registration by the Registrar of International Trusts.

Any variation of an international trust that would affect the information held by the trust agent corresponding to that particular trust must be filed with the trust agent.

Any variation of an international trust that would affect the information on the trusts register corresponding to that particular trust must be filed with the registrar of international trusts and shall be issued a numbered amended certificate of registration.

Any registered international trust that is terminated must have its certificate of registration returned for cancellation and shall have its entry on the trusts register also cancelled.

The trusts register shall not be open for general public inspection. Only a person authorized in writing by the trustee or the trust agent of an international trust may inspect the entry of that particular trust on the trusts register. The Registrar of International Trusts shall not disclose any information contained in the trusts register to any person without the trustee's or trust agent's written authorization except where a written request is made to him or her by: (a) the Director of Public Prosecutions, (b) the Director of the Financial Intelligence Unit, (c) the Commissioner of Police, or (d) other regulatory or enforcement authority, certifying that such information is reasonably required to facilitate a criminal investigation, prosecution or proceeding, whether in Belize or elsewhere.

## 2. Trust Agent

Any international trust shall at all times have a trust agent resident in Belize who shall be appointed by the trustee of that trust.

The trust agent shall accept service of all legal process on behalf of the trustee(s) and protector (if any), and shall be responsible for ensuring that the international trust at all times complies with the provisions of the Trusts Act as to registration or the regulations.

No person shall act or hold him or herself out as a trust agent unless he or she is the holder of a valid license to engage in trust business issued by the commission, and every person who contravenes this provision commits an offense and shall be liable to the penalties prescribed under the International Financial Services Commission Act.

Every trust agent shall maintain a record of international trusts containing the following information: (a) name of the trust, (b) date of settlement of the trust, (c) date of registration of the trust, (d) name(s) of the trustee(s), (e) name of settlor, (f) name of protector (if any), (g) names and addresses of all the beneficiaries, (h) initial funds settled, (i) additional funds settled, (j) changes in beneficiaries, (k) change of protector, and (l) original trust instrument and any amendments thereto.

There shall also be a register of trust agents maintained by the Registrar of International Trusts containing relevant details of the trust agent.

## 3. Exemptions of International Trusts

Only registered international trusts shall enjoy the following exemptions: (a) The trust shall be exempt from the provisions of the Income and Business Tax Act; (b) no estate, inheritance, succession, or gift tax or duty shall be payable with respect to the trust property by reason of the death of any person; and (c) all instruments relating to the trust property or to transactions carried out by the trustee on behalf of the trust shall be exempt from stamp duty.

The trustees of a registered international trust shall be regarded as Belize nonresidents for the purpose of the Exchange Control Regulations (1976) with regard to the trust property and to all transactions carried out by the trustee on behalf of the trust.

Chapter 8

# Bolivia[1]

A. Definition and Overview  129
B. The Grantor  131
C. The Trustee  131
D. The Beneficiary  133
E. Securitization  133
    1. Legal Framework  133
    2. The Stock Market Act  134
    3. Tax Treatment  136

In Bolivia, just like in most other Latin American jurisdictions, trusts acquire the status of a separate patrimony, distinct from that of the settlor, the trustee, and the beneficiary. However, notwithstanding the fact that the characteristics of trusts render them ideal vehicles to carry out securitization processes, Bolivian legislators did not employ it as the legal mechanism for securitization. To this end, they created securitization companies, which have an ordinary estate (that can be affected by the company's creditors) and as many special-purpose patrimonies as had been created by means of the transfer of assets of the originating companies (which take responsibility for the rights and liabilities of such patrimonies alone).

## A. DEFINITION AND OVERVIEW

Trust regulations are in title VII, chapter IV, section II, articles 1409 to 1427 of the Bolivian Commerce Code and in articles 3 and 9 of the Banks and Financial Institutions

---

1  This chapter was made possible thanks to Jaime Dunn, a prestigious lecturer on securitization in Latin America and general manager of *Nacional Financiera Boliviana Sociedad de Titularización* (NAFIBO ST; the leading securitization company in Bolivia), who read the manuscript and made an invaluable contribution.

Act (*Ley de Bancos y Entidades Financieras*). If these rules proves insufficient, the provisions that govern deposit and agency can be used, mutatis mutandis, for trusts.

Under article 1409 of the Bolivian Commerce Code, a trust is an agreement whereby a person, called settlor, conveys property to a bank, called trustee, which manages or makes disposition of it for the accomplishment of a certain end for the benefit of the former or a third party, called the beneficiary.

As can be seen, just like in most of the other jurisdictions under study, three legal positions exist under this agreement: namely, the grantor (transferring the property); the trustee (who undertakes to manage or make disposition of it for the accomplishment of a certain end); and the beneficiary, in whose benefit the trust is created.

Regarding the nature of the patrimony, the Commerce Code makes reference to the creation of a special-purpose patrimony, that is, it deems that the title transferred to the trustee by virtue of the trust (*fiducia*) does not come into the latter's estate, but rather that a special-purpose patrimony is created, with an intent or purpose in each case. Further, in line with all Latin American countries (but for Ecuadorian legislation), each special-purpose patrimony is not considered an entity with legal status.

Thus, article 1410 sets forth that the trust assets constitute a special-purpose patrimony, that it is no part of the so called "general guarantee" available to the trustee's creditors, and can only be affected by the duties deriving from the trust or its execution.

As regards the necessary formalities for the creation of a trust, an *inter vivos* trust must be recorded by a notary in a deed in accordance with the type of property, whereas the one created *mortis causa* must be so recorded by means of a will, in accordance with the regulations of the Bolivian Civil Code. As to the trust, which depends on a suspensive condition, it will not come into being if the condition does not occur in the term stated in the act of settlement.

Bolivian regulations prohibit

a. Secret trusts
b. Those trusts in which the benefit is vested in various persons who must successively be substituted because of the death of their predecessor (fiduciary substitution)
c. Those whose duration extends beyond thirty years, unless the beneficiary be a non-profit scientific, cultural, or technical assistance institution

Causes for the termination of trusts besides those prescribed by the Bolivian Civil Code

a. Expiration of the term stated in the trust instrument
b. Accomplishment of the resolutory condition to which the trust was subject
c. Death of the grantor or the beneficiary when the event has been expressly stipulated as cause of termination
d. Dissolution or liquidation of the trustee
e. Accomplishment or material impossibility of accomplishment of the purposes of the trust

f. Mutual agreement between grantor and beneficiary, without detriment to the trustee's rights (mainly to claim his or her fees for the original term of the trust)

g. Revocation of the grantor when he or she has reserved to him or herself that right in the trust instrument

h. Impossibility of substitution of the trustee for lack of another trustee

At the termination of the trust on any grounds, the trust property will revert to the grantor or, where appropriate, pass down to his or her heirs, except with an express statement to the contrary.

## B. THE GRANTOR

Concerning the rights of the grantor, the Code sets forth the following:

a. Those he or she has expressly reserved to him or herself in the trust contract

b. To revoke the trust when he or she has expressly reserved to him or herself this power in the trust contract

c. To require the removal of the trustee and to designate his or her substitute when the case may be

d. To secure the delivery of the assets at the termination of the trust period had no provision been made to the contrary in the trust instrument

e. To demand the rendering of accounting by the trustee

f. To sue the trustee

g. Generally, all the rights stated expressly and which are not incompatible with the nature of the trust

## C. THE TRUSTEE

As in many other Latin American countries, only banks are authorized to be trustees in Bolivia. In this respect, the Banks Superintendence (*Superintendencia de Bancos*) regulated trust transactions by means of its Circular SB/254/93 (July 12, 1993). This Circular has eight chapters: Application, Authorization, Organization, Operation, Capital, Accounting Requirements, Prohibitions, and Temporary Provisions.

The Commerce Code provides the following as powers of the trustee that are not delegable, apart from those prescribed in the trust instrument:

a. To perform with due diligence all necessary acts for the accomplishment of the object of the trust

b. To maintain the trust property segregated from his or her own and from those corresponding to other transactions of the same type and insure them when so stated in the trust instrument

c. To procure that the economic return from trust property is the best possible in compliance with the conditions stated in the trust instrument

d. To protect and defend the trust property against acts by third parties, even by the beneficiary or by the grantor him or herself
e. To transfer the property to the persons to whom it is due, according with the trust instrument or the law, once the trust has been terminated
f. To render accounts of their administration to the beneficiary or, if it be the case, to the grantor, every six months and at its conclusion

In the event that the trustee faces well-founded doubts as to the nature and scope of his or her duties, or should he or she be forced to cease in the functions stated in the trust instrument, or when circumstances demand, he or she is bound by law to consult or seek advice from the grantor or beneficiary or, where appropriate, he or she must do so from the administrative authority or the competent court.

Trustee's fees should be calculated in line with the regulations provided in the trust instrument. In the event of nonexistence of express guidelines, remuneration will be determined according with the fees approved by the competent administrative authority.

As under the law of most Latin American countries, the trustee could not acquire the ownership of any of the property under trust to avoid any conflict of interests. Put differently, the trustee cannot be the beneficiary or residual beneficiary of the trust assets.

Concerning the regulation relating to the prohibition placed on one person merging the capacities of trustee and beneficiary, the Bolivian Code prescribes that should such a situation obtain, then the beneficiary will not be permitted to enjoy the benefits flowing from the trust for as long as such a situation persists.

As regards the trustee's designation, the law provides for the case in which neither designation of the trustee nor establishment of the procedure for its designation has taken place, or for any other case in which that office is vacant. In such cases, the designation will be made by the beneficiary without altering the conditions of the trust or, where appropriate, by a court.

The law prescribes that the trustee may only resign his or her office on the grounds expressly stated in the agreement. However, lacking stipulation thereof, the following are assumed as warranted:

a. If the trust assets do not yield sufficient income to cover the stipulated fee in favor of the trustee
b. If the grantor, his or her heirs or the beneficiary refuse to pay such fee
c. If other causes established by a competent court exist

The trustee's resignation requires prior authorization from the competent administrative authority.

Conversely, the trustee can be removed by the competent court at the request of the grantor, the beneficiary, or the parties directly interested when involuntary tort, gross negligence, or neglect in his or her duties is verified, or when he or she does not consent to the inventory of the trust property, of the assets and liabilities and proceeds of the administration, or refuses to tender the security pledged in the trust agreement.

## D. THE BENEFICIARY

The beneficiary has the following rights, apart from those stated in the trust instrument and the law:

a. To demand that the trustee faithfully complies with his or her duties and, where appropriate, to sue him or her for his or her failure to do so
b. To claim trust property back into the trust when the trustee improperly abandoned it
c. To challenge the trustee's voidable acts within five years computed from the day he or she came into knowledge of the act that originated the action
d. To procure the removal of the trustee from the competent administrative authority, provided there exists just cause, and the appointment of an acting administrator as a preventative measure

The law expressly prescribes that the beneficiary's creditors could only claim the income obtained from the trust property. By the same token, they could not lay claims on such property unless their credits antedate the creation of the trust. However, the trust transaction held in fraud of creditors may be challenged by any prejudiced party.


## E. SECURITIZATION

Securitization has been growing in Bolivia since the first transaction in 2001, with 1 securitization patrimony in 2001 and 12 in 2008, which represents more than US$260 million administered by securitization companies.[2]


### 1. Legal Framework

The Stock Market Act, Law No. 1834 (*Ley del Mercado de Valores*) of March 31, 1998, aimed at regulating and promoting the stock market, devoted a section to securitization companies (*sociedades de titularización*) and securitization (*titularización*) (chapter VIII, articles 76–86).

Supreme Decree (*Decreto Supremo*) No. 25514 of September 17, 1999, laid down the general guidelines to regulate the organization and activities of securitization companies and the securitization process, set forth in the only chapter of title VIII of the Stock Market Act (Law No. 1834 mentioned in the previous paragraph). Also, the grounds for intervention and liquidation of the said companies were established, together with infractions and applicable penalties.

---

2    The detail of issuances (name of the security and year of issuance) is as follows: *Coboce* 001 (2001), *Soboce* 002 (2002), *Coboce* 003 (2003), *Concordia* (2004), *IC Norte* (2005), *INTI* (2006), *Terrasur* 007 (2006, 2007, and 2008), *Gas Electricidad* 008 (2007), *Liberty* 009 (2008), *Sinchi Wayra* 010 (2008), *Letras de Cambio ME* 012 (2007), *Letras de Cambio MN* 013 (2008), and *Sinchi Wayra* 015 (2008).

Administrative Resolution SPVS-IV No. 052 of February 14, 2000, by the Super-intendence of Pensions, Stock and Insurance (*Superintendencia de Pensiones, Valores y Seguros*) passed the regulations that aim at setting up the norms of prudence relevant to the securitization process. This resolution was amended by the Administrative Resolution SPVS-IV No. 488 of September 10, 2004, in the points related to minimum capital and hedge schemes. Finally, it was amended by Administrative Resolution SPVS-IV No. 1107 of December 2, 2005, which approved the regulation of issuances as a result of securitizations.

In this Resolution, the Specific Complementary Regulations on Securitization (*Reglamento de Disposiciones Complementarias Específicas Sobre Titularización*) were also passed with the aim of laying down the norms that securitization companies must comply with to secure authorization by the Stock Market Registry, as well as the authorization and inscription of the separate patrimony, of securities and the authoriza-tion of its public offering. These regulations also delineated the minimal requirements to be met by contracts and unilateral acts (creation of a trust by the sole declaration of the grantor who becomes the trustee of certain assets) for securitization.

By means of the Securities Superintendence Resolution SPVS-IV No. 212 of May 29, 2000, the accounting manual for securitization companies was created. Through Administrative Resolution SPVS-IV No. 245 of May 14, 2002, the rules applicable to securitization with banks as grantors were established. This resolution was ratified and complemented the Resolution of the Banks No. 026/2002 of May 5, 2002, modified by Resolution No. 121 of December 9, 2004.

## 2. The Stock Market Act

The Stock Market Act (Law No. 1834 mentioned before), like the Ecuadorian Stock Market Act, among others, provided the definition of securitization. To securitize involves constituting separate patrimonies under the administration of securitization companies with assets and property, present or future, designed to guarantee and pay for securities issued in favor of investors independent from the patrimony of the grantor, or the originating company (*empresa originadora*).

The separate patrimony is not a part of the estate of the originating company, nor of the securitization company. Therefore, neither the originating companies' creditors nor the securitization companies' creditors can affect the separate patrimony, which only responds to and guarantees the obligations deriving from the issuance of securities.

The securities issued as a consequence of the securitization process are deemed, to all legal effects and for the purpose of all types of transactions, as securities,[3] with all

---

3     Article II of Bolivian Law No. 1834 states that the term "security" will comprise certificated securities (paper ones) as well as uncertificated securities (records in books). The term "security" signifies: (a) the securities governed by the Commerce Code; (b) the securities issued by the Bolivian government and its agencies; (c) those transaction instruments in the Securities Market that comply with the following conditions: (i) that they be created and issued according to specific regulations; (ii) that they state the beneficiary of the resources obtained

the rights and duties pertaining to such, which can be placed and traded without any restrictions.

The participants in a securitization are

a. *The originator or originating company:* the person in whose benefit a separate patrimony is constituted and who undertakes to transfer to the securitization company the assets that will comprise that patrimony.
b. *The securitization company:* the recipients of the assets to be securitized, whose function it is to serve as a vehicle to carry out the issuance. Securitization companies are to be constituted as corporations with an exclusive corporate purpose, and they must include in their denomination the expression "Securitization Company." Securitization companies must obtain clearance for their operation from the Securities Superintendence (*Superintendencia de Valores*), having complied with the minimal corporate capital and the requirements and guarantees set forth by means of regulations. Similarly, they are subject to the supervision and control of the Securities Superintendence and are governed by the foregoing statutory and regulatory requirements. With a view to avoid conflicts of interest, securitization companies will not be allowed to take part in securitization processes of originating companies in which their shareholders, directors, administrators, or managers, as well as close relatives, hold a capital interest or relation, or some other form of participation in its administration and/or control.
c. *The investors:* the holders of the securities backed by the property that makes up the special-purpose patrimony.

Under the Stock Market Act, securitization processes can be structured from the following assets or property: public debt securities, listed corporate securities, loan portfolios, cash flows, agreements of sale of goods and services, leasing or factoring contracts, real estate property and projects, and the like, in accordance with the regulations.

According to the necessary expediency of business and movement of capitals, it has been provided that the transfer of assets or property to a securitization company does not require consent or notification by the respective transferred debtors, if any. The transfer of assets and property to a securitization company is absolute in legal as well as accounting terms, and is enforceable against third parties as from the signing of the transfer agreement, and the said property or assets cannot be applied to discharging liabilities in favor of creditors of the originating company nor of the debts of the securitization company. The transfer of the patrimony, with the ownership of the assets which compose it, comprises the transfer of the guarantees that back them, except for express agreement to the contrary.

As to the securities issued as a result of the securitization process, in the case of securities evidencing a debt or mixed with a participation right, they must bear risk-rating by an authorized risk-rating agency.

---

by the issuance; (iii) that its public offering be authorized by the Superintendent of Securities; (iv) that they evidence the existence of an effective obligation assumed by the issuer. Securities are freely transferable. Any limitation on their circulation is null and void.

Finally, the mechanism of securitization and the agreement, transfer, issuance, guarantees, risk-rating, administration procedures, as well as other requirements in the process, are governed by specific regulations.

## 3. Tax Treatment

It is important to emphasize that the transfer of the property or assets subject to securitization in charge of the securitization companies, as much at the outset as at the termination of the process, is exempt from several taxes, in accordance with the following legal framework:

a. Law No. 2064 of April 3, 2000, denominated the "Economic Reactivation Law." Under section 29(13), which modifies section 117 of the Stock Market Act (Law No. 1834), capital gains arising from the sale of listed securities in the stock market are exempted from value-added tax, tax complementary to the value-added tax, and the tax on companies income.
b. Law No. 2196 of May 2, 2001, denominated "Special Fund or Economic Reactivation Law." Section 12 establishes that capital gains, yields from investing in securities issued as a result of securitizations, and income of securitization patrimonies are not subject to the value-added tax, the tax complementary to the value-added tax, and the tax on companies income, the exemption including payments to foreign beneficiaries.
c. Supreme Decree No. 25514 of September 17, 1999, denominated "General Regulations that Rule the Organization and Activities of Securitization Companies and Securitizations." Section 28 clarifies that: (i) the exemption from value-added tax and the tax on financial transactions, established by the Stock Market Act (Law No. 1834) section 86 comprises the transfer of assets to the securitization company until the liquidation of the securitization patrimony; and (ii) the said section of the Stock Market Act (Law No. 1834) entails the exemption of any registration fee that would have been applicable to any registration in a public registry of a transfer of property because of a securitization process.
d. Law No. 3446 of July 21, 2006, section 9(i) that regulates the tax on financial transactions establishes that the credits and debits in the bank account of the securitization patrimony with the exception of the debits of sums actually collected by the originator or the beneficiary are exempted from this tax. This exemption was clarified by Supreme Decree No. 28815 of July 26, 2006, section 6(I) (j) (Regulating the Tax on Financial Transactions).

To summarize, the holder of securities issued because of a securitization is exempted from the value-added tax, the tax complementary to the value-added tax, the tax on financial transactions, the tax on companies income, and any withholding on payments to foreign beneficiaries. Furthermore, the bank accounts of the securitization patrimonies are exempted of the tax on financial transactions.

# Chapter 9

# Brazil[1]

A. Overview 137
B. Guarantee Trusts (*Alienação Fiduciaria en Garantía*) 138
   1. Trust Transfer in Guarantee of Personalty Ruled by Law No. 4.728 of
      1965—The Capital Markets Act (*Ley do Mercado de Capitais*) 142
   2. Realty Trust Transfer in Guarantee (Law No. 9.514 of 1997 Chapter II) 143
   3. Aeronautic Code 145
   4. Transfer of Creditors Rights in Guarantee 146
C. Realty Mutual Funds (Law No. 8.668 of 1993) 146
D. Inheritance Trust (*Fideicomisso or Substituição Fideicomissária*) 148
E. Securitization (Law No. 9.514 of 1997 Chapter I, Sections IV, V, and VI) 149
   1. CRI 149
   2. Securitization Trusts 150
   3. The Fiduciary Agent 152

## A. OVERVIEW

Unlike all other Latin American countries with trust laws, in which a general regulation of trusts allows its application to different purposes including the guarantee of obligations, Brazilian legislation provides separate legal regimes that regulate: (a) guarantee trusts (in its civil code and several acts), (b) securitization trusts,[2] (c) real estate trust,[3] and (d) a regimen similar to an inheritance trust (*fideicomisso* or

---

1    This chapter would not have been possible without the extraordinary help of Thaís Cíntia Cárnio, prestigious practicing corporate lawyer and professor. The excellent material she provided and her valuable guide to my understanding of Brazilian law (and her patience) cannot be acknowledged in its full dimension.

2    Securitization trust ruled by Law No. 9.514 of 1997.

3    Trust ownership of realty with the purpose of constituting real estate mutual funds ruled by Law No. 8.668 of 1993.

*substituição fideicomissária*) provided by sections 1951 to 1953 of the Civil Code. In other words, there is no general regimen of administration trust.[4]

The absence of a legal system to give certainty to the grantor and beneficiary's rights (particularly in the case of bankruptcy of the trustee) has meant a stumbling block to its development because (a) it does not permit transactions with independent investors because personal confidence placed in the trustee is everything, and (b) for large-scale or long-term transactions the trust, being an unregulated transaction, becomes unfeasible. Therefore, administration trust is almost unknown as a vehicle for legal businesses in Brazil.[5]

The most remarkable achievement of Brazilian law is that it has been able to respond to the demand for adequate guarantees that permit access to credit to people who otherwise would not enjoy this benefit.

It must be pointed out that a new Brazilian Civil Code (Act No. 10.406 of January 10, 2002)[6] entered into force on January 11, 2003. This Code included the regulation of guarantee trusts abrogating the rules that opposed to it.

## B. GUARANTEE TRUSTS (*ALIENAÇÃO FIDUCIARIA EN GARANTÍA*)

The Brazilian Civil Code rules on trust property in book III (*On the Right Over Assets*), title III (*On the Property*), chapter IX (*On the Trust Property*), sections 1361 to 1368A.

Diniz explained that in guarantee trust transfer (in Portuguese, *alienação fiduciaria en garantía*), the trustee becomes the owner of the assets transferred by the settlor. The resolution of the ownership happens at the moment in which the guarantee terminates, the assets coming back to the settlor. The settlor only acquires the property to guarantee his or her credit. The transfer of the property is related to a creditors' right, with its effects subordinated to the fulfillment of the obligation of the settlor–debtor.

---

4    De Oliveira explained that administration trusts (*fiducia cum amico*), similar to trusts in the United States, "tried to be part of the Brazilian Law in the Draft of Obligations Code drafted by [him] in 1965, but it did not find reception in the Draft of Civil Code of 1975." CELSO MARCELO DE OLIVEIRA, ALIENAÇÃO FIDUCIÁRIA EM GARANTIA 4 (2003).

       MELHIM NAMEM CHALHUB, NEGÓCIO FIDUCIÁRIO 66 (1998). The writer refers to two bills containing a general regulation of trusts but that, nevertheless, did not materialize into legislation.

5    Trust transactions not falling into any of the specific regimens mentioned above are unregulated contracts with permissibility that is currently being contested in Brazilian law. In favor of its legality, Chalhub claims that, even if scant, Brazilian case law acknowledges unregulated trust transaction deals as valid on freedom of contract grounds, as long as they do not conflict with public order or morals. Thus, Chalhub sees trust transactions as "the innominate legal transaction whereby a person (grantor) transfers property of something or title of a right to another (trustee), who undertakes to give it a certain end and, once that purpose is accomplished, transfers the property either right back to the grantor or to a beneficiary indicated in the trust instrument." CHALHUB, *supra* note 4, at 66–68.

6    This Code was drafted by a commission headed by the prestigious Brazilian jurist, Miguel Reale. It replaced the previous 1916 Code and several Acts on particular matters.

The trustee has to return the property to the settlor if the latter makes due payment of his or her obligation. The payment by the debtor represents the accomplishment of a resolutory condition that terminates the trust property with the settlor being the beneficiary.[7] The same author defined the guarantee trust transfer as a transfer made by a debtor to the creditor of a revocable property and an indirect possession of: (a) an infungible asset (Civil Code section 1361), (b) a fungible asset (Law No. 4.728/65 section 66-B(3) modified by Law No. 10.931/2004), or (c) an immovable asset (Law No. 9.514 sections 22–33), as guarantee of his or her obligation, the right of the creditor being one that terminates with the payment of the debtor.[8]

Any natural or legal person, even from the public sector, can be a settlor of a guarantee trust, as long as they have legal capacity and the right to transfer the asset to a third party.[9]

Section 1361 of the Civil Code provides that trust property is the revocable property of an infungible asset that a debtor, with the purpose of guarantee, transfers to a creditor. Trust property is constituted with the registry of the trust instrument in the Registry of Titles and Documents of the domicile of the debtor, or in the case of vehicles, in the competent governmental agency.[10] Trust property involves the splitting of possession, the debtor changing from owner to mere holder.

Section 1362 of the Civil Code provides that the trust instrument, which serves as title of the trust property, must detail: (a) the total amount of the debt or its assessment;

---

7    4 Maria Helena Diniz, Curso de Direito Civil Brasileiro 330 (23rd ed. 2008).

8    *Id.* at 583–584.

9    Before the modification of section 66 of Law No. 4.728/65 by Law No. 10.931 of 2004, there was a controversy around the legitimacy of being a creditor-trustee of personal property. The "strict position" maintained that only financial institutions can be such because of the status granted them in the Capital Markets Act, whereas a "broader view" posited that any individual or legal entity could be trustees in virtue of the absence of prohibition in the law. For a summary of opinions (in Portuguese) see Waldirio Bulgarelli, Contratos Mercantis 313 (11th ed. 1999). The author also quotes the complete text of the court rulings R.T. 400/199, R.T. 421/227, R.T. 439/134, where it is concluded that guarantee trusts are only to be used by financial institutions. *Also see* Diniz, *supra* note 7, at 587.

10   Judicial summary (*Súmula*) No. 92 issued by the Superior Court of Justice (S.T.J. [*Superior Tribunal de Justiça*]) of October 27, 1993, established that the trust transfer of a car not registered in the Registry of Vehicles cannot be opposed to a good faith (bona fide) third party. The same criteria emerge from judicial summary No. 489 issued by the Federal Supreme Court (S.T.F. [*Superior Tribunal Federal*]) of December 3, 1969.

     Under Brazilian law, a *Súmula* is a summary that records a specific or majority interpretation made by a court in relation to a particular matter. It has the double purpose of publishing the court criteria and of promoting the uniformity of court decisions. According to § 103-A of the Brazilian Constitution, *Súmulas* issued by the S.T.F. are binding for all other courts after their publication in the Official Gazette. It is worth noting that the Brazilian judiciary "comprises federal and state courts, and is headed by the Federal Supreme Court (STF). The STF is the final appeal court for federal and state courts on Federal Constitutional matters. . . . Under the STF are special courts. These are the final courts of appeal for nonconstitutional matters: Superior Court of Justice (STJ). This court hears appeals on how to interpret and apply federal law." BritCham Brazil, Doing Business in Brazil 25 (5th ed. 2005).

(b) the term for payment or the payment date; (c) the applicable interest rate;[11] and (d) the description of the asset transferred and the necessary elements for its identification.

The debtor can use the trust property at his or her own expense and risk, in accordance with the nature of the asset, being subject to the same obligations as a bailee (a) to guard the assets with the due diligence according to its nature and (b) to deliver the asset to the creditor if the debt is not paid when due.[12]

If when due, the debt is not paid,[13] the creditor must sell, not necessarily in a judicial process, the trust asset to third parties and apply the proceeds of the sale to the payment of his or her credit and the expenses incurred for its collection and deliver the balance (if any) to the debtor.[14] If the trust asset is sold, and the proceeds are not enough to cover the total amount of the debt and the collection expenses, the debtor remains responsible for the unpaid balance.[15] If a third party pays the debt, he or she subrogates, by this sole fact, in the credit and the trust property.[16]

Any stipulation that authorizes the trustee to keep the trust property if the debt is not paid when due is null and void. Nevertheless, after the due date of the obligation, the debtor can agree with the creditor the payment of the debt with the transfer of the trust assets.[17]

Trust property is, mutatis mutandis, subject to sections 1421, 1425, 1426, 1427, and 1436 of the Civil Code[18]—all sections of the Civil Code referring to mortgages and pledges. These sections applied to guarantee trusts may be summarized as follows:

a. The payment of one or more portions of a debt does not mean that the assets do not continue subject to the guarantee trust, even if the guarantee comprises several assets, unless there is an express disposition in the trust instrument.

b. Debts must be considered due: (i) if the trust asset is deteriorated or loses value, and the creditor requires the debtor to replace or improve such assets, and the debtor does not comply with such requirement; (ii) if the debtor becomes insolvent or goes bankrupt; (iii) if the debt is not paid by its due date. The creditor's voluntary collection of the debt payment means his or her resignation to the right to request the foreclosure of the guarantee; (iv) if the trust property is destroyed and it is not

---

11    Diniz explained that "usury is prohibited under Brazilian law (Law No. 1.521/51, section 4; Decree No. 22.626/33 amended by Decree-Law No. 182/38 and by Law No. 3.942/61), this is, the stipulation of an interest rate higher than 12% per annum. If there is no interest rate stipulation, it is understood that the parties agreed a 6% per year . . . (Decree-Law No. 22.626, section 1, paragraph 3), unless there is express stipulation that the loan is without interest." DINIZ, *supra* note 7, at 477.

12    Civil Code § 1363.

13    Judicial summaries (*Súmulas*) issued by the Superior Court of Justice: No. 72 of April 14, 1993; No. 76 of May 4, 1993; and No. 245 of April 17, 2001; require the delivery of a notification to the debtor demanding the payment of the debt.

14    Civil Code § 1364.

15    Civil Code § 1366.

16    Civil Code § 1368.

17    Civil Code § 1365.

18    Civil Code § 1367.

replaced by the debtor. In such case, the creditor has a preferential right to collect the insurance payment over the trust property; (v) if the trust asset is lost because of the action of a third party, and the debtor does not make a deposit of the amount necessary to pay the debt.

c. If the debt is considered due before its original due date, it would not include interest not accrued by then.

d. Unless there is an express stipulation, the third party who granted the guarantee is not subject to the obligation of replacing or improving it in the event that, such third party not being guilty, the trust asset deteriorates or loses its value.

e. The guarantee trust will terminate: (i) if the obligation guaranteed expires, (ii) if the trust asset is completely destroyed, (iii) by waiver of the creditor, (iv) by the concurrence in the same person of the capacities of creditor and debtor, and (v) in the sale of the trust property.

It is worth mentioning that although guarantee trusts could be deemed as abusive to the debtor,[19] in practice it allows debtors to get credit that they would normally not get were they to resort to traditional guarantees, which translates into the possibility of benefiting low-income social groups who could not otherwise access financed goods (mostly household appliances and automobiles).

To sum up, guarantee trusts afford a creditor an effective, expedient means to get at the financed funds in the event of nonpayment by the debtor. For his or her own part, the debtor can gain access to credit, and therefore goods, which he or she could not enjoy if he or she only had the traditional guarantees (i.e., pledge and mortgage), with the certainty that the asset will be his or hers with no restrictions if he or she complies with his or her obligations, regardless of the situation of the creditor.

Regarding the bankruptcy of the settlor (who has the tenancy of the trust assets), the Bankruptcy Law[20] (Law No. 11.101 of 2005) section 119, subparagraph IX, provides that patrimonies for specific purposes (such as trusts) will be subject to the applicable laws (trust legislation described in this chapter) its assets, rights, and obligations remaining separate from those of the bankrupt person up to the corresponding expiration or up to the fulfillment of its purposes, when the judicial administrator will accept the assets of the separate patrimony (if there is a positive balance) or will recognize a debt (if there is a negative balance of the patrimony).[21]

---

19  *See* BULGARELLI, *supra* note 9, at 311.

20  "After approximately 11 years of discussions in the Brazilian Congress, and as a result of a combined effort of law practitioners, economists, politicians and civil society as a whole, a new Brazilian bankruptcy law (Law No. 11.101/2005) was enacted on 9 February, 2005. . . . The previous bankruptcy law, which was in force from 21 June 1945 to 9 June 2005, was Decree-Law No. 7661/45." BRITCHAM BRAZIL, *supra* note 10, at 146.

21  Fàbio Ulhoa Coelho explained that if the settlor goes bankrupt, the trustee can request the restitution of the movable asset simply because the trustee is the owner of the asset. If the asset is an immovable one, the trustee can request becoming the full owner of the asset. Therefore, the trustee is not subject to the bankruptcy procedure with the obvious reduction of time and expenses. FÀBIO ULHOA COELHO, COMENTÁRIOS À NOVA LEY DE FALENCIAS E DE RECUPERAÇÃO DE EMPRESAS 131, 325–326 (6th ed. 2009).

By the time the Brazilian Civil Code entered into force (January 11, 2003), there were several special regimes of guarantee trusts, and there was a discussion on the abrogation of these regimens by the Civil Code. To finish with this discussion, Act No. 10.931 of 2004 included one section (1368A) that provides that the other kinds of trust property are subject to their specific Acts as long as the rules of the Civil Code are not incompatible with them. The following paragraphs will refer to these regimes in detail.

## 1. Trust Transfer in Guarantee of Personalty Ruled by Law No. 4.728 of 1965—The Capital Markets Act (*Ley do Mercado de Capitais*)

The Capital Markets Act section 66 was the first regulation of guarantee trust in Brazil.[22] The original section 66 of Law No. 4.728/65 (amended by Decree-Law No. 911 of 1969) was completely abrogated by Law No. 10.931 of 2004 that replaced the original text establishing a new section. The current title of the part of the law in which section 66 is included is "Guarantee Trust in the Financial and Capital Markets" (*Alienação Fiduciária em Garantia no Ambito do Mercado Financeiro e de Capitais*). The following section will discuss its main qualities.

The guarantee trust instrument executed within the financial and capital market must include, in addition to the requirements established by the Civil Code explained in the previous section, the interest rate, the penalties for default, the inflation adjustment index (if any), and other obligations and instructions.

If the trust property is not identified by numbers, marks, or other signs in the trust instrument, the trustee must prove to third parties the property of the trust assets that were held by the debtor.

The debtor that sells or transfers as guarantee to third parties, an asset that is trust property deposited with him, would be subject to the punishment provided by section 171, paragraph 2(I), of the Criminal Code (fine and imprisonment from one to five years).

---

22    De Oliveira says that "[guarantee] trust was introduced in Brazilian Law by section 66 of Law No. 4.728/65, it was a new [guarantee] scheme aimed to allow the facilitation of consumers credit, that can be used, as a credit, in a first instance, only by banks registered with the Brazilian Central Bank." OLIVEIRA, *supra* note 4, at 25.

   Along the same line of reasoning, Diniz said that "Law No. 4.728/65, Decree-Law No. 911/69, Law No. 6.071/74 and Law No. 9.514/97 (sections 22 to 33) introduced in [Brazilian] law the '[guarantee] trust,' turning its attention to the *fiducia cum creditore* of the Romans." DINIZ, *supra* note 7, at 583.

   Along these lines, Chalhub explained that "a process of modernization affecting the instruments of wealth circulation was started in Brazil, particularly in the early [19]60s, with the structuring of the capital market and the modernization of the financial market, in which contexts new instruments were created that would revolutionize our reality, opening up new perspectives in the economy and speeding up the pace of the country's industrialization." CHALHUB, *supra* note 4, at 264. Similar comments can be found in DINIZ, *supra* note 7, at 583.

Law No. 4.728 of 1965 section 66(3) states that fungible assets, rights over movable assets, and securities can be transferred to a guarantee trust. In such cases, the trust property remains in the possession of the trustee. This is different from the general case in which the assets are held by the debtor to be used as explained above. In the event of the default of the debtor of the guaranteed debt, the creditor–trustee can sell the asset and apply the proceeds to the payment of the said debt and the collection expenses and transfer the balance (if any) to the debtor with the corresponding documentation of the said sale.

In relation to the applicable laws, Law No. 4.728 of 1965 section 66 (4)–(6) provides that:

a. In relation to the guarantee trust over movable assets or securities, Law No. 9.514 of November 20, 1997, sections 18 to 20 are also applicable. The law and these sections are analyzed in the next paragraph.
b. The Civil Code sections 1421, 1425, 1426, 1435, and 1436 are also applicable (all these sections, with the exception of section 1435 have been summarized in the preceding section). Section 1435, "Of the Obligations of the Creditor Guaranteed with a Pledge," states that the creditor guaranteed with a pledge must: (i) keep the asset as bailee being responsible for the deterioration if it is caused by his or her negligence; (ii) defend the asset against third-party legal actions (for example, legal requests of attachment of the asset) or criminal acts (for example, robbery); (iii) attribute any rent arising from the asset to the expenses of the care of the assets, interest of the debt, and principal of the debt; (iv) deliver the asset to the debtor once the debt is paid; and (v) deliver to the debtor the balance of the proceeds of the sale in the event of default of the debtor.
c. The Civil Code section 644 does not apply to guarantee trust. This section provides that the bailee can keep the asset until his or her retribution, the expenses he or she incurred, and any damage suffered is paid by the bailor. Therefore, the trustee would not have the right to refuse the delivery of the assets based on the fact that his or her retribution and expenses have not been paid.

## 2. Realty Trust Transfer in Guarantee (Law No. 9.514 of 1997 Chapter II)

Law No. 9.514 of November 20, 1997, (amended by Law No. 10.031 of 2004 and Law No. 11.481 of 2007) rules the framework for guarantee trusts with regard to realty. Below is a summary of the principal points in chapter II of Law No. 9.514.

Section 22 of Law No. 9.514 of 1997 sets forth that the trust transfer regulated therein is the legal transaction whereby the debtor (the grantor of the guarantee trust), with the purpose of guarantee, agrees on the transfer of the revocable property in realty to the creditor, or trustee. Any natural or legal person can be creditor–trustee of a realty, it not being a prerogative of banks. The term "realty" used in this law is made up of finished immovable assets or ones under construction, and, in addition to property, it comprises the real right of use and habitation.

Trust ownership of immovable assets is established by filing the trust deed with the Real Estate Registry Office. With the creation of the trust ownership, there is a twofold division of the ownership, the grantor becoming direct owner and the trustee indirect owner of the immovable asset. Direct possession of the immovable property by the debtor makes him or her liable for taxes, rates, and duties, and for any damage occasioned on third parties.[23]

Under section 24 of Law No. 9.514 of 1997, trust deed must record:

a. The total amount of the debt
b. The date and terms of repayment of the loan
c. The rate of interest and expenses
d. A clause of creation of the trust property, with a description of the immovable asset subject to trust transfer
e. A clause that ensures the grantor, provided he or she complies with his or her duties, free use of the immovable asset
f. An indication, with a view to public auction, of the value of the immovable asset
g. The regulation of the auction procedures in the event of nonpayment, including the term during which the debtor will be compelled to regularize his or her debt

The trust property lasts until total settlement of the debt. The trustee then has a thirty-day period from satisfaction of the debt, under pain of fine, to issue the corresponding order (*termo de quitação* in Portuguese), so that the Real Estate Registry Office can cancel the trust ownership.[24]

If the grantor–debtor failed to comply with his or her duty, the asset would become the trustee's own property. In such cases, the law provides a regime of summons for the debtor, which awards him or her a grace period to redress the nonpayment, which ought to have been stipulated in the trust instrument. Once it has elapsed without the debtor regularizing his or her situation, the property will be put up for public auction according to due process of the law. Following this procedure, the property will be auctioned off at the price stipulated for that purpose in the trust instrument. In the event that it was sold, and a surplus was originated, it will be the grantor's. Nonetheless, should there be no bid for the stipulated value or a higher one, a second auction must be called. In the second auction, the offer that covers the debt and expenses (including taxes, among others) will be accepted, the remnant going to the debtor. However, if the bid did not cover the said sum, it is noteworthy that, unlike the system of trust transfer of personal assets (commented on earlier), the highest bid must be taken, and the outstanding part of the debt is deemed extinct without the grantor–debtor being held liable for it.

---

23  Law No. 9.514 of 1997.
      As regards the system for conveying realty in Brazil, Chalhub claims that "it is certainly an essential requirement for the creation of the trust ownership to file the trust transfer deed with the Real Estate Registry, since our system of real estate transfer adopts registry as the acquisition method of the property." CHALHUB, *supra* note 4, at 201.
24  Law No. 9.514 of 1997 § 25.

In the event of the grantor's insolvency, restitution of the transferred property is ensured to the trustee, in accordance with the relevant legislation.[25]

The cession of the loan, which was the object of the trust transfer in the guarantee, will involve the transfer to the assignee of all the rights and liabilities inherent to the trust property held in guarantee.[26] As an exception to the general rule, the debtor does not need to be notified of this transfer.[27]

The grantor, with express consent from the trustee, can transfer his or her rights over the property object of the guarantee trust, the purchaser assuming the corresponding responsibilities.[28]

The guarantor, or third party who paid the debt, will be subrogated automatically, both in the loan and in the trust ownership.[29]

Concerning taxation, it is worth noting that in the Federal Constitution of Brazil in its article 156, paragraph II it is established that there is tax liability on the "transfer *inter vivos,* by any onerous act, of personal assets, whether by nature or accession, and of real rights over immovable assets, except for those in guarantee."[30] Thus, this tax is not levied on trust transfers in guarantee.[31]

To sum up, at the time of the trust transfer in guarantee by the debtor (settlor) a trust property is vested in the creditor (trustee), which will become ordinary property on the sale of the immovable asset in the event of nonpayment by the debtor. Conversely, the debtor comes to have an ownership subject to a suspensive condition that will become full when his or her debt is paid off (the settlor is the beneficiary in the event of fulfillment of his or her obligation).

## 3. Aeronautic Code

There are other complementary regimens such as the one contained in the Aeronautic Code (Law No. 7565 of 1986) sections 148 to 152 that rule trust property in guarantee of aircraft.[32]

The Aeronautic Code section 148 provides that the trust transfer in guarantee transfer to the creditor the revocable property and the indirect possession of the aircraft and its equipment's, independently of the actual delivery (*tradição*), becoming the debtor,

---

25 Law No. 9.514 of 1997 § 32.

26 Law No. 9.514 of 1997 § 28.

27 Law No. 9.514 of 1997 § 35.

28 Law No. 9.514 of 1997 § 29.

29 Law No. 9.514 of 1997 § 31.

30 Constituição da República Federativa do Brasil 117 (B. Calheiros Bomfim ed., 9th ed. 1999).

31 This is a municipal rate born out of the splitting of the old state tax on transfer of realty (known as ITBI, acronym that in Portuguese stands for *imposto sobre a transmissão de bens imóveis*). Adilson Rodriguez Pires, Manual de Direito Tributário 91 (10th ed. 1990).

32 Defined by section 106 of the Brazilian Aeronautical Code as "all maneuverable equipment able to fly and transport persons and goods."

the holder, and bailee with all the responsibilities and duties of such under the civil and criminal law.

Section 149 of the same Code provides that the guarantee trust of an aircraft or its engines must be made in a deed that must include: (a) the amount of the debt, the interest rate, the fees allowed, the penalties for default, and the applicable inflation adjustment index; (b) the due date and the place determined for the payment; and (c) a description of the aircraft and its engines. If the transferred asset is an aircraft under construction or its components, the trust instrument must include the stage of the construction.

Trust transfer is valid only after the registration with the Brazilian Aeronautic Registry.[33]

In the event of default of the debtor, the creditor can sell the trust assets and collect its credit from the proceeds of the sale. If there is a positive balance, it must be delivered to the debtor. If there is a negative balance, the debtor must pay it. In the event of bankruptcy of the debtor, the creditor can request that the trust asset is delivered to him or her. The creditor has the right to request the judicial search and recovery of the trust asset.[34]

## 4. Transfer of Creditors Rights in Guarantee

Section 51 of Law No. 10.931 of 2004 provides that "notwithstanding the dispositions of the Civil Code, obligations in general can also be guaranteed, inclusive by third parties, by the trust transfer of creditors rights, deriving from immovable property sale contracts . . . and for the trust transfer of immovable property."

## C. REALTY MUTUAL FUNDS (LAW NO. 8.668 OF 1993)

Dos Santos explained that mutual funds "have the legal form of an open joint-ownership, forming into a communion of resources aimed at application in a diversified portfolio of assets and other operational modes available in the financial market. Their duration is indefinite."[35] In this same line of reasoning, Chalhub stated

---

33    Aeronautic Code § 150.
34    Aeronautic Code § 151.
35    José Evaristo Dos Santos, Mercado Financiero Brasilero 228 (1999).
      "Corporate entities or individuals domiciled abroad, foreign mutual funds and other foreign mutual investment entities may invest in quotas of Brazilian real estate investment funds. Real estate investment funds are closed-ended mutual funds for investing in real estate projects and properties. The Securities Commission (in Portuguese, *Comision de Valores Moviliarios* [CVM]) authorizes their creation and regulation. Quotas representing interest in mutual funds—a type of security—may be listed for trading on stock exchanges. The fund administrator holds the fund's assets as fiduciary, and must be a CVM-authorized financial institution. The administrator must manage the fund according to its articles of association and follow quota-holder general meeting decisions." BritCham Brazil, *supra* note 10, at 163.

that mutual funds "are organized under the form of joint ownership, defined by . . . the National Monetary Council as a communion of resources intended for application in securities . . . along these same lines are defined all other mutual funds, in whose legal configuration can be recognized a joint ownership of a special character."[36]

Law No. 8.668 of June 25, 1993, regulates real estate mutual funds and determines that the assets that constitute the mutual fund are the trust property of the fund manager.[37]

The purpose of this system is the protection of the unit holder to permit investment by independent third parties who base their participation in the transactions not only on their confidence in the entity that structures the fund but also in the existence of a proper legal regime.

Section 6 of Law No. 8.668 of 1993 sets forth that the corpus of the fund will be constituted by the assets and rights acquired by the managing company as trustee, complemented by section 7 of the Law, which establishes the independence of the trust property from that of the manager. Thus, the section sets forth that the trust property:

a. Is not a part of the own estate or ordinary assets of the managing company
b. Is not affected, either directly or indirectly, for any of the manager's obligations
c. Is not included in the list of assets or rights of the manager regarding judicial or extrajudicial liquidation
d. Cannot be given as security to the manager's creditors
e. Is not liable to execution by the manager's creditors
f. No encumbrance may be placed on it

Law No. 8.668 of 1993 section 7(2) provides that at the time of purchase the manager must record the restrictions enumerated above and will declare that the acquired asset makes up the real estate mutual fund. Furthermore, the Real Estate Registry Office will register the restrictions and representations of the manager.

The trustee will administer the assets taken in trust and dispose of them in the manner and according with the purposes set forth in the bylaws of the mutual fund or in the general meeting of unit holders, being liable in the event of gross or reckless misadministration, interests conflicts, failure to comply with the regulations or with the directions originating in the general meeting of unit holders.[38]

To sum up, the law created a trust ownership regime for mutual funds without altering the professional management in favor of a third party, which characterizes this investment vehicle.

---

36    CHALHUB, *supra* note 4, at 261–262.
37    Argentina adopted this very solution for mutual funds as regards real estate matters.
38    Law No. 8.668 of 1993 § 8.

## D. INHERITANCE TRUST (*FIDEICOMISSO* OR *SUBSTITUIÇÃO FIDEICOMISSÁRIA*)

The Brazilian Civil Code rules the inheritance trust (*substituição fideicomissária*) in book V (on successions), chapter IX (of the substitutions) sections 1951 to 1960. Sections 1947 to 1950 of the Code rules ordinary substitutions. The following sections will address the main subjects of substitutions and, in particular, trust substitutions.

Section 1947 defines ordinary substitution providing that the testator can substitute (i.e., appoint a substitute) for an heir in case he or she cannot or does not want to accept the inheritance. Section 1948 clarifies that it is valid to substitute several people by one person or vice versa. Finally, sections 1949 and 1950 establish that the substitute is subject to the same restrictions and has the same rights as the persona substituted by him or her.

Regarding trust substitution, the Civil Code provides that a testator may establish that an heir (called *fiduciário*) would have a trust property until the death of the heir, a certain date, or the accomplishment of certain condition. In such cases, the property would be transmitted to a remainder beneficiary (called *fideicomissário*).[39] The remainder beneficiary can only be persons not conceived at the moment of the death of the testator. If at the moment of the death of the testator the remainder beneficiary have been born, the remainder beneficiary would be the owner of the assets and the heir (*fiduciário*) would have the usufruct.[40]

The heir (*fiduciário*) has the property of the assets but subject to the restriction of transferring it to the remainder beneficiary. If the remainder beneficiary request it, the heir (*fiduciário*) must make an inventory of the assets and provide guarantees of his or her obligation of delivering the assets.[41]

Unless there is a stipulation in contrary in the will, if the heir (*fiduciário*) does not accept the inheritance, the remainder beneficiary can do it.[42] If the remainder beneficiary does not accept the inheritance, and there is not express stipulation in contrary in the will, the heir becomes full owner of the assets.[43]

If the remainder beneficiary dies before the heir (*fiduciário*) or before the accomplishment of the necessary condition for the transfer of assets from the heir (*fiduciário*) to the remainder beneficiary, then the heir (*fiduciário*) becomes full owner of the assets.[44]

Fiduciary substitution can only have one degree. Put differently, it is null and void to appoint a residual beneficiary of the residual beneficiary.[45] In such a case, the heir (*fiduciário*) would be the owner of the assets without restriction.[46]

---

39   Civil Code § 1951.
40   Civil Code § 1952.
41   Civil Code § 1953.
42   Civil Code § 1954.
43   Civil Code § 1955.
44   Civil Code § 1958.
45   Civil Code § 1959.
46   Civil Code § 1959.

In short, the Brazilian Civil Code allows an heir to appoint an heir. It is not a trustee because he or she can use the property in his or her own benefit with the sole restriction of transferring it to a third party at the moment of his or her death, at a certain date or at the moment of the accomplishment of a condition. Another main difference with a trustee, is that there are several cases in which the heir becomes full owner (holds an ownership without the restriction of transferring to a third party). Therefore, this legal institution is not a trust as understood under common-law jurisdictions. Diniz explained *fideicomisso*, expressing that it is a kind of revocable ownership (it can be used by the owner but is subject to a limited period of time) created *mortis causa* under which the heir has the duty to transfer the assets received as inheritance after certain conditions is accomplished.[47]

## E. SECURITIZATION (LAW NO. 9.514 OF 1997 CHAPTER I, SECTIONS IV, V, AND VI)

Within a broad concept of securitization, both real estate receivable certificates (in Portuguese, *certificados de recebíveis imobiliariário* or CRIs) and securitization companies should be analyzed. The following sections will examine their characteristics as contained in titles IV, V, and VI of Law No. 9.514 of 1997 (already mentioned before in this chapter but with a focus in other sections).

## 1. CRI

The CRI (*certificados de recebìveis imobiliariários*) is a registered debt security, freely negotiable, secured by real estate credits, which constitutes an assurance of payment of a sum of money. These securities can only be issued by securitization companies.[48] It can have a so-called "floating guarantee," which ensures a general privilege over the securitization company's assets but does not prevent dealing with the property making up those assets.

Section 8 of Law No. 9.514 of 1997 defines the securitization of real estate credits as the transaction whereby these credits are expressly linked to the issuance of a series of securities, by means of a deed (in Portuguese, *termo de securitização de créditos*), issued by a securitization company, in which the following is recorded:

a. Identification of the debtor and face value of each credit, together with identification of the realty that constitutes its security
b. Identification of the securities issued
c. If appropriate, description of other existing guarantees

---

47  Diniz, *supra* note 7, at 330–331.
48  Securitization companies were created by Law No. 9.514 of 1997. They are not financial institutions (no previous approval of the Brazilian Central Bank is needed), shall be incorporated under the corporation structure, and shall have as their purposes the acquisition and securitization of credits, and the issuance and release of CRIs.

## 2. Securitization Trusts

Strictly, securitization requires the creation of a separate patrimony that is only liable for the securities issued in relation to it and that allows obviating all analysis of the risks that could affect the trustee in his or her own business. Thus, Brazilian legislation provides for the possibility of securitization companies creating special-purpose patrimonies affected solely to certain debt securities.[49]

The securitization company will be able to establish a trust on the mortgages[50] to secure the issuance of CRIs—the trustee being a bank or a company authorized to this object, the beneficiaries being the purchasers of the issued securities.

The trust will be established by means of a unilateral statement (there is only one party in this deed) by the securitization company in the context of the *"termo de securitização"* of credits which, besides the elements set out in section 8 of Law No. 9.514 of 1997 as mentioned above, must include:[51]

a. The creation of the trust on the credits that secure the issue
b. The constitution of a separate patrimony made up of the total amount of credits under the trust arrangement securing the issue[52]
c. The application of credits as security of the issue of the respective series of securities
d. The naming of the trustee, with the definition of his or her duties and conditions of performance
e. The method of liquidation of the trust assets

The document in which the trust is created (in Portuguese, *termo de securitização de créditos*) must be entered in the Real Estate Registry where the respective properties are registered.[53]

Section 11 of Law No. 9.514 of 1997 expressly provides that the credits object of the trust:

a. Are a separate patrimony that is not confounded with that of the securitization company

---

49  Although securitization trusts are used in Brazil, it must be pointed out that most securitizations in Brazil are carried out with receivable investment funds (*Fundo de Investimento em Direitos Creditórios* [FIDC]) as legal vehicles. By the end of 2008 there were approximately 214 FIDC in operation with a consolidated net asset value of Brazilian Reais of 40,000 of millions.

50  The securitization of loans granted by banks required special authorization by the Brazilian Central Bank until 1998. In that year, Resolution No. 2.493/98 (replaced by Resolution No. 2.686/2000) allowed these transactions under certain general requirements. FERNANDO SCHWARZ GAGGINI, SECURITIZAÇÃO DE RECEBÍVEIS 31, 66–67 (2003).

51  Law No. 9.514 of 1997 § 10.

52  The creation of a separate patrimony means that in the event of bankruptcy of the securitization company its creditors cannot foreclose the assets of the trust and that it can continue under the administration of another securitization company. COELHO, *supra* note 21, at 297–298.

53  Last paragraph of § 10 of Law No. 9514 of 1997.

b. Should be kept separate from the assets of the securitization company until the redemption of all the securities of the series to which they were affected

c. Are destined exclusively to the payment of the securities to which they are affected, including payment of the respective administrative costs and of tax obligations

d. Are exempt from any action by creditors of the securitization company

e. Are not affected by insolvency of the securitization company.

f. Are not susceptible of constituting a security in favor of creditors of the securitization company

g. Will only be liable for the obligations inherent to the affected securities

Compliance with the items delineated in the previous paragraph entails that the securitization company must administer each separate trust, duly keep records of each one of them, and publish the respective financial statements. The securitization company will respond for the damage it could cause through failure to comply with statutory or regulatory requirements, through gross negligence or reckless misadministration, or through diversion in the trust purpose.[54]

Public offer of securities requires the previous approval of the Securities Commission.[55] Such securities can be registered or deposited with the *Cámara Brasileña de Liquidación y Custodia* (CBLC) that is a central depository entity that allows an efficient liquidation of transactions with securities.[56]

The beneficiaries (securities holders) can only pursue a claim against the loans of the particular trust that secures their securities, except that provision has been made expressly for other guarantees.

One of the aspects that is worth mentioning is that credit cessions to securitization companies are not subject to the notification requirements of the transferred debtor.[57]

---

54    Law No. 9.514 of 1997 § 12.

55    Law No. 6.385 of December 7, 1976 § 19.

  "No public offering of securities may be distributed in the market without prior registration with the Brazilian Securities and Exchange Commission (CVM). An offer of securities is public if: there is the use of selling or subscription lists, bulletins, pamphlets, prospectuses or announcements directed at the public; employees, agents or brokers are used to seed our subscribers or buyers for those securities; transactions are carried out in a store, office or other establishment open to the public; or there is the use of any kind of oral or written publicity to promote the sale or subscription of securities, especially by means of electronic communication or mass media. . . . Public offerings of securities in Brazil are currently governed by the CVM's Instruction No. 400, dated December 29, 2003 . . . which revoked the rules and regulations regarding public offering which had been in place since 1980." BRITCHAM BRAZIL, *supra* note 10, at 137–139.

  The control by the Securities Commission (in Portuguese, *Comision de Valores Moviliarios* [CVM]) has as its main objective the full disclosure of the relevant information. *See* GAGGINI, *supra* note 50, at 56. *Also see* VALDIR DE JESUS LAMEIRA, MERCADO DE CAPITAIS, 53 (2000).

56    LAMEIRA, *supra* note 55, at 116.

57    This regulation bears a parallelism with the regulations of Law No. 24441 in Argentina, which prescribe that notification will not be necessary for credit portfolio cessions with the purpose of securitization insofar as contractual provision exists in the instrument of the transferred credit.

The insufficiency of the assets of the trust will not bring about the declaration of bankruptcy, but a general meeting of beneficiaries will be summoned instead for administration and/or liquidation measures to be discussed. These may include, among other alternatives, the naming of a new administrator of the trust.[58]

Once the securities of the beneficiaries have been satisfied, the fiduciary agent (the representative of the beneficiaries in the terms explained below) will give his or her agreement so that the termination of the trust is registered, and the remaining credits are restored to the securitization company.[59]

## 3. The Fiduciary Agent[60]

The fiduciary agent is the entity conferred general powers of representation of the entire number of beneficiaries (securities holders). It is incumbent on him or her

a. To see that the beneficiaries' rights and interests are observed, accompanying the proceedings of the securitization company in the administration of the separate patrimony (trust).
b. To take any legal measures necessary for the defense of the beneficiaries' interests, including judicial foreclosure of the trust credits in the event that the securitization company does not do it. If the securitization company is insolvent, it must exercise the administration of the separate estate and summon an general meeting of beneficiaries to determine what steps should be followed.
c. To promote the liquidation of the trust in accordance with the trust instrument.
d. To execute the other tasks assigned to him or her in the trust instrument.

The fiduciary agent is responsible for the damage he or she could cause through not complying with legal or regulatory requirements, or through negligence or reckless misadministration.

---

58  Law No. 9.514 of 1997 § 14.
59  Law No. 9.514 of 1997 § 16.
60  Law No. 9.514 of 1997 § 13.

# Chapter 10

# Chile[1]

A. Overview 153
    1. Trust Property 154
B. The Trustee 156
C. The Beneficiary 156
D. Securitization 157
E. Securitization Companies 160
    1. Separate Patrimonies 161
    2. Full Disclosure 162
    3. Liquidation 163
F. Tax Treatment 164

## A. OVERVIEW

Unlike all the other Latin American countries in this book, Chile has no trust regulations. There is no such legal plan that allows the creation of a special-purpose patrimony, separate from the property of the grantor, the trustee, and the beneficiary.

Although the Chilean Civil Code regulates "trust property" in book II, title VIII regarding "limitations to ownership and primarily trust property," encompassing articles 732 through 763, this trust property does imply the creation of a special-purpose patrimony. Therefore, there are no clear rules regarding the legal actions for the fulfillment of the grantor's intent or the beneficiary rights. Furthermore, it is not clear whether the trust assets can be attacked by the trustee's creditors. Thus, the trust property regulated by the Chilean Civil Code is a completely different concept than the one prevailing in the common-law system. Because of the aforementioned reasons,

---

[1]    I am indebted to Alex Fischer and Gonzalo Suffiotti, two prestigious practicing lawyers, who read the manuscript and made valuable suggestions, provided material and guided my understanding of trusts and securitization in Chile.

it must be stressed that trust property is almost unused in Chile (a legal plan almost unknown to most lawyers).

With respect to securitization in Chile, the trust is not used because, as explained, it does not provide the necessary security to carry out a securitization process. Nevertheless, since the modification of the Stock Markets Act, Law No. 18045 (Official Gazette, October 22, 1981), there has been a special vehicle (securitization companies) that allows the creation of special-purpose patrimonies with the purpose of isolating assets and proceeding to their securitization (same legal design as Peru, Bolivia, and Brazil).

Below, the trust property will first be analyzed and then securitization companies.

## 1. Trust Property

In accordance with paragraph 1 of section 732 of the Chilean Civil Code, ownership can be limited in several manners, among is found the one limited by a condition (resolutory condition) which, once satisfied would imply the transfer of ownership to another person. Thus, trust property is that which is subject to the burden of passing to another person in the event of an occurring condition. The transfer of the property from the trustee to the beneficiary is called *restitution.*

As regards what assets can be transferred in trust property, section 734 of the Chilean Civil Code provides that a trust can only be constituted over the entirety of an inheritance or a fixed portion thereof, or over one or more specific things. Only the mentioned assets can be transferred in trust property. The reason for this limitation is that the trustee must transfer (restitute) to the beneficiary exactly the same thing transferred in trust property. Therefore, there cannot be a trust property of assets that cannot be identified (e.g., sums of money). Notwithstanding the restriction mentioned before, it can occur that a trust property over a fixed portion of an inheritance ends in a trust property on a sum of money that is a portion of such inheritance.

The Civil Code provides that trust property can only be constituted by an *inter vivos* act carried out by deed (with the participation of a public notary) or by a will. Furthermore, the creation of trust property that involves or affects realty must be filed with the Public Registry of Mortgages of the Real Estate Conservator of the local jurisdiction (*comuna*) in which the realty is located.

A person who at the time of creation of the trust property does not exist but is expected to exist at the end of the trust property could be a beneficiary.

Concerning the trust property duration, section 739 of the Civil Code provides that any condition on which the restitution of a trust property depends, and which takes longer than five years to be fulfilled, will be deemed failed, unless the death of the trustee is the condition on which occurrence termination of the trust property depends. These five years will be counted as from the transfer of the trust property from the grantor to the trustee.

The settlor of trust property can name not one but two or more trustees, and two or more beneficiaries.

In the Civil Code section 745, the creation of two or more successive trust properties is prohibited. Put differently, a trust is null and void in which, once the trust has been restored to a person, he or she acquires it with the encumbrance of restoring it to another at a later time. This is a way to avoid fiduciary substitutions in Chilean law. If they were actually created, the trust property acquired by one of the appointed beneficiaries would cause the expectancy of the others to be expired forever. It must be pointed out that this is an exception to the general rule in Chilean law (and almost all Latin American laws) that a prohibited stipulation is null and void.

When at trust property creation the trustee is not expressly designated, or when the appointed trustee is missing on any grounds, the condition being still pending, the settlor will enjoy the property if he or she is alive, or his or her heirs.

If provisions were made to the effect that the income of the assets held in trust property be reserved for the person who, by virtue of the occurrence or nonoccurrence of the condition, may acquire the ordinary property, the person who is to administer the assets will be a trust holder, who will only have the powers of a bailee.

Trust property can be alienated *inter vivos* and be conveyed *mortis causa,* but in either case with the charge of maintaining it undivided and subject to the encumbrance of restitution under the same conditions as they were in before. It will not be, however, alienable *inter vivos* when the settlor has barred its alienation, or conveyed by will or *ab intestato* when the day preset for distribution of the trust property is that of the death of the trustee; and, in this second case, if the trustee alienates it during the settlor's lifetime, it will always be his or her death that determines the day of distribution. This possibility of prohibiting the transfer of the assets under trust property is an exception to the general rule that such prohibitions are invalid. Similar rules may only be found in the Chilean law for the transfer of assets under usufruct (section 793, paragraph 3 of the Civil Code) and for the gratuitous transfer of assets (section 1432 of the Civil Code).

Where the settlor has passed the trust property to two or more persons, or when the rights of the trustee are transferred to two or more persons, the court can, at the request of any of them, entrust its administration to that person who gives better conservation assurances.

A trust property expires by reason of

a. Distribution of the assets under trust property
b. The resolution of the right of the grantor, such as when the trust property has been created on something that has been purchased under a repurchase agreement, and the option is exercised
c. The destruction of the trust property on which it is constituted
d. The resignation of the beneficiary prior to the day of distribution of the assets under trust property, without detriment to the rights of the substitutes
e. Absence of the condition, or its not having been fulfilled within the required period
f. The merger of the capacities of sole beneficiary with that of sole trustee

## B. THE TRUSTEE

The trustee of the trust property holds, on the assets under trust property, the rights and charges of the usufructary with the specific modifications established for the trust. In other words, the trustee of the trust property can take advantage of the trust property as the owner with the limitations imposed by the fact that he or she must deliver it to the beneficiary on the occurrence of a condition. The Civil Code clarifies that if, by reason of the trust property creation, the trustee is expressly conferred the right to enjoy the trust property at his or her discretion, he or she will not be held liable for any damage. And, if he or she is also conferred free disposition of the property, the beneficiary will only be entitled to claim what exists at the time of termination of the trust.

The trustee is under a duty to meet all extraordinary expenses for the conservation of the property, including payment of debts and mortgages owing on it; but, when the distribution of the assets under trust property takes place, he or she will be entitled to prior reimbursement of those expenses by the beneficiary, to the amount that with reasonable care and diligence they must have cost, and with these reductions:

a. If there has been investment in tangible works, such as dams, bridges, or walls, he or she will not be reimbursed in view of these works, but because of what they are worth at the moment of termination of the trust property.
b. If there has been investment in incorporeal objects, such as the raising of a mortgage or the costs of litigation, which could not have been avoided without compromising the rights of the beneficiary, a twentieth part will be deducted from the cost of the said objects for every year elapsed until restitution and, more than twenty having elapsed, nothing will be owing on this account.

The trustee is free to administer the assets comprised in the trust property, and is free to change their form, but maintaining their substance and value. He or she will be liable for the diminution and damage sustained by reason of his or her actions or fault. Section 44, paragraph 3 of the Civil Code provides that the trustee will be responsible for his or her lack of due diligence similar to that an ordinary person employs in his or her own business.

The trustee will be entitled to no claims because of unnecessary improvements, except when he or she has agreed on it with the beneficiary, to whom the restitution is to be made; but he or she may lay claim as compensation on the increase in value which the improvements have caused in the assets, to the amount of the compensation owed.

## C. THE BENEFICIARY

The beneficiary, pending the condition, has no right whatsoever on the trust property but the mere expectancy of acquiring it. He or she can, however, start the conservatory provisions that best benefit him or her if the trust property seemed jeopardized or to deteriorate in the hands of the trustee. The rightful ascendants of the beneficiary who still do not exist, but whose existence is expected will have the same rights; the representatives of the organizations and foundations interested; and the defender of religious benefactions if the trust property were in favor of a charitable organization.

The beneficiary who dies prior to restitution does not convey by will or *ab intestato* any rights over the trust property, nor even the mere expectancy, which is passed *ipso jure* to the substitute or substitutes appointed by the settlor, if there were any.

## D. SECURITIZATION

Securitization was not much developed at its outset (March 1994), because the law that regulated it did so in a limited manner. However, from the alterations introduced to Law No. 18045 by Law No. 19301 of the Securities Market Act, the concept was rendered even more flexible, which permitted a greater use of this financial mechanism.[2]

By means of the sanction of Law No. 19301, a large portion of the legal regulations of the capital market was modified, a response to the necessities of a more dynamic market. These changes fell on the Securities Market Act, Insurance Act, Pension Funds Act (that regulate the pension funds called *Administradoras de Fondos de Pensión* or *AFPs*), Mutual Funds Act ,and Investment Funds Act. They enabled the existence on the market of new investment instruments, among which stand out securitized debt securities, with a mechanism that is set out in the Securities Market Act.

In the reform of the Chilean Capital Market, two mechanisms were set forth to conduct the securitization of credits. On the one hand, a new title, "On Securitization Companies," was introduced through the Stock Market Act, which allowed securitization by means of the issuance of debt securities.

---

2    Regarding the development of the Chilean securitization market, Blujevich and Fabrizio explained that "Chile tapped the securitization arena in 1994 with an MBS [mortgage-backed security] deal. Since then, it has achieved a great development in this arena, which is reflected not only in the annual securitized figures but in the vast number of securitization players in the country and the number of deals closed per year. The Chilean securitization market shows a distinctive feature that somehow isolates itself from other Latin American markets, except the Mexican one. Although most local corporations in other Latin American countries have resorted to securitization structures to pave the road to access international financial markets, Chilean securitization is dominated by securitization of existing local currency-denominated assets. This is due, mainly, to Chile's economic, political and financial stability during the past two decades joined by a strong and stable domestic capital market's demand for this type of instrument represented, principally, by institutional investors. The high level of development of Chilean asset-backed securities is reflected not only in the volume of issuances, but also in the several securitizing companies active in the market. In Chile, the securitization activity has been concentrated mainly in mortgage-backed securities and housing leasing, given the high rate of growth of the real estate market in the country and the existence of a strong secondary mortgage market. Also, as the domestic capital markets evolved in Chile, new types of securities became available to investors, such as pools of auto and consumer loans, credit card voucher flows and future cash flows." Esteban C. Buljevich & Mariano A. Fabrizio, *Securitization in Latin America, in* EXPANSION AND DIVERSIFICATION IN SECURITIZATION YEARBOOK 2007, at 187 (Jan Job de Vries Robbé & Paul Ali, eds., 2008).

On the other hand, in the Mutual Funds Act, a Mutual Fund of Securitized Loans was established that allowed the issuance of participation certificates that represent an interest in a set of relatively homogeneous loans.[3] Mutual funds have a long tradition in the Chilean market. Nonetheless, Law No. 19301 introduced this type of fund. However, legislators did not treat these funds with the amount of detail with which they did with securitization companies, so that they included scant special regulations for these types of funds, referring rather to their own investment object without more extensive development regarding the effects and performance of this vehicle.

The principal regulations governing securitization in Chile are

a. Law No. 18045, the Securities Market Act, which since the sanction of Law No. 19301 regulates all aspects relating to securitization companies, underlying assets, and special aspects of the operation and the issuance of debt securities, the rights of the holders of the securities, and so forth

b. Law No. 18815 on mutual funds, which since the sanction of Law No. 19301 governs investment funds of securitized credits and Decree No. 864/90, which approved the regulations of Law No. 18815

c. Law No. 19281 of house leasing (with purchase option), including rules on the use of the rights arising from these agreements in favor of real estate companies

d. Decree-Law No. 3500 of Pension Funds Managers; Decreto con Fuerza de Ley (D.F.L.) No. 251 on Insurance Companies; Decree-Law No. 1092 on Insurance Benefit Companies, inasmuch as, after the application of Law No. 19301, it empowers these institutional subjects to invest in securities of securitization companies or quotas of mutual funds in securitized credits

e. Law No. 18046 of corporations, applicable subsidiarily to securitization companies and securitized loans mutual fund administrators, as both subjects are special-purpose corporations

f. Special rules of the Securities and Insurance Superintendence[4] (the Chilean equivalent of the U.S. Securities and Exchange Commission [SEC]) and of the Chilean Central Bank, particularly concerning securitization

What follows is an analysis of Chilean regulations with special stress on securitization companies and with reference, in the cases of loan mutual funds that can be securitized, to the general rules applicable to all mutual funds, for their more detailed development is beyond the scope of this book.

---

3   RIGOBERTO J. PARADA DAZA, INSTRUMENTOS DE FINANCIAMIENTO E INVERSIÓN 105 (2000).

4   The Securities and Insurance Superintendence (*Superintendencia de Valores y Seguros* [SVS]) is a government agency, with legal capacity and its own assets, which is linked to the government through the treasury department and has as its object the better control of the activities and entities that take part in the securities and insurance market in Chile. Thus, it is the SVS's duty to oversee the persons or institutions under its supervision from their inception to the end of their liquidation and to see to it that they comply with rules, statutes and other regulations which govern the operation of these markets.

In Chile, securitization has been limited to only certain assets which, because of express declaration of the law or by means of rules of a general character sanctioned by the Securities and Insurance Superintendence, may be acquired by securitization companies or securitized loans funds.

Regarding securitization companies, Law No. 18045 article 135 provides that for the performance of its corporate purpose the company may acquire mortgage securities and mortgage loans authorized by Decree-Law No. 3 of 1997 and other endorsable mortgage loans authorized by Decree-Law No. 3500 of 1980 and by Decree-Law No. 251 of 1931, assets and leasing agreements treated in Law No. 19281 article 17, credit and rights on payment flows arising from public works, infrastructure work of public use, national assets of public use or from the concessions of these assets or works, and other securities.

Included in the term "payment flows" is any cash flow from future road tolls, the guaranteed minimum income, subsidies, the rights issuing from exchange or collection guarantees, and all other payment flows inherent to federal government public works agreements that could be created or applied in the future. Furthermore, any obligation, existing or to be generated in the future, to pay one or more sums of money for the acquisition or use of assets or rendering of services is deemed a payment flow.

As regards securitized loans, mutual funds, in accordance with the provisions of Law No. 18815, can invest, within legal limits and like other classes of mutual funds, in securities issued by the government, Central Bank, or with a 100 percent government guarantee, securities evidencing money raised from financial institutions or guaranteed by them, bonds and commercial papers whose issuance has been registered with the Securities and Insurance Superintendence. Nevertheless, it is characteristic of this type of mutual fund to invest in credit or collection rights portfolios of those referred to in Law No. 18045 article 135, and also in leasing agreements governed by Law No. 19281.[5]

In connection with the manner in which these vehicles acquire credits, normally it is by means of delivery, which will be determined by the nature of the contract or security. Thus, Law No. 18045, Law No. 19281, and the D.F.L. No. 3, set up mechanisms that simplify the transfer of assets to be securitized regardless of the nature of the contract or security. As to securitization companies, agreements, loans and rights, or its securities, have a negotiable nature, even when among those assets were registered securities, in which case their acquisition, transfer and guarantee pledge can be affected by endorsement placed at the bottom, in the margin or on the back of the document whereon they appeared, whichever the form in which they had been issued originally.

Transfer or cession of the agreements, loans and rights, or of its securities, will be enforceable against their debtors from the date of the forming of the deed granting the issuing agreement with creation of a special-purpose patrimony or of its complementary deeds in which they are identified or determined. From that date, debtors will not be able to claim the grantee other legal defenses than those they bear against him or

---

5    Marianne Knaak Donoso, Factoring, Securitización, ADR's. Análisis, Regulación y Aplicación 150 (1998).

her, any other exception being unenforceable against him or her, whatever its origin or nature.

What has been said in the preceding paragraphs also holds true for transfers or alienation of agreements, loans, rights or of their securities made to entities or persons, constituted in Chile or overseas, who acquire them to issue debt securities designed to be placed exclusively abroad. These securities will not be filed with the Securities Registry.

Regarding mutual funds of credits susceptible to securitization, it should be added that no special rule exists in Law No. 18815 that indicates how assets are to be transferred although, because of the characteristics of the assets to be securitized, it would be effected by means of endorsement.

## E. SECURITIZATION COMPANIES

As mentioned, Law No. 19301 created a special vehicle designed for the securitization of assets different from the existing mutual funds. These companies must include in their names the word "securitization," will be subject to the control of the Securities and Insurance Superintendence and will be governed by the specific rules addressed in Law No. 18046 section 126 and following sections, and by the regulations applicable to listed corporations that will be addressed in the following paragraphs.

Securitization companies can administer directly the assets in the separate patrimonies under their administration or charge a bank, financial institution, administrator of endorsable mortgage loans, or other entities authorized by the Securities and Insurance Superintendence therewith.

In all cases, the securities making up the assets of the separate patrimonies must be handed over in custody to banks, financial institutions, securities deposit companies, or other entities expressly authorized by law.

The company can only issue debt securities backed by the acquired assets, participation certificates being reserved for securitized loan mutual funds.

Securitization companies will be incorporated as special purpose corporations. They are deemed to be companies having a single and specific object related to public interests, notwithstanding their private nature. In accordance with the provisions of section 132, these companies will have as their exclusive object "the acquisition of the loans referred to in section 135 (whose enumeration has been expounded), the acquisition of rights over payment flows and the issuance of short- or long-term debt securities." A Chilean author explained this specialization expressing that it is present in "four different dimensions, (i) laws that regulate the company, (ii) name of the company, (iii) object of the company, and (iv) capital of the company."[6]

As has already been pointed out, legislators have been restrictive when stating the assets to be securitized, the Securities and Insurance Superintendence can indicate other securities that can be additionally incorporated into this type of operation.

---

6    Mauricio Lopez, La Securitización y un Análisis Paralelo, 195 (2006).

# 1. Separate Patrimonies

Securitization companies may be holders of two or more patrimony units, their own estate, and as many patrimonies as securitizations they are carrying on. Thus, the assets of its own estate should be distinguished from the separate assets arising from each asset-backed issuance of debt securities, which creates a separate patrimony under section 132, which provides that "each issuance will give rise to the creation of a patrimony separate from the ordinary patrimony of the issuer." Further, section 137 provides that the debt securities issuance agreement with creation of a special-purpose patrimony must identify the assets, agreements, loans, and rights being part of it, in accordance with their nature. If they cannot be identified or determined in the agreement, their principal characteristics must be indicated, together with their degree of homogeneity, their number, term in which they will be acquired, and other indications that the Securities and Insurance Superintendence prescribes by means of general rules, as they should be identified or determined in one or more complementary deeds. Such deeds will be registered on the margin of the debt securities issuance agreement with creation of a special-purpose patrimony. A copy of the deed will be sent to the Securities and Insurance Superintendence within five days after its creation, attached to the securities issuance filing, for its filing with the Securities Registry.

Once the debt securities issuance agreement with creation of a special-purpose patrimony has been executed, the debt securities represent liabilities of the separate patrimony. The assets determined in the issuance agreement with creation of a separate patrimony or in the complementary deeds will be automatically part of the special-purpose patrimony thereof as from the date of the respective deed where they are determined.

The company must keep a special record for each separate patrimony that it constitutes, recording in it the debt securities that it issues.

The holders of debt securities issued by the securitization companies could only start legal actions against the assets of the separate patrimony that relates to such debt securities, unless there are real or personal sureties, granted by third parties or that encumber the ordinary patrimony of the company.

The cost of administration and custodianship of the separate patrimonies, the compensation of the representative of the holders of debt securities and other necessary expenses specifically indicated in the issuance deed (including the tax burden) will be charged to the special-purpose patrimony. The maximum amounts to be charged must be recorded in the respective deed.

To sum up, the securitization company will be the title holder of several patrimonies to affect certain assets to the payment of certain obligations. The general creditors of the company, whatever the origin or standing of their credits, will not be entitled to make them good with the assets of the separate patrimonies constituted by his or her debtor, nor affect them with liens, prohibitions, precautionary measures or encumbrances, except when they have come to be part of the ordinary patrimony in the cases permitted under this section.

Although, in principle, corporate creditors and those of the separate patrimonies can only follow their credits on the ordinary and separate patrimonies respectively, in the issuance deed, the creditors of the separate patrimony may be authorized so that they can collect, in any circumstance, the outstanding balance of their credits on the common patrimony with the rest of the general creditors.

Also, the law foresees cases where this patrimony separation principle is broken, allowing for the transfer of assets from one patrimony to another:

a. Payment of tax obligations of the company, whatever their nature or origin, will be the exclusive responsibility of the own estate of the company (ordinary patrimony) and not of the separate patrimonies that it has created. These patrimonies must contribute the necessary resources to the common patrimony of the company when it requires such compliance with the provisions of the final subsection of article 140.[7]

b. Once the debt securities issued against a separate patrimony have been paid, the assets and obligations that are part of the credits and remaining liabilities will pass to the own estate (ordinary patrimony) of the securitization company.

Securitization companies must not have more than 35 percent of assets in each of their separate patrimonies, which have been originated or sold by any one bank or financial company related to the securitization company. The same restriction applies to the administrators of securitized loans mutual funds referred to in Law No. 18815 with respect to the investment of each fund they administer.

The Chilean Central Bank, following a report by the Superintendence of Banks and Financial Institutions (*Superintendencia de Bancos e Instituciones Financieras*) required under article 35 of its Creation Act (*Ley Orgánica Constitucional*), will prescribe the conditions and determine the credits, investments, and rights over flows originating therefrom, which can be subject to sale or transfer by the banks or financial institutions to securitization companies or securitized credits mutual funds. Furthermore, it is the Superintendence's duty to control compliance with the rules dictated by the Chilean Central Bank (cf. Law No. 18045 article 136).

## 2. Full Disclosure

Law No. 18045 article 65 provides that the publicity, advertising, and broadcasting made by any media by issuers, securities intermediaries, securities exchanges, brokers associations, and whichever other persons or entities who participate in the issuance or placement of securities must not contain statements, allusions, or representations that may induce the public to error, misinterpretation, or confusion about the nature, pricing, profitability, redemption, liquidity, guarantees, or any other characteristics of the

---

7    This subsection provides that "the representative of the debt holders will not be entitled to decline the withdrawal from the respective separate patrimony of the necessary amount of money to pay off tax burdens or penalties arising from the results of the administration of such a separate patrimony or which affected the assets or debt securities of the separate patrimony." Final Subsection of Article 140 of Law No. 18045 (as amended by Law No. 19.301).

publicly offered securities or of its issuers. By the same token, the prospectuses or placement memoranda used for the publicity and advertising of a securities issuance must contain the entirety of the information that the Superintendence dictates and will not be disseminated if they have not been sent to the Securities Registry.

The Superintendence will be empowered to issue regulations conducive to ensuring compliance with the above rules and will be empowered to order the infractor or the CEO responsible for the mass medium that he or she modify or suspend the publicity in the event of infringement of the provisions of this article or of the general rules dictated by the agency to that effect, other applicable sanctions notwithstanding.

It is the Superintendence's duty to regulate, by means of general rules, matters in connection with the information duty that the representative of debt securities holders and the issuing company have before investors, the general public and the Superintendence.

## 3. Liquidation

The dissolution of a securitization company, its liquidation, and that of its separate patrimonies are governed by the rules laid down in title X of Law No. 18046 on corporations and by various regulations that refer to the subject specifically in relation to securitization companies in Law No. 18045, which shall presently be addressed.

In the event of dissolution of securitization companies, whatever the cause, which at the time of dissolution still retained separate patrimonies, the liquidation of the company will be executed by the Superintendence with all the powers conferred by law to carry out the liquidation of insurance companies. The liquidation of the company will bring about the liquidation of the separate patrimonies. The expenses of the liquidation of the company will be charged to its own estate (ordinary patrimony). From the time the company ceases to possess separate patrimonies, it will be in charge of the liquidation proceedings, in accordance with the general rules.

In all cases, the Superintendence can authorize the company to execute its own liquidation.

Once a separate patrimony has been declared in liquidation proceedings on any ground whatsoever, the liquidator will summon an extraordinary general meeting of securities holders, to be held within thirty days from the start of the proceedings, for it to decide on the rules of administration and patrimony liquidation, which will include the following:

a. Transfer of the separate patrimony as patrimonial unit to another trustee
b. Changes to the issuing agreement, which may include remission of a portion of the debts or modification of payment deadlines, methods, or initial terms
c. Manner of liquidation of the assets of the separate patrimony
d. Continuance of the administration of the separate patrimony until extinction of the assets that form it
e. Any other matter that is directed by the committee for the administration or liquidation of the separate patrimony

The liquidator will carry on the business until liquidation of the patrimony is accomplished, be it as a patrimonial unit or in installments or until the assets composing the separate patrimony become depleted. In all matters regarding the liquidation of the separate patrimony, in any manner it is performed, the regulations on corporate liquidation set forth by Law No. 18046 will be applicable in all appropriate points.

The securitization company may be declared bankrupt on the grounds prescribed in, and in accordance with, the regulations of Chilean law.

Bankruptcy of the company will only affect its ordinary patrimony and will not give rise to bankruptcy of the separate patrimonies that it had constituted. Nonetheless, bankruptcy of the issuing company and of its ordinary patrimony will entail the liquidation of the separate patrimonies that it may have constituted. The liquidation of one or more of these will not result in bankruptcy of the company, nor will the liquidation of the separate patrimonies.

When the company is declared bankrupt, the respective representative of the securities holders or who the committee of debt securities holders appoints, will administer and liquidate the separate patrimonies.

The securitization company cannot encumber, alienate, or promise to encumber or alienate the assets, agreements, credits, or rights identified or set forth in the issuance agreement or in its complementary deeds without consent from the representative of the debt securities holders, who may authorize or request the substitution of such assets, agreements, credits, and rights, provided the new assets are of similar characteristics to those which they substitute, as established in the corresponding agreement.

In accordance with the provisions of Law No. 18045 article 152, the Superintendence may revoke the authorization for the existence of the companies treated under this section, in accordance to its powers, in the event of fraudulent administration or gross misadministration.

## F. TAX TREATMENT

Issuance of debt securities by the securitization company will be exempt from the tax provided in section 1, subparagraph 3, Decree-Law No. 3475 of 1980 on fiscal and stamps duty (*Impuesto de Timbres y Estampillas*), so long as the assets of the corresponding separate patrimony are made up of documents that had already been taxed on issuance, distribution, or subscription, or were exempt from the said tax, to an amount at least equivalent to that of the bond debt corresponding to that patrimony. The final part of section 153, paragraph 1, of the Securities Market Act, provides that the said exception is applicable as long as the separate patrimony is constituted with instruments that were taxed when issued, granted or executed, or are exempted from the tax, in an amount at least equivalent to the amount of the amount of debt represented by bonds of the patrimony. This last provision has given place to a controversy and two interpretations: (a) the tax on the bonds issued on account of the securitization is due, for the total amount of it, if the amount of debt is higher than the nominal value of the assets transferred, taxed or exempted; or (b) the tax on the bonds issued as a result of the securitization is due only on the portion in which the debt is higher that the nominal value of the assets transferred.[8]

Payment of the tax obligations of the company, whatever their nature or origin, will be the exclusive responsibility of its ordinary patrimony and not of the separate patrimonies that it has created. Nevertheless, these patrimonies must contribute the necessary resources to the ordinary patrimony of the company when it is so required to comply with the tax burdens.

The difference between the purchase value of a securitized credit and its face value will not be deemed as income, which will be the result of comparing the acquisition cost of the credit, duly corrected, with that of its partial or definitive redemption, produced when effective collection thereof has been obtained, or the sale value. The expenses related with the income can be deducted. In particular, section 142 of the Securities Market Act provides that "administration costs and custody of the separate patrimony, the fee of the bondholders fiduciary representative and other specific expenses detailed in the issuance deed"[9] are deductible expenses.

To the intents of the provisions of the Income Tax Act article 31, the provisions and penalties pertaining to securitized credits that are past maturity, whether they form part of the separate patrimonies or not, and remissions thereof, be them due or not, will be deemed expenses under the first category of that law. The characteristics required by the provisions, remissions, and penalties, for the provisions of this rule to run, will be provided by the Securities and Insurance Superintendence after consultation with the Internal Tax Service (*Servicio de Impuestos Internos*).

Commissions and other remunerations, which the companies under this title pay to third parties for the administration and custodianship of the assets composing their separate patrimonies, in the terms prescribed by the first subsection of section 141, will be exempt from value-added tax. Nevertheless, tax authorities issued an opinion stating that the fee of the securitization contract includes the services of financial, operative, legal and tax analysis, the appointment of paying, custody and administration agents, auditors, fiduciary representative of the bondholders, rating agency, and so forth, and it is taxed, as is the issuance and placement of the securities originating in the securitization. This derives from the fact that all these services represent the performance of the activity of a financial entity.[10]

---

8    Lopez, *supra* note 6, at 261–262.
9    Article 142 of Law No. 18045 (as amended by Law No. 19301).
10   Ruling No. 327 of January 25, 2002.

## Chapter 11

# Colombia[1]

A. Overview 167
B. Commercial Trusts 169
    1. Legal Framework 170
    2. Special-Purpose Patrimony 171
    3. Real and Personal Relations Created by Trusts 171
    4. Formalities and Prohibited Stipulations of Trust Instruments 172
    5. Termination of the Trust 173
C. The Trustee 174
    1. Duties of the Trustee 174
    2. Resignation and Removal of the Trustee 175
D. The Grantor and the Beneficiary 176
E. Particular Cases and Experiences 177
    1. Real Estate Trusts 177
    2. Guarantee Trusts 177
    3. Investment Trusts and Mutual Funds 178
    4. Securitization Trusts 179
F. Tax Treatment 179

## A. OVERVIEW

In Colombia, there are five legal structures that must be considered when analyzing trusts. All of them are included under "Fiduciary Transactions" (*Negocios Fiduciarios*), which are defined as those fiduciary acts whereby a person delivers to another one or more assets, transferring or not ownership, for the latter to accomplish a specific

---

[1] I am indebted to María del Pilar Molina Grisales, Esq., for her valuable comments to the manuscript and her explanations of the trust market in Colombia, which made this chapter possible.

purpose with them, either in benefit of the settlor or of a third person. These five legal structures are

a. Civil trust property (*propiedad fiduciaria*) regulated by the Colombian Civil Code sections 794 to 822 (this chapter will refer to it as "Civil Trust Property" to avoid any confusion). The Colombian Civil Code section 794 provides that "it is called Civil Trust Property [to the property] that is subject to the burden of transferring it to a third person for the sole fact of the accomplishment of a condition. The creation of Civil Trust Property is called trust. This name is also given to the asset under Civil Trust Property. The transfer of the Civil Trust Property to the beneficiary is called restitution (*restitución*)." The Civil Trust Property, as in Chile and Ecuador, is not a separate patrimony but only some sort of limitation or burden over property transferred to a person (who is the civil trustee), who can use the property as an owner, but only until a condition is accomplished, when the property shall be transferred to the beneficiary. If the condition fails, the "civil trustee" becomes the full and sole owner of the property without any kind of burden or limitation on his or her ownership.
b. Fiduciary mandate (*encargo fiduciario*). Under this agreement, there is a delivery of assets but no transfer of property from one party to the other. Therefore, the recipient is a depositary (not a trustee) of the assets. This agreement is ruled by the regulations of the trust and those of the agency, in both cases if such rules are applicable to the nature of this contract.[2] In short, it is similar to an agency contract in common-law jurisdictions and in other civil-law jurisdictions.
c. Public sector trust (*fiducia pública*): In this kind of agreement, the so-called "settlor" is a governmental entity. This sole fact determines that the agreement qualifies as "public sector trust." The name is a misnomer because under section 32 of Law No. 80 of 1993, in the so-called "public sector trust," there is no transfer of the property of the public sector entity acting as "settlor," and no special-purpose patrimony is created. Therefore, there is no such thing as a trust, and in substance this agreement is, notwithstanding the name, a fiduciary mandate.
d. Trustee executor (*albaceazgo fiduciario*) is an almost unused agreement regulated by the Civil Code under which an executor is required to receive certain assets in trust at the moment of the death of the testator to be transferred to a third party. This is only applicable to half of the assets that are freely disposable (not subject to forced heirship rules) by the testator.
e. Commercial trust (*fiducia mercantil*) is regulated by the Commercial Code (here called "Commercial Trust"). This is an agreement under which a grantor transfers property to a trustee, creating a special-purpose patrimony that must be affected to the accomplishment of certain objectives determined by the grantor. As will be

---

2  Decree-Law No. 663 of 1993, denominated the Organic Regime of the Colombian Financial System (*Estatuto Orgánico del Sistema Financiero Colombiano*), provides in section 146, subsection 1, that the rules applicable to fiduciary mandates are those that rule the Commercial Trust, and those of the Commercial Code that rule the agency contract are subsidiary, as long as the former and the latter are compatible with the nature of the fiduciary mandate.

explained below, the Commercial Trust is the one that is most like the trust as it is known in common-law jurisdictions.

As the two legal schemes involving the transfer of property from a settlor to a trustee are the Civil Trust Property and the Commercial Trust, it is worth pointing out the main differences between them:

a.  Civil Trust Property could only be created by a deed, whereas Commercial Trusts could be created with less formalities.
b.  The settlor has no relevance at all once the Civil Trust Property is granted. In the Commercial Trust, the settlor can establish certain powers in his or her favor and is the natural residual beneficiary of the assets of the trust if the persons appointed as such do not accept, or for some reason cannot receive, the benefits.
c.  Civil Trust Property does not create a separate patrimony, the trust assets being property of the civil trustee and only subject to a restriction ("conditional owner"). Conversely, the Commercial Trust is a separate patrimony from the patrimony of the commercial trustee.
d.  Commercial Trusts always imply the payment of a fee to the trustee for his or her services as such, whereas in Civil Trust Property the trustee could act as such for free.
e.  In Civil Trust Property, the trustee could become the final owner of the trust assets, which is forbidden in Commercial Trusts.
f.  Any person could be a trustee in Civil Trust Properties, whereas only certain companies could be trustees of Commercial Trusts (as explained in detail below).

The rest of the chapter will be devoted to the Commercial Trust (the legal vehicle for business purposes in Colombia), concluding with a discussion of the securitization process by means of this mechanism in Colombia.

## B. COMMERCIAL TRUSTS

From a practical perspective, the importance of Commercial Trusts in Colombian economic life cannot be overlooked. Commercial Trusts started in 1971 with the creation of several companies with the sole purpose of acting as professional trustees, but it was in the 1990s that they saw a sharp increase in their pace of growth. Commercial Trusts are the legal vehicle for the development of big projects, such as infrastructure or construction, and for small construction projects and guarantee trusts. Other examples of uses of the Commercial Trusts include: (a) restructuring of companies under financial stress; (b) securitization of loan portfolios; (c) commercialization of social clubs, hotel suites, or housing; and (d) the administration and payment of social services subsidies or social health plans. Currently, there are 25 trustee companies, and the assets under trust administration represent in value one-third of the gross domestic product of Colombia.

## 1. Legal Framework

The Commercial Trust in Colombia has its first regulation in the Banking Regulation included in Law No. 45 of 1923,[3] a result of the Kemmerer mission,[4] which authorized banks to have a trust department and established the first definitions in relation to Commercial Trusts.[5] This was additional to the Civil Trust Property, which had already been in the Civil Code since 1886, as seen before.[6] Although not completely unused, trusts were not widespread because of several failures of this law. In this regard, Azuero said that "the development of the trust departments was precarious and the several doubts were never completely resolved by the scholars."[7]

In 1971 the current Commercial Code that regulates the Commercial Trust contract entered into force. This Code (Decree-Law No. 410 of 1971) defines the Commercial Trust, prescribing that "it is a legal transaction by virtue of which a person, called grantor or settlor, transfers one or more specified assets to another, called trustee, who undertakes to administer them or transfer them to achieve an aim set by the settlor, in benefit of the latter or a third party called beneficiary."[8]

In 1990, and as an answer to the criticism to Law No. 45 of 1923, a new law was passed (Law No. 45 of 1990) that modified the Commercial Code. Currently, the Commercial Trust is regulated by sections 1226 to 1244 of the Commercial Code.

Finally in 1994, Law No. 80 of 1993 entered into force. Denominated "Public Contracting Law" (*Ley de Contratación Pública*), it regulated the trusts created by governmental entities (public sector trust). As explained before, these "trusts" are fiduciary mandates, not actual trusts.

---

3     Section 7, subsection 2, of Law No. 45 of 1923 (not in force because of its derogation by Law No. 45 of 1990) provided that "for the effects of this law, any fiduciary transaction included in this law is understood as trust, and as trustee the individual or legal entity that is entrusted with it." This definition was heavily criticized by the Colombian scholars.

4     Rodrígues Azuero said that "Law 45 of 1923 on Banking Establishments was the result of the studies carried out by the Kemmerer Missión, which came to the country commissioned by the [g]overnment of President Pedro Nel Ospina with the purpose of studying that and other subjects, which also gave shape to other Acts (the General Audit of the Nation Act, Bank of the Republic, Negotiable Instruments, etc.)." Sergio Rodríguez Azuero, Negocios Fiduciarios: Su Significación en América Latina 54 (2005).

5     Rodríguez Azuero explained that the commercial trust in Colombia had its antecedents in the Anglo-Saxon trust as a consequence of the 1923 reorganization of financial regulations that generated, among others, Law No. 45 of that year. Sergio Rodríguez Azuero, Contratos Bancarios: Su Significación en América Latina 803 (2002).

6     Casas Sanz de Santa María explained that "unfortunately, in the translation of the project, what appeared to be minor mistakes were made, which in the long run had a decisive influence on the trust activity of banks being restricted within exceedingly narrow boundaries, which rendered the existence of the trust practically nonexistent," but "now the problem has been solved and we have a perfectly typified legal concept in the new Commerce Code." Eduardo Casas Sanz de Santamaría, La Fiducia 23 (2nd ed. 1997).

7     Azuero, *supra* note 4, at 56.

8     Comercial Code of Colombia, First Paragraph of Section 1226.

## 2. Special-Purpose Patrimony

In its first paragraph, section 1226 of the Colombian Commercial Code defines trust as "a legal transaction by virtue of which a person, called settlor, transfers one or more identified assets to another, called trustee, who subjects himself to the duty of administering or selling such assets to accomplish a purpose determined by the settlor, in favor of the settlor or a third party called beneficiary."

The definition involves the transfer of property from the settlor to the trustee (a fundamental requisite for the existence of a trust, which differentiates itself from the mere fiduciary mandate) and the existence of three parties: settlor, trustee, and beneficiary. As will be seen in this chapter, the settlor can name him or herself the beneficiary.

Trust property is a special-purpose patrimony that must be affected to the purposes of the trust established by the settlor in the trust instrument, separate of the own estate of the trustee, the settlor, and the beneficiaries. This derives from the following sections of the Commercial Code:

a. Section 1227 provides that trust property is no part of the general security of the trustee's creditors (it cannot be foreclosed by the trustee's creditors) and only guarantees the obligations contracted in the accomplishment of the purposes of the trust.
b. Section 1233 establishes that for all legal purposes the trust assets must be kept separate from the rest of the assets of the trustee (i.e., his or her own estate) and the trust property of other trusts and form a separate patrimony affected to the purposes established in the trust instrument.
c. Section 1238 lays down the rule that trust assets cannot be reached by the grantor's creditors unless his or her debts antedate the creation of the trust. The beneficiary's creditors can only pursue the returns that such assets produce. Nevertheless, the trust in fraud of third parties can be challenged by the interested parties. There have been several interpretations of this section, but a resolution (*circular externa*) of the Bank Superintendence made an official interpretation and established that the said section provides that it is legally impossible to request and obtain the foreclosure of trust assets for debts of the settlor and regulated the requirements to request the revocation of the trust transfer.

## 3. Real and Personal Relations Created by Trusts

The Colombian Constitutional Court (*Corte Constitucional de Colombia*) claimed that the two characteristic elements of the Commercial Trust in that country are as follows:

> The first may be defined as a real element, according to which the Commercial Trust constitutes a true transfer of ownership over the assets held in trust. In this connection, it should be added that, to some, the trust instrument in which no transfer of ownership but a mere handing over of assets is effected, does not constitute

the creation of a separate patrimony but amounts to a fiduciary mandate; whilst those cases in which the property is transferred and a special-purpose patrimony is constituted would be a true Commercial Trust (cf. Banks Superintendence resolution 007 of 1991) . . . both transfer of ownership and creation of a special-purpose patrimony are two elements without which the Commercial Trust agreement could not exist. A second element in this type of legal transaction is one [that] may be deemed as personal, in which the purposes established by the grantor for the administration of the assets by the trustee fall into the trust concept or into the confidence that the first reposes in the second—[that is,] in trust companies authorized by the Banks Superintendence—[]considering his abilities, his expertise[,] or his good will, with a fixed purpose or end, of whose product will benefit the settlor himself or a third party.[9]

From this extensive quotation, it may be concluded that in Colombia, just like in most jurisdictions, trusts involve as much a real right aspect touching on the transfer of an asset, as a personal aspect concerned with the duties undertaken by the trustee in favor of the beneficiary.

In the case quoted above, the Colombian Constitutional Court claimed that the antecedents of the Commercial Trust must be sought in the Anglo-Saxon trust, which found its full legal establishment in 1972 with the advent of the new Commerce Code.

## 4. Formalities and Prohibited Stipulations of Trust Instruments

With respect to the formalities of the trust instrument, the Commercial Code sets forth that the trust established *inter vivos* must be recorded by public notary in a deed and registered according to the nature of the assets. As for the trust established *mortis causa,* it must be carried out by will.

Commercial Trust instruments may be held without the formality of a public deed in such cases as are authorized by the national government by means of a general rule. Thus, the Executive Power passed Decree No. 847 of 1993, which prescribes that "Commercial Trust instruments formed by trust companies will not require the solemnity of a public deed where the assets held in trust are exclusively personal property . . . if the transfer of the ownership of the assets held in trust is subject to registration, the private document in which the agreement is recorded must be registered in the terms and conditions stated in the said regulation."[10]

The agreements recorded in a private document (without the participation of a public notary) and that correspond to assets with a transfer that is subject to registration must be filed with the Commercial Registry with jurisdiction in the grantor's

---

9   Judgment C-036 of 1995, Accumulated files D-647 & D-672, Unconstitutionality claim against article 32 (partial), 1993 Law No. 30 (Administrative Contracting General Statute [*Estatuto General de Contratación Administrativa*]), Santa Fe de Bogotá, March 1, 1995.

10   Section 1 of Decree No. 847 of 1993 (May 7, 1993).

domicile, above and beyond registration that must be performed in accordance with the law.

There is prohibition over

a. Secret trust transactions.
b. Those in which the benefit is granted to many persons successively (fiduciary substitution).
c. Those with a duration that is longer than twenty years. If it should exceed such a period, it will only be valid for that length of time. Exempted are trusts constituted in favor of persons under disability and charities or public utility entities.

As with many Latin American laws, any stipulations that prescribe that the trustee will acquire the ownership of the assets held in trust is null and void.[11]

## 5. Termination of the Trust

The causes of termination of the trust, among others, are the following:

a. Full accomplishment of its purposes or absolute impossibility of accomplishing it.
b. Expiration of its term or lapse of the maximum time prescribed by law.
c. Failure to comply with the resolutory condition to which it is subject.
d. When the suspensive condition, on whose occurrence depends the existence of the trust, is made impossible or is not performed within the stipulated term— Technically speaking, this is not a termination reason but the cause that the trust never existed (the suspensive condition refers to the condition that the creation, not the termination, of the trust is subordinated).
e. Death of the grantor or the beneficiary, when such an occurrence has been stated in the trust deed as cause of termination.
f. Dissolution of the trustee.
g. Action of creditors of the settlor for debts prior to the trust instrument.
h. Trust instrument declared nugatory.
i. Agreement between grantor and beneficiary without detriment to the trustee's rights.
j. Revocation of the trust by the grantor, when he or she has expressly reserved for him or herself that right.

Unless stipulation to the contrary in the trust instrument, at termination by any cause, the assets held under trust will devolve on the grantor or his or her heirs.

Finally, the competent court to hear the litigations in connection with the trust will be that of the trustee's domicile.

---

11    Commercial Code § 1244.

## C. THE TRUSTEE

Only trust companies that have as their sole activity being trustees and are especially authorized by the Banks Superintendence can be trustees.[12] Trustees are under the control of the Bank Superintendence, which regulates the necessary staff, accounting practices, allowed trust transactions, minimum capital, and level of liquidity of the trustee assets. Additionally, the Bank Superintendence has issued rules clarifying doubts, received complains of trustee's clients (even removed the trustees in certain cases), issues its opinion on the resignation of trustees and has answered the instruction request by trustees contemplated in section 1234 of the Commercial Code (which will be addressed in detail in the next paragraphs). In short, the Bank Superintendence has been very active in its ruling and supervisory activity, which is considered one of the key elements for the success of trust activity in Colombia.

Traditionally, trust instruments provide that any controversy that might arise will be subject to the arbitration of the Chamber of Commerce of Bogotá. Although in the last two years this has changed, and several trust instruments provide that any controversy will be subject to the Commercial Courts, a corpus of arbitral decisions has formed on the trustee's responsibilities. From these cases derives the standard of good professional services of the trustee, who must comply with the level of diligence of a good businessperson and must prove a high level of effort and knowledge to avoid being responsible for any damage to the trust property.

## 1. Duties of the Trustee

Apart from those indicated in the trust instrument, section 1234 of the Commercial Code establishes that the trustee has the following duties that he or she must not delegate:

a. To perform with reasonable diligence the necessary steps for the accomplishment of the object of the trust. To accomplish the purposes of the trust is the main obligation of the trustee.
b. To keep the assets object of the trust separate from his or her own and from those that pertain to other trusts.
c. To invest the assets originating in the trust in accordance with the requirements set forth in the trust deed, unless discretion has been permitted.

---

12  *Cf.* Section 1226 of the Commercial Code and section 6 of Law No. 45 of 1990. As Rodríguez Azuero explained, the rule that entered into force on January 1, 1972, (then abrogated by Law No. 45 of 1990) allowed banks and specialized companies to act as trustees. Nevertheless, reality has shown that it is the small specialized companies that have been the motor of trust growth. Banks considered their trust departments as a secondary activity, not as profitable as their core traditional business. The financial reform of 1990 forced banks to transform their trust departments into fully controlled special-purpose companies to go into the trust business. AZUERO, *supra* note 5, at 875.

d. To exercise his or her position as trustee for the safeguarding and defense of the assets held in trust against legal actions by third parties, by the beneficiary, and even by the settlor.

e. To request direction from the bank superintendent when he or she harbors well-founded doubts about the nature and scope of his or her duties. In these cases, the superintendent will summon the grantor and the beneficiary before making a decision on the course of action that the trustee must follow.

f. To procure the highest return of the assets held in trust, for which every transfer that he or she carries out will be for consideration, save indication to the contrary in the trust deed.

g. To transfer the assets to whom they are due, according to the trust deed or the law, once the trust has been concluded.

h. To render supported accounting of his or her administration to the beneficiary every six months.[13]

In regard to accounting, the difference between rendering supported accounting and simple reports should be borne in mind. In a supported accounting—as made clear by its name—the trustee must justify, argue, and demonstrate, with certainty, by dint of the relevant means, the performance of the task entrusted in the trust deed or in statutes, which procedure is provided in the law when it refers to the accounting to the trustee and/or the beneficiary.[14]

Instead, reports are more in the nature of mere communications by the trustee to bring to the knowledge of the interested parties the development and state of administration regarding certain activities or situations carried out by him or her. It does not presuppose, therefore, that such information is verified, but neither does it enjoy a status such as to discharge the trustee from his or her duties.

At the request of the grantor, beneficiary, or his or her ascendancy, the competent court can make the trustee liable to perform an inventory of the assets held in trust and to furnish a special security.

## 2. Resignation and Removal of the Trustee

Under section 1232 of the Commercial Code, the trustee will only be entitled to resigning his or her administration owing to the causes indicated in the trust instrument. Lacking such stipulation, the following are presumed causes that give rise to resignation:

a. The beneficiary refuses to or cannot receive the benefits in accordance with the trust instrument.

---

13   According to External Circular No. 6, enacted in 1991, of the Banks Superintendence, accounting is the detailed report of the administration of the trust assets, particularly regarding that which bears upon the tasks performed.

14   *Cf.* Resolution (*Circular Externa*) No. 6 of 1991 of the Bank Superintendence.

b. The assets held in trust do not yield sufficient income to cover the trustee's fees.

c. The grantor, his or her heirs or the beneficiary, where appropriate, refuses to pay such fee.

Resignation by the trustee requires the previous authorization of the bank superintendent. (There has been no case in which the said superintendent granted such authorization.)

In line with section 1239 of the Commercial Code, the trustee may be removed at the request of the interested party by the competent court if any of the following causes exist:

a. Incompatible interests with those of the beneficiary.

b. Incapacity or disability.

c. If involuntary tort or gross negligence is verified, or neglect in his or her capacity as trustee, or in whatsoever other transactions, his or her own or another person's, so that the good discharge of his or her administration is fundamentally doubted.

d. When he or she does not consent to verify the inventory of the assets held in trust or to furnish security or to take any other measure of a conservatory character that the court imposes on him. The trustee will answer even to slight guilt in the performance of his or her administration.

## D. THE GRANTOR AND THE BENEFICIARY

The settlor is the creator of the trust, who transfers the property and establishes the purposes of the trust. He or she can also reserve certain rights, such as revoking the trust or even appointing him or herself as beneficiary.[15] Unlike the settlor, the existence of the beneficiary is not necessary at the time of creation of the trust, but it must be possible and occur within the duration thereof for its purposes to have full effect.

In relation to the role of the grantor, section 1236 of the Commercial Code confers to him or her the following rights:

a. Those he or she had reserved for him or herself to be exercised directly on the assets held in trust

b. To revoke the trust, where he or she had reserved for him or herself that faculty in the deed of settlement, demand removal of the trustee and name a substitute, when appropriate

c. To secure restoring of assets at termination of the trust period, if not otherwise stated in the deed of settlement

d. To demand the rendering of accounting

---

15    The first sentence of the last paragraph of section 1226 of Commercial Code provides that "[t]he same person can be settlor and beneficiary."

e. To exercise legal liability action against the trustee

f. Ordinarily, all rights expressly stipulated that are not incompatible with the trustee's or the beneficiary's or with the nature of the trust

Regarding the rights of the beneficiary, section 1235 of the Commercial Code provides that the beneficiary will have, apart from those granted him or her in the trust instrument and the applicable laws, the following rights:

a. To demand from the trustee full performance of his or her duties and make good his or her responsibility for the trustee's compliance with the grantor's directions

b. To challenge acts voidable by the trustee, within five years from the day the beneficiary had notice of the act originating the action, and demand the return of the assets held in trust from whom may be holding them

c. To oppose any legal measure taken against the assets held in trust or because of obligations that do not affect them, in cases where trustee did not so do

d. To request from the bank superintendent the removal of the trustee with due cause and, as a preventive measure, the appointment of an acting administrator

The relevance of this section is that it allows the beneficiary (who is not the owner of the assets and whose creditors cannot foreclose the trust assets) to demand the return of the assets held in trust from whomever may be holding them (third parties that did not contract with the beneficiary but the trustee), and to oppose any legal measures taken against the assets held in trust or taken because of obligations that do not affect them, in cases where trustee did not so do. The law created a right by the trustee to carry out legal actions against third parties.

## E. PARTICULAR CASES AND EXPERIENCES

Some of the main kinds of trusts in Colombia are outlined in the following sections.

### 1. Real Estate Trusts

External Circular 6 of 1991 (*Circular Externa 6*) of the Banks Superintendence, defined the real estate trust as a trust in which real estate is transferred from the settlor to the trustee so that a project is developed, and the units are transferred to the beneficiaries. As in many other Latin American countries, this is one of the most popular kinds of trusts.

### 2. Guarantee Trusts

External Circular 6 of 1991 (*Circular Externa 6*) of the Banks Superintendence, defined guarantee trusts as that transaction by virtue of which a settlor transmits on a Commercial

Trust basis, ordinarily in an irrevocable fashion, ownership of one or many assets, or irrevocably conveys one or many assets in trust to a trust entity to secure with them and/or their income the performance of certain obligations in his or her charge or in the charge of third persons, designating the creditor of those beneficiary, who can request of the trustee the disposal or sale of the assets held in trust so that the value of the obligation or the balance may be discharged with their product, in accordance with the directions provided in the agreement. The debts thus secured enjoy, as far as the credit rating of the bank's portfolio is concerned, a status analogous to that of mortgages and pledges.

Decree No. 653 of 1993 sets forth that when the entire loan is secured by means of an irrevocable trust, the value of the realizable assets that are tendered as security cannot be below one and a half times the value of the loan and its interest.

The trust deed must lay down that the trustee should sell the assets that ensure payment in the event that the issuer defaults (he or she does not pay the securities holders the total amount of principal or interests in due time). With the proceeds of the sale, the trustee should pay the securities holders, either directly or by conduit of the payment agent.

There are several arbitral decisions regarding the responsibility of the trustee in cases where trust assets are not enough to satisfy the creditors' rights guaranteed with the trust. Therefore, trustees have increased the level of formality and ensured that the most strict procedures are applied, for example, valuation of the trust assets by third parties, sale of the assets in public auction, and so forth.

## 3. Investment Trusts and Mutual Funds

The Organic Financial System Act 29(2), states that an investment trust is any trust that is conducted by an authorized trustee with his or her clients for the benefit of the latter or of third parties designated by them, whose main aim is the possibility of investing or placing sums of money, in accordance with the directions imparted by the settlor. This kind of trust can be individual (one settlor) or collective (several settlors in the same trust). Collective investment trusts are mutual funds.

Colombia used the trust as a legal vehicle for the organization of mutual funds, differently from the undivided joint ownership model employed by Argentina and Uruguay (which was copied from the Luxembourg model several years ago), among others. In short, a "mutual fund" is deemed to be the "set of resources obtained on the occasion of the formation and execution of trust investment transactions, upon which the trustee exercises collective administration."[16]

Trustees can form ordinary mutual funds constituted by moneys received from many original or subsequent settlors for that purpose. In an ordinary mutual fund, resources must necessarily go toward investment in debt securities issued, accepted,

---

16    Decree No. 663 of 1993, Section 29, Paragraph 2, Subparagraph 4, called Organic Regulation of the Financial Sistem (in Spanish, *Estuto Orgánico del Sistema Financiero*). This definition is partially reproduced by Rule (*Circular Externa*) No. 7 of 1996 of the Banks Superintendency.

secured, or guaranteed in any other form by the government, other public entities, the Bank of the Republic, banking entities, financial corporations, savings and loan associations, commercial financing companies, savings banks, and high-ranking financial cooperative organizations, supervised by the Banks Superintendence; or any other title that is authorized by the said agency, provided the issuing companies accepting or securing those securities are not headquarters or subordinated to the bank.

No trustee can administer more than one ordinary mutual fund. However, they can integrate many special mutual funds, only by providing evidence of the necessary administrative capacity.

Finally, to prevent abuses in advertising the investments in mutual funds and to safeguard the independence of the mutual fund, it is prescribed that trust companies will refrain from guaranteeing, by any means, a fixed rate for the received resources, and also from ensuring returns through appreciation of the fund assets.

## 4. Securitization Trusts

In Colombian doctrine, Casas Sanz de Santamaría defined securitization as "the process whereby assets are converted into securities which are designed to circulate, [that is], to be sold to the public at large in the stock markets."[17]

Law No. 35 of 1993 sets forth in section 15, titled "Securitization," that the banks or the Securities Superintendences, as appropriate, will oversee within their legal competencies the securitization processes carried out by the entities under their control.

Decree No. 653 of 1993 establishes that trustees will be entitled to issue bonds acting on behalf of a Commercial Trust constituted by a plurality of companies. By the same token, the said entities will be entitled to issue bonds on behalf of two or more companies as long as a bank stands surety or becomes joint-and-several debtor of the issuance, and the administration of the issue is carried out by a trustee.

## F. TAX TREATMENT

The general rule in Colombia is that the trust is not subject to the income tax, but it must assess the tax every year on an accrual basis and issue the corresponding certificate. The gains arising from the trust property, as assessed by the trustee, must be considered by the beneficiaries of the trust in their yearly tax return. Put differently, the beneficiaries of the trust must declare for income tax purposes the benefits attributed by the trust each year. There have been exceptions to this principle:

a. The tax authorities denied the attribution of losses from the trust to the beneficiary.
b. If the assets are transferred for a consideration, the settlor will have to recognize the gain and not of the beneficiary (who is a mere purchaser of assets).

---

17    Casas Sanz de Santamaría, *supra* note 6, at 67.

c. In the event of securitization, the transfer of assets by the settlor in exchange for consideration is considered a sale by the settlor. Furthermore, the beneficiaries would be the holders of the securities that would undergo the tax treatment corresponding to interest (debt securities) or dividends (certificates of participation or similar securities).

d. If the beneficiary is not determinable, the trust becomes a taxpayer by itself and must assess and pay the tax. This rule has the obvious rationale of avoiding the loophole that would exist in the case of a trust that is not a taxpayer and a beneficiary who does not pay because it is not determined.

Trustees are subject to all formal obligations (e.g., drafting a tax return with the assessment of the tax and acting as withholding agent of any payment done by the trust).

Finally, regarding the tax on the patrimony, the beneficiary must declare his or her rights as beneficiary with mention of its value.[18]

---

18    Section 263 of the Tax Code (*Estatuto Tributario*).

# Chapter 12

# Costa Rica[1]

A. Overview 181
    1. Termination of the Trust 182
    2. Invalid Trusts 183
B. The Trustee 183
    1. Appointment 184
    2. Powers and Duties 184
    3. Investments Carried Out by the Trustee 186
C. The Beneficiary 187
D. Tax Treatment 187
E. Securitization 188
    1. *Peñas Blancas* Hydroelectric Project Securitization Trust 189
    2. Other Projects 190
F. Particular Cases and Experience 191
    1. Real Estate Trusts 191
    2. Conservation of Wildlife Trusts 191
    3. Guarantee Trusts 191
    4. Public Sector Trusts 191

## A. OVERVIEW

The trust was introduced in 1964 in the Commerce Code of Costa Rica following that of Mexico in its guidelines. Thus, Porras Zamora explained that "trusts in Costa Rica arise as a response to a necessity in view of the economic growth of [Costa Rica] in the 1970s. Although trusts had been in our Commerce Code as commercial agreements since 1964, it was not until 1971 that banks were permitted to offer this service thanks

---

1    This chapter has been possible thanks to the expert assistance of Lic. Jorge Porras Zamora, who presented me with a copy of his works (quoted in this chapter) and agreed to explain to me the main aspects of the commercial development of trusts in Costa Rica, and thanks to Lic. Luis Diego Castro, who generously provided assistance.

to the reform of [a]rticle 116 of the National Banking System's Organic Act [and] it has not been until the late 1980s and 1990s that it has taken on increased interest as a business."[2]

The significance of the trust in Costa Rica derives from the fact that it is "the country with the most trust transactions in Central America," has been the venue of the V Latin American Congress on Trusts (held in August 1995), but fundamentally from the fact that "to stress the importance of the trust as an ideal mechanism for the administration and management of any type of assets in Costa Rica is by now a truism."[3]

Regarding the legal framework, it must be pointed out that Costa Rica's Commerce Code (Law No. 3284) deals with trusts in book 2, title 1: "Obligations and Contracts," chapter 12, "On Trusts," which includes sections 633 through 662. Below, its principal features will be set out.

The Commerce Code section 633 provides that "by means of a trust, the grantor transfers to the trustee the property of assets or rights; the trustee is obligated to employ them for the accomplishment of ends both lawful and which have been provided in the trust deed."[4] It follows from this that trusts involve the transfer of ownership of a tangible or intangible asset to apply it to a specific end and, as will be seen later, for a limited length of time. Touching the assets that may be held in trust, latitude is absolute, as it is sufficient for the asset or right to be within the sphere of commerce (liable to be purchased and sold).

The Commercial Code establishes that "the assets held in trust will constitute a special-purpose patrimony, set apart for the purposes of the trust."[5]

The trust must be established in writing, by means of an *inter vivos* agreement or by will. In the case of assets subject to registration, they must be filed with the relevant registry in the name of the trustee.


## 1. Termination of the Trust

The trust will be terminated:

a. Owing to the accomplishment or the impossibility of the purpose wherefore it was created.
b. Owing to the accomplishment of the resolutory condition whereto it is subject.
c. By express agreement between grantor and beneficiary. In this case, the grantor may be opposed when rights of third parties originating during the trust's administration are left without guarantee.

---

2   Jorge Porras Zamora, El Fideicomiso en Costa Rica, Nociones y Productos Básicos 111 (1998).

3   Ronald Drake López, *Prologue* to El Fideicomiso en Costa Rica, Nociones y Productos Básicos 5 (1998).

4   Comercial Code, Section 633.

5   Comercial Code, last sentende of Section 634.

d. By the grantor's revocation when he or she has reserved for him or herself that right. If so, the rights of third parties acquired during the administration of the trust must be guaranteed.
e. Owing to vacancy in the office of trustee when substitution is impossible.

If the person to whom trust property must be conveyed once the trust has expired is indicated in the trust deed, that will be controlling. If no provisions were made, the property will be delivered to the grantor and, if the latter had died, delivery will be made to his or her heirs.

## 2. Invalid Trusts

The following are invalid trusts:

a. Trusts with secret purposes.
b. Trusts where the office of beneficiary is granted to several persons who must successively substitute each other at the death of his or her precedent, except the case in which substitution is carried out in favor of persons who are alive or already conceived at the grantor's death (this is the prohibition of fiduciary substitution explained in Chapter 1, Section A,1 and Section B, and in Chapter 5, Section D, 2 of this book).
c. Trusts whose duration is longer than thirty years, when the appointed beneficiary is a legal entity, except when it is the government or a scientific, cultural, or artistic nonprofit charitable association.
d. Trusts where the trustee is assigned profits, commissions, awards, or other economic advantages other than the fees stipulated in the trust deed. If such fees had not been stated, they will be fixed by the court, which will be advised by experts.

## B. THE TRUSTEE

Any individual or legal entity capable of acquiring rights and contracting obligations may be a trustee. Regarding legal entities, their trust deed must expressly empower them to obtain the trust property by agreement or will. It may be seen that a broad concept of capacity for grantorship–trusteeship exists, with the exception of legal entities that aspire to be trustees, which must have a special regulation in their bylaws. However, even taking account of the said exception, the model is one of broad freedom, because financial institution standing is not required and neither is registration.

Regarding banks acting as trustees, the National Banking System Organic Act Law No. 1644 (*Ley Orgánica del Sistema Bancario Nacional*), in title 3 "Transactions of Commercial Banks," chapter 10 "Other Transactions," provides in article 116 that "Commercial banks are entitled to carry out the following fiduciary duties . . . [m]ake trust agreements, in accordance with the provisions of the Commerce Code and other legal and regulatory rules."[6]

## 1. Appointment

Concerning appointment of the trustee, there is ample regulation by statute, which may be summarized thus:

a. The grantor may appoint several joint or successive trustees and establish the order and terms in which they should be substituted.
b. Except for stipulation to the contrary, the appointment of two or more trustees is presumed to be for their joint performance. Where two trustees have been appointed, discrepancy will be resolved by the court. If three or more trustees have been appointed, decisions will be made by a majority, and ties will be broken by the first appointed.
c. The trustee who dissents with the majority or has not participated in the decision-making process will only be liable for the actions by his or her cotrustees in the following contingencies: (i) if he or she delegates powers improperly; (ii) if he or she approves of, consents with, or covers up an infraction against the trust; or (iii) if, with guilt or gross negligence, he or she fails to exercise reasonable watchfulness over the actions of the other trustees.
d. If the office of trustee were vacant on any ground, the appointment of the substitute will be committed to the grantor, or failing that, to the court.
e. The trustee who substitutes another in his or her office is not liable for the acts of his or her predecessor, except in the following: (i) if his or her predecessor unlawfully acquired assets which his or her substitute knowingly retains; (ii) if he or she omits to carry out the necessary expedients to constrain his or her predecessor from delivering the trust assets to him; and (iii) if he or she refrains from advancing the necessary actions conducive to his or her predecessor compensating for any shortcomings in which his or her administration may have incurred.

## 2. Powers and Duties

Another aspect regulated at great length is that of the powers and duties of the trustee—the highlights are as follows:

a. The trustee will be prohibited from delegating his or her duties, but he or she may, under his or her responsibility, appoint the assistants and representatives demanded by certain matters.

---

6   In accordance with the reform introduced by article 189, Law No. 7732 of December 17, 1997, Regulatory of the Securities Market (*Ley Reguladora del Mercado de Valores*). This reform came into force two months after the publication of the Law on Tuesday, January 27, 1998, in the Official Bulletin No. 18. In addition, the quoted subsection was reformed in turn by article 1 of Law No. 4861 of October 19, 1971.

b. The trustee must carry out all necessary steps for the execution of the grantor's directions.

c. The trustee must earmark all trust property, register it, maintain it segregated from his or her personal property and from that corresponding to other trusts he or she may hold, and identify the trust in whose name he or she acts when administering. I believe that in the case where the trustee had not identified him or herself as acting for a certain trust, the counterparty could deem this as a direct obligation of the trustee.

d. The trustee has a duty to render an accounting of his or her administration to the beneficiary or to his or her representative, and where appropriate, to the grantor or the person he or she has appointed. Lacking provision to the contrary, this will be performed at least once a year.

e. The trustee is entitled to charge a fee with priority over other creditors, and to exercise the rights and acts legally necessary for safeguarding the trust and trust assets.

f. The trustee must employ in the discharge of his or her duties the care of a good paterfamilias.

g. The trustee who does not comply with statutes or the provisions contained in the trust instrument shall be removed from his or her office.

h. Once the trustee has assumed his or her office, he or she is not allowed to resign unless there is just cause, which the grantor or the court, if appropriate, will assess.

i. The trustee is prohibited from securing the income of the trust assets; if at termination of the trust there were uncollected or receivable credits, these will pass to the beneficiary.

j. The trustee will be liable for any loss sustained through his or her fault or negligence in the investment or management and care of the trust assets.

k. The trustee must pay the relevant taxes and duties on the trust assets. If he or she did not pay despite having the means, he or she will be jointly and severally liable.

l. Except when there is express authorization by the grantor, the trust assets cannot be encumbered. Notwithstanding the express prohibition of the grantor, the court may authorize the trustee to pledge assets in the event of and emergency that makes the raising of funds indispensable. To reach settlements or to submit certain matters to arbitration, the trustee will also require clearance from the court.

m. Where doubts existed regarding the scope of the trust deed or of the duties, rights or powers of the trustee, he or she or the beneficiary may appear before the court in review.

n. The trustee cannot be the beneficiary. Should these two roles coexist, the trustee will not be entitled to the trust's benefits for as long as the coexistence persists.

o. The Commerce Code makes no express provisions for the possibility of being grantor and trustee, such a possibility being accepted by the authors.[7] However, it is apparent from the wording of article 633, which states that "the grantor transfers

---

[7] "Regarding merger of grantor and trustee, it does not seem to represent an important conflict of interests; however, it should be admitted that such a coexistence of roles is hardly 'practical' for the purposes of the trust." ZAMORA, *supra* note 2, at 16.

to the trustee,"[8] that it implies not only the existence of two legal parties, but also of two different persons. Thus, as Porras Zamora pointed out, the solution is hardly "practical" because it implies the possibility of invalidation for lack of necessary independence between parties.

p. In the contingency of third parties claiming any rights over the trust property, or of those assets being threatened in some manner by reasons prior to the trust deed, banks, as trustees, were they in possession of information, must give notice to the grantor and the beneficiaries for them to exercise the relevant rights and actions, this being the only duty of banks in that sense. If the reasons were of a date later than the trust instrument, the provisions of article 644, subsection e of the Commerce Code will rule.[9]

q. In the relevant agreement, the establishment of controls may be agreed on regarding the management of trust assets. If "special committees" were set up with that end, the trustee, abiding by the regulations, will discharge his or her duty regarding the relevant transaction.

## 3. Investments Carried Out by the Trustee

Costa Rican legislation has set out in detail the aspects regarding investments carried out by the trustee. Thus,

a. In any transaction involving acquisition or substitution of assets or rights or investments of money or liquid funds, the trustee must abide strictly by the directions in the trust instrument. When the directions are not sufficiently accurate, or when the determination of the investment is left to the discretion of the trustee, the investment must be performed in securities affording the lowest risk. The trustee, in such cases, will not be able to invest in speculative securities; he or she is also prohibited from acquiring securities in companies in the process of incorporation or real estate to be sold. If he or she made loans in money, these will be exclusively with a first mortgage lien, and never for a sum in excess of 60 percent of the valuation of the realty, as performed by an expert.

b. To reduce the risk of possible investment losses, the trustee must diversify them and will be barred from investing in only one business more than the third part of the trust property, unless express authorization from the grantor.

c. The trustee will give notice to the beneficiary of all income receipt or liquidation proceeds carried out in performance of his or her duties within thirty days of collection. Within that time, he or she will notify any investment, acquisition or substitution of assets; notification may be omitted by express stipulation of the trust instrument or because of the nature of the trust.

---

8    Commercial Code, first part of Section 633.
9    The quoted subsection states that "the duties of the trustee are . . . [to] [e]xercise the rights and actions legally necessary for the defence of the trust and trust assets." Commercial Code, section 644, paragraph e).

TRUSTS IN LATIN AMERICA

## C. THE BENEFICIARY

In conjunction with the rights granted in the trust instrument, the beneficiary will have the following powers:

a. To demand from the trustee full compliance with his or her duties.
b. To claim the trust assets to restore them to the trust when they had improperly abandoned it.
c. Request the removal of the trustee when appropriate.
d. In the case that many beneficiaries exist who must be consulted, and if the trust instrument does not provide otherwise: (i) if they had the same rights, their decisions will be considered by majority of votes, computed by interests, and in the event of a tie, the court is to decide; (ii) if they were successive or had different classes of rights, in the event of discrepancies, the court will decide. In all cases, the trustees will take the urgent measures that the trust interest may require.

The trust in fraud of creditors may be challenged in the terms sanctioned by general legislation. There is a peculiar rule that establishes that a trust wherein the grantor is also the sole or main beneficiary is presumed created in fraud of creditors. Against this assumption, no more evidence will be admitted, but the fact that the benefits are sufficient to satisfy the obligation in favor of the creditor who challenges the trust, or that the grantor possesses other sufficient assets to pay.

## D. TAX TREATMENT

It is important to highlight the regulations relating to taxes and registration rates of the trust transfer, as they reflect the correct conception of it as a form of achieving an underlying business.

Ever since the modification introduced by Law No. 7558 of November 3, 1995, the Commerce Code provides that, should it be necessary to register in the Public Registry, and the assets given in trust to the trustee in his or her capacity as such, they will be exempt from any payment for registration rights and other taxes normally paid for such registration, for as long as the assets remain under the trust.

When the trustee conveys the trust property to a third party other than the original grantor, the full amount of charges for registration taxes and others due for that second registration shall be met.

It follows that in the event of creating a guarantee trust in which the asset returns to the debtor on the payment of the debt, neither the original conveyance of the asset nor its reinscription at the grantor's name would be encumbered by taxes or registration tax. This allows for a reduction of costs relating to the creation of guarantees.

As to direct taxes of the trust (such as income tax), the Costa Rican Treasury issued a ruling signed by General Director of Direct Taxation Lic. Jenny Phillips,[10] dated

---

10    Note included in ZAMORA, *supra* note 2, at 133.

January 7, 1997, stating that trusts are passive subjects of the tax burden under the same conditions as legal entities, being liable to the same rate, tax base, and use of the same forms. The trustee is jointly and severally liable for formal obligations (registration of the trust as taxpayer and submission of the pertinent affidavit, among others) and for substantial obligations (the payment of the tax). Also, where securities have been issued, the trustee–issuer shall proceed to carry out the corresponding withholding and pay it.

Although for several years, there has been a bill under the analysis of the Costa Rican Congress to establish worldwide source income taxation, currently Costa Rica only taxes the national source income. In other words, the trust would only be taxed for its Costa Rican source income.

In connection with bank trustees, the National Bank System Organic Act, Law No. 1644 (*Ley Orgánica del Sistema Bancario Nacional*), in title 3 "Commercial Banks Transactions" (*Operaciones de los Bancos Comerciales*), chapter 10 "Other Transactions" (*Otras Operaciones*), provides in the last part of section 116 that "with respect to income tax on the return of the assets in trust, the duty of banks as trustees is limited to notifying [the] Direct Taxation Agency, with a copy for the grantor, the benefits yielded as income of the trust assets, such a report being submitted even when the trust property is made up of securities [that] are exempt from income tax. If that should be the case, he shall so record it."

## E. SECURITIZATION

In discussing securitization in Part I, the definitions by Porras Zamora and the committee created by Decree-Law No. 27127-MP-MIVAH of June 27, 1998, to carry out a study on the "Securitization of Income-Related Unit Payment System in the Housing Sector" were discussed. Instead of expanding on those definitions here, the focus will be on the findings procured by the above-mentioned committee[11] and the relevant legislation.

The Committee found that "the solution to the housing problem in Costa Rica requires a steady flow of stable long-term resources which may be channeled to satisfy the needs for home financing of the Costa Ricans," and that "the world trend shows us that one of the best methods to obtain adequate resources for home financing is the securitization of mortgages, a mechanism which in Costa Rica will also contribute to solving the problem of the finance term matching between resources and loans granted, with which financial middlemen in this line of business have been traditionally faced. In this fashion, a novel attractive security for investing resources is made available to the financial market, emerging pension funds, mutual funds, insurance companies and like institutions in particular."[12]

---

11  Made up of Nuria Rodríguez Vásquez, Eugenia Meza Montoya, Oscar Alvarado Bogantes, Guillermo Carazo Ramírez, Rodolfo Mora Violabas, and Ronulfo Jiménez Rodríguez.

12  Inform of the *ad hoc* committee created by Decree-Law No. 27127-MP-MIVAH of June 27, 1998, to carry out a study on the "Securitization of Income-Related Unit Payment System in the Housing Sector," page 1.

It may be concluded from the preceding paragraph that the existence of a securitization market does not only facilitate a steady flow of funds for home financing, but also relieves mortgagors from suffering the finance terms mismatch (created by the fact that they are obtaining short-term financing, e.g., ninety days, and awarding long-term financing, e.g., ten or twenty years), and it also allows institutional investors to invest in long-term securities beneficial to the national economy.

Two of the items on which the Committee laid special emphasis are the need for the availability of a form of transfer of mortgages that does not require notification of the transferred debtors, and an adequate tax treatment not involving a cost that might spell out the impossibility of securitization.

With reference to the legal vehicle, using a trust with mortgages as underlying assets could be analyzed or, in the case of entities in the National Home Financing System (*Sistema Financiero Nacional para la Vivienda*) (SFNV), the application of a sui generis mechanism (called "mortgage participations") is possible, as set forth under article 119 of the SFNV Act. It should be borne in mind that the SFNV "is made up of the Home Mortgage Bank . . . which acts as a governing entity and second-level institution and by the Authorized Entities, currently formed by benefit company members, some public and private banks, one cooperative, many public organizations and one private foundation."[13]

Section 61 of Law No. 7983 of February 16, 2000, on workers' protection, places the limits of investment made by pension and labor capitalization operators (*operadoras de pensiones y capitalización laboral*). It states in its second paragraph that

> In all cases pension operators must invest not less than 15 [percent] of the funds in their deposits in the Mandatory Complementary Pension Regime [*Régimen Obligatorio de Pensiones Complementarias*], in securities with mortgage security, issued by the entities in the National Home Financing System and which offer a return at least equal to the average return on other investments made by the operators, in accordance with the regulations set forth by the Pension Superintendence [*Superintendencia de Pensiones*] in this respect . . . Investments in securities emerging from securitization processes authorized by the General Securities Superintendence [*Superintendencia General de Valores*] can be entered as part of the said 15 [percent].

From the quoted rule, it follows that as long as the said pension funds acquire greater volume of administered assets, they will be crucial to fuel securitization in Costa Rica.

## 1. *Peñas Blancas* Hydroelectric Project Securitization Trust

A very enlightening instance of securitization is to be found in the "Peñas Blancas Hydroelectric Project, Electric Infrastructure and Development Securitization Trust,"

---

13    Luis Fernando Céspedes Jiménez, Instrumentos Financieros y Subsidios en Vivienda Social. Brief handed to the author on his visit to the Costa Rican Home Mortgage Bank (BANHVI) (1998).

which was authorized in 2000 to issue up to US$70 million in 11 series, with terms fluctuating between 3 and 14 years. As stated in its issuance prospectus, the purpose of this trust is to "finance the building of the Peñas Blancas Hydroelectric Project, located between the San Ramón and San Carlos cantons in the province of Alajuela." Thus, "once construction of the hydroelectric plant has been finished, the trust will rent it out to the Costa Rican Electricity Board [*Instituto Costarricense de Electricidad*], or ICE, for its exploitation, according to the agreement signed previously to that effect. The income from this contract will constitute future flows of securitization funds."[14]

This trust offers an example of project finance set up by means of a trust with the issuance of securities. Investors finance the building of a hydroelectric dam that will be operated by the ICE, and which will generate the income for the repayment of the investment.

The originator of the trust is the ICE, a state agency with its main service as the provision of power (it generates 80 percent of Costa Rica's power) and telecommunications. It was created by Decree-Law No. 449 (passed on April 8, 1949), which was to be modified by Law No. 3226 of 1963 to include telecommunications in its object. The ICE seeks to expand and improve the power-generating capacity of the country. The trustee is the Costa Rican National Bank, founded in 1914 as the Costa Rican International Bank, which exercised the powers of central bank until its creation following World War II. This bank created its trust department in 1971 and currently administers many trusts. Finally, the direct beneficiaries are the holders of debt securities, and the ICE itself is the residual beneficiary.

## 2. Other Projects

After the Peñas Blancas Project, there was a new securitization of a US$140 million hydroelectric project called "Cariblanco" (US$170 million were originally authorized), also organized as a trust by the ICE with the same success. Furthermore, the ICE is working on a thermoelectric project (called Garabit), and other entities of the public sector (e.g., the University of Costa Rica, the administration of the Pacific Port, and some small local electric utilities cooperatives) have been working in similar schemes of financing of projects. Nevertheless, the difficulty to raise funds, the fact that securitization is a time-consuming process, and the costs involved all harm its development.

Finally, from the tax perspective, regarding payment of interest to foreign beneficiaries because of mortgages securitizations, the tax authorities have established that if the transaction is organized by a foreign bank acting as placement and payment agent in a foreign country, among other conditions, interest payments would not be subject to withholding.[15]

---

14   Offering Memorandum of the "Peñas Blancas Hydroelectric Project, Electric Infrastructure and Development Securitization Trust" (2000).

15   Ruling of the *Dirección General de Tributación*, August 14, 2001.

## F. PARTICULAR CASES AND EXPERIENCE

### 1. Real Estate Trusts

Real estate trusts are one of the main kinds of trusts in Costa Rica. Many of the projects that were developed during the real estate boom on the coast, such as hotels, condos, and marinas, have used trusts, either guarantee trusts or investment trusts with the participation of local and foreign investors.

### 2. Conservation of Wildlife Trusts

Wildlife conservation trusts are paradigmatic Costa Rican trusts. They are a perfect example of the successful use of trusts for public-interest objectives administered by private companies. During the 1980s, several debt conversions of external government debt were used for the financing of national parks, wildlife sanctuaries, conservation areas, and support to communities in projects aimed to protect the environment. Furthermore, in the 1990s this development continued with the contribution of foreign governments and international cooperation agencies.

### 3. Guarantee Trusts

As for guarantee trusts, the Commercial Code expressly states that "a trust may be created on assets or rights in [guarantee] of an obligation of the grantor with the beneficiary." This sole sentence avoids any argument on the legality of guarantee trusts in Costa Rica. Furthermore, the Commercial Code provides that "given the case, the trustee may proceed to the private sale or public auction of the assets in case of [nonpayment], in accordance with the provisions in the trust instrument." Again, a sole sentence makes a big difference, establishing the procedure to foreclose the trust assets and avoiding long (and useless) controversies such as those that exist in other countries.

### 4. Public Sector Trusts

The sole fact that the trustee is the government itself or a government-controlled bank does not mean that the trust is a public sector one. This will derive from the goals of the particular trust and the origin of the trust funds, not from the characteristics of the trustee.

Regarding trusts created by government agencies, it should be said that the General Control Agency (*Contraloría General de la República*) and the Governmental Corpus of Lawyers (*Procuraduría*) considered that the public administration could create trusts as long as there was no delegation of public powers of administration that should be complied with by the agency creating the trust.[16] In this same line, it was established that the creation of a trust in which the grantor is the government required express authorization by law, but, exceptionally, it could be done without such authorization as long as the following requirements were met:

a. The authorization could be derived from the applicable rules.
b. It should be strictly necessary for the fulfillment of the goals of the agency.
c. The trust is the right mechanism to fulfill the public interest involved.
d. The trust is not used to delegate the agency function.[17]

It must be pointed out that Law No. 8131 on the Financial Administration of the Republic and Public Budget (*Administración Financiera de la República y Presupuesto Público*), published on February 16, 2001, provides in its section 14 that public entities such as: (a) the executive power, the legislative power, the judicial power, the Supreme Court of Elections, its controlled and auxiliary entities; (b) the public administration and state-owned companies; (c) public universities; (d) municipalities; and (e) the Costa Rican Social Security Administrator, cannot create trusts contributing public assets unless there is an act that authorized to do so. Such act would regulate the conditions to be included in the trust deed. The aforementioned entities will have to subject themselves to the rules regarding the purchase of assets and the hiring or services and employees by the public sector. The trust instruments must be approved by the General Auditor of the Republic (*Contraloría General de la República*), which must also approve the right use of the funds, approve the budget, and issue the rules for the correct administration of such funds.

The ICE stands as an exception to the rule described in the previous paragraph. Section 9 of the Strengthening and Modernization of the ICE Act (*Ley de Fortalecimiento y Modernización del Instituto Costarricense de Electricidad*) establishes that the ICE may subscribe trust instruments for the development of its projects.[18] Therefore, the ICE can organize and act as grantor of trusts for the development of infrastructure projects without need of a specific act.

Finally, the explanation by the Executive Power of the bill sent to the congress, which was to become the Strengthening and Modernization of the ICE Act, states that the creation of trusts by the ICE allows the financing of projects provided the ICE has no indebtedness. It also explains that they expect to develop telecommunications projects under the securitization scheme already used for power-generation projects.

---

16 Ruling C-252–1987 December 15, 1987 and Legal Opinion OJ-055–1997 October 30, 1997 quoted in Ruling C-241–2001, September 5, 2001.

17 Ruling of the *Contraloría General de la República,* quoted in Ruling C-275–2001, October 4, 2001.

18 The relevant part of the section established that the ICE can agree to the creation of trusts with state-owned banks, securitization of cash flows, local or international issuances of securities, and credits from contractors. To secure the patrimony of the ICE, it will control the concessions, trademarks, and assets in every financing transaction of its projects.

# Chapter 13

# Ecuador[1]

A. Overview 193
B. Fiduciary Transactions: Civil Trust, Fiduciary Mandate, and Commercial Trust 194
C. Commercial Trusts 195
    1. Definition of Commercial Trust as a Special-Purpose Patrimony 196
    2. Commercial Trust Instrument 197
    3. Rendering of Accounts 199
D. The Grantor 199
E. The Trustee 200
    1. Resignation and Substitution 202
F. The Beneficiary 203
G. Tax Treatment 203
H. Securitization 204
I. Tax Treatment of Securitization 208

## A. OVERVIEW

In Ecuador, there are three legal structures included under "fiduciary transactions" that should be considered when analyzing trust in this country. These are: trust regulated by the Civil Code (Civil Trust), fiduciary mandate, and trust regulated by the Commercial Code (Commercial Trust). Commercial Trust is the one that is most like the trust as it is know in common-law jurisdictions. Therefore, the characteristics and differences of these legal structures will be briefly discussed, and then the rest of the chapter will be devoted to the Commercial Trust.

---

[1]   This chapter has been possible thanks to the expert assistance of Roberto González Torre, Esq., who generously guided my comprehension of the trust in Ecuador, read and commented on the manuscript, and presented me with a copy of his works (especially his book, EL FIDEICOMISO [2nd ed. 2000]). His observations proved invaluable as a result of his experience as a legal advisor of private trustees and public regulators on trust matters.

From a practical point of view the main uses of trusts in Ecuador have been: real estate trusts (that were adopted after the Colombian experience), guarantee trusts in favor of banks in structured finance, guarantee trusts with securities as underlying assets, cash flow trusts in which the debtor transfers the cash flow arising from the sales of assets (in most cases exportations) to a trustee who acts as paying agent in favor of a creditor, trust as vehicles of securitizations of commercial loans, credit card coupons, cash flow arising from electric utilities providers and local taxes. There is no use of testamentary trust, mainly because of the existence of a high forced heirship (as in other Latin American countries). Finally, the public sector made intensive use of trusts, particularly in relation to infrastructure projects.

## B. FIDUCIARY TRANSACTIONS: CIVIL TRUST, FIDUCIARY MANDATE, AND COMMERCIAL TRUST

Fiduciary transactions are generally defined as those acts of trust whereby a person delivers to another one or more assets, transferring or not ownership for the latter to accomplish a specific purpose with them, either in benefit of the settlor or of a third person. Where the transfer of the trust assets occurs, the trust is a Commercial Trust, which does not hold for fiduciary mandate, also instrumented based on regulations on agency as a model, where only the delivery of the assets exists but with no transfer of property. In short, if there is a transfer of property, it follows that there is a Civil Trust or a Commercial Trust. If there is no transfer of property but mere delivery of an asset, there is a fiduciary mandate (similar to an agency contract in common-law jurisdictions and in other civil-law jurisdictions).

Ecuadorian law distinguishes between Civil Trust and Commercial Trust. The Civil Trust, as in the case of Chile, is not a separate patrimony but only some sort of limitation or burden over property transferred to a person or corporation (which is the civil trustee), that can use the property as an owner but only until a condition is accomplished, when the property shall be transferred to the beneficiary (the conditional property represents by itself the burden or limitation known as *fideicomiso civil* or "civil trust property"). If the condition fails, the civil trustee becomes the full and sole owner of the property without any kind of burden or limitation on its ownership.

The main differences between Civil Trust and Commercial Trust are as follows:

a. Civil Trusts can be created by will whereas Commercial Trusts can only be created by contract.
b. Civil Trusts do not create a separate patrimony, the trust assets are property of the civil trustee, and they are only subject to a restriction ("conditional owner"). Conversely, Commercial Trust is a separate patrimony from the patrimony of the commercial trustee and, under Ecuadorian law, it has a limited legal personality. This characteristic is unique to Ecuadorian law, no other Latin American country considers trust as legal entity but a patrimony.
c. Commercial Trusts always imply the payment of a fee to the trustee for his or her services as such, whereas in Civil Trust the trustee can act as such for free.

d. In Civil Trusts the trustee can become the final owner of the trust assets—this is forbidden in Commercial Trusts.
e. Any person can be a trustee in Civil Trusts, whereas only certain companies can be trustees of Commercial Trusts (as explained in detail below).

To sum up, Ecuadorian law rules that

a. Civil Trusts in the Civil Code (similar to the ones of Chile, Colombia, and Venezuela because all of them are founded on the model of Andrés Bello, the Chilean jurist) involve the transfer of property, do not create a separate patrimony but restrict the ownership for the civil trustee.
b. In Commercial Trusts there is transfer of ownership and the creation of separate patrimony (with a limited legal personality situation that is unique to Ecuadorian Law).
c. In fiduciary mandates there is no transfer of ownership; this subclass bears a resemblance to agency.
d. Public Trusts are managed by public entities included in some special statutes.

The following sections examine Commercial Trusts (the legal vehicle for business purposes in Ecuador) and conclude with a discussion of the securitization process by means of this mechanism in Ecuador.

## C. COMMERCIAL TRUSTS

In Ecuador, Commercial Trusts are a regulated contract that was included in the Commercial Code in 1993. The inclusion was made by the reform to the Code set forth by the Securities Market Act, Law No. 31 (in particular title XV, which translates as "On Commercial Trusts and Fiduciary Mandate"). In addition, by mid-1998, trusts were regulated in greater detail by means of Law No. 107 also named the "Securities Market Act" (Official Record No. 367, July 23, 1998), which deepened updated, and replaced the rules of Law No. 31; and by means of the general regulations of Law No. 107, sanctioned by Decree No. 390 (Official Record No. 87, December 14, 1998).

Commercial Trusts are widespread as a vehicle for investments. Along this line, it is estimated that there are more than 500 commercial trusts registered with public registries, and more than tenfold not registered. Furthermore, the public companies supervisory authority promotes the commercial trust as a legal vehicle for the development of productive activities in Ecuador.[2]

Finally, owing to the special characteristics of the Commercial Trust, the law expressly excludes the application of Civil Trust rules (provided in books II and III of

---

2    Marcos Lopez Narvaez, *La Responsabilidad Fiduciaria in Derecho Societario: Memorias de las Primeras Jornadas Nacionales*, Oct. 22 & 23 ACADEMIA ECUATORIANA DE DERECHO Y EDINO, GUAYAQUIL 233 (2003).

the Civil Code) from the interpretation and effects of the Commercial Trust agreements, for having a different base and a different legal nature as explained above.

## 1. Definition of Commercial Trust as a Special-Purpose Patrimony

Article No. 109 of the Commercial Code defines the "commercial trust agreement" as that whereby one or more persons, called settlors or grantors, transfer temporarily and irrevocably the ownership of tangible or intangible, real or personal property, which exists or is expected to exist, to a special-purpose patrimony with its own legal personality, for the funds and trusts management company, which is its trustee and, as such, the legal representative of the special-purpose patrimony (trust), to comply with the specific objectives set forth in the trust deed, whether in favor of the settlor him or herself or of a third person named beneficiary.

The Commercial Trust, as a special-purpose patrimony, is a set of rights and duties affected to one purpose and is established by the trust agreement. Each Commercial Trust has an individual denomination stipulated by the settlor in the trust deed to differentiate it from others that the trustee may hold.

Ecuadorian law falls into the theory of special-purpose patrimony, which deems that the rights transferred to the trustee by virtue of the trust do not enter his or her property, but a special-purpose patrimony is created with its definite objectives or purposes. Nevertheless, as mentioned before and unlike all other Latin American legislations, Ecuadorian law deems each special-purpose patrimony (Commercial Trusts) as a legal entity with its own legal personality, the trustee being its legal representative who will exercise such functions in accordance with the directions stated by the settlor in the corresponding agreement.

Although a certain level of legal personality is granted to the Commercial Trust, Ecuadorian law establishes that the special-purpose patrimony (Commercial Trusts) is not and shall not be deemed a civil or commercial company but only as a legal entity capable of acquiring rights and contracting obligations through the trustee, in view of the directions stated in the agreement.

In short, the Ecuadorian Commercial Trust is a particular case in which although it has some characteristics of a legal entity, it is not a company. In any case, the law is clear that the special-purpose patrimony created by virtue of the trust deed (Commercial Trust) is separate from the individual property of the settlor, of the trustee and beneficiary, and of other Commercial Trusts held by the trustee.

As the special-purpose patrimony which it is, each Commercial Trust is made up of the assets, rights, credits, and obligations that are transferred by the settlor or that derive from the accomplishment of the purpose stated by the settlor. The property of the Commercial Trust answers for the obligations and liabilities contracted by the trustee on behalf of the Commercial Trust for the accomplishment of the aims set out in the agreement. Therefore, those who have credits against the Commercial Trust or at the holding of contracts with a trustee who acts on behalf of a Commercial Trust, will only be entitled to pursue the assets of the relevant Commercial Trust albeit not the trustee's own assets or the assets of other Commercial Trusts.

Liability for obligations contained in the special-purpose patrimony will be limited to the assets that have been transferred to the Commercial Trust, the own assets of the trustee being excluded. Furthermore, as a consequence of the creation of the special-purpose patrimony, the assets of the Commercial Trust cannot be attacked by the creditors of the settlor, nor by those of the beneficiary, except for provision to that effect in the trust deed.

In no case may those assets be attacked by the creditors of the trustee. The creditors of the beneficiary will be entitled to pursue the rights and benefits that are due to him or her in accordance with the trust deed. The beneficiary's creditors will be entitled to claim the rights and benefits owed to him or her in accordance with the trust deed.

The assets transferred to the special-purpose patrimony provide backing to all the obligations contracted by the Commercial Trust for the accomplishment of the objectives set by the settlor and may consequently be attacked by the creditors of the Commercial Trust.

Finally, it is worth pointing out that the Commercial Trust agreement entered into in fraud of third parties by the settlor, or in fraudulent agreement between him or her and the trustee, may be challenged in court by the interested parties by means of the relevant actions of nullity, sham, or any other provided in the law, as the case may be; notwithstanding the corresponding criminal action and liability.

## 2. Commercial Trust Instrument

The Commercial Trust shall be established by a notarized deed. The transfer of the property held in trust shall be effected according to the general provisions made in the statutes, considering the nature of the assets.

A Commercial Trust will be in force for a certain term, or it may subsist until the accomplishment of the stated purpose or of a condition. The duration of a Commercial Trust shall not be longer than eighty years, except for the following cases:

a. Where the resolutory condition of the Commercial Trust is the dissolution of a legal entity.
b. If Commercial Trusts are established with cultural or research purposes, altruistic or philanthropic, such as those having as an object the establishment of museums, libraries, scientific research, or cultural institutions, or of alleviating the situation of, orphans, senior citizens, the handicapped, interdict, poor or needy, they may subsist until accomplishment of the purpose wherefore they were created is feasible.

Commercial Trust agreements shall include at least the following:

a. Identification of the settlor or settlors and of the beneficiary or beneficiaries
b. An affidavit by the settlor stating that the assets or moneys transferred are of legitimate origin; that the agreement does not contain an unlawful cause or object and that it is not detrimental to creditors of the settlor or third parties
c. The transfer of the assets under Commercial Trust

d. The rights and duties of the original settlor, of the additional settlors—where such a possibility was provided for—of the trustee and of the beneficiary
e. The trustee's fee
f. The name of the Commercial Trust
g. The grounds for and methods of termination of the Commercial Trust
h. The grounds for the substitution of the trustee and the procedure to be followed therefore
i. The conditions for the management and delivery of assets, returns, benefits, and for the liquidation of the Commercial Trust

Apart from the enumerated elements, the agreement may include the power and the form whereby the trustee may issue participation certificates in the rights arising from the Commercial Trust agreement. These certificates constitute securities in accordance with the securitization rules issued by the National Securities Council, or CNV (*Consejo Nacional de Valores*) equivalent to the U.S. Securities and Exchange Commission (SEC). It may also include the existence of committees of beneficiaries, settlors, or other collegiate bodies necessary for the accomplishment of the purpose sought by the settlor.

No clauses shall be set forth that mean the imposition of illegal or inequitable conditions, such as:

a. Provisions diminishing the legal duties imposed on the trustee or increasing his or her legal powers in respects relevant to the settlor and/or the beneficiary. For example, those provisions that may exonerate the responsibility of the trustee, reserve the power to terminate the agreement before expiration, or to resign as trustee without previous agreement indicating expressly the reasons to do so and before the relevant administrative expedients are satisfied
b. Limitation of the legal rights of the settlor or the beneficiary, such as that of seeking redress of damage suffered, whether by failure to perform duties or because of the defective performance of the duties of the trustee
c. The determination of conditions that were not written in visible fonts on the first page of the agreement at the time of its execution, from which arises a consequence against the settlor or beneficiary, or which involves the transfer of prerogatives in favor of the trustee
d. Provisions with unfavorable effects for the settlor or beneficiary which are recorded with ambiguity, or in a confused or unclear fashion, and which, as a consequence, permit discrepancies to arise between the effects of the business that could be expected or foreseen and those actually resulting from the letter of the agreement
e. The possibility that the person who is under the obligation to perform the charged duties be a person other than the trustee, who is thus substituted as the obligee, unless because of the nature of the trust agreement it is necessary to entrust the office to experts in some given matters
f. Those that confer powers on the trustee to modify without need of consent one or more clauses, such as those that allow readjustment of the duties relating to the parties unilaterally

The following are grounds for the termination of Commercial Trusts, other than those provided in the trust agreement:

a. Accomplishment of the purpose of the Commercial Trust
b. Accomplishment of the conditions established in the Commercial Trust
c. Compliance with or failure of the resolutory condition
d. Termination of the Commercial Trust period
e. Absolute impossibility of accomplishing the purpose of the Commercial Trust
f. The final sentence passed by competent judicial authority
g. An agreement between settlor and trustee, provided it does not infringe the rights of the original settlor, of the additional settlors, of the beneficiary, of creditors of the Commercial Trust or of third parties
h. The bankruptcy or dissolution of the trustee, where there is no substitute

## 3. Rendering of Accounts

The rendering of accounts cannot be delegated to third persons, so that it is the trustee's duty to render a supported accounting of his or her administration. The burden of proof is on the trustee to demonstrate the right discharge of its duties, in accordance with the provisions of the trust deed and the general rules as stipulated by the National Securities Council.

The accounting rendered to the settlor and the beneficiary shall be in harmony with the information that the trustee should submit to the Corporations Superintendence (*Superintendencia de Compañías*)—particularly in those situations that considerably affect the normal course of the Commercial Trust. All the same, the legal representative of the trustee is obliged to report to the Corporations Superintendence the facts or situations that hamper the normal course of the trust transaction and that delay or may delay substantially its execution and/or termination, in a way that compromises gravely the securing of the pursued objects. Such notice shall be served within 15 days at the very latest following the event or the date in which he or she came to or should have come to the knowledge of the event. The National Securities Council will regulate the form and content of the reports on accountings that must be submitted at the Corporations Superintendence.

In addition, the person who has contractual rights arising from a trust agreement as original settlor, additional settlor, or beneficiary has a duty to record them in his or her books. Such accounting record is the exclusive responsibility of the beneficiaries, which have a fundamentally personal character, the trustee not being liable for omission or noncompliance with this rule, in according to the accounting rules passed by the Corporations Superintendence.

## D. THE GRANTOR

Any natural or legal person, whether private, public, or mixed; national or foreign; who could transfer the ownership of assets may be settlor of a Commercial Trust.

Where a third person other than the settlor joins in and accepts the provisions set forth in the Commercial Trust instrument, he or she will be called an additional settlor. This addition is possible in those agreements in which such a possibility has been expressly foreseen. The addition and acceptance by the additional settlors of the terms and conditions of a Commercial Trust agreement will be recorded in writing and will be filed by the trustee.

Although public sector institutions acting in such a capacity are bound by special regulations, they could be settlors of so-called "governmental trusts" or "public trusts."

The trustee in performance of Commercial Trust agreements may also transfer assets, whether it be to establish new Commercial Trusts or to increase the property of other existing trusts administered by him or herself or by another trustee.

The following are rights of the settlor of the Commercial Trust:

a. Those set forth in the trust deed
b. To demand from the trustee the performance of the purposes laid down in the Commercial Trust deed
c. To demand from the trustee the rendering of accounts, in accordance with the provisions of Ecuadorian law with the general rules sanctioned by the National Securities Council relating to trust activities and those provided in the deed
d. To exercise the necessary civil or criminal legal actions against the trustee even for involuntary tort or slight blame in the discharge of his or her duties


## E. THE TRUSTEE

The trustee of a Commercial Trust is under a duty to comply with the specific purposes set forth in the trust deed. The said trustees, called "fund and trust management companies" (*Administradoras de Fondos y Fideicomisos*) shall be incorporated as corporations and authorized to act as trustees. No other person could act as trustee of a Commercial Trust with the exception of certain government companies: the State Bank (*Banco del Estado*) and the National Finance Corporation (*Corporación Financiera Nacional*).

As has been said, the trustee exercises the legal representation of the Commercial Trust, so that he or she may act with all the rights and powers vested in the Commercial Trust before the courts, whether as plaintiff or defendant, before the competent authorities in all types of administrative or judicial proceedings and legal actions that should be performed for the defense of the trust assets, as well as demand the credits due to the trust and for the accomplishment of the purposes sought by the settlor.

It should be stressed that Ecuadorian legislation expressly prohibits the establishment of a Commercial Trust in which the trustee him or herself or his or her administrators, legal representatives or related companies are appointed as beneficiaries, whether principal or substitute.

Notwithstanding the obligations provided in the statutes, as well as those provided in the Commercial Trust deed, the trustee does not ensure with his or her performance that the objectives and purposes sought by the settlor are actually accomplished. Put differently, his or her liability is to act with reasonable diligence and professionalism to comply with the instructions set forth by the settlor with a view to attempt the accomplishment of the sought purposes, not to ensure a final result. The trustee is liable even for slight blame in the performance of his or her administration.

Additionally to the duties and obligations as funds administrator, the trustee has the following obligations, above and beyond the provisions set out in the Commercial Trust deed:

a. To administer with prudence and diligence the assets held in Commercial Trust, being able to execute all the acts and contracts necessary for the accomplishment of the purposes set forth by the settlor.
b. To maintain the Commercial Trust assets segregated from his or her own property and from that of other Commercial Trusts that he or she may hold, keeping to that effect separate books for each. The books of the Commercial Trust shall reflect the purpose pursued by the settlor and will be subject to generally accepted accounting principles.
c. To render an account of his or her administration, to the settlor or to the beneficiary, according to what the trust deed provides and with the frequency therein established and, in the absence of stipulation, it shall be carried out quarterly.
d. To transfer the assets to whom it is due according to the trust deed.
e. To terminate the Commercial Trust, as a result of the accomplishment of the objects provided in the trust deed.
f. To inform the Corporations Superintendence in the form and with the frequency that the National Securities Council stipulates by means of general rules.

Trustees are prohibited from:

a. Acquiring, alienating, or merging assets from one trust with its own assets
b. Merging assets from one trust with those from other trusts
c. Carrying out transactions outside the stock exchange when managing funds
d. Ensuring a result, yield, or rate of return
e. Transferring securities of its own ownership or issuance between the several trusts that it may administer
f. Giving or taking money from the trusts that it administers, whichever the cause, or tendering the same as security
g. Issuing securities and receiving money deposits
h. Participating in any way in the administration, counseling, management, or any other function that is not that of shareholder in those companies in which a trust holds investments
i. Being a shareholder of a securities dealer, trustee, risk-rating agency, external auditors, and other companies related to the mutual funds administrator

In addition, as trustees they shall not guarantee or secure the payment of benefits or fixed returns in relation to the assets they administer. However, according to the nature of the Commercial Trust, they may only estimate unsecured returns or benefits, fixed or variable, always stating that the obligations of the trustee do not guarantee the final benefit.

The trustee, for the duration of the Commercial Trust, shall not allow the beneficiary to appropriate the assets that he or she administers in accordance with the provisions of the trust deed.

Besides the prohibitions stated above, the trustee shall be barred from carrying out the activities assigned in this Ecuadorian law to securities dealers.

The administration organs of the trustees shall be those laid down in the articles of association. However, the trustee in its capacity as administrator in the case of carrying out the administration of investment trusts shall have an investment committee whose members must provide evidence of expertise of a minimum of three years in the financial, stock market, or like sectors. The investment committee will be charged with establishing the investment policies of the trust and see that it is complied with, apart from those set forth in the articles of association of the trustee.

The task of the trustees shall always give right to a fee in consideration that should be so recorded in the trust deed.


## 1. Resignation and Substitution

The trustee shall only be able to resign his or her office as long as he or she does not cause damage to the settlor, the beneficiary or third parties related to the Commercial Trust and because of the reasons expressly indicated in the Commercial Trust instrument. In the absence of specific stipulations, the following shall be deemed causes for resignation:

a. The beneficiary cannot or declines to, receive the benefits in accordance with the trust deed, except when the trustee had been instructed by the settlor to pay into Court, always at the expense of the settlor.
b. Nonpayment of the trustee's fee as agreed.

Unless agreement is reached between the parties, the trustee shall require previous authorization to resign from the Corporations Superintendence, who considering the provisions of the trust deed, can decide the actual delivery of the assets in the special-purpose patrimony to the settlor, the beneficiary, or to the substitute trustee provided in the trust deed, appointed by the beneficiary or by the Corporations Superintendent, as the case may be.

Where the trustee is substituted by reason of the grounds provided in the trust deed or in the statutes, the assets held in the Commercial Trust shall be delivered to the substitute in the same terms as stipulated in the trust deed. The substitute trustee shall not be held liable for the acts of his or her predecessor.

In the dissolution and liquidation process of a trustee, the regulations of the Corporations Act (*Ley de Compañías*) and its complementary regulations shall be applied.

The liquidation shall be executed by the Corporations Superintendence, which may authorize the trustee to conduct its own liquidation or that of the trusts.

## F. THE BENEFICIARY

Any natural or legal person, whether private, governmental or mixed, private with social or public utility, national or foreign, or an entity with legal status recorded as such in the trust deed by the settlor, or pursuant to that, if such a power was provided in the trust deed, may be beneficiary of a Commercial Trust. In addition, a person who at the moment of the creation of the trust does not exist but is expected to exist may be appointed as beneficiary.

Many beneficiaries of a trust may exist, the settlor being entitled to establish priorities among them and even appoint substitute beneficiaries. In the absence of stipulation, where there be no beneficiary or in the face of the resignation of the appointed beneficiary, and there being no substitute beneficiary or heirs to their titles, the settlor him or herself or his or her heirs, if that be the case, shall be held out as the beneficiary.

The beneficiary of a Commercial Trust is entitled to:

a. Exercise the rights set forth in the trust deed
b. Demand from the trustee compliance with the objectives set forth in the trust deed
c. Demand from the trustee a rendering of accounting, in accordance with the provisions of the Ecuadorian law and with the general rules issued by the National Securities Council on the trust activity and those provided in the clauses of the trust deed
d. Exercise the civil or criminal legal actions that could arise against the trustee for tort or gross or slight blame in the discharge of his or her duties
e. Challenge those agreements executed by the trustee against the directions and objectives of the Commercial Trust, within the terms prescribed in the statutes
f. Request the removal of the trustee on the grounds provided in the trust deed, as well as in cases of involuntary tort or slight blame in which the trustee has incurred, in accordance with the judicial sentence or judgment by arbitration, and in the case of dissolution or liquidation of the trustee

## G. TAX TREATMENT

In accordance with the provisions of the law, the trust transfer is not onerous nor is it gratuitous, because it does not bring about an economic gain for the settlor or for the trustee, and it takes place as a necessary means and effect for the latter to be able to comply with the objectives set forth by the former in the trust deed. Consequently, this kind of transfer to conform a trust is exempt from all types of taxes, rates, and contributions, because it does not constitute an event that generates tax liability nor indirect taxes provided in the laws that charges onerous and gratuitous transferences.

The ownership transference of realty carried out in favor of a Commercial Trust is exempt from stamp tax (*alcabala*) and registration duties, and from the corresponding additional taxes, as well as from the tax on profits originating in the buying and selling of urban property and their capital gain.

The transfers carried out by the trustee by returning the ownership to the settlor, whether that situation arise from failure of the condition provided in the trust deed, from any fortuitous situation or cases of force majeure or from contractual effects that determine that the assets be returned in the same conditions in which they were transferred, shall also enjoy the above-mentioned exemptions.

Free or onerous transfers that the trustee executes in favor of the beneficiaries in compliance with the objects set forth in the Commercial Trust deed will be taxed, provided the general provisions in the statutes so prescribe it. The trust transfer of ownership of personal property is exempt from value-added tax (VAT) and other indirect taxes. Such an exemption shall be applied in the case of return to the settlor in accordance with the case described in the previous paragraphs.

The Commercial Trust shall be a tax-withholding or collection agent with respect to the taxes that the trust is to withhold and receive in the terms of the tax law in force. To all subsequent effects, the liability of the trustee in relation to the trust which he or she administers shall be governed by the Tax Code (*Código Tributario*). The trustee shall be jointly and severally liable with the Commercial Trust for failure to comply with formal duties which, as withholding and collection agent, falls on the trust.

Regarding the trust tax treatment in relation to Ecuadorian income tax, according to the latest tax regulations issued by the Ecuadorian Internal Revenue Services, there are two alternatives: (a) if expressly established in the trust deed, the beneficiary would be responsible for the tax; or (b) if there is no express rule in the trust deed, the trust would be subject to the same income tax treatment as corporations or companies, the trustee being directly responsible for the tax payment.

## H. SECURITIZATION

The Securities Market Act expressly provides the possibility of employing the Commercial Trust as a vehicle to carry out securitizations backed exclusively by the trust assets and the corresponding credit enhancement mechanisms.

Thus, article 138 of the Act, defines securitization as the process whereby securities are issued that are apt to be placed and traded freely in the stock market and charged against a special-purpose patrimony. The securities issued as result of securitization processes constitute securities in terms of the Securities Market Act.[3]

The essential parties who must take part in a securitization process are the following:

*Originator:* This is one or more natural or legal persons, governmental, private or mixed, private with public or social utility, national or foreign, or entities with legal status, owners of assets or titles over flows capable of being securitized.

---

3    The Securities Market Act provides that the securities issued as a result of a securitization process may be bearer ones. The debt securities or mixed securities may have a coupon attached that acknowledges a fixed or variable financial yield, the coupons could be bearer ones, according to the characteristics of the securities whereto they are attached.

*Servicer:* This shall be a trustee, who apart from the powers laid down in the Commercial Trust deed, is charged with the following:

a. Obtaining the authorizations required for securitization processes in which the securities to be issued are to be placed by means of a public offering
b. Receiving the assets to be securitized from the settlor in representation of the special-purpose patrimony
c. Issuing securities, backed by the special-purpose patrimony
d. Placing the issued securities, by means of public offering
e. Administering the assets of the special-purpose patrimony, aiming at securing future flows, whether they be funds or securities
f. Distributing among the investors the returns obtained

The above-mentioned functions stated in items (a), (b), and (c) cannot be delegated. The delegation of the remaining functions shall be expressly stipulated in the Commercial Trust deed. The servicer shall always be held liable for all acts by third parties who perform the functions thus delegated.

The servicer must submit the public offering memorandum of the securities issued as a result of the securitization process to approval by the Corporations Superintendence. In the said public offering memorandum will be included information that allows investors to form a clear idea of the terms and conditions of the securities in which they will invest. The National Securities Council issued general rules that regulate the content of such a prospectus.

In all cases, the liability of the servicer does not extend beyond the good administration of the securitization process, therefore not being held liable for the results obtained, unless that process produces losses caused by involuntary tort or slight blame in the management's performance, declared as such in a court decision, in which case they shall be held liable in tort or even for slight blame.

*Special-purpose patrimony:* It is an independent patrimony formed initially by the assets transferred by the originator and, later, by the assets and liabilities resulting from, or integrated as a result of, the securitization process. From a legal point, such a special-purpose patrimony could be a mutual collective fund or a Commercial Trust that issues the securities to be publicly placed.

*Investors:* They are those who acquire and invest in securities issued as a result of a securitization process.

*Supervising committee:* It shall be made up of at least three members elected by the securities holders, holding no relationship with the servicer. The security holders from companies related to the servicer shall not be eligible as members of the said committee.

Whatever the special-purpose patrimony used to develop a securitization process, the assets or title overflows transferred by the originator shall be integrated into an independent patrimony, with its own financial statements, different from the individual patrimonies of the originator, of the servicer or of the investors.

The assets of the special-purpose patrimony cannot be seized nor can they be attacked by the originator's creditors, of the servicer or of the investors. The investors' creditors may lay claim on the rights and benefits due them with respect to the securities in which they invested. The special-purpose patrimony backs the corresponding securities issuance, so that the investors may only pursue their rights against the assets of the special-purpose patrimony, albeit not in the servicer's own assets. The securitized assets shall be exclusively affected to the accomplishment of the purpose of the securitization process.

The statutes provide that securitization processes may be developed from existing assets or from those expected to exist, which entail the expectation of generating ascertainable future flows, whether cash flow or securities, with respect to which its owner may dispose freely. In addition, no lien may bear on these assets, as well as no limitations on ownership, prohibitions to alienate, suspensive or resolutory conditions, nor should any tax, rate, or contribution be outstanding. The following are assets liable to securitization:

a. Governmental debt securities
b. Securities registered with the Stock Market Registry
c. Credit portfolios
d. Assets and real estate projects
e. Assets or projects capable of generating ascertainable future cash flows based on statistics of the last three years or in forecasts of at least three consecutive years, as the case may be

Notwithstanding the above listing, the Corporations Superintendence, pursuant to a rule sanctioned by the National Securities Council, may authorize the structuring of processes with assets other than the ones set out above.

The transference of assets from the originator to the special-purpose patrimony may be a trust transfer or a sale, according to the terms and conditions of each securitization process. When the transfer falls on personal assets, the formalities provided in the relevant statutes shall be observed.

Unless the securitization was structured in fraud of third parties, which must be decided by the competent court, the nullity, pretense, or ineffectiveness of the transfer cannot be declared, totally or partially, when this results in impossibility or difficulty of generating the projected future flow and, therefore, are detrimental to the investors, notwithstanding the civil or criminal actions that could ensue. Neither the originator nor the servicer may request the rescission of the transfer of realty by reason of gross injury.[4]

The securities issued as a result of securitization processes fall into three types:

a. Debt securities, whereby investors have the right to receive repayment of principal plus the corresponding financial yield, with the resources from the Commercial Trust and according to the terms and conditions of the issued securities. The special-purpose patrimony assets back the liabilities acquired with the investors,

---

4    It is considered that gross injury exists when there is lack of reasonable relationship between the asset sold and the consideration received.

it being the duty of the servicer to take the necessary steps to obtain the collection of the required cash flows for the timely servicing of the obligations evidenced in the issued securities.

b. Participation securities, whereby investors acquire a percentage of the special-purpose patrimony, *pro rata* of his or her investment, whereby he or she shares in the results, whether they are profits or losses, which that patrimony produces with respect to the securitization process.

c. Mixed securities, whereby investors acquire securities that combine the features of debt and participation securities, according to the terms and conditions of each securitization.

Thus, one special-purpose patrimony may back the issuance of different types of securities. Each given type of security may be made up by many series. The securities corresponding to each type or series, should there be any, shall acknowledge the same rights to investors, differences being possible in the rights granted to the several series. Whatever the type of securities issued, should situations arise that prevent the projected generation of future flows of funds or creditors' rights and, once depleted the resources of the special-purpose patrimony, investors must face the possible losses that ensue from such situations. The maximum issuance amount of any given securitization process shall be determined by the National Securities Council. Whatever the type of security issued, they may be redeemed in advance, totally by the servicer, in the cases expressly stated in the issuance conditions (*Reglamento de Gestión*).[5]

The National Securities Council regulates the contents of the information and frequency with which the servicer must make it available to the Corporations Superintendence and to investors.

The Securities Markets Act expressly provides the collateral mechanisms for the securitization process. Thus, considering the characteristics inherent to each securitization process, the servicer or the originator, as the case may be, shall furnish at least one of the following collateral mechanisms: (a) subordination of the issuance (creation of a subordinated and senior securities), (b) over-collateralization, (c) excess of funds flow, (d) replacement of nonperforming assets, (e) standby letters of credit, (f) guarantee granted by third parties, (g) bank guarantee or insurance policy, and (h) guarantee trust.[6]

All securities issued as a result of securitization shall be rated by at least one risk-rating agency of those legally authorized. The risk rating shall indicate which factors were taken account of to grant it and, additionally, reference must be made to the legality and method of transfer to the special-purpose patrimony. In no case must

---

5    Nevertheless, where the securitization results in losses occasioned by tort or slight blame in the performance of the servicer, declared as such by a court sentence, the investors may exercise the actions contemplated in the pertinent legal regulations with a view to obtaining the appropriate indemnifications. In case that there are gains not distributed in due time, the securities holders have a summary legal action.

6    This collateral mechanism involves the creation of a guarantee trust that serves the purpose of guaranteeing the securities purchased by the investors.

the risk rating consider the solvency of the originator or of the servicer or of any third party.

So that the servicer complies with the provisions of the Securities Market Act, complementary rules and internal regulations, he or she is under the surveillance of a Supervisory Committee that may summon him or her to an extraordinary general meeting of holders when it deems it necessary.

Trustees acting as servicers in securitization processes shall appoint a paying agent, which may be vested in the trustee him or herself or a financial institution subject to the control of Banks Superintendence. The paying agent shall not be part of the Supervision Committee. The Supervision Committee must inform the holder's meeting of its work and the results deriving from it. Notwithstanding, when during the course of its work, it detects failure to comply with the rules governing Commercial Trusts, it must bring this information into the knowledge of the Corporations Superintendence, in accordance with the regulations sanctioned by the National Securities Council to that effect.

Apart from compliance with the general rules stated above, the servicer resulting from portfolio securitization processes, from securitization of realty, from the securitization of real estate developments, and from the securitization of funds flows in general, it must comply with certain special regulations that should be analyzed on an individual basis.

The administration regulations of each securitization process shall contain the rules that will govern them, the following being indispensable:

a. Regime applicable to secure resources and/or future flows
b. Allocation of the remnant and/or the future flows, if any
c. Cases where anticipated redemption of the issued securities is necessary
d. Characteristics and manner of determining the breakeven point for the initiation of the project
e. All other requirements established by the National Securities Council by means of general rules

## I. TAX TREATMENT OF SECURITIZATION

Transfers of assets, whatever their nature, carried out with the object of developing securitization processes are exempt from all types of taxes, rates, and contributions, as well as from indirect taxes provided in the statutes that tax asset transfers. Transfers of realty carried out with the aforementioned object are exempt from and not subject to stamp tax (*alcabala*) and registration duties and from supplements thereof, as well as from the tax on returns originating in the buying and selling of urban property and capital gain thereof.

In addition, statutes provide that where the established breakeven point has not been achieved for the placing of securities issued as a result of securitization processes, and the servicer proceeds to return ownership of the realty to the originator, such restitution shall also take advantage the exemptions listed above.

The transfer of ownership to the special-purpose patrimony carried out with the aforesaid objective are exempt from and not subject to value-added tax (VAT) or other indirect taxes. The same exemption will apply in the case of the restitution of ownership of such special-purpose patrimony to the originator. Finally, income received by the special-purpose patrimony is subject to taxation, according to the nature of that income and the ordinary tax regime applicable thereto.

Chapter 14

# El Salvador[1]

A. Overview 211
B. The Grantor and the Beneficiary 214
C. The Trustee 214
    1. Appointment 215
    2. Rights and Duties 215
    3. Substitution 216
D. Tax Treatment 217

Arias explained that despite the multiple ends the trust could serve, in El Salvador it encountered many legal limitations that prevented it from booming as it should, and some of them, mainly in the tax field, constituted veritable stumbling blocks to its development. Therefore, Salvadorian trusts face most serious limitations to an efficient expansion.

## A. OVERVIEW

Regarding the legal framework, Arias pointed out that "the legal basis of trusts in El Salvador is contained in the Salvadorian Constitution (section 107, subparagraph 2); and the legal development of the concept appears in the Commerce Code of El Salvador (section 1233 and following) and the Banks Act [*Ley de Bancos*] (section 67 and following)"[2] among other regulations.

The Salvadorian National Constitution (in force since 1983) provides in section 107 that "any type of entailment is prohibited, except for: (1) trusts established in favor of

---

211

the State, municipalities, public entities, charitable or cultural institutions, and of the legally incapable; (2) trusts established for a period which does not exceed that prescribed by law and whose management is in charge of legally authorized banks or credit institutions; (3) the family assets regime." Furthermore, trusts are governed by the Salvadorian Commerce Code, sections 1233 to 1261.

The Commerce Code section 1233 sets forth that "trusts are established by manifestation of intent, whereby the grantor transfers the usufruct or use, wholly or partly, of certain assets in favor of the beneficiary, or establishes a given income or amount of money, entrusting the performance of such intention to the trustee, to whom the assets or rights are to be transferred in ownership albeit without the power to dispose of them, but rather in accordance with the precise directions given by the grantor in the trust instrument."

Trusts are classified into:

a. *Inter vivos* trusts, which are created by public deed, with all due formalities pertaining to *inter vivos* gifts. This type of trust may be subdivided into: (i) ordinary and (ii) for the issuance of securities. The latter category is associated with those trusts created with a commercial purpose and in favor of a collective and future beneficiary, allowing for the issuance of participation trust certificates, that is, securitization of the assets held in trust.
b. *Mortis causa* trusts, which must be created by a will.
c. Mixed trusts, which commence to be exercised during the grantor's lifetime and continue pursuant to his or her death. They must be created by public deed, with all due formalities of *inter vivos* trusts and ratified in the grantor's will, deeming the trust regulations as included therein as testamentary clauses, whether recording them completely or making clear and precise reference to the deed wherein they are contained. Mixed trusts are held to be *inter vivos,* so long as the grantor is alive.

The acceptance by the trustee perfects the existence of the trust. *Inter vivos* trusts are irrevocable thereafter, except where they were created for private purposes and express reservation was made in the trust instrument of the power to reform or revoke it. If the trust has the issuance of participation trust certificates as its object, it can only be irrevocable. In the cases of trusts for the issuance of securities, the grantor will probably be compensated for the transfer of the assets to the trust, because of which dynamics nothing but the irrevocability of this transaction is to be expected.

The trust is subject to a nondeferrable 25-year period; because once that time has elapsed, the assets under the agreement must return to the grantor or pass permanently to the beneficiary or another given person. This is an exception to the general rule in Latin America, which establishes a maximum period of time (in most cases twenty to thirty years), but with the possibility of extending it at the end of the period in all cases. Trusts in favor of the state, municipalities, public entities, charitable or cultural enterprises, and those of the legally incapable shall not be subject to this regulation and are permitted to last for as long as warranted by the objects for which they were created.

As long as the limitation described in the previous paragraph is not violated, the trust could have one underlying asset or the complete patrimony of an entity, and could be subject to a condition, up to a fixed date, for a certain period or for the life of the grantor, trustee or beneficiary. If the trust were subjected to a suspensive condition and that could necessarily not be fulfilled prior to 25 years, it shall be deemed as met from the date of the acceptance by the trustee. If, on the contrary, the condition can be realized prior or subsequent to 25 years, and it was not accomplished after the deadline, the trust shall not be.

The trust instrument must include, under penalty of impossibility of creating the trust:

a. The names of the grantor, trustee, and beneficiary, except for the beneficiary in the event of issuance of securities (the beneficiary would be whoever holds the securities).
b. The assets under the agreement (transferred from the grantor to the trustee or contributed by third parties).
c. The pertinent directions and the objects of creation, which shall not be contrary to morals or the law.

Trusts may be created over all types of assets, except those rights which, according to the law, are strictly personal to their titleholders or which are repugnant to trusts by reason of their very nature.

The assets given in trust are affected to the elected purpose of the trust as determined by the grantor. Only the rights and actions thus intended may be exercised with respect to them, those expressly reserved for him or herself by the grantor, those deriving from the trust itself for him or her and those legally acquired prior to the creation of the trust by the beneficiary or third parties.

Registration of the trust instrument and its modifications shall be filed with the Commerce Registry (*Registro de Comercio*), even where it must also be filed in the Real Estate Registry. The trusts created over real estate, as well as their revocations or modifications, must be registered in the Real Estate Registry. They will only be effective *erga omnes* from the date of filing with the Registry.

The trust expires in the event of

a. The accomplishment or impossibility of the purposes for which it was created
b. Failure to comply on a timely basis with the suspensive condition stated in the trust instrument
c. Fulfillment of the stipulated resolutory condition
d. Destruction of the trust assets
e. Revocation of the grantor's right over the trust assets
f. Revocation by the trustee, when he or she has expressly reserved that power
g. Death or resignation of the beneficiary, with the exception of those cases of beneficiary substitution, and of the cases in which the trust lasts for a fixed period of time and the right is conveyed to the heir of the beneficiary
h. Lapse of legal time (as explained, a nondeferrable 25-year period, except for trusts in favor of the state, municipalities, public entities, charitable or cultural enterprises, and those of the legally incapable, which shall not be subject to this regulation and are permitted to last for as long as warranted by the objects for which they were created)

## B. THE GRANTOR AND THE BENEFICIARY

Concerning the different roles, it is established that the grantor may create the trust in his or her benefit (be both grantor and beneficiary). The restriction established by the law is that the trustee shall not be beneficiary.

Conversely, any natural or legal person legally capable and worthy of inheriting the grantor may be a beneficiary. If the trust is created as the basis of the issuance of participation trust certificates, the beneficiary shall be composed of the plurality of certificate holders, to which the aforementioned incapabilities and unworthiness shall not apply.

No trust shall be created in which the benefit passes to another person after the death of the first beneficiary.[3] But if the trust were originally created in benefit of two or more persons, and if the grantor so indicated, the trust may be transferred to the survivor(s). This rule shall not apply to fiduciary securities.

The beneficiary shall be entitled to demand the execution of the trust to the trustee, to challenge the validity of the acts, which the latter performs to his or her detriment and to claim the assets which, as a result of these acts, had improperly abandoned the trust. To this end, he or she shall have access to the accounts of the trust.

Where the beneficiary is not determined, or he or she is incapable, the rights referred to in the above paragraph shall correspond to the ordinary representative, the legal representative or the attorney general's office, as the case may be.

If the trust is created for a fixed period of time for specific purposes which must be accomplished notwithstanding the death of the beneficiary or of the grantor, the rights and obligations of one and the other shall be transferred to their respective heirs.

The grantor may prohibit the beneficiary from the alienation or encumbrance of the income under the trust, in which case that income shall not be subject to claims or liens in benefit of the beneficiary's creditors; except where, through competent court, it be adjudged that a portion of the income of the beneficiary be applied to the cancellation of his or her obligations, at the instance of his or her creditors. The portion of the income allocated to the cancellation shall not reach a sum such that the remaining balance does not cover the reasonable sustenance of the beneficiary.

## C. THE TRUSTEE

Only banks or authorized credit institutions may be trustees, in accordance with the relevant statutes. Thus, the Salvadoran Banks Act provides that banks may accept or administer trusts, with prior authorization by the Superintendence. Transactions which are prohibited to banks generally, or which exceed the limits allowed them as banks, shall not be carried out in dealing with trusts.

---

3    This rule is consistent with the prohibition of fiduciary substitution in most Latin American codes, as explained in Chapter 1 when expounding the influence of the Napoleonic Code in Latin America.

To secure authorization by the Superintendence, banks must present the business plans, organization and policies to be applied in the different classes of trusts which they intend to offer the public. Within the first five days of each month, banks shall be obliged to inform the Superintendence in writing about the trusts they established the previous month. The Superintendence may contest any of those trusts within those thirty days from the date of submission of such information.

The trustee must guarantee the complete segregation of the patrimonies of the trusts from their own patrimonies, and each trust must have separate accounts.

## 1. Appointment

The grantor may appoint several trustees for them to carry out the trust jointly or successively, establishing the order and the conditions of substitution. Should the trustee bank not exist by the date the trust comes into effect, subsequently cease to exist, resign or be removed, another must be substituted by the Commercial Court. The competent court shall be that of the judiciary district where the trust assets were situated; if they were located in several places, the competent court will be that of the domicile of the beneficiary, even when there were no assets there; if the beneficiary resided outside El Salvador, or were undetermined, any of the courts in the capital of the Republic shall be competent.

The trustee appointed by the beneficiary or by the court is under a duty to accept the office and may only decline it or resign it for a reasonable cause, at the discretion of the Commerce Court from his or her place of residence. Reasons deemed reasonable shall only be:

a. That the beneficiary cannot or does not want to receive the benefits in the form indicated in the trust instrument
b. That the grantor, his or her heirs or the beneficiary, as appropriate, decline to pay the stipulated compensation in favor of the trustee
c. That the assets given in trust do not produce sufficient benefits to cover this compensation

The trustee may accept his or her office in the trust instrument or in a separate deed. In all cases, within 15 days from the date when the trustee comes into knowledge of the appointment, he or she must accept it or promote the expedients conducive to the determination of the grounds by reason of which he or she declines the office. The grantor and the beneficiary are entitled to force the trustee to comply with this regulation.

## 2. Rights and Duties

Any trust is remunerated. If the compensation is not fixed in the trust instrument, he or she shall be entitled to collect 5 percent of the net income produced by the trust assets.

Payment of the compensation may be in charge of the grantor, of his or her heirs or of the beneficiary, as stipulated in the trust instrument. If no provisions were made, the trustee may collect his or her due directly from the income of the trust assets.

The Commerce Code states that the trustee must abide by the clauses of the trust instrument, considering the purposes of the trust and not the interest of the trustee. Thus, the beneficiary may challenge the acts of the trustee that exceed the functional limits set down in the trust instrument.

The trustee may not alienate or encumber the trust assets if he or she were not so authorized in the trust instrument. When the execution of the trust necessarily calls for the alienation or encumbrance of the assets, the court, at the request of the trustee and with the intervention of the attorney general's office, must authorize it.

If the directions of the grantor were not sufficiently accurate, or when the determination of the funds investment was left at the discretion of the trustee, it shall be carried out in Salvadorian securities which, at the discretion of the institution, are the most secure.

As for liability, the trustee shall be liable for the losses or injury arising from not performing his or her office with due diligence.

Conversely, it is prescribed that the trustee shall discharge his or her duties by means of delegates specially appointed, for whose acts they shall be liable directly and unlimitedly, notwithstanding the civil liabilities incurred personally. The Financial System Superintendence (*Superintendencia del Sistema Financiero*) may veto the appointment of the officials carried out by the institution. The delegates may appoint special proxies within the limits of their own powers.

The trustee may be obliged to tender security at the request of the attorney general's office, of the grantor, of the beneficiary, of the legal representative of the latter, or of his or her ascendants when he or she is in his or her mother's womb, or of the ordinary representative of the holders of participation trust certificates.

At termination of the trust, the trustee is under a duty to render an accounting of his or her administration and to return the trust assets.


## 3. Substitution

The trustee shall be substituted: (a) if he or she embezzled or administered the trust assets negligently or fraudulently, and/or (b) when at the grantor's request, the beneficiary or the attorney general's office, did not render an accounting of his or her administration within 15 days; or (c) when he or she was declared by a judge guilty of losses or injury sustained by the trust assets. In such cases, or if the trust funds suffered losses, the grantor, the beneficiary or the attorney general's office may start the due legal actions, in summary process, to preserve the assets.

In the event of the substitution of the trustee, the realty held in trust or acquired in the course of the trust that is registered to his or her name shall be registered by transfer to the name of the substitute who replaced him. The substituted trustee shall deliver to the substitute the entirety of the assets held in trust or acquired in the course of the trust, together with the corresponding documentation. For the registration of the trust assets to be valid in favor of the trustee substitute, his or her appointment and the instrument where his or her acceptance is recorded must be attached.

## D. TAX TREATMENT

Article 22 of the Salvadorian Income Tax Act (*Ley del Impuesto sobre la Renta*) establishes that the income obtained by reason of the trust shall count like the income of natural persons, from the date of its creation to the deadline of the ordinary fiscal year. At termination, computation must be done of the income obtained in the period from the date in which the fiscal year commenced until the date of its expiry.

In addition, article 20 of the VAT Act (*Ley del Impuesto al Valor Agregado*) states that trusts are subjects of the burden.

Finally, article 1 of the Salvadorian Real Estate Transfer Tax Act (*Ley del Impuesto a la Transferencia de Bienes Raíces*) relating to trusts provides that the transfer of realty by *inter vivos* acts is taxed, with the exception of the *inter vivos* trust in favor of the grantor, when the trust assets devolve to him after the designated period.

# Chapter 15

# Guatemala[1]

A. Overview  220
    1. Definition  220
    2. Trust Creation Formalities  220
    3. Separate Patrimony  221
    4. Termination and Maximum Period of Trusts  222
    5. Prohibited Trusts  223
B. The Grantor  223
C. The Trustee  223
    1. Rights and Duties  224
    2. Causes of Removal  225
D. The Beneficiary and the Residual Beneficiary  225
    1. Rights of the Beneficiary  225
E. Tax Treatment  226
F. Public Sector Trusts  226
G. Particular Cases and Experience  227
    1. Housing Promotion Trusts  227
    2. Agriculture Promotion Trusts  227
    3. Guarantee Trusts  228
H. Securitization and Investment Trust Agreement  228

---

1    This chapter would have not been possible without the valuable cooperation of Luis Augusto
     Zelaya Estradé, Esq., prestigious practicing lawyer and professor, who read the manuscript
     and corrected several points and provided a complete compilation of the relevant regulatory
     material.

## A. OVERVIEW

The trust was first regulated, without defining it, in the National Constitution of the Republic of Guatemala in 1945 (not in force today), which in its section 28 established that

> Anyone can freely dispose of his assets, as long as doing so does not contravene the law. The fiduciary substitutions (*vinculaciones*) are totally prohibited, as any mortmain institution, with the exception of the foundations destined to charity, artistic or scientific establishments or purposes, which must be approved by the government. The creation of trusts is authorized which do not last in excess of 25 years; in all cases carried on by a bank or credit institution authorized to do business in the Republic. This authorization does not extend in any form to religious or monastic congregations, nor to priests or ministers of any religion. The term can only be extended when it is in favor of the incurably sick or the legally incapable.

The current Civil Code (Decree-Law No. 106 promulgated on September 14, 1963) was used to regulate trust property in its sections 560 to 570 of chapter IV, "Of the Trust Property," included in title II (Of the Property) within book II, related to property and other real rights. This chapter was abrogated by section 1, paragraph 4 of the Decree No. 2-70 of the National Congress, which regulates the Commercial Trust.

Nowadays, the trust is regulated by chapter V of the *Book on Obligations and Commercial Contracts of the Commerce Code of Guatemala* in sections 766 to 793, in which its fundamentals are set out. Additionally, Decree No. 34-96 of the National Congress, related to Securities and Goods, regulates the investment trust in its section 75, and Decree No. 18-2002 of Financial Supervision establishes the Superintendence of Banks as the regulator of banks, which are the sole authorized trustees in Guatemala.

## 1. Definition

Although an express legal definition does not exist as to what should be construed as a trust, according to the features of the agreement, as defined in section 766 of the Commercial Code, the trust agreement could be said to be that whereby a person (the grantor) transfers certain goods and rights to another (the trustee), who receives them with the obligatory restriction of carrying out only those acts necessary to accomplish the trust objects, applying them to a given end.

## 2. Trust Creation Formalities

As to the method of creation of a trust, it may be established by an agreement or by means of a will. In the latter case, the regulations of the Commerce Code provide that once the legitimacy of the will creating a trust is established, an inventory and assessment of the trust assets will be made with the intervention of the trustee. Should the trustee not be named in the will, the court will designate the person proposed by the beneficiary and, failing that, the court will proceed to make the appointment.

In the case of the trust created by agreement, it must be recorded by public deed in the act of subscription. The exception to this rule is the investment trust regulated by section 75 of Decree No. 34-96 of the National Congress related to securities and goods, which does not require a deed but just a private instrument (an agreement executed by both parties).[2] In any case, the acceptance by the trustee should be recorded in the act, together with the estimated value of the property.

Also, there is a possibility of Civil Court Judges of the First Instance constituting trusts at the request of the interested party and with the favorable opinion of the attorney general's office in those cases where, by law, they may appoint persons to undertake the administration of property. In these instances, the court-appointed trustee will only be the administrator of the property.

## 3. Separate Patrimony

Regarding third-party effects arising from the creation of a trust, article 776 provides that the trust has effects against third parties:

a. From the time of the filing of the trust instrument with the Registry, in the case of realty, real rights, and other such assets subject to registration
b. From the time the transfer is completed in accordance with the document evidencing the obligation or the law, in the case of credits or nonendorsable obligations
c. From the date of the endorsement or registration, if appropriate, in the case of registered or bearer securities, or movables subject to registration
d. From the date in the trust instrument, in the case of realty not subject to registration
e. From the time when the actual delivery is effected, in the case of bearer securities

---

2    Section 75 of Decree No. 34-96 established that: "[b]anks and private financing companies may agree with the agents [on] the delegation of their functions as trustees. The delegate trustee may carry on all the activities of a trustee and will be, jointly with the delegating entity, responsible for his acts. Banks, private financing companies and the delegated trustees may be trustees of trusts created with the purpose of investing in publicly offered securities. If as a result of the creation of the trust the issuance of trust certificates is agreed, its public offer must be registered with the Public Registry and the certificated may be listed in a stock exchange. In such a case, the tax treatment would be the same as that of the bonds of private financing companies. The constitutional instrument of the investment trust, as its amendments, may be done in a private instrument [not a deed but just an agreement executed by both parties]; and the issuance and sale of the trust certificates would be subject to the requirements established by this law of securities issued by corporations."

f. From the time of publication of the Decree in the Official Gazette, with due notification to the interested parties, in the case of industrial, commercial, or agricultural businesses

As regards the special-purpose patrimony created by the agreement, wherein lies the very nature of the trust, the Code expressly provides in section 777 that the trust property only responds

a. For the obligations relating to the termination of the trust
b. For the rights that the grantor has reserved for him or herself
c. For the rights deriving from the trust for the grantor
d. For the rights lawfully acquired by third parties, including, without limitation, tax and labor
e. For the rights acquired by the beneficiary with priority to, or during the life of, the trust

## 4. Termination and Maximum Period of Trusts

Concerning the termination of the trust, the Commercial Code provides in section 787 that it expires by reason of

a. The accomplishment of the object for which it was created
b. The accomplishment of its object becoming impossible
c. The accomplishment of its resolutory condition
d. Express agreement between the grantor and the beneficiary
e. Revocation by the grantor, when he or she has expressly reserved for him or herself that right in the trust instrument
f. Resignation, declination, or nonacceptance by the trustee, where substitution of the trustee is not possible
g. Lapse of maximum period of 25 years, unless the beneficiary is an incompetent or terminally ill person, or a social-assistance institution
h. A court sentence

At termination, the trust property in the hands of the trustee must be delivered to the corresponding persons, according to the provisions of the trust instrument or court sentence, should there be one; and, in its absence, to the grantor or his or her heirs, in the instances pointed out in items (b), (c), (d), (e), and (f) above, and to the beneficiary in the instances set out under (a) and (g) above.

The maximum legal duration of trusts created for a period longer than 25 years is construed to be that maximum and will be valid, unless the beneficiary is a state unit, a nonprofit social, cultural, scientific, or artistic assistance institution or an incompetent or terminally ill person. In such cases, the period of the trust may be indefinite.

## 5. Prohibited Trusts

Like other Latin American legislations, Guatemalan legislation prescribes the nullity of certain types of trusts, such as

a. Those created in secret
b. Those in which the benefit is granted to many persons successively, who must substitute their predecessor by reason of his or her death, unless the substitution is effected in favor of persons in living or *in ventre mare* at the grantor's death (in other words, Guatemalan law prohibits testamentary substitution)

## B. THE GRANTOR

Under section 767 of the Commerce Code, the grantor must have legal capacity to alienate his or her property, and the beneficiary, to enjoy the benefit of the trust. The said Code prescribes that those persons who are disqualified or unworthy to inherit may not be beneficiaries of a testamentary trust.

Conversely, the Commercial Code empowers the legal representatives of minors, incompetents, and the absent, to create a trust by means of a court authorization. It may also be created by means of a legal representative but only with a power of attorney with that specific purpose.

## C. THE TRUSTEE

Only banks established in the country, credit institutions, and "private investment companies"[3] with authorization by the Monetary Committee (*Junta Monetaria*) may become trustees. The Bank Superintendence, which is under the jurisdiction of the Monetary Committee, is the supervisory authority in those cases where the trustee is a bank or finance institution.[4]

---

3    These companies are regulated by Decree-Law No. 208 and Resolution No. 7556 of the Monetary Committee. Article 1 of Decree-Law No. 208 defined them as those "banking institutions acting as financial intermediaries specializing in investment bank transactions, which promote the creation of productive companies by means of raising and channelling internal and external medium- and long-term resources, which they invest in these companies, whether directly by acquiring shares or a stake, or indirectly by furnishing loans for their organization, development, modification, transformation or merger, so long as they further the development and diversification of production."

4    The Bank Superintendence, regulated by Decree No. 18-200, acts under the general supervision of the Monetary Committee and is the regulator and controlling entity of the Bank of Guatemala, banks, financial entities, credit institutions, securing entities, insurance companies, general deposits, exchange companies, financial holdings, and companies owned by financial entities.

One or more trustees may be designated, in which case they may act jointly or successively, according to the provisions of the trust instrument.

## 1. Rights and Duties

The trustee may carry out all acts necessary for the accomplishment of the objects of the trust, but for the sale, gift, or encumbrance of the trust assets an express power is required, which should be recorded in the trust instrument. If the execution of the trust becomes impossible or manifestly detrimental without alienating or encumbering the assets, and the trustee is not expressly empowered to that end, he or she will be entitled to seek court authorization.

If the trustee alienates or encumbers the assets abusing the powers granted by the agreement or instrument, the grantor or the beneficiary may demand him or her to respond for the damages deriving from the negotiation, as well as provide for his or her removal and the imposition on the trustee of all due penalties.

The trustee enjoys the following rights:

a. To exercise the powers and carry on all the outlays required by the execution of the trust, except for the limitations established by law or in the trust instrument.
b. To exercise all the actions required by the defense of the trust assets.
c. To grant special power of attorneys in relation to the trust purposes.
d. To receive compensation for his or her services, collecting his or her remuneration from the trust's income, preferably. The trustee's fees may be the responsibility of the grantor, the beneficiary, or both with the trustee enjoying preferred status over all other creditors for the collection of fees, credits, and expenses originating in the trust, which should be effected with trust assets.
e. All others requisite to the accomplishment of the object of the trust.

Except for express authorization to the contrary provided in the trust instrument by the grantor, the trustee may only invest in bonds and debt securities widely known to be creditworthy, issued or guaranteed by the government, public entities, financial institutions, banks operating in the country, and private companies whose issuances the Securities Commission has rated as "investment grade."

The trustee is charged with the following duties:

a. To execute the trust according to its constitution and objects.
b. To discharge his or her office with due diligence. The trustee will only be allowed to resign it on justified grounds, which must be qualified by a court.
c. To come into possession of the trust assets in the terms of the trust instrument and watch for their safety and preservation.
d. To keep a detailed account of his or her administration, separately from his or her other operations and render accountings and reports to whom they are due, at least on a yearly basis or when the grantor or the beneficiary should require it.
e. All others inherent to the nature of his or her position.

f. The trustee must clarify that he or she acts in such a capacity, in every act or contract that he or she enters into in the execution of the trust.

## 2. Causes of Removal

Finally, under section 786 of the Commercial Code, the following are the grounds for removal of the trustee:

a. Not complying with the directions contained in the trust instrument
b. Not performing his or her office with due diligence
c. Holding interests that are contrary to those of the trust

The removal of the trustee does not terminate the trust unless his or her substitution is impossible.

## D. THE BENEFICIARY AND THE RESIDUAL BENEFICIARY

The Commercial Code provides that the beneficiary may be any person who has the legal capacity to acquire rights at the time when he or she is entitled to commence enjoyment of the benefits arising from trust property. In addition, it is not a requirement for the trust to be valid that the beneficiary be individually appointed, so long as the trust instrument sets forth the rules for his or her subsequent appointment, the grantor being permitted to appoint him or herself in that capacity.

Under Guatemalan law, the trustee may never be the beneficiary of the same trust (prohibition that is also applicable to guarantee trusts).

## 1. Rights of the Beneficiary

The Commercial Code enumerates the following as the beneficiary's rights:

a. To exercise those deriving from the agreement or trust instrument
b. To demand from the trustee the execution of the trust
c. To request the removal of the trustee on the grounds set out in section 786 of the Commercial Code (which were discussed earlier in Causes of Removal)
d. To challenge the acts that the trustee carries out in bad faith or infringing the provisions regulating the trust and claim the civil recovery of the assets which, as a result of these acts, have left the trust
e. To supervise him or herself or by means of any other persons appointed by him or her at any time the books, accounts, and documentation of the trust, as well as having it audited

A point to be borne in mind is that the rights that the beneficiary may have in the trust are not available to his or her creditors, but the income received by the beneficiary is.

The trust assets may be recorded as having preference over the rights of the beneficiaries at termination of the trust. Where assets that are not subject to registration are involved, the trustee must serve notification to bear this fact in mind at the time of liquidation.

Where no definite beneficiary exists, the rights of the beneficiary fall on the attorney general's office.

## E. TAX TREATMENT

The Commerce Code section 792 provides that the trust instrument and the trust transfer of assets to the trustee are free from tax. Similarly, the return of assets to the trustee at trust termination is tax-exempt.

Further, the contract or act whereby the trustee disposes of or transfers realty to the beneficiary or to third parties will be subject to all the taxes in force at the date of the act or contract, but in the case of testamentary trusts, regarding realty, the tax will be graduated according to the degree of kinship of the grantor with the corresponding beneficiary.

## F. PUBLIC SECTOR TRUSTS

The Budget Organic Act (Decree No. 101-97) regulated for the very first time the possibility to create and administer trusts with governmental assets. Section 33 provides that financial resources that the state allocate with the obligation of reimbursement to its decentralized and autonomous entities for investment in social-benefit projects, and which produce a financial return, may be given in trust. Furthermore, Social Funds may carry on its projects under trust. Trusts will have as trustee any bank of the national banking system. Additionally, the Budget Organic Act section 59, in its relevant part, establishes that the banks that act as trustees in the trusts created by governmental agencies will render accountings on a monthly basis.

In its section 41, the General Budget of Returns and Expenses for Fiscal Year 2006 Act (also valid for fiscal year 2008) provides that the entities of the central governmental administration and decentralized governmental administration that create trusts to carry on projects, and in the cases established in treaties with International Financial Organisms, must fulfill the following:

a. Obtain a favorable opinion of the Ministry of Public Finances, before the creation or amendment of the trust
b. Subject itself to the condition that the Public Credit Committee of the Ministry of Public Finances may control the trust whenever it is considered necessary
c. To register the trust in the Accounting Integrated System (*Sistema de Contabilidad Integrada* [SICOIN])
d. To provide a monthly financial report, including a detailed accounting of returns and expenses, to the Ministry of Public Finances

e. To establish in the trust instrument the obligation of the trustee to provide a copy of the financial statements on a monthly basis, as well as any other information that is requested

f. To select the bank acting as trustee based on its financial solidity, liquidity, and profitability

g. To immediately deposit in the account denominated "Government of the Republic— Ordinary Funds" the proceeds arising from the liquidation of trusts

The Municipal Code (Decree No. 12-2002) allows municipalities to obtain funds in trust.

Finally, in the case of trusts with public sector funds as underlying asset, the General Accounting Auditor (*Contraloría General de Cuentas*) is the governmental control body of all public sector trusts. This entity must report to the Ministry of Public Finances. This control is independent of the one that is carried on by the Bank Superintendence or by a particular audit that the government may determine.

## G. PARTICULAR CASES AND EXPERIENCE

In Guatemala, the trust is a legal institution that has been used repeatedly, not only to implement new banking transactions and management of new investment projects, but also as a tool with a very important social function.

## 1. Housing Promotion Trusts

Trusts exist, for example, aimed at the construction of housing by the government of Guatemala, which allow for the erection of low-cost housing developments with financing that is generally provided by international development institutions, such as the Central American Bank of Economic Integration (*Banco Centroamericano de Integración Económica* [BCIE]). Furthermore, there are several cases of trusts that administer the funds for the conservation and improvement of the national road system (created by Decree No. 134-1996 of the National Congress).

## 2. Agriculture Promotion Trusts

The Agriculture and Nutrition Ministry (MAGA), as a representative of the Guatemalan state, has acted as grantor in many trusts with the object of reactivating and modernizing agricultural activity. Among the trusts are

a. Reactivation and Modernization Agricultural Activity National Fund (*Fondo Nacional para la Reactivación y Modernización de la Actividad Agropecuaria* [FONAGRO])

b. Sierra of the Cuchumatanes Rural Development Project (*Proyecto para el Desarrollo Rural de la Sierra de los Cuchumatanes*)

c.  Land Fund, Peace Agreement (*Fondo de Tierras, Acuerdo de Paz*)
d.  Sustainable Rural Development Project in Ecologically Endangered Areas in the Trifinio Area Region of Guatemala (*Proyecto para el Desarrollo Rural Sostenible en Zonas de Fragilidad Ecológica en la Región del Trifinio Area de Guatemala*–[PRODERT])

## 3.  Guarantee Trusts

In this type of trust, the trustee bank receives assets for guaranteeing the payment of obligations, where the creditor acts as a beneficiary in the event of nonpayment.

The Commercial Code establishes that, in the case of guarantee trusts, and should the debtor incur nonpayment, the trustee may promote the sale of the trust assets in a public auction before a notary public, rendering null and void any other agreement authorizing the trustee to otherwise deliver the assets to the creditor. The trustee of a guarantee trust must be a different person from the creditor. Banking operations with a trust guarantee will be assimilated to credits with real guarantees.

## H.  SECURITIZATION AND INVESTMENT TRUST AGREEMENT

Although there have been no securitization transactions in Guatemala, there is a growing interest in them.

There is not one law that specifically regulates the process of securitization in the Republic of Guatemala. Only the power of trustees to issue trust certificates backed by the trust assets is contemplated in the Commerce Code. These trust certificates have the status of credit securities and only bestow on their holders one or several of the following rights: (a) a percentage of the income of the trust assets; (b) a percentage of the title to said assets, or to the price they fetch by disposing of them; (c) title over a given part of the realty under trust.

As mentioned before in this chapter, the Securities and Goods Market Act (*Ley de Mercados de Valores y Mercancías*) (Decree No. 34-96), under title VII, chapter VI, regulates the investment trust contract. In this connection, article 77 provides that the banks and financial companies may act as trustees of trusts created for investment in publicly offered securities. Also, it provides that, if the issuance of trust certificates is agreed as a result of the creation of the trust, its public offering must be filed at the Registry and, in turn, the trustee must request its registration for it to be quoted in the Exchange, in which case the tax regime of the respective certificates will be the same as that applicable to the bonds issued by private financial companies.

Both the investment trust instrument and its modifications may be recorded by private document, and the issuance and placement of the trust certificates referred to in this article will be subject to only the requirements established by this law to carry out a public offering of securities issued by commercial companies.

As can be seen, although by means of this procedure the grantor could obtain liquidity from nonliquid assets, a wider regulation would be required to create a better legal frame, so that new investments can be lured to the capital market. To achieve this, and considering that the bases of the trust in Guatemala have already been laid and that the vehicle is rather well-known, it would be profitable to consider the adaptation of the trust such as it exists today in Guatemala to the model of financial trust existing, for example, in Argentina and Uruguay.

Finally, certain types of companies called "private financial companies" are empowered to issue securities backed by assets (a type of assets-backed securities). In this way, they issue bonds with specific guarantees (backed by mortgages or pledges) or with general ones (backed by the entire assets). Although bonds with specific guarantees are guaranteed by a credit portfolio, the assets affected to the guarantee remain as the issuer's property.

There is not as yet in Guatemala an appropriate special vehicle to carry out a pure asset securitization, whether through financial trusts (as is the case with Argentina) or securitization companies, after the manner of those created in Bolivia, Ecuador, Chile, and Peru.

Therefore, it is necessary, in view of the popularity and progress made by the trust, to adapt the trust, which would become an excellent mechanism for asset securitization in Guatemala.

# Chapter 16

# Honduras[1]

A. Overview  232
B. The Grantor and the Beneficiary  233
C. The Trustee  234
D. Securitization  237
E. Tax Treatment  239

Honduras included the trust in its legislation in 1950 with the entrance into force of the current Commercial Code. Trust regulations were based on the Mexican law that was in force in the same year.

Trusts were not used at all for several decades, but they are growing and are being used as collateral (guarantee trusts), as legal vehicles of real estate developments, and as part of project finance schemes in infrastructure projects. Currently, it is estimated that there are more than 300 trusts with assets estimated in more than US$1 billion (out of which, approximately one-half are guarantee trusts), the trust activity growing at a fast pace.

Regarding the legal framework, it is important to note that in 1995 a financial legislation reform took place that led to the passing of the Banks and Insurance National Committee Act (*Ley de la Comisión Nacional de Bancos y Seguros*) (Decree No. 155/95 of October 24, 1995) creating the entity regulating financial intermediation activities, and the Financial System Institutions Act (*Ley de Instituciones del Sistema Financiero*) (Decree No. 170/95 of October 31, 1995), which regulates the organization, operation, and liquidation of institutions related to financial intermediation.

By virtue of this reform, the control of banking transactions, which were in the hands of the Honduran Central Bank, was transferred to the Banks and Insurance Committee. In its turn, the Financial System Institutions Act introduced supplementary

---

1  I am indebted to the invaluable assistance of Lic. Ricardo Antonio Montes Belot, who compiled the relevant regulatory material and explained the general framework of trusts in Honduras.

regulations to govern trusts and other financial transactions. This act states that it will regulate trusts, in conjunction with the rules of the Commerce Code (Decree No. 73 of February 16, 1950) and the decrees of the Honduran Central Bank, pursuant to a decision by the Banks and Insurance National Committee. Regulations relating to trusts in the Commerce Code of Honduras, like many other Latin American trust laws, derived from the Mexican legislation in force between 1930 and 1945.

Finally, securitizations are governed by article 253 of the Securities Market Act (Decree No. 8/2001 of February 20, 2001).

## A. OVERVIEW

Article 1033 of the Commerce Code defines trusts as "a legal transaction by virtue of which the bank authorized to operate as trustee is granted the ownership over some given assets, with the mandatory limitation of performing only those acts dictated by the discharge of its lawful and definite object."[2]

The trust may be established by an *inter vivos* act or by will, according to circumstances, and as a unilateral act (emerging only from the declaration of one person), or as an agreement between two or more people.

The trust involves the transfer of certain assets in favor of the trustee and, consequently, the trustee shall be deemed the owner of the rights or assets held in trust.

The trustee shall exercise ownership over the assets and rights granted in trust, in accordance with the following conditions:

a. Such powers shall be exercised toward the purposes that must be carried out, not in the benefit of the trustee.
b. The economic benefit of the trust assets shall fall on the beneficiary.
c. The beneficiary may challenge the acts of the trustee that exceed the functional limits of the office.
d. The assets and rights must return to the grantor after a maximum of thirty years or pass definitely to the beneficiary or to a given person, except for the trusts created in favor of public or charitable legal persons.

Consent in the creation of the trust must be express.

Any class of assets and titles may be object of a trust, except for those, which in accordance with the law, belong strictly to its holder (assets that cannot be transferred because of legal restrictions).

Trust property is affected to the intended purposes, and consequently, only the titles and actions that refer to the said object may be exercised with respect to them, unless the trustee expressly reserves for him or herself those deriving from the trust itself, or those relating to such assets as were acquired legally, prior to the creation of the trust, by the beneficiary or by third parties.

---

2    Commerce Code, Section 1033.

Trusts established in fraud of third parties may be challenged by the interested parties.

Trusts may be established to serve any purpose conceivable as a legal activity, provided they are lawful and definite.

The following are prohibited:

a. Secret trusts
b. Those in which the benefits are granted to several persons successively, who must substitute their predecessor because of his or her death, unless where substitution is carried out in favor of persons who are alive or conceived at the time of the grantor
c. Those whose duration is in excess of thirty years, when a noncharitable or nonpublic entity is appointed as beneficiary

The trust expires by reason of

a. The accomplishment of the object for which it was created
b. The impossibility of that object
c. The impossibility of complying with the suspensive condition on which it is dependent or not having obtained within the period stipulated at the creation of the trust, or in the absence of that, within twenty years following its creation
d. Compliance with the resolutory condition to which it is subject
e. Express agreement between grantor and beneficiary
f. Revocation done by the grantor when he or she reserved for him or herself that right when the trust was created
g. When the trustee ceases in his or her office, and substitution is not possible

Once the trust has expired, such assets under it as remain in the hands of the trustee shall be returned to the grantor or his or her heirs. In the case of real estate, the transfer will be produced by the registration with the Public Registry of the trust instrument.

## B. THE GRANTOR AND THE BENEFICIARY

The grantor may create the trust in his or her favor, but the trustee may never be the beneficiary.

Any natural or legal person capable of effecting the application of assets implied by the trust may be a grantor, as well as the competent judicial or administrative authorities, where it is the duty of these authorities, or of the persons by them appointed, to exercise custodianship, preservation, administration, liquidation, distribution, or alienation of these assets.

Any natural or legal persons who have the necessary capacity to receive the benefits the trust implies can be a beneficiary. The grantor may assign several beneficiaries to receive simultaneously or successively the benefit of the trust. Where there are two or more beneficiaries, and their will must be consulted, provided it is not stipulated in the trust instrument, decisions shall be made on a majority basis, computing representations, not persons. In the event of a tie, the civil judge from the domicile of the trustee shall decide.

The trust shall be valid even if it is created without determination of a beneficiary in particular, as long as its object is lawful and definite.

The beneficiary shall have, besides those rights conferred on him or her by virtue of the trust instrument, the right to demand its execution to the trustee; that of attacking the validity of the acts he or she carries out in his or her detriment, in bad faith or in excess of the powers which by virtue of the act of settlement or of the statutes he or she is entitled to carry out and, when it is due, that of making civil recovery of the assets, which as a result of those acts, have abandoned the trust. Where there is no definite beneficiary, or he or she is legally incapable, the rights as beneficiary will fall on the person who exercises custody, or the guardian or curator, or on the attorney general's office, depending on the case.

The following rights are vested in the grantor:

a. Those he or she reserved for him or herself to exercise directly over the trust assets.
b. Revoking the trust according to the aforementioned provisions and demanding the removal of the trustee. When the trustee, when requested, does not render an accounting of his or her administration within a period of 15 days, or when he or she is declared by a court guilty of the losses or injuries sustained by the trust property, or liable for those losses or injuries for gross negligence, his or her removal shall be enforced.
c. Appointing a new trustee in the scenario described above.
d. Securing the return of the assets at termination of the trust, if no provisions had been made otherwise.
e. Demanding an accounting.
f. Instituting civil or criminal actions against the trustee.
g. All those expressly indicated and not incompatible with the minimum legal rights of the trustee, or of the beneficiary, or with the nature of the trust.

## C. THE TRUSTEE

As in most Latin American countries, there is a restriction on the persons who may act as trustees. In the case of Honduras, only authorized banking institutions may act as such.

Where at trust creation no bank is appointed, that elected by the beneficiary shall be deemed effective, or in his or her absence the civil judge of the location of the assets, or the most valuable asset should they be located in several places.

The grantor may appoint many trustees for them to jointly or successively execute the trust, setting the order and terms in which they will be substituted. Except for the provisions of the trust instrument, when the trustee does not accept, either through resignation or removal he or she ceases in the performance of his or her office, another shall be appointed in replacement. Such a substitution being impossible, the trust will expire.

The trustee appointed by the beneficiary or by the court is obliged to accept the office, and may only decline or resign with sufficient cause, as determined by the civil judge of the domicile of the trustee. Only the following are to be deemed as sufficient cause:

a. That the beneficiary cannot, or declines to, receive the benefits or assets in accordance with the trust instrument
b. That the grantor, his or her heirs, or the beneficiary, as it may be, decline to pay the stipulated compensation to the trustee
c. That the assets or rights held in trust do not yield sufficient product to cover these compensations

Concerning the consideration in favor of the trustee, the Commercial Code provides that the trustee shall be compensated. The payment of the compensation may be charged to the grantor, his or her heirs, or the beneficiary. The beneficiary may also be authorized to directly collect the agreed amount out of the product of the assets held in trust.

The trustee shall have all the rights and actions required for the execution of the trust, except for statutory provisions and the limitations established at trust creation. It shall be obliged to perform the trust in accordance with the trust instrument and must at all times act as an independent businessperson, being responsible for the losses or injuries that the assets sustain through his or her fault.

The trustee shall perform his or her duties and shall exercise his or her powers by means of one or more officials specially appointed to the effect, and for whose acts its office shall be liable either directly or indirectly, notwithstanding the civil or criminal liabilities which they incur personally.

The Banks Superintendence may at any time veto the appointment of the officials the trustee has made, or decide on their removal. It shall suffice to accredit the status of these officials with the registration of the act, where record is kept of the appointment by the committee or testimony of the general power of attorney granted him or her by the trustee, even when there is no mention in the act or in the power of attorney of the subject matter or business in which they hold the representation.

The agents of the trustee may appoint general or special agents and even substitute, if they are authorized to do so. In this case, the substitution must be communicated to the Banks Superintendence, so that their right of veto may be exercised.

As established in the Credit Securities and Transactions General Act of Mexico (*Ley General de Títulos y Operaciones de Crédito*), in the act of settlement of the trust, or in its reforms requiring the beneficiary's consent, the grantors may provide the creation of a technical or funds distribution committee, furnish the rules for its operation and determine its powers. When the trustee acts abiding by the provisions or agreements of this committee, it shall be free of any liability.

In any kind of transaction involving acquisition or substitution of assets, or investment of money or liquid funds, the trustee must strictly abide by the directions of the grantor. When the directions of the trust were not sufficiently precise, or when the investment decisions were left to the discretion of the trustee, they shall be carried out, necessarily, in securities that offer the greatest assurance in the trustee's judgment, the investment and the legal notification to the registry being executed in the shortest possible period.

In any kind of transaction involving receiving or disposing of liquid funds that are not to be applied immediately to a specific object and with respect to which neither the law nor the trust instrument determined the use whereto they must be put, the trustee will invest them in the manner most adequate to its objects, which represents the greatest security to the beneficiary or to the end whereto they are intended, taking special account of the investment and its income. When the buying and selling of securities, currency, merchandise, or other goods object of a regular organized market is concerned (such as a stock exchange), and with respect to which, when directing a given transaction, the date or the quotation at which they shall be made were not recorded, the transactions shall be carried out 48 hours subsequent to the date when the transaction was directed or when the availability of the assets was had. If the market conditions did not allow for the transaction to be carried out within this period, it will be executed as soon as possible. In the event of the market having suffered in detriment of the client a variation which represents no less than 10 percent of the value of the assets after the date when the transaction was directed, the trustee must request, through the quickest means, ratification or rectification of the directions, unless that was impossible because of the nature of the trust or that it had been dispensed expressly with this duty or also when, in the trustee's judgment, any further delay in the execution could bring about more serious damage.

Of any income, product, or revenues of liquidation received that the trustee carries out in the discharge of its duties, it will notify the beneficiary within 48 hours following collection. Likewise, it will notify within the same period any investment, acquisition, or substitution of assets, communicating the details for the identification of those assets. Where, because of the nature of the trust or of an express provision of the grantor, this notification must be suppressed, the institution must, within such a period, record the transaction, with the said details, in a special registry, foliated and sealed, which the trustee shall keep in rigorous secret.

The violation of the confidentiality proper to this type of transaction, even before the authorities or courts in trials or claims other than those brought by the grantor or beneficiary against the trustee, or vice versa, shall make the institution liable for the damages occasioned, without precluding the corresponding criminal liabilities.

For its part, article 46 of the Financial System Institutions Act provides that the trust funds must be managed in strict accordance with the provisions of the trust instrument, and may be invested in fixed-term savings accounts, securities, short- and long-term credit transactions and others approved by the Honduran Central Bank. Trustees may not invest the liquid resources managed in trust in their own credit transactions as banks. In the cases where the trust instruments so allow investing those resources in loans, the trustee shall assume the credit risk.

## D. SECURITIZATION

The Securities Market Act defines securitization as the process whereby a patrimony is constituted with the sole object to back the payment of the titles granted to the holders of the issued securities, charged to that patrimony. Additionally, it includes the transfer of the assets to that patrimony and the issuance of the relevant securities.

Also, private banks, savings and loans associations, and financial institutions are barred from housing stock exchange dealers, leasing companies, or any other auxiliary credit business or business different from financial services, in the same premises where they carry out their authorized activities. They are also forbidden from using names, colors, or distinctive signs that may somehow misrepresent that the financial institution is responsible for the said transactions or that it guarantees them.

The processes of securitization are authorized, and it is up to the Banks and Insurance National Committee to issue, according to internationally accepted norms, the special regulations concerning such processes. It is also its duty to exercise the control and supervision of the natural and legal persons involved in the securitization processes. The Banks and Insurance National Committee is also empowered to issue the rules to which the said persons must subject their performance.

In an effort to avoid the repetition of unsuccessful securitizations that affected the image of the vehicle with the general public, Circular D-41199, Regulation 419-I2/99 of the Board of Directors of the Honduran Central Bank prescribed that, notwithstanding all other legal regulations applicable to trusts, those that permit the issuance of participation certificates shall be subject to the following regulations:

a. In each trust, the powers must be established clearly, among other things, for the trustee to carry out the issuance and placing of such securities.

b. The projects of creation of each trust in which the issuance of certificates is authorized must be submitted to the Banks and Insurance National Committee for its knowledge and other relevant ends.

c. The face value of the issues including outstanding interest, should there be any, must not be in excess of 60 percent of the value of the trust assets as determined by a valuation expert, duly registered with the Banks and Insurance National Committee, except in those cases where, considering the characteristics of such assets, the said Committee authorizes a higher percentage. In addition, the value of such assets must not include revaluations done prior to the creation of the trust, unless they are progress in works or development of the project object of the trust.

d. The resources obtained by means of the placing of securities may only be used to accomplish the objects stated in the trust.

e. The maturity period (redemption) of the securities must not be shorter than the period foreseen for the recovery of the resources; except when within the rules and restrictions to that effect set forth by the Banks and Insurance National Committee, the trustee bank grants the trust a standby credit for those cases in which the investors decide to renew the investment.

f. Only fixed-income participation certificates may be issued when evidence exists that the trust assets are capable of generating sufficient income for their payment, or when it is foreseen that the resources obtained for the placement of securities will raise sufficient income for the distribution of such yields.

g. The trustee is under an obligation to prepare and submit for review to the Banks and Insurance National Committee a prospectus of the participation securities for the knowledge of the purchasers and its due publicity, which shall contain at least the following:

    i. A detailed account of the trust assets

    ii. A financial statement of the trust duly audited by external auditors

    iii. Clear indication that the certificate participation is not a certificate of deposit

    iv. The warning that the securities only have the backing of the trust

    v. Clarification that the trustee bank does not guarantee the fiduciary participation securities

    vi. The powers of the trustee bank to effect the issuance of such securities

    vii. Any further information that the Banks and Insurance National Committee considers necessary

h. Prominent in the issued participation certificates must be recorded the name of the trust, the warning that the trustee bank is not liable for the payment of the obligations and that they are only backed by the trust assets and by the income generated by them, as well as any further information that the Banks and Insurance National Committee deems indispensable.

i. Each trust must keep accounts separate from those of the trustee and of other trusts established, under the rules prescribed by the Banks and Insurance National Committee.

j. The banks acting as trustees must furnish audited financial statements of each trust and of the grantors to the Banks and Insurance National Committee with the frequency established by the said Committee, as well as the additional information required by it.

k. If a trustee undertakes to pay off the obligations of a trust or the redemption of participation certificates without indicating that payment will be made by the trust, those obligations shall be deemed the bank's, according to the restrictions provided for its transactions under the Financial Institutions System Act.

l. No bank shall accept the participation certificates issued by the trusts where it is a trustee as guarantee of its loans.

m. No bank shall be a trustee when the trust involves the issuance of participation certificates, if the grantor or the beneficiaries bear any relationship with the bank.

Regarding the entrance into force of the preceding rule, it is said that any issuance of participation certificates, from the time this rule comes into force, must comply with the regulations herein contained and, with respect to the trusts created with priority to this rule coming into effect, trustee banks that issued participation certificates must take any necessary measures, in the period set forth by the Banks and Insurance National Committee, for such trusts to comply with the rules hereby set forth.

## E. TAX TREATMENT

Income tax was first established by decree on November 10, 1949, and became effective in 1950. It was an adaptation of the Mexican income tax law. The current law was promulgated by Decree-Law No. 25 of December 20, 1963.

Income tax finds its constitutional basis in section 351 of the Honduran Constitution, which establishes that "the tax system will be ruled by the principles of legality (no taxation without representation), proportionality, generality, and equity, according to the economic capacity of the taxpayer",[3] and under section 109, which lays down the rule that "taxes will not be confiscatory. No one shall be subject to the payment of taxes that had not been legally established by the National Congress, in ordinary sessions."[4]

Section 20 of the Tax Code establishes that taxpayers are, among others, the entities, organizations, or legal arrangements that constitute a functional or patrimonial unit affected to a certain purpose. Furthermore, section 12 of the Income Tax Law provides that the "patrimonies administered by any person due to an instruction, trust or affected to certain purposes" are taxpayers of income tax.

Honduras adopted the worldwide income principle. Therefore, trusts created in Honduras must pay taxes for their income of Honduran and foreign source.

Although it clearly derives from the applicable rules that trusts are taxpayers, there are several doubts regarding tax treatment of trusts, and the most accepted practice is to consider the trust as some sort of pass-through entity, the grantor being responsible for paying taxes.

Regarding tax rates, individuals are subject to progressive rates from 0 percent to 25 percent, and legal entities are subject to a flat 30 percent (which is the result of a tax rate of 25 percent plus an additional 5 percent). Capital gains are subject to a 10 percent rate both for individuals and legal entities. Interests are subject to a 10 percent withholding tax, and no income tax is applicable to the beneficiary of the payment. Payments to foreign beneficiaries are subject to rates that vary from 5 up to 35 percent, and it must be stressed that there are no tax treaties in place to avoid double taxation. There is a net worth tax of 1 percent that is a tax credit computable against income tax. Finally, there is a 12 percent sale tax.

---

3     Constitution of Honduras, section 351.
4     Constitution of Honduras, first and second paragraphs of section 109.

# Chapter 17

# Mexico[1]

A. Overview  242
   1. Formalities, Registration, and Enforceability of Trust Instruments  244
   2. Trust Termination  245
B. The Grantor  247
   1. The Technical Committee  247
C. The Beneficiary  248
D. The Trustee  249
   1. Credit Institutions  249
   2. General Rules on Trustees  252
   3. Relevant Case Law  253
E. Guarantee Trusts  254
F. Experience and Particular Cases  258
   1. Trusts in the Restricted Zones (*Fideicomisos de Zonas Prohibidas*)  258
   2. Governmental or Public Sector Trusts  260
   3. Trust of Shares of Financial Entities under Restructuring  260
G. Securitization  261
H. Income Tax  265

Compared with the rest of Latin America, Mexico has seen a very long tradition of the use of trusts.[2] As explained in detail in Chapter 2 (Section A1) about the antecedents of trusts in Latin America, despite several attempts in the first decades of the twentieth

---

1    This chapter was possible thanks to the valuable comments of Adolfo González Olhovich. who guided my understanding of Mexican law and the trust market and provided an excellent compilation of legal and case law material.

2    It was said, back in 1998, that "trusts are business transactions which for more than sixty years have been carried out by our country's banking institutions, and also since 1993, with some restrictions, by stock exchange agents, insurance institutions and surety companies." Sergio Monserrit Ortíz Soltero, El Fideicomiso Mexicano, at ix (1998).

century, an example being the Trust Banks Act of June 30, 1926,[3] trusts were regulated by the Securities and Credit Transactions General Act (*Ley General de Títulos y Operaciones de Crédito* or LGTOC) passed in 1932 and amended several times since then.[4] Summarizing the explanation in Chapter 2, the Mexican trust was modeled by Pablo Macedo (who was a member of the committee appointed to draw up the 1932 LGTOC) after the U.S. trust,[5] influenced by the works of Pierre Lepaulle.[6]

## A. OVERVIEW

The LGTOC defines trust in section 381, where it establishes that by virtue of a trust the grantor transmits to the trustee the property of some assets to be applied to a given lawful purpose, entrusting the performance of that end to the trustee.[7]

On the legal nature of trusts, Mexican doctrine is consistent in holding that "it is an agreement, a legal relationship between two or more persons, because there must always be a grantor and a trustee; that relationship establishes rights and duties between two parties."[8] Thus, case law stated that "it is true that trusts are perfected through the appointment and acceptance by the trustee of such an office; this being so for, in accordance with section 346 [current section 381 quoted earlier] of the LGTOC, the trustee shall realize the objects of the trust."[9] And also expressed that "a trust is an agreement

---

3   It is noteworthy that no trust was established under this act.

4   The Mexican "trust corresponds to the U.S. legal notion of a trust and was first introduced in Mexico in its Credit Institutions Act of 1924. However, it was not until 1932, in the General Act of Credit Instruments and Credit Operations, that it was recognized as a valid, autonomous legal transaction." Jorge A. Vargas, *Fideicomisos: Real Estate Trusts in Mexico's Restricted Zone, in* 1 Mexican Law: A Treatise for Legal Practitioners and International Investors 352 (Jorge A. Vargas, ed., 1998).

5   A comparative analysis of the U.S. trust and the Mexican one is attempted in Miguel Acosta Romero & Pablo Roberto Almazán Alaniz, Tratado teórico práctico de fideicomiso 12 (3rd ed. 1999).

   For a comparison between Mexican and U.S. law, see Jorge A. Vargas, *Contrasting Legal Differences Between the U.S. and Mexico: Legal Actors, Sources, Courts and Federal Agencies, in* 1 Mexican Law: A Treatise for Legal Practitioners and International Investors 1–45 (Jorge A. Vargas, ed., 1998).

6   According to the claims of Acosta Romero and Almazán Alaniz, quoting Rodolfo Batiza, the authors point as a first antecedent of the Mexican trust to one created in North America, on realty located in Mexico, in favor of North American trustees as mortgage creditors, and in the benefit of the holders of the bonds issued to finance the construction of railways by the Mexican railroad companies. Romero & Alaniz, *supra* note 5, at 17.

7   Villagordoa Lozano defined trusts as "the fiduciary transaction whereby the grantor transfers title to given assets and rights to the trustee, who is under a duty to dispose of the assets and exercise the rights for the performance of the purposes set forth in the benefit of the beneficiary." José Manuel Villagordoa Lozano, Doctrina General del Fideicomiso 141 (3rd ed. 1998).

8   Romero & Alaniz, *supra* note 5, at 189.

9   First Collegiate Civil Court, Third Circuit. *Amparo directo* No. 951/91. Banco Mexicano Somex, SNC, April 9, 1992. Semanario Judicial de la Federación [S.J.F.], Vol. X, Nov. 1992, p. 259 (Mex.).

wherein the assets are intended for the object of the transaction, and representation in defense of the interests falls on the trustee. . . . That is why it is erroneous to claim that we are in the presence of a moral company or person, since trusts are agreements and, as such, they cannot be deemed as collective legal persons."[10] Finally, it has been said that a trust "is a legal transaction whereby the grantor applies one or more assets to a given object in the benefit of another, entrusting its performance to a bank receiving ownership of the assets, which implies the creation of a patrimony distinct from that of the parties under the agreement, which means that the title to the trust assets passes from the ownership of the grantor to that of the trustee; so that it may be concluded that trusts involve the constitution of a real right which is not affected by the procedural action of the seizure, for they are not rights or credits of the same nature."[11]

With respect to the transfer of the ownership of the assets to the trust, and as follows from the provisions of the LGTOC, for a trust to exist, a transfer of assets must be carried out, for unless this happens, in the terms of such a regulation, it is not a trust but some other fiduciary service. Put differently, the assets must abandon the patrimony of the grantor to enter the trusts' separate patrimony so that a trust exists.

Under the second paragraph of section 386 of the LGTOC, trust assets shall be deemed affected to the intended trust purposes only and, hence, only the rights and actions relating to those purposes may be exercised, except: (a) those expressly reserved by the grantor, (b) those deriving for him or her from the trust itself, or (c) those acquired legally over those assets, prior to the creation of the trust, by the beneficiary or by third parties. The trustee must record and keep trust assets separately from his or her own estate.

Along this line of reasoning, case law stated that

> A trust is a legal transaction whereby the grantor constitutes a special-purpose patrimony, whose title is granted to the trustee, for the accomplishment of a given object, but when it is claimed that this is a special-purpose patrimony, what is said in particular is that it is different from the own patrimonies of the trust parties, [that is,] it is different from the patrimonies of the grantor, of the trustee and of the beneficiary. It is a special-purpose patrimony affected to a given object, under title and execution of the trustee, who holds all the rights and actions aimed at the performance of the trust, naturally in accordance with its establishment rules and regulations. The assets given in trust are transferred, therefore, out of the patrimony of the grantor, to remain as separate or special-purpose, under legal title of the trustee, inasmuch as it is necessary for compliance with the objects of the aforementioned application, objects according to which (and in accordance to what was agreed), that title holder may appear in court as a plaintiff, or as a defendant, as well as sell, rent, transfer, etcetera.[12]

---

10 Third Collegiate Civil Court, First Circuit. Action in review No. 153/95. Nacional Financiera, SNC, as trustee of INFOTEC. January 26, 1995.

11 Third Collegiate Civil Court, Third Circuit. Action in review No. 653/91. Cristino Alcalá Barba. February 13, 1992. Semanario Judicial de la Federación [S.J.F.], Vol. X, July 1992, p. 362 (Mex.).

12 *Amparo directo* No. 5567/74. Banco Internacional Inmobiliario, SA, June 15, 1979. Quoted by Romero Alaniz, *supra* note 5, at 548.

As to the assets that may be object of a trust, the LGTOC provides in the first paragraph of its section 386 that they may be of all classes and titles, except those which, by law, are strictly personal to its title holder.

The LGTOC provides in section 394 that the following are forbidden:

a. Secret trusts.
b. Those in which the benefit is granted to several persons in succession who must be substituted for death of the predecessor, unless the substitution is carried out in favor of persons in being or already conceived, at the death of the grantor.
c. Those whose duration is longer than fifty years, when a legal person is appointed as beneficiary who is not a public person or a charitable institution. However, they may be established for a period above fifty years when the object of the trust is the upkeep of nonprofit science or art museums. Section 85 of the Credit Institutions Act provides an exception to this rule for trusts created by the federal government and declared of "public interest by it."

## 1. Formalities, Registration, and Enforceability of Trust Instruments

The LGTOC section 387 provides the creation of the trust must always be recorded in writing.

Trusts whose object falls on realty must be registered with the Property Department of the Public Registry of the place where the assets are located. The trust shall be effective against third persons, in this case, after the date of registration in the Registry.[13]

Conversely, trusts falling on personalty shall come into effect against third parties from the date the following requirements are met:[14]

a. Where a nonnegotiable credit or personal right is concerned, from the time the debtor is notified of the trust
b. Where a certificated security is concerned, because it is indorsed to the trustee, and record is made in the issuer's accounts, where appropriate
c. Where a tangible asset or bearer securities are concerned, from the time they are in the possession of the trustee

The LGTOC provides in the final paragraph of section 386 that the trust created in fraud of third parties may at any time be challenged for nullity by the interested parties.

Regarding the effects of section 388, even in the case that the trustee has not accepted its office, case law has established that

It is true that trusts are perfected with the appointment and acceptance of the trustee in charge; and this is so because, under the provisions of section 346 [current

---

13    LGTOC § 388.
14    LGTOC § 389.

section 381 quoted earlier] of the LGTOC, it shall be the trustee that will accomplish the objects of the trust. Nevertheless, that does not prevent, under section 353 [current section 388] of the named Act, the trust instrument from becoming effective against third parties with respect to trust assets from the time when it is recorded in the Real Estate Public Registry, although the trustee which is to execute it had not been named at the time of the creation. . . . Hence, the interpretation and broadness that must be conferred upon the term "Trust" referred in the named section 353 [current section 388], spanning [sic] from the trust instrument which, once recorded in the Public Registry, shall come into effect against third parties, as it is understood that as from that event the trust assets formally abandon the grantor's patrimony, which they do physically once the trustee agrees to act as such.[15]

Finally, trusts established in fraud of third parties may at any time be challenged as null by the interested parties.[16]

## 2. Trust Termination

As concerns trust termination, LGTOC provides the grounds for expiration in its section 392:

a. Accomplishment of the object for which the trust was created
b. Impossibility of complying with that object
c. Impossibility of meeting the suspensive condition whereon it depends, or failure to be complied with within the period stipulated at creation or, absent that, within a period of twenty years following its creation
d. Accomplishment of the resolutory condition to which it was subjected
e. Written agreement between grantor, trustee, and beneficiary
f. Revocation made by the grantor, when he or she has expressly reserved that right in the trust instrument
g. In the case ruled by the final paragraph of section 386 of the LGTOC (a trust established in fraud of third parties that is challenged as null by the interested parties)
h. In the case ruled by section 392 bis of the LGTOC

Section 392 bis of the LGTOC establishes that in the event that the trustee could not collect his or her fees, established in the trust instrument, for three or more years, the trustee can terminate the trust without responsibility. In such a case, the trustee must notify the settlor and the beneficiary of his or her decision to terminate the trust based on the lack of payment of his or her fees and establish a 15-day period so that they can make the payment. If the fees are not paid within the said period, the trustee must transfer the trust assets to the settlor or the beneficiary in accordance with the

---

15  First Collegiate Court, Third Circuit. *Amparo directo* No. 951/91. Banco Mexicano Somex, SNC, April 9, 1992. Semanario Judicial de la Federación [S.J.F.], Vol. X, Nov. 1992, p. 259 (Mex.).

16  LGTOC § 386 last paragraph.

instructions in the trust instrument. In the event that, after reasonable efforts following the procedure established by section 1070 of the Commercial Code,[17] the trustee does not know where to notify the settlor and the beneficiary, the trustee may (a) in the case of liquid assets, transfer them to the global account ruled by section 61 of the Credit Institutions Act (*Ley de Instituciones de Crédito*),[18] and (b) if the assets are not liquid ones, they can be liquidated and transferred to the said global account.

Regarding other grounds for termination not provided under the law,[19] those may be: (a) lapse of period to which the trust is subject (which currently is a maximum of fifty years and used to be thirty years), (b) total destruction of the trust assets, (c) resignation of the sole beneficiary, (d) merging of the capacities of trustee and the sole beneficiary, except for those cases specially provided, and (e) termination of the office of the trustee and impossibility of substitution.[20]

Touching on the termination of trusts, case law has held that

> Seeing that the object for which the trust instrument originating the action (real estate development) was established could not be accomplished without securing the building permit and the permit of land use in the stipulated period, which the defendant contracted as obligations, as well as that the said period has already elapsed, which leads to [considering that] the said trust was conditioned to the named securing of licenses and permits; since such an event could or could not occur[,] it is possible to conclude that since no such requisite was fulfilled, this triggers the grounds for termination of the trust, provided in [section 392] of the LGTOC, which prescribes that the trust expires [because of] the suspensive condition not taking place within the period stipulated at the creation of the trust.[21]

Once the trust has expired, the assets still in the hands of the trustee shall be restored by it to the grantor or the beneficiary, according to the trust instrument instructions. In the event of doubt, the competent judge shall determine the destination of the assets. For this return to be effective, in the case of realty or of real rights over them, it shall suffice that the trustee so declares it, and that this declaration is filed with the Real Estate Registry where the trust had been registered. Trustees shall pay compensation to the beneficiaries for any act done in bad faith or in excess of his or her faculties in the execution of the trust that damaged the beneficiaries.[22]

In addition, the trustee is entitled to demand a releasing document and payment of the fees and expenses due him or her, ensuring that the payment of taxes, dues, or any

---

17   Section 1070 of the Commercial Code provides that the information regarding the address must be requested to the Official Registry of Persons and should there not be in such registry any information regarding the address or if such information is not correct, an advertisement must be published for three consecutive days in a national and in a local newspaper.

18   Basically, after three years in such account, if the amount is a low one, the assets became state-owned assets.

19   *See* Romero & Alaniz, *supra* note 5, at 334.

20   *Cf.* LGTOC § 385 last paragraph.

21   Fifth Collegiate Civil Court, First Circuit, *Amparo directo* No. 5425/95, Inmobiliaria Holsa, SA de CV, November 16, 1995. Semanario Judicial de la Federación y su Gaceta [S.J.F.G.], Vol. III, Jan. 1996, p. 290 (Mex.).

22   LGTOC § 393.

other tax burden generated by the trust, as well as any liability related to personnel had the trustee hired any, has been duly covered.[23]

## B. THE GRANTOR

Section 384 of the LGTOC provides that only: (a) natural or legal persons who have the necessary capacity to transfer the property to the trust; and (b) competent judiciary and administrative authorities, can be settlors.

As to the rights of the grantor, he or she may reserve some given rights at the creation of the trust. Among them, for example, is the right to revoke the trust[24] and the right to request an accounting from the trustee.[25] The grantor also has the power to appoint a technical committee[26] in the trust instrument and provide the rules for its operation.

## 1. The Technical Committee

According to Acosta Romero and Almazán Alaniz, the origin of the technical committee is unknown. It was the Credit Institutions and Auxiliary Organizations General Act of May 31, 1941, that the included the provision relating to this body, which is reproduced almost entirely by the Credit Institutions Act article 80. These authors claimed that they believe the Technical Committee "to be reminiscent of American Law, in which trustees seek assistance from skilled, proficient and competent persons to distribute funds which are delivered to them, thus covering their responsibility," adding with respect to the banking use of the concept that "it is not in every trust that there exists a Technical Committee but only in those whose management makes it necessary and whose trust property is so important that the grantor deems it convenient to establish this Technical Committee." Finally, the authors conclude that that in private trusts unlike public sector trusts it is not a frequent practice in Mexico.[27]

Monserrit Ortíz Soltero explained that the technical committee "is a body with no legal status, composed of a given number of natural and/or legal persons, created by the grantor and/or the beneficiary of the trust at the trust instrument, or in its modifications, in order to define criteria, provide for contractual lacunae, foresee, and possibly

---

23 ROMERO & ALANIZ, *supra* note 5, at 344.
24 *Cf.* LGTOC § 392 (already quoted).
25 The second paragraph of section 84 of the Credit Institutions Act (*Ley de Instituciones de Crédito*) reads: "Legal actions to request an accounting, to demand the liability of credit institutions and to request the removal shall fall on the beneficiaries or their legal representatives, in any case in the measure of their interests, and in the absence of these on the attorney general's office, notwithstanding the possibility of the grantor reserving for himself the right to exercise this action in the act of settlement or in its modifications."
26 ROMERO & ALANIZ, *supra* note 5, at 138.
27 ROMERO & ALANIZ, *supra* note 5, at 141–142.

solve, controversies which may exist between the parties, in the view of the diversity of the interests of the beneficiaries."[28]

## C. THE BENEFICIARY

As to those who may become beneficiaries, the LGTOC sets forth in its section 382 that any natural or legal person who has the necessary capacity to receive the benefit entailed by the trust can be a beneficiary. The beneficiary can be appointed in the trust instrument or in a subsequent act of the settlor. Trusts shall be valid even when they are created with no mention of the beneficiary, as long as their object be lawful and definite, and there is evidence of the acceptance of the office by the trustee.

The third and fourth paragraphs of section 382 of the LGTOC set forth that the trust that is created in favor of the trustee is null and void, except for those guarantee trusts where, on creation, the ownership of the trust assets is transferred in guarantee of commercial loans granted by the trustee. In this hypothesis, the parties must agree to the terms and conditions to settle any possible conflict of interests among them.

The grantor may appoint several beneficiaries, so that they simultaneously or successively receive, the benefit of the trust, with the limitation established in section 394 of the LGTOC (in cases where trust instrument establishes that the benefit is granted to several persons in succession who must be substituted for death of the predecessor, the substitution must be carried out in favor of persons in being or already conceived at the death of the grantor). Where a trust is established with two or more beneficiaries and their will should be consulted, as long as it is not provided in the trust instrument, the decisions shall be made by the majority of votes computed by representation, not by persons. In the event of a draw, the court in the first instance from the place of residence of the trustee shall decide.[29]

The beneficiary, in addition to the rights granted to him or her in the trust instrument, shall be entitled to: (a) demand the execution of the trust purposes from the trustee; (b) challenge the validity of the acts that the trustee makes to his or her detriment, in bad faith or in excess of the powers which, by virtue of the trust instrument or of the law, are his or her, and (c) where appropriate, that of making civil recovery of the assets which, as a result of those acts, have abandoned the trust property. When no definite trustee exists or when he or she is incapable, the rights mentioned before shall fall on the person who exercises custodianship, the custodian or the attorney general's office, as the case may be.[30]

Regarding the nature of the rights of the beneficiaries, case law stated that "the beneficiaries could never have title to the realty in view of the legal nature of the trust instrument. Thus, if at a given time such a trust still being in effect, the rights that the beneficiaries held in that capacity could be singled out for seizure, by reason of their being in the beneficiaries' patrimony, the same does not hold for the property in the

---

28    SOLTERO, *supra* note 2, at 124.
29    LGTOC § 383.
30    LGTOC § 390.

realty under the trust, whose legal title, under express provision of the law, is reserved to the trustee."[31]

As mentioned before, under section 84 of the Credit Institutions Act, the beneficiary has the right to request from the trustee the rendering of an account of his or her administration within a period of 15 business days.

## D. THE TRUSTEE

Regarding who can act as a trustee in Mexico, section 385 of the LFTOC lays down the fundamental rule: Only legal persons expressly authorized by law can be trustees. Along this line, credit institutions are expressly authorized by the Credit Institutions Act. Further, insurance companies[32] and stock exchange brokers,[33] even if more restrictively, may also be trustees under the statutes governing them.

## 1. Credit Institutions

The Credit Institutions Act (*Ley de Instituciones de Crédito*) section 46 establishes that "credit institutions can only carry on the following activities . . . XV. To carry out trust transactions included in LGTOC." Therefore, credit institutions are allowed to act as trustee in Mexico subject to the regulation established in the Act that is briefly commented on in the following paragraphs.

Section 79 of the Credit Institutions Act provides for trust transactions that credit institutions shall keep separate books for each agreement, recording therein and in their own books funds and other assets, securities or rights entrusted to them, as well as the increases or decreases because of the trust income or expenses, respectively. Invariably, the balances of the accounts in the books of the credit institution must

---

31 First Collegiate Court, Fifth Circuit. Semanario Judicial de la Federación [S.J.F.], Vol. XIV, Dec. 1994. Action in review No. 90/94. Víctor Genaro Padilla Ruiz. August 11, 1994 (Mex.).

32 Section 34, subsection IV, of the Insurance Institutions and Mutual Society General Act (*Ley General de Instituciones y Sociedades Mutualistas de Seguros*) provides that insurance companies can only be trustees in transactions related to the insurance activity, regarding administration trusts with insurance payments as underlying assets. Furthermore, insurance companies can be trustees of guarantee trusts (as explained in Secton E of this chapter). In the case of life insurance companies, businesses trusts will be considered related that have as their main purpose the administration of individual pension funds, annuities, insurance payments, and employee retirement plans. Insurance companies are subject to the LGTOC rules described in this chapter.

33 Sections 183 to 187 of the Securities Market Act (*Ley de Mercado de Valores*) provide the rules applicable to stock exchange brokers (*casas de bolsa*) when being trustees. The main points of the said sections are similar to the ones described for credit institutions in this chapter, the difference being that unlike credit institutions, which have no limits to the trusts they can accept as trustees, section 183 of the Securities Market Act provides that stock exchange brokers can only be trustees in transactions related to their activity. Stock exchange brokers are subject to the LGTOC rules described in this chapter.

coincide with those of the separate books. The last paragraph of the above article prescribes that "in no case shall these assets be affected to other liabilities than those deriving from the trust, agency, commission or custodianship itself, or those to which third parties are entitled against them under the law."

Section 80 of the Credit Institutions Act has several fundamental rules:

a. Credit institutions must carry out their activities and faculties as trustees through fiduciary delegates (*delegados fiduciarios*).[34]
b. The credit institution will be responsible for the damages caused because of the lack of fulfillment of the terms and conditions established in the trust instrument of the law.[35]
c. The trust instrument or subsequent instruments may establish a technical committee, its rules, and faculties. If the credit institution acts following the opinions of such committee, it would be free of any responsibility.

The personnel of credit institutions directly or exclusively employed in the operation of trusts shall not form part of the institution's staff but, on a case-by-case basis, shall be deemed at the service of the trust. Nonetheless, any right those persons have under the law they may exercise against the credit institution, which, if appropriate, in compliance with the regulations issued by the competent authority, shall affect, in the necessary measure, the material trust assets.[36]

When the credit institution, on request, does not render an accounting of its administration within a period of 15 working days, or when it is declared by a court guilty of the losses or damage suffered by the trust assets, or liable for those losses or damage for gross negligence, its removal as trustee shall be appropriate.[37]

The actions to request the rendering of accounting and demand the liability of the credit institutions and to seek their removal shall fall on the beneficiary or his or her legal representatives, in any case in the measure of their interest, and in their absence on the attorney general's office, notwithstanding the possibility of the grantor reserving in the trust instrument or its modifications the right to exercise this action.[38]

---

34    Acosta Romero and Almazán Alaniz define the fiduciary delegate as "the official(s) appointed by the institutions, especially to be in charge of the performance of trusts." ROMERO & ALANIZ, *supra* note 5, at 117.

       Monserrit Ortiz Soltero defined the fiduciary delegate as "the natural person, generally an expert in law, who maintains a work relationship of subordination with the trustee and who binds it, through his signature, in any legal act which entails the establishment, modification or execution of trusts, agencies or commercial commissions." SOLTERO, *supra* note 2, at 111.

35    With respect to the civil liability of the trustee, it has been maintained that "banking institutions shall be open to civil liability for the damage caused for failure to comply with the terms and conditions of the trust . . . agreement, or the law." Eighth Collegiate Civil Court, First Circuit. *Amparo directo* No. 331/98. Banco Unión SA. April 27, 1998. Semanario Judicial de la Federación [S.J.F.], Vol. XI, Mar. 2000 (Mex.).

36    Credit Institutions Act § 82.

37    Credit Institutions Act § 84 ¶ 1.

38    Credit Institutions Act § 84 ¶ 2.

In the event of resignation, the provisions of section 385, final paragraph of the LGTOC, shall be applied.[39] The paragraph provides: "except for the provisions of the trust instrument, when the trustee does not accept, either through resignation or removal, cessation in the discharge of his duties, a substitute must be appointed. This substitution proving impossible, the trust shall expire."

Regarding the prohibitions on the credit institutions in their capacity as trustees, section 106 of the Credit Institutions Act forbids them from carrying out the following transactions, among others:

a. Guarantee to the settlors the nonpayment of the credits granted, or of the securities acquired, except when their fault, or securing the returns for the funds whose investment was entrusted to them. If at the termination of the trust established for the granting of credit, these had not been paid by the debtors, the trustee must transfer them to the grantor or beneficiary, as the case may be, refraining from covering the amounts due. The named prohibitions shall be visibly inserted in the trust instrument, apart from a statement by the trustee to the effect that he or she unmistakably put their content in the knowledge of the persons from whom he or she has received assets for investment.

b. To be trustees of trusts where the trust accepts deposits from the general public, with the exception of trusts created by the federal government or that issue securities registered with the National Registry of Securities in accordance with the Securities Market Act.

c. To be trustees of trusts included in the second paragraph of section 88 of the Investment Companies Act.[40]

d. To be trustees of trusts aimed to evade limitations or prohibitions contained in financial laws.

e. Use funds or securities from the trusts intended for the granting of credits, in which the trustee has the discretional power in the granting of those credits to carry out transactions by virtue of which its fiduciary delegates result or may result debtors; the members of the administrative or executive council, as it may be the case, even substitutes, whether in office or not, the employees and officers of the institution, external auditors of the institution; the members of the technical committee of the relevant trust; the ascendants or descendants or spouses of the named persons; the companies in whose shareholders general meetings the named persons have a majority, and also those persons that the Bank of Mexico determines by means of general regulations.

---

39   Credit Institutions Act § 84 ¶ 3.

40   Section 88 of the Investment Companies Act (*Ley de Sociedades de Inversión*) refers to trusts whose purpose is to invest or administer any kind of securities, offering to indeterminate persons participation in the gains or losses of the proceeds. It will be considered for the purposes of the law that there are indeterminate persons if at trust creation, the persons that will be settlors and beneficiaries are not determinate, or it is allowed to adhere to the trust after the creation. These trusts could only be administered by duly authorized investment companies.

f. To administer rural properties, except for the case of trusts for production or guarantee trusts.

g. To be trustee of trusts that administer funds that are contributed on a regular basis by consumers for the purchase of certain assets.

h. To provide to third parties the information obtained from the celebration of the transaction with the client, unless there is written express approval of the client.

Section 122 bis 22 of the Credit Institutions Act provides that in the event of liquidation of a bank, the liquidator must provide the replacement of the said bank as trustee based on an agreement with another bank.

## 2. General Rules on Trustees

The second and third paragraphs of section 385 of LGTOC provides that the same trust might have several trustees for them to jointly or successively execute the trust instructions, establishing the order and conditions in which they are to be succeeded.[41] Except for the provisions of the trust instrument, when the trustee does not accept cessation in the discharge of his or her duties, either through resignation or removal, a substitute must be appointed. This substitution proving impossible, the trust shall expire.

As has been stated before, when the trust is created the grantor appoints the trustee. Nonetheless, where the trust is established, and no trustee is appointed nominally, the one elected by the beneficiary shall be deemed appointed, or in his or her absence, by the court of the first instance from the place where the assets are located, from among the institutions expressly authorized under the law. This does not mean that the trustee is under a duty to discharge his or her duties without his or her appointment and no consent. The trustee must express his or her consent to be obligated to perform his or her duties.

The trustee shall have all the rights and actions required for the execution of the trust, except the regulations or restrictions established therefore, at the time of the creation of the trust.[42] It has been said that "although it is true that the LGTOC does not state specifically the acts or powers which the trustee may execute or exercise, it is clearly understood that the trustee must follow the directions which he or she receives to that effect from the grantor, the beneficiary or the Technical Committee, by means of buying and selling, exchange, donation or any other act involving the transfer of ownership."[43]

In regard to the duties of the trustee, it is worth pointing out that his or her principal obligation consists, under the second part of section 391 of the LGTOC, in complying

---

41  Acosta Romero and Almazán Alaniz claimed that "to appoint several trustees for them to act in such capacity in one trust, instead of profiting would harm the smooth working and swiftness in decision-making and policies to be followed." ROMERO & ALANIZ, *supra* note 5, at 240.

42  First part of section 391 of the LGTOC.

43  ROMERO & ALANIZ, *supra* note 5, at 240.

with the trust instrument instructions. Moreover, the trustee may not excuse him or herself or resign his or her charge but for grave grounds in the view of the court of the first instance from his or her domicile and must always act as a good paterfamilias, being responsible for the losses or damages that the assets sustain through his or her fault.

In the hypothesis that a technical committee is set up, the trustee is obliged to comply loyally with the directions that the committee issues validly. As mentioned before, section 80 of the Credit Institutions Act sets forth that when the credit institution acts abiding by the decisions and agreements of this committee, it will be free of all liability.

## 3. Relevant Case Law

In terms of defense of the trust assets, case law has established that

> When it is necessary to defend the property or possession of the trust asset, the representation of the trust shall fall upon an agent empowered by the trustee. It must be concluded that it is up to the latter to defend the trust assets, on account of all rights and actions required for the execution of the trust being vested in it, owing to which fact the trustee, as titleholder, may appear in court as plaintiff or defendant, as well as sell, rent, transfer and carry out other like acts, since such rights and acts cannot be constrained to the ordinary acts aimed at securing the objects of the trust but must also include the acts whose object it is to defend the trust assets against the actions of those who alter, hamper, or prevent the accomplishment of these ends, as this is implied in its broad sense by carrying out the object of the trust. Therefore, the beneficiary, in the present hypothesis, lacks legitimization to defend the property or possession of the trust assets.[44]

Moreover, it has been stated that

> The exercise of the actions and the defense brought against the trust are restricted to the defense of its patrimony and falls on the trustee. . . . [T]he said trustee is the owner of the trust assets, for the grantor conveys to him their trust title, with the restrictions imposed in the trust itself. However, when the termination action of a trust is exercised by a grantor or beneficiary, the other grantors or beneficiaries are passively legitimized . . . since such action affects the trust instrument directly, for that action is clearly not directed against the trust assets but aimed at terminating the trust, [that is,] the agreement itself, which was held by a plurality of subjects and, therefore, it proves indisputably that . . . each and every contracting party forming the legal relationship must be heard, whose fundamental interest is for the trust not to be declared terminated, as intended by the plaintiff.[45]

---

44  Third Court. Contradiction of thesis No. 6/90. Among those upheld by the First and Third Collegiate Civil Courts, First Circuit. June 25, 1990. Semanario Judicial de la Federación [S.J.F.], Vol. VI, Pt. I, p. 197 (Mex.).

45  Fifth Collegiate Civil Court, First Circuit. Action in review No. 255/89. Miguel Ángel Bornacini Hervella. March 30, 1989. Semanario Judicial de la Federación [S.J.F.], Vol. III, Second Part-1, January–June 1989, p. 348 (Mex.).

Touching the powers of the trustee, case law has established that

> If in a trust instrument it is established that the trustee shall have the obligation of appointing a person with sufficient powers in order for him to exercise the rights deriving from [the trust instrument] and proceeds to their defense, and also that in case of emergency the trustee may carry out the indispensable acts to preserve and defend the trust assets, it is evident that the defense of such assets falls on the attorney appointed by the said beneficiary and exceptionally, [that is,] in case of emergency, it could be done by the trustee. Hence, it is deemed that it is not necessary to institute proceedings against the trustee, even when the claimed resolution affects part of the trust assets because the moving party of the action is precisely the attorney of the beneficiary.[46]

In regard to the legal interest to challenge the acts infringing on the trust, it has been claimed that "because a trust is an agreement whereby one person transfers to a trustee part of his assets for the accomplishment of a lawful purpose, which that person himself states in the relevant instrument, it is clear that the titleholder of the assets or rights conveyed is the trustee, and it is this trustee that has a duty to control the discharge of the obligations or objects of the trust . . . and that is the reason [the trustee] is the only one legitimized to take legal action for any act of authority which" damages the trust property.[47]

Finally, in regard to the autonomy of the patrimony and the legitimization for the defense of the ownership of the trust assets, it has been said that

> The trust assets abandon the patrimony of the grantor, to remain as autonomous patrimony under the title of the trustee, for the accomplishment of a given object, but in specifying the autonomous nature of the trust assets, thus it is distinguished from the patrimonies proper to the parties taking part in the trust, [that is,] it is diverse from the patrimonies of the grantor, the trustee and the beneficiary . . . given that the . . . asset [whose property is discussed in the trial] is held in trust under its title and execution, such institution is the one legitimized to appear in court as plaintiff or defendant, due to its being vested with all the rights and actions aimed at the execution of the trust.[48]

## E. GUARANTEE TRUSTS

Guarantee trusts are ruled by sections 395 to 407 of the LGTOC, and general rules of trusts are applicable as long as they are not opposed to the rules contained in the said sections.[49]

---

46  Third Collegiate Civil Court, Third Circuit *Amparo directo* No. 2506/98. Stela Solar Uno, SA de CV. September 13, 1999. Semanario Judicial de la Federación [S.J.F.], Vol. XI, Feb. 2000 (Mex.).

47  First Collegiate Civil Court, Fifth Circuit. Action in review 175/88. Banco de Mexico, SNC. Nov. 9, 1988. Semanario Judicial de la Federación [S.J.F.], Vol. IV, Second Part-1, July–December 1989, p. 258 (Mex.).

48  Fifth Collegiate Civil Court, First Circuit. *Amparo directo* No. 465/90. Gelasio Guerrero Licea. June 7, 1990. Semanario Judicial de la Federación [S.J.F.], Vol. V, Second Part-1, January–June 1990, p. 497 (Mex.).

49  LGTOC § 407.

One of the most particular aspects of guarantee trusts in Mexico is that they have broader criteria than the ones applicable to administration trusts, to determine who may be a trustee. Section 395 of the LGTOC establishes that the following can be trustees of trusts that have as purpose the guarantee to the beneficiary of the trust, the fulfillment of an obligation, and his or her preference of payment:

a. Credit institutions
b. Insurance institutions
c. Bail institutions
d. Stock exchange brokers
e. Financial corporations of multiple objects included in section 87-B of the General Organizations and Auxiliary Activities of Credit Act (*Ley General de Organizaciones y Actividades Auxiliares de Crédito*)[50]
f. General depositaries
g. Credit unions

Those trustees mentioned in points (b), (c), (d), and (f) are subject to section 85 bis of the Institutions of Credit Act. The section currently provides that the entities mentioned before in points (b), (c), (d), and (e) require the previous authorization, and a minimum capital to be determined by the federal government. Nevertheless, this rule will change on July 18, 2013, and the said requirements will be applicable to entities mentioned in points (b), (c), (d), and (f).

The trustees of guarantee trusts can be at the same time beneficiaries of the trust if the trust has as its purpose to guarantee credits of the trustee. In such a case, the parties must agree to the terms and conditions to settle possible interest conflicts.[51]

The same trust can guarantee, simultaneously or successively, several obligations of the settlor, with the same or with different creditors. Each creditor or beneficiary must notify (by public notary, within five working days of such circumstance) to the trustee the moment in which his or her credit has been paid. After such notification, the settlor can appoint a new beneficiary or terminate the trust. If the said notification were not delivered in due time, the beneficiary would be responsible for any damage caused to the settlor.[52]

---

50    Section 87-B provides that granting of credits, such as the execution of leasing or financial factoring, can be carried out on a habitual and professional basis by any person without need of authorization by the federal government. Those corporations that have bylaws that provide as their main object carrying out one or several of the activities mentioned before on a habitual and professional basis will be considered financial corporations of multiple purposes. Such corporations are divided into: (i) regulated financial corporations of multiple purposes, which are owned by financial institutions and fall under the control of the National Commission of Banking and Securities (*Comisión Nacional Bancaria y de Valores*), and (ii) nonregulated financial corporations of multiple purposes, which are not owned by financial institutions and are not under the control of the National Commission of Banking and Securities.

51    LGTOC § 396.

52    LGTOC § 379.

Regarding guarantee trusts on movable assets, it can be established in the trust instrument that the settlor has the right to:

a. Use the trust assets, even to combine them or to use them to produce other assets, as long as the value of the asset is not reduced and the produced assets become part of the trust assets.
b. Collect and use the benefits of the trust assets.
c. Instruct the trustee to sell the trust assets, without responsibility of the trustee, as long as such sale is in line with the ordinary business of the settlor. In such a case, the proceeds of the sale will replace the sold assets in the guarantee trust. This right would terminate in the event of default or insolvency of the settlor or debtor.[53]

In relation to the stipulation of the trust instrument mentioned in the previous paragraph, the parties must agree to the following in the creation of the trust:

a. The location where the trust assets must remain
b. The minimum consideration that the trustee must receive for the sale of the assets
c. The person or persons, or the kind or persons, to whom the trustee can sell the assets based on instructions of the settlor, and the destination of the proceeds of the sale
d. The information that the settlor must deliver to the beneficiary on the transformation, sale, or transfer of the trust assets
e. The procedure to assess the value of the trust assets
f. The procedure to review the relation with the value of the trust assets and the value of the debt in cases where trust assets increase its value

In the event of breach of any of these stipulations, the credit would be considered due at that moment.[54]

The parties can agree that the possession of the trust assets is held by the settlor or third parties. In such a case, the settlor or the third party: (a) would be a bailee and would be subject to the obligation of taking care of the assets as it they were its own assets, (b) is subject to the obligation not to use them in any other way that the one established in the trust instrument, (c) is responsible for the damages to third parties caused when using the trust assets (this responsibility cannot be requested to the trustee), and (d) the settlor must pay the conservation and administration expenses. In the event of loss or deterioration of the trust assets, the beneficiary has the right to request to the settlor the contribution of new assets to the trust or the payment of the debt guaranteed with the trust assets.[55]

---

53    LGTOC § 398.
54    LGTOC § 399.
55    LGTOC § 400.

The loss, damage, or deterioration of the trust assets must be suffered by the person in possession of them, who is subject to the obligation of allowing the other parties to inspect its general condition, quantity, and weight.[56] If expressly stipulated in the contract, and should the market value of the trust assets become lower than the amount of the debt, the debtor shall contribute more assets to the trust, or the debt will be considered due at that moment.[57]

In the event of default by the debtor, if the bailee denies the restitution of the trust assets, the judicial enforcement of such restitution would be subject to fifth book, third bis title, of the Commercial Code.[58] This title of the Commercial Code establishes a summary process to recover the property, and if so elected by the trustee or creditor, to keep the assets in payment of the debt.

Under the guarantee trust, the parties may agree to the procedure under which the trustee can sell the trust assets, as long as the following is established in the trust instrument:

a. The trustee must sell the trust assets when he or she receives from the beneficiaries or creditors a notification of the default of the debtor and a request to proceed with such sale.
b. The trustee provides a copy of the aforementioned notification to the settlor or debtor, who can only oppose the sale if he or she proves, with the corresponding instruments, that he or she paid the debt or that he or she obtained an extension of the due date in his or her favor.
c. The terms to carry out the said procedure.

The said procedure must be described in a special section of the trust instrument that must be signed by the settlor in particular (additional to the signature of the whole document). If there were no particular terms and conditions for the sale in the agreement, the procedure follow that of the fifth book, third bis title, of the Commercial Code already mentioned.[59]

In short, a guarantee trust instrument that meets all the property transfer requirements allows the secured party, in the event of default, the sale of the trust property without going through a court proceeding.

Finally, as the trust implies a transfer of property from the grantor to the trustee and not a mere pledge or certain restriction to the debtor, in the event of bankruptcy of the debtor, the creditor will be in a far better condition with the possibility of selling the asset privately to satisfy his or her credit.

---

56    LGTOC § 406 established imprisonment and a fine to the one that, being in possession of the trust assets, should sell, pledge, or deteriorate them against the law.
57    LGTOC § 401.
58    LGTOC § 402.
59    LGTOC § 403 and the Credit Institutions Act § 83.

## F. EXPERIENCE AND PARTICULAR CASES

### 1. Trusts in the Restricted Zones (*Fideicomisos de Zonas Prohibidas*)[60]

This trust is established so that alien persons may use and enjoy realty in Mexico in those areas considered restricted, lying in the 100-kilometer strip along the borders and the 50-kilometer area on the coasts of the country, without acquiring direct ownership over it, that is, without properly being owners, for a maximum period of fifty years, which may be renewed for equal periods, as long as the purpose of the trust asset is for tourist-housing activities.

The Political Constitution of the United States of Mexico bars aliens from acquiring direct ownership over the property in that area, called restricted or prohibited, and the only manner by virtue of which they may make use of the property in that area in their benefit is by means of the creation of a trust, whereby the trustee acquires direct ownership over that realty, which is placed at the disposal of the aliens, in their double capacity as grantor and beneficiary, who may use and enjoy it for as long as the trust, or its modifications, is in effect. Once the trust is terminated, the trustee shall transfer it to whom the foreign grantor indicates, such beneficiary receiving the price agreed on with the purchaser.

The foreign investor shares in all the advantages of the nature of the beneficiary, with the only restriction that he or she shall not be able to acquire the realty directly despite even being able to rent out the property and receive the income from periodic payments arising from that rent.

Some modes of this class are the trust in barred areas, created with tourist ends and the trust for the cross-border assembly plant industry.[61]

---

60    For a complete description of the "Restricted Zone" regulations and the trust as a legal mechanism for foreign acquisitions in such zone, see Jorge A. Vargas, *Fideicomisos: Real Estate Trusts in Mexico's Restricted Zone, in* 1 Mexican Law: A Treatise for Legal Practitioners and International Investors 352 (Jorge A. Vargas, ed., 1998). This author explained that "[the] trust represents the practical solution adopted by Mexico in 1971 to attract direct foreign investment to its coastal and border areas without violating the prohibition contained in Article 27 of the Constitution. In simple terms, the first paragraph of this article, enacted in 1917, provides that foreigners may not acquire real estate in those areas under [any] circumstances. Ownership in the commercially sought locations—legally labelled as the Restricted Zones—is exclusively reserved to Mexicans, whether these are individuals or legal entities with no foreign investments." Nevertheless, it should be stressed that "the Foreign Investment Act of 1993 . . . allowed Mexican companies with foreign investors," if certain conditions are met, "to acquire the direct ownership of real estate located in the Restricted Zone."

61    According to Acosta Romero and Almazán Alaniz, the cross-border assembly industry was initiated in 1965, when the Border Industrialization Plan (*Plan de Industrialización Fronteriza*) was set in motion, which resulted in the building of the first plant, mainly along the border with the United States. These are companies set up under Mexican law with 100 percent foreign investment and with benefits for Mexico, such as job creation, industrial training, and so forth. "Such companies require the trust to use and enjoy the land where they erect their industrial premises for the accomplishment of their objects, allowing them for long-term planning and absolute security in the use of the relevant property." Romero & Alaniz, *supra* note 5, at 433.

In line with this, it is worth pointing out that the Foreign Investment Act (*Ley de Inversiones Extranjeras*) establishes in section 11 that permission from the Foreign Affairs Office is required before credit institutions acquire property as trustees over real property located within the restricted area, when the purpose of the trust is to permit the better use of such assets without constituting real rights over them, and the beneficiaries are: (a) Mexican companies without an aliens exclusion clause; and (b) alien natural or moral persons. The maximum period of time of these trusts is fifty years, but they can be renewed.[62]

Additionally, the Foreign Investment and Foreign Investment National Registry Act Regulations (*Reglamento de la Ley de Inversión Extranjera y del Registro Nacional de Inversiones Extranjeras*) sets forth that, in regard to foreign natural or moral persons, the Foreign Affairs Office will grant the permissions when the application complies with the relevant requirements, and when the trust realty is intended, among others, for: (a) industrial parks; (b) hotels; (c) industrial premises; (d) shopping malls; (c) research centers; (d) tourist developments, as long as they do not involve property intended for residential purposes; (e) tourist marinas; (f) wharfs and industrial and commercial premises on them; and (g) premises intended for the production, transformation, packing, preservation, transportation, or storage of agricultural, timber, and fishing production.

The trust agreements established under the permissions envisaged in the Foreign Investment Act must subject themselves to the following conditions:

a. That the corresponding public instrument provides that foreign beneficiaries agree to consider themselves Mexican regarding their rights as beneficiaries and to not invoke, therefore, the protection of their governments.

b. That for as long as the trust is in effect, the trustee retains title to the realty held in trust without granting rights in rem to the beneficiaries.

c. That the trustee submits a report once a year to the Foreign Affairs Office on the authorized trusts in the event of trustee substitution, as well as on the appointment of substitute beneficiaries or transfer of beneficiary rights in favor of foreign natural or moral persons, or of Mexican companies with an alien admission clause, in the case of realty purchased with housing purposes.

d. That the beneficiaries undertake to inform the trustee about the accomplishment of the trust objects, and that the latter undertakes to inform the Foreign Affairs Office about the matter, when it is requested, provided there exist reasons to assume a breach of the contract under which the permission was granted.

e. In the event of failure to comply with, or violation of, any of the conditions established in the corresponding permission, the trustee will be granted a sixty business-day period to amend or rectify them, computed as from the date of notification of the said irregularities by the Foreign Affairs Office; otherwise, the trust must be terminated.

f. That the trustee secures with priority permission by the Foreign Affairs Office in the event of extension of the subject matter and change of the objects of the trust.

---

62  Foreign Investment Act § 13.

g. That the trustee undertakes to notify the termination of the trust to the Foreign Affairs Office within forty business days of its termination date.

h. That the parties to the agreement undertake to terminate the trust at the request of the Foreign Affairs Office, within 180 business days computed as from the date of notification of the requirement; in the event of failure to comply with, or violation of, any of the conditions set forth in the relevant permission.

## 2. Governmental or Public Sector Trusts

The Mexican federal government, the Federal District government, or those of the federative entities or states, create public trusts to favor certain sectors of the economy, for the privatization of government assets or to carry out certain infrastructure developments.[63]

There are several acts that provide particular rules for public trusts and their control. As an example, the main rules for public trusts under the Credit Institutions Act are commented on here.

Section 3 of the Credit Institutions Act provides that the Mexican Banking System would be integrated by the Bank of Mexico, the institutions of multiple banking, the institutions of development banking, and the public trusts created by the federal government, which carry out financial activities, such as the self-regulated banking entities. It would be understood that public trusts for the economic development, which have as their main purpose to grant loans on a habitual and professional basis or the assumption of third-party obligations, carry out financial activities under the terms of the Credit Institution Act. Such transactions must represent more than 50 percent of the assets of the trust. All public trusts for the economic development may receive concessions on the same basis as other state entities.

Section 134 bis 4 of the same Act establishes that the Treasury and Public Credit Secretary (*Secretaría de Hacienda y Crédito Público*) will publish each year a list of public trusts that are considered part of the Mexican Banking System. Such trusts will be subject to the National Banking and Securities Commission (*Comisión Nacional Bancaria y de Valores*) supervision and will be the competent authority to issue the general regulations to rule the accounting standards of these trusts.

## 3. Trust of Shares of Financial Entities under Restructuring

Sections 29 bis 2, 29 bis 3, and 29 bis 4 provide the creation of a trust with at least 65 percent of the shares of banks under financial stress, as requisite to be allowed to go on with their financial entity activity.

---

63    State governments created trusts for the administration of local taxes to administer the resources from local taxes so as to earmark them for different programs and projects of the state, which collected them, or of a given economic sector, in accordance to the directions issued by the technical committee of the trust made up of representatives from the political, social, and private state sectors.

## G. SECURITIZATION

Mexico is the biggest securitization market in Latin America, and it has been very active in the securitization of several assets, such as mortgages, cash flow, consumer loans, and taxes (e.g., the State of Veracruz securitized state taxes on vehicles in 2006).[64]

The trust is the legal scheme under which securitizations are conducted in Mexico, in particular the issuance of "trust participation certificates" ruled by sections 228(a) to 228(v) of the LGTOC that is described in the following paragraphs.

The LGTOC defines the concept of participation certificates in section 228(a), where it provides that they are credit securities evidencing

a.  The right to a percentage of the income or yield of the trust assets of any type that the issuing trustee holds in irrevocable trust to that end;
b.  The right to receive a percentage of the ownership of the trust assets; or
c.  The right to a percentage of the proceeds from the sale of the trust assets.

In the cases of subsections (b) and (c), the total rights of the trust certificate-holders of each issuance will be equal to the percentage represented at the time of issuance by its total nominal worth in relation to the commercial worth of the corresponding trust assets set by the expert's report carried out pursuant to article 228(h) of the LGTOC. Where on the sale of the trust assets their commercial value were diminished, without being lower than the nominal amount of the trust certificates, the attribution or liquidation proceeds in cash will be paid to the holders up to a value equal to the nominal one in their certificates; and if the commercial value of the trust assets were lower than the total nominal value of the issuance, they will be entitled to the entire application of the assets or net income of their sale.

Section 228(a) bis states that the "housing certificates" (*certificados de vivienda*) are the securities that represent: (a) the right to the property of a house, with the payment of the total of installments agreed as consideration; (b) to use the house during the life of the said certificates; and (c) in the event of abandonment of the house, the right to get back a portion of the paid installments.

Only credit institutions authorized to be trustees can issue trust certificates.[65]

Trust certificates can be issued based on trusts with any kind or underlying assets, including commercial and industrial establishments considered as economic units.[66]

---

64  Within asset securitization in the housing sector, two fundamental structures are employed in the Mexican experience. On the one hand, the securitization of accounts payable transferred by a construction company to a trust and, on the other hand, the so-called mortgage securitization by means of the issuance of certificates of participation in trusts backed by existing or future mortgages, creditworthiness depending on the issuance of the flows generated by the mortgages. Another use of securitization in Mexico is the transaction conducted by banks to dispose of delinquent portfolios.

65  LGTOC § 228(b) ¶ 2.

66  LGTOC § 228(c).

In accordance with the provisions of the LGTOC section 228(d), participation certificates are classed as ordinary, when the trust assets subjected to the issuance are movable, and real estate certificates, when the trust assets are real property.

In the case of real estate certificates, the certificate-holders can use the real estate property that is in the trust according to the terms and conditions established in the issuance instrument.[67]

The issuing trustee, with the consent and approval of the common representative of the certificate holders, when appropriate, may arrange and obtain loans for the improvement and increase of the real property subject to the issuance, issuing therefore "trust indebtedness certificates." Trust indebtedness certificates are debt securities against the corresponding trust. Their payment is preferred to the participation certificates of that trust.[68]

If the trustee is authorized to carry out financial transactions under the corresponding Act, he or she can secure the certificated holders a minimum income.[69]

The total nominal value of the issuance would be determined after the expert report of the *Nacional Financiera S.A.* (if the trust has movable assets) and the *Banco Nacional Hipotecario Urbano y de Obras Públicas* (if the trust has immovable assets). The said entities, to issue their reports and determine the amount of the issuance, shall consider as base the commercial value of the assets to be transferred to the trust, and if the certificates were redeemable ones, they have to consider a margin of security between the value of the assets and the value of the issuance. The expert report is final and biding.[70]

Certificates are classed into redeemables (*amortizables*) and nonredeemables (*no amortizables*).[71] Redeemable participation certificates confer on their holders, besides the right to a quota of the corresponding income or yield, that to reimbursement of the face value of the securities. In the event of the issuing trustee not paying the face value of the certificates on maturity, their holders will be entitled to the rights set forth in subsections (b) and (c) and the final paragraph of section 228(a) of the LGTOC mentioned before (a right to a percentage of the trust assets or to the proceeds of the trust assets).[72]

In the case of nonredeemable participation certificates, the issuing trustee is not obliged to pay their face value to the holders at any time. At the termination of the trust originating the issuance, and in accordance with the resolutions of the general meeting of certificate-holders, the issuing company will proceed to the awarding and sale of the trust assets and the distribution of its net income under article 228(a).[73]

The certificates can be nominative or bearer ones, or nominative with bearer coupons. They must be issued in series in nominal value of 100 pesos or multiples. Certificates of the same series must have the same rights.[74]

---

67    LGTOC § 228(e).
68    LGTOC § 228(f).
69    LGTOC § 228(g).
70    LGTOC § 228(h).
71    LGTOC § 228(i).
72    LGTOC § 228(j).
73    LGTOC § 228(k).
74    LGTOC § 228(l).

As regards the formal aspects of the issuance of the certificates, section 228(m) of the LGTOC prescribes that it will be carried out subsequent to a unilateral manifestation of intent by the issuing trustee set down in a public deed, where the following will be recorded:

a. The name, object, and domicile of the issuing company
b. An account of the trust instrument that is the base of the issuance of the trust certificates
c. An adequate description of the trust assets subject to the issuance
d. The expert's report set forth by section 228(h) (mentioned above)
e. The amount of the issuance, specifying the number and value of the certificates to be issued, and of the series and subseries, if appropriate
f. The nature of the securities and the rights they will confer
g. The denomination of the securities
h. Where applicable, the minimum guaranteed yield
i. The period indicated for the payment of income or yields, and if the certificates were redeemable, the periods, terms and conditions and method of redemption
j. The registration data necessary for the identification of the trust assets subject to the issuance and of its antecedents
k. The appointment of the common representative of the certificate-holders and his or her acceptance, with his or her statement: (i) of having verified the creation of the trust, base of the issuance; and (ii) of having verified the existence of the trust assets and the authenticity of the expert's report carried out under article 228(h) (mentioned above)

It is also worth pointing out that in the case that certificates are offered for sale to the public, the publicity thereof will contain the said details.

The terms and conditions of the certificates of participation, the issuance instrument, the certificates themselves, and any amendment, must be approved by the National Banking Commission (*Comisión Nacional Bancaria*). The said commission must be present at the moment of the execution of the issuance instrument.[75]

If in the issuance instrument it is established that the certificates are redeemable by draw, section 222 of the LGTOC is applicable.[76] The said section provides that draws must be carried out with a public notary and with the presence of the common representative of the certificate-holders. The issuer must publish the result of the draw in the Official Gazette of the Federation and in a newspaper of its domicile, and make the payment of the certificates within a month of the draw.

Section 228(q) provides that a common representative of the certificate-holders must be appointed. His or her fees must be paid by the issuer, he or she cannot resign his or her office without the authorization of a judge based on serious reasons, but it can be removed at any moment by the certificate holders.

---

75   LGTOC § 228(o).
76   LGTOC § 228(p).

Under the LGTOC section 228(r), the common representative of the certificate-holders will act as their agent, with the following duties and powers, apart from those expressly indicated in the issuance instrument:

a. To verify the terms of the trust instrument that is the base of the issuance
b. To verify the existence of the trust assets or rights, and where applicable, that the buildings and the assets included in the trust are insured, as long as the issuance is not redeemed totally for its value or for the amount of the circulating certificates, when the latter is less than the former
c. To receive and retain the corresponding funds as receiver and employ them for the payment of the acquired assets or of their construction in the terms stated in the issuance instrument, when its amount or part of it must be aimed at the purchase or construction of assets
d. To authorize with his or her signature the certificates to be issued
e. To exercise all actions or rights vested in the group of certificate-holders relating to the payment of interests or principal owed or by virtue of the collaterals indicated in the issuance, as well as those required by the performance of the duties and functions stated in this section
f. To attend any possible draws
g. To summon and preside over the general meeting of certificate-holders and execute their decisions
h. To gather from the issuing trustee officials all reports and details that he or she needs for the exercise of his or her powers, including those related to the financial situation of the trust originating the issuance

The general meeting of the certificate-holders represents all the certificate-holders and their decisions, if according to the Law and the applicable stipulations of the issuance instruments, are binding to all certificate holders, even the absent and the ones who voted against.[77]

The trust originating the issuance will not expire as long as there are outstanding certificates or of participation against the trust assets.[78]

The LGTOC section 228(u) establishes that the holders of certificates will have, mutatis mutandis, the rights provided by sections 223 and 224 of the Act. The main points of the sections mentioned before can be summarized (and adapted to certificate holders) as follows:

a. Each of the holders may start legal actions by him or herself, unless it contravenes a valid resolution of the general meeting, or the general representative already started the same legal action, to challenge the validity of a certificate holders' general meeting summon or decision, to request the payments due, to request to the general representative to carry out the necessary actions in protection of the general

---

77    LGTOC § 228(s).
78    LGTOC § 228(t).

interest of the certificate holders, or to request to the general representative to respond for his or her negligence.

b. The nullity of the issuance would have as effect the obligation of the issuer to restitute to the certificate holder any amount paid by the latter to the former.

Section 228(v) of the LGTOC provides that the possibility to start legal actions for the collection of the coupons of the certificates shall expire 3 years as from maturity. The actions for the collection of redeemable certificates shall be limited to a 5-year period from the date when the stipulated periods to redeem them expire, or, in the event of draw, as from the date when the list of drawn certificates are published by the Official Gazette of the Federation (*Diario Oficial de la Federación*). The limitation of the actions for cash collection or attribution of trust assets, in the case of nonredeemable certificates, shall be governed by the rules of ordinary law, and the corresponding term shall commence as from the date stipulated by the general meeting of holders that is cognizant of the termination of the relevant trust. Finally, in the event of expiration, in all cases, it shall be in favor of the patrimony of the Health and Assistance Office (*Secretaría de Salubridad y Asistencia*).

## H. INCOME TAX

Section 13 of the Income Tax Law (*Ley del Impuesto sobre la Renta*) provides that if commercial activities are carried out by a trust, the trustee must assess the tax under the commercial corporations rules and must pay the tax on behalf of the beneficiaries.

The beneficiaries must include the income arising from their participation in the trust in their tax return and consider as a tax credit the tax paid by the trustee. In cases where trust has a net operating loss (NOL), such NOL can only be applied against future benefits of the trust. If at the moment of the termination of the trust there is an NOL, such NOL can be distributed (and computed) by the beneficiaries against any income of the beneficiary. Any asset contributed to the beneficiary to the trust without receiving a consideration (other than his or her rights as beneficiary) would be considered by the trust at the same cost that it had for the settlor or beneficiary.

Foreign beneficiaries are subject to withholding on the income arising from the trust.

The benefits arising from trusts would not be attributable to Mexican individuals acting as settlors or beneficiaries, as long as the trust is a charitable one, or the purpose of the trust is to provide the resources for the education of the descendents of the settlor.

In the case of trusts in which the purpose is to rent immovable assets, any income of the trust would be considered an income of the settlor, unless it is an irrevocable trust, and the settlor has no right to receive the assets, in which case the income of the trust would be considered income of the beneficiary. The trustee must inform the tax authorities about the beneficiaries of the trust, the amount of income, and make provisory payments of the tax.

According to the Fiscal Code of the Federation (*Código Fiscal de la Federación*), the transfer of assets to a trustee is not a sale. Section 14 of the Code established the exceptions to this rule providing that alienation of assets are, among others,

a. That carried out through the trust, in the following cases: (i) in the act whereby the grantor appoints or undertakes to appoint a beneficiary other than him or herself and provided he or she is not entitled to reacquire the assets from the trustee, and (ii) in the act whereby the grantor loses the right to reacquire the assets from the trustee, had he or she reserved such a right
b. The transfer of the rights over trust property, at any of the following times: (i) in the act whereby the appointed beneficiary transfers his or her rights or instructs the trustee for him or her to transfer the ownership of the assets to a third party. In these cases, the beneficiary shall be deemed to acquire the assets in the act of appointment and to alienate them at the time of transferring his or her rights or of giving such directions, and (ii) in the act whereby the grantor transfers his or her rights if among these is included that the assets be transferred in his or her favor.

# Chapter 18

# Panama[1]

A. Overview 269
  1. Trust Instrument 270
  2. Separation of Trust Patrimony 271
  3. Beneficiaries 271
  4. Termination of the Trust 272
  5. Trust Confidentiality and "Know Your Client" Rules 272
  6. Applicable Legislation and Change of Jurisdiction of the Trust 273
  7. Trust for the Liquidation of Corporations 273
B. The Trustee 273
C. Tax Treatment 276
  1. Panamanian Source Income 276
  2. Tax Rates 277
  3. Trusts with Assets Outside of Panama 277
  4. Trusts with Panamanian Source Income 277
  5. Pension Funds 278
  6. Guarantee Trusts 278
D. Private-Interest Foundations 279
  1. Main Regulations of the Foundations Act 279
  2. The Foundational Act 281
  3. The Foundation Council and Controlling Bodies (Protector) 283
  4. Termination of the Foundation 286
  5. Change of Domicile of the Foundation (*Redomiciliation*) 286
  6. Taxation 287

---

1    I want to thank to Dayra Berbey de Rojas, TEP, for her wonderful help and the material provided for this chapter.

Although Panama boasts Latin American's first trust law (Law No. 9 of 1925, written by Ricardo J. Alfaro, replaced by Law No. 17 of 1941, which was in turn replaced by current trust Law No. 1 of 1984),[2] it was not until the enactment of the current law in 1984 that the trust began to be actually used. Therefore, three different periods could be established:[3]

a. From 1925 to 1941 (Law No. 9 of 1925), the trust was not used.[4] This law was a consequence of Alfaro's work and the so-called "Kemmerer mission."[5]
b. From 1941 to 1984 (Law No. 17 of 1941), the trust was not used.
c. From 1984 (Law No. 1 of 1984),[6] this law has been actively used, which explains the fact that currently there are 56 professional trust companies in Panama[7] (also, anyone can be a trustee as long as it is not a professional practice).

Trusts in Panama are peculiar in that they serve not only as a local but also as an offshore transaction vehicle. Tejada Mora put it graphically when he stated that "in the case of Panama, our business and services legislation (including trusts) uses bifocals: [I]t looks locally and at once adjusts itself to deal with assets and transactions moving at an international level."[8] Mora stated that current Panamanian law acknowledges the existence of trusts "in terms substantially equal to those countries under

---

2    Besides being one of the main Latin American jurists in relation to the adoption of the trust in Latin America, Dr. Alfaro was President of Panama, a member of the team of jurists that drafted the charter of the United Nations, and a member of the Hague International Court of Justice. EDUARDO FERRER M., THE TRUST UNDER THE LEGISLATION OF THE REPUBLIC OF PANAMA 3 (2nd ed. 1999).

3    *Cf.* LUIS A. CHALHOUB MORENO, CASUÍSTICA DEL FIDEICOMISO SOMETIDA AL ANÁLISIS DE LOS TRIBUNALES PANAMEÑOS 9 (2005).

4    Eduardo Ferrer explained that "the trust institution, as introduced in Dr. Alfaro's legislation, never became popular in Panama. It remained a seldom used legal instrument. Most Panamanian jurists believed that, besides the cultural considerations that account for the lack of familiarity with the concept and its use, the law drafted by Dr. Alfaro was so rigid that it became of not much practical value." FERRER, *supra* note 2, at 4.

    Similar comments are made by Juan A. Tejada Mora: "Any commercial use [of the trust under Law No. 9 of 1925], if any, must have been very exceptional." Juan A. Tejada Mora, *Notas Sobre el Fideicomiso de Garantía Como Alternativa a las Garantías Reales en Panamá*, *in* ALGUNAS CONFERENCIAS SOBRE EL FIDEICOMISO, LAS FUNDACIONES DE INTERÉS PRIVADO Y SUS USOS EN PANAMÁ 14 (2005).

5    Eduardo Ferrer explained that "Mr. Kemmerer was a well-known advisor to the government of the United States who visited some Latin American countries on a good-will mission during the year of 1921. . . . The report [drafted after the visits], which was sent to all the governments visited, made an emphatic recommendation for the adoption of the Trust in Latin American countries." FERRER, *supra* note 2, at 3.

6    Drafted by the practicing lawyer and professor Dr. José Angel Noriega. MORA, *supra* note 4, at 14.

7    DAYRA BERBEY DE ROJAS, *Panama in* STEP DIRECTORY AND YEARBOOK 2008, at 433 (Society of Trust and Estate Practitioners–STEP, 2008).

8    Juan A. Tejada Mora, *Adaptación del Trust y de las Fundaciones de Interés Privado en Panamá para servicio de Latinoamérica*, paper presented at the VII LATIN AMERICAN CONGRESS ON TRUSTS, Cancún (Mexico) 9 (1997).

common law—terms mostly gathered in the Hague Convention relating to [legislation applicable to trusts (July 1, 1985)]."[9]

One particularity of Panama is that the trust coexists with private-interest foundations that have similar estate-planning functions, as will be seen in detail in the last part of this chapter.

## A. OVERVIEW

Regulations on trusts are embodied in Law No. 1 of January 5, 1984 (Official Gazette No. 19971 of January 10, 1984) (hereinafter referred to as the "Trust Law") and Decree No. 16 of October 3, 1984 (Official Gazette No. 20165 of October 18, 1984).

Article 1 of the Trust Law defines trusts stating that "they are legal acts by virtue of which a person called the grantor transfers assets to another person called the trustee for him to administer or dispose of those assets in favor of a beneficiary, who may be the grantor himself." The second paragraph of this article sets forth a particular regime for trusts created by governmental entities, which "may retain assets of their own in trust and act as trustees of those assets for the performance of their [the entity's] objects, by means of a declaration carried out in accordance with the formalities of this statute." In short, the grantor could not be the trustee unless it is a governmental entity.

Regarding the assets that can be transferred to the trust, the said statute states that "the trust may be created upon assets of any type, present or future. Assets may be added to the trust by the grantor or by a third person, after the creation of the trust, with the consent of the trustee." Furthermore, "the trust may be created upon ascertainable assets or upon the entirety or portion of a property."

The Trust Law requires that the intent to create a trust be declared expressly and in writing, so that no verbal, constructive, or implied trust may arise.[10] Nevertheless, there are cases of trust creation as a result of a law provision, as in the case of the liquidation of corporations, which will be analyzed below.

There exists the widest latitude as concerns the objects of the trust, as long as they are not in contravention of morals, law, or public order. Trusts may be subjected to a condition or period.

---

9   *Id.*

10   This rule was ratified by the Panamanian Supreme Court, Civil Room, January 27, 1972 stating that "in Panamanian legislation it is necessary for the person who creates the trust to establish it in an express fashion. It cannot be done implicitly. . . . Trust is never assumed because it is a restriction against freedom. Thus, scholars have created the rule in *dubio semper contra fideicomiso*, due to which, in the event of doubt the freedom to dispose [assets] instead of the existence of a trust must be chosen. Therefore, trusts must be express ones. . . . It is established in the doctrine that a trust cannot be created with mere assumptions because the terms of the trust must always be clear and express ones, although no specific expressions are necessary." In this same line of reasoning, the same court, on July 14, 1999, stated that the sole use of the expression "fiduciary administrator" does not imply the creation of a trust. Both court decisions are included in: MORENO, *supra* note 3, at 9.

As a general rule, trusts are irrevocable unless express provision to the contrary is made in the trust instrument.

The Superintendence of Banks of Panama is the regulatory body of trustees and trust activity that grants licenses to professional trustees.

Finally, regarding the uses of the trust, it can be said that local ones are mainly guarantee trusts, and offshore ones are used for estate planning, asset protection, and tax planning.[11]

## 1. Trust Instrument

The trust instrument must contain the following:

a. The complete and clear designation of the grantor, the trustee, and the beneficiary, as well as that of the substitute of the trustee and beneficiary, if any. Where future beneficiaries or classes of beneficiaries are involved, they must be properly identified.
b. The description of the assets or property, or portion thereof, subject to the trust.
c. The express declaration of intent to create the trust.
d. The powers and duties of the trustee, as well as the prohibitions and restrictions to which he or she is subjected.
e. The rules of accrual, distribution, or disposition of the assets, income, and benefits of the trust assets.
f. Place and date of creation.
g. The appointment of a residing agent in the Republic of Panama who will be a lawyer or law firm, who must approve the trust instrument.
h. The domicile of the trust in the Republic of Panama.
i. An express declaration to the effect that the trust is created in accordance with the laws of the Republic of Panama.

As to the form of *inter vivos* trusts, the general rule is that it may be created by public or private deed, with the signatures authenticated by a notary. Nevertheless, trusts on realty located in the Republic of Panama must be created by public deed. Conversely, the trust that takes effect after the death of the grantor must be created through a will, or, where the trustee is authorized to conduct the trust business professionally, by means of a private deed without the formalities of a will. The First Superior Tribunal of the First Judicial Circuit stated on August 6, 2003 that "the law allows *mortis causa* trusts by means of a private deed if the trustee is authorized to conduct the trust business . . . In case of the death of the settlor . . . a succession judicial process is not required, but it must be understood that the assets object of the trust pass automatically to the trustee . . . In this line of reasoning, once the death of the settlor has

---

11    Berbey de Rojas, *supra* note 7.

happened . . . , the trustee . . . acquires all the rights of the settlor as owner" of the assets.[12]

The trust without an object or purpose, or which has an object that is unlawful, or is created by incapable persons is null and void. Nonetheless, the nullity of one or more clauses of the trust instrument will not leave the trust without effect, unless the accomplishment of its object is made impossible as a result of such a nullity.

Effects against third parties will only arise as from the time the signatures of the grantor and trustee have been authenticated by a Panamanian notary public. Where the trust has realty located in the Republic of Panama as its object, effects against third parties will arise as from the date of registration of the trust deed in the Public Record Office.

## 2. Separation of Trust Patrimony

One of the most consequential regulations is the one providing the segregation of the trust assets. It reads: "The trust corpus will constitute a separate property from the personal assets of the trustee for all legal purposes and will not be seized or attached, except for obligations incurred or for damages produced in acts related to the execution of the trust, or by third parties when they had transferred or retained the assets by fraud and to the detriment of their rights." This rule was applied by the Panamanian Supreme Court, Civil Room, October 7, 2004, stating that the trust assets cannot be seized or subject to attachment, with the exception of obligations incurred by, or damage caused in occasion of, the execution of the trust instructions, or in cases where assets are transferred in fraud of third parties. Additionally, it was applied by the First Superior Tribunal of the First Judicial Circuit on December 2, 2003, stating that even in the case of the transfer of a car to a guarantee trust that was not registered with the Registry of Property of Vehicles, the fact that a trust instrument with signatures certified by a public notary exists, was considered good enough to repeal the claim of a third party over the car.[13]

## 3. Beneficiaries

The trustee may appoint substitute beneficiaries, whether successive or not. In revocable trusts, the beneficiary may be replaced, or new beneficiaries may be appointed, at any moment, by the grantor, or by a person authorized by the grantor to conduct the substitution or appointment, with the same formalities with which the trust instrument was granted. Where one or more nonexistent beneficiaries are designated, or a class of ascertainable beneficiaries, this designation will only be effective if one or many of the beneficiaries should exist or be determined during the life of the trust.

---

12    Court decision included in MORENO, *supra* note 3, at 9.
13    Both court decisions are included in: *Id.*

## 4. Termination of the Trust

The trust expires by reason of

a. Accomplishment of its objects.
b. Impossibility of accomplishment of its objects.
c. Resignation or death of the beneficiary, without substitute.
d. Loss or total destruction of the trust assets.
e. Merging of the capacities of sole trustee and sole beneficiary in one single person.
f. Any cause established in the trust instrument or applicable laws.

Item (e) clearly shows that Panamanian law enshrines the same principle as U.S. law when it deems as a sine qua non condition for the existence of a trust that there is a division between the formal owner (trustee) and the economic beneficiary of the property (beneficiary). Where both merge, outright ownership exists and, consequently, it makes no sense to speak of the existence of a trust.

The trust having been terminated without the existence of a beneficiary to receive the assets subject to trust, and there not being in the trust instrument a disposition to indicate the use to which those assets should be put, the trustee must transfer them to the National Treasury and submit a final accounting to the approval of the competent court.

## 5. Trust Confidentiality and "Know Your Client" Rules

Confidentiality is one of the key elements in Panamanian law. Tejada Mora held that "another protection enjoyed by Panamanian trusts is the strict confidentiality which safeguards them. With the exception of realty located in Panamanian territory, there is no public record of trust instruments," and he added that the notary authenticating the signatures "does not retain a copy of the document nor does he keep a record of the parties whose signatures have been authenticated."[14]

In keeping with the above discussion, article 37 of Law No. 1 of 1984 provides that "the trustee and his agents or employees, state organizations authorized by law to conduct inspections or gather documents relating to fiduciary transactions and their respective officials, as well as those persons involved in those transactions on account of their profession or trade, must observe confidentiality about them and comply with the current statutory dispositions on the matter in the Republic of Panama"; and that "violation of this disposition will be penalized with imprisonment of up to six months and fine." What has been said does not preclude the information that should be disclosed to the official authorities and the inspections that they must conduct as required by law.

Executive Decree No. 16 of October 3, 1984, which regulates trust law sets forth in articles 19 through 22, among other items, that "the obligation to observe fiduciary

---

14    Mora, *supra* note 4, at 19.

confidentiality is maintained even when the trust or the professional or labor relationship is terminated or the fiduciary license has been cancelled," an equal obligation of observing confidentiality existing on the part of the administrative and judicial authorities.

Regarding anti–money laundering provisions, it must be stressed that

> Decree [No.] 213 of [October 3, 2000] gave powers to the Superintendence of Banks to carry out inspections of trust companies. During the latter part of 2000, the Superintendence of Banks created the Specialized Fiduciary Unit (SFU) to undertake inspections of trust activities . . . Law [No.] 42 of 2000 and the Superintendence of Banks' Agreement [No.] 12-2005 require trust companies to comply with "Know Your Client" rules set forth by [these] owners, including letters of reference and proof of domicile. Information on clients must be kept confidential, unless a capital-laundering, drug-trafficking or terrorism investigation is in process. Every trust transaction in cash for [US$]10,000 or more, and any suspicious transaction, must be reported to the Superintendence of Banks, which in turn reports it to the Financial Intelligence Unit (FIU). An existing trust must have all reporting requirements on file.[15]

## 6. Applicable Legislation and Change of Jurisdiction of the Trust

The law sets forth that the trusts created in accordance with the statutes of the Republic of Panama shall be governed by Panamanian law. Nevertheless, trusts may subject themselves in their execution to a foreign law if the trust instrument so provides.

The trust, as well as its assets, may be transferred or subjected to the laws or jurisdiction of another country, as established in the trust instrument. In turn, trusts created in accordance with a foreign law may opt for Panamanian law, as long as the grantor and the trustee or the latter alone, if so provided in the trust instrument, make a declaration to that effect, subjecting themselves to the legal requirements and formalities set forth in this law for the creation of the trust.

## 7. Trust for the Liquidation of Corporations

Section 86 of Law No. 32 (which rules Panamanian Corporations) refers to Law No. 17 (1941) (the former law on trusts). Therefore, the directors of a corporation become trustees because of law mandate at the moment of the liquidation of a corporation.

## B. THE TRUSTEE

The general rule is the freedom to be a trustee. The law provides that "natural or legal persons may become trustees." However, the relevant license must be secured if the

---

15    BERBEY DE ROJAS, *supra* note 7, at 434.

activity as trustee is pursued professionally. In this last case, it is requisite to comply with the requirements set forth in Executive Decree No. 16 of October 3, 1984 (Official Gazette No. 20165 of October 18, 1984) relating to minimum guarantees and moral and professional qualification.[16] Furthermore, the use of the expression "*fideicomiso*," "trust" or the translation to any language in the denomination of a company requires previous authorization.[17]

The grantor may appoint one or more trustees. Unless the trust instrument provides otherwise, if two trustees should be appointed, they must act jointly, and if no more than two were appointed, these two must act by majority. Furthermore, the grantor may appoint one or more substitutes to replace the trustee. In revocable trusts, the trustee may be replaced or new trustees may be appointed at any time by the grantor or by the person whom he or she has authorized to carry out the replacement or appointment with the same formalities with which the trust instrument was granted.

In the event of death, subsequent incapacity, removal, or resignation by the trustee, if he or she should have no substitute, the competent court may appoint a substitute at the request of the trustee, the grantor or, in the absence of the latter, at the request of the beneficiaries or of the attorney general's office if the beneficiaries were minors or incompetents, and he or she will order the transfer of the trust assets to the substitute thus appointed. This request must be carried out within a period not in excess of three years after the vacancy in the trusteeship was produced, as once this period elapses without the said request being carried out, the trust will be terminated.

The person appointed as trustee is not under the obligation to accept the office, his or her duties starting only on his or her acceptance in writing.

It is deemed that the trustee is entitled to compensation although the free provision of his or her services may be established. In principle, the trustee's compensation will be as stipulated in the trust instrument. Should no stipulation exist, it will be fixed at the amount normally paid in the domicile where the trust is established.

The trustee may resign his or her position when he or she has been expressly authorized by the trust instrument. In the absence of express authorization, he or she may resign with the approval of the court, with justified cause, but such a resignation will only be effective as from the time a new substitute trustee is appointed, and he or she has accepted the position.

A fundamental point deals with the powers of the trustee in relation to the trust assets. The trustee will possess all the actions and rights inherent to ownership but will be subject to the objects of the trust and the conditions and obligations imposed by statutes and the trust instrument. In this respect, the law states that the trustee will

---

16   Article 2(c) defined the trustee as "the natural or legal person to whom the assets are transferred so that he executes the intent of the trust"; and in subsection (d) it defined "trustee company" as "the banks, insurance companies, lawyers and any natural or legal person engaging professionally and habitually in the exercise of the fiduciary business, with prior authorization." Executive Decree No. 16 of October 3, 1984.

17   This rule was ratified by the Panamanian Supreme Court, Civil Room, September 18, 1985, stating that "the law requires [] all persons interested in being a trustee to use the word trust (*fideicomiso*) or its related expression in any language to obtain previous authorization." Court decision included in MORENO, *supra* note 3, at 9.

dispose of the trust property as established in the trust instrument. Included in the instrument must be, under pain of nullity, the powers and duties of the trustee.

In the present wording of article 28 of the Trust Law, its regulatory decree prescribes that if the grantor does not state otherwise in the trust instrument, it is prohibited for the trustee to

a. Invest the trust assets in: (i) stock of the trustee and other assets in its property, or (ii) stock or assets of companies in which the trustee holds an interest or in those where its directors or dignitaries are partners, directors, dignitaries, advisors, or counselors, unless the shares are of companies registered in the National Securities Committee of Panama, or shares offered to the public with the authorization of the equivalent governing authority abroad, with prior authorization from the National Banking Committee.
b. Grant loans with funds originating in the trusts to its dignitaries, directors, shareholders, employees, or subsidiary, affiliate, or companies otherwise related to the trustee.
c. Acquire trust assets directly or through a third person.

Regarding the liability of the trustee, he or she will be liable for the losses or damage of the trust assets arising from not having employed in its execution the care of a good paterfamilias.

The trust instrument may establish restrictions on the trustee's liability, but in no case will such restrictions exempt the trustee from his or her liability for losses or damage produced through gross fault or tort.

Where there are many trustees, they will be jointly and severally liable for the execution of the trust, unless otherwise stipulated in the trust instrument. Panamanian law, just like most Latin American legislations, uses the standard of the good paterfamilias and prohibits the dispensation of fraud and grave fault. In addition, as will be seen below, noncompliance with this standard results in the removal of the trustee.

The trustee must give an accounting of his or her administration as established in the trust instrument, and should the instrument lack provision to that effect, the accounting must be to the grantor or to the existing beneficiaries, at least once a year and at termination of the trust. If the accounting was not objected to in the period stipulated in the trust instrument and, lacking that, in a period of 90 days from receipt, the accounting will be deemed tacitly approved. Whether the accounting is tacitly or expressly approved, the trustee will stand free of all liability before the grantor and the present or future beneficiaries for all the acts performed in the period of the accounting. However, such an approval will not exempt the trustee from the liability for damage caused through his or her fault or fraud in his or her administration of the trust.

The trustee may be removed by recourse to law, by means of summary action:

a. If he or she held incompatible interests with those of the beneficiary or residual beneficiary
b. If he or she administered the trust assets without the diligence of a good paterfamilias

c. If he or she were sentenced for crimes against property or public faith
d. As from the moment that his or her incapacity occurs or he or she is made unable to execute the trust
e. Because of his or her insolvency, or voluntary or involuntary bankruptcy, or because of the administrative intervention of an authorized person to exercise the trust business

The judicial removal of the trustee may be requested by the grantor, the beneficiaries, or the representative of the attorney general's office in defense of the minor or legally incapable beneficiaries, or in the interest of public interests.

Finally, in the case where the trustee must be replaced by a substitute or is dissolved, the trust assets must be transferred to the substitute by the outgoing trustee, or in the absence of such transfer, by means of judicial decision.

## C. TAX TREATMENT

Unlike most Latin American countries (with the exception of, for example, Costa Rica and Uruguay), Panama has a national source income taxation system. Therefore, only income of Panamanian source is taxed no matter: (a) the nationality, domicile, or tax residency of the beneficiary; (b) the place of execution of the contracts involved; or (c) the place of payment or collection.

Panama has treaties to avoid double taxation in relation to the commercial use of ships and/or airplanes with several countries, including the United States.

## 1. Panamanian Source Income

Among other cases, Panamanian source income is considered the one arising from: (a) commercial services and professional activities carried on in Panama; (b) real estate property or natural resources located in Panama; (c) rights or things economically used in Panama, including funds invested in Panama (this includes interest, dividends, profits arising from branches located in Panama, the lease of assets located in Panama, annuities, etc.); (d) any income arising from the transport or telecommunication between Panama and abroad; (e) insurance over risks located in Panama; and (f) 50 percent of copyright payments and other royalties.

The following, among others, will be considered foreign source income, and therefore not taxed in Panama: (a) invoicing from Panama for the sale of goods for an amount higher than the one that was invoiced to the Panamanian entity, as long as the goods are outside of Panama or are located in Panamanian ports or airports in a transit only status; (b) to manage from Panama transactions that are executed or have effects abroad; (c) rendering of services outside of Panama, as long as they are not related to taxable activities in Panama; (d) the distributions of profits or dividends to partners or shareholders, as long as such profits or dividends arise from foreign source income; (e) interest arising from loans with foreign persons that do not apply their funds in

Panama; (f) interest and fees paid by entities that do not have Panamanian source income, including the ones arising from sea commerce of ships legally registered in Panama; (g) trusts created with underlying assets located abroad, funds deposited by persons who do not have Panamanian source income and securities issued by companies that do not have Panamanian source income, even in the case of those funds and securities being deposited in Panama; (h) insurance over risks located outside of Panama; and (i) the proceeds of the sale of shares of a Panamanian company in case such company only has foreign source income.

## 2. Tax Rates

Individuals are subject to rates that range from 0 percent up to 27 percent (the latter applicable if the taxable basis is higher than US$30,000). Corporations are subject to a 30 percent tax rate if they have taxable income higher than US$100,000 (if they have a lower taxable income, they are taxed as individuals).

Dividends payments arising from Panamanian source income are subject to a 10 percent withholding rate if shares are registered, and to a 20 percent withholding rate if shares are bearer shares. If during a given year there is no dividends distribution, or the amount distributed as dividends is lower than 40 percent of the net income of the year, 4 percent of the income of the company must be paid.

## 3. Trusts with Assets Outside of Panama

Section 35 of Law No. 1 of 1984 provides that "all acts concerning the creation, modification or termination of a trust as well as the transfer, transmission or encumbrance of trust property and the proceeds from such property or any other act regarding the same, shall be exempted from any tax, assessment, toll or any charge, providing that the trust involves: (1) property located abroad; (2) money deposited by natural or legal persons whose income does not derive from a Panamanian source or is not taxable in Panama; or (3) shares or securities of any kind, issued by a corporation which is not derived from a Panamanian source, even when such money, shares or securities are deposited in the Republic of Panama."

Notwithstanding, any trust will be subject to an annual rate that it must pay on its creation and within three months of every anniversary of its creation. Nonpayment of this rate will give rise to surcharges and, on the third year of nonpayment, dissolution of the trust.

## 4. Trusts with Panamanian Source Income

Section 15 of Law No. 1 of 1984 establishes that "the assets of the trust shall make up a separate patrimony apart from the trustee's personal estate for all legal purposes and may not be seized or attached, except for obligations incurred or for damages caused by virtue of the execution of the trust, or by third persons whenever the property has been transferred or withheld with fraud and in prejudice to their rights. *Consequently, the trustee shall separately pay all the taxes, surcharges or any other charges incurred by the assets given in trust*" (emphasis added).

Originally, section 7 of Decree No. 60 of 1965 (not in force), regulating income tax, established that "any natural or legal person, independently of its nationality, domicile or residence, that perceives Panamanian source income, is a taxpayer of income tax and must comply with the obligations established by the Tax Code and this Decree. Estates are taxpayers up to the attribution of the assets [to heirs]. Trusts are also taxpayers in which the grantor renounces permanently to all the attributes of property, with the exception of trusts created under section 37 of this Decree." The section mentioned referred to pension funds for employees of the taxpayer. Nevertheless, these rules did not have any use in practice.

Currently, section 81 of Decree No. 170 of 1993 establishes that "taxpayers are the natural or legal persons, independently of their nationality, domicile or residence, that perceive Panamanian source income. Trusts and estates are also taxpayers up to the attribution of the assets [to heirs] . . . In the case of trusts . . . the trustee is the taxpayer and must assess the tax under the rules applicable to natural persons." In short, the trust must pay the tax as an individual, and the trustee is responsible for such payment.

The advantages of the payment as a natural person are: (a) the lower progressive rate in comparison with the flat rate applicable to companies (up to 27 percent instead of a flat 30 percent); and (b) no tax on dividends or profits distributions (as it arises from Ruling (*nota*) No. 201-01-1975 of December 28, 2005, of the Panamanian Tax Authorities).

## 5. Pension Funds

Section 27 of Decree 170 of 1993 provides that contributions to create pension funds for employees can be deducted as expenses by the employer if they are created with a trust with such exclusive purpose, which is administered separately from the ordinary activities of the company by trustees duly authorized and regulated by Law No. 1 of 1984. Employees may make their own contributions, but they may not deduct more than 10 percent of their gross annual income. The beneficiary may pay the tax when he or she receives the payment from the trust.

## 6. Guarantee Trusts

The Tax Authorities (Ruling No. 201-01-490, May 25, 2000) stated that the transfer of assets to the trustee and the devolution of such assets by the trustee to the grantor or beneficiary in a guarantee trust once the guaranteed obligation is paid, are exempted from the Tax on the Transfer of Movable Assets and the Tax on the Transfer of Immovable Assets established by Law No. 75 of 1976 and Law No. 106 of 1974.

## D. PRIVATE-INTEREST FOUNDATIONS

As mentioned before, trusts are "accompanied" by private-interest foundations, which in Panama perform a role similar to that of asset-protection trusts. As explained in Section G of Chapter 4 when comparing trusts with foundations, unlike most jurisdictions in Latin America, which only feature public-interest or public-utility foundations, Panama recognizes private-interest foundations in favor of designated subjects (usually members of a family). Such foundations have been contemplated under Law No. 25 of June 12, 1995 (which is referrerd to here as the "Foundations Act," and which was based on Liechtenstein's legislation[18] on the subject). The Foundations Act is complemented by Decree No. 417 of August 8, 1995, that regulates the registration of foundations with the Public Registry in Panama and Resolution No. 201-847 (enacted on July 5, 1995, and published on September 19, 1995).

Unlike trusts, which are merely separated property (not legal entities), these foundations are legal entities. They differ from corporations in that they do not have shareholders, nor are they owned by third persons such as unit holders, joint-tenants, and so forth. Their object is to benefit the persons designated by the founder in the terms and conditions he or she establishes. Thus, the protection of assets and estate planning is permitted.

## 1. Main Regulations of the Foundations Act

Section 1 of the Foundations Act provides that "foundations can be created by individuals or legal entities, acting directly or through third parties." This provision of the Foundations Act expressly allows the creation of "shelf foundations" by individuals who then transfer the rights and duties of the founder to an individual or legal entity that desires to have such a foundation, but with the confidentiality of the name of the founder. Furthermore, it must be considered that the registration with the Public Registry only involves the foundational act but not the regulations (similar to a letter of wishes), which is a confidential instrument. Nevertheless, the founder can choose to register the regulations if he or she desires to do so. The usual practice is to include the name of the beneficiaries in the regulations to keep this information confidential.

---

18    Eduardo Ferrer M. explained that the team of jurists that drafted the Foundations Act, which was led by Rogelio Fábrega Zarak and had himself as a member, analyzed Luxembourg Law and determined that there was no need of a distinction between family foundations and mixed foundations (whose beneficiaries are members of a family and third parties). Therefore, Panamanian private-interest foundations are the same whether the beneficiaries are members of a family or not. He also explained that Oyden Ortega Durán was the legislator who presented and defended the draft in the National Assembly, a draft which was in turn approved by all the political parties. EDUARDO FERRER M., LA FUNDACIÓN DE INTERÉS PRIVADO BAJO LA LEGISLACIÓN DE LA REPÚBLICA DE PANAMÁ, at xi (2003).

Additionally, section 1 also establishes that "the creation of a foundation implies the affectation of a patrimony to certain objectives or purposes expressed in the foundational act. The initial patrimony can be increased by the founder or by any other person." Certainly, this provision helps to understand the parallelism between private-interest foundations and asset-protection trusts, both are legal schemes allowing the creation of a patrimony affected to certain purposes.

Section 2 of the Foundations Act provides that "[private-interest] foundations will be regulated by the foundational act and its regulations, by the provisions of this Act and other applicable legal and regulatory rules. Provisions of title II of book I of the Civil Code shall not be applicable to these foundations." The main point of this section is to clarify that public-interest foundations rules are not applicable to private-interest foundations. One of the main differences is that public-interest foundations require the approval of the government to be created, whereas private-interest foundations only require registration (as an ordinary corporation).

Section 3 stipulates that "private-interest foundations cannot pursue profit-making aims. Nevertheless, they can develop commercial activities on a nonregular basis, or exercise the rights arising from shares of corporations that are part of the patrimony of the foundation, as long as the proceeds of such activities are applied exclusively to the purposes of the foundation." In other words, the foundation cannot develop a commercial activity as an operative corporation, but it can be a holding company and get paid dividends and vote (among other rights and duties as shareholder) and sell its shares. An obvious consequence of this section is that foundations cannot request any license to carry on commercial activities (e.g., banks, insurance companies, professional trustees, etc.).

Section 4 states that "[private-interest] foundations may be created to have effects [after] their creation or after the death of the founder, by any of the following means: [(1)] By private instrument signed by the founder, with the signature certified by public notary of the place of the creation[; (2)] by public instrument registered by the public notary of the jurisdiction of the creation of the foundation. No matter the means of creation of the foundation, the formalities of this Act must be fulfilled. In case the foundation is created, by private or public deed, to have effects after the death of the founder, the formalities of will shall not be required." The main point of this section is that Panamanian private-interest foundations could be created in any place of the world as long as the signature of the founder is certified by a public notary.

Section 26 provides that any beneficiary of the foundation can challenge the acts of the foundation that damage his or her rights, denouncing this circumstance to the protector or to any other controlling bodies if they exist, or in absence of such bodies, with a legal action with the judge of the domicile of the foundation.

Sections 34 and 35 establishes the obligation to keep secret the transactions of the foundations with the exception of the information regarding antilaundry rules, in particular the ones emerging from Decree No. 468 of 1994, which rules the obligation of lawyers to apply "know your client" rules to avoid illegal activities in relation to severe criminal offenses.

Finally, section 36 clarifies that the foundational act may establish that any controversy must be settled by arbitration under the procedure ruled by the foundational act itself. This allows the founder to avoid legal actions with the local judges, which may be inconvenient because of the language of the founder (other than Spanish), the distance to Panama, or other reasons (i.e., lack of familiarity with Panamanian law).

## 2. The Foundational Act

Section 5 of the Foundations Act states the content that must be included in the foundational act:

1. The name of the foundation in any language as long as it is written with the Latin alphabet. The name cannot be the same as, or similar to, the name of any other existing foundation in Panama and must include the word "foundation."
2. The initial patrimony of the foundation in any currency. This patrimony cannot be lower than [US$]10,000.
3. The name and address of the members of the foundation council (*consejo de la fundación*).
4. The domicile of the foundation.
5. The name and domicile of the registered agent (*agente residente*) of the foundation in Panama, who must be a lawyer of a [] firm, who must approve the foundational act before its registration with the Public Registry.
6. The purposes of the foundation.
7. The procedure to appoint the beneficiaries of the foundation. The founder could be the beneficiary or one of the beneficiaries.
8. If the founder desires to do so in the future, the right to modify the foundational act.
9. The duration of the foundation.
10. The destiny of the assets of the foundation and the procedure for the liquidation in case of dissolution.
11. Any other clause that the founder desires to include.

The name of the foundation may be in English. Furthermore, it can be the same as that of a corporation in Panama (the same name can be used for the foundation and the corporation in which the foundation is the shareholder).

There is no need to contribute the minimum initial patrimony (in U.S. dollars) before the creation of the foundation. Therefore, it is enough to state the obligation of the founder to make such contribution. If the contribution is not actually paid, after signing the foundational act, the founder would be a debtor of the foundation (this is reinforced and clarified by section 10 of the Foundations Act).

The founder can be a member of the council of the foundation, and it can be established in the foundational act that all or certain decisions require the unanimous consent of all the members of the council. This allows the founder to control the foundation. The obvious caveat is that this would probably have tax consequences in the jurisdiction of the founder, whose tax authorities may consider that there was no "actual transfer of property" to the foundation. The same proviso could be made regarding the bankruptcy remoteness analysis of the foundation vis-a-vis the founder's creditors.

In Panama it is possible to establish that the foundation will have no limit in time. Put differently, a perpetual foundation is possible.

Section 6 provides that "the foundational act, as any amendment to it, must be in any language that uses the Latin alphabet and complies with the rules regarding the registration of acts and titles with the Public Registry, including [that previously] notarized by a public notary in Panama. If the foundational act or its amendments are not in Spanish, they must be notarized, with the translation made by a Panamanian Public Translator."

In short, if a private-interest foundation is created outside of Panama in English, Panamanian law requires the translation of such document to Spanish and the notarization by a Panamanian public notary. As the foundational act is a document that states the basic rules, the translation does not represent a problem. Once again, it must be stressed that the most sensitive document is the regulations (or letter of wishes), which does not need registration (therefore, no translation is needed of the regulations). In short, private-interest foundations can be created around the world without any difficulty if their foundational act and regulations are written in English.

"The amendments of the foundational act, if they are permitted, must be done and signed according [to] the rules of the Foundations Act itself. The amendment must include the date, the name of the persons [who] sign it and the signatures certified by a public notary of the place of the execution."[19]

Section 9 provides in its first part that "the registration of the foundational act in the Public Registry would grant legal personality without need of any legal or administrative authorization. The registration with the Public Registry additionally constitutes a means of publicity vis a vis third parties." As mentioned, this is clearly a substantial difference with the public-interest foundation, which requires the express authorization of the government.

Section 11 states that "for all legal effects, the assets of the foundation are a patrimony separate from the assets of the founder. Therefore, the assets of the foundation cannot be seized, subject to attachment, nor be the object of legal actions or injunctions, except for obligations incurred or for damages caused on occasion of carrying on the purposes of the foundation, or due to legitimate rights of the beneficiaries." This section does not state anything different from the obvious conclusion of the circumstance that the foundation is a legal person different from the founder and the beneficiaries. Nevertheless, the intention of avoiding any doubt is apparent. This section was amended by means of Law No. 32 (August 2006) to clarify that the foundation council of a private-interest foundation can approve all kinds of guarantees over the foundation assets, because of obligations of the foundation or third parties.

"Foundations are irrevocable, unless: (1) The foundational act has not been registered with the Public Registry. (2) It is otherwise established in the foundational act in an express fashion. (3) For any of the revocation reasons of the donations. The transfers that are made to foundations are irrevocable by the transferor, unless it is

---

19    Foundations Act § 7.

otherwise established in the transfer instrument in an express fashion."[20] The last sentence is applicable to the case where someone different from the founder makes a transfer. Regarding the causes of revocation of the donations, the main ones are a criminal offense by the beneficiary against the founder and the lack of fulfillment by the beneficiary of the conditions established by the founder to enjoy his or her rights as beneficiary.

Section 13 complements the previous one providing that the foundations created to have effects after the death of the founder can be revoked by him or her during all his or her lifetime. The heirs of the founder would not have the right to revoke the foundation, or the transfers to the foundation, even if it is not registered with the Public Registry.

The main section regarding the estate planning purposes of the foundation is section 14. It provides that "the existence of heirship rules in the founder's or beneficiaries' domicile cannot be brought to challenge the foundation, nor shall it affect the validity nor prevent the accomplishment of its objects, in the manner set forth in the foundational act of settlement or its bylaws." In other words, Panamanian judges shall not declare the nullity of any foundation based on forced heirship rules in the jurisdiction of the founder or of the beneficiaries. This is a key provision if it is considered that one of the main reasons to create a foundation is to plan the administration and distribution of the estate of the founder. An exception in Latin America, Panama does not have forced heirship rules. This provision makes the Panamanian foundation an exceptionally good vehicle for estate planning in comparison to forced heirship rules.

Section 15 deals with the transfer to a foundation in fraud of creditors of the transferor, stating that such transfer could be challenged for a three-year period after the transfer of the assets to the foundation.

Finally, section 16 provides that all sorts of assets, existing or future ones, can be transferred to a trust. The formalities of each kind of assets must be observed.

## 3. The Foundation Council and Controlling Bodies (Protector)

Section 17 is a key one in relation to the government of the foundation. It provides that all foundations "must have a foundation council (*consejo de la fundación*), whose powers and responsibilities shall be established by the foundational act or in its regulations. Unless it is a legal entity, the number of members of the foundation council shall not be less than three (3)." At first glance, the foundation council is similar to the directors of a corporation, but as the foundation has no shareholders, there are substantial differences. If the founder is not alive, and there is no protector, the foundation council must interpret the foundational act and regulations. Put differently, the role of the foundation council is similar to the one of the trustee.

Section 18 establishes that

> The [foundation council] will be in charge of the accomplishment of the purposes and objectives of the foundation. Unless otherwise expressed in the foundational

---

20    Foundations Act § 12.

act or in the regulations, the [foundation council] will have the following general obligations and duties: (1) Administer the assets of the foundation, according [to] the foundational act and regulations. (2) Execute acts, contracts, or legal business that result [and are] convenient or necessary to accomplish the purposes of the foundation, and to include in the contracts, agreements, and other instruments and obligations, necessary and convenient clauses and conditions, that adjust to the purposes of the foundation and that are not contrary to the law, morals, good customs, or public order. (3) To inform to the beneficiaries of the foundation of the patrimonial situation of the foundation, according with the foundational act and the regulations. (4) To convey to the beneficiaries of the foundation the assets established in their favor by the foundational act or regulations. (5) To carry on the acts or contracts allowed to the foundation by this [law] and other applicable regulations.[21]

Regarding the appointment of a protector and the subordination of the foundation council to him or her, section 19 provides that "the foundational act or the regulations may stipulate that the members of the [foundation council] can only exercise their faculties with the previous authorization of a protector, committee or any other controlling body, appointed by the founder or by the majority of founders. The members of the [foundation council] shall not be responsible for the losses or deterioration of the assets of the foundation, nor for the damages caused if the said authorization was duly obtained." In other words, the foundation council could be subordinated to a third party, and in such a case the council is not responsible for the actions carried on following instructions.

In relation to the rendering of accounts, section 20 of the Foundations Law expresses that

Unless otherwise established in the foundational act or its regulations, the [foundation council] must render accounts of its management of the foundation to the beneficiaries, and if established, to the controlling body. If the foundational act or its regulations do not establish otherwise, the rendering of accounts must be annual. If the accounts rendered are not challenged within the period of time established by the foundational act or its regulations, or if such period is not established within 90 days of its reception, it will be considered that the accountings are approved . . . Once the accounts have been approved, the members of the [foundation council] shall be liberated of the responsibility of its management, unless they did not act as good paterfamilias. The approval does not liberate them vis a vis the beneficiaries or third parties with interests in the foundation if the damages are caused due to gross negligence or with intention on occasion of the management of the foundation.[22]

"In the foundational act, the founder could reserve for himself, or for third parties, the right to remove the members of the [foundation council], or to appoint or add

---

21    Foundations Act § 18.
22    Foundations Act § 20.

new members."[23] This allows the founder, or the person determined by the founder, to control the foundation.

If the rights explained in the previous section are not exercised, the legal solution is provided by section 22, laying down the rule that

> If the foundational act or the regulations do not establish the right or the causes to remove the members of the [foundation council], these members could be removed through a judicial process . . . due to the following causes: (1) If the interest of the [foundation council] members are incompatible with the interests of the beneficiaries or the founder. (2) If the [foundation council] members manage the assets of the foundation without the due diligence of a good paterfamilias. (3) If the [foundation council] members are considered guilty of criminal offenses against the property or the good faith of the general public. During the legal process, the members of the [foundation council] can be suspended in their functions. (4) Due to legal incapacity or impossibility to accomplish the purposes of the foundation. (5) Due to the fact that the members of the [foundation council] are subject to insolvency, bankruptcy, or other judicial process of debt restructuring.[24]

Section 23 complements the previous one providing that the beneficiaries and the founder can request a judge to remove the members of the foundation council. If the beneficiaries are minors or legally incapable, they can be represented by the person who has their custody. The sentence that determines the removal of the members must appoint new ones with the necessary skills to manage the foundation.

Section 24 deals with the controlling body regime, laying down that the foundational act or its regulations can provide the creation of a controlling body that may be integrated by legal or natural persons, such as auditors, protectors, and the like. The functions of the controlling body must be included in the foundational act or the regulations and may include:

a. Oversee the accomplishment of the purposes of the foundation by the foundation council and the rights and interests of the beneficiaries.
b. To require the rendering of accounts by the foundation council.
c. Modify the purposes and objectives of the foundation if they are impossible or too difficult to accomplish.
d. To appoint new members to the foundation council as a result of transitory or permanent absence or expiration of the period of any of the members, or to increase the number of members of the foundation council.
e. To approve the decisions of the foundation council detailed in the foundational act or its regulations.
f. To custody the assets of the foundation and to control that they are applied to the purposes detailed in the foundational act.
g. To exclude beneficiaries of the foundation and to add others, according to the rules of the foundational act or the regulations.

---

23   Foundations Act § 21.
24   Foundations Act § 22.

As it is derived from the enunciation above, the protector (or like controlling body) can have the broadest powers, including the determination of the beneficiaries of the foundation. Section 24 must be read jointly with section 19. Together they provide the legal framework so that the protector can rule the foundation. For non-Panamanian founders, these rules are particularly important because there is no requirement of nationality or residence in relation to the protector (as there is for the members of the foundation council). Therefore, a foreign founder can appoint a foreign protector and provide in the regulations (which may be kept as a confidential document) that the protector would rule the foundation, and the foundation council shall not be responsible as long as it follows the instruction of the protector.

## 4. Termination of the Foundation

Section 25 provides that the foundation is dissolved:

a. At the date established as the termination date in the foundational act.
b. If the purposes of the foundation are accomplished or become impossible.
c. Because of its insolvency, bankruptcy, or judicial declaration of debt restructuring.
d. Given the total loss of the assets of the foundation.
e. At revocation (if such possibility was expressly included in the foundational act, as established in sections 12 and 13 above).
f. For any other cause established in the foundational act or in the Foundations Act.

This section provides certain causes that would operate independently of the desire of the founder (i.e., the insolvency of the foundation), but it makes it clear that the founder is free to establish any cause of termination of the foundation according to his or her wishes. The sole requirement that must be kept in mind is the one contained in section 5, namely, to prescribe the destiny of the assets in the event of dissolution. In short, the founder is free to establish any cause of termination as long as the destiny of the assets is clearly described.

## 5. Change of Domicile of the Foundation (*Redomiciliation*)

Section 28 provides that foundations created under foreign law may continue as Panamanian foundations. In other words, foreign private-interest foundations (such as those in Liechtenstein or Curacao) might change their domicile and applicable law to Panama. Sections 29 and 30 complements the previous one stating that such foreign foundations that desire to change their domicile to Panama must submit

a. A "certificate of continuation" issued by its internal government body (i.e., foundation council), which must include the name and date of creation of the foundation, the information regarding its registration in its country of origin, the express declaration of its desire to continue as a Panamanian foundation, and the requirements to create a Panamanian private-interest foundation included in section 5 of the Foundation Act.

b. A copy of the original foundational act (although the wording of the Foundations Act is not as clear as desirable, the translation of this point follows the most reasonable interpretation based on the antecedents of the Act and actual practice in Panama).

c. A power of attorney to a Panamanian lawyer to make the necessary filings in Panama.

To avoid any possibility that the change of domicile is used as a means to avoid responsibilities in the jurisdiction of origin of the private-interest foundation, section 32 establishes that the responsibilities, duties and rights of the foundation, acquired before the change of domicile or applicable legislation, will go on, as any legal process against the foundation or which the foundation started against third parties, without being affected by the change of law or domicile.

Panamanian law also allows the change of domicile (and applicable law) from Panama to another jurisdiction that allows this procedure. Section 23 expresses that foundations created under the Panamanian Foundations Act, and the assets of such foundations, can change their jurisdiction and applicable law, according with its foundational act and regulations.

## 6. Taxation

Section 27 of the Foundations Acts states the tax regime of foundations providing that the creation, amendment, or termination of the foundation shall be exempted of any tax, contribution, or council tax of any kind or nature, as shall be the transfer or creation of a lien over the assets of the foundation and the income arising from such assets or any other act over them, as long as such assets are

a. Assets located outside of Panama.

b. A deposit of money made by individuals or legal entities that have no Panamanian source income or whose income is not taxable in Panama for any reason.

c. Shares or securities of any kind, issued by companies that have no Panamanian source income, or its income is not taxable in Panama for any reason, even if such shares or securities are deposited in Panama.

This section is analogous to the one of Law No. 1 of 1984 (Trust Act) and provides a tax shield for any foundation with assets outside of Panama. Therefore, Panamanian private-interest foundations have no tax costs in Panama when used by foreign founders for their non-Panamanian assets.

# Chapter 19

# Paraguay[1]

A. Overview  290
   1. Legal Framework  290
   2. Central Bank of Paraguay as Trust Regulator  291
   3. Transference of Assets to a Trust  292
   4. Illegal Trusts  293
   5. Separation of the Trust Patrimony  293
   6. Termination and Liquidation of Trusts  294
B. The Grantor  296
C. The Trustee  297
   1. Trustee Substitution  297
   2. Rights and Powers of the Trustee  298
   3. Duties of the Trustee  298
   4. Trustee's Fees  301
   5. Trustee Resignation  301
D. The Beneficiary and the Residual Beneficiary  302
E. Securitization Companies  303
F. Tax Treatment  305
   1. Value-Added Tax  305
   2. Stamp Duty  306
   3. Notary Rights  306
G. Particular Cases and Experience  306
   1. Investment Trusts  306
   2. Guarantee Trusts  308
   3. Real Estate Trusts  308
   4. Securitization Trusts  308

---

[1]   I wish to thank Dr. Christian Borja Terán, MBA, for his comments on the manuscript of this chapter and his explanations and material on the trust and securitization market in Paraguay, which proved invaluable.

## A. OVERVIEW

Unlike Argentina, Uruguay, and other South American countries where the 2001–2002 crisis—which entailed the fall of the financial system as a whole—created the conditions for the spread of the trust, in Paraguay the crisis affected the trust in an adverse fashion. The explanation is that mutual funds, which had been used until the crisis, were restructured (with heavy losses for the investors) based on the Trust Law. Furthermore because of the crisis, two companies in dire financial straits were administered through administration and guarantee trusts. These two trusts (called *Caballeros Vargas*[2] and *Pechugon*[3]) are two successful cases of trusts, especially if it is considered that in one of them the first trustee was liquidated as a result of his own financial difficulties, and the trust was transferred smoothly to a second trustee who continued with the administration process in favor of the beneficiaries of the trust.

Although all the experiences described above led to the association of trusts with insolvency and bankruptcy in the mind of the general public, who were not too familiar with trusts, it is worth mentioning that since the last quarter of 2006, the use of trusts has been growing steadily. In particular, since then, there has been a securitization transaction every two months. This increase in the use of trusts helped to create a new image of the trust as vehicle of securitizations and business, not just a scheme for reorganizations caused by insolvency. The trust was most used in 2008; an estimate reckoned a fourfold growth in the volume of business over the previous years. Several real estate trusts are currently in progress, and it is most likely that there will be some testamentary trusts in the future.

It is worth mentioning that no case law will be quoted in this chapter simply because there is no case law regarding trusts or trustees in Paraguay. The closest judicial decisions are the ones regarding guarantee deposits (called "warrants"), with rules that have been fully respected by case law.

## 1. Legal Framework

Trusts are governed by the 1996 Law No. 921 on Fiduciary Transactions and Resolution No. 6 (November 22, 2004), issued by the Superintendence of Banks (a department of the Central Bank of Paraguay).[4] As will be seen in detail, the Paraguayan trust could be considered "overregulated," and several amendments are under study to simplify these rules in favor of the creation of a trust market.

Law No. 921 provides in article 1 that "by virtue of the fiduciary transaction, a person, called the grantor or settlor, delivers to another, called the trustee, one or

---

2   Created in 2001, with estimated liquidation in 2017. The trustee was replaced in 2003.
3   Created in 2002 and liquidated in 2007.
4   As you will see in the last part of this chapter, one of the main points of this Resolution is that a guarantee for an amount of 10 percent of the net worth of any investment trust must be created with liquid assets of the trustee. This rule led to the avoidance of investment trusts in Paraguay.

more specified assets, transferring to him or not the title over that property, with the object that the latter administers the assets or alienates them and accomplishes with them a certain object, whether in the benefit of the former or of a third person, called the beneficiary. The fiduciary transaction involving conveyance of the title of the trust assets is called a trust; otherwise, it is called fiduciary charge." As can be seen, the methodology used by Paraguay is similar to that captured by Ecuador in article 112 of the Securities Market Act (*Ley de Mercado de Valores*) in that the fiduciary transaction is the class, and the Commercial Trust and the fiduciary mandate are its subclasses, stressing that in both cases (Ecuador and Paraguay), there was an influence of Colombian jurists.

Summarizing, Paraguay has two fiduciary transactions:

a. Commercial trusts (referred to here simply as trusts), in which a special-purpose patrimony is created, as explained in detail in this chapter.
b. Fiduciary mandates, in which there is no transfer of property and no special-purpose patrimony, and as a logical consequence, no trust. In short, this is an agency contract that could be complemented with a bailment in case certain assets are necessary for the accomplishment of the acts by the agent (referred to here as fiduciary mandates, not as trusts). In case such bailment exists, the assets must be intended for the accomplishment of the object stated in the instrument of the fiduciary mandate.

Requirements relating to trusts and, secondarily, the Civil Code regulations governing the agreement of agency will be applied, where appropriate, to fiduciary mandates, as long as both are compatible with the nature of these transactions and do not run against the special stipulations provided in Law No. 921 and its regulation.

Finally, Law No. 2334 of 2003, which regulates the Guarantee Regime of Deposits in Financial Entities, established the use of trusts as vehicles for the securitization of assets of financial entities under liquidation.

## 2. Central Bank of Paraguay as Trust Regulator

In relation to the regulator of the trust, Law No. 921 provides that it is the duty of the Central Bank of Paraguay:

a. To regulate fiduciary and permissible transactions, issuing the necessary directions on the manner the requirements contained therein must be satisfied, setting the technical and legal criteria, which facilitate their compliance and indicating the procedures for their correct application. As explained, the Superintendence of Banks (*Superintendencia de Bancos*) issued resolution No. 6 of November 22, 2004.
b. To qualify, appointed by the court or at the request of the interested party, certain activities or transactions as fiduciary by reason of their nature and content, and instruct that the persons carrying them out come under the provisions of Law No. 921 and its rules, without the necessity of instituting any disciplinary action.

The decision will be adopted by means of a resolution motivated at least summarily in the fundamental facts and applicable rules, which will be of immediate enforcement, so that the resources appropriate against it by the administrative channel will not suspend its enforceability.

c.  It will be the duty of the Banks Superintendence to dictate the overall rules to which the accounting of fiduciary transactions must subject itself, notwithstanding the autonomy recognized of the trustee to select and employ ancillary methods, provided they are not at odds, directly or indirectly, with the general rules dictated by that body.[5]

## 3. Transference of Assets to a Trust

Any type of assets or rights, existing or future ones, whose delivery is not prohibited by law may be subject to fiduciary transactions.

Fiduciary transactions may be constituted or held by means of an *inter vivos* act, pursuant to the following rules:

a.  If the fiduciary transaction does not involve the transfer of title of the trust assets (fiduciary mandate and not a trust), its execution will not be subject to the observance of any special solemnity or formality, but material delivery must take place, which will be recorded in writing.

b.  If the fiduciary transaction has as its object the transfer of the title of personalty exclusively, it will be perfected by the mere consent of the contracting parties expressed through a written agreement and the physical delivery of the assets.

c.  If the transfer of the title of the trust assets is subject to registry (e.g., a car), the trust transfer must be recorded in a public deed, which will be registered in the public registry in which the assets are recorded.

d.  If there is realty within the property whose title is being transferred, the trust transfer will not be perfected as long as the corresponding public deed has not been furnished, and the registration of the deed has not been effected in the relevant registry.

The aforementioned registration will be effected in accordance with what the general recordation regulations establish on the matter. To effect such a registration, the respective registries will specify that the manner of acquisition of the title entails a trust transfer of assets. As will be seen latter in this chapter, this kind of transaction has a particular tax treatment.

In the event of a trust by testamentary act, the general rules of the law of wills control.

---

5   For example, Rules No. 0322/99 (July 30, 1999) and No. 00048/2002 (March 5, 2002). Currently, the accounting rules for trusts are regulated by resolution No. 6 of November 22, 2004, issued by the Superintendence of Banks (*Superintendencia de Bancos*).

The fiduciary transaction will only be effective against third parties as from the time when the requirements laid down by statute are met, in accordance with the type and nature of the trust assets.

## 4. Illegal Trusts

Fiduciary transactions will be null and void under these circumstances:

a. When the grantor and trustee, or the trustee and the beneficiary, are the same person. As can be seen, there is no legal possibility that a person subject certain assets of his or her property to trust by a declaration of trust. Grantor and trustee must be two different persons.
b. When they infringe a regulation whose observance is in the interests of public order or traditional moral standard.
c. When they fall on assets or rights whose delivery is prohibited by law.
d. When the grantor is under legal incapacity.

Fiduciary transactions will be voidable in the following cases:

a. When the benefit is granted to several persons successively who must be substituted by death of the predecessor, unless the substitution is effected in favor of persons who are alive or in being at the death of the grantor. This rule prevents the creation of a succession order different from the one established by public policy inheritance laws.
b. When its duration is in excess of thirty years, but only as to the excess term. Fiduciary transactions held in favor of people under legal incapacity or of charitable or public utility entities are exempted of this maximum time period. In other words, trusts can only last for thirty years unless they are charitable trusts or in favor or people under legal incapacity.

Law No. 921 states that fiduciary transactions cannot be the means to carry out transactions that the grantor cannot carry out directly in accordance with the law.

## 5. Separation of the Trust Patrimony

For all legal purposes, in trusts the transfer of the title to trust property gives rise to the formation of a special-purpose or separate patrimony, which is affected to the accomplishment of the object stated by the grantor in the trust instrument.

The trust assets are not part of the estate of the trustee. Along this line of reasoning, Law No. 921 specifies that the trust assets and those that replace them cannot be affected by the creditors of the trustee and do not belong to the corpus of assets of his or her liquidation. Such assets only guarantee the obligations incurred by the trustee in pursuit of the object stipulated by the grantor in the trust instrument.

To avoid any confusion and make these rules fully applicable and operative in practice, the trustee must at all times state the capacity in which he or she acts. The aim of such clarification is to avoid the possibility that a counterparty of a contract executed by the trustee argues that he or she understood in good faith that the assets that he or she considered, could be seized in the event of default of the trustee's obligations, were the general estate of the trustee or the assets of other trusts.

The assets comprising the special-purpose patrimony may not be followed in a court of law by the grantor's creditors, but the trust assets held in fraud of third persons may be challenged by the interested parties.

The creditors of the beneficiary may only follow the income produced by the trust assets.

On no account may the trust assets, not even cash, mingle with the trustee's own assets, nor with those relating to other fiduciary transactions. The trustee may not record as his or her own the assets that he or she has received by virtue of a fiduciary transaction.

So as to make a reasonable presentation of the financial situation and the result of the transactions for the accomplishment of the object, for each fiduciary transaction held, the trustee must prepare the following basic financial statements: (a) balance sheet of the fiduciary transaction; and (b) profit and loss statement.

The basic financial statements must be accompanied by the respective explanatory notes as an integral part of the statements. The explanatory notes must be clear and accurate, and their content will limit themselves to disclose the necessary information for a better interpretation of the figures in the basic financial statements, or which, not having any direct bearing on the statements, may be indispensable for their correct construction.

## 6. Termination and Liquidation of Trusts

In addition to those provided in the trust instrument, the fiduciary transaction terminates or expires as a result of the occurrence of any of the following grounds:

a. Full accomplishment of its object
b. Outright impossibility of accomplishing the object stated in the trust instrument
c. Lapse of the period or having reached the maximum duration provided in the law (thirty years, except for charitable trusts or in favor of people under legal incapacity)
d. Compliance with the resolutory condition to which the trust is subject
e. Impossibility of the suspensive condition on which occurrence centers the existence of the trust or to its failure to obtain within the period stated
f. Dissolution and liquidation of the trustee
g. Removal of the trustee ordered by a court of law in the cases provided under the law
h. Mutual agreement between the grantor and the trustee without detriment to the rights of the beneficiary
i. Declaration of outright nullity of the trust instrument

j.  Impossibility of substituting the trustee when the existence of the substitute trustee has not been foreseen in the trust instrument
k.  Revocation of the fiduciary transaction effected by the grantor when he or she has expressly reserved that right in the trust instrument
l.  Resignation by the trustee without detriment to the rights of the grantor and the beneficiary

When any of the grounds for expiry or termination of the trust is present, only the trustee may carry out the necessary acts for its immediate liquidation. The liquidation of the fiduciary transaction will be subject to the following procedure:

a.  The trustee must prepare an inventory of the trust property, which will include an itemized account of the assets and liabilities originating in the execution of the fiduciary transaction.
b.  The trustee will notify the grantor and the beneficiary, as the case may be, of the state of liquidation in which the fiduciary transaction is, having expired or terminated.
c.  The trustee will proceed to collect the credits deriving from the execution of the fiduciary transaction, if any, and to carry out the necessary expedients to satisfy the debts affecting the trust property. The liabilities having been cancelled, the remnant of the trust property, if any, will be returned to the persons to whom it is due, in accordance with the act of settlement or the law.
d.  As long as the liabilities have not been totally cancelled, the trustee must not return any portion of the trust assets to the person to whom they are due in accordance with the act of settlement or the law. However, such portion of the assets may be returned as exceeds double the inventoried liabilities outstanding at the time of the return.
e.  Having undergone the procedure described in the previous subsections, the trustee will immediately summon the grantor and the beneficiary, as the case may be, so that they approve the final accounts of the liquidation. If notice having been served, the grantor fails to attend, or the beneficiary or both, the trustee will summon them again within ten days, and if any of them does not attend, the accounts will be deemed approved, which will not be liable to be challenged at a later date.
f.  Having approved the final account of the liquidation, the trustee will return to the grantor or his or her heirs, as the case may be, what they are due. For the return to be effective between the parties and against third parties, the same requirements must be met as stated in this very law for the creation of the fiduciary transaction.

The litigation deriving from the fiduciary transaction will be the jurisdiction of the civil and commercial court of the trustee's domicile.

In the act of settlement, it may be stipulated that any conflict arising between the grantor and the trustee or the beneficiary, as the case may be, by reason of the existence, construction, development or termination of the fiduciary transaction, be subjected to arbitration. To these effects, the trust instrument shall expressly state the substantive and adjective or procedural regulations whereto the arbitration will be submitted and, in their absence, the arbitration rules prescribed in the law shall be applied.

## B. THE GRANTOR

Grantors can be: (a) individuals or legal entities who have the capacity to transfer assets; or (b) the competent judicial or administrative authorities, when dealing with assets whose custodianship, administration, liquidation, distribution, or alienation is their duty or that of the persons appointed by them to that effect.

The grantor will have the following rights and powers:

a. Those he or she has reserved to exercise directly on the trust assets
b. To enhance or approve the enhancement of the trust assets as effected by a third party, including the extension of the trust object and purpose of the fiduciary transaction; any enhancement or modification required for validity conformity with the formalities required for fiduciary transactions
c. To appoint one or more beneficiaries and to designate one or more substitutes in the event they cannot act in that capacity in the fiduciary transaction
d. To designate one or more trustees for their successive execution of the fiduciary transaction, setting the order and conditions for substitution
e. To designate one or more substitutes of the trustee for his or her replacement in the event of manifest impossibility
f. To revoke the fiduciary transaction, when he or she has expressly reserved this power at trust creation (the general rule is the irrevocability of the trust)
g. To request the removal of the trustee on the grounds provided in Law No. 921 (as explained in the next section)
h. To secure the return of the trust assets on termination of the fiduciary transaction, if those assets were not to pass to a third beneficiary or if the trust instrument had not provided otherwise
i. To set the suspensive or resolutory condition to which the fiduciary transaction will be subject
j. To demand periodic itemized and documented reports from the trustee regarding the results of the entrusted administration
k. To demand from the trustee that, at termination of the fiduciary transaction, for any reason, he or she gives an account of his or her administration
l. To demand from the trustee an inventory of the trust assets
m. Generally, all rights and powers expressly stipulated in his or her favor that are not incompatible with those of the trustee, the beneficiary or the nature of the fiduciary transaction

Further to the provisions in the act of settlement of the fiduciary transaction, the grantor's obligations are as follows:

a. To deliver the trust assets to the trustee
b. To state the purpose for which the trust assets are intended
c. To pay the trustee his or her fees as stipulated in the trust instrument
d. To keep the trust indemnified from defects or hidden faults of the trust assets (both material defects and also legal claims on the assets from third parties) with causes

that existed prior to the fiduciary transaction and which do not permit their application to the object stated in the trust instrument; and others as laid down in the law

Finally, sections 60 and 61 of resolution No. 6 of November 22, 2004, issued by the Superintendence of Banks establish that banks can only be grantors if the trust assets are real estate property or loan portfolios with qualification 4 or 5, according to the qualification rules of the Paraguayan Central Bank and certain rules regarding recording in financial statements and recognition of gains and losses as a result of the trust transfer.

## C. THE TRUSTEE

Only specialized departments of banks[6] and corporations with the exclusive purpose of being trustees and authorized by the Central Bank of Paraguay may act as trustees. From a practical perspective, it must be stressed that currently there are four trustees who actually perform such role and three more authorized but without activity, all of them being banks (none of them is a specially authorized corporation).

To obtain authorization to operate, trustees must at least prove compliance with the following special requirements:

a. To be incorporated as companies with the exclusive object of being trustees. The rationale of this requirement is to avoid that the problems emerging from other activities damage the performance of the services as trustee and to facilitate control by the Central Bank.
b. To possess paid-in capital equal, at least, to that demanded for the incorporation of a financial company. This is a burdensome requirement and the main reason for the inexistence of this kind of corporations.
c. To have a technical, administrative and human infrastructure sufficient to perform adequately the administration and management of the trust assets, in accordance with what in this matter is established by the Central Bank of Paraguay by means of general rules.

As explained before, under Paraguayan law, in no case will the role of grantor or beneficiary merge with that of trustee in a fiduciary transaction.

## 1. Trustee Substitution

When the grantor appoints one or more trustees for their successive execution of the trust, the outgoing trustee will give a documented account of his or her administration

---

6    Section 40 of Law No. 861/96 that regulates banks, financial entities, and other credit entities provides that banks can be trustees subject to Paraguayan Central Bank regulations (the same rule for other financial entities other than banks can be found in section 73 of the Law). Additionally, section 42 of the same Law established that banks must create special departments or subsidiaries to perform trust services.

and will give a copy of the evidentiary documentation to the substitute trustee, who must acknowledge receipt of it and declare his or her approval or disapproval, regardless of the grantor's power to contest such an accounting.

If the grantor or the substitute trustee oppose the accounting presented by the outgoing trustee, the latter will continue in office until the controversy is settled, either in court or out of court.

The person who is designated substitute trustee must formalize his or her acceptance in writing to the grantor and the initial trustee, and his or her signature be certified by public notary, which will be attached to the trust instrument.

The substitute trustee will not be held liable for the acts of the outgoing trustee, except that he or she covers up for them in bad faith or that he or she does not adopt the necessary corrective measures on a timely basis.

## 2. Rights and Powers of the Trustee

Further to the provisions of the trust instrument, the trustee will have the following rights and powers:

a. To conduct and execute all acts and contracts necessary for the accomplishment of the purpose stated by the grantor in the trust instrument.
b. To freely administer the trust assets in compliance with the object stated in the trust instrument. The form of the trust assets may be altered, but not their integrity and value. These powers would be limited if the grantor had reserved certain rights on the creation of the trust to exercise them directly on those assets.
c. To collect the fees agreed with the grantor, in the terms, amount, and form provided in the trust instrument.
d. To obtain payment of the compensations stipulated in his or her favor in the trust instrument, as well as reimbursement of all reasonable expenses conducive to the accomplishment of the object of the trust.
e. To resign his or her administration on the grounds stated in the trust instrument and, absent that, in Law No. 921.
f. Others that derive of the rules of Law No. 921.

## 3. Duties of the Trustee

In addition to those provided in the trust instrument, the following duties and obligations of the trustee cannot be delegated:

a. To show diligence in all acts necessary for the accomplishment of the object stated in the trust instrument, carrying out all the acts of administration and alienation of the trust assets requisite to that end.
b. To invest or place the trust assets in the form and with the requirements provided in the trust instrument, unless discretion has been granted.

c. To watch over the corresponding security and liquidity of the investments or placements made with the trust assets.

d. To collect interests, dividends, and any other yields generated by the investments and placements made with the trust assets.

e. To seek the highest returns from the trust assets, for which any act of disposition that he or she carries out will always be onerous and for profit, unless otherwise stated in the trust instrument. In other words, donations by the trustee are prohibited unless expressly authorized by the trust instrument.

f. To keep trust assets and the assets deriving from the execution of the trust separated from his or her own and from those from other trusts, in such a manner that at any time it may be known if a given asset or property belongs to the trustee or is a part of the assets and property under the trust. When the trust assets are, in part or entirely, in the form of amounts of money, these sums may remain deposited in banks' checking or savings accounts with clear identification of the trust to which the checking or savings account is attached. The bank's checking account or the savings deposit, as the case may be, may be opened or constituted in the trustee itself, so long as it is duly authorized by the Paraguayan Central Bank to raise resources from the public under any of such modes. In every case, banks' checking accounts or savings deposits will be eminently temporary in accordance with the object of the corresponding trust.

g. To keep separate accounts to show the financial situation and results of each trust in particular, in accordance with the administrative and legal provisions governing the matter. In every case, such accounts must be conducted in conformity with generally accepted accounting regulations and principles.

h. To keep updated and in order, the information and documentation relating to the transactions carried out in pursuance of the object stated in the trust instrument.

i. To exercise the rights and legal actions necessary for the protection and defense of the trust assets.

j. To oppose any preventive or execution measure taken against the trust assets or by reason of obligations that do not affect them.

k. To return the trust assets to the grantor or his or her heirs or to the beneficiary, as the case may be, at termination of the trust term on any ground, its liquidation having been effected, as prescribed by law. Any stipulation (whether included in the trust instrument or in any other agreement or declaration) which, directly or indirectly, provides that the trustee will acquire permanently, by reason of the trust, the ownership of the entirety or a portion of the trust assets will not be valid and will be deemed as not stipulated.

l. To request directions from the grantor or the Banks Superintendence when he or she has well-founded doubts as to the nature and scope of his or her obligations, or when he or she must stray away from the authorizations in the trust instrument, when circumstances so require. If directions are requested from the Banks Superintendence, it will previously summon the grantor and the beneficiary.

m. To provide the grantor and the beneficiary, at least every three months, with an itemized and documented report on the results of the entrusted administration.

n. To render a documented account of his or her administration to the grantor and beneficiary, as the case may be, at termination of the trust on any ground.

o. To furnish the Central Bank of Paraguay or any other competent authority in pursuance of its functions with the complete and truthful information that it may request.

p. To conduct the inventory of the trust assets at the request of the grantor, the beneficiary, or his or her ascendants if one does not exist.

The trustee's duty is to display all his or her effort, knowledge, and diligence for the accomplishment of the object stated in the trust instrument, but under no circumstances could it be understood that he or she has the obligation to guarantee a result. Consequently, the losses originated in the accomplishment of the object stated in the trust instrument, provided they are not attributable to negligence or lack of prudence of the trustee in the administration of the trust assets, will affect the grantor or the beneficiary, as the case may be.

In the performance of his or her administration duties, the trustee will refrain from

a. Conducting transactions of any kind and nature with him or herself or for his or her own benefit (self-dealing), or that of the members of his or her own board of directors, or that of his or her presidents, or that of his or her managers or, in general, that of the persons with legal representation powers. The Central Bank of Paraguay may authorize, by means of general rules, the performance of certain transactions when there is no conflict of interests involved.

b. Conducting with the trust assets transactions of any type and nature whereby the members of the board of directors, presidents, managers, administrators and, in general, employees, syndics, and internal or external auditors, or headquarters, or the companies controlled by these persons become, or may become, debtors.

c. Granting loans under any concept with the trust assets, except when they originate in securities repurchase agreements (repos) or debt document discount transactions generally.

d. Pledging, granting guarantees, or imposing any other burden compromising the trust assets and, generally, the assets deriving from the execution of the fiduciary transaction, except for acts intended to guarantee loans secured for the acquisition of those assets or in the development of privatization processes.

e. Conducting with the trust assets, transactions of any type or nature dealing with securities with issuance or placing that is administered or assisted by the trustee him or herself.

f. Investing the trust assets in securities or documents issued, accepted, or guaranteed in any other form by the trustee him or herself, except when the transaction is conducted through the stock exchange, and so long as it is not a concerted practice which, directly or indirectly, aims at producing, or actually produces, the effect of preventing, restricting, or distorting the free interaction of loyal competition in the market.

g. Delegating in any manner to third persons, the performance of the entrusted duties, unless it is indispensable by virtue of the nature of such duties to do so to persons specializing in certain fields.

h. Accepting trust agreements or the rights contained therein as guarantee of loans granted to the grantor or beneficiary.

i. Investing the trust assets in the financing or execution of projects or undertakings of any nature with administration that is conducted by the trustee him or herself.

Finally, regarding the trustee criminal responsibility, it worth mentioning that section 192 of the Criminal Code of Paraguay provides the concept of "breach of trust" penalizing the person who, based on an agreement, assumed the responsibility of protecting a property interest relevant for a third party and caused, or not prevented, damage to his or her property within the scope of protection that was entrusted him. It is our understanding that, should the conditions obtain, the trustee would be liable to criminal charges.

## 4. Trustee's Fees

Unless expressly stipulated to the contrary in the trust instrument, the trustee will collect by reason of his or her administration the fees expressly agreed on in the trust instrument from the trust assets.

In the case that no fee is established in the trust instrument, the trustee has the right to collect the ordinary compensation for this class of services or that which is determined by experts, considering the nature and scope of the administration entrusted.

When the fiduciary transaction expires or terminates prior to the accomplishment of its object, the trustee will be entitled to a compensation to be fixed by taking account of the value of the services rendered and the total compensation agreed on for the sake of the entrusted administration. If the contractually agreed-on compensation is manifestly inordinate, the grantor may request a reduction from a court or an arbiter, as the case may be, proving that the ordinary compensation for that type of administration entrusted is notably lower than that agreed on in the trust instrument, or proving the disproportion by means of experts, absent ordinary compensation. The reduction may not be requested when the compensation was willingly paid by the grantor subsequent to the expiry or termination of the fiduciary transaction.

In none of the cases mentioned above, will a method of compensation be used that involves the guarantee of a result or the obligation of the trustee to procure the highest possible return of the trust assets. The compensation also may not consist, wholly or partly, of the earnings, profits, or benefits ultimately to be generated by the trust assets.

## 5. Trustee Resignation

The trustee may request the Banks Superintendent's authorization to resign or excuse him or herself from performance of the entrusted administration on the grounds stipulated contractually. Lacking contractual stipulation, the following are deemed justified grounds:

a. That the beneficiary may not, or declines to, receive the considerations established in his or her favor under the trust instrument
b. That the trust assets do not yield sufficient income to cover the compensations stipulated in favor of the trustee
c. That the grantor, his or her heirs, or the beneficiary, as the case may be, decline to pay for such compensations

At the grantor's or beneficiary's request and on justified grounds in the opinion of the Banks Superintendent, the latter may remove the trustee from his or her office and, if it be the case, order the appointment of an acting trustee as preventive measure, so that he or she may continue with the execution of the trust.

The trustee will also be removed from his or her office by the competent court at the request of the interested party and when one of these grounds is present:

a. Legal incapacity;
b. When he or she has interests that are incompatible with those of the grantor or the beneficiary
c. When tort or gross negligence is proven, or neglect in the performance of his or her duties as trustee or in any other transactions, whether they be his or her own or that of other persons, in such a way that the good result of the entrusted administration is fundamentally doubted
d. When he or she declines to verify the inventory of the trust assets, or to take the conservatory measures imposed by the competent court

Judicial requests for the removal of the trustee will be dealt with by means of summary proceedings, subsequent to the summoning of the grantor and the beneficiary.

The trustee will be responsible for even slight blame for the damages that he or she occasions the grantor or the beneficiary through lack of diligence and care in the discharge of the entrusted administration.


## D. THE BENEFICIARY AND THE RESIDUAL BENEFICIARY

Natural or legal persons with the capacity to enjoy the economic considerations or benefits that the trust entails may be beneficiaries or residual beneficiaries.

The grantor him or herself or a third person could be beneficiary or residual beneficiary. If the beneficiary is a third person, the benefit can be revoked by the grantor as long as there is no express or tacit acceptance of the benefit by the beneficiary.

The trust may be carried out in favor of one or many beneficiaries or residual beneficiaries. The trust carried out without appointing a beneficiary or residual beneficiary is valid, so long as it is purpose is lawful and definite. Also valid is the fiduciary transaction in which no beneficiary or residual beneficiary exists at the time of creation, so long as his or her existence is possible, and his or her appointment is carried out within its duration, so that its objects may have full effects.

In addition to the powers and rights conferred by the trust instrument, the beneficiary or residual beneficiary has the following powers and rights:

a. To demand the faithful and timely performance of the obligations of the grantor deriving from the fiduciary transaction and the law, and to make good the liabilities for noncompliance with those obligations.
b. To challenge voidable acts carried out by the trustee, within five years computed as from the day the beneficiary came into knowledge of it. This term will not run for minors and the legally incapable, but as from their coming of age or the date when their barring ceases.
c. To oppose any illegitimate preventive or foreclosure measure taken against the trust assets or by reason of obligations not related to them if the trustee does not do so.
d. To request the Banks Superintendent, on justified grounds, the removal of the trustee and, as preventive measure, the appointment of an acting trustee to continue executing the trust.
e. To demand that the trustee takes an inventory of the trust assets.

## E. SECURITIZATION COMPANIES

Law No. 1036 of 1997 creates and governs securitization companies. Despite this Act having been in force for more than 10 years now, there is not a single securitization company in Paraguay. The main reason is that the requirement of capital to create a securitization company is the same as is required to create a bank.

Securitization companies are those that have as their exclusive object the acquisition of credit portfolios and the issuance on such credit portfolios of short-, medium- and long-term publicly offered debt securities.

Unlike trustees that are controlled by the Paraguayan Central Bank, securitization companies are authorized and controlled by the National Securities Commission (*Comisión Nacional de Valores* [CNV]),[7] which keeps records.

These companies must fulfill the following requirements:

a. To be incorporated and to have securitization as their exclusive activity.
b. To issue registered shares exclusively, with negotiation that will be informed to the National Securities Commission.
c. To include in their registered name the term "securitization."
d. To have a paid-in capital in cash to a certain amount equal to the one required of banks. For the effective period of the authorization, 50 percent of the minimum

---

7   The CNV is a decentralized entity that is related to the Public Administration through the Minister of Industry and Commerce, created by Law No. 94 of the December 20, 1991, which was in turn replaced by the current law that rules Paraguay's capital market (Law No. 1284/98).

paid-in capital of securitization companies may not be affected by liens, inhibitions, or attachments.

e. To have an adequate infrastructure and resources.

The company will be held liable for the damages produced in the administration of the special-purpose patrimonies it administers. This liability may be claimed by any securities holder.

The property of the company is different from, and does not merge with, the separate estates that are administered by it. Each company may manage more than one separate estate.

Once the debt securities agreement with the creation of special-purpose patrimony is set up, the assets and obligations that are determined in it will be a part of its assets and liabilities. As from that date, the company may not encumber or alienate the assets in it.

The separate patrimonies constituted by a securitization company have the following characteristics:

a. The creditors of the securitization company, whatever the origin or nature of its credits, may only lay claim on the assets that make up the assets of the separate patrimonies, or that are affected with liens, inhibitions, precautionary measures, or attachments, when they have come to form part of the corporate property.

b. On the assets making up a separate property, only payment of obligations originating in the debt securities issued on that separate property may be followed, not withstanding above item a.

c. The debt securities issued by securitization companies constitute, in favor of their holders, a security right over the corresponding separate property, regardless of the personal or real securities granted by third parties encumbering the corporate property of the issuing company.

d. The creditors of the separate property are made up exclusively by the holders of debt securities making up the corresponding issue and, where appropriate, by the custodian of the securities in the property, the representative of the securities holders, and the administrator of the assets of the property, so long as compensation is due them.

Despite what has been laid out in the aforementioned items, the issuance agreement must provide that the creditors of the separate property may collect under any circumstances the unpaid balance of their credits on the corporate property of the securitization company, pari passu with the other creditors. In such circumstances, and in the event of the declaration of bankruptcy of the company, the creditors of the separate property will be recognized as ordinary creditors of the company.

Once the debt securities issued against a separate property have been paid, the assets and obligations making up the remaining assets and liabilities will pass to the corporate property of the issuing company. An action by a representative of the securities holders who has wide powers for their defense is provided.

The accounts of the corporate property of the company and the accounts of each of the separate patrimonies administered by the company must be kept independent.

## F. TAX TREATMENT

Law No. 921 states that any income received by the trustee as compensation or commission for services rendered by virtue of fiduciary transactions is subject to Income Tax. Additionally, the income will be subject to tax which, at the termination or expiry of the fiduciary transaction on any ground, may be produced by the trust assets, whether it flows from financial yields, interests, dividends, technically established valuations of the assets and property deriving from the execution of the fiduciary transaction, or from any other income. This income will be taxed on the beneficiary or residual beneficiary, except in these cases:

a. When they derive from the formation and execution of fiduciary transactions with an object to the granting of loans, and the grantor or beneficiary of the transactions is a government unit, or when the loans are granted for the fulfillment of social benefit or public utility plans and schemes
b. When they derive from the conduction and execution of fiduciary transactions that have as their object the administration of voluntary pension and disability funds and those complementary to the public pension systems
c. When they derive from fiduciary transactions that have as their object the link to ordinary mutual investment funds or to special mutual investment funds, which have as their object the development of social benefit or public utility plans and schemes
d. When they derive from fiduciary transactions that have as their object investment in debt securities issued, guaranteed, accepted, or secured in any other form by the treasury, other state entities, or the Central Bank of Paraguay
e. When they derive from the conduction and execution of fiduciary transactions that have as their object the advancement of securitization processes structured on debt securities issued, accepted, guaranteed, or secured in any other form by the treasury, other state entities, or the Central Bank of Paraguay, or structured with the object of financing the development of energy activity, infrastructure works, or provision of services, that is, to ensure the fulfillment of plans and schemes of economic, social, sanitary, and educational development, as well as allied matters deemed top priorities by the national government
f. When they derive from investment in securities issued in the development of fiduciary transactions that have as their object securitization processes

## 1. Value-Added Tax

In connection with value-added tax, it is provided that to all appropriate tax purposes, fiduciary transactions and the transactions under Law No. 921 are excluded from the concept of alienation and, consequently, will be exempt from value-added tax.

Also exempt from this tax will be such fiduciary services as the law authorizes banks, financial institutions, and fiduciary companies to offer, including the compensation received for the entrusted administration.

## 2. Stamp Duty

In addition, the following are exempt from the Acts and Documents Tax:

a. Public and private instruments where the creation, modification, termination, or liquidation of a fiduciary transaction are recorded
b. The public or private documents where are recorded the legal transactions and transactions executed by the trustee in performance of the object stated in the trust instrument
c. The securities issued in the course of fiduciary transactions that have as their object the structuring of asset mobilization or securitization processes

## 3. Notary Rights

In fiduciary transactions that convey title recorded in public deed, the notary rights will be liquidated based on the value of the fee to be received by the trustee for his or her administration (and not the value of the assets transferred to the trust). This rule will apply in regard to those acts and contracts that the trustee must hold for the accomplishment of the object indicated in the trust instrument, or when he or she must return the trust assets to the grantor, to his or her heirs, or to the beneficiary, as the case may be, the fiduciary transaction having been terminated on any grounds. Although what would happen is not expressly established in cases where the right to receive the assets from the trust is transferred from the original beneficiary to a new one, it is understood by many trustees that the transfer of assets to the new beneficiary would be subject to the special treatment.

## G. PARTICULAR CASES AND EXPERIENCE

As mentioned before, Resolution No. 6 (November 22, 2004), is the main regulation issued by the Superintendence of Banks for trusts and trustees in Paraguay. In these final chapter sections, the specific rules for the different types of trusts will be addressed.

## 1. Investment Trusts

Investment trust is defined by Resolution No. 6 as the trust in which the main objective is, or there is a possibility that, sums of money are invested according with the instructions of the grantor. Investment trusts can be classified as follows:

a. Single investment trust: This kind of trust is subject to specific regulations. In particular: (i) the precise trust instrument instructions of the grantor cannot be printed in the model of contract used by the trustee; (ii) it is prohibited to make loans with the trust assets to the trustee or any related party, or to any other trust administered by the same trustee; (iii) to invest the trust assets in securities issued by the trustee or any other related party; and (iv) to guarantee a fixed rate of return due to the trustee administration.

b. Collective investment trust: This kind of trust includes mutual funds (*fondos comunes de inversión*) that are defined as the collection of assets received by a financial entity as the result of the execution of trusts of collective administration. Every mutual fund must have its regulations of investments approved by the Paraguayan Central Bank that must include, among other, the following items: (i) name of the trustee and of the mutual fund, (ii) the trustee rights and duties, (iii) the subscription and redemption procedure, and (iv) the policy of investments of the mutual fund. There are several rules in relation to the fees of the trustee and the regulation of the transactions that the mutual fund can enter into.

One of the most relevant restrictions established by Resolution No. 6 is that the amount of assets under trust administration cannot be higher than 15 times the capital of the Bank acting as trustee of such assets as determined by section 43 of Law No. 861/96, which is the General Law of Banks, Financial Entities, and Other Credit Entities.[8]

Law No. 921 establishes that the Central Bank of Paraguay may demand the furnishing of an additional capital as guarantee of the correct administration and management of the trust assets, which will be represented by the investments or assets that the Central Bank authorizes by means of general rules and which, in addition, must be recorded separately in conformity with the directions issued by the Central Bank.

In view of the legal nature and economic function of the trust transactions in Law No. 921, the trustees are not under an obligation to make forced investments or to retain deposits at the Central Bank of Paraguay as legal reserves. However, to safeguard the economic interests of the grantors and of the beneficiaries appointed by them, the Central Bank of Paraguay may order at any time that the trustees constitute special securities or guarantees in the cases it deems appropriate and in the amounts it establishes.

The Central Bank of Paraguay determined that any trustee of an investment fund, either individual or collective, must create a reserve with his or her assets (not trust assets, but his or her own estate) for the amount equivalent to 10 percent of the value of the assets under administration. The reserve must be constituted by deposits with the Central Bank of Paraguay or certain public securities issued or guaranteed by the said Central Bank. As has been said, this rule halted the development of the investment trust.

---

8   This section established that capital must be determined as follows: paid-in capital plus reserves, plus the computable portion of subordinated debt, minus the participation in subsidiaries and foreign banks, plus gains of the current or previous years, minus losses of the current or previous years, plus certain accounting reserves for the valuation of assets.

## 2. Guarantee Trusts

The guarantee trust is defined by Resolution No. 6 as the trust transaction under which the grantor transfers, on an irrevocable basis, the property of assets with the aim of securing certain obligations, actual or future ones, either of the grantor or of a third party, in favor of one or more creditors of such obligations, with the instruction that in the event of default of the debtor of the obligation the trust assets are sold and the obligation paid.

The guarantee trust instrument must include a detail of the secured obligations, including the description of any condition and due date, and the procedure to be followed by the trustee to sell the trust assets in the event of default. The procedure must include a notification to the grantor for him or her to comply with the obligation or prove that he or she has already complied.

Unlike in other Latin American countries, in Paraguay, in no case could the guarantee trust be established to secure obligations in which the trustee is a creditor.

## 3. Real Estate Trusts

Defined as a trust with the aim of being the vehicle of a real estate project in which the grantor transfers a real estate property with the instruction to the trustee to develop the project and sell the units to third parties.

Among the restrictions established by Resolution No. 6, the most relevant one is the rule that establishes that the construction cannot be started unless the financing of the project is obtained.

Finally, the financial statements of this kind of trust must be complemented with information on the characteristics of the project, number, and kind of units to be constructed, construction company in charge of the project, estimation of costs of the project, sources of financing, percentage of completion of the construction, and so forth.

## 4. Securitization Trusts

The securitization trust (also called trust for the "mobilization" of assets) is defined as the legal scheme that turns illiquid assets liquid through the issuance of bonds in the capital markets. The assets that can be securitized are: credits portfolios, public bonds, securities, immovable assets, and cash flows as long as they can be estimated based on data of the last three years. The securities to be issued can be debt securities, participation securities, or mixed securities.

Regarding securitization trusts, although Law No. 1284, which regulates the Securities Market, establishes that a risk-rating is needed to obtain the public offer authorization, as there are no authorized rating agencies in Paraguay (because of too-strict regulations and the prohibition that foreign rating agencies rate securities in Paraguay if they do not have an authorized subsidiary in Paraguay), the few trust securities that were issued did not have a risk-rating. Currently, there is a bill to reform the Rating Agencies Act (Law No. 1056/97), and there is one rating agency that filed with the Banks Superintendence to be authorized to rate issuances.

Resolution No. 6 establishes that the Central Bank will not authorize a securitization in cases where the grantor is a financial entity and the Central Bank finds that the securitization would affect its financial strength, or the risks to be assumed by it are too high, if the conditions of the financial market are not the right ones, or if for any reason the Central Bank finds that it is a scheme of abuse of the aims of securitization.

Finally, regarding credit enhancement mechanisms, the following are ruled by Resolution No. 6: (a) subordination of certain securities, (b) over-collateralization, (c) replacement of defaulting credits, (d) standby letters of credit, (e) guarantees granted by third parties, and (f) guarantee trusts.

# Chapter 20

# Peru[1]

A. Overview 312
   1. Trust as a Separate Patrimony 313
   2. Formalities of the Trust Instrument 313
   3. Duration of a Trust 314
   4. Invalid Trusts 314
   5. Termination of Trusts 315
   6. Testamentary Trusts 315
   7. Guarantee Trusts 316
B. The Trustee 316
   1. Rights and Duties of the Trustee 317
C. The Grantor and the Beneficiary 319
   1. The Beneficiary 319
D. Securitization 320
   1. Securitization Trusts 322
   2. Formalities of the Securitization Trust Instrument 322
E. Securitization Companies 323
   1. Separate Patrimony 325
   2. Securities Backed with the Securitization Trust Assets 325
   3. Termination of the Trust 326
   4. Special-Purpose Companies 327
   5. Securities Offering and Risk-Rating 328

1    This chapter was possible thanks to the expert assistance of several colleagues in Peru. In particular, Lic. Arturo Tuesta M., one of the most prestigious tax and corporate lawyers of Peru, who read the manuscript, made valuable comments, and provided material that is included in the tax treatment part of this chapter; Lic. José Manuel Peschiera R., who explained the main characteristics of Peruvian trusts; Lic. Paulo Comitre Berry, general manager of the main trustee of Peru, who explained to me several practical aspects of the Peruvian trust market and shed light on certain legal aspects; and Raúl De Negri, who provided valuable information on the trust market. I am indebted to all of them.

F. Tax Treatment  328
  1. Income Tax  329
  2. General Sales Tax  330
  3. Municipal Taxes  330

The first Civil Code of Peru (1852) did not contain any reference to trusts. The reason could be, just like in other Latin American contemporary civil codes, the confusion of trusts with the "fiduciary substitutions" expressly prohibited by the Napoleonic Civil Code (the main source of most Latin American Civil Codes). Furthermore, the Civil Code of 1936 equally ignored trusts, and the same occurred with the one currently in force since 1984.

Decree-Law No. 770, the Banking, Financial and Insurance Institutions General Act (*Ley General de Instituciones Bancarias, Financieras y de Seguros*), was the first to rule in its title I "Multiple Banks," chapter IV "Instruments and Contracts," the concept of "trust" as it is known today.

Currently, trusts are regulated in Peru by title III "Trusts," chapter II, Act No. 26702, called "Financial and Insurance Systems General Act and Banks and Insurance Superintendence Organic Act" (*Ley General del Sistema Financiero y del Sistema de Seguros y Orgánica de la Superintendencia de Banca y Seguros*), which will be referred to here at the Trust Act. The Trust Act was enacted in 1996 and was modified by Law No. 27008 (1998) and Law No. 27102 (1999). Regarding record with public registries of the assets of the trust, the Trust Law is complemented by the Resolution of the National Superintendence of National Registries No. 316-2008 (published by the Official Gazette on November 27, 2008).[2]

Additionally, the Securities Market Act (*Ley de Mercado de Valores*) uses the concept of "securitization trust," availing itself to develop the process of the special-purpose patrimony that constitutes a trust with these characteristics, which will be discussed after analyzing the trust regulated by the Financial and Insurance Systems General Act.

## A. OVERVIEW

Under the Trust Act, trust is defined as a legal relationship whereby the grantor transfers assets to another person, called the trustee, for the constitution of a trust , and affected to the accomplishment of a specified object in favor of the grantor or of a third person, called the beneficiary. According to the above definition, and comparable to other jurisdictions, it may be noted that there are three legal positions: (a) the grantor, who transfers the assets to the trust; (a) the trustee, who holds the trust property; and (c) the beneficiary, in favor of whom the trust is created.

---

2    In the course of the discussion of this resolution, I was honored with an invitation to lecture on the registration of trust property, and I had the chance to discuss several issues with the members of the Peruvian Public Registry, in particular, the comparison between the Argentine registration system of trust property and the Peruvian one.

# 1. Trust as a Separate Patrimony

Trust property constitutes a special-purpose property, different from the own estate of the trustee, but under his or her administration. As a result, the Trust Act provides that the trustee must keep separate accounts for each trust under its administration in books that are duly authenticated, apart from the corresponding registers and accounts in the trustees' books.

Trust assets and activities do not generate charges to the corresponding own estate of the trustee, unless liability for misadministration has been allocated by a judge, as well as for the amount of the relevant damages.

Trust property is not available for the obligations of the trustee or the grantor and his or her heirs and, with respect to the obligations of the beneficiaries, such liability is only enforceable upon the income or the considerations at their disposal, if appropriate. When the trustee does not oppose the measures affecting the trust property, the grantor or any beneficiary may do so. Both parties are empowered to contribute in the defense if the trustee has not enforced its opposition.

The assets in the trust property are affected to the payment of the obligations and liabilities that the trustee incurs as a result of the acts it carries out for the accomplishment of the object for which the trust was created and, generally, in accordance with the provisions of the trust instrument. In the absence of a regulation to the contrary, the trustee, the grantor, and the beneficiary are not responsible for the obligations of the trust.

By virtue of the fact that the trustees may only be financial institutions, the law clarifies that minimum capital requirements are not applicable to the liquid part of the funds making up the trust, the Banks Superintendence being the body in charge of dictating general rules on the several types of trust transactions.

In the event that the trust is created in fraud of creditors, the Trust Act provides that the action to nullify the transfer to the trust effected in their fraud expires six months subsequent to publication in the Official Gazette, for three consecutive days, of a notice informing of the alienation. In all cases, that expiration operates two months subsequent to the time the creditor has been notified personally of the creation of the trust.

# 2. Formalities of the Trust Instrument

The creation of the trust could be by contract between the grantor and the trustee, by means of private instrument (an agreement signed by both parties), or in a deed with the intervention of a notary public. It also arises by unilateral intent of the grantor if stated by will.

To enforce the trust against third parties, it is required that if the assets and rights transferred can be registered with the public registry, this is actually done, and that any other legal requirement for the transfer of property is fulfilled (for example the actual delivery of movable assets or endorsement of securities).

Finally, when the trust instrument entails the transfer of personalty to the trust, it can be registered in the Risk Head Office of the Superintendence (*Central de Riesgos de la Superintendencia*), at the grantor's discretion.

## 3. Duration of a Trust

As to the maximum period of a trust, section 251 of the Trust Act provides that it is thirty years, with the following exceptions:

a. In life trusts in favor of named beneficiaries born or in being at the time of trust creation, the period is extended to the death of the last of the beneficiaries.
b. In cultural trusts with the object of establishing museums, libraries, archaeological, historical, or artistic research institutes, the period may be indefinite, and the trust exists as long as it is feasible to accomplish the object for which it was created.
c. In philanthropic trusts with the object of furthering the situation of the insane, orphans, abandoned senior citizens, and the destitute, the period may likewise be indefinite, and the trust exists as long as it is feasible to accomplish the object for which it was created.

In the cases where the trust period must be extended beyond the legal maximum, so as not to injure the interests of third parties, the Superintendence may authorize its validity for such a period as is strictly necessary for the accomplishment of the foreseen objects.

If the trust is established for a longer period than permitted by law (and no exception is applicable), the excess period is deemed unrecorded, except for cultural, philanthropic, and life trusts (Trust Law section 151).


## 4. Invalid Trusts

In accordance with section 265 of the Trust Act, the trust is null and void:

a. If it infringes the requirement set forth in section 243 of the Trust Act. This section provides that, notwithstanding other requirements, for the trust instrument to be valid, the grantor must have the capacity to dispose the assets being transmitted.
b. If its object is unlawful or impossible.
c. If the trustee itself is appointed beneficiary, except with securitization trusts. Put differently, the trust where the trustee is at once the beneficiary is only held to be valid in the case of asset-securitization trusts, which will be addressed further on.
d. If all of the beneficiaries are legally barred from receiving the benefits of the trust—if this bar only falls on part of the beneficiaries, the trust is valid with respect to the remaining ones.
e. If all of the assets that must form the trust are out of commerce (there is a legal prohibition to sell them)—if one or more of the assets that are to make up the trust are out of commerce, but not all of them, the trust is valid and arises with the remaining assets.

## 5. Termination of Trusts

Regarding the grounds of trust termination, these are

a. Justified resignation by the trustee, accepted by the Superintendence.
b. Liquidation of the trustee.
c. Removal of the trustee.
d. Express resignation by all of the beneficiaries of the benefits of the trust.
e. Loss of the trust assets or of a substantial part in the opinion of the trustee.
f. Accomplishment of the object for which the trust was created.
g. Impossibility to accomplish its object.
h. Agreed resolution between grantor and trustee, with the approval of the beneficiaries in the case contemplated in the first paragraph of section 250 of the Trust Act, which provides that "if the beneficiary is a party to the contract, he acquires in his own name the rights therein established in his favor, which cannot be altered without his consent."
i. Revocation by the grantor, prior to delivery of the assets to the trustee, or prior to compliance with the legal requirements, and in any case prior to the acceptance by the trustee. If the revocation is partial, the trust is enforced with the assets that do come into the trust property.
j. Expiration of its period.

In the cases of items (a), (b), and (c), the grounds run if in the term of six months, another trustee is not found to accept the office.

Further, if the trust instrument does not name the person to whom the assets will be returned at the termination of the trust, the said assets will be returned to the grantor or his or her heirs. An exception is made of the trusts addressed in section 244 of the Trust Act, in which the assets, in the amount that affected the forced portion of a certain heir (based on the forced heirship rules), are delivered to him or his or her successors.

## 6. Testamentary Trusts

Peruvian law provides that inter *vivos trusts* are agreements between the settlor and the trustee. However, in the case of *mortis causa* trusts (testamentary trusts), the law does not prescribe acceptance of the appointed trustee nor of the beneficiaries as a requirement for the validity of a testamentary trust instrument. In other words, testamentary trusts, like wills, are valid and enforceable with the sole expression of the person that produced it. If the trustee declined its appointment, it must put forth a substitute, and if no other trustee took on the charge, the trust expires. This type of trust is deemed created as from the inception of probate proceedings.

If the rights arising from the forced heirship rules have been affected by the trust, the forced heirs of the grantor may demand the return of the assets placed in trust in the part that damaged their forced portions. Nevertheless, the trustee company has the power to elect, among the trust assets, those subject to the return. The exception to this rule is the case of the forced portion of minor or legally incompetent heirs. In such a case, the grantor may place under trust the assets that are part of the forced portion of his or her minor or incompetent heirs, as long as the trust is in their own benefit and for as long as their minority or incapacity persists.

The trustee, in all cases, must provide for the maintenance of the minor or incompetent and charge the income or benefits to the trust.

## 7. Guarantee Trusts

Unlike most of the legislations examined in this book, Peruvian trust law handles the guarantee trust expressly in its section 274. It provides that the company granting loans with a guarantee trust constituted with a third-party trustee will reimburse an unpaid loan with the proceeds from the execution of the trust property, as provided in the trust instrument or with the very trust property where this consists of money, in this latter case informing the Superintendence. Unlike Uruguay (where this is permitted in the case of bank trustees) and other countries where the situation is not clear, the Trust Act expressly provides that in this type of trust the capacities of trustee and creditor may not merge in one person.

The relevance of this rule is that it avoids any discussion on the validity of guarantee trusts in Peru. In fact, guarantee trusts are one of the most widespread in the Peruvian market.

## B. THE TRUSTEE

Regarding those who can act as trustees, section 242 of the Trust Act provides that the following are authorized to act as trustees:

a. Financial Development Corporation Inc. (*Corporación Financiera de Desarrollo S.A.* [COFIDE]), a state-owned financial institution
b. Banking companies, financial companies, municipal savings and credit banks, municipal people's credit banks, entities for the development of small- and micro-sized companies (EDPYMEs), savings and credit cooperatives authorized to raise resources from the public, rural savings and credit banks, exchange services companies, and funds transfer companies
c. Trust companies (corporations that have as their sole object and activity to be trustees)
d. Insurance and reinsurance companies

From a practical point of view, it must be said that for several years, until 2008, the sole professional trustee in Peru was *La Fiduciaria*, when *FiduPerú* started its operations.

In relation to securitization trusts, as pointed out in the Securities Market Act, the companies in the financial market must constitute securitizing companies, as will be covered further below.

For each trust under its administration, the trustee (which under Peruvian law is always a corporation) must appoint an individual called the "trust factor" (*factor fiduciario*), who personally assumes its management, as well as liability for the acts, contracts, and operations relating to that trust. The company is severally and jointly liable for the acts which, with respect to the trust, the trust factor and the trustee's employees carry out, except for the provisions of the second paragraph of section 259 of the Trust Law. That section provides that the trustee that incurs in nonperformance of its duties by reason of fraud or gross fault must reimburse the value of the losses to the trust property, plus an indemnity for the damages occasioned, further to the corresponding liability.

The same individual may be trust factor to many trusts. The appointment of the trust factor must be informed to the Superintendence body empowered to order its removal at any time.

If the nature or the number of operations, acts, and contracts relating to the assets of one trust or required for the accomplishment of its object warrant it, the trustee may appoint an administrative committee of the trust. Such a committee must be made up of no fewer than three nor more than seven members, and its work and powers must be regulated by the trustee subject to the rules in the trust instrument. The trustee may employ ad hoc staff for each trust. Such staff may only exercise their rights against the assets of the relevant trust, and the validity of their work relation is subordinated to the subsistence of the trust that determined their employment. The employment contracts must be recorded in writing. If the trust instrument provides the existence of a committee, general meeting, or other governing body, its decisions may not modify the trust purpose.

Trustees have trust property, which confers on them full powers, including those to administer, use, dispose, and make civil recovery of the assets in the trust property, all of which are exercised pursuant to the object for which the trust was created, and in conformity with the restrictions set forth in the trust instrument. Depending on the nature of the trust, the grantor and his or her heirs have a personal credit right against the trust (not a direct right over the trust property like the trustee's, but a right to receive from the trustee certain benefits with the trust property).

The trustee may only dispose of the trust assets as stated in the provisions of the trust instrument. The disposition acts carried out in infringement of the trust instrument provisions are voidable, if the purchaser did not act in good faith, except when the transfer was conducted in the stock exchange. Action may be started by any of the beneficiaries, the grantor, or even the trustee itself.

## 1. Rights and Duties of the Trustee

Under section 256 of the Trust Act, the trustee is bound to

a. Protect and administer the assets and rights in the trust property with the diligence and conscientiousness of a careful businessperson and loyal administrator

b. Defend the trust property, safeguarding it both from physical damage and from legal actions or extrajudicial acts that might affect or impair its integrity
c. Protect with insurance policies the risks incurred by the trust assets as agreed on in the trust instrument
d. Comply with the charges aiming at the accomplishment of the object of the trust, carrying out the required acts, contracts, operations, investments, or transactions with the same diligence that the trustee applies to its own matters
e. Keep the inventory and accounts of each trust in accordance with the law and conform to the tax obligations of the trust property, both substantive and procedural
f. Prepare balance sheets and financial statements for each trust, at least once every semester, as well as an annual report, and make those documents available to the grantors and beneficiaries, apart from their submission to the Superintendence
g. Keep secret all operations, acts, contracts, documents, and information relating to the trusts with the same scope that this law imposes for banking secrecy
h. Notify the beneficiaries of the existence of assets and services available in his or her favor, within the term of ten days after the benefit is good
i. Return to the grantor or his or her heirs, at termination of the trust, the remaining trust property, unless, having complied with the trust transfer, delivery is due to the beneficiaries or to other persons
j. Transfer to the new trustee, in the event of subrogation, the resources, assets, and rights of the trust
k. Render an account of his or her performance to the grantors and to the Superintendence at termination of the trust

In the event of fraud or grave blame, the Superintendence may order the removal of the trustee and appoint a substitute, if the grantor did not do so within the period accorded.

In accordance with the provisions of section 257 of the Trust Act, the trustee is prohibited from securing or otherwise guaranteeing the grantor or the beneficiaries the results of the trust or of the operations, acts, and contracts carried out with the trust assets. An agreement to the contrary is null, as well as the guarantees and commitments agreed on in infringement of the provisions of the said section.

Also, the trustee is prohibited by law from conducting operations, acts, and contracts with the trusts' funds and assets in the benefit of certain subjects, namely

a. The trustee itself
b. Its directors and employees and, if any, the members of the committee in charge of the trust
c. The trust factor
d. The employees in its trust department of a financial institution and those employed for the relevant trust
e. Its external auditors, including the partners in the firm and the professionals engaged in auditing activities of the trustee

These impairments extend to the spouse and relatives of the said persons, as well as to the legal persons with which the spouse and relatives jointly and personally hold a participation superior to 50 percent. The transactions carried out in breach of the listed prohibitions are null and void.

By virtue of section 261 of the Trust Act, the trustee enjoys the following rights:

a. To collect compensation for its services as laid down in the trust instrument or, in the absence of such a provision, one not in excess of 1 percent of the market value of the trust assets
b. Seek reimbursement with trust resources of the expenses incurred in the administration of the trust property and in the accomplishment of its object

In the event of liquidation of the trustee, the Trust Act provides that those who have a lawful interest are entitled to identify and recover the existing trust assets and rights, at any stage of the process, for not being a part of the trust property.

The Trust Law grants a first preference credit to the beneficiary over the assets of the trustee for the value of the lost or unascertainable rights of the trust.

## C. THE GRANTOR AND THE BENEFICIARY

The primary obligation which the Trust Act mentions concerning the grantor or his or her heirs, is that of bringing into the trust property the assets and rights stated in the trust contract, in the stipulated time and place. The sole requirement to be a grantor is to have the legal capacity to carry out the transfer of the assets.

## 1. The Beneficiary

The Trust Act provides that a valid trust may be created in favor of

a. Indefinite persons who meet certain conditions or requirements, or the public at large, so long as the required qualifications to enjoy the benefits of the trust or the rules to grant them are recorded in the trust instrument
b. The grantor him or herself, that is, the so-called trustee-beneficiary trust
c. Persons who must successively substitute for each other, as a result of death of the predecessor or some other event, so long as the substitution is carried out in favor of persons existing at the time the right of the first appointee is made good (this is a way to limit the fiduciary substitution that is explained in Chapter 1, Section A1 and Section B, and in Chapter 5, Section D2)

If the beneficiary is a party to the contract, he or she acquires the rights therein set forth in his or her favor, which may not be modified without his or her consent. Nevertheless, in all other cases, the grantor may agree on the modifications he or she deems appropriate with the trustee, and even the termination of the trust, unless this injures the rights of third parties.

To modify or terminate the trust instrument, the heirs of the grantor require, in all cases, the undivided consent of the beneficiaries or, if these were indefinite, approval from the Superintendent.

The beneficiaries are entitled to demand from the trustee the benefits generated by the trust property or from the principal itself, according to the provisions of the trust instrument and, if it was issued, as is indicated in the participation certificate. The action may be exercised by any of the interested beneficiaries, for the portion of the benefits due him or her and in favor of common interest.

The definite beneficiaries, the grantors, and their respective successors may transfer their rights to persons who are not barred by statute or by the provisions of the trust instrument.

Where the beneficiaries are five or more, they must hold general meetings subject to the rules established for corporate bond holders assemblies by sections 236, 237, and 238 of the General Corporations Act (*Ley General de Sociedades*), unless the trust instrument stipulated differently on the matter.

The general meetings mentioned in the previous paragraph have as their object:

a. To appoint representatives or attorneys-in-law who act to safeguard the common interest of the beneficiaries.
b. To approve modifications in the terms of the trust, when the consent of the beneficiaries were necessary, so long as they are not minors or legally incapable people and therefore unable to personally participate in the assemblies.
c. To adopt other measures and decisions in favor of the common interest of its members.
d. In the cases of trusts with indefinite beneficiaries, the representation is assumed by the Superintendence.

## D. SECURITIZATION

The first securitization transaction took place in 1998, and the securitization market has been active since then. Some underlying assets have been future cash flows related with sales of services rendered by the grantor or proceeds from sales of the grantor (basically sales made by the grantor, a supermarket), real estate projects, and Peruvian government bonds.[3]

Under section 260 of the Trust Act, any issuance of securities backed by a trust asset is subject to the provisions of the Securities Market Act. Furthermore, the Securities Market Act of Peru (Legislative Decree No. 861) prescribes in chapter I, title XI, Special Rules Pertaining to Securitization Processes (*Normas Especiales Relativas a Procesos de Titulización*), the provisions associated with these processes

---

3    The figures of securitization issuances for the last years are as follows: 2003: US$91.4 million; 2004: US$142.9 million and Peruvian *soles* 52.2 million; 2005: US$241 million and Peruvian *soles* 80 million; 2006: US$50 million and Peruvian *soles* 210 million; and 2007: US$40 million and Peruvian *soles* 231 million.

and securitization vehicles. The provisions of title XI under study set forth rules to which the persons conducting securitization processes must subject themselves. In the cases where a securitization process is effected partially in Peruvian territory, the rules in this title will be applicable, unless there is an agreement to the contrary, exclusively to those acts conducted in the country.

Peruvian law defines securitization in section 291 of the Trust Act, which provides that "securitization is the process whereby a property is constituted whose exclusive object is to back the payment of the rights conferred on the titleholders of securities issued on such a property. It also encompasses the transfer of assets to the said property and the issuance of the respective securities."

The Trust Act defines the terms involved in this type of process, stating that for the purposes of the regulations relating to securitization processes, the following will be understood by:

a.  Assets: the liquid assets and all manner of property and rights
b.  Credit assets: the rights, whether evidenced in securities or not, which confer their titleholder the right to receive sums of money
c.  Enhancer: the person who grants additional guarantees for the payment of the securities issued in a securitization
d.  Originator: the person in whose interest a special-purpose property is created, who undertakes to transfer the assets that will compose it
e.  Special-purpose patrimony: that which serves as backing to the payment of the securities issued in a securitization
f.  Backing: the guarantee or source of funds for the payment of the rights conferred by the issued securities in securitization
g.  Servicer: the person who executes the payment of the considerations relating to the assets making up a special-purpose property

It is the duty of the National Corporations and Securities Supervisory (*Comisión Nacional Supervisora de Empresas y Valores* [CONASEV]) to rule and exercise the control and surveillance of the natural and legal persons participating in securitizations. The CONASEV is the public institution in charge of supervising and controlling compliance with the Securities Market Act (the Peruvian equivalent to the U.S. Securities and Exchange Commission [SEC]).

According to the provisions of the Securities Market Act, securitization may be conducted from the following special-purpose patrimonies:

a.  Trust property (securitization trusts)
b.  Property of special-purpose companies
c.  Others that are appropriate, as stated by the CONASEV by means of general rules

Which is to say that, apart from the securitization trust, special-purpose companies may be created for asset securitization. To form part of exclusive-purpose patrimonies, any assets upon which their titleholder may dispose freely, may be transferred. By means of general rules, the CONASEV is also empowered to set restraints on the use of certain categories of assets. The transfer of assets to the trust is carried out by means of the corresponding legal means pursuant to their nature.

As a way to protect the investors in a securitization, section 298 of the Trust Act provides that the following may not be declared: (a) nullity because of simulation, (b) annulment, or (c) invalidity for fraud of the instrument whereby one or more persons constitute a special-purpose patrimony and transfer assets to such patrimony, if such declaration may damage: (a) those subscribing or acquiring the securities by public offering, or (b) having subscribed or acquired them by virtue of a private negotiation, had acted in good faith. It is considered that the holders of securities are damaged when payment of the considerations due to the securities titleholders becomes impossible, the likelihood of such payment is impaired, or, in all cases, when a downgrade in the assigned risk-rating is produced.

## 1. Securitization Trusts

Under section 301 of the Trust Act, in securitization trusts a person, called grantor, undertakes to carry out the transfer of a set of assets in favor of the trustee for the creation of a special-purpose patrimony, called trust property, subject to the ownership of the latter and affected to the specific object of supporting the rights evidenced in securities, with the subscription or acquisition or purchase that grants their titleholder the status of beneficiary.

It should be noted that only securitizing companies can be trustees in securitization trusts. Securitizing companies are under the control and surveillance of the CONASEV, must have authorization of organization and operation issued by that governmental body and be registered in the Registry. The securitization company may hold one or more trust estates under its ownership.

The securitization company, by means of a unilateral act (in which there is only one party that records his or her intention), may also create patrimonies. By virtue of such acts, the company undertakes to establish a trust (separate patrimony under his or her trust ownership) with a set of assets, merging in that case the capacities as grantor and trustee. Such assets and the gains and income deriving from them will not be available to return to the property of the securitization company until the object for which the trust was created is accomplished, except for an express stipulation to the contrary. As mentioned in other chapters, this is the securitization model of several countries (e.g., Bolivia, Brazil, and Chile), but it is against the general rule in Latin America that the grantor cannot be a trustee.

## 2. Formalities of the Securitization Trust Instrument

Under section 308 of the Trust Act, the trust instrument must be recorded in public deed, and cannot be modified without prior consent from the beneficiary. The public deed must record at least for

a. The specific purpose for which the trust is created, which may not be any other than that of serving as backing of a securities issuance.

b. The itemized statement of the assets to be transferred, indicating whether they are in the transferor's property or, on the contrary, they are third-party assets to be acquired or future assets; in these latter cases, the party assuming the risk of their acquisition or existence must be indicated. Whether the assets are subject to any encumbrance or attachments, or whether they are under controversy or legal arbitration or administrative litigation must also be recorded. Should that itemized statement prove impossible at the time of trust creation, the description of the requirements and characteristics that the assets must meet will be recorded.
c. Method and period of transfer of the assets that will make up the trust property.
d. Denomination of the trust property.
e. The rights, obligations and powers of the grantor, the securitization company and the beneficiary, with indication of
  i. The terms and conditions of the securities issuance that it will secure, especially all regarding voting rights among the different series or classes of securities issued
  ii. The power of the securitization company to delegate certain functions on the grantor or third persons, as well as the restrictions on their disposition and administration powers regarding the assets in the trust property
  iii. Grounds and powers to decide the removal of the securitization company
  iv. Powers and procedure for election of the substitute trustee in the event of resignation, liquidation, or removal of the securitization company
f. Additional guarantees that the grantor, the securitization company, or third persons may have established, or, if it be the case, those to be established in the exercise of the trust ownership.
g. Conditions or periods, the latter's indeterminacy being possible.
h. The object of the assets at termination of the trust.

## E. SECURITIZATION COMPANIES

The securitization company is a corporation of indefinite duration whose exclusive object is to serve as trustee in securitization processes, apart from engaging in the acquisition of assets to create patrimonies that back the issuance of securities. The Trust Act expressly provides that securitizing companies must include in their registered name the phrase "securitization company." Under the provisions of article 303 of the Trust Act, its minimum corporate capital is 750,000 Peruvian nuevos soles, which must be entirely subscribed and paid prior to the start of activities. In no case may the net capital of the securitization companies be inferior to the amount of the corporate capital prescribed in the previous paragraph. Such a minimum capital must be increased according to the number and amount of the trusts, in compliance with the regulations dictated to that effect by the CONASEV.

For each trust, the securitization company appoints an individual, called trust factor, who personally assumes its management. Additionally, when circumstances call for it, the securitization company may appoint an administration general meeting, to whose decisions the trust factor is subject. The securitization company will be jointly and severally liable with the members of the administration general meeting for the acts carried out in execution of its decisions as to the trust. If the existence of the administration general meeting or like organ, has been provided in the trust instrument at the instance of the grantor, the joint and several liability addressed in the above paragraph is assumed by the latter, not by the securitization company.

The Trust Act provides that the following cannot be founders, directors, managers, representatives, trust factors, or members of the administration general meeting or like body:

a. Those disqualified or barred by the relevant laws
b. The directors, advisors, officials, and other employees with the CONASEV and their relatives
c. Those who, at any time, have been found guilty of a crime by the commission
d. Those declared in bankruptcy, despite that proceedings were dismissed, or insolvency, for as long as that status persists
e. Those removed by the CONASEV, the Superintendence, or any other government agency or unit from the office of directors, managers, or representatives of a company subject to its control or surveillance

By virtue of the trust, and apart from those stated in the trust instrument and in the Trust Act, the securitization company is under the following obligations:

a. To keep the trust assets separate from those in its own property and from those in other patrimonies
b. To summon a general meeting of beneficiaries when required by beneficiaries representing at least one-fifth of the rights guaranteed by the trust property; or to request directions when so required by circumstances
c. To perform its duties in accordance with the terms of the trust instrument
d. To produce its own financial statements and those of each separate estate under its administration with the periodicity and requirements prescribed by the CONASEV
e. Others set forth by the CONASEV

The resignation of the securitization company will only be valid with the approval of the grantor and beneficiary. In all cases, the resignation will take effect as from the transfer of the trust property to the new trustee. Any agreement to the contrary is null and void.

In its turn, section 320 of the Trust Act, relating to the removal of the securitization company, provides that the power of the parties to decide the removal of the securitization company is subject to the provisions of the trust instrument. Notwithstanding powers granted to the trustees, or agreement by the parties empowered to decide such a removal, this can be resolved by the CONASEV where the existence of fraud or gross fault had been proved. The removal request before CONASEV may be petitioned by the grantors, beneficiaries representing at least one-fifth of the rights supported by the trust property, or anyone with a lawful interest in cases where the latter did not so petition.

The agreements associated with the removal and acceptance of the resignation of the securitization company, when it comes to the designation of agents and attorneys, as well as those relating to modification of the trust terms, must be adopted by beneficiaries representing at least the absolute majority of the rights conferred by the issued securities.

In the absence of an appointed representative, or declination by the securitization company, the CONASEV, at the request of titleholders representing at least one-fifth of the rights backed by the trust property, may summon the general meeting of beneficiaries.

According to section 319 of the Trust Act, the dissolution and liquidation of the securitization company will only affect its own property and not the trust property.

When a securitization company starts dissolution and liquidation proceedings, it is the CONASEV's duty to appoint the person or persons who will act as liquidator.

In the event of lost or unascertainable trust property assets, a preferred status is enjoyed by the beneficiary as regards credit against the assets of the liquidation of the securitization company, which is exercised pursuant to the order of precedence laid down in the law.

## 1. Separate Patrimony

The trust instrument, once the due formalities have been complied with, generates a special-purpose patrimony, different from the securitization company's own property, the grantor's, the beneficiary's, and that of the person appointed as receiver of the remaining trust assets. On such property, the securitization company exercises a trust property, which grants it full powers, including its administration, disposition, and civil recovery of the assets in the trust property, which are exercised in accordance with the purpose for which the trust was created and observing the restraints set down in the trust agreement.

The registrations and other instruments where are recorded the acts effected by virtue of the trust ownership must state such a fact, indicating the corresponding trust name (or other identification means).

If it were so stated in the trust instrument, the provisions of the previous paragraph are applicable to the other assets acquired with the proceeds of the trust assets or with the income of their disposition.

Furthermore, the assets of the trust are affected to the payment of the obligations and liabilities incurred by the securitization company acting as trustee of such trust in pursuance of the object for which the trust was created and, generally, in accordance with the trust instrument. The assets in the trustee's, grantor's, or beneficiary's own property are not affected to such payment, unless otherwise agreed on.

## 2. Securities Backed with the Securitization Trust Assets

Under the provisions of section 314 of the Trust Act and the trust instrument, the securitization company issues securities freely marketable, evidencing rights backed by the trust property. Such securities confer on their holder the status of beneficiaries of the trust. The securities may be issued as registered or bearer securities, and they may be evidenced by registration in books. Section 309 of the Trust Act provides that, when the securities are subject to public offering, the trust instrument will be registered in the Public Registry and for each trust, the following data will be recorded within thirty days of the granting of the public deed:

a. The modifications that may have been introduced
b. The guarantees and other agreements relating to the rights granted by the trust
c. The appointment of the persons exercising the fiduciary ownership in representation of the securitization company
d. The termination of the trust

The rights of the securities backed with the trust assets may be of the following classes:

a. Of credit content, where both the principal and interest are paid with the resources from the trust property
b. Of participation, where a quota of the resources originating in the trust property is conferred on the titleholder

Securities in which the rights in the above items are combined may be issued, as can security certificates evidencing one or more securities. The trust property may also back securities evidencing third-party issuer's credit rights if it had so been established in the trust instrument.

The Trust Act also provides the possibility that a trust property may back different classes of securities. When each class includes series, the values making up each series must grant equal rights, and differences may be established between the rights conferred by various series. Should there be no series, the values included in a given class must confer equal rights.


## 3. Termination of the Trust

When a trust enters into a dissolution and liquidation process, it is the duty of the CONASEV to appoint the person or persons who will act as liquidator.

The dissolution and liquidation of the trust property does not affect the securitization company's own property nor does it affect the other trusts.

In the event of insolvency of the trust, had an alternative mechanism not been foreseen that safeguards the rights of the interested parties and those of the third parties authorized by the Trust Act to claim payment of their rights with the trust property, the stipulations of the regulations relating to corporate asset restructuring will be followed, where appropriate.

The trust ownership of a securitization company expires by reason of the following:

a. Resignation
b. Entering into a dissolution and liquidation process
c. Removal

In these hypotheses, the securitization company, or whoever is in charge of its liquidation, is obligated to transfer the assets of the trust property to the substitute trustee, handing over the instruments and contributing to the relevant registrations.

Once the period fixed by regulations has elapsed without the person who shall assume as trustee being appointed, such designation will be in the hands of the CONASEV. The appointment may only fall on another securitization company. Where exceptional circumstances exist, the appointment may fall on a bank, with the authorization of the CONASEV.

The termination of the trust because of accomplishment of its object having occurred, the trustee will be obligated to deliver the trust assets to the residual beneficiary of the extinguished property, handing over the instruments and contributing to the relevant registrations.

## 4. Special-Purpose Companies

As already said, securitization may also be developed by property of special-purpose companies. Special-purpose companies are primarily governed by the provisions of the Trust Act and, where applicable, by the rules applicable to corporations. These types of companies are corporations whose assets are basically constituted by credits, and whose corporate object confines its business to the acquisition of such assets and to the issuance and payment of securities guaranteed by its property. Special-purpose companies are subject to the control and surveillance of the CONASEV and must be registered at the Registry when the securities they issue are, or are to be, subject to public offering. As these companies are not used in practice, the following comments are brief.

As set forth in section 327 of the Trust Act, concerning special-purpose companies,

a. They do not require plurality of shareholders for their creation (unlike most corporate laws in Latin America, which require at least two shareholders).
b. Their designation or registered name must include the phrase "special-purpose company."
c. Their corporate object must indicate that their activity is confined to the acquisition of credit assets and the issuance of securities, and they may not conduct other activities that are not directly linked to this object, nor raise resources from the public.
d. The type of credit assets to be acquired by the company must be stated clearly and precisely in its bylaws.
e. The rules relating to the distribution of earnings must indicate the restrictions that could be agreed on as to the allocation of dividends.

The administration's regime must include the restrictions and liabilities to which the company's administrators are subject in their performance, as well as the power of the securities holders to appoint at least one of the members of their board of directors.

## 5. Securities Offering and Risk-Rating

The securities guaranteed by the exclusive-purpose patrimonies (whether it is securitization trusts or special-purpose companies) may be subject to public or private offering.

When the securities are subject to public offering, the provisions of title III of the Securities Market Act are to be followed. Also applicable are the other rules relating to the public offering of securities.

As to the securities guaranteed by an exclusive-purpose patrimony, when so agreed on, it is possible to subordinate the payment of the consideration due its titleholders to the payment of another present or future obligation guaranteed by the same exclusive-purpose patrimony. This subordination remains valid in the event of liquidation of the exclusive-purpose patrimony.

To the purposes of risk-rating of the securities issued in a securitization, the risk-rating agencies must carry out their classification based on an analysis of the exclusive-purpose patrimony guaranteeing them, as well as the quality of the used securitization structure. A risk-rating agency may not assume the rating of the issued securities in a securitization when it is deemed related to, or holds an interest in, the originator or the enhancer. Likewise, the members of the risk-rating agency, the managers and officials responsible for carrying out the rating studies, who hold an interest or are related to those persons, must refrain from participating in the corresponding risk-rating process.

Finally, the Trust Act provides that, taking account of the securitization structure employed, the hired risk-rating agency keeps updated the analyses of the activities and of the financial situation of the originator, the issuer, and the enhancer, as the case may be, in reliance of the essential information, public or confidential, and keeping due confidentiality.

## F. TAX TREATMENT[4]

Notwithstanding any position regarding the status of Peru as a centralized or federal country from a political point of view, Peru is certainly not a federal country from a tax perspective. Put differently, unlike federal countries that have three levels of taxation, national or federal taxes, estate or provincial taxes, and county taxes—Peru only has two levels of taxation, federal or national taxes and county or municipal taxes. The main difference between the municipal taxes and the provincial or estate taxes is the lack of autonomy of the former to establish and regulate its own taxes.

The following sections will examine income tax and general sales tax (the two main national taxes) and the municipal taxes (stamp tax, real estate tax, and car tax).

---

4    This part of the chapter is based on material provided by Lic. Arturo Tuesta M., widely considered the most prestigious expert on trust taxation in Peru.

## 1. Income Tax

Up to December 2003, trusts did not pay income tax. The grantor was considered the owner of the assets (and there were no tax effects regarding the transference of assets to the trust), and the trustee was responsible for the payment of the income tax on the income arising from the trust assets.

The treatment of securitization trusts was different. Securitization trusts were considered income-tax taxpayers (as corporations) up to fiscal year 2002. From 2003 to 2004, they were pass-through entities, and any income arising from the securitization trust assets was attributed to the beneficiary of the trust.

Since fiscal year 2004, both kinds of trusts (ordinary trusts and securitization trusts) have been unified, and both became pass-through entities, and any income arising from the securitization trust assets has been attributed to the beneficiary of the trust (with certain exceptions in particular cases).

Finally in fiscal year 2009, the rules for both kinds of trusts are the following:

a. Trusts are different tax entities from the grantor, the trustee, and the beneficiary, who must have their own accounting, but are not taxpayers.
b. Trusts assess the income, but for tax purposes it is allocated, in the case of ordinary trusts, to the grantor (with the exception of testamentary trusts, which for obvious reasons, allocate income to the beneficiaries); and in the case of securitization trusts, to the beneficiary of the income.
c. Income attributed to the grantor or the beneficiary must be qualified by the trustee as taxable or exempted. If they are taxable, a withholding is applicable, which varies depending on the characteristics of the beneficiary of the income. If the receptor of the income is a legal entity resident in Peru, 30 percent is withheld; if a natural person, not involved in commercial activities, resident in Peru, 5 percent is withheld; if a foreign beneficiary, 30 percent is withheld (a reduction for individuals who are foreign beneficiaries is in place for 2010).
d. Trustees are responsible for the due payment of the taxes of the trust.

Regarding the transfer of assets to the trust, if it is established in the trust instrument that they will return to the grantor once the trust is terminated, the transfer has no tax effects, and the trust must consider the assets at the same value as the one used by the grantor. In such a case, it is reasonable to understand that if the grantor is subject to particular tax rules (e.g., exemptions as a result of carrying on a promoted activity or special amortization rules), such tax rules are applicable to the trust. If the asset does not come back to the grantor, the transfer to the trust is a sale for income tax effects.

Guarantee trusts, charitable trusts, trusts with cultural purposes, and lifelong trusts are not subject to the rules explained before, as they are not considered separate entities for tax purposes. They are considered as if the assets had never been transferred by the grantor to the trustee. This special tax treatment has two exceptions: (a) guarantee trusts with cash flows as underlying assets (no special rationale explains this exception); and (b) in cases where trustee must sell the underlying assets in a foreclosure procedure because of the default of the obligation guaranteed with the trust assets.

Regarding securitization trusts, it is established that the difference between the nominal value of the credits transferred to the trust and the actual amount of cash received as consideration for the transfer (discount made by the securitization trust that represents the securitization trust income) is considered an expense that must be deducted proportionally during the period of time that lasts the securitization trust (as any other financial expense for financing). Furthermore, it was expressly clarified that the transfer of assets as collateral has no tax effects at all.

## 2. General Sales Tax

Securitization trusts are subject to the general sales tax and must declare and pay any tax arising from their transactions.

Ordinary trusts are not subjects of the tax, nor is the transfer of assets to the trust subject to this tax. Therefore, the grantor is subject to the tax for any taxable event done by the trustee with the trust assets.

## 3. Municipal Taxes

Unlike national taxes, there are no specific rules regarding trusts or trust property at the municipal level of taxation.

Regarding the Stamp Tax (*Impuesto de Alcabala*), it taxes the transfer of real estate property. As it is reasonable to understand that the word "property" refers to ordinary property and not trust property, it can be argued that this tax is not applicable to the transfer of real estate to trusts. Nevertheless, it is reasonable to restrict this interpretation to the case of transfer done by a grantor, not by third parties who sell real estate to the trust receiving as consideration a sum of money.

In relation to the Real Estate Tax (*Impuesto Predial*) and the Vehicle Tax (*Impuesto al Patrimonio Vehicular*), although the case of trusts is a debatable one, it is reasonable to understand that real estate and cars transferred to a trust are subject to the tax.

# Chapter 21

# Uruguay[1]

A. Overview 332
    1. Definition of Trust 333
    2. Trust as a Separate Special-Purpose Patrimony 334
    3. Assets That May Be Transferred to a Trust 335
    4. Trust as Agreement, Separate Patrimony, and Trust Property 335
        a. Trust Agreement 335
        b. Trust Property 336
    5. Registration of the Trust Instrument 336
    6. Termination 337
    7. Insufficiency of the Trust Assets 339
B. The Grantor 340
C. The Trustee 340
    1. Registry of Professional Trustees 341
    2. Penalties 341
    3. Multiple Trustees and Trustee Substitution 342
    4. Standard of Trust Services 342
    5. Duties of the Trustee 342
    6. Prohibitions That Affect the Trustee 343
    7. Trustee's Fees 343
    8. Termination of the Office of the Trustee 344
D. The Beneficiary 345
E. Guarantee Trusts 346
    1. The Montevideo Airport Guarantee Trust 347
F. Testamentary Trusts 347
    1. Forced Heirship in Uruguay 347

---

[1]   This chapter was possible because of the kind help of CPA and MBA Daniel Porcaro, who explained several aspects of Uruguayan trusts and provided some excellent material on their tax treatment.

G. Financial Trusts 349
    1. Securitization in Uruguay Before the Trust Law 349
    2. Current Situation 350
    3. Trust Securities 351
    4. The Trust Securities Holders' Meeting 351
H. Tax Treatment 352
    1. Nonfinancial Trusts 353
    2. Financial Trusts 353
    3. Guarantee Trusts 353
    4. Offshore Trusts 354
    5. Tax Benefits 354
    6. Tax Treatment and Responsibility of the Trustee 354
    7. Foreign Beneficiaries 354
    8. Tax Secret 355

## A. OVERVIEW

Law No. 17703 entered into force on November 26, 2003 (published in the Official Gazette on November 4, 2003). This law introduced the trust into Uruguayan law, being complemented by Regulatory Decree No. 516, amended by Decree No. 46/04 (hereinafter the "Trust Law" and the "Decree"), and also regulated by rules 1892, 1889, 1895, and 2004/041 of the Uruguayan Central Bank (BCU). Before the Trust Law, Uruguayan law did not regulate the trust, and it was not possible to create a separate special-purpose patrimony with assets that could not be attacked by the creditors of the grantor, trustee, and beneficiary.[2]

Because of the restriction to bank financing and the recession that took place in 2002, the need of creating a new instrument was obvious, which allowed the flow of funds to productive activities. In this scenario, the bill that then became the Trust Law was sent by the president to the legislative assembly in November 20, 2002.[3] This bill was based on the Argentine one and became the Trust Law, with the amendments made during the debate in the Legislative Assembly,[4] Uruguay being the last country in Latin America to include the trust in their legal systems (Argentina being the penultimate).

As explained by Uruguayan jurists, the creation of the trust has as its main objective to facilitate the access to financing, which practically disappeared during the 2002 banking crisis. At the end of that year, the government sent to parliament a "Promotion

---

2    Before the Trust Law, Uruguayan law only had tangential mentions to trusts. Thus, it has been said that trusts in Uruguayan law "are not regulated expressly with a general character" and that "Articles 783, 865, and 866 of the Civil Code prohibit testamentary trusts expressly." GLADIS FERNÁNDEZ FORMIGO, ESTUDIO SOBRE EL FIDEICOMISO, 33 (2000). No other mention to the concept is to be found.

3    Daniel Porcaro and Nicolas Malumian published a comment to this bill under the title "Fideicomiso en Uruguay: Análisis del Proyecto de Ley," in Montevideo (Uruguay), May, 2003.

4    *Cf.* GUSTAVO ORDOQUI CASTILLA, EL FIDEICOMISO 1 (2nd ed. 2004).

of Financing Bill," which created the Uruguayan trust and a special kind of securities guaranteed with movable assets deposited with a third party. Parliament first enacted the Trust Law. One of the aims of the Trust Law was that institutional investors (mainly pension funds) were able to make investments in productive projects.[5] Along the same line, another jurist said that Uruguay accepted the trust as a consequence of the worst financial stress suffered during its history and the need to gain new forms of financing for industrial and commercial activities.[6] As it follows from these opinions, the trust is seen as an investment vehicle that allows the flow of funds from investors to developers of productive projects.

The trust was already used, but it was not as widespread as in other countries. One of the milestones was the issuance of bonds by the Uruguayan corporation that held the concession of the airport serving the city of Montevideo (Carrasco Airport) to finance a brand new terminal, guaranteed with a guarantee trust with the cash flow of the airport as underlying asset. This was the biggest issuance in the history of Uruguay.

Furthermore, as the Uruguayan tax system is a local source-based one, only Uruguayan source income is taxed, leaving room to trusts for activities outside of Uruguay. The tax treatment of the trust changed with the Tax Reform Act No. 18083, which entered into force on July 1, 2007. The tax treatment of the trust in Uruguay will be dealt with in the last section of this chapter.

## 1. Definition of Trust

Section 1 of the Trust Law defines trust as the agreement that creates trust property over rights, over things or credits that are transmitted from the grantor to the trustee, who should act in relation to such trust property according to the instructions of the grantor in the benefit of a person called beneficiary, determined in the trust agreement, and once a period of time or a condition is accomplished, the trustee transfers the property to the grantor or the beneficiary. In other words, a trust is created by a contract or a will that involves the transfer of assets from the grantor to the trustee to create a separate special-purpose patrimony.

Although the Trust Law uses the expression "person" for the beneficiary, it should be stressed that this does not mean that the grantor or even the trustee, in certain cases that will be described in detail, could be the beneficiary of the trust. Furthermore, there could be several beneficiaries, not just one. There will always be a settlor, a trustee, and a beneficiary, but not always would they be three persons because one person could have more than one role, or more than one person could exercise the same role (i.e., several persons being beneficiaries). Along this line, section 1247 of the Uruguayan Civil Code states that each party of a contract could be constituted by one or several people.

---

5    ALEJANDRO HERNÁNDEZ MAESTRONI, GIANNI GUTIÉRREZ PRIETO & FERNANDO FOTI FAROPPA, FIDEICOMISO: ASPECTOS LEGALES, TRIBUTARIOS Y CONTABLES 13–14 (2004).

6    CASTILLA, *supra* note 4.

Regarding the transfer of property, in the event of a trust created by unilateral declaration (or self-declaration), there is no transfer, because only one person acts as grantor and trustee. In these cases (addressed in detail in this chapter), the grantor-trustee creates a restriction over certain assets that are his or her property in favor of the beneficiary.

## 2. Trust as a Separate Special-Purpose Patrimony

The Trust Law establishes that "the assets and rights transferred to a trust are a [special-purpose] patrimony, separate and independent of the patrimonies of the grantor, the trustee and the beneficiary." In keeping with this rule, the Trust Law states that

a. Trust assets are exempted from the legal actions of the trustee's creditors.
b. The beneficiary's creditors cannot affect the trust assets but can affect the beneficiary's rights against the trust.
c. If the trust was created by an *inter vivos* agreement (contract), the grantor's creditors cannot affect the trust assets, with the exception of fraud (according to article 1296, the action to claim that the transfer was a fraud expires one year after the registration of the agreement).
d. The assets of the person acting as trustee would not be affected by the obligations of the trust, which would only be satisfied with the trust assets.
e. If the trustee is a married person, the trust assets would not be considered income of the couple, but the payment for the trustee's services will qualify as such.

In short, the trust assets would not be subject to any action arising from obligations or responsibilities of the grantor, the trustee, or the beneficiaries.

The trust patrimony is the property that is subject to a special purpose by the trust instrument. At the very outset, the assets transferred by the grantor are exactly the same as the trust assets. Nevertheless, as soon as the trust patrimony is created, it starts to evolve and to differ from the original situation. For example, if a real estate property was transferred, and it was rented, a credit would accrue (the rent payments), and several debts would accrue (i.e., property taxes).

Section 7 of the Trust Law establishes that trust assets are subject to sections 189, 190, and 191 of Law No. 16060, which rules Uruguayan corporations. The sections mentioned before are the ones related to the disregard of the legal entity and as applied to the trust can be summarized as follows:

a. Separation of the trust patrimony can be disregarded if it can be proved that this legal scheme is used in fraud of public policies, the law, or third parties.
b. If the trust is considered in fraud of third parties, this judicial declaration would only benefit the parties involved in the judicial action and would respect the rights of a third-party who acted on a good faith basis.

## 3. Assets That May Be Transferred to a Trust

Regarding the assets that could be transferred to a trust, the Trust Law states that the *inter vivos* trust (trust established by contract) could have as trust asset any kind of assets or rights, existing or future ones, including the transfer as a whole of all the assets of an individual (as in a testamentary trust, in which all the assets of an individual are transferred to the trust on his or her death) or a corporation (as in the transfer of the going concern of a corporation). The points to be stressed here are (a) Uruguayan law expressly states that the total of the assets of an individual or corporation as a whole can be transferred to a trust (a situation not expressly established in other Latin American laws, which gave rise to different opinions); and (b) it is expressly established that future assets (such as cash flows from credits not existing at the moment of the creation of the trust) can be transferred to a trust.

Trust Law requires (item a of section 4 and the second paragraph of section 6) that the trust instrument determines the trust assets, and if such determination is not possible, a description of the assets to be transferred should be included.

## 4. Trust as Agreement, Separate Patrimony, and Trust Property

As explained in Part I, the word "trust" can refer to: (a) the separate patrimony; (b) the trust contract that transfers property from the grantor to the trustee, creating and regulating the trust patrimony; and (c) the trust property as a kind of property. The trust as a patrimony has already been discussed, so the following sections will address the concepts of trust contract and trust property under Uruguayan law.

a. *Trust Agreement* As mentioned before, section 1 of Trust Law defines the trust contract as the agreement by which the trust property is created. Furthermore, section 2 states that trusts can be created by *inter vivos* agreements or wills, and that the *inter vivos* trust is an innominate contract that should be in writing to be valid and that it has the power to transfer the property from the grantor to the trustee. The comments that arise from these sections are that (a) there is no doubt that the trust is a contract, and (b) it should be in writing. This requirement obviously excludes oral trust agreements, but it can also be understood as excluding implied trusts. (c) Although the Trust Law regulates the trust contract, it says it is an innominate contract, which is at the very least difficult to understand, but in any case it does not affect the effects, validity, legitimacy, or enforceability of the contract.

Additionally, the Trust Law states that a deed (*escritura pública*) and registration with a public registry would be necessary if the assets required such formality for its transfer. In particular, the Decree expresses that a deed would be necessary for any trust that has real estate property as underlying asset.

Under section 4 of the Trust Law, the trust contract must have certain clauses. The question that arises is what would happen in the event that these clauses were missing. To make this point clear, each mandatory clause and the effect if the contract lacks it will be examined.

a. Individualization of the trust assets, and if such individualization were not possible at the time the trust contract is executed, the description of the trust assets: As there is no trust without trust assets, it is hard to find a trust contract in which there is no individualization or description of the trust assets. If the contract does not establish any asset transfer (present or future) to the trustee, there is no trust, but some other contract.

b. The procedure under which the assets could be transferred to the trust in the future: It is understood that this clause relates to the regulation of the participation of new grantors in the trust (i.e., the possibility that the trust allows inclusion of a new grantor, or the prohibition to do so).

c. The period of time or the condition that will determine the termination of the trust. In cases where this is not established, the Trust Law provides the solution and states that the trust will last for thirty years.

d. Rights, duties, and procedure to replace the trustee. It is obvious that the complete lack of regulation of the duties of the trustee would mean that the trust contract would be invalid as a result of lack of determination of the object of the contract (the trustee has no instructions at all, therefore no valid trust exists). Regarding the substitution process, the Trust Law provides supplementary rules that will be applicable, therefore the lack of these rules in the contract does not mean that it is an invalid one.

*b. Trust Property* Trust property is the right that the trustee has over the trust assets that is created (and regulated) by the trust contract or will. It is a *ius in rem* (direct right between a person and a thing), but with the particularity that the owner (trustee) does not have a full and complete right, but a limited one ,as he or she is the owner of the assets in the benefit of a third party (the beneficiary).

The beneficiary has no *ius in rem,* but a *ius in personam,* a right against the trust to obtain the benefit established in his or her favor. The beneficiary is not the owner of the assets of the trust.

Finally, a terminological comment is in place. The Trust Law uses the expression "trust dominium" in sections 7, 8, 25, and 39 and "trust property" in sections 1, 2, 4, 6, 7 and 22. Therefore, it should be considered whether there is any difference, or whether both expressions could be considered synonymous. Section 486 of the Uruguayan Civil Code states that "dominium" (also called "property") is the right to use and dispose of a thing as desired, as long it is not against the law or third-parties' rights, and section 489 of the same Code clarifies that dominium or property is a quality of the thing, a link between a person and a thing that cannot be broken without an act of the person. In short, the expressions "trust property" and "trust dominium" should be considered synonymous.

## 5. Registration of the Trust Instrument

The Trust Law has a rule that is peculiar to Uruguay: The trust instrument must be registered with the Uruguayan Ministry of Education and Culture. This registration is additional to the one that should be done in cases where the underlying assets require the registration of their ownership. For example, in the case of a real estate property transferred to a trust, there will be a double registration: (a) with the Registry of Immovable Property, and (b) with the Ministry of Education and Culture.

Section 17 of the Trust Law establishes that the trust will be valid and enforceable regarding third parties once registered. Therefore, any action of the trustee in violation of the trust instrument would not affect the beneficiary or residual beneficiary of the trust. If the trust is not registered, any restriction to the powers of the trustee in relation to the trust property would not be enforceable unless it can be proved that the third party who contracted with the trustee knew that he or she was acting beyond his or her powers, or that this situation was notorious.

The registration is indexed on the basis of the name of the trustee and the beneficiaries, and the required information is: (a) name, address, nationality, and ID number of trustee and grantor; (b) period of time or condition of termination; (c) destiny of the assets at the termination of the trust; (d) rights and duties of the trustee; and (e) procedure to replace the trustee.

## 6. Termination

According to section 33 of the Trust Law, the following are the causes of termination of the trust:

a.  The accomplishment of the purposes of the trust or the complete impossibility to accomplish them:

    If it is considered that a trust is a special-purpose patrimony, it is obvious that the accomplishment or the complete impossibility to accomplish the purposes of the trust would mean that the trust is senseless and must be terminated.

    Law regulations regarding maximum duration of trusts have been the object of scholars' debate. Some considered that the contract could not establish a period longer than thirty years,[7] others supported the idea that the thirty-year period must be considered only if there is no maximum period of time established in the contract (our position).

    If a condition is established to terminate the trust, it will be considered fulfilled after thirty years of the execution of the trust instrument.

b.  The agreement between the grantor and the beneficiary, notwithstanding the rights of the trustee:

    This section of the Law assumes that if the person who created the trust and the person who receives the benefits of it agree to terminate the trust, there is no reason to object such agreement. The sole caveat to this rule is that the trustee has the right to receive a fee during the life of the trust, and he or she has a right to receive a compensation for the reduction of the duration of these services.

---

7    *Cf.* MAESTRONI ET AL., *supra* note 5, at 44 & 50.

c. The incapacity of the trust to pay its obligations, unless it is a financial trust:

 The rule has an obvious rationale. If there are no means to accomplish the trust objectives, there is no reason for the existence of the trust. The exception of the financial trust is because in the case of this kind of trust, the lack of means would trigger a trust securities meeting that would be in charge of making the decision of terminating the financial trust.

d. If expressly established in the trust instruments, the trust could be terminated by the decision of the grantor:

 The general rule in Uruguay (as in most Latin American countries) is that *inter vivos* trusts are irrevocable. Nevertheless, the Law allows the grantor to include in the trust instrument the right to revoke the trust. In such a case, the rights of the beneficiary would be revocable ones and would be subject to the decision of the grantor to terminate with the trust.

 Emphasis should be laid on the fact that trusts created by will are always revocable, regardless of there not being an express clause in the instrument. Section 779 of the Uruguayan Civil Code expresses that "wills are essentially revocable acts." The same criteria emerges from sections 998 to 1005, the first of which holds that all wills are revocable by the testator until his or her death and that any restriction to this right is null and void.[8]

e. By resolution of the trust debt securities holders' meeting under the conditions established by section 32 of Trust Law:

 Section 32 of the Trust Law establishes that the trust debt securities holders' meeting, with a simple majority vote of the debt securities holders, considering the nominal value of the outstanding trust securities (not per capita vote), could resolve several issues. From the joint interpretation of section 32 and the paragraph under analysis, it is evident that the trust securities holders' meeting can terminate with the trust with a majority vote.

 In cases where the trust issued certificates of participation, although the law does not mention them expressly, it is reasonable to understand that their vote would be necessary to terminate the trust. Section G (Financial Trusts) will examine this again.

f. Due to death or legal incapacity of the trustee declared by a judge, unless the trust instrument appoints a substitute trustee:

 This clause assumes that if the trustee is an individual, unless the substitution of the trustee is expressly regulated in the trust instrument, the trustee is essential for the trust. Therefore, if the trustee dies or his or her legal incapacity is declared, the trust is terminated. This is a particular rule of Uruguay that does not have a counterpart in other Latin American regulations.

---

8 Other relevant rules regarding the revocation of wills are:

  § 999: A will could not be expressly revoked, but by another will.

  § 1,001: If the will that revokes a previous will is revoked, the first will does not gain force again unless the testator expressly states it so.

  § 1005: A will is not revoked by the sole fact that there is a newer will unless the newest will expressly states so or contains clauses that are contradictory with the previous will.

Other Latin American legislations consider that the incapability of the trustee to continue as such simply means that the trust assets are transferred to another trustee, and the trust is not affected.

As an obvious conclusion, if an individual is appointed as trustee, his or her replacement must be ruled in the trust instrument to avoid that his or her death or declaration of legal incapacity frustrates the objectives of the trust.

g. Any other cause expressly included in the trust instrument:

This clause only underlines the freedom to establish any circumstance as the reason to terminate the trust (obviously within the limits of time remarked on in clause a of this section).

As mentioned when analyzing the contents of the trust instrument, it must rule the destiny of the assets when the trust is terminated. Nevertheless, if nothing is established in the trust instrument, the general rule is that once the trust is terminated, the trustee must assign the trust assets to the grantor or his or her successors unless the trust instrument states otherwise (e.g., the assignment of the trust assets to a beneficiary different from the trustee).

In cases where the trust is terminated because of the death or declaration of legal incapacity of the trustee (without the trust instrument providing for the appointment of a substitute), the transfer of the trust assets to the grantor is *ipso iure* (by the mere operation of law), and no agreement is needed between the trustee and the grantor. The rationale of the rule is self-evident: As the trustee is dead or legally incapable, it is impossible for him or her to execute the agreement by him or herself, and the appointment of a representative means a delay that could adversely affect the trust assets.

The general rule (i.e., assignment of assets to the grantor or the person established as residual beneficiary in the trust instrument) is not applicable in the event of termination of the trust because of insufficiency of the trust assets to pay the trust obligations. In the following point, it will be seen that in such a case the trust assets must be liquidated and the proceeds devoted to pay the trust obligations in accordance with bankruptcy law rules.

The Trust Law rules that "in no case could the trust assets become the permanent property of the trustee." Nevertheless, if the trustee was the grantor (trust created by the sole unilateral declaration of the grantor), this rule would make no sense, the interpretation of this rule in the guarantee trust being debatable, as will be addressed when dealing with this kind of trust later in this chapter. In any case, the rationale of the rule is to avoid any conflict of interests between the trustee and the beneficiary of the trust.

## 7. Insufficiency of the Trust Assets

The insufficiency of the trust assets to comply with the obligations of the trust will not allow the declaration of bankruptcy, voluntary bankruptcy procedure, or judicial liquidation. In such a case, and if the grantor or the beneficiary does not provide further assets to avoid the termination of the trust according to the trust instrument rules, the trustee will make a private (nonjudicial) liquidation. The trust assets must be sold and the proceeds delivered to the creditors according with the ranking established by bankruptcy law.

In the event of financial trusts, a trust debt securities holders' special meeting must be called by the trustee (as is explained with further detail in this chapter in section G, Financial Trusts), and if there is any conflict, an arbitral process would be applicable.

## B. THE GRANTOR

Although all Latin American laws allow the existence of more than one grantor in a trust (a common situation because the trust is used as a legal vehicle for projects that involve several investors), but do so without an express rule, Uruguayan law makes it clear in an express manner, stating that "there could be a plurality of grantors."[9]

This plurality could be the result of many situations, the main ones being

a. Several persons transfer as grantors the joint property of an asset to a trust.
b. Several persons transfer several assets at the execution of the trust, or they do it during a certain period of time (e.g., the subscription period for a construction trust until all the units to be constructed have been correlated with a grantor of cash and beneficiary of the unit).

The trust in which the grantor is the same person as the trustee, in other words, the trust created by the sole declaration of the grantor, is known as trust by "unilateral act." This name is caused by the fact that the creation of the trust is not an agreement between two parties, but the sole declaration of one party (unilateral, as opposed to a bilateral agreement).

Uruguayan law defines contract in section 1247 of the Civil Code as an agreement by which a party creates an obligation in favor of another party, or both parties are mutually obliged to do something, not to do something, or to convey something, making it clear that a party could be one or several persons. Therefore, the declaration made only by the trustee is not a contract because it does not involve two parties.

A trust could only be created by unilateral act if it is a financial one. This will be explained in further detail in the financial trust subtitle in this chapter.

## C. THE TRUSTEE

The general rule under Uruguayan law is that any individual or corporation could be a trustee. The exceptions are that an authorization is required to be a financial trustee (a trustee of a financial trust) or a professional trustee. Any natural or legal person who is trustee of five or more trusts in any calendar year will be considered a professional trustee.

---

9   Trust Law, last paragraph of section 1.

To summarize, trustees can be classified in the following three categories:

a. Ordinary trustees: any legal or natural person can be the trustee of less than five nonfinancial trusts without being subject to any registration requirement.
b. Professional trustees must be banks or persons registered with the Central Bank of Uruguay.
c. Financial trustees must be banks or mutual funds administrators registered with the Central Bank of Uruguay.

## 1. Registry of Professional Trustees

The Trust Law provides that the Central Bank of Uruguay is in charge of the professional trustees' registry, in which natural or legal persons wishing to be professional trustees must register.

If the trustee to be registered is a corporation, it must have nominative shares and inform the data of the shareholders and directors (including a description of their patrimony), inform any professional insurance, submit the last three audited financial statements, and keep this information updated at least semiannually or five days after there is a substantial change. All the information provided for the registration is available to the general public.

Once the request is made to the Central Bank, it has thirty days to answer it (unless an information requirement is issued by the Central Bank), and if the request goes unanswered in this period of time, the trustee is considered registered.

Foreign corporations that will only be trustees of assets located outside of Uruguay are exempted from the requirements described in this subtitle.

## 2. Penalties

The Trust Law refers to sanctions established by regulations of the Law that govern financial activities in Uruguay. From the joint interpretation of both the Trust Law and the referred law, it follows that any person who violates the Trust Law and its regulations would be subject to a criminal offense action (if applicable) and

a. Admonition (*observación*)
b. Severe admonition (*apercibimiento*)
c. Fine
d. Appointment of an auditor, and eventually replacement of the directors with the ones appointed by the Central Bank
e. Prohibition to continue with the trustee activity for a certain period of time
f. Revocation of the professional trustee authorization

If the Central Bank considers that anyone is acting as a professional trustee without the necessary authorization, it can request all the relevant information and documentation.

If such information and/or documentation is not submitted within ten days after the request, the Central Bank shall assume that this is professional trustee illegal activity and order the termination of such activity.

## 3. Multiple Trustees and Trustee Substitution

Section 13 of the Trust Law provides that in cases where the grantor appoints several trustees to act in succession, the grantor must determine the order and the conditions under which the first trustee is replaced.

The Trust Law clarifies that there can be several grantors and several beneficiaries, but it does not mention the possibility of having several trustees acting simultaneously. Although not expressly regulated, it is reasonable to understand that there can be cotrustees acting together as long as their responsibilities are clearly regulated by the trust instrument.

Finally, the Trust Law provides that the grantor can reserve for him or herself the right to appoint a new trustee during the life of the trust.

## 4. Standard of Trust Services

The trustee must accomplish his or her duties arising from the trust instrument or the Law with the prudence and diligence of a good businessperson who acts based on his or her fiduciary duties. If the trustee fails to accomplish his or her duties with due diligence, he or she will be responsible in relation to the grantor and the beneficiary, and he or she will have to repair any damage that his or her lack of due diligence may have caused.

The trustee cannot be exempted from his or her responsibility for damages caused as a result of his or her willful misconduct or slight blame or his or her dependents.

## 5. Duties of the Trustee

The Trust Law provides the following duties of the trustee:

a. Rendering of accounts: The trust deed cannot provide against the obligation of the trustee to render accounts to the grantor and the beneficiary at least once a year. As rendering accounts is the sole way the trustee can be freed of his or her responsibility, the Trust Law provides mechanisms for the tacit approval of the accounts and its effects. Once the accounts are rendered, if they are not objected by one or more of the recipients (the grantor and the beneficiary) within the period of time established by the trust deed (and if such period is not established in the trust instrument within a ninety-day period), the accounts will be considered approved unless there is fraud or willful omission of substantial information. The approval of the accounts would mean that the trustee is free of responsibility in relation to the grantor and the beneficiaries (present of future ones) for the period covered by the accounts rendered.

b. Protection of trust assets: The trustee must protect the trust assets against claims of third parties or even the beneficiary. Judges may authorize the grantor or the beneficiary to protect the trust assets if such defense is necessary, and the trustee is reluctant to do it.

c. Separate accounting: The trustee must have a separate accounting of the assets and obligations of the trust patrimony. If the trustee is a trustee of several trusts, each trust must have its own accounting.

d. Transfer of the trust assets at the moment of termination of the trust: The trustee must transfer the trust assets to the grantor or the beneficiary at the moment of termination of the trust, or to the replacing trustee in the event of substitution of trustees.

e. Trustee confidentiality: The trustee must keep secret of the transactions, agreements, documents, and information that are related to the trust.

## 6. Prohibitions That Affect the Trustee

The Trust Law provides that the trustee cannot:

a. Guarantee in any way to the grantor or the beneficiary the result of the trust or any transaction that is done with the trust assets. In other words, the trustee cannot ensure a result, yield, or rate of return.

b. Carry on transactions with the trust assets in his or her own benefit or the benefit of his or her directors, management, relatives, or any other legal entity in which they have a relevant position of management or control.

c. Carry on any transaction in which the trustee has any interest lacking the joint and express authorization of the grantor and the beneficiary.

These rules can be found in most Latin American countries and are based on the idea that the trustee must carry on his or her duties in favor of the beneficiary, and his or her sole interest must be his or her fees.

## 7. Trustee's Fees

The Trust Law provides that unless the trust instrument states otherwise, the trustee has the right to the payment of all his or her expenses and a fee. If the fee is not established in the trust instrument, it must be established by the competent judge taking into account the kind of trust and the amount of trust assets. Which is to say, that there is a legal assumption that the trustee is acting as such for a fee and not for free. In any case, from a practical point of view, it is hard to think of a trust in which the fees of the trustee are not expressly waived or established.

## 8. Termination of the Office of the Trustee

The trustee shall terminate his or her office in the following cases:

a. If the trustee is an individual, because of death, legal incapacity, or incapacity to carry on commercial activity declared by a judge. In these cases, the transfer of property to the new trustee, the grantor or the beneficiary (according to the trust instrument) is *ipso iure* (no need of agreement, but by the sole effect of law).
b. If the trustee is a legal entity, because of dissolution, declaration of bankruptcy, voluntary bankruptcy procedure, or judicial liquidation.
c. By removal of the grantor if he or she reserved this right in the trust deed. In such a case, the trustee must appoint the new trustee so that the removal of the current one is effective. The grantor can delegate this right to a third party (similar to a protector in the common law), who can make the decision of replacing the trustee according to his or her criteria.
d. By removal of the trustee decided by a judge, based on the requirement of the grantor, the beneficiary, or creditors representing 50 percent or more of the outstanding debts, in all cases as a result of the breach of the trustee's duties.
e. By resignation of the trustee if this possibility is expressly contemplated in the trust instrument and according to the causes established in it. If the trust deed does not provide this possibility, the trustee can only resign if: (i) the beneficiary refuses to receive the benefits of the trust; or (ii) the trust assets are not enough for the payment of the trustee's fees, and the grantor and the beneficiary refuse to pay the trustee's fees. The resignation will only be effective after the transfer of the trust assets to the new trustee.

Although not expressly stated by the Trust Law, the general principles of Uruguayan Law would allow a trustee to resign in the event of force majeure, such as severe illness (if the trustee is an individual).

Once the trustee's office is terminated (and assuming that the trust deed does not provide that in such a case, the trust must be dissolved), if a substitute is appointed in the trust instrument he or she must be called to continue the trust. If no one is appointed, but the grantor reserved for him or herself or a third party the right to appoint a new trustee, such person must be requested to appoint the new trustee. If the previously mentioned courses of action were impossible for whatever reason (e.g., no substitute trustee appointed in the trust instrument, the appointed trustee does not exist anymore, or the grantor who must appoint the substitute trustee cannot be contacted), the sole residual solution is to request a judge to appoint the new trustee.

Nevertheless, in cases where a request of appointing a new trustee is submitted to a judge, he or she could understand that the trust aims were only achievable by the original trustee and that no substitute trustee must be appointed, but that the trust must be dissolved. Therefore, this point must be made very clear in the trust instrument to avoid any future inconvenience.

## D. THE BENEFICIARY

The beneficiary can be defined as the person, determined in the trust deed or determinable based on the characteristics defined by the trust instrument, who obtains the benefits of the trust assets. As mentioned before, section 23 of the Trust Law provides that the trust instrument must appoint the beneficiary, who could be a legal or natural person.

In the case of *inter vivos* trusts, the beneficiary could be an unborn person. In such a case, the trust instrument must contain the precise description of the characteristics of the future beneficiary to allow its identification in the future. Furthermore, the trust would be subject to the condition of the actual future existence of the beneficiary, and it would be considered without effects if such beneficiary were not born within one year of the execution of the trust instrument.

There has been a long debate among Latin American scholars in relation to the role of the beneficiary as party of the *inter vivos* trust or as a third party (i.e., if the trust is an agreement in his or her favor). Whether the first or the second position is chosen, the beneficiary must accept the contract executing it (or by similar means, such as a letter stating that he or she was able to read it, and he or she accepts it). From a practical point of view, it must be kept in mind that in an *inter vivos* trust, the general rule is that the beneficiary is not receiving his or her benefits for free. The beneficiary is either the original grantor making a contribution to the trust, or he or she has paid for such right to someone who transferred the rights as beneficiary. Therefore, the case in which the beneficiary does not participate in the discussion and execution of the trust agreement is, at least, an exceptional one. In short, most beneficiaries participate in the trust agreement execution, but in the rare cases in which this does not happen, the beneficiary will have to accept the trust set up in his or her favor.

Section 1256 of the Uruguayan Civil Code provides that if someone stipulates any benefit in favor of a third party, even if he or she has no right to represent such third party, this third party can request this benefit if he or she accepted it and notified such acceptance before the benefit was revoked. The key point to be considered that arises from this section is that in the case that the beneficiary did not participate in the execution of the trust agreement, the benefits in his or her favor can be revoked until they are accepted.

The Trust Law expressly makes it clear that sections 835, 841, and 1038 of the Uruguayan Civil Code are applicable to testamentary trusts. The first of these sections provides that the successor must exist by the time of the initiation of the succession process.

Section 835 of the Uruguayan Civil Code must be read jointly with section 834. Both sections provide that anyone can be a beneficiary of a will unless expressly excluded by law. The persons excluded are: (a) the ones that are not conceived by the time of the initiation of the succession process or those who, being conceived, are not born with aptitude to live or actually live for at least 24 hours; and (b) associations or corporations not allowed by law.

Finally, section 841 of the Code provides that any clause in a will is null and void if in favor of those who cannot be beneficiaries of a will, regardless of whether it is a pretended sale, or a third party is used as intermediary.

Two or more beneficiaries could be appointed so that they act as beneficiaries together or successively, with the exception that it is prohibited to appoint several beneficiaries to replace each other after their predecessor's death.

If several beneficiaries are appointed jointly, and for any reason one or many of them does accept the benefits of the trust (i.e., because of death, the beneficiary is never born, the beneficiary is unwilling to accept), unless something different is stipulated in the trust instrument, the remaining beneficiaries must receive an equal part of the benefits corresponding to the beneficiary or beneficiaries who did not accept the benefits of the trust.

The Trust Law states that the trust that appoints the trustee as beneficiary is null and void, with the sole exception of guarantee trusts in which the trustee and lender is an Uruguayan financial institution.

In fact, if the trustee is the sole beneficiary, the trust is nonexistent because the property of the assets and the benefits of such property merge in the same person. But guarantee trusts present a special case. The grantor is the trustee's debtor and keeps using the trust assets and obtaining the benefits of such assets, but if he or she defaulted his or her debt, the assets would be sold and the debt paid. The Trust Law recognizes this particular case (guarantee trust) and allows merging the roles of trustee and beneficiary (the debtor being the residual beneficiary of all the assets that were not used to pay his or her debt). Nevertheless, to prevent abuses, this possibility is restricted to financial institutions under the control of the Uruguayan Central Bank.

## E. GUARANTEE TRUSTS

The original draft of the Trust Law sent by the president to parliament did not mention the guarantee trust. During the parliamentary discussion, two sections were added that refer expressly to the guarantee trust. Besides the provisions of such sections, they are very relevant because they avoided any future discussion in relation to the legitimacy and legality of the guarantee trust. In order words, it is very hard to construe the guarantee trust as illegal when it is expressly regulated by the Trust Law.

The sections of the Trust Law that refer to the guarantee trust are: (a) section 9, paragraph b, which, as explained in the previous point, provides that a trust that appoints the trustee as beneficiary is null and void, with the sole exception of guarantee trusts in which the trustee and lender is a Uruguayan financial institution; and (b) section 42, which regulates certain tax issues of the guarantee trust, which will be dealt with in the last part of this chapter.

The foreclosure agreement that allows the creditor to keep the asset pledged as payment of the debt that is guaranteed by such asset is generally understood as *pactum commissorium*. This agreement is prohibited in most Latin American countries in relation to mortgages (*hipotecas*) and pledges (*prendas*). In the particular case of Uruguayan law, section 2338 of the Uruguayan Civil Code establishes that a clause is null and void that authorizes the creditor to become the owner of the asset subject to mortgage or to sell it in other form than a public auction. Additionally, section 2301 of the Code provides that the creditor cannot become the owner of a pledged asset unless expressly approved by the debtor.

The sections mentioned in the previous paragraph are not applicable to the guarantee trust, but it must be kept in mind that section 33 of the Trust Law provides that in no case the trustee shall become the owner of the trust assets. Put differently, the trustee may not transform his or her trust property into a full (ordinary) property. This rule is understood as a prohibition of the *pactum comissorium* for the guarantee trust. Therefore, in the event of a guarantee trust in which the trustee is the creditor (as explained, this is only legal if the trustee or creditor is a financial institution), if the debtor defaults his or her obligations, it is reasonable to understand that the trustee must sell the assets and get paid with the proceeds.

## 1. The Montevideo Airport Guarantee Trust

The most important single issuance of corporate bonds in the history of Uruguay was in April 2007 for an amount of US$87 million. It was carried out by an Uruguayan corporation called *Puertas del Sur,* which has the concession of Carrasco's airport, which serves the city of Montevideo (Uruguay's capital city). The proceeds of the placement are currently being used for the new terminal of the airport. This issuance was guaranteed with a guarantee trust on the cash flow produced by the airport services.

## F. TESTAMENTARY TRUSTS

Section 779 of the Uruguayan Civil Code establishes that a will is an essentially revocable instrument by which an individual disposes, according to the applicable law, a portion or all his or her assets, to take effect after his or her death.

Regarding the formalities of the will, it may be "open" or "closed." It is open if the public notary and the witnesses know the dispositions of the will, and it is closed if there is no legal obligation that the public notary and the witnesses should know such dispositions.

## 1. Forced Heirship in Uruguay

Section 884 of the Uruguayan Civil Code defines forced heirship portion (legitime) as the portion of the assets that the law allocates to certain heirs, independently of the grantor's will, which the grantor cannot deprive without fair and proved cause.

The main points of sections 885 to 895 of the Code are

a. Sons, daughters and parents have a right to their forced heirship portion.
b. To one son or daughter appertains a forced portion of half of the assets.
c. If two sons or daughters, the forced portion is of two-thirds.

d. If three or more sons and daughters, the forced portion is of three-fourths.
e. If any son or daughter dies before the succession process is started, their sons or daughters can represent them.
f. If there are no sons or daughters, half of the assets would be the parents' forced portion.
g. If there are several forced heirs (e.g., several sons and daughters), the forced portion is divided in equal parts.

The part of the assets not affected by the forced heirship can be disposed in the will and be the underlying asset of a testamentary trust. The forced portion cannot be pledged, subjected to condition, or any other lien by the grantor.

Section 10 of the Trust Law establishes that testamentary trusts cannot affect forced heirship, and in case that they do affect it, the trust instrument must be modified to be according to law. If an heir is the beneficiary of a trust created by the grantor while the grantor was alive, any benefit arising from such trust would be considered a donation.

The Trust Law provides that testamentary trusts are prohibited and are null and void in which several beneficiaries are appointed and replace one another as a result of the death of their predecessor. The rationale of the prohibition is to prevent using the trust as a means to alter inheritance rights established by law.

Before the enactment of the Trust Law, section 865 of the Civil Code established that "all trusts are void, no matter their form," because the trust was regarded as a method of creating inheritance privileges different from the legal regulations. This section was abrogated by the Trust Law which, needless to say, holds a different concept of trusts as its underlying idea.

Furthermore, section 866 of the Civil Code was modified and now reads, in its relevant part, "the following clauses are null and void . . . the one that, not creating a trust, has as objective to provide that one or all the assets must be used or invested according to the grantor's instructions. In other words, if the grantor's will is to create certain investment rules, these rules must be contained in a testamentary trust."

Section 2 of the Trust Law states that "testamentary trusts provide the trustee with a personal right to claim from the heirs the assignment of the assets and rights that are its object, except in the case the trust property is on an asset clearly determined. In such a case, the trustee acquires the trust property after the death of the grantor."

Section 7 of the Trust Law stipulates that in the cases that the testamentary trust is created with determined assets, the trust assets would be subject to the legal claim of the grantor's creditors as follows:

a. The trust assets could only be affected if at the time of the initiation of the succession process, there are not enough assets to pay the grantor's debts.
b. The trust assets would only be subject to the payment of debts if the heir does not pay them.
c. The trust would only be responsible for the portion of the debt that corresponds according to the portion of the grantor's asset that the trustee received.

If the testamentary trust is created with the total or a percentage of the grantor's assets, the trust assets would be subject to the legal claims of the grantor's creditors. The trustee must make an inventory of the assets transferred to the trust and notify the creditors of the undivided estate.

## G. FINANCIAL TRUSTS

The Trust Law defines financial trust as the trust agreement that stipulates as beneficiaries the holders of certificates of participation of the trust property, trust debt securities backed with the trust assets, or mixed securities that grant credit rights and participation rights as residual beneficiaries. Several comments must be made in relation to this definition:

a. It is worth clarifying that although the name of the securities issued by the financial trust is "certificates of participation in the trust property," the trustee holds title over the trust property and the holders of the certificates are only beneficiaries of the trust.
b. It seems unnecessary to name the debt securities as "debt securities backed with the trust assets" because it is obvious enough to call them "debt securities."
c. The expression that states that there could be mixed securities that grant credit rights and "participation rights as residual beneficiaries" is confusing because they can grant other rights as beneficiaries other than residual beneficiaries.
d. Finally, the definition does not mention that a financial trust requires a financial trustee.

In short, a financial trust, is a trust that: (i) has as beneficiaries the holders of securities (that could represent a creditor's right or a right to the benefits arising from the trust), and (ii) has a trustee that qualifies as financial trustee.

## 1. Securitization in Uruguay Before the Trust Law

Before the Trust Law, the sole legal vehicles for securitizations were closed-end funds (regulated by Law No. 16774 of 1996 [Mutual Funds, Securitization, and Factoring, hereinafter "Mutual Funds Law"], amended by Law No. 17202 of 1999), but they were not used at all basically because of market conditions in Uruguay and uncertainties of a fiscal nature, which were amended as from 2001.

The Mutual Funds Law defines investment funds in section 1 as "the special-purpose patrimony, made up by contributions from natural or legal persons under the regime of the present law (Law No. 16774), for its investment in securities and other assets," making it clear that "investment funds do not constitute companies, lack legal status and must be administered by a funds management company which is vested with the powers of ownership without being the owner, so that, in the name of the contributors, it carries out an adequate distribution of its assets, taking account of risks and returns."

The nature of the special-purpose patrimony is materialized in the rules that set forth that it will not be held liable for the contributors' debts nor for the administering or receiving companies. The creditors of the fund will not be able to make good their credits against the contributors, whose liability is confined to their contributions. The contributors to the mutual funds are joint owners of the assets comprising its property, which will remain undivided for the whole length of their existence. The prohibition to divide the property of an investment fund does not cease at the request of one or more of the undivided joint owners, his or her heirs, or creditors, who may not request its dissolution for the period set for its existence in the fund's regulations.

In brief, before the Trust Law, securitization was contemplated in Uruguayan law by means of the concept of the mutual investment funds. However, it was confined to secured credits, which lent it a very limited field of development.

## 2. Current Situation

Unlike the Mutual Funds Law that only allowed the securitization of mortgages (and left it to a regulation that was never enacted the possibility to securitize unsecured loans), the Trust Law does not establish any limitation regarding the assets that can be securitized with a financial trust. This means that even cash flows can be securitized with a financial trust.[10] The Trust Law expressly regulates the securitization of local taxes, allowing it as long as the objective of the trust is to finance public infrastructure, and the local legislative power is notified.

To give some idea of the volume of securitizations in Uruguay, it can be mentioned that in 2008 there was one issuance of trust securities for a total amount of approximately US$5 million and two issuances of negotiable obligations (corporate bonds) guaranteed with guarantee trusts for a total amount of approximately US$37.65 million. In 2007 the figures were: five issuances of trust securities for a total amount of approximately US$123 million and six issuances of negotiable obligations guaranteed with guarantee trust for a total amount of approximately US$137 million (including the issuance of US$87 million already commented on in Section E1 of this chapter).

As mentioned before, and unlike ordinary trusts, financial trusts can be created by the sole declaration of the grantor (called unilateral act, as opposed to an agreement that requires two parties, and as such is a bilateral act), as long as the trust securities are publicly placed.

As noted when dealing with the regulations of trustees, the Trust Law restricts the possibility of being a financial trustee (a trustee of a financial trust) to Uruguayan financial entities, administrators of pension funds (*administradoras de fondos de pensión*), and companies expressly authorized to be financial trustees. To be a financial trustee, registration with the Uruguayan Central Bank is needed providing full

---

10   *Cf.* Maestroni et al., *supra* note 5, at 73.

information on several issues in relation to shareholders, directors, managers, and so forth, which will become available on the webpage of the said institution.

The transfer of credits to a financial trustee is subject to a special regime that provides a much faster and practical procedure than the general one and, in cases where trust securities are publicly placed, there are no actions available against the grantor to request that the assets transferred to the trust are considered not transferred under claims of fraud. These exceptions to the general rules aims to facilitate securitization of credits and give a higher degree of certainty to the holders of trust securities backed with the trust assets.

## 3. Trust Securities

The Trust Law clarifies that trust securities qualify as securities under Uruguayan law and are ruled by Decree-Law No. 14701 of 1977, the general regulation of securities in Uruguay. Furthermore, the public offer of trust securities is ruled by Law No. 16749 of 1996. Therefore, any public offer of trust securities requires the previous authorization of the Uruguayan Central Bank.

Regarding the possible investors, the Trust Law provides that pension funds can purchase trust securities as long as the trust develops an activity in Uruguay or has underlying assets located in Uruguay. Law No. 16713 regulates the Uruguayan social security system and, in particular, provided the creation of the main pension funds called AFAPs (*Administradoras de Fondos de Ahorro Previsional*). Section 92 of the Law defines AFAPs as legal entities of the private sector under the scheme of a corporation (*sociedad anónima*) that administers a pension fund that is a separate patrimony of the one of the AFAP. It is reasonable to understand that the concept of trust did not exist by the time this Law was enacted, therefore, although the description is the one of a trust (special-purpose separate patrimony) the AFAPs Law does not use the word "trust." In relation to the investments of the AFAPs, paragraph (e) of section 123 allows AFAPs to invest in securities that represent investments in real estate, industrial, forestry or other productive sectors, and paragraph (d) of the same section allows the investment in securities of Uruguayan companies that were authorized by the Central Bank to be publicly placed. Furthermore, the Trust Law states that trust securities could be considered included in such investments.

In short, AFAPs can invest in financial trust securities as long as the trust has as its objective to develop an activity in Uruguay.

## 4. The Trust Securities Holders' Meeting

In the event of lack of resources of the trust to face its obligations, or in the event of contingencies that could affect the financial position of the trust in the future, the trustee must summon the trust securities holders to hold a meeting and determine the steps to be followed to continue or liquidate the trust.

The trust securities holders meeting with the vote of the majority of the nominal value of the securities may determine

a. To transfer the trust assets to another trustee. This is tantamount to saying that the meeting can change the trustee.
b. To change the conditions of the securities to refinance them.
c. To continue without changes.
d. To establish the way to liquidate the trust assets.
e. To appoint a liquidator different from the trustee.
f. Any other action that the meeting finds wise.

Although the Trust Law does not mention the holders of the certificates of participation but only the trust debt holders, a decision that affects the former made exclusively by the latter would not be legitimate. Therefore, the participation and vote of both is highly advisable.

Finally, the rules of shareholders meetings are the applicable rule for all the issues not expressly considered by the Trust Law.


## H. TAX TREATMENT

Income Tax in Uruguay is not one but three different taxes, all of them based on the Uruguayan territorial principle. Therefore, only Uruguayan source income is taxed in Uruguay, and foreign source income obtained by any person in Uruguay is not taxed. The main taxes on income are:

• Income Tax on Economic Activities (*Impuesto a la Renta de las Actividades Económicas* [IRAE]): It taxes the Uruguayan net income of companies at a 25 percent tax rate.
• Individual Income Tax (*Impuesto a la Renta de las Personas Físicas* [IRPF]): It taxes the income of individuals.
• Nonresidents Income Tax (*Impuesto a la Renta de los No Residentes* [IRNR]): it taxes non-Uruguayan residents' income.

Both IRPF and IRNR general tax rate is 12 percent with special tax rates for income of financial activities and for personal labor (in the latter case, there is a progressive rate that ranges from 0 percent to 25 percent).

There is a specific tax on the sale or transfer of immovable property by individuals as a result of the death of the owner of such property called Tax on Patrimonial Transfers (*Impuesto a las Trasmisiones Patrimoniales* [ITP]).

These taxes are complemented with a Tax on Personal Assets (*Impuesto al Patrimonio* [IP]) that is levied on assets located in Uruguay belonging to individuals, families, or undivided estate located in Uruguay as long the assets have a value higher than approximately US$100 for individuals and US$200 for families. Furthermore, assets located in Uruguay of persons subject to IRAE and offshore legal entities without a permanent establishment in Uruguay are subject to a tax on these assets at a 1.5 percent tax rate.

Value-added tax (VAT) in Uruguay is the highest of all Latin American countries with a 22 percent tax rate. It taxes the sale of assets, the importation of assets, the rendering of services, and construction.

Finally, it should be stressed that Uruguay has a strict banking secret rule.

## 1. Nonfinancial Trusts

Trusts, with the exception of guarantee trusts, are taxpayers of all national taxes. Therefore, trusts, with the exception of guarantee trusts, are subject to IRAE and IP, just the same as an Uruguayan corporation. Furthermore, trusts are subject to VAT depending on the activity developed.

## 2. Financial Trusts

As a general rule, financial trusts are subject to the same rules as ordinary trusts mentioned in the previous paragraph. However, the financial trust is created to invest in credit rights to serve as a securitization vehicle. The trust is subject to the IRAE and is a withholding agent of the IRPF or IRNR, which must be paid by the securities holders. Regarding IP, the tax rate is higher (2.8 percent instead of 1.5 percent), but the taxable basis is much lower because all the debts of the trust can be deducted from it (in other words, tax is not calculated over the assets, but over the net worth of the trust). Finally, VAT treatment of interests paid to the trust is the same as it would be if the credit were on the originator. The rationale is to prevent the loss of the benefit (exemption) that was granted in favor of the debtor.

## 3. Guarantee Trusts

As long as the trust is not a means to transfer assets from the grantor to the beneficiary, the guarantee trust is considered inexistent for tax purposes. Therefore, the grantor must consider that the assets transferred to the trust belong to him or her, as if they had never been transferred.

If for any reason the trusts are sold to a third party or transferred to the beneficiary of the guarantee (e.g., because the grantor did not pay his or her obligation, and the asset is transferred to the credit as a payment), there has been a sale for tax purposes.

Section 42 of the Trust Law expressly exempts from ITP the transfer of real estate to a guarantee trust and the transfer of the same real estate to the grantor when the trust is liquidated. If because of the default of the grantor the real estate must be transferred to the creditor or a third party, ITP would be applicable.

## 4. Offshore Trusts

Section 37 of the Trust Law provides that trusts created abroad with assets in Uruguay, even if grantor and beneficiary are not Uruguayan residents, shall be subject to the same rules as local trusts.

## 5. Tax Benefits

The tax exemptions applicable to trusts are

a. Financial trusts with publicly placed bonds authorized by the Uruguayan Central Bank are exempted from ITP, VAT, and other taxes levied on the sales of assets.
b. The president of Uruguay may decide to apply the aforementioned exemptions to ordinary trusts.
c. Certain benefits of the Investments Act are applicable to trusts that carry on industrial, agricultural, or livestock farming activities.
d. Trusts located in "free zones" (such as Zonamérica, Montevideo's tax-free zone) are excepted from all national taxes; wages are exempted from social security duties; import and export rights are not applicable; there is to be no exchange control and promotional utilities fees.
e. Section 43 of the Trust Law deals with the so-called "special beneficiaries," which are insurance companies and certain pension funds, stating that the president of Uruguay may exempt the securities of trusts in cases where these beneficiaries invest in such securities.

## 6. Tax Treatment and Responsibility of the Trustee

Trustees' fees are subject to IRAE and VAT.

The trustee is responsible for the taxes of the trust in cases where his or her fault or his or her intentionality is proved. If the trustee is negligent, but he or she does not incur fraud or any intentional tax criminal offense, his or her responsibility is restricted to the amount of the value of the assets under administration. On the contrary, where his or her intention to commit tax evasion is proved, he or she will have unlimited responsibility.

This responsibility has been understood as relating to taxes strictly speaking, not including fines or interest.

## 7. Foreign Beneficiaries

Foreign holders of trust securities shall be subject to IRNR. The general tax rate is 12 percent. In the event of publicly placed debt securities, the tax rate is reduced to 3 percent, and in the case of benefits arising from ordinary trusts it is be 7 percent, and the taxable basis would only be the amount subject to IRAE. In other words, if the trust only obtained foreign income, it would not pay IRAE, nor would the beneficiary pay IRNR.

Any asset or right located in Uruguay shall be subject to IP each December 31.

## 8. Tax Secret

Tax authorities' tax secret rule is established by section 47 of the Tax Code and binds both each member of the Tax Authority Office and tax authorities as a group. The sole exceptions are other Uruguayan tax authorities and judges in criminal offense, and minority and customs issues. Uruguayan tax authorities express their opinion that there being no tax treaty establishing the exchange of information with any other tax authority of any other country, they cannot make such information exchange.

# Chapter 22

# Venezuela[1]

A. Overview 358
   1. Testamentary Trusts 359
   2. Termination 360
   3. Competent Courts and Sanctions 360
B. The Trustee 361
   1. Duties of the Trustee 362
   2. Acceptance, Removal, and Resignation 364
   3. Regulation of Investments 364
C. The Grantor and the Beneficiary 366
   1. The Beneficiary 366
D. Particular Cases and Experience 367
   1. Club Administration Trusts 367
   2. Realty Trusts 367
   3. Savings Funds Trusts (*Fideicomiso de Fondos de Ahorro*) 367
   4. Savings Bank Trusts (*Fideicomisos de Caja de Ahorro*) 367
   5. Social Benefits Trusts (*Fideicomiso de Prestaciones Sociales de Antigüedad*) 368
   6. Trusts for Carrying Out Projects 368
   7. Guarantee Trusts 368
   8. Investment Trusts 368
   9. Housing Plan Trusts 369
   10. Retirement Plan Trusts 369
   11. Life Insurance Trusts 369

---

1    I am indebted to the invaluable contribution of María del Carmen Barroso, who read the manuscript and made several suggestions, supplied me with material touching the current regulations on trusts in this country, and explained the main uses of trusts in Venezuela.

In Venezuela, trusts are regulated by the Trust Act (*Ley de Fideicomiso*), whose entrance into force dates back to 1956 (Extraordinary Official Gazette No. 496 of August 17, 1956), but it has not been actively used until more recently. In fact in 1999, Turuhpial Cariello expressed that "the trust is one of the few bank contracts fully regulated in detail by our law, notwithstanding it is still practically unknown. If when lecturing I forget to say that the Trust Law that my students must purchase for the course dates back to 1956, many of them come back the following class without purchasing the law because they think that the bookseller tried to sell them an old and abrogated law."[2] Nevertheless, the same author explained that the situation described was changing: "[T]he financial institutions realized the exceptional flexibility of the trust for fulfilling private and social benefit purposes." He also said that he envisioned a development of the trust for family needs, the development of the public sector trust for public works and services, and as collective schemes of investment.[3] The author was right, as currently public sector trusts and so-called "social benefits trusts" (which will be addressed in detail at the end of this chapter), among others, are intensively used.

In relation to the legal framework antecedents, it should be remembered that the concept of the trust in Venezuela has its first antecedents in the Civil Code, but in reference only to inheritance matters and to features completely different from those created by the Trusts Act.

To complete the current legal framework, it should be mentioned that by means of Decree No. 3228 of October 28, 1993, the president of Venezuela, in the exercise of extraordinary measures in economic and financial matters granted by statute, issued the Banks and Other Financial Institutions General Act (*Ley General de Bancos y Otras Instituciones Financieras*), which regulated in its second section of chapter IV, title I, the trust transactions permitted to banking institutions. Afterwards, by means of the Decree with Rank, Value and Force of Law No. 6287 of July 31, 2008 (Extraordinary Official Gazette No. 5892, July 31, 2008), denominated "Partial Reform of Banks and Other Financial Institutions General Act" (*Ley de Reforma Parcial de la Ley General de Bancos y Otras Instituciones Financieras*), establishes in sections 47 to 66 of the law the regulation of trusts with banks as trustees.

## A. OVERVIEW

Section 1 of the Trust Act defines trusts as a legal relationship whereby a person called grantor transfers one or more assets to another person, called trustee, who undertakes to use it in the benefit of the latter or a third person, called beneficiary. According to this, and like that in other jurisdictions, there exist three intervening parties to this legal relationship: (a) the grantor, who transfers the assets to the trust; (b) the trustee, who administers the trust, and (c) the beneficiary, in favor of whom the trust is created. Of course, this does not necessarily means that there should be three different persons.

---

2    Héctor Turuphial Cariello, El Fideicomiso 11 (2000).
3    *Id.* at 12.

The trust may be constituted on all types of assets, except those which, according to the law, are strictly personal to the owner.

The assets transferred from the grantor to the trustee and those replacing them cannot be attacked by the trustee's creditors. Put differently, a separate estate is created by the trustee. It is also established that, unless otherwise dictated by statute, the trustee is subject to meeting the obligations deriving from the trust or its management with such assets and may oppose any preventive or execution measure issued at the request of creditors who proceed by virtue of credits not deriving from the trust or its execution.

The *inter vivos* trust must be recorded in a deed. The grantor's consent must also be granted in a deed, in the trust instrument or in a separate act.

The transfer to the trustee by an *inter vivos* act of personalty or realty rights will only take effect against third parties as from the time when the recording of the trust instrument is recorded in the relevant registry. Likewise, if dealing with such assets or rights, the recording will be conducted in the Public Registry at termination of the trust or in the case of trustee substitution.

When the creation, modification, or termination of the trust is of a commercial nature for the grantor, or for the trustee, so long as with respect to him or her there was an act of commerce, whatever the nature of the assets given in trust, recording in the Commercial Registry of the jurisdiction will be carried out in all cases, with all due publication formalities required by the Commerce Code.

The duration of the trust created in favor of a legal person may not be in excess of thirty years.

## 1. Testamentary Trusts

The trust may be created by will, so that it takes effect after the grantor's death. In that case, the trustee must manifest his or her acceptance or declination before the trust's court.

The trustee who accepted a testamentary transfer of assets as heir of all the assets of the grantor is only liable for inherited debts with such assets and those substituting them when, at the outset of the trust, he or she presented an inventory of the trust assets.

Moreover, notwithstanding the provisions of the Civil Code on forced heirship portions, the testator may arrange the creation of a trust on such forced portion, or a part of it, in favor of the heirs apparent so long as they have repeatedly done acts of wastefulness or are so insolvent as to severely jeopardize their future acquisitions. In that case, despite the provisions of the trust instrument, the benefited heirs apparent will be entitled to receive the income of the trust assets, at least, on a half-yearly basis.

The creation of the trust on the forced portion (legitime), or a part of it, is not valid if at the testator's death the heirs apparent have permanently abandoned their wasteful life or are not in the insolvent status originating the testator's provisions; and in all cases, the trust is terminated if this comes about subsequently.

At termination of the trust on the forced portion (legitime), or a part of it, the trust assets will be transferred to the heirs apparent or to their heirs.

The creation of trusts in favor of legally incapable persons for the duration of their incapacity is deemed valid, as regards their own forced portion (legitime).

The exception to the rule is the prohibition against the creation of trusts granting benefits gratuitously to incompetent persons by will or through a gift.

So long as the trust assets comprise a minor's forced portion (legitime), even when the trust instrument provides otherwise, the trustee will pay the income at least on a half-yearly basis to the father or the mother who has the legal usufruct of the child's assets.

The trust assets pertaining to the forced portion (legitime) of the legally incapable must necessarily be transferred to him or her at the termination of his or her incapacity, or in any other case of termination of the trust.

## 2. Termination

In accordance with the Trusts Act, the trust will terminate by reason of

a. Accomplishment of the object for which it was created, or its impossibility
b. Expiration of the period or fulfillment of the resolutory condition to which it may be subject
c. Resignation of all beneficiaries to their rights deriving from the trust
d. Revocation by the grantor, when he or she has reserved that power
e. Lack of trustee, if it is impossible to substitute him or her

The trust being terminated and pending obligations having been satisfied, the trustee remains obligated to transfer the trust assets to the person provided in the trust instrument or the law, and to render an accounting of his or her administration.

Should the trustee not comply with his or her obligation of conveying the trust assets, the other beneficiary may demand the transfer and claim a compensation for the damages occasioned to him or her by the trustee. The sentence will produce the legal transfer of the property from the trustee to the beneficiary without need of further actions by the trustee.

The grantor who had reserved the right to revoke the trust and the persons who must receive the assets at its termination enjoy, even when they are not beneficiaries during the life of the trust, the rights prescribed for the latter.

## 3. Competent Courts and Sanctions

Regarding the competent judge, the Trust Act establishes that it is the duty of the civil jurisdiction to hear all controversies regarding the creation, management, and termination of the trust, unless its creation is an act of commerce for the grantor, in which case it will be in the hands of the commercial jurisdiction.

To the effects of the Trust Act, the trust's court imports

a. In the case of trust created by will, the court of the place of the succession procedure, and if that had been carried out outside of Venezuela, the court of the place where the greater part of the grantor's assets, which exists in the national territory is located.

b. In the case of an *inter vivos* trust, the court of the domicile of the grantor at the time of the creation, unless the latter elected another place for the administration of the trust assets, in which case the court of that domicile will be competent.

The administrators of banks and insurance companies that in detriment of the beneficiaries and residual beneficiaries willingly perform acts in violation of the resulting obligations of the trust will be penalized with imprisonment from one to five years.

## B. THE TRUSTEE

Section 12 of the Trust Act provides that only banking institutions and insurance companies may be trustees if incorporated in the country and are authorized to that effect by the National Executive, by Decree of the Ministry of Economy or Promotion. Such an authorization will be governed by section 32 of the Banks and Other Financial Institutions General Act; the second paragraph of section 24 of the National Savings and Loan System Act, and by those regulations issued by the National Executive for insurance companies.[4]

Thus, the Banks and Other Financial Institutions General Act section 32 provides that commercial banks,[5] mortgage banks,[6] investment banks,[7] and universal banks[8]

---

4     As regards insurance companies, Decree No. 561 of June 14, 1966, provided that insurance companies incorporated in the country that intend to act as fiduciaries must seek prior authorization from the Ministry of Promotion which, in view of the national interest, may grant it by means of a Decree of the Insurance Superintendence, published in the Official Bulletin of the Republic of Venezuela. Furthermore, it was provided that those companies authorized to act as trustees must submit monthly a detailed account of the assets received in trust and of their object to the Insurance Superintendence. Additionally, it was provided that the insurance companies authorized to act as fiduciaries will have a trust services department, and all of its operations will be recorded separately and published in the balance sheet under a separate heading, according to the directions dictated by the Insurance Superintendence.

5     According to the Banks and Other Financial Institutions General Act § 38, commercial banks are those that have as an object the conducting of financial intermediation transactions and other financial transactions and services compatible with their nature, with the restrictions set forth in the Act.

6     The Banks and Other Financial Institutions General Act § 45 provides that mortgage banks will have as an object to grant mortgage-backed loans and conduct the financial transactions and services compatible with their nature, with the restrictions set forth in the Act.

7     Investment banks are those that have as an object participation in the placing of capitals, finance production, construction, and investment projects, to participate in the financing of operations in the capital markets and, generally, to carry out other activities compatible with their nature as investment banks, with the restrictions set forth in the Banks and Other Financial Institutions General Act § 55.

8     Universal banks are those that may conduct all the operations which, in accordance with the provisions of the Banks and Other Financial Institutions General Act, may be effected by specialized banks and financial institutions (Banks and Other Financial Institutions General Act § 95).

require the authorization of the Superintendence of Banks and Other Financial Institutions to act as trustees in accordance with the Trusts Act, as well as to carry out agencies, commissions, and other fiduciary charges.[9]

This Act provides in its section 50 that the institutions authorized to act as trustees in the terms of the Trusts Act will have a trust department. Also, the Act provides that all of the transactions will be recorded separately and will be published along with the balance sheet, under a separate heading, according to the directions dictated by the Superintendence.

As with the majority of Latin American legislations, the Venezuelan Trust Act expressly provides in section 23 that the trustee may not be the beneficiary.

In the trust instrument, the grantor may appoint the trustee and one or more substitutes for the event that the former did not accept the appointment or ceased in his or her duties. Absent such regulations, the court must appoint the trustee or his or her substitute at the request of any beneficiary. There will be only one trustee for each trust.

## 1. Duties of the Trustee

Apart from the obligations set down in the trust instrument and the applicable law, the trustee is bound to

a. Carry out all the necessary acts for the accomplishment of the trust object.
b. Keep the trust assets duly separated from his or her other assets and from those corresponding to other trusts.
c. Render an accounting of his or her administration to the beneficiary, at least on an annual basis.[10]

The trustee will perform his or her duties with the care of a diligent administrator and may appoint, under his or her own responsibility, the assistants and representatives required by the execution of the trust. The Trust Act also provides that in no case may he or she delegate his or her powers.

It should be noted that the Banks and Other Financial Institutions General Act provides that when, in accordance with the regulations governing the trust, liquid funds originating in or resulting from the trust remain in the possession of the trustee, such an institution must keep them in cash or deposit them in a special account. Moreover,

---

9   However, it is worth underscoring that the exception to the rule providing that only banks may be trustees, the Family Protection Act (*Ley de Protección Familiar*), prescribes that to the effects of the obligor's assets necessary for the performance of his or her alimentary duties, a trust may be created on those assets in favor of the beneficiary, and the court is authorized to appoint as trustee any person who is capable of entering into contracts.

10  It should be noted that under section 37 of the Banks and Other Financial Institutions General Act, the Superintendence may request from the financial institutions the periodic submission of a detailed account of the assets received in trust.

authorized institutions may not invest the funds received in trust or by means of other fiduciary mandates in

a. Their own shares or obligations and other assets of their property.
b. Shares, obligations, and assets of banks and other financial institutions with which balance consolidation or combination is established.
c. Obligations, shares, or assets of companies not registered in the National Securities Registry where they have an interest; or where their executives participate as managers, partners, or advisors.
d. Obligations, shares, or assets of companies registered in the National Securities Registry in which they have an interest superior to 20 percent of the corporate assets, or when their executives have an interest in such companies superior to 20 percent of the corporate assets, or when their executives participate in the administration of such companies in a proportion of one-fourth (1/4) or more of the total amount of the Managing Assemblies.
e. Obligations, shares or assets of companies with which they have agreed on reciprocal investment mechanisms

By reasons of monetary policies, the Central Bank of Venezuela may prohibit or restrict the investment abroad of the funds received in trust or managed for a third party, including agencies, commissions, and other charges, as well as investment carried out in the country in foreign currency or in foreign-denominated securities, according to the rules dictated to the effect. The Superintendence, with the prior opinion of the Central Bank of Venezuela, may set regulations regarding the financial information, accounting standards, and control of trust operations, as well as agencies, commissions, and other fiduciary mandates.

The law grants the trustee a solution when he or she has well-grounded doubts as to the nature and scope of his or her duties. Thus, the trustee may request directions from the trust's court that, before deciding, will hear the beneficiary or his or her legal representative, or both, if the former is older than 15 years of age and is in full command of his or her faculties.

Further, when the trustee has to deviate from the directions in the trust instrument by reason of a change in circumstances unforeseen by the grantor, he or she must request directions from the trust's court. In cases of proved emergency, the court must decide summarily.

Any act conducted by the trustee in contravention of his or her duties are voidable, so long as the act is a gratuitous one or has been effected with third parties who were, or should have been, in knowledge of the trustee's duties. Apart from the provisions of paragraph 2, article 24, of the Trust Act,[11] and notwithstanding his or her fault, the act

---

11   Such a regulation provides that the beneficiary will enjoy, along with the rights granted him or her by the act of settlement and the law, the right to "challenge voidable acts by the trustee, within five years computed as from the day when the beneficiary has come into knowledge of the act originating the legal action, and demand the return of the trust assets to whom they are due. This period will not run for minors and the interdit, but as from their majority or as from the time when their barring ceases." Trust Act, paragraph 2 of section 24.

may be attempted by the trustee or by the person acting for him or her, in the benefit of the beneficiary.

Any beneficiary will be compensated, and when the amount of such compensation is not stipulated in the trust instrument, the respective court will after hearing the beneficiary. The compensation fixed by the court will not be in excess of 15 percent of the liquid income of the trust assets.

Finally, it is worth remarking on a very peculiar rule of Venezuelan law. That is section 51 of the Banks and Other Financial Institutions General Act (amended as commented on in the first part of this chapter), which establishes that the value of the assets under trust administration cannot be more than five times the patrimony of the bank acting as trustee. This is a rule unique in Latin America that severely affects the development of the trust in Venezuela.

## 2. Acceptance, Removal, and Resignation

The trustee may accept or decline the trust. At the instance of any beneficiary, the trust's court will indicate a reasonable period within which he or she must manifest his or her acceptance or excuse. Nonappearance in court will be deemed a declination.

Resignation of the trust requires prior authorization by the corresponding court, which will not grant it but in the presence of, in its opinion, grave circumstances.

Banking institutions and insurance companies will cease their fiduciary duties as well owing to dissolution, bankruptcy, or removal from their capacity by the trust's court on grave grounds.

In leaving his or her office through resignation or any other cause, the trustee must transfer the trust assets to his or her substitute, if any; the provisions of section 27 of the Trust Act[12] will be applicable here. The substitute will be liable with such assets for all the obligations that could have been enforced against the trustee as to those assets.

## 3. Regulation of Investments

Investments by trustees are regulated by section 53 of the Banks and Other Financial Institutions General Act (amended by Decree with Rank, Value and Force of Law, denominated as Partial Reform, published in the Extraordinary Public Gazette No. 5892 [July 31, 2009]), and by Resolution No. 179-2000 (May 30, 2002) of the Superintendence

---

12   Section 27, already commented on before, provides that the trust being terminated and out-standing obligations having been satisfied, the trustee remains obligated to transfer the trust assets to the corresponding person in accordance with the trust instrument or the law, and to render him or her an accounting of his or her administration. If the trustee does not comply with the obligation of transferring the trust assets, the beneficiary may claim the transfer and claim damages occasioned by the trustee's omission.

of Banks and Other Financial Institutions (hereinafter the "Resolution"), which is addressed here.

Section 53 establishes that trustees may not carry on the following transactions, among others, with the trust assets:

a. Grant loans, unless the loans are granted to the beneficiaries, or the trust administers public funds
b. Guarantee with or encumber the trust assets without the express authorization of the settlor or the beneficiary
c. Carry on repos with the trust securities unless authorized by the Superintendence of Banks
d. Carry out transactions with or invest in companies related to the trustee unless authorized by the Superintendence of Banks
e. Purchase the shares or assets of the trustee

Section 1 of the Resolution provides that trust instruments must not suffer such a lack of regulations as to prevent its adequate management or fulfillment, or be object of subjective interpretations. Furthermore, trust instruments must clearly state that the trustee will not be responsible for the losses of the trust if the trustee has accomplished his or her obligations with the due diligence of a diligent administrator.

Section 2 requires that all trustees have adequate software and qualified staff who must detect the risks involved in each trust to be able to take corrective measures on time. Besides, the staff must seek compliance with the manuals, procedures, and mechanisms for the trust area of the bank and the auditing area.

Section 3 states that if a financial institution, acting as trustee, accepts assets to be administered on behalf of third parties, it must be clearly stated in the contract that the bank is not assuming any financial or economic risk. Otherwise, the bank must assume the assets and liabilities as its own and apply all the banking regulations.

Section 4 lays down the rule that financial institutions acting as trustees cannot guarantee or assure the principal or yield of the trust assets under its administration. The Trust must be kept as a relation based on trust in the trustee and a diligent administration.

Section 5 provides that financial institutions that publicly offered, or will offer, asset-backed securities, must comply with securitization rules (mainly a registry) and obtain the authorization of the National Securities Commission (*Comisión Nacional de Valores*).

Section 6 outlines that the trust instruments of investment trusts focused on certain assets must include the alternatives that the trustee would give to the investors, so that the grantor and/or beneficiary chooses the one that they find more interesting, the latter assuming the risks of the investment. The trust instrument must state in a clear fashion the risks of the investments, and if there is change in the circumstances, the Superintendence of Banks and the beneficiary of the trust must be informed of such change.

Section 7 and 9 must be considered together. They establish that if the Superintendence determines that a financial institution acting as trustee is assuming financial or economic risks or assuring in any way the returns of the investment, however they do it, such financial institution must register such transactions as its own credits and debts according to the rules of bank accounting in Venezuela.

Section 8, complementing the Trust Act rules, regulates that all financial institutions acting as trustees must submit to the beneficiary and the grantor a semiannual accounting including, without limitation, the financial statement of the period and a detail of the invested assets, gains, and losses of the period; the trustee's fees; and any circumstance that might mean a deterioration of the assets of the trust.

Finally, section 10 provides that any financial institution that requests the authorization to act as trustee must submit to the Banks Superintendence the following:

a. Manual of rules and procedures of the trustee
b. Accounting rules and practices of the trusts
c. Trustee software
d. Description and résumé of the staff of the financial institution's trust area
e. Forecast of the activity, assets under trust, expenses, and returns
f. Business plan
g. Draft of trust instruments

## C. THE GRANTOR AND THE BENEFICIARY

The law sets no restrictions to act as grantor in a trust.

### 1. The Beneficiary

A trust may be created in favor of one or several beneficiaries. The trustee may constitute it in his or her own favor (grantor-beneficiary trust).

The trust may be created in the benefit of several persons who must be successively substituted, whether by reason of the predecessor's death or for any other reason, so long as the substitution is carried out in favor of persons in being when the first beneficiary's right is obtained (this is a way to avoid the fiduciary substitution explained in Chapter 1, Section A1 and Section B, and in Chapter 5, Section D2).

The beneficiary will enjoy, apart from those provided by the trust instrument and the applicable law, the following rights:

a. To demand from the trustee the faithful performance of his or her duties and to press liability for their noncompliance.
b. To void all voidable acts carried out by the trustee within five years computed as from the day when the beneficiary came into knowledge of the act originating the action, and to demand the return of the trust assets from whom it may concern. This period will not run for minors and the interdict, but as from their majority or the time when their barring ceases.
c. To oppose any preventive or execution measure taken against the trust assets for obligations not affecting them, in case the trustee did not so do.

d. To request, on justified grounds, the removal of the trustee and, as a preventive measure, in the opinion of the trust's court, the appointment of an acting administrator.

When the beneficiary is a different person than the grantor, the latter may exclude, with effects against third parties, the transfer of the beneficiary's right to the income of the trust assets or a part of them. However, such income will remain subject to the execution of the beneficiary's creditors, except that that and other of his or her income does not suffice for his or her upkeep, in which case the court will fix the amount of income which is not subject to attachment.

## D. PARTICULAR CASES AND EXPERIENCE

To exemplify the use of trusts in Venezuela, a few particular cases of special importance in this country will now be considered.

### 1. Club Administration Trusts

A trust is created between one or more club(s) promoting a company or companies (grantor) and the banking entity, which offers itself as trustee to sell the shares and the premises of the said club, for those moneys to be applied to the payment of the works carried out in the benefit of the beneficiaries.

### 2. Realty Trusts

Realty trusts consist of a contract subscribed by a construction or development company, which transfers a plot of land and project in ownership to the trustee for him or her to administer the payments originating in the presale, making payment for terminated works and investments on the remnant in the benefit of the grantor or beneficiaries.

### 3. Savings Funds Trusts (*Fideicomiso de Fondos de Ahorro*)

Savings fund trusts consist of a contract between such employees as unite to create a fund with a portion of their salary. Such funds will be transferred through the trust and administered and invested by the banking entity with the object of benefiting themselves or those appointed by them in the contract as beneficiaries.

### 4. Savings Bank Trusts (*Fideicomisos de Caja de Ahorro*)

In a savings bank trust, a contract is signed whereby a savings bank civil association acts as grantor and the banking entity as trustee, to stimulate and administer the savings of the member workers who will be its beneficiaries. Both institutions will be governed by the provisions of their respective bylaws.

## 5. Social Benefits Trusts (*Fideicomiso de Prestaciones Sociales de Antigüedad*)

A social benefits trust is one of the most widely used kinds of trusts in Venezuela and is almost unique in Latin America.

Decree No. 124 of May 31, 1975, established the right of the employee to receive compensation proportional to the time that he or she or she was an employee after termination of the labor relationship, no matter the reason. Furthermore, Decree No. 869 of April 15, 1975, established that this right to compensation must be backed with assets of the employer that can be transferred to a trust. In such a case, these assets must be invested, and the income arising from such investments are exempted from income tax.[13] Additionally, these assets can be used as collateral for certain loans to the employee. Currently, these kinds of trusts are regulated by section 108 of the Labor Law, which establishes that the employer must contribute five days' monthly wage (salary) to the trust.

In short, the social benefits trust has the employee as beneficiary, lasts the same period of time as the labor relation, and has as underlying assets the contributions made by the employer during the period of the labor relation.

## 6. Trusts for Carrying Out Projects

Funds are transferred to a trust with the instruction to the trustee to pay the contractor as long as certain advances in the project are achieved. This gives comfort to both the contractor and the person that must pay him or her.

## 7. Guarantee Trusts

As explained, guarantee trusts are used as a guarantee of an obligation of the grantor or a third party.

## 8. Investment Trusts

Investment trusts are trust contracts, regulated in the Venezuelan law, which have an aim to obtain financial returns from the assets of the trust.

---

13   ATILIO ROJAS, EL FIDEICOMISO, FIDUCIA O TRUST EN AMÉRICA 422 (2008).

## 9. Housing Plan Trusts

The objective of a housing plan trust is to administer funds and make payments to contractors to construct housing. Usually the funds are contributed in a great portion by a public sector entity.

## 10. Retirement Plan Trusts

Retirement plan trusts are trusts to which a working person makes contributions to form a fund and makes investments to receive an annuity when he or she retires.

## 11. Life Insurance Trusts

In a life insurance trust, the trustee is the beneficiary of an insurance policy of the grantor to administer the benefits of the policy in favor of his or her or her family or other beneficiaries.

# Bibliography

- Adilson Rodriguez Pires, Manual de Direito Tributário (10th ed. 1990).
- Alejandro Hernández Maestroni, Gianni Gutiérrez Prieto & Fernando Foti Faroppa, Fideicomiso: Aspectos Legales, Tributarios y Contables (2004).
- Alfred E. von Overbeck, *Explanatory Report on the 1985 Hague Trusts Convention, in* 2 The Proceedings of the Fifteenth Session (1984): Trusts—Applicable Law and Recognition 371 (1985).
- 1 American Law Institute, Restatement of the Law Second, Trusts (1959).
- American Law Institute, Restatement of the Law of Trusts (1935).
- Ami Morris Hess, George Gleason Bogert & George Taylor Bogert, The Law of Trusts and Trustees (3rd ed. 2007).
- Antonio Domingo Aznar, El Fideicomiso y la Sustitución Fideicomisaria (1999)
- Atilio Rojas, El Fideicomiso, Fiducia o Trust en América (2008).
- Diane Audino, Rosario Buendía & Kevin Kime, *Los Seguros de Riesgo Político Pueden Mejorar las Transacciones Estructuradas, in* Titulización en América Latina 2000, 43 (2001).
- Constituçao da República Federativa do Brasil (B. Calheiros Bomfim ed., 9th ed. 1999).
- Benedetta Ubertazzi, *The Trust in Spanish and Italian Private International Law—Part II*, Tr. & Trustees 13 (1), 7–13 (2007).
- Benedetta Ubertazzi, *The Trust in Spanish and Italian Private International Law—Part I,* Tr. & Trustees 12 (10), 14–19 (2006).
- Black´s Law Dictionary (6th ed. 1990).
- BritCham Brazil, Doing Business in Brazil (5th ed. 2005).
- Celso Marcelo De Oliveira, Alienação Fiduciária em Garantia (2003).
- Daniel Porcaro & Nicolas Malumian, Fideicomiso en Uruguay: Análisis del Proyecto de Ley (2003).
- Denis Kleinfeld, *Choosing an Offshore Jurisdiction, in* 1 Asset Protection Strategies: Planning with Domestic and Offshore Entities 73–86 (Alexander A. Bove, Jr., ed., 2005).
- E. H. Burn & G. J. Virgo, Trusts & Trustees: Cases & Materials (6th ed. 2002).
- Eduardo Casas Sanz de Santamaría, La Fiducia (2nd ed. 1997).
- Eduardo Ferrer M., La Fundación de Interés Privado Bajo la Legislación de la República de Panamá (2003).
- Eduardo Ferrer M., The Trust Under the Legislation of the Republic of Panama (2nd ed. 1999).
- Elías P. Guastavino, La Propiedad Participada y sus Fideicomisos (1994).
- Esteban C. Buljevich & Mariano A. Fabrizio, *Securitization in Latin America, in* Expansion and Diversification in Securitization Yearbook 2007 179–92 (Jan Job de Vries Robbé & Paul Ali eds., 2008).
- Fàbio Ulhoa Coelho, Comentários à Nova Ley de Falencias e de Recuperação de Empresas (6th ed. 2009).
- Fernando Schwarz Gaggini, Securitização de Recebíveis (2003).

- Francisco Armando Arias & Lic. Zygmunt Brett, *Marco Legal del Fideicomiso en El Salvador* (brief) (1998).
- Gladis Fernández Formigo, *Estudio Sobre El Fideicomiso* (brief, 2000).
- Glen CH Wilson, *Belize, in* STEP DIRECTORY AND YEARBOOK 2009 563–64 (Society of Trust and Estate Practitioners, 2008).
- GUSTAVO ORDOQUI CASTILLA, EL FIDEICOMISO (2nd ed. 2004).
- HÉCTOR TURUPHIAL CARIELLO, EL FIDEICOMISO (2000).
- HELA CHEIKHROUHOU, W. BRITT GWINNER, JOHN POLLNER, EMANUEL SALINAS, SOPHIE SIRTAINE & DIMITRI VITTAS, STRUCTURE FINANCE IN LATIN AMERICA: CHANNELING PENSION FUNDS TO HOUSING, INFRASTRUCTURE, AND SMALL BUSINESSES (2007).
- Herbert F. Goodrich, *Introduction, in* 1 RESTATEMENT OF THE LAW SECOND, TRUSTS, at vii & ix (American Law Institute, 1959).
- HILLAIRE BELLOC, HISTORIA DE INGLATERRA: DESDE LOS ORÍGENES HASTA EL SIGLO, XX (2008).
- William Draper Lewis, *Introduction, in* RESTATEMENT OF THE LAW OF TRUSTS i (American Law Institute, 1935).
- Jacob Gyntelberg, Eli Remolona & Camilo E. Tovar, *Securitization in Asia and Latin America Compared, in* EXPANSION AND DIVERSIFICATION IN SECURITIZATION YEARBOOK 2007 383–404 (Jan Job de Vries Robbé & Paul Ali eds., 2008).
- JAMES V. CALVI & SUSAN COLEMAN, AMERICAN LAW AND LEGAL SYSTEMS (4th ed. 2000).
- JOAQUÍN DE ARESPACOCHAGA, EL TRUST, LA FIDUCIA Y FIGURAS AFINES (2000).
- John H. Langbein, *The Contractarian Basis of the Law of Trusts*, 105 YALE L.J. (1995).
- John H. Langbein, *The Secret Life of Trust: The Trust as an Instrument of Commerce*, 107 YALE L.J. (1997).
- JOHN HENRY MERRYMAN, THE CIVIL LAW TRADITION: AN INTRODUCTION TO THE LEGAL SYSTEMS OF WESTERN EUROPE AND LATIN AMERICA (2nd ed. 1985).
- Jorge A. Vargas, *Fideicomisos: Real Estate Trusts in Mexico's Restricted Zone, in* MEXICAN LAW: A TREATISE FOR LEGAL PRACTITIONERS AND INTERNATIONAL INVESTORS 1 352 (Jorge A. Vargas ed., 1998).
- JORGE PORRAS ZAMORA, EL FIDEICOMISO EN COSTA RICA, NOCIONES Y PRODUCTOS BÁSICOS (1998).
- JORGE R. HAYZUS, FIDEICOMISO (2000).
- JOSÉ EVARISTO DOS SANTOS, MERCADO FINANCIERO BRASILERO (1999).
- JOSÉ MANUEL VILLAGORDOA, LOZANO, DOCTRINA GENERAL DEL FIDEICOMISO (3rd ed. 1998).
- Juan A. Tejada Mora, *Adaptación del Trust y de las Fundaciones de Interés Privado en Panamá para Servicio de Latinoamérica*, paper presented at the VII LATIN AMERICAN CONGRESS ON TRUSTS, Cancún (Mexico) (1997).
- Juan A. Tejada Mora, *Notas Sobre el Fideicomiso de Garantía Como Alternativa a las Garantías Reales en Panamá, in* ALGUNAS CONFERENCIAS SOBRE EL FIDEICOMISO, LAS FUNDACIONES DE INTERÉS PRIVADO Y SUS USOS EN PANAMÁ 7–58 (2005).
- L. A. SHERIDAN, THE LAW OF TRUSTS (12th ed. 1993).
- Laurent Chambaz, *Is France Adopting Trust Wholesale? The Answer Is "Not, But . . ."* 13(7) TR. & TRUSTEES 255 (2007).
- LAWRENCE M. FRIEDMAN, A HISTORY OF AMERICAN LAW (2nd ed. 1985).
- Luigi Belluzzo & Alessandro Belluzzo, *Trusts Find a Tax Rule within the Italian Financial Bill 2007* 13(7) TR. & TRUSTEES 262 (2007).
- Luis A. Chalhoub M., *Estudio Comparativo entre el Fideicomiso y la Fundación de Interés Privado en la Legislación Panameña, in* ALGUNAS CONFERENCIAS SOBRE EL FIDEICOMISO, LAS FUNDACIONES DE INTERÉS PRIVADO Y SUS USOS EN PANAMÁ 87–103 (2005).
- Dayra Berbey de Rojas, *Panama, in* STEP DIRECTORY AND YEARBOOK 2009, at 455 (Society of Trust and Estate Practitioners, 2008).
- LUIS A. CHALHOUB MORENO, CASUÍSTICA DEL FIDEICOMISO SOMETIDA AL ANÁLISIS DE LOS TRIBUNALES PANAMEÑOS (2005).
- Luis Fernando Céspedes Jiménez, *Instrumentos Financieros y Subsidios en Vivienda Social* (brief, Costa Rican Home Mortgage Bank [BANHVI] 1998).
- LUIS RODOLFO ARGÜELLO, MANUAL DE DERECHO ROMANO: HISTORIA E INSTITUCIONES (3rd ed. 2007).

- Marcos Lopez Narvaez, *La Responsabilidad Fiduciaria in Derecho Societario: Memorias de las Primeras Jornadas Nacionales,* Oct. 22 & 23 ACADEMIA ECUATORIANA DE DERECHO Y EDINO, GUAYAQUIL (2003).
- 4 MARIA HELENA DINIZ, CURSO DE DIREITO CIVIL BRASILEIRO (23rd ed. 2008).
- MARIANNE KNAAK DONOSO, FACTORING, SECURITIZACIÓN, ADR´S. ANÁLISIS, REGULACIÓN Y APLICACIÓN (1998).
- Mario A. Bonfanti, *Significado Actual del Fideicomiso* 780 J.A. (1999-III).
- MARIO A. CARREGAL, EL FIDEICOMISO: REGULACIÓN JURÍDICA Y POSIBILIDADES PRÁCTICAS (1982).
- MAURICIO LOPEZ, LA SECURITIZACIÓN Y UN ANÁLISIS PARALELO (2006).
- MIGUEL ACOSTA ROMERO & PABLO R. ALMAZÁN ALANIZ, TRATADO TEÓRICO PRÁCTICO DE FIDEICOMISO (1999).
- Nicola Saccardo, *Taxation of Trusts in Italy* 6(4) TR. Q. REV. (2008).
- NICOLAS MALUMIAN & FEDERICO BARREDO, OBLIGACIONES NEGOCIABLES (2008).
- NICOLAS MALUMIAN & FEDERICO BARREDO, OFERTA PÚBLICA DE VALORES NEGOCIABLES (2007).
- PAUL JOHNSON, EL NACIMIENTO DEL MUNDO MODERNO (1999).
- PIERRE LEPAULLE, TRATADO TEÓRICO PRÁCTICO DE LOS TRUSTS: EN DERECHO INTERNO, EN DERECHO FISCAL Y EN DERECHO INTERNACIONAL (1975).
- RICARDO D. RABINOVICH-BERKMAN, DERECHO ROMANO (2001).
- RICARDO J. ALFARO, EL FIDEICOMISO: ESTUDIO SOBRE LA NECESIDAD Y CONVENIENCIA DE INTRODUCIR EN LA LEGISLACIÓN DE LOS PUEBLOS LATINOS UNA INSTITUCIÓN NUEVA, SEMEJANTE AL TRUST DEL DERECHO INGLÉS (1920).
- Richard W. Hompesch II, *Domestic Asset Protection Trusts—More Might Than First Appears, in* 1 ASSET PROTECTION STRATEGIES: PLANNING WITH DOMESTIC AND OFFSHORE ENTITIES 11 (Alexander A. Bove, Jr., ed., 2005).
- RIGOBERTO J. PARADA DAZA, INSTRUMENTOS DE FINANCIAMIENTO E INVERSIÓN (2000).
- ROBERTO GONZÁLEZ TORRE, EL FIDEICOMISO (2nd ed. 2000).
- Ronald Drake López, *Prologue* to EL FIDEICOMISO EN COSTA RICA, NOCIONES Y PRODUCTOS BÁSICOS 5–7 (1998).
- SERGIO MONSERRIT ORTÍZ SOLTERO, EL FIDEICOMISO MEXICANO (1998).
- SERGIO RODRÍGUEZ AZUERO, CONTRATOS BANCARIOS: SU SIGNIFICACIÓN EN AMÉRICA LATINA (2002).
- SERGIO RODRÍGUEZ AZUERO, NEGOCIOS FIDUCIARIOS: SU SIGNIFICACIÓN EN AMÉRICA LATINA (2005).
- Sonia Martin, *Trusts in American Law and Some of Their Substitutes in Spanish Law: Part II* 13(7) TR. & TRUSTEES 242 (2007).
- VALDIR DE JESUS LAMEIRA, MERCADO DE CAPITAIS (2000).
- WALDIRIO BULGARELLI, CONTRATOS MERCANTIS (11th ed. 1999).
- Wendy Warren, *Anti-Forced Heirship Regimes*, 16(10) STEPJOURNAL 51.

# Index

## A

*Actio fiduciae contraria,* 6
Adjustable rate mortgages (ARMs), 49
*Administradoras de Fondos de
    Pensión* (AFPs), 51
Administration trusts, 71–73
    business trusts, 72–73
    charitable trusts, 72
Adoption of trust statutes in Latin American
    countries, 16–19
Aeronautic Code
    Brazil, 145–46
AFH legal regimes. *See* Anti-forced heirships
    (AFH) legal regimes
AFPs. *See Administradoras de Fondos de
    Pensión* (AFPs)
Agency, 63–64
Agriculture promotion trusts
    Guatemala, 227–28
Alfaro Law, 18
Alfaro, Ricardo J., 17–20, 268
American Bar Association
    Executive Committee, 12n36
American Society of International
    Law, 12n36
Anglo-Saxon trust, 8n17, 19, 172
    Latin American trusts compared, 23–27
        civil-law traditions, 23–24
        common-law traditions, 23–24
        sources of trust law in Latin
            America, 26–27
        U.S. trusts and Latin American trusts,
            differences, 24–26
Antecedents, 3–13
    Anglo Saxon trust, 172
    Argentina, 84–85
    continental civil law,
        evolution of trust, 7–8
    England, trusts in, 8–11

Roman law, 3–7
United States, trusts in, 11–13
Anti-forced heirships (AFH) legal regimes
    Belize, 108n4
Appointment of trustee
    Belize, 118–19
    Costa Rica, 184
    El Salvador, 215
Argentina, 83–106. *See also* Argentina Law
    No. 24441 (Construction Financing Act);
    Argentine Civil Code; Argentine
    Commercial Code
    antecedents, 84–85
    Bankruptcy Act, 101
    beneficiary, 95–97
        residual beneficiary, 96–97
    *Caja de Valores S.A.,* 56n16
    Corporate Capital Trust Fund, 104
    "cost contribution" real estate trusts, 105
    Criminal Code, 42n41, 94
    criminal responsibility of trustee, 94
    Decree No. 286/95, 104
    Decree No. 675/97, 104
    Executive Power by Decree 468, 85
    federal income tax, 105–6
    *fideicomisario,* 96–97
    financial trustee, 95
    Financial Trustee Registry, 95
    financial trust instrument, 99–101, 106
    forced heirship, 86–87
    grantor, 88–89
    gross revenue tax, 106
    hybrid securities, 103
    *inter vivos* acts, 96
    Law No. 18061 (Financial
        Institutions Act), 85
    Law No. 21526 (Financial
        Institutions Act), 85
    Law No. 23696, 85

Argentina (*cont.*)
  Law No. 24441 (Construction
      Financing Act), 84–87
  liquidation of trust, 101
  *Message of Presentation,* presidential, 85
  minimum presumed income tax, 106
  *mortis causa,* 96
  mutual funds, use of trusts to create, 80
  National Mortgage Bank, 98
  National Securities Commission, 89, 97, 106
  Ordinary Trustees Public Registry, 89
  ordinary trusts, 105–6
  overview, 84–88
  personal wealth tax, 106
  public sector trusts, 75, 104
  *Requirements of the Trust Agreement,* 99
  residual beneficiary, 96–97
  Resolution 296/97, 33*n*31
  rights and duties of trustee, 90–92
  securitization, 47*n*2, 97–99
  separate patrimony, trust as, 92–93
  sole beneficiaries, 34*n*32
  stamp tax, 106
  tax treatment, 45, 105–6
    federal income tax, 105–6
    gross revenue tax, 106
    minimum presumed income tax, 106
    personal wealth tax, 106
    stamp tax, 106
    value-added tax, 106
  termination of Office of the Trustee, 94–95
  transference of credits to the trust, 99–100
  trust agreement, requirements, 87–88
  trust assets insufficiency, 100–101
  trustee, 30–31, 34*n*32, 89–95
    criminal responsibility of, 94
    financial trustee, 95
    rights and duties of, 90–92
    separate patrimony, trust as, 92–93
    termination of Office of the
        Trustee, 94–95
  trust securities, 101–4
  value-added tax, 106
Argentina Law No. 24441 (Construction
    Financing Act)
  beneficiary, 96
  criminal responsibility of trustee, 94
  definition, 86–87
  financial trust, 97, 99–101
  generally, 84–85
  grantor, 88
  residual beneficiary, 96–97
  rights and duties of trustee, 90–92
  separate patrimony, trust as, 92

  sources for drafting, 85–86
  termination of office of trustee, 94
  trustee, 89
  trust securities, 101–3
Argentine Civil Code (1869)
  Article 2662, 84*n*1
  beneficiary, 95
  fiduciary property, xxiii*n*2
  rights and duties of trustee, 90
  separate patrimony, trust as, 93
Argentine Commercial Code
  rights and duties of trustee, 91
ARMs. *See* Adjustable rate mortgages (ARMs)
Assets. *See* Trust assets
Association of American Law Schools, 12*n*36
Augustus, 4
Autonomy of patrimony
  Mexico, 254

B
Backup servers, 56
Bahamas
  forced heirship, 108*n*4
Bailment, 62–63
*Banco de Inversión y Comercio Exterior SA*
    (BICE), 104
Bank of the Argentine Nation, 104
Bankruptcy
  Chile, 164
  Uruguay, 339–40
Belize, 107–28. *See also* Belize International
    Trust; Belize Trust Fund; Belize Trusts Act
  anti-forced heirships (AFH) legal
      regimes, 108*n*4
  applicable law for trusts, 109–10
  appointment of trustee, 118–19
  assets transferred in trust, 113
  Bankruptcy Act, 111
  beneficiary, 113–15
  breach of trust, 124–25
  case law, 125–26
  charitable trusts, 115, 116
  creation of trust, 110
  "determining event," beneficiary, 114
  disclosure, 126
  duration of trust, 110
  duties of trustee, 120–22
  failure of trust, 115–17
  fees, 123–24
  fiduciaries, change of, 126
  Income and Business Tax Act, 128
  independence from foreign laws, 111–12
  International Financial Service
      Commission, 126

international trusts
  exemptions, 128
  trust agent, 127
invalid trusts, 110–11
Law of Property Act, 111
letter of wishes, 114–15
noncharitable trusts, 115
overview, 108–13
powers of the court, 112–13
powers of trustee, 118–20
protector, 117–26
Reciprocal Enforcement of
    Judgments Act, 111–12
reimbursement of expenses, 123–24
removal of trustee, 118–19
revocation of trust, 115–17
settlor, 117
Statute of Elizabeth, 112
termination of the trust, 115–17
trust agent, 127
trustee, 117–26
  appointment, 118–19
  breach of trust, 124
  described, 31
  duties of, 120–22
  fees, 123–24
  powers of, 118–20
  reimbursement of expenses, 123–24
  removal of, 118–19
  resignation of, 118–19
  variation of trusts, 117
Belize International Trust, 108, 126–28
  exemptions, 128
  register of international trusts,
    creation of, 126–27
  trust agent, 127
Belize Trust Fund, 125–26
Belize Trusts Act (1992), 108
  breach of trust, 124
  definition, 109
  duties of trustee, 120–22
  establishment of trust, 110n6
  powers of trustee, 118–19
Belizian trust. See Belize
Beneficiary
  Argentina, 95–97
    residual beneficiary, 96–97
  Belize, 113–15
  Bolivia, 133
  Chile, 156–57
  Colombia, 176–77
  Costa Rica, 187
  described, 32
  Ecuador, 203

El Salvador, 214
Guatemala
  residual beneficiary, 225–26
  rights of beneficiary, 225–26
Honduras, 233–34
Mexico, 248–49
Panama, 271
Paraguay, 302–3
Peru, 319–20
sole trustee as, termination of the trust, 38
termination of the trust, agreement between
    grantor and, 35
Uruguay, 345–46
  foreign beneficiaries, 354–55
Venezuela, 366–67
Best efforts
  trustee as securities underwriter, 59
BICE. See Banco de Inversión y Comercio
  Exterior SA (BICE)
Bogotá
  Chamber of Commerce, 174
Bolivia, 129–36. See also Bolivian Civil Code
  Administrative Resolution SPVS-IV
    No. 052, 134
  Administrative Resolution SPVS-IV
    No. 107, 134
  Administrative Resolution SPVS-IV
    No. 212, 134
  Administrative Resolution SPVS-IV
    No. 245, 134
  Administrative Resolution SPVS-IV
    No. 488, 134
  Banks Superintendence, 131
  beneficiary, 133
  Circular SB/254/93, 131
  definition, 129–31
  fiduciary substitution, 78
  grantor, 131
  Law No. 1834, 134n3
  Law No. 2064, 136
  Law No. 2196, 136
  Law No. 3446, 136
  legal framework, 133–34
  overview, 129–31
  prohibited types of trust, 130
  Resolution of the Banks No. 026/2002, 134
  securitization, 133–36
    legal framework, 133–34
    Stock Market Act, 134–36
    tax treatment, 136
  Specific Complementary Regulations on
    Securitization, 134
  Stock Market Act, Law No. 1834, 133–36
  Stock Market Registry, 134

Bolivia, 129–36. *See also* Bolivian
  Civil Code (*cont.*)
  Superintendence of Pensions, Stock and
    Insurance, 134
  Supreme Decree No. 25514, 133, 136
  Supreme Decree No. 28815, 136
  tax treatment, 136
  trustee, 31, 131–32
Bolivian Civil Code
  prohibited types of trust, 130
Brazil, 137–52. *See also* Brazilian Civil
  Code; Brazilian Code of 1916; Brazilian
  Constitution; Brazilian Criminal Code
  Bankruptcy Law, 141
  *Companhia Brasileira de Liquidação e
    Custódia* (CBLC), 151
  Capital Markets Act, 139*n*9, 142
  Central Bank, 150*n*50
  CETIP, 56*n*16
  CRI *(certificados de recebíveis
    imobiliários),* 150
  Decree-Law No. 911/69, 142
  exception to general trust regulation
    trend, xxiv
  Federal Constitution of Brazil, 145
  Federal Supreme Court (STF), 139*n*10
  FIDC, 150*n*49
  *fideicomisso,* 137, 148–49
  fiduciary agent, 152
  fiduciary substitution, 78, 137, 148–49
  foreign mutual funds, 146*n*35
  guarantee trusts, 138–46
    Aeronautic Code, 145–46
    creditors, transfer of rights in
      guarantee, 146
    realty trust transfer in guarantee, 143–45
    trust transfer in guaranty of
      personalty, 142–43
  inheritance trust, 148–49
  Law No. 4.728 of 1965, 139, 143
  Law No. 8.668 of 1993, 146–47
  Law No. 9.514 of 1997, 139,
    143–45, 149–52
  Law No. 10.031 of 2004, 143
  Law No. 10.931 of 2004, 139
  Law No. 11.101 of 2005, 141
  Law No. 11.481 of 2007, 143
  Law No. 7576 of 1986, 145
  mutual funds, 146–47
    use of trusts to create, 80
  National Monetary Council, 147
  Official Gazette of the Federation, 139*n*10
  overview, 137–38
  realty mutual funds, 146–47

Securities and Exchange Commission
    (CVM), 151*n*55
  Securities Commission, 146*n*35, 151
  securitization, 47*n*2, 48*n*4, 149–52
    CRI *(certificados de recebíveis
      imobiliários),* 149
    fiduciary agent, 152
    securitization trusts, 150–52
  securitization trusts, 150–52
  separate patrimony, creation of, 150*n*52
  Súmulas, 27*n*26, 139*n*10
  *Supremo Tribunal Federal,* 27*n*26
  trust substitution, 148–49
  usury, 140*n*11
Brazilian Civil Code
  fiduciary substitution, 78
  guarantee trusts, 138–40, 142
  new Code, 137
  trust transfer in guarantee of
    personalty, 142–43
Brazilian Code of 1916, 7*n*13
Brazilian Constitution, 139*n*10
Brazilian Criminal Code, 142
Breach of trust
  Belize, 124–25
Buenos Aires City
  gross revenue tax, 106
Business trusts, 72–73

C
Canada
  Civil Code of Quebec, 85
Capital Markets Act
  Brazil, 142
Case law
  Belize, 125–26
Cash flow
  and trusts, 53
Cedel, 104
Certificates
  Brazil, 149, 150
  Mexico, 261–64
  Panama, 286–87
Charitable foundations, 67–69
Charitable trusts, 72
  Belize, 115, 116
Chile, 153–65. *See also* Chilean Capital
  Market; Chilean Central Bank;
  Chilean Civil Code
  bankruptcy, 164
  beneficiary, 156–57
  civil trust property, 168
  commissions, 165
  Creation Act, 162

Decree-Law No. 3 of 1997, 159
Decree-Law No. 251 of 1931, 159
Decree-Law No. 3475 of 1980, 164
Decree-Law No. 3500 of 1980, 158, 159
fiduciary substitution, 78
fiscal and stamps duty, 164
full disclosure, 162–63
Insurance Act, 157
Internal Tax Service, 165
*inter vivos* trusts, 155
Investment Funds Act, 157
Law No. 18045, 86, 154, 157–59, 162, 164
Law No. 18046, 158, 160, 163–64
Law No. 18815, 158–60, 162
Law No. 19281, 158, 159
Law No. 19301, 157, 158
liquidation, 163–64
*mortis causa,* 155
Mutual Funds Act, 157, 158
no legal regulation of trust, xxiv
overview, 153–55
payment flows, 159
Pension Funds Act, 157
Public Registry of Mortgages of the Real
    Estate Conservator, 154
restitution, 154
Securities Market Act, 85–86, 157,
    158, 164–65
securitization, 154, 157–60
securitization companies, 160–64
    full disclosure, 162–63
    liquidation, 163–64
    separate patrimonies, 161
separate patrimony, 163–64
special-purpose patrimony, 161
stamp tax, 164
Stock Market Act, 154, 157
Superintendence of Banks and Financial
    Institutions, 162, 165
tax treatment, 164–65
trustee, 156
trust property, 154–55
Chilean Capital Market, 157
Chilean Central Bank, 162
Chilean Civil Code
    trustee, 156
    trust property, 153–55
Civil Code. *See specific country*
Civil-law traditions
    Anglo-Saxon and Latin American trusts
        compared, 23–24
Civil trust
    Ecuador, 194–95
Civil trust property

Chile, 168
Colombia, 168, 169
Ecuador, 168
Club administration trusts
    Venezuela, 367
CMOs. *See* Collateralized mortgage obligations
    (CMOs)
Collateralized mortgage obligations (CMOs), 49
Colombia, 167–80. *See also* Colombian
    Commercial Code; Colombian Constitutional
    Court
    agency, 64
    Banking Regulation, 170
    Banks Superintendence, 175*n*13, 177–78
    beneficiary, 176–77
    civil trust property, 168, 169
    Commerce Code, 85
    Commercial Registry, 172
    commercial trust, 168–73
        formalities, 172–73
        legal framework, 170
        prohibited stipulations of trust instruments,
            172–73
        real and personal relations created by
            trusts, 171–72
        special-purpose patrimony, 171
        termination of the trust, 173
    Decree-Law 410 of 1971, 170
    Decree-Law No. 663 of 1993, 168*n*2
    Decree No. 653 of 1993, 178, 179
    Decree No. 847 of 1993, 172
    duties of trustee, 174–75
    External Circular No. 6 of 1991,
        175*n*13, 177–78
    fiduciary mandate, 168
    fiduciary substitution, 78
    formalities of trust instruments, 172–73
    grantor, 176–77
    guarantee trusts, 73, 177–78
    investment trusts, 178–79
    Kemmerer mission, 170
    Law No. 35 of 1993, 179
    Law No. 45 of 1923, 170
    Law No. 45 of 1990, 170, 174*n*12
    Law No. 80 of 1993, 168, 170
    legal framework, commercial trust, 170
    mutual funds, 178–79
    Organic Regime of the Colombian Financial
        System, 168*n*2
    overview, 167–69
    personal relations created by trusts, 171–72
    prohibited stipulations of trust
        instruments, 172–73
    Public Contracting Law, 170

Colombia (*cont.*)
  public sector trust, 168
  real estate trusts, 177
  real relations created by trusts, 171–72
  resignation and removal of trustee, 175–76
  securitization, 47*n*2
  securitization trusts, 179
  special-purpose patrimony, 171
  tax treatment, 45, 179–80
  termination of the trust, 173
  trustee, 174–76
    described, 31
    duties of, 174–75
    resignation and removal of
      trustee, 175–76
    trustee executor, 168
Colombian Commercial Code
  commercial trusts, 170–72
  grantor and beneficiary, 176–77
  resignation and removal of trustee, 175–76
  trustee, 174
Colombian Constitutional Court, 171–72
Commercial trust
  Colombia, 168–73
    formalities, 172–73
    legal framework, 170
    prohibited stipulations of trust instruments,
      172–73
    real and personal relations created by
      trusts, 171–72
    special-purpose patrimony, 171
    termination of the trust, 173
  Ecuador, 195–99
    beneficiary, 203
    fiduciary transactions, 194–95
    instrument, 197–99
    rendering of accounts, 199
    special-purpose patrimony, definition as,
      196–97
    tax treatment, 204
    trustee, 200–201
Commissions
  Chile, 165
Common-law traditions
  Anglo-Saxon and Latin American trusts
    compared, 23–24
Competent courts
  Venezuela, 360–61
Confidentiality
  Honduras, 236
  Panama, 272–73
  Uruguay, 343
Consumers Protection Law No. 24.240, 24*n*19
Continental civil law, evolution of trust, 7–8

Convention on the Law Applicable to
  Agency, 64
Corporate Capital Trust Fund
  Argentina, 104
Corporation, 66–67
Costa Rica, 181–92
  appointment of trustee, 184
  beneficiary, 187
  "Cariblanco" project, 190
  Commerce Code, 73, 181–82
    powers and duties of trustee, 185
    trustee, 184
  Commercial Code
    guarantee trusts, 191
  Decree-Law No. 27127-MP-MIVAH, 188
  Direct Taxation Agency, 188
  Executive Decree
    No. 27127--MP-MIVAH, 51*n*7
  fiduciary substitution, 78
  Financial Administration of the Republic and
    Public budget, 192
  Garabit project, 190
  General Auditor of the Republic, 192
  General Control Agency, 191
  General Securities Superintendence, 189
  Government Corpus of Lawyers, 191
  guarantee trusts, 73, 191
  housing sector, 188
  ICE Act, 192
  invalid trusts, 183
  investments carried out by trustee, 186
  Law No. 1644, 183, 188
  Law No. 3284, 182
  Law No. 7732, 184*n*6
  Law No. 7983, 189
  Law No. 8131, 192
  Mandatory Complementary Pension
    Regime, 189
  merger of grantor and trustee, 185*n*7
  National Banking System's
    Organic Act, 182, 183
    Law No. 1644, 183, 188
  National Home Financing
    System (SFNV), 189
  overview, 181–82
  Pacific Port administration, 190
  *Peñas Blancas* Hydroelectric Project
    Securitization Trust, 189–90
  Pension Superintendence, 189
  powers and duties of trustee, 184–85
  public sector trusts, 75, 191–92
  real estate trusts, 191
  securitization, 51*n*7, 188–90
    "Cariblanco" project, 190

Garabit project, 190
Pacific Port administration, 190
*Peñas Blancas* Hydroelectric Project
    Securitization Trust, 189–90
tax treatment, 187–88
termination of the trust, 182–83
trustee, 183–86
    appointment, 184
    described, 31
    investments carried out by, 186
    powers and duties, 184–86
wildlife trusts, 191
"Cost contribution" real estate trusts
    Argentina, 105
Creation of trust
    Belize, 110
    Chile, 162
    Guatemala, 220–21
    Mexico, 244
    ways of, 34–35
Credit enhancement
    and securitization, 54–56
Credit institutions
    Mexico, 248–52
Credit-linked obligations, 47n2
Cree, Enrique C., 17
CRI *(certificados de recebíveis imobiliários),*
    149, 150
Criminal Code
    Argentina, 42n41, 94
    Brazil, 142
    Paraguay, 301
Criminal responsibility of trustee
    Argentina, 42, 94

D

Death of trustee
    termination of the trust, 38
Debt
    liability for trust debt, trustee's, 41–42
Department of Housing and Urban
    Development (HUD), 50
Department of Veterans Affairs (VA), 48, 50
Deposit
    irregular deposit, 62–63
    regular deposit, 62
    trust, differences, 62–63
Depository Trust Company (DTC), 56n16
Derivatives, 56
Direct investment funds
    and securitization, 53–54
Disclosure
    Chile, full disclosure, 162–63
    public offer of trust securities, 57

DTC. *See* Depository Trust Company (DTC)
Durán, Oyden, 279n18
Duration of a trust
    Peru, 314
Duties of trustee. *See specific country*
Dynastic trusts, 8n17
Dynasty use of trusts, 79

E

Ecuador, 193–209
    agency, 64
    Banks Superintendence, 207
    beneficiary, 203
    civil trust
        fiduciary transactions, 194–95
        property, 168
    commercial trust, 195–99
        beneficiary, 203
        fiduciary transactions, 194–95
        instrument, 197–99
        rendering of accounts, 199
        special-purpose patrimony, definition as,
            196–97
        tax treatment, 204
        trustee, 200–201
    Corporations Act, 202
    Corporations Superintendence, 199, 205
    Decree No. 390, 195
    fiduciary mandate, 194–95
    fiduciary transactions, 194–95
    grantor, 199–200
    Law No. 31, 195
    mixed securities, 206
    National Finance Corporation, 200
    National Securities Council (CNV), 198, 199,
        205, 206
    Official Record No. 87, 195
    Official Record No. 367, 195
    overview, 193–94
    Securities Market Act, 195, 204, 206–7, 291
    securitization, 204–8
        debt securities, 205–6
        investors, 205
        mixed securities, 206
        originator, 204
        participation securities, 206
        servicer, 205
        special-purpose patrimony, 205–6
        supervising committee, 205
        tax treatment, 207–8
    special-purpose patrimony, 205–6
        commercial trust defined as, 196–97
    stamp tax, 203, 207
    Supervision Committee, 207

Ecuador (*cont.*)
  Tax Code, 204
  tax treatment, 45, 203–4
    securitization, 207–8
  trustee, 200–202
    commercial trust, 200–201
    described, 31
    fund and trust management
      companies, 200
    resignation, 202
    substitution, 202
    trustee substitution, 202
Ecuadorian Stock Market Act, 134
El Salvador, 211–17
  Banks Act, 211
  beneficiary, 214
  Commerce Code, 211–12, 216
  Commerce Registry, 213
  Financial System Superintendence, 216
  grantor, 214
  *inter vivos* trusts, 212
  mixed trusts, 212
  *mortis causa,* 212
  overview, 211–13
  Real Estate Registry, 213
  rights and duties of trustee, 215–16
  Salvadorian Banks Act, 214
  Salvadorian Income Tax Act, 217
  Salvadorian National Constitution, 211–12
  Salvadorian Real Estate Transfer
    Tax Act, 217
  tax treatment, 217
  trustee, 214–17
    appointment, 215
    described, 31
    rights and duties, 215–16
    substitution, 216–17
    trustee substitution, 216–17
  VAT Act, 217
Emergency Home Finance Act (title III), 49n5
Enforceability of trust instruments
  Mexico, 244–45
England, trusts in, 8–11
  *feoffee* (trustee), 10
  *inter vivos* trusts, 9
  Judicatura Acts (1873-1875), 10n27
  *mortis causa,* 9
  mortmain acts, 9n24
  Norman Conquest, 9
  Statute of Mortmains, 9n24
  Statute of Uses, 9–11
Entities for the development of small- and
  micro-sized companies (EDPYMEs)
  Peru, 316

Estañol, Jorge Vera, 17
Euroclear, 56n16, 104

F
Failure of trust
  Belize, 115–17
Fannie Mae. *See* Federal National Mortgage
  Association (Fannie Mae)
Federal Home Loan Mortgage Corporation
  (Freddie Mac), 49n5, 50
Federal Housing Administration (FHA), 48, 50
Federal income tax. *See specific country*
Federal National Mortgage Association
  (Fannie Mae), 48–50
Fees
  trustee, 42–43
    Belize, 123–24
    Paraguay, 301
    Uruguay, 343
*Feoffee* (trustee), 10
FHA. *See* Federal Housing Administration
  (FHA)
*Fideicomisario*
  Argentina, 96–97
*Fideicomisso*
  Brazil, 137, 148–49
*Fideicomissum,* 4–5
  derivation of term, xxiv, 3
  development of, 8
  fiduciary substitution, 77, 79
*Fiducia,* xxiv, 5–6
  derivation of term, 3
  disuse, fall into, 6–7
  fiduciary substitution, 79
  use of term, 7n13
*Fiducia cum amico,* 6
*Fiducia cum creditore,* 6
Fiduciary agent
  Brazil, 152
Fiduciary duties. *See also Fiducia*
  concept of, 3n1
Fiduciary mandate, 64
  Colombia, 168
  Ecuador, 194–95
Fiduciary substitution, 79
  Bolivia, 78
  Brazil, 78, 137, 148–49
  Chile, 78
  Colombia, 78
  Costa Rica, 78
  and trust, distinction, 76–79
Fiduciary transactions
  Ecuador, 194–95
  Paraguay, 291

*FiduPerú*, 316
Financial factoring
  Mexico, 255*n*50
Financial trust
  Argentina, 99–101
  Uruguay, 349–52
    current situation, 350–51
    securitization before Trust Law, 349–50
    tax treatment, 353
    trust securities, 352
    trust securities holders' meeting, 351–52
Financial trustee
  Argentina, 95, 106
Firm commitment
  trustee as securities underwriter, 58
Firstborn child, replacement of beneficiary, 77–78
Firstborn son, continental civil law, 7
Fiscal and stamps duty
  Chile, 164
Fitch Ratings (2006)
  securitization, 47*n*2
Forced heirship, 76. *See also* Anti-forced heirships (AFH) legal regimes
  Argentina, 86–87
  Bahamas, 108*n*4
  Peru, 315
  Uruguay, 347–49
Foreign investors
  Mexico, 258–60
Foreign mutual funds
  Brazil, 146*n*35
Formalities of the trust instrument
  Colombia, 172–73
  Peru, 313
Foundations, 67–69
  private-interest foundations, 68–69
Foundations Acts, 67
France
  Law No. 2007-211, xxiv*n*4, 8
Fraud
  antifraud legal proceeding, 36–37
  Mexico, 244
  termination of the trust, 37
Freddie Mac. *See* Federal Home Loan Mortgage Corporation (Freddie Mac)
French law, ancient
  evolution of trust, 7
French Revolution, 8

G

General aspects of trusts. *See also* Antecedents; Latin America, trusts in (generally); Securitization

  trusts versus other types of contractual arrangements, 61–69
  types of trusts, 71–80
German law, ancient
  evolution of trust, 7
Germany
  no trust regulation, xxv*n*4
Ginnie Mae, 48, 50
Good businessperson, good paterfamilias, or diligent administrator
  trustee duties and responsibilities, 39–41, 90
Governmental trusts, 74–75
  Mexico, 260
Grantor
  Argentina, 88–89
  Bolivia, 131
  Colombia, 176–77
  described, 29–30
  Ecuador, 199–200
  El Salvador, 214
  Guatemala, 223
  Honduras, 233–34
  Mexico, 247–48
    technical committee, 247–48
  multiple grantors, 88
  Paraguay, 296–97
  Peru, 319–20
  termination of the trust
    agreement between beneficiary and, 35
    revocation by grantor, 36
  Uruguay, 340
  Venezuela, 366–67
Grantor-beneficiary
  described, 32–33
Grantor-trustee (declaration of trust)
  described, 33
Gratuitous transfers, law of, 25*n*21
Gross revenue tax
  Argentina, 106
  Buenos Aires City, 106
Guarantee deposits
  Paraguay, 289
Guarantee trusts, 64–65, 73–74
  Brazil, 138–46
    Aeronautic Code, 145–46
    creditors, transfer of rights in guarantee, 145
    realty trust transfer in guarantee, 143–45
    trust transfer in guaranty of personalty, 142–43
  Colombia, 73, 177–78
  Costa Rica, 73, 75, 191
  Guatemala, 228
  Mexico, 73, 254–57

Guarantee trusts (*cont.*)
  Panama, 278
  Paraguay, 308
  Peru, 316
  Uruguay, 316, 346–47
    Montevideo (Carrasco Airport) guarantee
      trust, 333, 347, 354
    tax treatment, 353
  Venezuela, 368
Guatemala, 219–29
  Accounting Integrated System
    (SICOIN), 226
  Agriculture and Nutrition
    Ministry (MAGA), 227
  agriculture promotion trusts, 227–28
  Bank Superintendence, 227
  beneficiary
    residual beneficiary, 225–26
    rights of, 225–26
  Budget Organic Act, 226
  Central American Bank of Economic
    Integration, 227
  Civil Code, 220
  Civil Court Judges of the
    First Instance, 221
  Commerce Code, 223, 226
  Commercial Code, 223, 225, 228
  Decree-Law No. 106, 220
  Decree-Law No. 208, 223n3
  Decree No. 12-2002, 227
  Decree No. 34-96, 220–22, 228
  Decree No. 101-97, 226
  Decree No. 134-1996, 227
  definition of trust, 220
  General Accounting Auditor, 227
  General Budget of Returns and Expenses
    for Fiscal Year 2006 Act, 226
  Government of the Republic--Ordinary
    Funds, 227
  grantor, 223
  guarantee trusts, 228
  housing promotion trusts, 227
  investment trust agreement, 228–29
  Land Fund, Peace Agreement, 228
  maximum period of trusts, 222
  Ministry of Public Finances, 226, 227
  Monetary Committee,
    Resolution No. 7556, 223n3
  Municipal Code, 227
  National Congress, 221, 227
  overview, 220
  prohibited trusts, 223
  Public Credit Committee of the Ministry of
    Public Finances, 226
  public sector trusts, 226–27

  Reactivation and Modernization
    Agricultural Activity National
    Fund, 227
  removal of trustee, 225
  Securities and Goods Market Act, 228
  securitization, 228–29
  separate patrimony, 221–22
  Sierra of the Cuchumatanes Rural
    Development Project, 227
  Social Funds, 226
  Sustainable Rural Development Project in
    Ecologically Endangered Areas in the
    Trinity Region in the Area of
    Guatemala, 228
  tax treatment, 45, 226
  termination of the trust, 222
  trust creation formalities, 220–21
  trustee, 223–25
    described, 31
    removal, causes of, 225
    rights and duties, 224–25

H
Hague Conference on Private International
  Law, 27–28
Hague Convention on the Law Applicable
  to Trusts and on their Recognitions, 27–29,
  69, 76
Henry VIII (king of England), 10
Honduras, 231–39
  Banks and Insurance National Committee,
    232, 237–38
  Banks and Insurance National Committee
    Act, 231
  beneficiary, 233–34
  Circular D-41199, 237
  Commerce Code, 232
  Commercial Code, 235
  confidentiality, 236
  Constitution, 239
  Decree-Law No. 25, 239
  Decree No. 170/95, 231
  Financial System Institutions Act, 231–32,
    236, 238
  grantor, 233–34
  Honduran Central Bank, 231–32, 237
  liquidation, 236
  overview, 232–33
  Regulation 419-I2/99, 237
  secret trusts, 233
  Securities Market Act, 237
  securitization, 237–38
  tax treatment, 45, 239
  trustee, 234–36
    described, 31

Housing and Urban Securitization
Act, 48
Housing plan trusts
Venezuela, 369
Housing promotion trusts
Guatemala, 227
Housing sector
Costa Rica, 188
Mexico, 261*n*64
HUD. *See* Department of Housing and Urban
Development (HUD)
Hybrid securities
Argentina, 103
*Hyphoteca* (mortgage), 6, 7*n*12

I

Illegal trusts
Paraguay, 293
Immovable assets, tax on sale or transfer of
Panama, 278
Uruguay, 352
Incapacity of trustee
termination of the trust, 38
Income tax. *See specific country*
Individualization of trust assets
Uruguay, 336
Inheritance trust
Brazil, 148–49
Insolvency
termination of the trust, 37
Insufficiency of trust assets
Uruguay, 339–40
*Inter vivos* acts
Argentina, 96
*Inter vivos* trusts, 9, 64
Chile, 155
El Salvador, 212
Peru, 315
Uruguay, 334, 345
Venezuela, 359, 361
Invalid trusts
Belize, 110–11
Costa Rica, 183
Peru, 314
Investments carried out by trustee
Costa Rica, 186
Investment trust agreement
Guatemala, 228–29
Investment trusts
Colombia, 178–79
Paraguay, 306–7
collective investment trusts, 307
single investment trusts, 306–7
Venezuela, 368
Irrevocable agency instruction, theory of, 20

Italy
no trust regulation, xxv*n*4

J

Judicatura Acts (1873-1875), 10*n*27
Jurisdiction of the trust, change of
Panama, 273
*Jus in rem,* 65

K

Kemmerer mission, 170, 268
"Know your client rules"
Panama, 272–73

L

Latin American Congress on Trusts, 182
Latin America, trusts in (generally). *See also
specific topics*
adoption of trust statutes in Latin American
countries, 16–19
Anglo-Saxon and Latin American trusts
compared, 23–27
creation of trust, 34–35
Hague Conference on Private International
Law, 27–28
Hague Convention on the Law Applicable
to Trusts and on their Recognitions,
27–29
nature of trust, 19–23
parties to trust agreement, 29–34
tax treatment, compared, 43–46
termination of the trust, 35–38
trustee, responsibilities, rights, and duties of,
39–43, 90–92
Law No. 24441 (Argentina). *See* Argentina
Law No. 24441 (Construction
Financing Act)
Leasing
Mexico, 255*n*50
Legislative Assembly, 77
Lepaulle, Pierre, 17, 18, 21, 242
Letter of wishes
Belize, 114–15
LGTOC. *See* Securities and Credit Transactions
General Act (LGTOC)
Life insurance trusts
Venezuela, 369
Liquidation
Argentina, 101
Chile, 163–64
Honduras, 236
Panama, 273
Paraguay, 294–95
Luxembourg Law, 279*n*18

M

Macedo, Pablo, 17–19
Maximum period of trusts
    Guatemala, 222
MBS program. *See* Mortgage-backed security
    (MBS) program
Mexican jurists, adaptation of U.S. trust to
    Latin American civil law, 16–19
Mexico, 241–66
    adoption of trust, xxiii
    amortizables, 262
    asset transfers, 243
    autonomy of patrimony, 254
    *Banco Nacional Hipotecario Urbano y de
        Obras Públicas,* 262
    Bank of Mexico, 260
    beneficiary, 248–49
    Border Industrialization Plan, 258n61
    case law, 243
    certificates, 261–64
    Commercial Code, 246
    creation of trust, 244
    Credit and Banking Establishments General
        Law, 17–18
    credit institutions, 248–52
    Credit Institutions Act, 246, 247, 249–53, 260
    Credit Institutions and Auxiliary
        Organizations General Act of May 31,
        1941, 247
    Credit Securities and Transactions General
        Act of the United States of Mexico, 85, 235
    Deposit of Values, 56n16
    enforceability of trust instruments, 244–45
    experience, 258–60
    fiduciary delegate, defined, 250n34
    financial entities under restructuring,
        shares of, 260
    financial factoring, 255n50
    Fiscal Code of the Federation, 266
    Foreign Affairs Office, 259–60
    Foreign Investment Act, 259
    Foreign Investment and Foreign Investment
        National Registry Act, 259
    foreign investors, 258–60
    formalities, 244–45
    fraud, 244
    General Organizations and Auxiliary
        Activities of Credit Act, 255
    governmental trusts, 260
    grantor, 247–48
        technical committee, 247–48
    guarantee trusts, 73, 254–57
    Health and Assistance Office, 265
    housing sector, securitization, 261n64

    income tax, 265–66
    Institutions of Credit Act, 255
    Insurance Institutions and Mutual Society
        General Act, 249n32
    Investment Companies Act, 251n40
    leasing, 255n50
    Mexican Banking System, 260
    mortgage securitization, 261
    *Nacional Financiera S.A.,* 262
    National Banking and Securities
        Commission, 260
    National Banking Commission, 263
    National Commission of Banking and
        Securities, 255n50
    net operating loss (NOL), 265–66
    Official Gazette of the Federation,
        263, 265
    overview, 242–47
    Political Constitution of the United States of
        Mexico, 258
    protector, described, 32
    public sector trusts, 75, 260
    railways, 242n6
    real estate certificates, 262
    Real Estate Public Registry, 245, 246
    registration of trust instruments, 244–45
    restricted zones, 258–60
    restructuring, shares of financial entities
        under, 260
    secret trusts, 244
    Securities and Credit Transactions General
        Act (LGTOC), 242–43
    Securities and Credit Transactions General
        Law, 17
    Securities Market Act, 249n33
    securitization, 47n2, 48n3, 261–65
        housing certificates, 261
        housing sector, 261n64
        mortgage securitization, 261
    technical committee, 247–48
    termination of the trust, 245–47
    Treasury and Public Credit Secretary, 260
    trust assets, 256–57
    Trust Banks Act of June 30, 1926, 242
    Trust Banks Law, 18
    trust certificates, 261–64
    trustee, 248–54
        autonomy of patrimony, 254
        case law, 253–54
        credit institutions, 248–52
        described, 31
        general rules, 252–53
Minimum presumed income tax
    Argentina, 106

Mixed securities
    Ecuador, 206
Mixed trusts
    El Salvador, 212
Mortgage-backed security (MBS)
    program, 50
Mortgages, 64–65
Mortgage securitization, 48–50
    adjustable rate mortgages (ARMs), 49
    collateralized mortgage
        obligations (CMOs), 49
    Department of Housing and Urban
        Development (HUD), 50
    Department of Veterans
        Affairs (VA), 48, 50
    Emergency Home Finance Act
        (title III), 49n5
    Federal Home Loan Mortgage Corporation
        (Freddie Mac), 49n5, 50
    Federal Housing Administration
        (FHA), 48, 50
    Federal National Mortgage Association
        (Fannie Mae), 48–50
    Ginnie Mae, 48, 50
    Housing and Urban Securitization Act, 48
    Mexico, 261
    mortgage-backed security (MBS)
        program, 50
    National Housing Act (1934), 48
    real estate mortgage investment conduits
        (REMICs), 49
    Rural Housing Service (RHS), 50
    Serviceman's Readjustment Act (1944), 48
*Mortis causa,* 4, 9
    Argentina, 96
    Chile, 155
    El Salvador, 212
    Peru, 315
Mortmain acts, 9n24
Municipal taxes
    Peru, 330
Mutual funds
    Brazil, 146–47
    Colombia, 178–79
    trusts used to create, 80

N

Napoleonic Code, 7–8, 77
*National Conference of Commissioners on
    Uniform State Laws,* 12n36, 13
National Housing Act (1934), 48
Nature of Latin American trust, 19–23
    irrevocable agency instruction,
        theory of, 20

trust agreement, 22–23
trustee's special-purpose patrimony,
    theory of, 21–23
trust property, 22–23
unfolded property, theory of, 20
unholder special-purpose patrimony,
    theory of, 20–21
Net operating loss (NOL)
    Mexico, 265–66
New York Stock Exchange, 49
Nixon, Richard M., 49
NOL. *See* Net operating loss (NOL)
Noncharitable trusts
    Belize, 115
Nonfinancial trusts
    Uruguay, 353
Norman Conquest, 9
Notary rights
    Paraguay, 306

O

Obregón, Toribio Esquivel, 17
Official Gazette of the Federation
    Brazil, 139n10
    Mexico, 263, 265
    Peru, 313
    Uruguay, 332
Offshore trusts
    Uruguay, 354
OPIC, 55n14
Ordinary trusts
    Argentina, 105–6
    Peru, 329

P

Pacific Stock Exchange, 49
*Pactum commissorium*
    Uruguay, 346
*Pactum fiduciae,* 5–6
Panama, 267–87
    assets outside of Panama,
        trusts with, 277
    Banks' Agreement No. 12-2005, 273
    beneficiaries, 271
    confidentiality, 272–73
    Decree No. 16, 269, 272–74
    Decree No. 60 of 1965, 278
    Decree No. 170 of 1993, 278
    Decree No. 212 of 2000, 273
    Decree No. 468 of 1994, 280
    Financial Intelligence Unit (FIU), 273
    First Superior Tribunal of the First Judicial
        Circuit, 270–71
    Foundational Act, 281–83

Panama (*cont.*)
  foundation council and controlling
    bodies, 283–86
  Foundations Acts, 279–81, 287
  Foundations Law, 284
  guarantee trusts, tax treatment, 278
  immovable assets, tax on sale or
    transfer of, 278
  jurisdiction of the trust, change of, 273
  Kemmerer mission, 268
  "know your client rules," 272–73
  Law No. 1 of 1941, 268
  Law No. 1 of 1984 ("Trust Law"), 268–69,
    272, 275, 277–78, 287
  Law No. 9 of 1925, 268
  Law No. 17 of 1941, 85, 268, 273
  Law No. 32 of 2006, 282
  Law No. 42 of 2000, 273
  Law No. 75 of 1976, 278
  Law No. 106 of 1974, 278
  legislation, applicable, 273
  liquidation of corporations, trust for, 273
  Luxembourg Law, 279n18
  National Assembly, 279n18
  overview, 269–73
  pension funds, tax treatment, 278
  private-interest foundations, 279–87
    certificate of continuation, 286–87
    change of domicile of the foundation,
      286–87
    Foundational Act, 281–83
    foundation council and controlling bodies,
      283–86
    Foundations Acts, 279–81, 287
    Foundations Law, 284
    Panamanian Foundations Act, 287
    taxation, 287
    termination of the foundation, 286
  Registry of Property of Vehicles, 271
  separation of trust patrimony, 271
  source income, 276–78
    trusts with, 277–78
  Specialized Fiduciary Unit (SFU), 273
  Supreme Court, 269n10, 274n17
  Tax Authorities, 278
  Tax on the Transfer of Immovable
    Assets, 278
  Tax on the Transfer of Movable
    Assets, 278
  tax treatment, 276–78
    assets outside of Panama, trusts with, 277
    guarantee trusts, 278
    pension funds, 278
    private-interest foundations, 287

  source income, 276–78
    tax rates, 277
  termination of the trust, 272
  testamentary trusts, 76
  trustee, 273–76
    described, 31
  trust instrument, 270–71
Panamanian Private Foundation, 108
Panamanian trust, 108
*Pandectistas,* 8
Paraguay, 289–309
  Acts and Documents Tax, 306
  agency, 64
  Banks Superintendence, 291–92, 299,
    301, 303
  beneficiary, 302–3
  capital, determination of, 307n8
  Central Bank of Paraguay, 291–92, 297, 300,
    305, 307, 309
  Civil Code, 291
  Commercial Trust, 291
  Criminal Code of Paraguay, 301
  experience, 306–9
  fiduciary transactions, 291
  General Law of Banks, 307
  grantor, 296–97
  guarantee deposits, 289
  Guarantee Regime of Deposits, 291
  guarantee trusts, 308
  illegal trusts, 293
  investment trusts, 306–7
    collective investment trusts, 307
    single investment trusts, 306–7
  Law No. 861 of 1996, 297n6, 307
  Law No. 921 of 1996, 290–93, 298, 305, 307
  Law No. 1036, 303
  Law No. 1056 of 1997, 309
  Law No. 1284, 308
  Law No. 2334 of 2003, 291
  legal framework, 290–91
  liquidation of trusts, 294–95
  National Securities commission, 303
  notary rights, 306
  Paraguayan Central Bank, 297, 303, 307
  Rating Agencies Act, 309
  real estate trusts, 308
  residual beneficiary, 302–3
  Resolution No. 6, 291, 306, 308–9
  Securities Market, 308
  securitization companies, 303–4
  securitization trusts, 308–9
  separation of the trust patrimony, 293–94
  stamp duty, 306
  tax treatment, 305–6

Acts and Documents Tax, 306
  notary rights, 306
  stamp duty, 306
  value-added tax, 305
termination of the trust, 294–95
transference of assets to a trust, 292–93
trustee, 297–302
  described, 31
  duties of the trustee, 298–301
  fees, 301
  resignation, 301–2
  rights and powers of the trustee, 298
trustee substitution, 297–98
trust for the mobilization of assets, 308–9
value-added tax, 305
warrants, 289
Parties to trust agreement, 29–34
  beneficiary, 32
  coexistence of various roles in same person,
    32–34
  grantor, 29–30
  grantor-beneficiary, 32–33
  grantor-trustee (declaration of trust), 33
  protector, 32
  trustee, 30–32
  trustee-beneficiary, 34
Pasquel, Roberto Molina, 18
Penalties
  Uruguay, 341–42
  Venezuela, 360–61
*Peñas Blancas* Hydroelectric Project
  Securitization Trust, 189–90
Pension funds
  Panama, 278
  Uruguay, 352
Performance risk, 53
Personal relations created by trusts
  Colombia, 171–72
Personal wealth tax
  Argentina, 106
Peru, 311–30
  Act No. 26702, 312
  beneficiary, 319–20
  CAVALI ILCV S.A., 56*n*16
  Civil Code of Peru (1852), 312
  Decree Law 770, 312
  duration of a trust, 314
  entities for the development of small- and
    micro-sized companies
    (EDPYMEs), 316
  Financial Development Corporation Inc.
    (COFIDE), 316
  forced heirship, 315
  formalities of the trust instrument, 313

General Corporations Act, 330
grantor, 319–20
guarantee trusts, 316
income tax, 329–30
*inter vivos* trusts, 315
invalid trusts, 314
Law No. 27008 (1998), 312
Law No. 27102 (1999), 312
Legislative Decree No. 861, 320
*mortis causa,* 315
municipal taxes, 330
Napoleonic Civil Code, 312
National Corporations and Securities
  Supervisory (CONASEV), 321–27
Official Gazette of the Federation, 313
ordinary trusts, 329
Peruvian Public Registry, 312*n*2
real estate tax, 330
Resolution of the National Superintendence
  of National Registries No. 316-2008, 312
rights and duties of trustee, 317–19
Risk Head Office of the
  Superintendence, 313
risk-rating, 328
sales tax, 330
Securities Market Act, 312, 320–21, 328
securitization, 320–23
  formalities of the securitization trusts
    instrument, 322–23
  special Rules Pertaining to Securitization
    Processes, 320–21
securitization companies, 323–28
  risk-rating, 328
  securities offering, 328
  securitization trusts assets, securities
    backed with, 325–26
  separate patrimony, 325
  special-purpose companies, 327
  termination of the trust, 326–27
securitization trusts, 322, 329
  assets, securities backed with, 325–26
separate patrimony, 313, 325
special-purpose companies, 327
stamp tax, 330
tax treatment, 45, 328–30
  income tax, 329–30
  municipal taxes, 330
  real estate tax, 330
  sales tax, 330
  stamp tax, 330
  vehicle tax, 330
termination of the trust, 315, 326–27
testamentary trusts, 315–16
Trust Act, 312–28

Peru (*cont.*)
trustee, 316–19
described, 31
rights and duties of, 317–19
"trust factor," 317
trustee-beneficiary trust, 319
Trust Law, 319
trust taxes, responsibility of trustee for, 46
vehicle tax, 330
*Pignus* (pledge), 6, 7*n*12
Pledges, 64–65
Portugal
Law No. 9514, 51*n*7
securitization, 51*n*7
securitization trusts, 150
Powers of trustee
Belize, 118–119
Costa Rica, 184–85
Paraguay, 298
Private-interest foundations, 68–69
Panama, 279–87
certificate of continuation, 286–87
change of domicile of the foundation,
286–87
Foundational Act, 281–83
foundation council and controlling bodies,
283–86
Foundations Acts, 279–81, 287
Foundations Law, 284
Panamanian Foundations Act, 287
taxation, 287
termination of the foundation, 286
Prohibited stipulations of trust instruments
Colombia, 172–73
Prohibited trusts
Guatemala, 223
Project finance vehicle, 79–80
Projects, trusts for carrying out
Venezuela, 368
Protection of trust assets
Uruguay, 343
Protector
Belize, 117–26
described, 32
*Prudent Investor Rule,* 12–13
Public offer of trust securities, 56–59
full disclosure, 57
previous authorization, 57–58
trustee as securities underwriter, 58–59
Public sector trusts, 74–75
Argentina, 75, 104
Colombia, 168
Costa Rica, 191–92
Guatemala, 226–27

Mexico, 75, 260
*sui generis* legal procedures, 104

R
Railways
Mexico, 242*n*6
Real estate certificates
Mexico, 262
Real estate mortgage investment conduits
(REMICs), 49
Real estate projects
and securitization, 53–54
Real estate tax
Peru, 330
Real estate trusts
Colombia, 177
Costa Rica, 191
Paraguay, 308
Real relations created by trusts
Colombia, 171–72
Realty mutual funds
Brazil, 146–47
Realty trusts
Venezuela, 367
Registration of the trust instrument
Mexico, 244–45
Uruguay, 336–37
Reimbursement of expenses
Belize, 123–24
trustees, 42–43
Remainder property, 65
REMICs. *See* Real estate mortgage investment
conduits (REMICs)
Removal of trustee. *See specific country*
Rendering of accounts, 41
Ecuador, 199
Uruguay, 342–43
Republic of Panama. *See* Panama
Residual beneficiary
Argentina, 96–97
Guatemala, 225–26
Paraguay, 302–3
Resignation and removal of trustee. *See specific
country*
Responsibilities of trustee. *See specific
country*
*Restatement of the Law Second, Trusts,* 12,
25*n*21, 27
*Restatement of the Law Third, Trusts,* 12, 26
*Restatement of the Law, Trusts,* 12
Restitution
Chile, 154
Restricted zones
Mexico, 258–60

Restructuring, shares of financial entities under
  Mexico, 260
Retirement plan trusts
  Venezuela, 369
Revocation of trust
  Belize, 115–17
RHS. *See* Rural Housing Service (RHS)
Rights and duties of trustee. *See specific*
  *country*
Risk-rating
  Peru, 328
Risks
  and securitization, 52–54
Roman law, xxiv, 3–7. *See also Fideicomissum;*
  *Fiducia; Pactum fiduciae*
  *actio fiduciae contraria,* 6
  *fiducia cum amico,* 6
  *fiducia cum creditore,* 6
  *hyphoteca* (mortgage), 6, 7n12
  *pignus* (pledge), 6, 7n12
Rule against perpetuities
  defined, 110n7
Rural Housing Service (RHS), 50

S

Sales tax
  Peru, 330
*Salman,* 8
Sanctions. *See* Penalties
Sarsfield, Damalcio Vélez, 84n1
Savings bank trusts
  Venezuela, 367–68
Savings fund trusts
  Venezuela, 367
SEC. *See* Securities and Exchange Commission
  (SEC)
Secret trusts
  Honduras, 233
  Mexico, 244
Securities and Credit Transactions General Act
  (LGTOC)
  asset transfers, 243
  beneficiary, 248
  creation of trust, 244–45
  forbidden trusts, 244
  fraud, 244
  generally, 17, 235
  grantor, 247
  guarantee trusts, 254–55
  modification, 85–86
  securitization, 261–65
  termination of the trust, 245–46
  trust, defined, 242
  trustee, 249, 251–52

Securities and Exchange
  Commission (SEC), 158
Securities Market Act
  Chile, 85–86, 157, 158, 164–65
  Ecuador, 195, 204, 206–7, 291
  Honduras, 237
  Mexico, 249n33
  Peru, 312, 320–21, 328
Securitization, 47–59
  advantages, 51–52
  Argentina, 47n2, 97–99
  Bolivia, 133–36
    legal framework, 133–34
    Stock Market Act, 134–36
    tax treatment, 136
  Brazil, 47n2, 48n4, 149–52
    CRI *(certificados de recebíveis*
     *imobiliários),* 149
    fiduciary agent, 152
    securitization trusts, 150–52
  cash flow, trusts and, 53
  Chile, 154, 157–60
  Colombia, 47n2
  Costa Rica, 51n7, 188–90
    "Cariblanco" project, 190
    Garabit project, 190
    Pacific Port administration, 190
    *Peñas Blancas* Hydroelectric Project
     Securitization Trust, 189–90
  credit enhancement, 54–56
  credit-linked obligations, 47n2
  definition, 51–52
  direct investment funds, 53–54
  domestic securitization,
    development of, 47n2
  Ecuador, 204–8
    debt securities, 205–6
    investors, 205
    mixed securities, 206
    originator, 204
    participation securities, 206
    servicer, 205
    special-purpose
     patrimony, 205–6
    supervising committee, 205
    tax treatment, 207–8
  Guatemala, 228–29
  Honduras, 237–38
  Mexico, 47n2, 48n3, 261–65
    housing certificates, 261
    housing sector, 261n64
    mortgage securitization, 261
  mortgage securitization. *See* Mortgage
    securitization

Securitization (*cont.*)
    Peru, 320–23
        formalities of the securitization trusts
            instrument, 322–23
        securitization trusts, 322
        special Rules Pertaining to Securitization
            Processes, 320–21
    Portugal, 51*n*7
    public offer of trust securities, 56–59
    real estate projects, 53–54
    risks, 52–54
    Uruguay, 51
        before Trust Law, 349–50
Securitization companies
    Chile, 160–64
        full disclosure, 162–63
        liquidation, 163–64
        separate patrimonies, 161
    Paraguay, 303–4
    Peru, 323–28
        risk-rating, 328
        securities offering, 328
        securitization companies, 326–27
        securitization trusts assets, securities
            backed with, 325–26
        separate patrimony, 325
        special-purpose companies, 327
Securitization trusts
    Brazil, 150–52
    Colombia, 179
    Paraguay, 308–9
    Peru, 329
    Portugal, 150
Senatus Consultum, 5*n*5
Separate accounting
    Uruguay, 343
Separate patrimony
    Argentina, 92–93
    Brazil, 150*n*52
    Chile, 161, 163–64
    Guatemala, 221–22
    Peru, 325
    Uruguay, 335–36
Separate special-purpose patrimony
    Uruguay, 334
Separation of the trust patrimony
    Panama, 271
    Paraguay, 293–94
Serviceman's Readjustment Act (1944), 48
Settlor
    Belize, 117
    legal actions by creditor, termination of the
        trust, 36–37
Simulated agreements, 61–62

Social benefits trusts
    Venezuela, 368
*Sociedad Hipoteca Federal*
    (Mexico), 48*n*3
Sole trustee as sole beneficiary
    termination of the trust, 38
Source income
    Panama, 276–78
        trusts with source income, 277–78
Sources of trust law in Latin America, 26–27
Spain
    no trust regulation, xxv*n*4
Special-purpose companies
    Peru, 327
Special-purpose patrimony
    Chile, 161
    Colombia, 171
    Ecuador, 205–6
        commercial trust defined as, 196–97
    theory of, 21–23
    Uruguay, 350
Stamp tax
    Argentina, 106
    Chile, 164
    Ecuador, 203, 207
    Paraguay, 306
    Peru, 330
Statute of Mortmains, 9*n*24
Statute of Uses (England), 9–11
Stock Market Act
    Bolivia, 134–36
    Chile, 154, 157
    Ecuador, 134
*Substituiçao fideicomissária. See* Fiduciary
    substitution
*Sui generis* legal procedures, 104
Súmulas, Brazil, 27*n*26, 139*n*10
*Supremo Tribunal Federal,* 27*n*26
Switzerland
    no trust regulation, xxv*n*4
    taxation of trusts and trustees, xxv*n*4

T
"Tailor made" trust securities
    Argentina, 103
Tax secret
    Uruguay, 355
Tax treatment, 43–46. *See also specific types
    of tax*
    Argentina, 45, 105–6
        federal income tax, 105–6
        gross revenue tax, 106
        minimum presumed income tax, 106
        personal wealth tax, 106

stamp tax, 106
value-added tax, 106
Bolivia, 136
Chile, 164–65
Colombia, 45, 179–80
Costa Rica, 187–88
Ecuador, 45, 203–4
  securitization, 207–8
El Salvador, 217
Guatemala, 45, 226
Honduras, 45, 239
Panama, 276–78
  assets outside of Panama, trusts with, 277
  guarantee trusts, 278
  pension funds, 278
  private-interest foundations, 287
  source income, 276–78
  tax rates, 277
Paraguay, 305–6
  Acts and Documents Tax, 306
  notary rights, 306
  stamp duty, 306
  value-added tax, 305
Peru, 45, 328–30
  income tax, 329–30
  municipal taxes, 330
  real estate tax, 330
  sales tax, 330
  stamp tax, 330
  vehicle tax, 330
trustee, responsibility for trust taxes, 46
Uruguay, 45, 352–55
  financial trusts, 353
  foreign beneficiaries, 354–55
  free zones, 354
  guarantee trusts, 353
  Income Tax on Economic Activities
    (IRAE), 352, 353
  Individual Income Tax (IRPF), 352, 353
  nonfinancial trusts, 353
  Nonresidents Income
    Tax (IRNR), 352–55
  offshore trusts, 354
  special beneficiaries, 354
  Tax Authority Office, 355
  tax benefits, 354
  Tax Code, 355
  Tax on Patrimonial Transfers (ITP), 352,
    353
  Tax on Personal Assets (IP), 352–53
  tax secret, 355
  trustee, responsibility of, 354
  value-added tax, 353
value-added tax, 45

Termination of Office of the Trustee, 43
  Argentina, 94–95
  Uruguay, 43, 344
Termination of the trust, 35–38
  accomplishment of, 35
  antifraud legal proceeding, 36–37
  Belize, 115–17
  Colombia, 173
  Costa Rica, 182–83
  death of trustee, 38
  effects of, 38
  expiration of period, 35
  fraudulent acts, 37
  fulfillment of condition, 35
  grantor and beneficiary, agreement
    between, 35
  Guatemala, 222
  impossibility, 35
  incapacity of trustee, 38
  insolvency, 37
  legal actions by creditors of
    settlor, 36–37
  Mexico, 245–47
  Panama, 272
  Paraguay, 294–95
  Peru, 315, 326–27
  revocation by grantor, 36
  sole trustee as sole beneficiary, 38
  trust assets, insufficiency, 36
  Uruguay, 337–39
    separation of trust assets, 343
  Venezuela, 360
  ways of, 35–38
Testamentary trust, 75–79. *See also* Forced
  heirship
  fiduciary substitution and trust,
    distinction, 76–79
  Panama, 76
  Peru, 315–16
  Uruguay, 76, 347–49
Transference of credits to the trust
  Argentina, 99–100
*Treuhand,* 8
Troubled financial entities, trusts used to
  rebuild, 80
Trust Act
  Peru, 312–28
  Venezuela, 358, 360–64, 366
Trust agent
  Belize, 127
Trust agreement, 22–23. *See also* Parties to
  trust agreement
  Argentina, 87–88
  Uruguay, 335–36

Trust assets
  adequate identification of by trustee, 41
  Argentina, insufficiency, 100–101
  Belize, transfers in trust, 113
  foreclosure extrajudicially, 65
  insufficiency
    Argentina, 100–101
    termination of the trust, 36
  Mexico, 256–57
  Uruguay, 335
Trust certificates
  Mexico, 261–64
Trustee. *See also specific topic*
  Argentina, 89–95
    criminal responsibility of trustee, 94
    financial trustee, 95
    rights and duties of, 90–92
    separate patrimony, trust as, 92–93
    termination of Office of the Trustee, 94–95
  Belize, 117–26
    appointment, 118–19
    breach of trust, 124
    duties of, 120–22
    fees, 123–24
    powers of, 119–20
    reimbursement of expenses, 123–24
    removal of, 118–19
    resignation of, 118–19
  Bolivia, 131–32
  Chile, 156
  Colombia, 174–76
    duties of trustee, 174–75
    resignation and removal of trustee, 175–76
  Costa Rica, 183–86
    appointment, 184
    investments carried out by trustee, 186
    powers and duties, 184–86
  criminal responsibility, 42, 94
  death of, termination of the trust, 38
  described, 30–32
  Ecuador, 200–202
    commercial trust, 200–201
    fund and trust management
      companies, 200
    resignation, 202
    substitution, 202
  El Salvador, 214–17
    appointment, 215
    rights and duties, 215–16
    substitution, 216–17
  fees, 42–43
  good businessperson, good paterfamilias, or
    diligent administrator, 39–41, 90
  Guatemala, 223–25

  removal, causes of, 225
  rights and duties, 224–25
  Honduras, 234–36
  incapacity of, termination of the trust, 38
  liability for trust debt, 41–42
  Mexico, 248–54
    autonomy of patrimony, 254
    case law, 253–54
    credit institutions, 248–52
    general rules, 252–53
  Panama, 273–76
  Paraguay, 297–302
    duties of the trustee, 298–301
    fees, 301
    resignation, 301–2
    trustee rights and powers of the trustee, 298
    trustee substitution, 297–98
  Peru, 316–19
    rights and duties of, 317–19
    "trust factor," 317
  reimbursement of expenses, 42–43
  rendering of accounts, 41
  responsibilities, rights, and duties of, 39–43,
    46, 90–92
  as securities underwriter, 58–59
  sole trustee as sole beneficiary, termination of
    the trust, 38
  termination of Office of the Trustee,
    43, 94–95
  trust assets, adequate identification of, 41
  trust secret, 42
  trust taxes, responsibility for, 46
  Uruguay, 89, 340–43
    confidentiality, 343
    death of trustee, 338
    duties of the trustee, 342–43
    fees, 343
    multiple trustees, 342
    penalties, 341–42
    prohibitions affecting, 343
    protection of trust assets, 343
    registry of professional trustees, 341
    rendering of accounts, 342–43
    separate accounting, 343
    separation of trust assets at moment of
      termination of the trust, 343
    standard of trust services, 342
    tax treatment, 354
    termination of Office of the Trustee,
      43, 344
    termination of the trust, 343
    trustee substitution, 342
  Venezuela, 361–66
    acceptance, 364

duties of the trustee, 362–64
　removal, 364
　resignation, 364
Trustee-beneficiary
　described, 34
　Peru, 319
Trustee executor
　Colombia, 168
Trustee substitution
　Ecuador, 202
　El Salvador, 216–17
　Paraguay, 297–98
　Uruguay, 342
Trust for the mobilization of assets
　Paraguay, 308–9
Trust instrument
　Panama, 270–71
Trust Law
　Panama, 268–69, 272, 275, 277–78, 287
　Peru, 319
　Uruguay, 332–39, 341–46, 348–54
　Venezuela, 358
Trust property, 22–23
　Chile, 154–55
　Uruguay, 336
Trust secret, 42
Trust securities. *See also* Public offer of trust
　securities
　Argentina, 101–4
　how issued, 104
　Uruguay, 352
Trust securities holders' meeting
　Uruguay, 351–52
Types of trusts, 71–80

U

Underwriter
　trustee as securities underwriter, 58–59
Unfolded property, theory of, 20
Unholder special-purpose patrimony, theory of,
　20–21
*Uniform and Principal Act,* 13
*Uniform Commercial Code,* 13
*Uniform fiduciaries Act,* 13
*Uniform Probate Guide,* 13
Uniform Trust Code, 26
　agency, 63
　good businessperson, good paterfamilias, or
　　diligent administrator, 40
*Uniform Trustees Act,* 13
*Uniform Trustee's Powers Act,* 13
United States, trusts in, 11–13
　"black letter" sections of *Restatements,*
　　12n37, 27

Latin American trusts, differences, 24–26
*Prudent Investor Rule,* 12–13
*Restatement of the Law, Trusts,* 12
Uruguay, 331–55
　*Administradoras de Fondos Ahorro*
　　*Previsional* (AFAPs), 51, 352
　*Administradoras de Fondos de Pensión*
　　(AFPs), 51
　agency, 63
　assets transferred to trust, 335
　bankruptcy, 339–40
　beneficiary, 345–46
　　foreign beneficiaries, 354–55
　Civil Code, 333, 336, 340, 345–48
　confidentiality, 343
　Decree-Law No. 14701 of 1977, 352
　Decree No. 46/04, 332
　definition of trust, 333–34
　fees, 343
　financial trusts, 349–52
　　current situation, 350–51
　　securitization before Trust Law, 349–50
　　tax treatment, 353
　　trust securities, 352
　　trust securities holders' meeting, 351–52
　forced heirship, 347–49
　free zones, 354
　grantor, 340
　guarantee trusts, 316, 346–47
　　Montevideo (Carrasco Airport) guarantee
　　　trust, 333, 347, 354
　　tax treatment, 353
　immovable assets, tax on sale or
　　transfer of, 352
　Income Tax on Economic Activities (IRAE),
　　352, 353
　Individual Income Tax (IRPF), 352, 353
　individualization of trust assets, 336
　insufficiency of trust assets, 339–40
　*inter vivos* trusts, 334, 345
　Law No. 16060, 334
　Law No. 16713, 352
　Law No. 16774, 349
　Law No. 17202 of 1999, 349
　Law No. 17703, 332
　Legislative Assembly, 332
　Ministry of Education and Culture, 336–37
　Montevideo (Carrasco Airport) guarantee
　　trust, 333, 347, 354
　Mutual Funds Law, 349–50
　nonfinancial trusts, tax treatment, 353
　Nonresidents Income Tax (IRNR), 352–55
　Official Gazette of the Federation, 332
　offshore trusts, 354

Uruguay (*cont.*)
overview, 332–409
*pactum commissorium,* 346
penalties, trustee, 341–42
pension funds, 352
prohibitions affecting, 343
"Promotion of Financing Bill," 332–33
protection of trust assets, 343
*Puertas del Sur,* 347
registration of the trust instrument, 336–37
registry of professional trustees, 341
Regulatory Decree No. 516, 332
rendering of accounts, 342–43
securitization, 51
before Trust Law, 349–50
separate accounting, 343
separate patrimony, 335–36
separate special-purpose patrimony,
trust as, 334
separation of trust assets at moment of
termination of the trust, 343
special beneficiaries, 354
special-purpose patrimony, 350
Tax Authority Office, 355
tax benefits, 354
Tax Code, 355
Tax on Patrimonial Transfers (ITP), 352, 353
Tax on Personal Assets (IP), 352–53
Tax Reform Act No. 18083, 333
tax secret, 355
tax treatment, 45, 352–55
financial trusts, 353
foreign beneficiaries, 354–55
free zones, 354
guarantee trusts, 353
Income Tax on Economic Activities
(IRAE), 352, 353
Individual Income Tax (IRPF), 352, 353
nonfinancial trusts, 353
Nonresidents Income Tax (IRNR), 352–55
offshore trusts, 354
special beneficiaries, 354
Tax Authority Office, 355
tax benefits, 354
Tax Code, 355
Tax on Patrimonial Transfers (ITP),
352, 353
Tax on Personal Assets (IP), 352–53
tax secret, 355
trustee, responsibility of, 354
value-added tax, 353
termination of Office of the Trustee, 43, 344
termination of the trust, 337–39, 343
testamentary trusts, 76, 347–49

trust agreement, 335–36
trustee, 89, 340–43
confidentiality, 343
death of, 338
described, 31
duties of the trustee, 342–43
fees, 343
multiple trustees, 342
penalties, 341–42
prohibitions affecting, 343
protection of trust assets, 343
registry of professional trustees, 341
rendering of accounts, 342–43
separate accounting, 343
separation of trust assets at moment of
termination of the trust, 343
standard of trust services, 342
tax treatment, 354
termination of Office of the Trustee,
43, 344
termination of the trust, 343
trustee substitution, 342
Trust Law, 332–39, 341–46, 348–54
trust property, 336
trust securities, 352
trust securities holders' meeting, 351–52
unilateral act, 350
Uruguayan Central Bank (BCU),
332, 341–42, 346, 350
value-added tax, 353
U.S. Federal Reserve System, 56*n*16
U.S. Securities and Exchange Commission,
56*n*16
Usufruct, 65–66
Usury
Brazil, 140*n*11

V

VA. *See* Department of Veterans Affairs (VA)
Value-added tax, 45
Argentina, 106
Paraguay, 305
Uruguay, 353
Vehicle tax
Peru, 330
Venezuela, 357–69
Banks and Other Financial Institutions
General Act, 358, 361–62, 364
beneficiary, 366–67
Central Bank of Venezuela, 363
Civil Code, 358–59
club administration trusts, 367
Commerce Code, 359
commerce registry, 359

competent courts, 360–61
DECEVAL, 56n16
Decree No. 124 of May 1975, 368
Decree No. 561, 361n4
Decree No. 869 of April 1975, 368
Decree of the Ministry of Economy or
    Promotion, 361
Decree with Rank, Value and Force of Law
    No. 6287 of 2008, 358, 364
experience, 367–69
Extraordinary Official Gazette No. 496 of
    1956, 358, 364
Family Protection Act, 362n9
grantor, 366–67
guarantee trusts, 368
housing plan trusts, 369
inter vivos trusts, 359, 361
investment trusts, 368
Labor Law, 368
life insurance trusts, 369
Managing Assemblies, 363
National Executive for insurance
    companies, 361
National Savings and Loan System Act, 361
National Securities Commission, 365
National Securities Registry, 363
Official Bulletin of the Republic of
    Venezuela, 361n4
overview, 358–61
penalties, 360–61

projects, trusts for carrying out, 368
public registry, 359
realty trusts, 367
Resolution 179-2000, 364–75
retirement plan trusts, 369
savings bank trusts, 367–68
savings fund trusts, 367
social benefits trusts, 368
Superintendence of Banks and Other
    Financial Institutions, 364–66
termination of the trust, 360
testamentary trusts, 359–60
Trust Act, 358, 360–64, 366
trustee, 361–66
    acceptance, 364
    described, 32
    duties of the trustee, 362–64
    removal, 364
    resignation, 364
Trust Law, 358
universal banks, 361n8

W

"Waterfall," trust securities, 103
Wildlife trusts
    Costa Rica, 191

Z

Zamora, Porras, 181, 188